THIRTEENTH EDITION

Modern Real Estate Practice

FILLMORE W. GALATY
WELLINGTON J. ALLAWAY
ROBERT C. KYLE

**Real Estate
Education Company**
a division of Dearborn Financial Publishing, Inc.

Publisher: Carol L. Luitjens
Acquisitions Editor: Margaret M. Maloney
Project Editor: Janet Webster
Art and Design Manager: Lucy Jenkins
Cover Design: James A. Buddenbaum
Interior Design: Daniel Christmas, Design Alliance Inc.

© 1959, 1963, 1965, 1968, 1971, 1973, 1975, 1978, 1982, 1985, 1988, 1991, 1994 by Dearborn Financial Publishing, Inc.

Published by Real Estate Education Company/Chicago
a division of Dearborn Financial Publishing, Inc.

94   95   96   10   9   8   7   6   5   4

Library of Congress Cataloging-in-Publication Data

Galaty, Fillmore W.
    Modern real estate practice \ Fillmore W. Galaty, Wellington J.
Allaway, Robert C. Kyle.—13th ed.
        p.   cm.
    Includes index.
    ISBN 0-79310-704-0
    1. Real estate business—Law and legislation—United States.
2. Vendors and purchasers—United States.   3. Real property—United
States.   I. Allaway, Wellington J.   II. Kyle, Robert C.
III. Title.
KF2042.R4G34   1993
346.7304′37—dc20
[347.306437]   93-36187
                                                                CIP

Contents

16   Leases   226

Part Two:
PRACTICES

17   Property Management   245

Acknowledgments

The authors would like to thank Laurel D. McAdams, GRI, of Pittsburgh, Pennsylvania, who served as development writer for the Thirteenth Edition of Modern Real Estate Practice. Mrs. McAdams is Senior Advisor and faculty member for the real estate program at Robert Morris College in Pittsburgh. She is a licensed real estate broker, specializing in real estate education, conducts seminars on civil rights law and chairs the Volunteer Education Advisory Committee to the Pennsylvania State Real Estate Commission.

The authors would like to thank the following people who served as reviewers for the thirteenth edition: Christopher Ashe, Learning Unlimited; Floyd M. Baird, RPA, SMA, Liberty Trust Company; Elyse Berns, ERA Real Estate Institute; Maurice A. Boren, National Institute of Real Estate; Leona Busby, Long & Foster Institute of Real Estate; William Carmody, College of Du Page; Gerald Cortesi, Triton College; Mark Dennison, J.D., Dennison Legal Services; Lee Dillenbeck, Elgin Community College; Charles R. Hermanek, Shannon & Luchs Academy of Real Estate; Donna Lee Higgins, GRI, CRS, O'Conor, Piper & Flynn; Robert P. Hurley, University of Connecticut; Deborah K. Hutson, GRI, Grempler Realty, Inc.; David January, MAI, SRA; Craig Larabee, Larabee School of Real Estate; Helen Crites Lewis, Shannon & Luchs; John D. Mayfield, Jr., The Southeast Real Estate Prep School; Jean Metzler, Metzler Enterprises; Sharon A. Millett; C. Edward Neeley, South Carolina School of Real Estate; Edward P. Norris, Norris School of Real Estate; L. K. O'Drudy, University of Virginia & National Institute of Real Estate; Marcia Russell, T. A. Russell & Company; Susan Shadley, Coldwell Banker-Eagle Rock; Priscilla W. Sheeley, Long & Foster; Marie S. Spodek, DREI, GRI, Charleston Trident Association of REALTORS® School; Dawn M. Svenningsen, Dabbs Academy of Real Estate, Inc.; John A. Tirone, J.D., Oakland University; Paul W. Turner, Memphis State University; Roger Weeks, Central Piedmont Community College.

The authors also thank the following educators for their valuable assistance:

Joan D. Acuff, Professional Dynamics Institute
Michael B. Agron, St. Mary's College
Charles G. Albrecht, Pikes Peak Community College
Carl V. Allen, Murrell Real Estate

Robert H. Allen, Educational Seminar Service, Inc.
Richard Angelo, St. Joseph's University
James A. Anselmi, Academy Real Estate School
Helen E. Archer, Coldwell Banker Institute of Real Estate
Donald P. Ash, Delaware School of Real Estate
Debbie Ashbrook, Coldwell Banker Mid-America Group School of Real Estate
L. William Bailey, CCIM, Professional Real Estate Programs
Keith R. Ballweg, Park Place Real Estate School
Sonona M. Bazemore, Farrall Institute, Inc.
Wayne F. Bender, MacCormac Junior College
Elyse Berns, ERA Real Estate Institute
Scott Berns, ERA Real Estate Institute
Louis Berolatti, Lincoln Trail College
James L. Black, Southern Ohio College
Paul R. Blaser, Northeast Community College
Donald E. Bodley, Ph.D., Eastern Kentucky University
David Boone, Memphis State University
Richard Bowen, Jr., Lincoln Land Community College
Tom Bowen, Professional School of Real Estate
Joan Brawley, GRI, CRS, DREI, College of Southern Idaho
Robert M. Brenner, J.D., Western Nebraska Tech Community College
Sherri Browning, Milotte Associates Real Estate School
Leona Busby, Long & Foster Institute of Real Estate
Jean L. Cannata, Greater Brockton Real Estate Institute
Gabe Caporale, Triton College
Mike Chastain, North Lake College
Steven Cherin, Truman College
Barbara Christoff, Gateway Technical College
Jackie Clift, Success Real Estate School
Roger D. Colestock, Indiana Vocational Technical College
M. Dan Coogan, J. Everett Light Career Center
Bo Cooper, Pierce College
Florence Darr, Suburban Real Estate Academy
James DeLee, Ph.D., Louisiana Real Estate School
Ralph DeMartino, GRI, Paducah Community College
Carol De Rossett, Academy of Real Estate
Robert Dell, Harris Real Estate School
Colleen Deininger, Kenosha School of Real Estate
David M. DiBrito, St. Cloud Technical
Anthony J. DiChiara, Niagra University
Harry L. Dickey, Mesa Community College
Lee Dillenbeck, Elgin Community College
Tom Durkin, Hall Institute of Real Estate
Robbie A. Earhart, CRS, GRI, Mississippi University for Women
Kathy Elliott, Wor-Wic Tech Community College
Stephen Elliott, Ph.D., Northwestern State University
Ward Elliott, Ward Elliott Institute of Real Estate
Alfred E. Fabian, Ivy Tech College
David Finley, Town & Country School of Real Estate
Samuel F. Fusaro, Sr., Brookdale Community College
James M. Gillespie, CRS, Brigham-Williams Real Estate Institute
Paul M. Gilligan, Coldwell Banker School of Real Estate
Jack Given, Indiana Vocational Technical College
Thomas A. Gosnell, GRI, Frederick Community College

Andrew J. Grod, South Suburban College
Linda H. Hamm, Columbia Academy of Real Estate
Phil Hardwick, Millsaps College
Ferne Harmon, SAD #6, Noble High School
Elizabeth M. Hazell, Christiana School of Real Estate
Carl Hemmeler, Columbus Real Estate Technology
Ray Henry, Arizona Institute of Real Estate
Russell S. Hicks, The Real Estate School
Donna Higgins, O'Conor, Piper & Flynn School of Real Estate
Byron K. Hiller, Real Estate, Real Estate Advanced Learning &
    Training Institute
John Wayne Hite, Blue Ridge Community College
Thomas B. Hoffman, IVCC
Fred Horn, St. Xavier University
Joan Horner, Kopka School of Real Estate
Gerald Hosemann, Hinds Community College
Patricia Hubbard, Jefferson County Board of Education
Leon E. Hustad, Las Vegas School of Real Estate
William Jackson, Jackson School of Real Estate
Ford Jensen, Ford Jensen Real Estate School
Aage Jensen, New York Institute for Real Estate Studies, Inc.
Mary Ellen Johnson, Sally McMahon School of Real Estate
Bill Joyce, University of Nebraska
Jane G. Kaplan, New York Technical College
F. Jeffrey Keil, J. Sargeant Reynolds Community College
Les Kepner, Danville Area Community College
Arthur L. Kevorkian, Central Connecticut State University
Teresa Keyes, Real Estate School of Nevada
Barbara Knudsen, Coldwell Banker
Craig Larabee, Larabee School of Real Estate & Insurance
Cheryl Lawrence, T. A. Edison
Melvin G. Lee, Southeastern Community College
Mark Lewkovich, Martin T. Marbry Real Estate School
Mark Lee Levine, University of Denver
Richard S. Linkemer, American School of Real Estate
Ronald A. Long, GRI, Metropolitan Real Estate School
Frank McGrath, Ph.D., St. Augustine College
James L. McNutt, CREA, GRI, Valley Realty & Investment Inc.
Denise Mancini, J. W. Riker
Pamela Martin, Olive-Harvey College
Mary Lois Massa, State Technical Institute
Anil B. Mavalankar, Truman College
John Mayfield, Jr., The Southeast Real Prep School
Beverly McCormick, Morehead State University
Marce Mehren, Western Wisconsin Technical College
Lorraine Meighan, Champion Institute of Real Estate
Ruth E. Mercer, Kansas School of Real Estate
Thomas L. Meyer, Cape Girardeau Missouri School of Real Estate
John Michaels, Oakton Community College
Wayne R. Michelsen, Oakton Community College
Denise I. Mitchell, Abillty School of Real Estate
Jeff Mitchell, Village Real Estate Education Co.
John A. Morgan, National Real Estate School
Richard D. Morrison, Dona Ana Branch Community College

Theresa A. Morse, Theresa A. Morse School of Real Estate
Clem W. Mundel, Skogman Pre-License School
K. Murray, Central Community College
Dee Muzingo, Professional Real Estate Education
Theodore Napper, Guilford Technical Community College
Carl Edward Neeley, South Carolina School of Real Estate
Gary L. Nelson, Dakota County Technical College
Heather L. Niebauer, Portage Lakes Career Center
Elizabeth J. H. Nolan, Southeastern Oklahoma State
Marc Normand, New Hampshire Vocational Technical College
Ron Nyhus, Chippewa Valley Technical College
Jim Oakley, Truman College
Paul Olsen, Wesley College
S. H. Peckham, Professional School of Real Estate & Insurance
Joyce Pence, Kirkwood Community College
Ted A. Perszyk, Milwaukee Area Technical College
Robert Polston, Morton College
Jerry Prock, University of Texas—Pan American
Ervin A. Pruitt, Greenville Technical College
Vivian B. Ready, Sullivan Vo-Tech
Sibyl Reece, Northwest Community College
Betty Reed, Alabama Institute of Real Estate
Marilyn Reeves, Century 21 Northern California/Northern Nevada
Sharon Reinking, GRI, Traverse City Board of Realtors School of Real Estate
John Reino, Greenfield Community College
John D. Rinehart, The Real Estate Institute of York County, Inc.
Carl Roberts, Central Community College—Platte Campus
Robbie Robison, Allegany Community College
Hugh J. Rode, Utah Valley Community College
Eston L. Rodgers, Jr., Greenville Technical College
Jack Rodgers, National Real Estate Institute, Inc.
Kathy Roosa, Kathy Roosa School of Real Estate
Irvin J. Roth, Chicago State University
Larry Rowan, Coldwell Banker
Charles K. Russelburg, Daviess County Senior Vocational Technical College
Alan Russell, Triton College
Mary I. Ruth, Mt. Wachsusett Community College
Robert W. Ruthenberg, National Real Estate Schools—Blue Island Branch
Bob Rydarczyk, The Real Estate School
Lawrence Sager, Madison Area Technical College
Patricia A. Salyers, GRI, Moraine Valley Community College
Ruth Scharer, Yorktown Pre-License School
Andrea Schmidt, Landmark-Prudential Real Estate
Bonnie H. Sheer, Esq., Goldey-Beacom College
Elizabeth Skidmore, Allegany Community College
Edward J. Smith, Ed Smith Real Estate School
Kathryn Smith, Smith Real Estate School
Thomas A. Smythe, Sauk Valley Community College
Bob Snow, The Real Estate Academy
Margaret E. Sprencz, Dyke College
Paul C. Sprencz, Lorain Business College
Paul L. Stansel, Ph.D., Troy State University
W. Leonard Still, Spartanburg Technical College
Charles Storey, Progressive School of Real Estate

Calvin Streza, Portage Lakes Career Center
Nancy Strohbusch, Southwest Wisconsin Technical College
Edwin J. Stuart, Southeastern Oklahoma State University
Don Sullivan, Kentucky Academy of Real Estate
Dawn M. Svenningsen, Dabbs Academy of Real Estate, Inc.
David A. Tarantul, Hall Institute of Real Estate
William A. Tarter, Greenville Technical College
Marsha A. Temirian, Pat Crilley Schools
Christina Teusch, Carlson Pre-License School
Paul J. Thiel, South Carolina School of Real Estate
Dave Thompson, College of Lake County
Irene Thornburg, Ancilla College
Edward H. Tracy, Indiana Real Estate Institute
Ron Tremmel, Rend Lake College
Charles A. Trester, Northeast Wisconsin Technical College
Richard L. Turney, Adams State College
Betty Van Boening, Mid-Plains Technical Community College
Randall S. van Reken, Southern Nevada School of Real Estate
John W. Vincent, Piedmont Tech
John A. Vincze, South Central Community College
Joseph C. Wall, Jr., L. K. Farrall Institute
James E. Walsh, Tidewater Community College
Linea Warmke, Ohio University
Sheryl Marra Watson, Nebraska School of Real Estate
Wilma L. Watteau, IVTC South Central
Roger A. Weeks, Central Piedmont Community College
Grant J. Wells, Ph.D., Ball State University
Sally Wells, Columbia College
Paul Wessel, South Suburban College
Jim Westfall, Mohave Community College
Ginger G. Westin, Real Estate Masters
Mary Wezeman, Coldwell Banker Real Estate School
Margaret Wheatley, Grempler Real Estate Institute
Ted Wilkinson, Jr., CRS, GRI, Waubonsee Community College
O. D. Williams, DREI, Real Estate School of Santa Fe
Candace T. Wilson, Southeastern Illinois College
Jerry L. Wooten, Tucker School of Real Estate
Eric S. Worner, Parkland College
David W. Yang, Ph.D., University of Arkansas—Pine Bluff

Thanks also are extended to the many real estate professionals who have contributed to earlier editions of the book. Each new edition builds on the foundation they have helped us develop.

Furthermore, special credit is extended to the following people or groups for permission to use materials or forms: Floyd M. Baird; Kermit Burton, Alpha Enterprises; Judith Deickler, Diane Flannigan, Founders Title Insurance Agency, Inc.; Yvette Fleeger, Peter Cook Mortgage Company; The Forms Committee, Arizona Association of REALTORS®, National Association of Environmental Risk Auditors; Robert Rucker, Arizona Regional Multiple Listing Service; John Reilly; William L. Ventolo, Jr., Vista Environmental Information, Inc.; and Martha R. Williams. The sample forms may not be applicable to all jurisdictions and are subject to pertinent changes in the law.

Finally, the authors would like to extend their appreciation to the entire staff of Real Estate Education Company for their execution of this Thirteenth Edition. Special assistance has been provided by Margaret Maloney, Acquisitions Editor; Janet Webster, Project Editor; Lucy Jenkins, Art and Design Manager; Christine Benton, Copy Editor.

Fillmore W. Galaty
Wellington J. Allaway
Robert C. Kyle

Preface

Since its first printing in 1959, *Modern Real Estate Practice* has provided hundreds of thousands of people with valuable real estate information. Whether they were using the book to prepare for taking a state licensing examination, or for a college or university program, or just for their own personal knowledge, they knew that *Modern Real Estate Practice* set the standard for contemporary information in an easy-to-read format.

This thirteenth edition has been revised in response to extensive research to make the book as sensitive as possible to the needs of the reader. With each edition, there are refinements in the organization of material, study aids and text writing to enhance the understanding of information that is currently relevant for today's real estate practitioner. The real estate industry is undergoing significant changes because of increased awareness of the needs and rights of consumers, the growing importance of environmental issues and the enactment of new laws and regulations that respond to these concerns. The major changes in this edition reflect these developments by expanding the discussion of the law of agency and the responsibilities and services a licensee provides to clients and customers, including disclosure of agency representation and property conditions; revising mortgage loan programs, appraisal certification requirements and RESPA procedures; and expanding discussion of fair housing laws, professional ethics and environmental issues throughout.

There are a number of useful study aids that set *Modern Real Estate Practice* apart from other books of its kind. The end-of-chapter questions are written in the style followed by many professional testing agencies plus two sample examinations that enable the reader to gauge his or her understanding of the material. The glossary is revised to include terminology and definitions that are common to the practice of real estate in the 1990s. Additional aids include the Mathematics Review and the Environmental Issues Appendix. The selection of illustrations and figures in each chapter is revised to provide increased understanding, eliminating those which reviewers have suggested are not particularly useful to the reader.

The text is only a tool. It is intended to introduce the reader to a variety of real estate concepts, theories and specialties in practice. The instructor is encouraged to supplement the text material with classroom discussions, using practical examples and exhibits of forms and other documents common in that area. The reader is encouraged to pursue further study through additional publications and discussions with industry practitioners. Education is a continuous process in which the reader and instructor are active participants.

Supplements for *Modern Real Estate Practice* have been developed for more than 30 states, detailing laws, principles and practices specific to the real estate business in those particular states. A *Study Guide for Modern Real Estate Practice* contains additional review questions and study problems to further assist the student in his or her real estate education. In addition, a comprehensive *Instructor's Manual,* including some of the figures that previously appeared in *Modern Real Estate Practice*, a computerized test bank, interactive exam prep software, Key Point Review audio tapes and transparencies, are available to instructors as companions to this text. Contact Real Estate Education Company for further details about these materials.

Comments always are appreciated; they assist in evaluating the current edition and formulating policy for future editions. Any comments should be directed to Carol Luitjens, Vice-President, Real Estate Education Company, a division of Dearborn Financial Publishing, Inc., 520 North Dearborn, Chicago, Illinois 60610.

Part One

PRINCIPLES

Introduction to the Real Estate Business

1

THE REAL ESTATE BUSINESS IS "BIG" BUSINESS

In our modern world some type of real estate transaction occurs at every moment: A commercial leasing company rents space in a mall to an electronics store. The owner of a building rents an apartment to a retired couple. An appraiser gives an expert opinion of the value of 100 acres of farmland now that the tract is surrounded by residential subdivisions. A bank lends money to a professional corporation so it can purchase a medical office building. And, of course, the typical American family sells its old house and buys a bigger new home.

All of this adds up to big business—billions of dollars' worth of sales alone every year in the United States. The services of millions of highly trained individuals are required. Not only home buyers and sellers but also attorneys, banks, trust companies, abstract and title insurance companies, architects, surveyors, accountants, tax experts and many others depend on the skills and knowledge of today's real estate practitioner.

REAL ESTATE—A BUSINESS OF MANY SPECIALIZATIONS

Despite the size and complexity of the real estate business, many people think of it as being made up of only brokers and salespeople. Actually today's real estate industry employs millions of specialists as well. Appraisal, property management, financing, subdivision and development, counseling and education are all separate businesses within the real estate field. Every real estate professional must have a basic knowledge of these specialties to be successful.

Real Estate Professions

Brokerage. Brokerage is the business of bringing people together in a real estate transaction. The **broker** acts as an agent who is the intermediary between two or more people in the negotiation of the sale, purchase or rental of property. Usually one of the parties (or both) agrees to pay the broker to act as his or her agent. The compensation may be a flat fee, hourly rate or a percentage of the amount of the transaction. Fees and percentages are *not* fixed in the marketplace; they are negotiated between the agent and the client. There may be a **salesperson** working on behalf of the broker who provides services to the client. Brokerage is further discussed in Chapter 4.

Appraisal. Appraisal is the process of estimating a property's value. Although their training will give brokers some understanding of the valuation process, property that is financed or sold by court order requires the expertise of a qualified appraiser. Appraisers must have sound judgment and detailed knowledge of the methods of valuation and usually must meet state licensing or certification requirements. Appraisers are paid a fee, the size of which depends on their expertise and the complexity of the appraisal task. Appraisal is covered in Chapter 18.

Property management. A property manager is hired to operate property for its owner, relieving the owner of that responsibility. Management tasks might include soliciting tenants, collecting rents, altering or constructing new space for tenants, ordering repairs and generally maintaining the property. In the case of an apartment building, that might mean supervising maintenance to keep the structure in good shape as well as marketing to ensure the highest possible occupancy and rents. The scope of the work depends on the terms of the individual employment contract, known as a *management agreement.* Whatever tasks are specified, the underlying responsibility of the property manager is to protect the owner's investment and maximize the owner's returns. Property management is discussed in Chapter 17.

Financing. Financing is the business of providing funds for a real estate transaction. Most transactions are financed by means of a mortgage loan or a trust deed loan secured by the property. Individuals involved in financing real estate work in a variety of settings, such as commercial banks, savings and loan associations, mortgage banking and mortgage brokerage companies. Financing is examined in Chapters 14 and 15.

Subdivision and development. Subdivision involves splitting a large parcel of real estate into smaller ones. The subdivider must survey the land, both before and after the splitting is done, and draft a map of the newly created parcels, often referred to as a *plat map.* Development involves the construction of improvements on the land. These improvements fall into two categories. Offsite improvements, such as water lines and storm sewers under city streets, are made on public lands to serve the new development. On-site improvements, such as a new home or a swimming pool, are made on individual parcels. While subdivision and development normally are related—particularly in the area of new housing—they are independent processes that can occur separately. Subdivision and development are discussed further in Chapters 19 and 20.

Counseling. Counseling involves providing clients with competent independent advice based on sound judgment. A real estate counselor attempts to give clients direction in choosing among alternative courses of action regarding the purchase, use and investment of property. It is their responsibility to increase the client's knowledge.

Education. Real estate education is available to both practitioners and consumers. Colleges and universities, private schools and trade organizations conduct courses and seminars on all aspects of the business, from the principles of a prelicensing program to the technical aspects of tax and exchange law.

Other areas. Many other real estate careers are available, and practitioners will find that real estate specialists are needed in numerous business settings. Lawyers specializing in real estate are always in demand. Large corporations with extensive land holdings often have real estate and/or property tax departments. Specialists in real estate finance can work for mortgage banking firms, government agencies and mortgage brokers as well as banks and S&Ls. Local governments must staff both zoning boards and assessing offices.

Professional Organizations

Of the many trade organizations serving the real estate business, the largest is the National Association of REALTORS® (NAR). NAR sponsors various affiliate organizations that offer professional designations to brokers, salespeople and others who complete required courses. Members subscribe to a code of ethics and are entitled to be known as REALTORS® or REALTORS-ASSOCIATES®.

Among the many other professional associations is the National Association of Real Estate Brokers (NAREB), whose members also subscribe to a code of ethics. Members of NAREB are known as Realtists. Other professional associations include the Appraisal Institute, the National Association of Independent Fee Appraisers and the Real Estate Educators Association.

Types of Real Property

Just as there are areas of specialization within the real estate industry, there are different types of property in which to specialize. Real estate can generally be classified as follows:

- Residential—all property used for housing, from acreage to small city. In single-family and multifamily, in urban, suburban and rural areas

- Commercial—business property, including office space, shopping centers, fronts, theaters. hotels and parking facilities

- Industrial—warehouses, factories, land in industrial districts and power plants

- Agricultural—farms, timberland, ranches and orchards

- Special-purpose—churches, schools, cemeteries and government-held lands

The market for each of these types of property can be subdivided into the sale market, which involves the transfer of title and ownership rights, and the rental market, in which space is transferred temporarily by lease.

IN PRACTICE...

Although a real estate firm or person can perform all the services listed earlier (unless restricted by licensure) and handle all classes of property, this is rarely done except in small towns. Most firms specialize to some degree, especially in urban areas. In some cases a licensee may perform only one service for one type of property, such as residential sales or commercial leasing.

THE REAL ESTATE MARKET

In literal terms a **market** is a place where goods can be bought and sold. The function of the market is to provide a setting in which supply and demand can establish market value, making it advantageous for buyers and sellers to trade.

Supply and Demand

Supply and demand are the economic forces that set prices for products. As they interact in the market, prices go up or down. Essentially, *when supply increases, prices decrease; when demand increases, so do prices.* Greater supply means producers need to attract more buyers, so they lower prices. Greater demand means producers can raise their prices because buyers are competing for the product.

Supply and demand in the real estate market. Two characteristics of real estate govern the way the market reacts to the pressures of supply and demand: uniqueness and immobility (see Chapter 2). Despite the fact that several units in one development may be built to the same specifications, each parcel has its own geographic location. Therefore, no two parcels are ever exactly alike. Real estate is also immobile, as, generally, are property buyers (with the exception of retirees with regard to their residences). This means that property cannot be relocated to satisfy demand where supply is low. Nor can buyers always relocate to an area with greater supply. For these reasons real estate tends to be made up of local markets. In these well-defined small areas, real estate offices can keep track of what type of property is in demand and what types are available.

Also because of real estate's uniqueness and immobility, the market generally adjusts slowly to the forces of supply and demand. Though a house offered for resale can be withdrawn in response to low demand and high supply, it is much more likely that oversupply will result in lower prices. When supply is low, on the other hand, a high demand may not be met immediately because development and construction are lengthy processes. Development may, in fact, occur in uneven spurts of activity due to these factors.

Even when supply and demand can be forecast with some accuracy, natural disasters such as hurricanes and earthquakes can disrupt market trends. In those cases communities face formidable challenges to meet the unanticipated demand of dislocated families and businesses whose properties are damaged or destroyed.

Factors Affecting Supply

Factors that tend to affect supply in the real estate market include the labor force, construction costs, government controls and financial policies.

Labor force and construction costs. Any shortage of skilled labor or building materials or increase in cost of materials can decrease the amount of new construction. Higher construction costs will be passed along to buyers and tenants. There is a limit to how much more they are willing to pay. Technological advances that result in cheaper materials and more efficient means of construction tend to counteract some price increases.

Government controls and financial policies. Government monetary policy can have a substantial impact on the real estate market. The Federal Reserve Board, as well as such government agencies as the Federal Housing Administration (FHA), the Government National Mortgage Association (GNMA) and the Federal Home Loan Mortgage Corporation (FHLMC), can affect the amount of money available to lenders for mortgage loans (see Chapter 15).

The government fiscal policies also influence how much money is available for real estate investment. For example, taxation takes money out of circulation.

The government puts money into circulation through spending programs ranging from welfare to farm subsidies.

Real estate taxation is one of the primary sources of revenue for local governments. Policies on taxation of real estate can have either positive or negative effects. High taxes may deter investors. On the other hand, tax incentives can attract new businesses and industries. And, of course, along with these enterprises come increased employment and expanded residential real estate markets.

Local governments also can influence supply by applying land-use controls. Communities use building codes and zoning ordinances to control and encourage the highest potential use of land, which stabilizes real estate values and markets. Community amenities such as churches, schools and parks also shape the market.

Factors Affecting Demand

Factors that tend to affect demand in the real estate market include population, demographics and employment and wage levels.

Population. Shelter is a basic human need, so the need for housing grows as the population grows. Although the total population of the country continues to increase, the demand for real estate increases faster in some areas than in others. The Sunbelt, for example, is still attracting mobile retirees, but community incentives have succeeded in drawing businesses and young families, as well. Similar local controls have also made other areas attractive for newcomers.

In other locations growth has ceased altogether or population has plummeted. The local airbase or manufacturing plant might close. The result can be a dwindling population or a mass exodus, with an accompanying drop in demand for real estate.

Demographics. The makeup of the population—demographics—affects demand as strongly as simple numbers. Family size and the ratio of adults to children, the number of people moving into retirement care facilities and retirement communities, the effect of "doubling up" (two or more families using one housing unit) and the changing number of single-parent households all contribute to the amount and type of housing needed. Another factor is the number of young people who would prefer to rent or own their own residences but share with roommates or remain in their parents' homes for economic reasons.

Employment and wage levels. Whether to buy or rent and how much to spend on housing are inextricably related to income. Therefore, when job opportunities are scarce or wage levels low, demand for real estate usually drops. The market might, in fact, be affected drastically by the actions of a major employer in a small community. So licensees must keep abreast of employers' plans.

Licensees should also be aware of economic trends. How people use their income depends on consumer confidence, which is based not only on perceived job security but also on the availability of credit and the impact of inflation.

●   ●   ●   ●   ●   ●   ●

KEY TERMS   broker   salesperson   demand   supply   market

SUMMARY   Although brokerage is the most widely recognized real estate activity, many
other services are also provided by the industry, such as appraisal, property management, property development, counseling, property financing and education
Most real estate firms specialize in only one or two of these areas. However, the
highly complex and competitive nature of our society requires that a real estate
person be an expert in a number of fields.

Real property can be classified by its general use as residential, commercial, industrial, agricultural or special-purpose. Although many brokers deal with more
than one type of real property, they usually specialize to some degree.

A market is a place where goods and services can be bought and sold and price
levels established. Because of its unique characteristics, real estate is relatively
slow to adjust to the forces of supply and demand.

The supply of and demand for real estate are affected by many factors, including changes in population numbers and demographics, wage and employment
levels, construction costs and availability of labor and governmental monetary
policy and controls.

Questions

1. Commercial real estate includes all of the following *except*
   a. office buildings for sale.
   b. apartments for rent.
   c. retail space for lease.
   d. fast-food restaurants.

2. In general, when the supply of a certain commodity increases,
   a. prices tend to rise.
   b. prices tend to drop.
   c. demand tends to rise.
   d. demand tends to drop.

3. All of the following factors tend to affect supply *except*
   a. the labor force.
   b. construction costs.
   c. government controls.
   d. demographics.

4. Which of the following is an example of special-purpose real estate?
   a. An apartment building
   b. A public library
   c. A shopping center
   d. An industrial park

2 Real Property and the Law

LAND, REAL ESTATE AND REAL PROPERTY

The words *land*, *real estate* and *real property* are often used interchangeably. For a full understanding of the nature of real estate and the laws that affect it, however, licensees need to be aware of the subtle yet important differences in meaning.

Land

Land is defined as *the earth's surface extending downward to the center of the earth and upward to infinity, including things permanently attached by nature, such as trees and water.* (See Figure 2.1.)

The term *land* thus refers to not only the surface of the earth but also the underlying soil and things that are naturally attached to the land, such as boulders and plants. Land includes the minerals and substances far below the earth's surface, together with the air above the land up into space. These are known respectively as the subsurface and airspace.

Real Estate

Real estate is defined as *land at, above and below the earth's surface, including all things permanently attached to it, whether natural or artificial.* (See Figure 2.1.)

The term *real estate* is somewhat broader than the term land; it incudes not only the natural components of the land but also all man-made improvements. An **improvement** is any artificial thing attached to land, such as a building or a fence. Land is also referred to as *improved* by streets, utilities, sewers and other additions that make it suitable for building.

Real Property

Real property is defined as *the interests, benefits and rights inherent in the ownership of real estate.* (See Figure 2.1.)

The term *real property* is broader than either *land* or *real estate*. It includes the physical surface of the land, what lies above and below it, what is permanently attached to it, as well as the *bundle of legal rights (legal rights of ownership)* that attach to ownership of a parcel of real estate. Real property includes not

Figure 2.1
Land, Real Estate
and Real Property

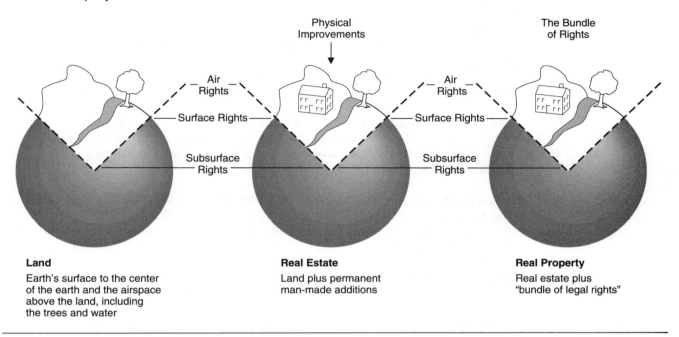

Land	Real Estate	Real Property
Earth's surface to the center of the earth and the airspace above the land, including the trees and water	Land plus permanent man-made additions	Real estate plus "bundle of legal rights"

only the surface, subsurface and airspace but also the surface rights, subsurface rights and air rights, all of which can be owned by different individuals.

IN PRACTICE...

When people talk about buying or selling homes, office buildings, land and the like, they usually call these things real estate. For all practical purposes, the term is synonymous with real property as defined here. Thus, in everyday usage, real estate includes the legal rights of ownership specified in the definition of real property. Sometimes the term realty *is used instead.*

Subsurface and air rights. **Subsurface rights** are the rights to the natural resources lying below the earth's surface. A transfer of **surface rights,** *the right to use the surface of the earth,* may be accomplished without transfer of subsurface rights. For example, a landowner may sell the rights to any oil and gas found in the land to an oil company. Later the same landowner can sell the remaining interest to a purchaser and reserve the rights to all coal that may be found in the land. After these sales, three parties have ownership interests in this real estate: (1) the oil company owns all oil and gas, (2) the seller owns all coal and (3) the purchaser owns the rights to the remaining real estate.

The rights to use the air above the land, provided the rights have not been preempted by law, may be sold or leased independently of the land. **Air rights** can be an important part of real estate, particularly in cases where air rights over railroads must be purchased to construct office buildings, such as the Pan-

Am Building in New York City and the Merchandise Mart in Chicago. To construct such a building, the developer must purchase not only the air rights but also numerous small portions of the land's surface for the building's foundation supports.

Before air travel was common, a property's air rights were considered to be unlimited. Today, however, the courts permit reasonable interference with these rights, such that is necessary for aircraft, as long as the owner's right to use and occupy the land is not unduly lessened. Governments and airport authorities often purchase adjacent air rights to provide approach patterns for air traffic.

With the continuing development of solar electric power, air rights may be redefined by the courts to include solar access rights. Tall buildings that block sunlight from smaller solar-powered buildings may be ruled as interfering with the smaller buildings' sun rights.

In summary, one parcel of real estate may be owned by many people, each holding a separate right to a different part of the real estate. There may be (1) an owner of the surface rights, (2) an owner of the subsurface mineral rights, (3) an owner of the subsurface gas and oil rights and (4) an owner of the air rights. The rights of each owner must be respected equally. A purchaser should be aware of ownership by others.

| IN PRACTICE. . . | *The land and subsurface may be contaminated by a variety of chemical substances. Increasing awareness of these environmental hazards and subsequent federal and state legislation impact the ownership and development of real estate today. See "Environmental Issues and the Real Estate Transaction" in the appendix for a discussion of these issues.* |

REAL PROPERTY VERSUS PERSONAL PROPERTY

Personal property, sometimes called *personalty*, is *all property that does not fit the definition of real property*. An important distinction between the two is that personal property is movable. Items of personal property, also referred to as **chattels**, include such tangibles as chairs, tables, clothing, money, bonds and bank accounts.

The distinction between real and personal property is not always obvious. A mobile home, for example, is generally considered personal property even though its mobility may be limited to a single trip to a mobile-home park. A mobile home may, however, be considered real property if it is permanently affixed to land as prescribed by state law. Real estate licensees should be familiar with local laws before attempting to sell mobile homes. Some states permit only mobile home dealers to sell them.

Trees and crops generally fall into one of two classes. Trees, perennial shrubbery and grasses that do not require annual cultivation are considered real property. Annual plantings or crops of wheat, corn, vegetables and fruit, known as *emblements*, are generally considered personal property. But as long as an annual crop is growing, it will be transferred as part of the real property unless other provisions are made in the sales contract. The former owner or tenant is entitled to the harvest from the crops that result from their labor.

Figure 2.2
Real versus
Personal Property

Real Estate	Personal Property	Fixture	Trade Fixture
Land and anything permamently attached to it	Movable items not attached to real estate; items severed from real estate	Item of personal property converted to real estate by attaching it to the real estate with the intention that it become permanently a part thereof	Item of personal property attached to real estate that is owned by a tenant and is used in a business; legally removable by tenant

An item of real property can be changed to personal property by **severance**. For example, a growing tree is real estate until the owner cuts down the tree and thereby severs it from the earth. Similarly, an apple becomes personal property once it is picked from a tree, and a crop of wheat becomes personal property once it is harvested.

It is also possible to change personal property into real property. If a landowner buys cement, stones and sand and constructs a concrete walk on the land, the components of the concrete, which were originally personal property, are converted into real property. They have become a permanent improvement on the land. This process is called *annexation*.

Classifications of Fixtures

In considering the differences between real and personal property, it is important to be able to distinguish between a *fixture* and personal property. (See Figure 2.2.)

Fixtures. A **fixture** is *an article that was once personal property but has been so affixed to land or a building that the law construes it to be part of the real estate*. Examples are heating plants, elevator equipment in high-rise buildings, radiators, kitchen cabinets, light fixtures and plumbing fixtures. Almost any item that has been added as a *permanent part* of a building is considered a fixture.

Legal tests of a fixture. Courts use four basic tests to determine whether an item is a fixture (and therefore part of the real property) or personal property:

1. Intention: Did the person who installed the item intend it to remain permanently or to be removable?

2. Method of annexation: How permanently was the item attached? Can it be removed without causing damage?

3. Adaptation to real estate: Is the item being used as real property or personal property?

4. Agreement: Have the parties agreed on whether the item is real or personal property?

Although these tests seem simple, court decisions have been inconsistent. Articles that appear to be permanently affixed have sometimes been ruled to be personal property, while items that do not appear to be permanently attached have been ruled as fixtures. It is important that an owner clarify what is to be sold with the real estate at the very beginning of the sales process.

At the time the property is listed, the seller and listing salesperson should discuss which items are intended to be included in the sale. The written sales contract between the buyer and the seller should list all articles that are being included in the sale, particularly if there is any doubt as to whether they are personal property or fixtures. Articles that might be included are television satellite dishes, built-in appliances, built-in bookcases and wall-to-wall carpeting, wood stoves, chandeliers and ceiling fans and hot tubs. It is also expected that the landscaping will remain as is.

Trade fixtures. An article owned by a tenant and attached to a rented space or building or used in conducting a business is a **trade fixture** or a *chattel fixture*. Examples of trade fixtures are bowling alleys, store shelves, bars and restaurant equipment. Agricultural fixtures, such as chicken coops and toolsheds, are also included in this definition. Trade fixtures must be removed on or before the last day the property is rented. The tenant is responsible for any damage caused by the removal of a fixture. Trade fixtures that are not removed become the real property of the landlord. Acquiring the property in this way is known as **accession**.

Trade fixtures differ from fixtures generally in these ways:

- Fixtures belong to the owner of the real estate, but trade fixtures are usually owned and installed by a tenant for the tenant's use.

- Fixtures are considered a permanent part of a building, but trade fixtures are removable. Trade fixtures may be attached to a building so that they appear to be fixtures. Due to the landlord-tenant relationship, however, trade fixtures may be removed before the expiration of the lease and the rented space must be restored to substantially its original condition, except for reasonable wear and tear.

- Fixtures are legally construed to be real property, and are included in any sale or mortgage of the real property. Trade fixtures are legally construed to be personal property and are not included in the sale or mortgage of real property except by special agreement.

CHARACTERISTICS OF REAL ESTATE

Real estate possesses seven basic characteristics that define its nature and affect its use. These characteristics fall into two broad categories—economic characteristics and physical characteristics (see Figure 2.3).

Economic Characteristics

The economic characteristics of land affect its investment value.

**Figure 2.3
Characteristics
of Real Estate**

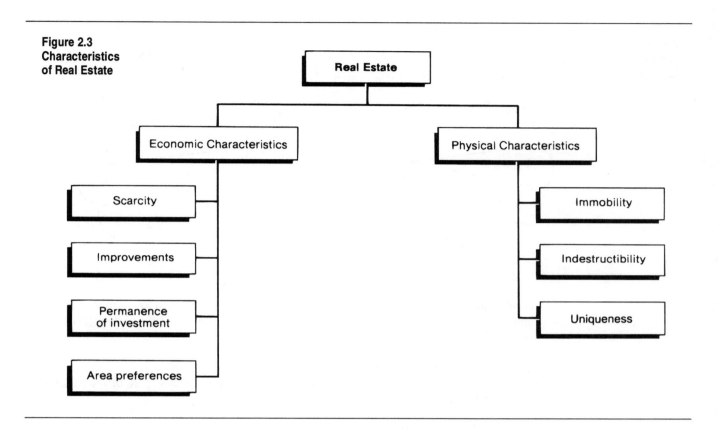

Scarcity. Although we usually do not think of land as a rare commodity, the total supply is in fact fixed. While a considerable amount remains unused or uninhabited, the supply in a given location or of a particular quality is generally considered to be limited.

Improvements. Building an improvement on one parcel of land can affect the value and use not only of neighboring tracts but also on whole communities. For example, constructing a new shopping center or selecting a site for an atomic reactor can change the value of land in a large area.

Permanence of investment. The capital and labor used to build an improvement represent a large fixed investment. Although even a well-built structure can be razed to make way for a newer building or other use of the land, improvements such as drainage, electricity, water and sewerage remain. The return on such investments tends to be long-term and relatively stable.

Area preference. This economic characteristic, sometimes called *situs,* does not refer to a geographic location but rather to people's choices for a given area. It is the unique quality of people's preferences that results in different values for similar units. *Area preference is the most important economic characteristic of land.*

**Physical
Characteristics**

Land also has certain physical characteristics that set it apart from other commodities.

**Figure 2.4
The Bundle of
Legal Rights**

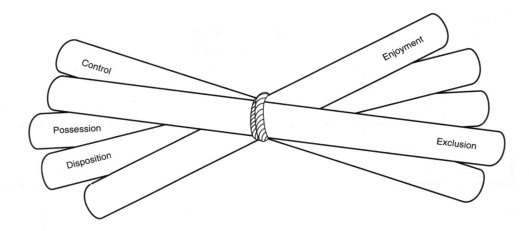

Land is immobile. It is true that some of the substances of land are removable and that topography can be changed, but *the geographic location of any given parcel of land can never be changed.* It is fixed.

Land is indestructible. Land is also *indestructible.* This permanence of land, coupled with the long-term nature of the improvements, tends to stabilize investments in land.

The fact that land is indestructible does not, however, change the fact that the improvements on land depreciate and can become obsolete, thereby reducing values—perhaps dramatically. This gradual depreciation should not be confused with the fact that the *economic desirability* of a given location can change.

Land is unique. No two parcels of land are ever exactly the same. Although there may be substantial similarity, *all parcels differ geographically,* because each parcel has its own location. There is no substitute for an individual parcel because each is unique. The uniqueness of land is also referred to as its *heterogeneity* or *nonhomogeneity.*

OWNERSHIP OF REAL PROPERTY

The unique nature of real estate has given rise to a unique set of laws and rights. Even the simplest of real estate transactions brings into play a body of complex laws, and licensees must understand not only the effect of the law but also how the law defines real property. Real property is often described as a **bundle of legal rights.** In other words, a purchaser of real estate is actually buying the rights of ownership held by the seller. These rights (see Figure 2.4) include the right of possession, the right to control the property within the framework of the law, the right of enjoyment (to use the property in any legal manner), the right of exclusion (to keep others from entering or using the property) and the right of disposition (to sell, will or otherwise dispose of the property).

The concept of a bundle of rights comes from old English law. When the populace could not commonly read and write, a seller transferred property by giving the purchaser a bundle of bound sticks from a tree on the property. This process was referred to as a *livery of seisin.* The purchaser who held the bundle also owned the tree from which the sticks came and the land to which the tree was attached. Because the rights of ownership can be separated and individually transferred, the sticks became symbolic of those rights.

A person who acquires real estate owns the property subject to any rights retained by the seller or held or acquired by other persons. For example, as discussed earlier, a landowner may sell real estate while retaining the rights to certain minerals or natural resources. Likewise, a lending institution that holds a mortgage on real estate has the right to force a sale of the property if the loan is not repaid. The various rights in real estate will be discussed in detail later in the text.

Buying or selling real estate is usually the biggest financial transaction of a person's life. The buyer typically pays out more cash, undertakes more debt and has a deeper personal interest in this transaction than in any other purchase made during his or her lifetime. The real estate also is likely to have been the seller's biggest single investment in terms of money and work. Although there are people for whom the sale or purchase of real estate is a routine matter, for most it is a very important, emotional and complicated affair. Therefore the real estate licensees aiding in this transaction must pay strict attention to the applicable laws to assist in the successful transfer of the property.

REAL ESTATE LAW

The average citizen generally thinks of laws as rules laid down by the state to govern conduct. *Real estate brokers and salespeople must have a broader and better understanding of the sources of law and how various laws affect real estate.*

Laws Affecting Real Estate Practice

The specific areas that are important to the real estate practitioner include the *law of contracts,* the *general property law,* the *law of agency* (which covers the obligations of brokers to the persons who engage their services) and the *real estate license law,* all of which will be discussed in this text.

A real estate practitioner cannot be an expert in all areas of real estate law but should know and understand the basic principles of the law. Just as important is the ability to recognize problems that should be referred to a competent attorney. An attorney is a person trained and licensed to prepare documents defining or transferring rights in property and to give advice or counsel on matters of law. *Under no circumstances may a broker or salesperson act as an attorney unless separately licensed and representing a client in that capacity.*

All phases of a real estate transaction should be handled with extreme care. Carelessness in handling negotiations and the documents connected with a real estate sale can result in disputes. In many cases expensive legal actions could have been avoided if the parties handling negotiations had exercised greater care and employed competent legal counsel.

Real estate license laws. Because brokers and salespeople are involved with other people's real estate and money, the need for regulation of their activities has long been recognized. To protect the public from fraud, dishonesty or incompetence in the buying and selling of real estate, all 50 states, the District of Columbia and all Canadian provinces have passed laws that require real estate brokers and salespeople to be licensed. The license laws of the various states are similar in many respects but differ in some details.

In most cases applicants must have certain specific personal and educational qualifications and must pass an examination to assure a minimal level of competency for the business for which they are seeking licensure. In addition, to qualify for license renewal licensees must follow certain standards of business conduct. Some states also require licensees to complete continuing education courses. Chapter 13 more fully describes the state license laws and required standards.

•   •   •   •   •   •   •

KEY TERMS

accession	personal property
air rights	real estate
bundle of legal rights	real property
chattel	severance
fixture	subsurface rights
improvement	surface rights
land	trade fixture

SUMMARY

Although most people think of land as the surface of the earth, land is the earth's surface and also the mineral deposits under the earth and the air above it. The term real estate further expands this definition to include all natural and man-made improvements attached to the land. Real property describes real estate plus the bundle of legal rights associated with its ownership.

The different rights to the same parcel of real estate may be owned and controlled by different parties, one owning the surface rights, one owning the air rights and another owning the subsurface rights.

All property that does not fit the definition of real estate is classified as personal property, or chattels. When articles of personal property are affixed to land, they may become fixtures and as such are considered a part of the real estate. However, personal property attached to real estate by a tenant for business purposes is classified as a trade, or chattel, fixture and remains personal property.

The special nature of land as an investment is apparent in both its economic and physical characteristics. The economic characteristics are scarcity, improvements, permanence of investment and area preferences. Physically, land is immobile, indestructible and unique.

Even the simplest real estate transactions reflect a complex body of laws. A purchaser of real estate actually purchases from the seller the legal rights to use the land in certain ways.

Every state and Canadian province has some type of licensing requirement for real estate brokers and salespeople. Students should become familiar with the licensing requirements of their states.

Questions

1. Which of the following best defines *real estate?*
   a. Land and the air above it
   b. Land and the buildings permanently affixed to it
   c. Land and all things permanently affixed to it
   d. Land and the mineral rights in the land

2. A broker lists a building for sale in which a restaurant is a tenant. How will the restaurant's refrigeration and cooking equipment, booths and counters be handled in the sale of the building?
   a. The restaurant business will be sold when the building is sold.
   b. The restaurant equipment will not be involved in the sale of the building.
   c. The restaurant equipment and booths and counters are fixtures and will be sold with the building.
   d. The equipment will be valued separately and added to the sale price of the building.

3. The term *nonhomogeneity* refers to
   a. scarcity.
   b. immobility.
   c. uniqueness.
   d. indestructibility.

4. The bundle of legal rights is included in
   a. land.   c. real property.
   b. real estate.   d. trade fixtures.

5. The bundle of legal rights includes all of the following *except*
   a. the right to exclude someone from the property.
   b. the right to enjoy the property within the framework of the law.
   c. the right to sell or otherwise convey the property.
   d. the right to use the property for any purpose, legal or otherwise.

6. All of the following would be considered real estate *except*
   a. fences.   c. growing trees.
   b. buildings.   d. farm equipment.

7. All of the following would be considerations for an item being real property *except*
   a. the cost of the item when it was purchased.
   b. the method of its attachment to other real property.
   c. the intended use of the item by its owner.
   d. the manner in which the item is actually used with other real property.

8. Which of the following is *not* an economic characteristic of real estate?
   a. Indestructibility
   b. Improvements
   c. Area preferences
   d. Scarcity

9. Real property can be converted into personal property through
   a. severance.   c. conversion.
   b. accession.   d. inference.

10. When the buyer moved into a newly pur-
    chased home, the buyer discovered that the
    seller had taken the electric lighting fixtures
    that were installed over the vanity in the
    bathroom. The buyer was disturbed because
    the seller did not indicate that these fixtures
    were not included in the sale. Which of the
    following is true?
    a. Lighting fixtures are normally
        considered to be real estate.
    b. The lighting fixtures belong to the seller
        because he installed them.
    c. These lighting fixtures are considered
        trade fixtures.
    d. Lighting fixtures are normally consid-
        ered personal property.

11. A buyer purchases a parcel of land and sells
    the rights to minerals located in the ground
    to an exploration company. This means that
    the buyer now owns all but which of the fol-
    lowing rights to this property?
    a. Air rights
    b. Surface rights
    c. Subsurface rights
    d. Air and subsurface rights

Concepts of Home Ownership

3

HOME OWNERSHIP

People buy their own homes for psychological as well as financial reasons. To many, home ownership is a sign of financial stability. It is an investment that can appreciate in value and provide federal income tax deductions. Home ownership also has benefits that may be less tangible but are viewed as no less valuable. It can give the owner a sense of belonging to the community, and it often is a source of pride.

In the past most homes were single-family dwellings bought by married couples with small children. Today, however, social, demographic and economic changes have altered the residential real estate market considerably. For example, many real estate buyers today are *single* men and women. Many are *empty nesters,* married couples whose housing needs change after their children move away from home. Others are married couples who choose not to have children or unmarried couples living together.

Types of Housing

As our society evolves, the needs of its home buyers become more specialized. The following paragraphs describe the types of housing currently available to meet these diverse needs. Some of these types are not only innovative uses of real estate but also incorporate a variety of ownership concepts.

Apartment complexes, groups of apartment buildings with any number of units in each building, continue to be popular. The buildings may be low-rise or high-rise, and the amenities may include parking as well as clubhouses, swimming pools and even golf courses.

The *condominium* is a popular form of residential ownership, particularly for people who want the security of owning property but not the responsibilities of caring for and maintaining a house. Owners of condominium apartments or townhouses—which share party walls with other units—share ownership of common facilities, such as halls, elevators, swimming pools, club houses, tennis courts and surrounding grounds. Management and maintenance of building exteriors and common facilities are provided by agreement, with expenses paid out of monthly assessments charged to owners. Office buildings and shopping centers may also be established as condominiums, allowing businesses to build equity in the space they occupy while avoiding unpredictable rent increases. The condominium form of ownership is discussed in detail in Chapter 7.

A *cooperative* is similar to a condominium because it has units within a larger building with common walls and facilities. The owners, however, do not actually own the units. Instead they buy shares of stock in the corporation that holds title to the building. In return for stock, they receive a *proprietary lease* entitling them to occupy a particular unit. Like condominium unit owners, cooperative unit owners pay their share of the building's expenses. Cooperatives are discussed further in Chapter 7.

Planned unit developments (PUDs), sometimes called master-planned communities, merge such diverse land uses as housing, recreation and commercial units in one self-contained development. PUDs are planned under special cluster zoning ordinances. These ordinances permit maximum use of open space by reducing lot sizes and street areas. Owners do not have direct ownership interest in the common areas. A community association is formed to maintain these areas with fees collected from the owners.

Converted-use properties are factories, office buildings, hotels, schools, churches and other structures that have been converted to residential use. Usually the property was abandoned and bought by developers who found it both aesthetically and economically appealing to renovate it for use as rental or condominium units. An abandoned warehouse may be transformed into luxury loft condominium units, a closed hotel may become an apartment building and an old factory may become a shopping complex.

Retirement communities, many of them in temperate climates, are often structured as PUDs. They may provide shopping, recreational opportunities and health care facilities in addition to residential units.

Because of recent amendments to the fair housing laws, retirement communities cannot exclude families with children *unless* they meet the legal requirements for "housing for older persons." This is defined as housing to be occupied solely by persons 62 years of age or older or housing in which at least 80 percent of the units are to be occupied by at least one person who is 55 years of age or older. The laws also require that there must be facilities and services to meet the physical, recreational and social needs of older persons.

High-rise developments, sometimes called mixed-use developments (MUDs), combine office space, stores, theaters and apartment units. MUDs usually are self-contained, offering laundry facilities, restaurants, food stores, valet shops, beauty parlors, barbershops, swimming pools and other attractive and convenient features. The most successful developments also take advantage of natural assets such as rivers, lakes and forest preserves.

Mobile homes were once considered useful only as temporary residences or for travel. But in times of high-priced housing, they are often used as principal residences or stationary vacation homes. Relatively low cost, coupled with the increased living space available in the newer, double-wide and triple-wide models, has made mobile homes more attractive. Increased sales have in turn resulted in growing numbers of mobile-home parks in some communities. These parks offer complete residential environments with permanent community facilities as well as semipermanent foundations and hookups for gas, water and electricity.

Modular homes are also gaining popularity as the price of newly constructed homes rises. Each room, preassembled at the factory, is lowered into place on the building site by a crane; workers later finish the structure and connect plumbing and wiring. Entire developments can be built at a fraction of the time and cost of conventional construction.

Through *time-shares* purchasers share ownership of one vacation home. Each owner is entitled to use the property for a certain period of time each year, usually one week. In addition to the purchase price, each owner pays an annual maintenance fee. Due to high initial marketing costs and an uncertain resale market, time-share resale prices can be significantly lower than their original purchase prices.

FACTORS INFLUENCING HOME OWNERSHIP

After 35 years of steady advances the percentage of housing units occupied by their owners fluctuated during the 1980s and 1990s. The high inflation of the 1970s caused housing prices to rise rapidly, but individual incomes failed to keep pace. As a result, the average home price in some markets is beyond the means of many single wage earners and even some two-income households.

In some areas, however, the recession of the early 1990s slowed the rapid price increases and appreciation of the 1980s, causing housing values to flatten or even decrease. The general economic climate and employment conditions in some of these markets, however, have inhibited the ability of many individuals to take advantage of the more affordable housing prices.

Housing affordability has become a major issue. Home ownership has declined most severely among the young and low to moderate income purchasers. First-time buyers, for example, often have difficulty saving the down payment and closing costs needed for a conventional loan. Real estate and related industry groups are working with Congress, state legislatures and local government bodies to develop solutions that will increase the availability of suitable and affordable housing for all segments of the population.

Certainly not all people should own homes. Home ownership involves substantial commitment and responsibility, and the flexibility of renting suits some individuals' needs. People whose work requires frequent moves or whose financial position is uncertain will particularly benefit from renting. Renting also provides more leisure time by freeing tenants from management and maintenance.

Those who choose the responsibilities of home ownership must evaluate many factors before they make a final decision to purchase a particular property.

Mortgage Terms

Mortgage terms and payment plans have been liberalized since the 1920s, helping many people buy homes. For instance, the amount of a conventional mortgage loan in relation to property value (the loan-to-value ratio) has increased from 40 percent in the 1920s to as much as 95 percent today thanks to private mortgage insurance. Low-down-payment mortgage loans also are available under programs sponsored by the Federal Housing Administration (FHA) and the Department of Veterans Affairs (commonly called *VA*, in deference to the original Veterans Administration).

An increasing number of creative mortgage loan programs are being offered by various government agencies and local lenders. Loan terms have increased from 15 to 30 years. Adjustable-rate loans, whose lower initial interest rate makes it possible for many buyers to qualify for a mortgage loan, are now common. Specific programs may offer lower closing costs or deferred interest or principal payments for purchasers in targeted neighborhoods or for first-time buyers. Many innovative loans are tailored to suit the young buyer, who may need a lower interest rate to qualify now but whose income is expected to increase in coming years.

Ownership Expenses and Ability to Pay

Home ownership involves many expenses, such as charges for utilities (electricity, natural gas, water), trash removal, sewer charges and maintenance and repairs. Owners must also pay for real estate taxes and property insurance, as well as the interest due on the mortgage loan.

To determine whether a prospective buyer can afford a certain purchase, lenders traditionally have used a "rule of thumb" formula. The monthly cost of buying and maintaining a home (mortgage payments plus tax and insurance impounds) should not exceed 28 percent of gross (pretax) monthly income. The payments on all debts should not exceed 36 percent of monthly income. These formulas may vary, however, depending on the type of loan program and the borrower's earnings, credit history, number of dependents and other factors.

Investment Considerations

Purchasing a home offers several financial advantages. First, if the property's value increases, a sale could bring in more money than the owner paid—a long-term gain. Second, as the total mortgage debt is reduced through monthly payments, the owner's interest—called **equity**—increases. A tenant accumulates nothing except a good credit rating by paying the rent on time; a homeowner's mortgage payments build equity and thus net worth. Equity builds even further when the property's value rises. Third are the tax deductions available to homeowners but not to renters.

Tax Benefits

To encourage home ownership the federal government allows homeowners certain income tax advantages. Homeowners may deduct from their income some or all of the mortgage interest paid as well as real estate taxes and certain other expenses. They may even defer or eliminate tax on the profit received from selling the home. In fact tax considerations are among the most important in any decision to purchase a home. (See Table 3.1.)

Tax deductions. Homeowners may deduct from their gross income

- mortgage interest payments on first and second homes that meet the definition of "qualified residence interest"
- real estate taxes (but *not* interest paid on overdue taxes)
- certain loan origination fees
- certain loan discount points and

Table 3.1 Homeowners' Tax Benefits	**Income Tax Deductions**	**Age 55 or Older**
	Loan interest on first and second homes, subject to limitation Loan origination fees Some loan discount points Loan prepayment penalties Real estate taxes	Once in lifetime, homeowner may exclude up to $125,000 of profit or gain on sale of home owned and used as principal residence for at least three years during last five years before sale
	Deferment of Tax on Profit	
	Tax on some or all of profit on sale postponed if another personal residence is purchased within 24 months before or after sale	

- loan prepayment penalties.

"Qualified residence interest" is limited as follows: All debt secured by a principal and second residence and incurred to acquire, construct or substantially improve those residences—called *acquisition indebtedness*—must equal no more than $1 million. Home equity loans—loans secured by the property and in amounts not exceeding the owner's equity in the property—may not be more than $100,000.

Capital gain. **Capital gain** is the *profit* realized from the sale or exchange of an asset, including real property. To stimulate investment, Congress at various times has allowed part of a taxpayer's capital gain to be free from income tax.

Deferment of tax on capital gain. All or part of the gain (profit) on the sale of a personal residence is exempt from immediate taxation if another residence is bought and occupied within 24 months (before or after) the sale of the old residence.

If the new home's value is equal to or greater than that of the house sold, tax on the entire gain may be *deferred*. This means that the gain *will* become taxable when the property is sold in a taxable transaction, such as when another home is not purchased.

55 or older exclusion. Taxpayers aged 55 or older are entitled to a one-time exclusion from taxation of up to $125,000 of the gain from the sale or exchange of property used as the taxpayer's principal residence for at least three of the last five years preceding the sale or exchange.

Each homeowner may exclude gains from taxation under this provision *only once in a lifetime,* even if the total gain excluded is less than the $125,000 limit. When this exclusion is taken by a married couple selling a home, *both parties* have given up their once-in-a-lifetime exclusion. In the case of divorce or death and remarriage, the individual is not entitled to a second exclusion even if the new spouse has not claimed the exclusion.

The Internal Revenue Service, a certified public accountant or some other tax specialist should be consulted for further information on these and other income tax issues. IRS regulations are subject to frequent revision and official interpretation. A real estate licensee should not attempt to give tax or legal advice to clients or customers.

HOMEOWNER'S INSURANCE

Most homeowners see the wisdom in protecting an investment as sizable as their home by insuring it. Lenders, to lessen their own risk of loss when the debt is secured by the property, usually require homeowners to have such insurance. Owners could purchase individual policies to insure them against destruction of the property by fire or windstorm, injury to others on the premises and theft of personal property owned by the homeowner or family members. Most, however, choose to buy a packaged **homeowner's insurance policy** to cover all these risks.

These policies also insure the homeowner against liability for injury and personal property damage suffered by guests or resident employees. Such **liability coverage** protects an owner whose acts or negligence cause injury to another. It covers the voluntary medical payments and funeral expenses of guests or resident employees who have accidents on the insured property, but it does not include benefits due under any workers' compensation or occupational disease law.

Characteristics of Homeowners' Packages

Although coverage provided may vary, all homeowners' policies have three common characteristics.

First, they all have *fixed ratios of coverage.* That is, each type of coverage, such as on household contents and other items, must be a fixed percentage of the amount of insurance on the building itself. The amount of contents coverage may be increased but it cannot be reduced below the standard percentage.

Second, homeowners' policies have an *indivisible premium,* which means the homeowner must pay for the whole package and may not choose to exclude certain perils from coverage.

Finally, *first- and third-party insurance*—the liability coverage discussed earlier—covers not only actual damage or loss but also the homeowner's legal liability for losses, damages or injuries.

There are four major forms of homeowners' policies. The basic form provides property coverage against

- fire or lightning
- glass breakage
- windstorm or hail
- explosion
- riot or civil commotion
- damage by aircraft
- damage from vehicles
- damage from smoke

- vandalism and malicious mischief
- theft and
- loss of property removed from the premises when endangered by fire or other perils.

A broad-form policy also covers

- falling objects
- weight of ice, snow or sleet
- collapse of the building or any part of it
- bursting, cracking, burning or bulging of a steam or hot water heating system or of appliances used to heat water
- accidental discharge, leakage or overflow of water or steam from within a plumbing, heating or air-conditioning system
- freezing of plumbing, heating and air-conditioning systems and domestic appliances and
- injury to electrical appliances, devices, fixtures and wiring from short circuits or other accidentally generated currents.

Further coverage is available from policies that cover almost all possible perils.

Other policies include a broad-form policy designed specifically for apartment renters and a broad-form policy for condominium owners. Apartment and condominium policies generally provide fire and windstorm, theft and public liability coverage for injuries or losses sustained within the unit. However, they do not usually cover losses or damages to the structure. The structure is insured by either the landlord or the condominium owners' association (except, in condominium ownership, for additions or alterations made by the unit owner and not covered by the association's master policy).

Claims

Most homeowners' insurance policies contain a **coinsurance clause.** This provision usually requires the owner to maintain insurance equal to at least 80 percent of the **replacement cost** of the dwelling (not including the price of the land). An owner who has this type of a policy may make a claim for the full cost of the repair or replacement of the damaged property without deduction for depreciation.

For example, a home that has a replacement cost of $100,000 is damaged by fire, and the estimated cost to repair the damage is $71,000. By carrying at least $80,000 insurance on the dwelling (80% of $100,000) the homeowner can file a claim for the full $71,000.

If the homeowner carries less than 80 percent of the full replacement cost, however, the claim will be handled in one of two ways. The loss will be settled either for the *actual cash value* (replacement cost less depreciation) or prorated by dividing the percentage of replacement cost actually covered by the policy by the minimum coverage requirement (usually 80 percent). For example, if a building is insured for only 60 percent of its value, the policy will pay only 75 percent of any claim filed (60% ÷ 80% = 75%). Therefore, the insurance company will pay only $53,250 of the $71,000 loss (75% of $71,000).

In any event, the total settlement cannot exceed the face value of the policy. Because of coinsurance clauses, homeowners should periodically review all policies to be certain that the coverage equals at least 80 percent of the current replacement cost of their homes.

Most policies also have a **subrogation clause** that applies when the insured collects for damage from the insurance company. It provides that any rights the insured may have to sue the person who caused the damage will be assigned to the insurance company. The insurer may pursue legal action to collect the amount paid out from the party at fault. The clause prevents the insured from collecting twice for the same damage.

FEDERAL FLOOD INSURANCE PROGRAM

The National Flood Insurance Act of 1968 was enacted by Congress to help owners of property in flood-prone areas by subsidizing flood insurance and by taking land use and control measures to improve future management for flood-plain areas. The Department of Housing and Urban Development (HUD) administers the flood program. The Army Corps of Engineers has prepared maps that identify specific flood-prone areas throughout the country. Owners in flood-prone areas must obtain flood insurance to finance property by federal or federally related mortgages, loans, grants or guarantees. If they do not obtain the insurance (either because they don't want it or because they don't qualify as a result of their communities' not having properly entered the program) they are not eligible for this financial assistance.

In designated areas, flood insurance coverage is required on all types of buildings—residential, commercial, industrial and agricultural—for either the value of the property or the amount of the mortgage loan, subject to the maximum limits available. Policies are written annually and can be purchased from any licensed property insurance broker, the National Flood Insurance Program or the designated servicing companies in each state.

•   •   •   •   •   •   •

KEY TERMS

capital gain
coinsurance clause
equity
homeowner's insurance policy

liability coverage
replacement cost
subrogation clause

SUMMARY

In addition to single-family homes, current trends in home ownership include apartment complexes, condominiums, cooperatives, planned unit developments, retirement communities, high-rise developments, converted-use properties, modular homes, mobile homes and time-shares.

Prospective buyers should be aware of both the advantages and disadvantages of home ownership. While a homeowner gains financial security and pride of ownership, the costs of ownership—both the initial price and the continuing expenses—must be considered.

One of the income tax benefits available to homeowners is the ability to deduct mortgage interest payments (with certain limitations) and property taxes from their federal income tax returns. Income tax on the gain from a sale may be deferred if the homeowner purchases and occupies another residence within 24 months before or after the sale. Homeowners aged 55 or older are given additional benefits.

To protect their investment in real estate most homeowners purchase insurance. A standard homeowner's insurance policy covers fire, theft and liability and can be extended to cover many types of less common risks. Another type of insurance, which covers personal property only, is available to people who live in apartments and condominiums.

Many homeowners' policies contain a coinsurance clause that requires the policyholder to maintain insurance in an amount equal to 80 percent of the replacement cost of the home. If this percentage is not met, the policyholder may not be reimbursed for the full repair costs if a loss occurs.

A subrogation clause enables an insurer to sue the party responsible for damage to the insured's property.

In addition to homeowner's insurance, the federal government makes flood insurance mandatory for people living in flood-prone areas who wish to obtain federally regulated or federally insured mortgage loans.

Questions

1. The real cost of owning a home includes certain costs or expenses that many people tend to overlook. Which one of the following is *not* a cost or expense of owning a home?

   a. Interest paid on borrowed capital
   b. Homeowner's insurance
   c. Maintenance and repairs
   d. Taxes on personal property

2. When a person buys a house using a mortgage loan, the difference between the amount owed on the property and its market value represents the homeowner's

   a. tax basis.   c. replacement cost.
   b. equity.   d. capital gain.

3. A building that is remodeled into residential units and is no longer used for the purpose for which it was originally built is a(n)

   a. converted-use property.
   b. example of urban homesteading.
   c. planned unit development.
   d. modular home.

4. In a homeowner's insurance policy *coinsurance* refers to

   a. the specific form of policy purchased by the owner.
   b. the stipulation that the homeowner must purchase insurance coverage equal to at least 80 percent of the replacement cost of the structure to collect the full insured amount in the event of a loss.
   c. the stipulation that the homeowner must purchase fire insurance coverage equal to at least 70 percent of the replacement cost of the structure to collect the full insured amount in the event of a loss.
   d. Combined coverage for fire and flood damage.

5. Federal income tax laws do not allow a homeowner to deduct which of the following expenses from gross income?

   a. Mortgage origination fees
   b. Real estate taxes
   c. Routine home improvements
   d. Mortgage prepayment penalties

6. A town house may be associated with which of the following types of housing?

   a. High-rise development
   b. Condominium
   c. Mobile home
   d. Ranch house

7. V, age 38, sells his home of eight years and realizes a $25,000 gain from the sale. Income tax on the profit from the sale of his home may be

   a. taxed at a lower rate because of his age.
   b. deducted from the purchase of another home.
   c. reduced by the amount of mortgage interest paid over the life of the ownership.
   d. eliminated by claiming the once-in-a-lifetime exclusion.

8. F, age 62, sells the home she has occupied for the last 15 years and realizes a $52,000 gain from the sale. Income tax on the profit from the sale of her home may be

   a. taxed at a lower rate because of her age.
   b. deducted from the purchase of another home.
   c. reduced by the amount of mortgage interest paid over the life of the ownership.
   d. eliminated by claiming the once-in-a-lifetime exclusion.

9. A typical homeowner's insurance policy covers all of the following *except*
   a. the cost of medical expenses for a person injured in the policyholder's home.
   b. theft.
   c. vandalism.
   d. flood damage.

10. The profit a homeowner receives from the sale of his or her residence
    a. is the homeowner's tax basis.
    b. is deferred from immediate taxation if a replacement residence is purchased within certain time limits.
    c. is always considered "taxable gain" for tax purposes.
    d. can be excluded from taxation for a couple if one spouse has not previously taken the over-55 exclusion.

11. A homeowner sold his house for $127,500. Selling expenses were $750; the house had been purchased new three years earlier for $75,000. What is the homeowner's gain on this transaction?
    a. $53,250
    b. $52,500
    c. $51,750
    d. $75,000

12. In question 11, how much of the gain will be subject to income tax?
    a. $51,750
    b. $20,700
    c. $21,300
    d. $21,000

4

Real Estate Brokerage and Agency

INTRODUCTION TO BROKERAGE AND AGENCY

The nature of real estate brokerage services, particularly those provided in residential sales transactions, has changed significantly in recent years. Through the 1950s real estate brokerage firms were primarily one-office, minimally staffed, family-run operations. The broker listed an owner's property for sale and found a buyer without assistance from other companies. Then the sale was negotiated and closed. It was relatively clear that the broker represented the seller's interests.

In the 1960s, however, the way buyers and sellers are brought together in a transaction began to change. Brokers started to share information about properties they had listed, resulting in two brokers cooperating with one another to sell a property. The brokers formalized this exchange of information by creating multiple-listing services (MLSs). The MLS expedited sales by increasing exposure to potential buyers and thus became a widely used industry service.

Unfortunately, confusion arises about who the broker represents in these cooperative transactions. With two different brokers involved in a sale, the natural assumption was that there is a clear division of responsibility. The broker who has the property listed for sale represents the seller; and the broker who finds the buyer represents that party. However, this was *not* the case. In these shared transactions, both brokers represented the seller.

Such misunderstandings ultimately led buyers to question exactly how their interests were being protected. This is part of a growing trend in which all consumers are demanding that their rights be protected so that they can make informed decisions. In many states lawmakers have departed from the common law doctrine of caveat emptor—let the buyer beware—toward greater consumer protection. Buyers are seeking not only accurate, factual information but also advice, particularly as real estate transactions have become much more complex. They view the real estate licensee as the expert on whom they can rely to guide them. Today, buyers are seeking representation.

The basic framework of the law that governs the legal responsibilities of the broker to the people who he or she represents—known as the *law of agency*—has not changed. But its *application* has. Brokers are reevaluating their services. They are determining whether they are going to represent the seller, the buyer

**Figure 4.1
Definitions in
Agency Law**

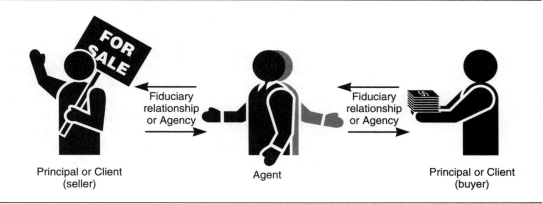

Principal or Client   Agent   Principal or Client
(seller)   (buyer)

or both, if that is permitted by state law, in the sale or rental of a property. They must also decide how they will cooperate with other brokers on a transaction, depending on which party each broker is representing. In short, the brokerage business is undergoing many changes as brokers focus on ways to enhance their services to buyers and sellers.

**Definitions in
Agency Law**

Real estate brokers and salespersons are commonly referred to as "agents." Legally, however, the term refers to strictly defined legal relationships. In the case of real estate, it is a relationship with buyers and sellers. In the **law of agency**, the body of law that governs these relationships, the following terms have specific definitions. (See Figure 4.1.)

- **Agent**—the individual who is authorized to and consents to represent the interests of another person. In the real estate business the broker of the firm is the agent.

- **Principal**—the individual who hires and delegates to the agent the responsibility of representing his or her interests. In the real estate business this is the buyer or seller.

- **Agency**—the fiduciary relationship between the principal and the agent

- **Fiduciary**—the relationship in which the agent is placed in the position of trust and confidence to the principal

- **Client**—the principal

- **Customer**—the third party for whom some level of service is provided

The principal-agent relationship evolved from the master-servant relationship under English common law. The servant owed absolute loyalty to the master. This loyalty superseded the servant's personal interest as well as loyalty the servant might owe to others. The agent owes the principal similar loyalty. As masters used the services of servants to accomplish what they could not or did not want to do for themselves, the principal uses the services of the agent. The agent is regarded as an expert on whom the principal can rely for specialized professional advice.

There is a distinction between the level of the services that the agent provides to a client and a customer. The *client* is the principal to whom the agent gives *advice* and *counsel.* The agent is entrusted with certain *confidential information* and has *fiduciary responsibilities* (discussed in greater detail later) to the principal. In contrast, the *customer* is entitled to factual information and fair and honest dealings as a consumer but does not receive advice and counsel or confidential information about the principal. The agent works *for* the principal and *with* the customer. Essentially, the agent is an advocate for the principal.

The relationship between the principal and agent must be *consensual*: the principal *delegates* authority; the agent *consents* to act. The parties must mutually agree to form the relationship. An agent may be authorized by the principal to use the assistance of others. These persons are **subagents** of the principal.

Real Estate Brokerage

Before discussing the intricacies of agency, it is important to look more closely at the people who provide the client and customer services in a real estate agency relationship.

As mentioned in Chapter 1, **brokerage** is the business of bringing parties together for the purpose of selling, renting or exchanging property. Buyers and sellers in many fields of business employ brokers to facilitate complex business transactions. In real estate a *broker* is defined as a person who is licensed to buy, sell, exchange or lease real property for others and to charge a fee for those services. The broker is employed by an agreement between the parties that creates the agency relationship and defines the scope of the broker's authority to act on behalf of the employer. A brokerage business may be established as a sole proprietorship, a corporation or a partnership with another broker. The real estate *salesperson* works on behalf of and is licensed to represent the broker.

The *principal* who employs the broker may be a seller, a prospective buyer, an owner who wishes to lease property or a person seeking property to rent. The real estate broker acts as the *agent* of the principal. When the broker successfully performs the service for which he or she was employed, the principal usually compensates the broker with a commission or fee. Generally, that service is negotiating a transaction with a prospective purchaser, seller, lessor or lessee who is ready, willing and able to complete the contract.

Seller as Principal

If a seller contracts with a broker to market the seller's real estate, the broker becomes an *agent* of the seller; the seller is the *principal,* the broker's *client.* A buyer who contacts the broker to review properties listed with the broker's firm is the broker's *customer*, unless the buyer enters into an agreement for agency representation. Though obligated to deal fairly with all parties to a transaction and to comply with all aspects of the license law, the broker is strictly accountable *only to the principal*—in this case the seller. The customer (in this case the buyer) represents himself or herself.

The listing contract usually authorizes the broker to use licensees employed by the broker as well as the services of other, cooperating brokers in marketing the seller's real estate. Cooperating brokers assist the broker (agent) as *subagents.* The relationship of a salesperson or an associate broker to an employing broker is also an agency. These licensees are thus agents of the broker in addition to being subagents of the principal.

Buyer as Principal

Whereas a real estate broker has commonly been hired by a seller to locate a buyer for the seller's real property, the practice of buyers hiring brokers to find real estate with certain characteristics or usable for specific purposes is becoming more common. In this situation the broker and the buyer usually draw up an agreement that details the nature of the property desired, the amount of the broker's compensation and how it is to be paid. The buyer becomes the *principal,* the broker's client. In this case the broker, as *agent,* is strictly accountable to the buyer. The seller is the customer.

Owner as Principal

An owner may employ a broker to market, lease, maintain and/or manage the owner's property. This arrangement is known as *property management.* The broker becomes the agent of the property owner through a property management agreement. The broker has a fiduciary responsibility to the client-owner to provide services within the scope of that agreement. The owner may employ a broker only to market the property to prospective tenants. In this case, the broker's responsibility is to find suitable tenants for the owner's property. Property management is discussed further in Chapter 17.

LAW OF AGENCY

The *law of agency* defines the rights and duties of the principal and the agent. It applies to a variety of business transactions. In real estate transactions contract law and the real estate licensing laws, in addition to the law of agency, interpret the relationship between licensees and their clients.

Types of Agency

The authorized activity of an agent will be as simple or as complex as the principal dictates. An agent may be classified as a general agent or a special agent, based on the authority delegated.

A **general agent** is empowered to represent the principal in a *broad range of matters* and may bind the principal to any contracts within the scope of the agent's authority. This type of agency can be created by a general power of attorney, which makes the agent an *attorney-in-fact.* The broker does *not* typically have this scope of authority as an agent in real estate transactions.

A **special agent** is authorized to represent the principal in *one specific act or business transaction, under detailed instructions.* A real estate broker is usually a special agent. If hired by a seller, the broker's duty is limited to finding a ready, willing and able buyer for the property. As a special agent, the broker is *not authorized* to bind the principal to any contract. The principals must bind themselves to the terms of contracts. A *special power of attorney* is another means of authorizing an agent to carry out only a specified act or acts.

Creation of Agency

Agents are employed for their expertise. However, providing services does not in itself create an agency relationship. As previously mentioned, no agency exists without *mutual consent* between the principal and the agent. The agent consents to undertake certain duties on behalf of the principal, subject to the principal's control. The principal authorizes the agent to perform these acts when dealing with others.

Express agency. Principal and agent may make an **express agreement**, in which the parties state the contract's terms and express their intention either orally or in writing. An agency relationship between a seller and a broker is generally created by a written employment contract, commonly referred to as a **listing agreement**, which authorizes the broker to find a buyer or tenant for the owner's property. Although a written listing agreement is usually preferred, some states consider an oral agreement binding. An agency relationship between a buyer and a broker is created by a **buyer-agency agreement.** Similar to a listing agreement, it stipulates the activities and responsibilities the buyer expects from the broker in finding the appropriate property for purchase or rent.

Implied agency. A written contract is not necessary to create an agency relationship. An agency may be created by **implied agreement.** This occurs when the *actions* of the parties indicate that they have mutually consented to an agency. A person acts on behalf of another as agent; the other person, as principal, delegates the authority to act. The parties may not have consciously planned to create an agency relationship. Nonetheless, it can result *unintentionally, inadvertently* or *accidentally* by their actions.

Even though licensees may be required to disclose to the parties whom they represent, it is often difficult for customers to understand the complexities of the law of agency. Buyers can easily assume that when they contact a salesperson to show them property, the salesperson becomes "their agent." Though, under a listing contract, the salesperson *legally* represents the seller. An implied agency with the buyer can result if the words and conduct of the salesperson do not dispel this assumption. Otherwise one agency relationship is created in conflict with another. Dual representation, which will be discussed in greater detail later, may occur even though it was not intended.

Compensation. Because the source of compensation does not determine agency, the agent does not necessarily represent the person who pays the commission. In fact, agency can exist even if there is no fee involved (a gratuitous agency). Buyers and sellers can make any agreement they choose about compensating the broker, regardless of which one is the agent's principal. For example, the seller could agree to pay a commission to the broker who is the buyer's agent. The written agency agreement should state how the agent is being compensated.

Termination of Agency

An agency may be terminated at any time (except in the case of an agency coupled with an interest, discussed in the following paragraph), for any of the following reasons:

- Death or incapacity of either party (notice of death is not necessary)
- Destruction or condemnation of the property
- Expiration of the terms of the agency
- Mutual agreement by all parties to the contract
- Breach by one of the parties, such as abandonment by the agent or revocation by the principal (in which case the breaching party might be liable for damages)

- By operation of law, as in a bankruptcy of the principal (bankruptcy terminates the agency contract and title to the property transfers to a court-appointed receiver)

- Completion, performance or fulfillment of the purpose for which the agency was created

An **agency coupled with an interest** is an agency relationship in which the agent is given an interest in the subject of the agency, such as the property being sold. Such an agency *cannot be revoked by the principal or be terminated upon the principal's death.* For example, a broker might agree to supply the financing for a condominium development in exchange for the exclusive right to sell the completed units. Since this is an agency coupled with an interest, the developer would not be able to revoke the listing agreement after the broker provided the financing.

Fiduciary Responsibilities

The employment agreement usually authorizes the broker to act for the principal. The law of agency requires the broker to make a reasonable effort to carry out the assumed agency duties successfully. It does not guarantee that the broker will be *able* to perform. The agent's fiduciary relationship of trust and confidence with the principal does, however, mandate that the broker owes the principal certain specific duties. *These duties are not simply moral or ethical; they are the law—the law of agency.* The agent owes the principal the duties of *care, obedience, accounting, loyalty* and *disclosure,* easily remembered by the acronym COALD (see Figure 4.2). Figure 4.3 shows the differences between client and customer services provided to a buyer.

Care. The broker must exercise a reasonable degree of care while transacting business entrusted to the broker by the principal. The principal expects the agent's skill and expertise in real estate matters to be superior to that of the average person. The most fundamental way in which the broker exercises care is to use that skill and knowledge in the principal's behalf. The broker should know all facts that are pertinent to the principal's affairs, such as the physical characteristics of the property being transferred and the type of financing being used.

If the broker represents the seller, care and skill include helping the seller arrive at an appropriate and realistic listing price, discovering facts that affect the seller and disclosing them and properly presenting the contracts that the seller signs. It also means making reasonable efforts to market the property such as advertising and holding open houses, and helping the seller evaluate the terms and conditions of offers to purchase.

A broker who represents the buyer will be expected to help the buyer locate suitable property and evaluate property values, neighborhood and property conditions, financing alternatives and offers and counteroffers with the buyer's interest in mind.

A broker who does not make a reasonable effort to properly represent the interests of the principal could possibly be found negligent. The broker is liable to the principal for any loss resulting from the broker's negligence or carelessness.

Obedience. The fiduciary relationship obligates the broker to act in good faith at all times, obeying the principal's instructions in accordance with the contract.

Figure 4.2
Agent's
Responsibilities

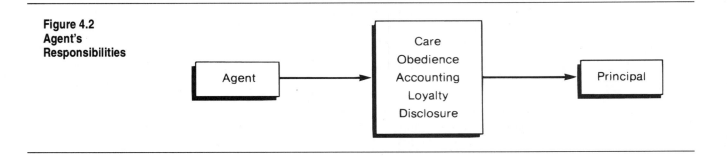

That obedience is not absolute, however. The broker *may not* obey any instructions that are unlawful or unethical. For example, the broker may not follow instructions to make the property unavailable to members of a minority group or to conceal a defect in the property. Because illegal acts do not serve the principal's best interests, obeying such instructions violates the broker's duty of loyalty. On the other hand, a broker who exceeds the authority assigned in the contract will be liable for any losses that the principal suffers as a result.

Accounting. The broker must be able to report the status of all funds received from or on behalf of the principal. Most state real estate license laws require brokers to give accurate copies of all documents to all parties affected by them and to keep copies on file for a specified period of time. Generally the license laws also require the broker to deposit immediately, or within 24 to 48 hours, all funds entrusted to the broker in a special trust, or escrow, account. Commingling such monies with the broker's personal or general business funds is illegal.

Loyalty. The broker owes the principal the utmost loyalty. That means placing the principal's interests above those of all others, including self-interest. *Confidentiality* about the *personal* affairs of the principal is a key element of loyalty and the relationship is similar to that between a client and an attorney. An agent may not, for example, disclose the principal's financial condition. When the principal is the seller, the broker may not reveal that the principal will accept less than the listing price or is anxious to sell unless authorized to make the later disclosure. If the principal is the buyer, the broker may not disclose that the principal will pay more than the offered price or any similar facts that might harm the principal's bargaining position. The broker, however, must disclose material facts about the *property*.

Because the agent may not act out of self-interest, the agent must conduct the negotiation of a sales contract without regard to the amount the broker will earn in commission. All states forbid brokers or salespeople to buy property listed with them for their own accounts or for accounts in which they have a personal interest without first disclosing that interest and receiving the principal's consent. Likewise, by law neither brokers nor salespeople may sell property in which they have a personal interest without informing the purchaser of that interest.

Disclosure. It is the broker's duty to keep the principal informed of all facts or information that could affect the transaction. Duty of disclosure includes relevant information or *material facts* that the agent knows or *should have known*. The agent is obligated to discover facts that a reasonable person would feel are important in choosing a course of action, regardless of whether they are

Figure 4.3
Customer-Level
vs. Client-Level
Service

THE SELLING BROKER

Customer-Level Service as Subagent	Client-Level Service as Buyer's Broker

RESPONSIBILITIES

Be honest with buyer but owe greater responsibility to seller, including duty of skill and care to promote and safeguard seller's best interest.

Be honest to seller, but owe greater responsibility to buyer, including duty of skill and care to promote and safeguard buyer's best interest.

EARNEST MONEY DEPOSIT

Collect amount sufficient to protect seller.

Suggest minimum amount, perhaps a note; put money in interest-bearing account; suggest that forfeiture of earnest money be sole remedy if buyer defaults.

SELLER FINANCING

Can discuss, but should not encourage, financing terms and contract provisions unfavorable to seller, such as (1) no due-on-sale clause, (2) no deficiency judgment (nonrecourse), (3) unsecured note. If a corporate buyer, suggest seller require personal guaranty.

Suggest terms in best interest of buyer, such as low down payment, deferred interest, long maturity dates, no due-on-sale clause, long grace period, nonrecourse.

DISCLOSURE

Disclose to seller pertinent facts (which might not be able to disclose if a buyer's broker) such as (1) buyer's willingness to offer higher price and/or better terms, (2) buyer's urgency to buy, (3) buyer's plans to resell at profit or resubdivide to increase value, (4) buyer is sister of broker.

Disclose to buyer pertinent facts (which might not be able to disclose if subagent of seller) such as (1) seller near bankruptcy or foreclosure, (2) property overpriced, (3) other properties available at a better buy, (4) negative features, such as poor traffic flow, (5) construction of chemical plant down street that may affect property value.

NONDISCLOSURE

Refrain from disclosing to buyer facts that may compromise seller's position (seller's pending divorce) unless under a legal duty to disclose (zoning violation).

Refrain from disclosing to seller such facts regarding buyer's position as fact buyer has options on three adjoining parcels. No duty to disclose name of buyer or that broker is loaning buyer money to make down payment.

PROPERTY CONDITION

Suggest use of "as is" clause, if appropriate to protect seller (still must specify hidden defects).

Require that seller sign property condition statement and confirm representations of condition; require soil, termite inspections, if appropriate; look for negative features and use them to negotiate better price and terms.

DOCUMENTS

Give buyer a copy of important documents, such as mortgage to be assumed, declaration of restrictions, title report, condominium bylaws and house rules.

Research and explain significant portions of important documents affecting transaction, such as prepayment penalties, subordination, right of first refusal; refer buyer to expert advisers when appropriate.

NEGOTIATION

Use negotiating strategy and bargaining talents in seller's best interest.

Use negotiating strategy and bargaining talents in buyer's best interest.

Source: *Agency Relationships in Real Estate,* by John Reilly. © 1987 Dearborn Financial Publishing.

Figure 4.3
(continued)

Customer-Level Service as Subagent	Client-Level Service as Buyer's Broker

SHOWING

Show buyer properties in which broker's commission is protected, such as in-house or MLS-listed properties. Pick best times to show property. Emphasize attributes and amenities.

Search for best properties for buyer to inspect, widening marketplace to "For Sale by Owner,," lender owned (REO), probate sales and unlisted properties. View property at different times to find negative features, such as evening noise, afternoon sun, traffic congestion.

PROPERTY GOALS

Find buyer the type of property buyer seeks; more concerned with *sale* of seller's property that fits buyer's stated objectives.

Counsel buyer as to developing accurate objectives; may find that buyer who wants apartment building might be better with duplex at half the price or that buyer looking for vacant lot would benefit more from an investment in improved property.

OFFERS

Can help prepare and transmit buyer's offer on behalf of seller; must reveal to seller that buyer has prepared two offers, in case first offer not accepted.

Help buyer prepare strongest offer; can suggest buyer prepare two offers and have broker submit lower offer first without revealing fact of second offer.

POSSESSION DATES

Consider what is best date for seller in terms of moving out, notice to existing tenants, impact on insurance and risk of loss provision.

Consider what is best for buyer in terms of moving in, storage, favorable risk of loss provision if fire destroys property prior to closing.

DEFAULT

Discuss remedies upon default by either party. Point out to seller any attempt by buyer to limit liability (nonrecourse, deposit money is sole liquidated damages).

Suggest seller's remedy be limited to retention of deposit money; consider having seller pay buyer's expenses and cancellation charges if seller defaults.

BIDDING

Can bid for own account against buyer/customer but should disclose to buyer and seller.

Cannot bid for own account against buyer *client.*

EFFICIENCY

Don't expend much time and effort, as in an open listing, because in competition with the listing broker, seller and other brokers to sell buyer a property before someone else does.

Work at an "exclusive listing" efficiency, realizing that broker's role is to assist buyer in locating and acquiring best property, not to sell the buyer any *one* property.

APPRAISAL

Unless asked, no duty to disclose low appraisal or fact broker sold similar unit yesterday for $10,000 less.

Suggest independent appraisal be used to negotiate lower price offer; review seller's comparables from buyer's perspective.

BONUS

Cannot agree to accept bonus from buyer for obtaining reduction in listed price.

Can receive incentive fee for negotiating reduction in listed price.

TERMINATION

Easier to terminate a subagency relationship (as when broker decides to bid on property).

Legal and ethical implications of agency relationship and certain duties may continue even after clearly documented termination.

favorable or unfavorable to the principal's position. The broker may be held liable for damages for failure to disclose such information. For example, an agent for the seller has a duty to disclose

- all offers;
- the identity of the prospective purchasers, including the agent's relationship, if any, to them (such as a relative or the broker's being a participating purchaser);
- the ability of the purchaser to complete the sale or offer a higher price;
- any interest the broker has in the buyer (such as the buyer's asking the broker to manage the property after it is purchased); or
- the buyer's intention to resell the property for a profit.

An agent for the buyer must disclose deficiencies of a property, as well as sales contract provisions and financing that do not suit the buyer's needs. The broker would suggest the lowest price that the buyer should pay based on comparable values, regardless of the listing price. The agent would disclose information about how long a property has been listed or why the seller is selling that would affect the buyer's ability to negotiate the lowest purchase price. This information, if the agent is representing the seller, violates the fiduciary to the seller.

AGENCY RELATIONSHIPS

A variety of agency relationships may be created. The distinction among them is not always clear. When consumers feel their individual interests have not been adequately protected, licensees may face legal and ethical problems. The broker must decide the agency policy and procedures for the firm, who is going to be represented, disclose the agency alternatives to each party, then act according to the agency relationship defined.

Single Agency

In single agency the broker represents *either* the buyer *or* the seller in a transaction. The agent represents *one* client; any third party is a customer. In the past, particularly in residential sales, brokers almost always represented the seller. The broker served the seller as the client. In this case, prospective buyers do not have a client-based relationship with anyone. Rather, they are the customers (the third parties), to whom licensees are responsible only within the scope of their legal and ethical responsibilities to consumers. Consequently buyers must take responsibility for protecting their own interests in a transaction—in essence, they are not being represented by anyone other than themselves. Brokers may choose to represent buyers as their clients. In single agency, in this case, sellers are the customers. Because of the growing awareness that buyers, also, deserve the degree of representation available in a client-based relationship, more buyers are seeking brokers to represent them.

A single agency broker may represent both sellers and buyers. However, in single agency, the broker does not represent both in the same transaction. This limitation avoids conflicts and results in client-based service and loyalty to only one client. The broker must establish policies for the firm that define for whom the client-services will be performed.

Subagency. A subagency is created when one broker, usually the seller's agent, appoints other brokers (with the authority of the seller) to assist in performing client-based functions on the principal's behalf. These *cooperating brokers* have the same fiduciary obligations to the seller as the *listing broker,* assisting in producing a ready, willing and able buyer for the property. This arrangement is typically created through a multiple-listing service. The listing broker now becomes liable for the conduct of all of the cooperating brokers and their salespeople in protecting the fiduciary responsibility to the seller. (See Figure 4.4.)

As mentioned earlier, the participation of more than one broker leads many buyers to assume erroneously that a *selling broker* (who has not listed the property) is representing them in a client-based relationship. To receive client-based services, however, the buyers would have to *engage the services* of this broker as their representative. The resulting relationship would not be subagency but *single* agency: the selling broker would represent the buyer, and the listing broker would represent the seller.

Dual Agency

In **dual agency** the broker represents two principals in the same transaction. It requires the agent to be equally loyal to two separate principals at the same time. Because agency originates with the broker, dual agency arises when the broker is the agent of the buyer *and* either the agent or subagent of the seller. The salespeople, as agents of the broker, have fiduciary responsibilities to the same principals as well. The challenge is to fulfill the fiduciary obligations to one principal without compromising the other principal, especially when their interests are not only separate but may also be opposite. Although serving two principals at the same time may appear to be impossible under the strictest terms in the law of agency, there are lawful ways for the broker to accomplish this task.

Disclosed Dual Agency. Real estate licensing laws in some states permit dual agency with very specific conditions. These laws require that buyers and seller be *informed* and *consent* to the broker representing both of them in the same transaction. Although the possibility of conflict of interest still exists, the disclosure is intended to minimize the risk for the broker and ensure that both principals are aware of its effect on their respective interests. The disclosure alerts the principals that they may have to assume greater responsibility for protecting their interests than they otherwise would if they had independent representation. The broker must reconcile how, as agent, he or she will discharge the fiduciary duties to both principals, particularly providing loyalty and protecting confidential information. Armed with sufficient information, it is assumed the principals can make informed decisions before agreeing to the dual representation.

There is considerable debate about whether brokers can properly represent both buyers and sellers in the same transaction, even though the dual agency is disclosed. Recently, several states have passed laws in an attempt to avoid dual agency, particularly when the buyer-principal wants to purchase a property listed by the same broker-agent (known as an in-house sale). Under these laws the broker can designate certain licensees within the firm who are the *legal representatives* of a principal. The broker would not be considered a dual agent as long as the designated legal representative for each principal in the transaction is not the same salesperson. In effect, these laws create a split-agency, which is quite a departure from the common doctrines of the law of agency. It is ex-

**Figure 4.4
Subagency
Relationship
Chart**

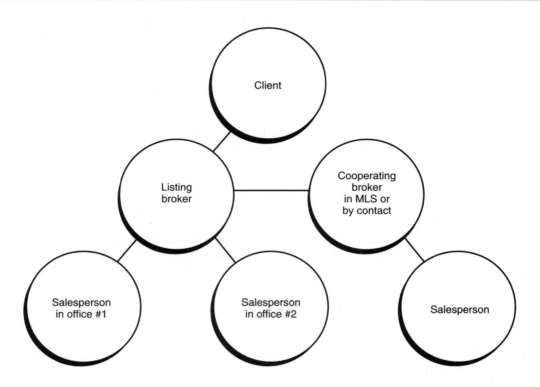

Agency relationship = Any one step between circles
Subagency relationship = More than one step

pected that there will be a number of other legislative developments as the
states wrestle with the issue of dual agency.

Undisclosed dual agency. A broker may not intend to create a dual agency. However, by a salesperson's words and actions it may occur *unintentionally* or *inadvertently*. Sometimes the cause is carelessness. Other times the salesperson does
not fully understand his or her fiduciary responsibilities. Some salespeople lose
sight of other responsibilities when they focus intensely on bringing buyers and
sellers together. For example, a salesperson representing the seller might tell a
buyer that the seller will accept less than the listing price. Or the salesperson
might promise to persuade the seller to accept an offer that is in the buyer's interest. Giving the buyer any specific advice on how much to offer can lead the
buyer to believe that the salesperson is an advocate for the buyer. These actions
create an *implied* agency with the buyer and violate the duties of loyalty and
confidentiality to the principal-seller. Because neither party has been informed
of that situation and been given the opportunity to seek separate representation,
the interests of both are jeopardized. This undisclosed dual agency is a violation
of licensing laws. It can result in the rescission of the sales contract, forfeiture
of commission or filing of a suit for damages.

**Disclosure of
Agency**

Requiring disclosure of agency relationships is an acknowledgment that all consumers deserve to be informed about how their interests are protected in real

estate transactions. In many states brokers are required to reveal for whom they provide client-based services. Understanding the scope of the service a party can expect from the broker allows customers to make an informed decision about whether to seek their own representation.

Many states have enacted mandatory agency disclosure laws. These laws stipulate when, how and to whom disclosures must be made. They may, for instance, dictate that a particular type of written form be used. The laws might state what information an agent must provide to gain informed consent where disclosed dual agency is permitted. The laws might even go so far as to require that all agency alternatives be explained, including the brokerage firm's policies regarding its services.

In fact, whether the law requires it or not, licensees should explain to both buyers and sellers what agency alternatives exist, how client and customer services differ and how these services impact the interests of each party. Once a client-based relationship is established, it is critical that the customer be informed about how this will impact the customer's interests. As mentioned, if the broker is representing two principals in the same transaction, the impact on both parties must be explained.

AGENT'S RESPONSIBILITIES TO THIRD PARTIES

Even though an agent's primary responsibility is to the principal, the agent also has duties to third parties. The duties to the third party or customer include:

- Reasonable care and skill in performance

- Honest and fair dealing

- Disclosure of all facts that the licensee knows or should reasonably be expected to know that materially affect the value or desirability of the property

As part of the recent trend toward public protection of purchasers, some states now have statutes requiring disclosure of property conditions to prospective buyers. Prepurchase structural inspections, termite infestation reports or other protective documentation may also be used.

Environmental Hazards

Disclosure of environmental health hazards, which can render properties unsalable, also may be required. Frequently the buyer or the buyer's mortgage lender will request inspections or tests to determine the presence or level of risk. Licensees are urged to obtain advice from state and local authorities responsible for environmental regulation whenever toxic waste dumping, contaminated soil or water, nearby chemical or nuclear facilities or health hazards such as radon, asbestos and lead paint may be present.

Opinion vs. Fact

Whatever the specific topic, brokers, salespeople and other staff members must be careful about the statements they make. They must be sure that the customer understands whether the statement is an opinion or a fact. Statements of opinion are only permissible as long as they are offered *as opinions* and without any intention to deceive.

Statements of fact, however, must be accurate. Exaggeration of a property's benefits is called **puffing.** While puffing is legal, licensees must ensure that none of their statements can be interpreted as *fraudulent.* **Fraud** is the *intentional* misrepresentation of a material fact in such a way as to harm or take advantage of another person. That includes not only making false statements about a property, but also intentionally concealing or failing to disclose important facts.

If a contract to purchase real estate is obtained as a result of fraudulent misstatements, the contract may be disaffirmed or renounced by the purchaser. In such a case the broker will not only lose a commission but also can be liable for damages if either party suffers loss because of a broker's misrepresentations. What if the broker's misstatements are based on the owner's own inaccurate statements to the broker? If the broker had no independent duty to investigate their accuracy, the broker may be entitled to a commission even if the buyer rescinds the sales contract.

Latent Defects

The seller has a duty to discover and disclose any latent defects that threaten structural soundness or personal safety. *A latent defect is a hidden structural defect that would not be discovered by ordinary inspection.* Examples are cases in which a house was built over a ditch that was covered with decaying timber, a buried drain tile caused water to accumulate or a driveway was built partly on adjoining property. Buyers have been able either to rescind the sales contract or to receive damages when such defects have not been revealed. The courts have also decided in favor of the buyer when the seller neglected to reveal violations of zoning or building codes.

Stigmatized Properties

In recent years questions have been raised about stigmatized properties, properties that society has branded as undesirable because of events that occurred there. Typically the stigma is a criminal event, such as a homicide, a shooting, illegal drug manufacturing, gang-related activity, or some other tragedy such as a suicide. Because of the potential liability to a broker for inadequately researching the facts concerning a property's condition, and the responsibility to disclose material facts, brokers should seek competent counsel when dealing with a stigmatized property. Some states have laws regarding the disclosure of information about stigmatized properties. In other states the broker's responsibility may be difficult to define because the issue is not a physical defect but the perception that a property is undesirable.

IN PRACTICE. . .

Because real estate licensees have, under the law, enormous exposure to liability, some brokers purchase what are known as errors and omissions insurance policies *for their firms. Similar to malpractice in the medical field, such policies generally cover liability for errors, mistakes and negligence in the usual listing and selling activities of a real estate office. Individual salespeople, likewise, should be insured. Licensing laws in several states require errors and omissions insurance for brokers and, in some cases, for the individual salespeople as well. However, no insurance will protect a licensee from litigation arising from criminal acts. Also, insurance companies normally exclude coverage for violation of civil rights laws.*

PRINCIPAL'S DUTIES

An agency agreement is like any other contract in that each party has duties and obligations to the other. An agency agreement is an *employment contract* that defines the compensation the agent will receive for professional services. In a listing agreement, for example, the owner is obligated to pay and an agent is entitled to receive a fee when the broker produces a "ready, willing and able buyer." In a buyer agency agreement, the agent is entitled to a commission when the buyer purchases a property as stipulated in the agreement. In a property management agreement, the owner agrees to compensate the broker for the services provided and any expenses incurred on behalf of the principal.

Beyond compensation, the principal has a duty not to hinder the agent's ability to fulfill the fiduciary obligations. That is, the principal must cooperate with the agent, dealing with the agent in good faith.

NATURE OF THE BROKERAGE BUSINESS

As discussed so far in this chapter, real estate brokerage is based on agency relationships that impose certain duties on both the agent and the principal. Because fiduciary obligations cannot be taken lightly, it is crucial that brokers exercise their right to reject any proposed agency relationship that in their judgment violates the high ethical standards of the office. It is, in fact, up to the broker to set effective policies for every aspect of the brokerage operation: hiring of employees and salespeople, determination of compensation, direction of staff and sales activities as well as procedures to follow in carrying out agency duties.

Real Estate License Laws

The state's real estate licensing laws and regulations serve as a framework for brokerage operations by defining the authority and responsibility of brokers and salespeople and by addressing many aspects of the day-to-day business operations. For example, the laws require that the firm have a definite, regular place of business. They also govern the placement of business signs and set requirements for establishing and maintaining branch offices. The laws dictate proper accounting and advertising procedures, correct handling of escrow accounts and the specific manner of execution and retention of documents involved in real estate transactions.

Broker-Salesperson Relationship

Although brokerage firms vary widely in size, few brokers today perform their agency duties without the assistance of salespeople. Consequently much of the business's success hinges on the broker-salesperson relationship.

A *real estate salesperson* is any person licensed to perform real estate activities on behalf of a licensed real estate broker. The broker is fully responsible for the actions performed in the course of the real estate business by all persons licensed under the broker. In turn, *all of a salesperson's activities must be performed in the name of the supervising broker.* The salesperson can carry out *only* those responsibilities assigned by the broker with whom he or she is licensed and can receive compensation *only* from that broker. As an agent of the broker the salesperson has no authority to make contracts with or receive compensation from any other party, whether the principal, another broker, the buyer or the seller.

Independent contractor versus employee. The agreement between a broker and a salesperson should be documented in a written and signed contract that defines the obligations and responsibilities of the relationship. State license laws generally treat the salesperson as the employee of the broker, regardless of whether the salesperson is considered, for tax purposes, to be an employee or an independent contractor. The broker is liable for the acts of the salesperson within the scope of the employment agreement. Whether a salesperson is treated as an employee or an independent contractor will affect the structure of the salesperson's work responsibilities and the broker's liability to pay and withhold taxes from the salesperson's earnings. (See Figure 4.5.)

A broker can exercise certain *controls* over salespeople who are employees. The broker may require an **employee** to follow rules governing such matters as working hours, office routine, attendance at sales meetings and dress codes. As an employer, a broker is required by the federal government to withhold social security tax and income tax from wages paid to employees. The broker is also required to pay unemployment compensation tax on wages paid to one or more employees, as defined by state and federal laws. In addition, employees might receive benefits such as health insurance, profit-sharing plans and workers' compensation.

A broker's relationship with an independent contractor is very different. As an **independent contractor,** a salesperson operates more independently than an employee. The broker may not control the salesperson's activities in the same way. The broker may control *what* the independent contractor will do but not *how* it will be done. The broker cannot *require* the independent contractor to keep specific office hours or attend sales meetings. Independent contractors are responsible for paying their own income and social security taxes and provide their own health insurance. Independent contractors receive nothing from brokers that could be construed as an employee benefit.

IN PRACTICE...	*The Internal Revenue Service often investigates the independent contractor/ employee situation in real estate offices. Under the qualified real estate agent category in the Internal Revenue Code, meeting three requirements can establish an independent contractor status: The individual must have a current real estate license; he or she must have a written contract with the broker that contains the following clause: "The salesperson will not be treated as an employee with respect to the services performed by such salesperson as a real estate agent for federal tax purposes"; and 90 percent or more of the individual's income as a licensee must be based on sales production and not on the number of hours worked. The broker should have a standardized agreement drawn and reviewed by an attorney to ensure its compliance with these federal dictates. The broker should also be aware that written agreements mean little to an IRS auditor if the actions of the parties contradict the document's provisions.*

Broker's Compensation

The broker's compensation is specified in the listing, buyer agency, management agreement or other contract with the principal. License laws may stipulate that a written agreement set forth the compensation that will be paid. Compensation can be in the form of a **commission** or brokerage fee computed as a percent-

**Figure 4.5
Independent
Contractor versus
Employee**

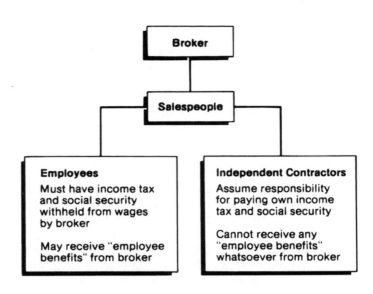

age of the total amount of money involved (sales price), a flat fee or an hourly rate. The amount of a broker's commission is *negotiable in every case.* Attempting, however subtly, to impose uniform commission rates is a clear violation of state and federal antitrust laws (discussed later in this chapter). A broker may, however, set the minimum rate that is acceptable for that broker's firm. The important point is for broker and client to agree on a rate before the agency relationship is established.

Commission is usually considered to be earned when the work for which the broker was hired has been accomplished. Most sales commissions are *payable* when the sale is consummated by *delivery of the seller's deed.* This provision is generally included in the listing agreement or in the real estate sales contract. When the sales or listing agreement specifies no time for the payment of the broker's commission, the commission generally is *earned* when a completed sales contract has been executed by a ready, willing and able buyer; it has been accepted and executed by the seller; and copies of the contract are in the possession of all parties.

To be entitled to a sales commission, an agent must be a licensed broker, be the procuring cause of the sale and have been employed by the principal under a valid contract. To be considered the **procuring cause** of sale, the broker must have taken action to start or to cause a chain of events that resulted in the sale. A broker who causes or completes such action without a contract or promise to be paid is a *volunteer* and may not legally claim compensation.

Once a seller accepts an offer from a ready, willing and able buyer, the seller is technically liable for the broker's commission. A **ready, willing and able buyer** is one who is *prepared to buy on the seller's terms and ready to take positive steps toward consummation of the transaction.* Courts may prevent the broker from receiving a commission if the broker knew the buyer was unable to perform. If the transaction is *not* consummated, the broker may still be entitled to a commission if the seller

- has a change of mind and refuses to sell
- has a spouse who refuses to sign the deed
- has a title with uncorrected defects
- commits fraud with respect to the transaction
- is unable to deliver possession within a reasonable time
- insists on terms not in the listing (for example, the right to restrict the use of the property) or
- has a mutual agreement with the buyer to cancel the transaction.

In other words, a *broker is generally due a commission if a sale is not consummated because of the principal's default.*

In many states it is illegal for a broker to pay a commission to anyone *other than* the salesperson licensed with the broker or to another broker. Fees, commission or other compensation cannot be paid to unlicensed persons for services requiring a real estate license. Other compensation includes gifts of certain items of personal property such as a new television, or other premiums, such as vacations. This is not to be confused with referral fees paid between brokers for "leads," which are legal as long as the individuals are licensed.

Salesperson's Compensation

The compensation of a salesperson is set by a mutual agreement between the broker and the salesperson. A broker may agree to pay a salary or a share or percentage of the commissions from transactions originated by a salesperson. In some cases a salesperson may draw from an account against earned shares of commissions. Some brokers require salespeople to pay all or part of the expenses of advertising listed properties.

Some firms have adopted a *100-percent commission plan.* Salespersons in these offices pay a monthly service charge to their broker to cover the costs of office space, telephones and supervision in return for 100 percent of the commissions from the sales they negotiate. The 100 percent commission salespersons pay all of their own expenses.

However the salesperson's compensation is structured, only the employing broker can pay it. The commission must first be paid to the employing broker for payment to the salesperson, unless otherwise permitted by license laws and agreed to by the employing broker.

MATH CONCEPT
Sharing Commissions

A commission might be shared by many people: the listing broker, the listing salesperson, the selling broker and the selling salesperson. Drawing a diagram can help you determine which person is entitled to receive what amount of the total commission.

Salesperson E, while working for broker H, took a listing on a $73,000 house at a 6% commission rate. Salesperson T, while working for broker M, found the buyer for the property. If the property sold for the listed price, the listing broker and the seller broker shared the commission equally, and the selling broker kept 45% of what he received, how much did salesperson T receive? (If the broker retained 45% of the total commission that he received, his salesperson would receive the balance: 100%–45% = 55%.)

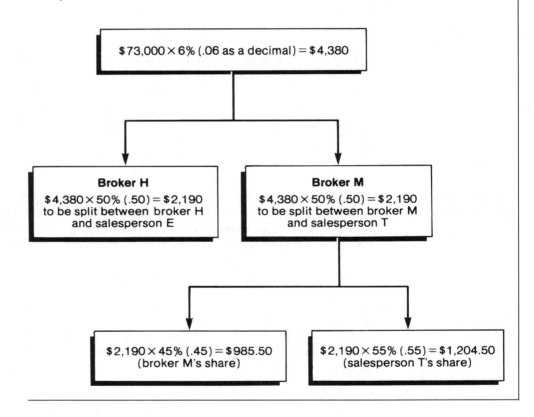

Legal Rights and Obligations

As each contract is prepared for signature during a real estate transaction, the broker should advise the parties of the desirability of securing legal counsel to protect their interests. As mentioned earlier, *only an attorney can offer legal advice.* Licensees who are not attorneys are prohibited from practicing law.

In recent years bar associations and real estate organizations have discussed how the legal rights and obligations of the parties in a real estate transaction can be protected. These matters have been brought before the supreme courts of some states. The courts uniformly recognize that a real estate broker must be able to secure some form of contract between a buyer and seller to document the transaction and provide for payment of the broker's commission. As a result, the bar associations and real estate commissions in many states have approved a special form of sales contract that must be used by real estate brokers. Brokers are prohibited from using any other form of contract. In some instances the license of a broker who does so can be revoked.

Antitrust Laws

The real estate industry is subject to federal and state **antitrust laws.** Generally, these laws prohibit monopolies and contracts, combinations and conspiracies that unreasonably restrain trade. The most common antitrust violations are price fixing, group boycotting and allocation of customers or markets.

Price-fixing is the practice of setting prices for products or services rather than letting competition in the open market establish those prices. In real estate it occurs when brokers agree to set sales commissions, fees or management rates, and it *is illegal.* Brokers must independently determine commission rates or fees only for their own firms. These decisions must be based on the broker's business judgment and revenue requirements without input from other brokers.

Multiple-listing organizations, Boards of REALTORS® and other professional organizations may not set fees or commission splits. Nor are they allowed to deny membership to brokers based on the fees the brokers charge. Either practice could lead the public to believe that the industry sanctions not only the unethical practice of withholding cooperation from certain brokers but also the illegal practice of restricting open-market competition.

The broker's challenge is to avoid any *impression* of attempts at price-fixing as well as the actual practice. Hinting in any way to prospective clients that there is a "going rate" of commission or fee implies that rates are in fact standardized. Brokers must clarify to clients that the rate stated is only what *their* firm charges. Likewise, discussions of rates among licensees from different firms could be construed as a price-fixing activity and should be avoided scrupulously.

Group boycotting occurs when two or more businesses conspire against other businesses or agree to withhold their patronage to reduce competition. It is also illegal under the antitrust laws.

Allocation of customers or markets involves an agreement between brokers to divide their markets and refrain from competing for each other's business. Allocations may be made on a geographic basis, with brokers agreeing to specific territories within which they will operate exclusively. The division may occur by markets, such as by price range. These agreements conspire to eliminate competition.

The penalties for such acts are severe. For example, under the Sherman Antitrust Act people who fix prices or allocate markets may be found guilty of a misdemeanor punishable by a maximum $100,000 fine and three years in prison. For corporations the penalty may be as high as $1 million. In a civil suit a person who has suffered a loss because of the antitrust activities of a guilty party may recover triple the value of the actual damages plus attorney's fees and costs.

•   •   •   •   •   •   •

KEY TERMS

agency   fraud
agency coupled with an interest   general agent
agent   implied agreement
antitrust laws   independent contractor
brokerage   law of agency
buyer-agency agreement   listing agreement
client   principal
commission   procuring cause
customer   puffing
dual agency   ready, willing and able buyer
employee   special agent
express agreement   subagent
fiduciary relationship

SUMMARY

Real estate brokerage is the bringing together, for a fee or commission, of people who wish to buy, sell, exchange or lease real estate. An important part of real estate brokerage is the law of agency. A real estate broker is the agent, hired by the seller or buyer to sell or find a particular parcel of real estate. The person who hires the broker is the principal. The principal and the agent have a fiduciary relationship, under which the agent owes the principal the duties of care, obedience, accounting, loyalty and disclosure. The agent may seek the participation of subagents to assist the broker in serving the principal.

The law of agency governs the principal-agent relationship. Agency relationships may be expressed either by the words of the parties or written agreement or implied by their actions. In single-agency relationships the broker/agent represents one party, either the buyer or the seller, in the transaction. If the agent elicits the assistance of other brokers who cooperate in the transaction, the other brokers are subagents of the principal.

Representing two opposing parties in the same transaction is dual agency. Licensees must be careful not to create a dual agency when none was intended. This unintentional or inadvertent dual agency can result in the sales contract being rescinded and commission being forfeited or a suit in court. Disclosed dual agency requires that both principals be informed and consent to the broker's multiple representation. In any case the prospective parties in the transaction should be informed about the agency alternatives and how client versus customer level services differ. Many states have mandatory agency disclosure laws. The source of compensation for the client services does not determine the party who is being represented.

Licensees have certain duties and obligations to their customers as well. Consumers are entitled to fair and honest dealings and information that is necessary for them to make informed decisions. This includes disclosing accurate information about the property. Some states have mandatory property disclosure laws.

The broker's compensation in a real estate sale may take the form of a commission, a flat fee or an hourly rate. The broker is considered to have earned a commission when he or she procures a ready, willing and able buyer for a seller.

A broker may hire salespeople to assist in this work. The salesperson works on the broker's behalf as either an employee or an independent contractor.

Many of the general operations of a real estate brokerage are regulated by the real estate license laws. In addition, state and federal antitrust laws prohibit brokers from conspiring to fix prices or allocate customers or markets.

Questions

1. A person who has the authority to enter into contracts concerning all business affairs of another is called a(n)

   a. ~~general agent.~~   c. special agent.
   b. secret agent.   d. attorney.

2. The term *fiduciary* refers to

   a. the sale of real property.
   b. principles by which a real estate seller must conduct his or her business.
   c. one who has legal power to act on behalf of another.
   d. ~~the principal-agent relationship.~~

3. The relationship between broker and seller is generally a

   a. ~~special agency.~~
   b. general agency.
   c. secret agency.
   d. universal agency.

4. A real estate broker acting as the agent of the seller

   a. is obligated to render faithful service to the seller.
   b. can make a profit if possible in addition to the commission.
   c. can agree to a change in price without the seller's approval.
   d. can accept a commission from the buyer without the seller's approval.

5. The statement "To recover a commission for brokerage services, a broker must be employed" means that

   a. the broker must work in a real estate office.
   b. ~~the seller must have made an agreement to pay a commission to the broker for selling the property.~~
   c. the broker must have asked the seller the price of the property and then found a ready, willing and able buyer.
   d. the broker must have a salesperson employed in the office.

6. A broker is entitled to collect a commission from both the seller and the buyer when

   a. the broker holds a state license.
   b. the buyer and the seller are related.
   c. ~~both parties give informed consent to such a transaction.~~
   d. both parties have attorneys.

7. An agency relationship may be terminated by all *except* which of the following means?

   a. The owner decides not to sell the house.
   b. ~~The broker discovers that the market value of the property is such that he or she will not make an adequate commission.~~
   c. The owner dies.
   d. The broker secures a ready, willing and able buyer for the seller's property.

8. Under the law of agency a real estate broker owes all of the following to the principal *except*

   a. care.   c. disclosure.
   b. obedience.   d. advertising.

9. A broker may lose the right to a commission in a real estate transaction if he or she
   a. did not advertise the property.
   b. was not licensed when employed as an agent.
   c. did not personally market and sell the listing.
   d. did not cooperate with other brokers.

10. A real estate broker hired by an owner to sell a parcel of real estate must comply with
   a. any instructions of the owner.
   b. any instructions of the buyer.
   c. the concept of caveat emptor.
   d. the law of agency.

11. While in the employ of a real estate broker a salesperson has the authority to
   a. act as an agent for the seller.
   b. assume responsibilities assigned by the broker.
   c. accept a commission from another broker.
   d. advertise the property on his or her own behalf.

12. A real estate broker learns that her neighbor wishes to sell his house. The broker knows the property well and is able to persuade a buyer to make an offer for the property. The broker then asks the neighbor if she can present an offer to him, and the neighbor agrees. At this point
   a. the neighbor is not obligated to pay the broker a commission.
   b. the buyer is obligated to pay the broker for locating the property.
   c. the neighbor must pay the broker a commission.
   d. the broker has become a subagent of the neighbor.

13. A real estate broker who engages salespeople as independent contractors must
   a. withhold income tax from all commissions earned by them.
   b. require them to participate in office insurance plans offered to other salespeople hired as employees.
   c. withhold social security from all commissions earned by them.
   d. refrain from controlling how the salesperson conducts his or her business activities.

14. A salesperson was listing a seller's house. The seller informed the salesperson that he would not sell to a member of a particular religious sect. The salesperson would be wise to do any of the following *except*
   a. accept the listing and ignore the seller's comment.
   b. explain the fair housing laws to the seller.
   c. discuss the situation with his broker.
   d. refuse the listing.

15. Broker D lists K's residence for $87,000. K's employer has transferred her to another state, and she must sell her house quickly. To expedite the sale, D tells a prospective purchaser that K will accept at least $5,000 less for the property. Based on these facts, all of the following statements are true *except*
   a. D has violated his agency responsibilities to K.
   b. D should not have disclosed this information regardless of its accuracy.
   c. D should have disclosed only the lowest price that K would accept.
   d. D has a special agency relationship with K.

16. A broker would have the right to dictate which of the following to an independent contractor who was working for him?
   a. The number of hours that the person would have to work
   b. The schedule that the person would have to follow
   c. The minimum acceptable dress code for the office
   d. The commission rate that the person would earn

17. A buyer who is a client of the broker wants to purchase a house that the broker has listed for sale. Which of the following is true?

    a. If the listing salesperson and selling salesperson are two different people, there is no problem.
    b. The broker should refer the buyer to another broker to negotiate the sale.
    c. The seller and buyer must be informed and agree to the broker's representing both of them.
    d. The buyer should not have been shown a house listed by the broker.

18. If a property that is listed for sale is placed in an MLS, this usually establishes for other brokers

    a. an implied agency.
    b. subagency.
    c. dual agency.
    d. single agency.

5

Listing Agreements

LISTING PROPERTY

Just as a supermarket without inventory will have no customers, the real estate broker without inventory will have no customers. To acquire inventory most brokers obtain listings of properties for sale, although some work with properties for lease, rent, exchange or option.

As discussed in Chapter 4, a listing agreement creates a *special agency* relationship between the principal (the owner of the property) and the broker (the agent). As agent the broker is authorized to represent the principal and the principal's real estate to third parties, including obtaining and submitting offers for the property.

The listing agreement is an *employment contract* rather than a real estate contract. It is a contract for the personal professional services of the broker, not the transfer of real estate. In most states, either by their statute of frauds or by specific rule from their real estate licensing authority, the listing must be in writing to be enforceable in court. However, oral listings are permitted in some jurisdictions.

Under the law of agency and the real estate license laws, only a broker can act as agent to list, sell or rent another person's real estate and provide other services to a principal. A salesperson who performs these acts does so only in the name and under the supervision of the broker. Throughout this chapter, unless otherwise stated, the terms *broker, agent* and *firm* are intended to include both the broker and a salesperson working under the broker. However, the parties to a listing contract are the seller and the broker.

TYPES OF LISTING AGREEMENTS

There are several different types of listing agreements. The type of contract determines the specific rights and obligations of the parties.

Exclusive-Right-to-Sell Listing

In an **exclusive-right-to-sell listing** one broker is appointed as the sole agent of the seller. The broker is given the exclusive right, or *authorization,* to market the seller's property. If the property is sold while the listing is in effect, the seller must pay the broker a commission *regardless of who sells the property.* In other words, if the seller finds a buyer without the broker's assistance, the seller must *still* pay the broker a commission. Brokers strongly favor this form of listing agreement because it offers the broker the greatest opportunity to receive a commission. In turn the seller can benefit because the broker feels freer to spend money for multiple-listing service fees, marketing, advertising, brochures, fliers, open houses and other selling expenses.

Exclusive-Agency Listing

In an **exclusive-agency listing** *one* broker is authorized to act as the exclusive agent of the principal. However, the seller *retains the right to sell the property by himself or herself* without obligation to the broker. The seller is obligated to pay a commission to the broker only if the broker or a subagent of the broker has been the procuring cause of a sale.

Open Listing

In an **open listing** (also known in some areas as a *nonexclusive listing* or a *general listing*), the seller retains the right to employ any number of brokers as agents. The brokers can act simultaneously, and the seller is obligated to pay a commission only to that broker who successfully produces a ready, willing and able buyer. If the seller personally sells the property *without the aid of any of the brokers,* the seller is not obligated to pay commission. A listing contract that does not specifically provide otherwise ordinarily creates an open listing. An advertisement of property "for sale by owner" may indicate "brokers protected" or in some other way invite offers brought by brokers. Such an invitation does not by itself create a listing agreement. The terms of even an open listing still must be negotiated.

Special Listing Provisions

Multiple listing. A *multiple-listing clause* may be included in an exclusive listing. It is used by brokers who are members of **multiple-listing services** (MLSs). These are marketing organizations whose broker members make their own exclusive listings available through other brokers and gain access to other brokers' listed properties as well.

A multiple-listing service offers advantages to both the broker and the seller. Brokers develop a sizable inventory of properties to be sold and are assured a portion of the commission if they list a property or participate in the sale of another broker's listing. Sellers gain because their property is exposed to a larger market.

The contractual obligations among the member brokers of a multiple-listing organization vary widely. Most provide that upon sale of the property *the commission is divided between the listing broker and the selling broker.* Terms for division of the commission are agreed upon individually by the brokers, however, rather than by multilist agreement.

Under most MLS contracts the broker is not only authorized but *obligated* to turn new listings over to the multiple-listing service within a specific period of time. The length of time during which the listing broker can offer a property exclusively without notifying the other member brokers varies but usually is less than 72 hours.

Under the provisions of most multiple-listing services a participating broker agrees to offer unilateral subagency to any other member brokers who attempt to sell the listing broker's property. The broker must have the written consent of the seller to offer such subagency. If a broker chooses to be an agent for the buyer on a property in the multiple-listing service, that broker must notify the listing broker before any communication with the seller takes place. The brokers must determine the appropriate way to proceed to protect their fiduciaries.

IN PRACTICE. . .	*MLSs offer brokers benefits beyond broad exposure to listings. Through computers most MLSs offer instant access to information on which properties are on and off the market. They are equally helpful to the licensee who needs to make a competitive market analysis to determine the value of a particular property and thus arrive at a listing price for it. Computerization also helps the buyer select a property within the community that best satisfies the buyer's needs.*

Net listing. A **net listing** provision specifies that the seller will receive a net amount of money from any sale, with the excess being given to the listing broker as commission. The broker is free to offer the property at any price higher than that net amount. However, net listings can create a conflict of interest between the broker's fiduciary responsibility to the seller and the broker's profit motive. Therefore, net listings are illegal in many states and are discouraged by real estate licensing authorities and trade associations in most others.

Option listing. An **option listing** provision gives the broker the right to purchase the listed property. Use of an option listing may open the broker to charges of fraud unless the broker is scrupulous in fulfilling all obligations to the property owner. In some states a broker who chooses to exercise such an option must first inform the property owner of the broker's profit in the transaction and secure *in writing* the owner's agreement to it. An option listing is different from an option contract, which will be discussed in Chapter 10.

TERMINATION OF LISTINGS

Agency between a broker and a seller can be ended for several reasons, which were listed in Chapter 4. Most obviously, a listing agreement is terminated when its purpose is fulfilled, such as when a buyer or tenant is procured for the property. The agreement also can be ended when its term expires without a successful transfer. Sometimes property is destroyed—perhaps by a hurricane or mudslide—or its use is changed by some force outside the owner's control, such as a zoning change or condemnation by eminent domain (see Chapter 6). Or title to it may be transferred by operation of law, as in the case of the owner's bankruptcy. In those cases there is no property for the broker to market, so the listing agreement ends. The broker and seller can simply mutually agree to end the listing, or one party may end it. If either party dies or becomes incapacitated, the listing is terminated. It is also terminated if either the broker or seller breaches or cancels the contract, but that party might be liable to the other for damages.

A listing agreement is a *personal service contract*. Its success depends on the personal efforts of the broker who is a party to the agreement. The broker cannot turn the listing over to another broker without the principal's written consent. Failing to perform any work toward its fulfillment or revoking the agreement, constitutes abandonment of the listing. The property owner cannot force the broker to comply in that event but can sue the broker for damages.

The property owner might also fail to fulfill the terms of the agreement. A property owner who refuses to cooperate with reasonable requests of the broker, such as allowing tours of the property by prospective buyers or refuses to proceed with a sales contract could be liable for damages to the broker.

The preceding are examples of breaches of contract by the broker or owner. The contract could also be cancelled by either party. However, the canceling party could be liable for damages to the other party.

Expiration of Listing Period

All listings should specify a definite period of time during which the broker is to be employed. *In most states failure to specify a definite termination date in a listing is grounds for suspension or revocation of the real estate license.*

The courts have discouraged the use of automatic extension clauses in exclusive listings and have even outlawed them in some states. Many listing contract forms specifically provide that there can be no automatic extensions of the agreement. An example of an automatic extension is a listing that provides for a base period of 90 days and "continues thereafter until terminated by either party hereto by 30 days' notice in writing." Some courts have held that such an extended period is an open listing rather than part of the original exclusive-agency listing.

Some listing contracts contain a "broker protection clause." This clause provides that the property owner will pay the listing broker a commission if, within a specified number of days after the listing expires, the owner transfers the property to someone the broker originally introduced to the owner. This clause protects a broker who was the procuring cause from losing a commission because the transaction was completed after the listing expired. The times for such clauses usually parallel the terms of the listing agreement; for example, a six-month listing may carry a broker protection clause of six months after the listing's expiration. To protect the owner and prevent any liability of the owner for two separate commissions, most of these clauses stipulate that they cannot be enforced if the property is relisted under a new contract either with the original listing broker or with another broker.

THE LISTING PROCESS

Prior to signing a contract, the broker and seller must discuss a variety of issues. The seller's most critical concerns typically will be the selling price of the property and the net amount the seller can expect to receive from the sale. The broker has several professional tools to provide information about a property's value and to calculate the proceeds from a sale. Most sellers will ask other questions as well: How quickly will the property sell? What services will the broker provide during the listing period? This is the broker's opportunity to explain the various types of listing agreements, the ramifications of agency relationships and the marketing services the broker provides. At the end of this process the seller should feel comfortable with the decision to list with this broker.

Similarly, before the listing agreement is finalized, the broker should feel well equipped to fulfill the fiduciary obligations that the agreement will impose. The seller should have provided comprehensive information about the property and the personal concerns of the seller so that the broker can accept the listing with confidence that its purpose can be served.

Pricing the Property

While it is the responsibility of the broker or salesperson to advise and assist, it is ultimately the *seller* who must determine the listing price for the property. Because the average seller does not usually have the background to make an informed decision about a reasonable listing price, real estate agents must be prepared to offer their knowledge, information and expertise.

A broker or salesperson can help the seller determine a listing price for the property by using a **competitive market analysis (CMA).** This is a comparison of the prices of recently sold properties that are similar in location, style and amenities to the property of the listing seller. If no adequate comparisons can be made, or if the property is unique in some way, the seller may prefer that a formal real estate appraisal—a detailed estimate of a property's value—be prepared by a professional appraiser.

Whether a CMA or a formal appraisal is used, the figure sought is the property's market value. **Market value,** discussed in Chapter 18, is *the most probable price property would bring in an arm's-length transaction under normal conditions on the open market*. A broker performing a CMA will estimate market value as likely to fall within a range of figures (for example, $135,000 to $140,000). A CMA, however, should not be confused with an appraisal.

While it is the property owner's privilege to set whatever listing price he or she chooses, a broker should reject any listing in which the price is substantially exaggerated or severely out of line with the indications of the CMA or appraisal. These tools are the best indications of what a buyer will likely pay for the property. An unrealistic listing price will make it difficult for the broker to properly market the seller's property.

Seller's Return

Through simple calculations the broker can show the seller roughly how much the seller will net from a given sales price or what sales price will produce a certain net. The mathematical examples show the net the seller would receive after the sales commission. In addition there are other expenses that the seller incurs (see Chapter 23).

MATH
CONCEPT
Calculating
Sales Prices,
Commissions
and Nets to
Seller

When a property sells, the sales price is equal to 100% of the money being transferred. Therefore, if a broker is to receive a 6% commission, 94% will be left for the seller's other expenses and equity.

To calculate a commission using a sales price of $80,000 and a commission rate of 6% (.06 as a decimal), multiply the sales price by the commission rate:

$$\$80,000 \times 6\% = \$80,000 \times .06 = \$4,800 \text{ commission}$$

To calculate a sales price using a commission of $4,550 and a commission rate of 7% (.07 as a decimal), divide the commission by the commission rate:

$$\$4,550 \div 7\% = \$4,550 \div .07 = \$65,000 \text{ sales price}$$

To calculate a commission rate using a commission of $3,200 and a sales price of $64,000, divide the commission by the sales price:

$$\$3,200 \div \$64,000 = .05 \text{ as a decimal} = 5\% \text{ commission rate}$$

To calculate the net to the seller using a sales price of $85,000 and a commission rate of 8% (.08 as a decimal), multiply the sales price by *100% minus the commission rate:*

$$\$85,000 \times (100\% - 8\%) = \$85,000 \times .92 = \$78,200$$

The same result could be achieved by calculating the commission ($85,000 × .08 = $6,800) and deducting it from the sales price ($85,000 − $6,800 = $78,200). However, this involves unnecessary extra calculations.

Sales price × commission rate = commission
Commission ÷ commission rate = sales price
Commission ÷ sales price = commission rate
Sales price × (100% − commission rate) = net to seller

Information Needed for Listing Agreements

Once the real estate licensee and the owner have agreed on a listing price consistent with the owner's wishes and what the market will bear, the licensee obtains specific detailed information on the property. Obtaining as much factual information on the property as possible assures that most contingencies can be anticipated and provided for. This is particularly important when the listing will be shared with other brokers through a multiple-listing service and other licensees must rely on the information taken by the lister.

Information generally includes (where appropriate):

• the names and relationships, if any, of the owners;

• the street address of the property;

• the size of the improvements (residence, garage, carport, patio, etc.);

- the age of the improvements and their type of construction;

- the number and the sizes of the rooms ("room count");

- the size of the lot, including its dimensions;

- existing loans, including the name and address of each lender, the type of loan, the loan number, the loan balance, the interest rate, the monthly payment and what it includes (principal, interest, real estate tax impounds, hazard insurance impounds, mortgage insurance premiums), whether the loan may be assumed by the buyer and under what circumstances, whether the loan may be prepaid without penalty, etc.;

- the possibility of seller financing;

- the amount of any outstanding special assessments and whether they will be paid by the seller or assumed by the buyer;

- the zoning classification of the property;

- the current (or most recent year's) property taxes;

- the neighborhood (schools, parks and recreational areas, churches, public transportation, etc.);

- any real property to be removed from the premises by the seller and any personal property to be included in the sale for the buyer (both the listing contract and the subsequent purchase contract should be explicit on these points);

- any additional information that would make the property more appealing and marketable; and

- any required disclosures concerning agency representation and property conditions.

Disclosures

Disclosure of agency relationships and property conditions has become the focus of consumer safeguards in the 1990s. As discussed in Chapter 4, most states have enacted laws requiring agents to disclose whose interest the agent legally represents, a particularly confusing issue when subagents are involved in the transaction. It is important that the seller be informed of the company's policies regarding cooperation with subagents and any potential for the property to be shown by an agent for the buyer.

Chapter 4 also mentioned that seller disclosure of property conditions is required by law in several states with more states expected to adopt such laws in coming years. These disclosures normally cover a wide range of structural, mechanical and other conditions that a prospective purchaser should know about to make an informed decision. Frequently, the laws require the seller to complete a standardized form. It is the licensee's responsibility to see that the seller complies with these disclosures. Agents should caution sellers to make truthful disclosures to avoid litigation arising from fraudulent or careless misrepresentations.

THE LISTING CONTRACT FORM

A wide variety of listing contract forms is available today. Some brokers draft their own contracts, some use forms prepared by their multiple-listing service and some use forms produced by their state real estate licensing authority. Some have a separate information sheet (also known as a profile or data sheet) for recording many of the foregoing property features, including room sizes, lot sizes and taxes. That sheet is "wed" to a second form containing the contractual obligations between the seller and the broker: listing price, duration of the agreement, signatures of the parties and so forth. Others use a single form. Regardless of which form is used, most listing contracts require similar information because the same considerations arise in almost all real estate transactions. A sample form is presented in Figure 5.1 or licensees should review a form that is used in their area. Refer to state laws for any specific requirements of listing contracts. Some of the considerations covered in a typical contract are discussed in the following paragraphs.

The type of listing agreement. Is the contract an exclusive-right-to-sell listing (the most common type of listing), an exclusive-agency listing or an open listing? This is the section of the contract in which the principal gives the broker the authority to act on the principal's behalf.

The broker's authority and responsibilities. According to the terms of the contract, will the broker be able to place a sign on the property and advertise and market the property? A major consideration is whether the broker will be allowed to authorize subagents through a multiple-listing service. Will the contract allow the broker to show the property at reasonable times and upon reasonable notice to the seller and place a lockbox on the property? May the broker accept earnest money deposits on behalf of the seller and what are the broker's responsibilities for holding escrow funds? Without the written consent of the seller, the broker cannot undertake any of these or similar activities.

The names of all parties to the contract. Anyone having an interest in the property must be identified and should sign the listing for it to be valid. If the property is owned under one of the forms of concurrent ownership discussed in Chapter 7, that fact should be clearly established. If one or more of the owners is married, it is wise to obtain the spouse's consent and signature on the contract to release the appropriate marital rights. If the property is in the possession of a tenant, that should be disclosed and instructions given on how the property is to be shown to a prospective buyer.

The brokerage firm. The brokerage company name, the employing broker and, if appropriate, the salesperson taking the listing must all be identified.

The listing price. This is the proposed gross sales price. The seller's net proceeds will be reduced by unpaid real estate taxes, special assessments, mortgage and trust deed debts and any other outstanding obligations.

Real property and personal property. This section identifies the personal property that will be left with the real estate when it is sold and the items of real property that the seller expects to remove at the time of the sale. Each item should be explicitly identified (brand name, serial number, color). Some of these items may later become points of negotiation when a ready, willing and able buyer is found for the property. Typical items to consider include major appliances, swimming pool and spa equipment, fireplace accessories, storage sheds, stacked firewood and stored heating oil.

**Figure 5.1
Sample Listing
Agreement**

**EXCLUSIVE AUTHORIZATION AND RIGHT TO SELL
RESIDENTIAL**
This is Intended to be a Legally Binding Contract

Type **ER**

Legal I.D. 347954

1. **Exclusive Right to Sell.** In consideration of the acceptance by the undersigned licensed Arizona real estate broker ("Broker") of the terms of
2. this Contract and Broker's promise to endeavor to effect a sale of the property described below (the "Property"), I or we, as owner(s) (the
3. "Owner") employ and grant Broker the exclusive and irrevocable right commencing on _____ , 19 _____ , and expiring at
4. midnight on _____ , 19 _____ to sell, exchange, option or rent the Property described in lines 5 through 8.

5. **The Property.** For purposes of this Contract, the "Property" means the real property in _____ County, Arizona described
6. below, plus all fixtures and improvements thereon, all appurtenances incident thereto and all personal property described in lines 11 through 17.

7. _____
                                                        Legal Description

8. _____
                                                        Street Address

9. **Price.** The listing price shall be $ _____ , to be paid as described in the Owner's Data Entry Form, or such other price
10. and terms as are accepted by Owner.

11. **Fixtures and Personal Property.** Except as provided in the Data Entry Form, the property includes the following fixtures or personal property:
12. All existing storage sheds, heating and cooling equipment, built-in appliances, light fixtures, window and door screens, sun screens, storm
13. windows and doors, towel, curtain and drapery rods, attached carpeting, draperies and other window coverings, fireplace equipment, pool
14. and spa equipment (including any mechanical or other cleaning systems), garage door openers and controls, irrigation systems, fire
15. warning and security systems, fences, ceiling fans and attached antennas.

16. **Additional Property and Leased Equipment.** The property may include additional personal property and exclude leased equipment as
17. described in the Data Entry Form.

18. **Access and Lockbox.** Owner authorizes Broker to install and use a Lockbox containing a key to the Property. ☐ yes ☐ no. Owner
19. acknowledges that a Lockbox and any other keys left with or available to Broker will permit access to the Property by Broker, Broker's
20. subagents and buyers' agents, together with potential purchasers, even when Owner is absent; that neither the Arizona Regional Multiple
21. Listing Service ("ARMLS"), nor any Board of REALTORS®, nor any broker is insuring Owner against theft, loss or vandalism resulting from any
22. such access; that Owner is responsible for obtaining appropriate insurance; and that Owner will obtain and provide to Broker written per-
23. mission from the occupant of the Property, if it is a person other than Owner.

24. **Sign.** Broker is authorized to place Broker's "For Sale" and "Sold" Signs, as appropriate, on the Property.

25. **Home Protection Plan.** Owner acknowledges that home protection plans are available and that such plans may provide additional protection
26. and benefits to Owner and any purchaser of the Property. Owner agrees to provide at his expense a home protection plan promptly after
27. the execution of this Contract ☐ yes ☐ no.

28. **Additional Terms.** _____
29. _____
30. _____

31. **Compensation to Broker.** Owner agrees to compensate Broker as follows:
32. a. If Broker produces a ready, willing and able purchaser in accordance with this Contract, or if a sale or exchange of the Property is made
33. by Owner or through any other agent, or otherwise, during the term of this exclusive listing, for services rendered, Owner agrees to pay
34. Broker a commission of _____ .
35. The same amount of commission shall be payable to Broker if, without the consent of Broker, the Property is withdrawn from this listing,
36. otherwise withdrawn from sale, or transferred or conveyed by Owner.
37. b. Owner agrees not to rent the Property during the term of this Contract without Broker's prior knowledge and consent and, if the Property
38. is rented, Owner agrees to pay Broker a rental commission of _____
39. If during the terms of such rental or within _____ after its termination, the tenant, or any of such tenant's heirs, executors, or assigns
40. shall buy the Property from Owner, the commission described in line 34 shall be deemed as earned by and payable to Broker.
41. c. If within _____ days after the expiration of this Contract, a sale, exchange or option is made by Owner to any person to
42. whom the Property has been shown by Broker or any agent of Broker, or with whom Broker or any agent of Broker has negotiated
43. concerning the sale of the Property, the same fee shall be payable unless this Contract has been renewed or the Property has been relisted
44. on an exclusive basis with another real estate broker.
45. d. Owner authorizes Broker to cooperate with other brokers and to divide with other brokers all such compensation in any manner acceptable
46. to Broker.
47. e. Owner will instruct the escrow company to pay all such commissions to Broker as a condition to closing and irrevocably assigns Owner's
48. proceeds to Broker at close of escrow to the extent necessary therefor. If completion of the sale is prevented by default of Owner, or with
49. the consent of Owner, the entire fee shall be paid directly by Owner. If the earnest deposit is forfeited for any other reason, Owner shall
50. pay a brokerage fee equal to one-half of the earnest deposit, provided such payment shall not exceed the full amount of the fee. Nothing in
51. this paragraph shall be construed as limiting applicable provisions of law relating to when commissions are earned or payable.

52. **TERMS ON REVERSE.** THE TERMS AND CONDITIONS ON THE REVERSE SIDE HEREOF PLUS ALL INFORMATION ON THE DATA
53. ENTRY FORM ARE INCORPORATED HEREIN BY REFERENCE.

54. **Receipt of Copy.** Broker and Owner acknowledge receipt of a copy of this Contract.

55. COMMISSIONS PAYABLE FOR THE SALE, LEASING OR MANAGEMENT OF PROPERTY ARE NOT SET BY ANY BOARD OF REALTORS®
56. OR MULTIPLE LISTING SERVICE OR IN ANY MANNER OTHER THAN BY NEGOTIATION BETWEEN THE BROKER AND THE CLIENT.

57. _____
        Owner   Address   Date

58. _____
        Owner   City/Zip   Phone

59. In consideration of Owner's representations and promises in this Contract, Broker agrees to endeavor to effect a sale, exchange or option
60. in accordance with this Contract and further agrees to file this listing for publication by a local Board of REALTORS® and dissemination to the
61. Users of ARMLS.

62. _____
        Listing Office   By (Signature)   Phone

63. Accepted by: _____   Date: _____
                        Broker

64. Broker's File/Log No. _____ Manager's Initials _____ Broker's Initials _____ Date _____

NO REPRESENTATION IS MADE AS TO THE LEGAL VALIDITY OR ADEQUACY OF ANY PROVISION OR THE TAX CONSEQUENCES THEREOF. IF YOU DESIRE LEGAL OR TAX ADVICE,
CONSULT YOUR ATTORNEY OR TAX ADVISOR.

Copyright © 1989 by Arizona Regional Multiple Listing Service   FOR USE WITH DATA ENTRY FORM NUMBER 1, 2 & 3

                                                                                                                7/89

BROKER

**Figure 5.1
(continued)**

65. **Multiple Listing Service.** Broker is a member of a local Board of REALTORS®, which is a member of ARMLS. This listing information will be
66. provided to ARMLS to be published and disseminated to its Users. Broker is authorized to offer subagency and to appoint subagents and to
67. report the sale, exchange, option or rental of the Property, and its price, terms and financing, to a local Board of REALTORS® for dis-
68. semination to and use by authorized ARMLS Users and to the public.

69. **Role of Broker.** Owner acknowledges that Broker is not responsible for the custody or condition of the Property or for its management,
70. maintenance, upkeep or repair.

71. **Title.** Owner agrees to furnish marketable title by warranty deed and an Owner's policy of title insurance in the full amount of the
72. purchase price.

73. **Cooperation by Owner.** Owner agrees to make available to Broker and prospective purchasers all data, records and documents pertaining
74. to the Property, to allow Broker, and any other broker who is a subagent of Broker to show the Property at reasonable times and upon
75. reasonable notice and to commit no act which might tend to obstruct Broker's performance hereunder. Owner shall not deal directly with any
76. prospective purchaser of the Property during the term of this Contract and shall refer all prospective purchasers to Broker during the term
77. hereof. Owner agrees to cooperate with Broker on any offers to purchase the Property. Owner also authorizes Broker to permit a broker who
78. is a buyer's agent to show the Property at such times and on such terms as are acceptable to Owner or Broker.

79. **Warranties by Owner.** Owner represents and warrants, as follows:

80. a. Owner is the Owner of record of the Property and has full authority to execute this Contract.

81. b. All information concerning the Property in this Contract, including the Data Entry Form relating to the Property, or otherwise provided by
82. Owner to Broker or any purchaser or prospective purchaser of the Property is, or will be at the time made, and shall be at the closing, true,
83. correct and complete. Owner agrees to notify Broker promptly if there is any material change in such information during the term of
84. this Contract.

85. c. Except as otherwise provided in this Contract, Owner warrants that Owner shall maintain and repair the Property so that, at the earlier of
86. possession or the close of escrow: the property shall be at least in substantially the same condition as on the effective date of this Contract;
87. the roof will be water-tight; all heating, cooling, plumbing and electrical systems and built-in appliances will be in working condition; and
88. if the Property has a swimming pool and/or spa, the motors, filter systems (and heaters, if so equipped) will be in working condition. Owner
89. warrants that prior to the close of escrow, payment in full will have been made for all labor, materials, machinery, fixtures or tools furnished
90. within the 120 days immediately preceding the close of escrow in connection with the construction, alteration or repair of any structure on
91. or improvement to the Property. Prior to the close of escrow, Owner shall grant the purchaser or purchaser's representatives reasonable
92. access to enter and inspect the Property.

93. d. The information in this Contract, if any, pertaining to a public sewer system, septic tank or other sanitation system is correct.

94. e. Owner will disclose to any potential purchaser all facts known to him concerning adverse conditions or latent defects in, to or affecting
95. the Property.

96. f. At his expense, Owner will place in escrow a wood-infestation inspection report by a licensed pest control contractor which, when considered
97. in its entirety, indicates that all residences and buildings attached to the Property are free from evidence of current infestation by any
98. wood-destroying organisms.

99. **Indemnification.** Owner agrees to indemnify and hold Broker, all Boards of REALTORS®, ARMLS, and all other cooperating brokers harmless
100. against any and all claims, liability, damage or loss arising from any misrepresentation or breach of warranty by Owner in this Contract, any
101. incorrect information supplied by Owner and any facts concerning the Property not disclosed by Owner, including without limitation, any
102. facts known to Owner relating to adverse conditions or latent defects.

103. **Attorneys Fees.** In any action or proceeding to enforce any provision of this Contract, or for damages sustained by reason of its breach, the
104. prevailing party shall be entitled to reasonable attorneys fees, as set by the court or arbitrator and not by a jury, and to all other related
105. expenses, such as expert witness fees, fees paid to investigators and court costs. Additionally, if any Broker reasonably hires an attorney to
106. enforce the collection of any commission payable pursuant to this Contract, and is successful in collecting some or all of such commission
107. without commencing an action or proceeding, Owner agrees to pay such Broker's reasonable attorneys fees and costs.

108. **Deposits.** Owner authorizes Broker to accept earnest deposits on behalf of Owner and to issue receipts for such earnest deposits.

109. **Recommendations.** If any broker recommends a builder or contractor or any other person or entity to Owner for any purpose, such recom-
110. mendation will be independently investigated and evaluated by Owner, who hereby acknowledges that any decision to enter into any
111. contractual arrangements with any such person or entity recommended by any Broker will be based solely upon such independent investiga-
112. tion and evaluation.

113. **FIRPTA.** Upon Broker's request, Owner agrees to complete, sign and deliver to escrow company a certificate concerning whether Owner is a
114. foreign person or nonresident alien pursuant to the Foreign Investment in Real Property Tax Act of 1980 (FIRPTA).

115. **Subsequent Offer.** Upon Owner's acceptance of an offer with respect to the Property, Owner waives his right to receive any subsequent offer
116. with respect to the Property until after forfeiture by the offeror or other nullification of the contract with the offeror.

117. **Entire Agreement.** This Contract, any attached exhibits and any addenda or supplements signed by the parties, shall constitute the entire
118. agreement between Owner and Broker and supersede any other written or oral agreements between Owner and Broker. This Contract can be
119. modified only by a writing signed by Owner and Broker.

120. **Equal Opportunity.** The Property is offered without respect to ancestry, race, religion, color, sex, handicap, marital status, familial status, age
121. or national origin.

122. **Construction of Language.** The language of this Contract shall be construed according to its fair meaning and not strictly for or against
123. either party. Words used in the masculine, feminine or neuter shall apply to either gender or the neuter, as appropriate. All singular and plural
124. words shall be interpreted to refer to the number consistent with circumstances and context.

Leased equipment. Is any leased equipment—security systems, cable television boxes, water softeners, special antennas—going to be left with the property? If so, the seller is responsible for notifying the equipment's lessor of the change of property ownership.

The description of the premises. In addition to the street address, the legal description, lot size and tax parcel number may be required for future insertion into a purchase offer.

The proposed dates for the closing and for the buyer's possession. These should be based on an anticipated sale date, with adequate time allowed for the paperwork involved (including the buyer's qualification for any financing) and the physical moves to be arranged by the seller and the buyer.

The closing. Who will handle the closing of the transaction, such as a closing attorney, title company or escrow company? Will the designated party complete the settlement statements and disburse the funds? Will he or she file the proper forms, such as documents to be recorded, documents to be sent the Internal Revenue Service and documents to be submitted for registering foreign owners?

The evidence of ownership. How will the title be transferred to the buyer? Most commonly used are a warranty deed and either a title insurance policy or an abstract and legal opinion.

Encumbrances. What liens will be paid in full at the closing by the seller and what liens will be assumed by the buyer?

Homeowner warranty program. Is a homeowner warranty plan available? What items does the warranty cover? Is the seller willing to pay for it? If not, will it be available to the buyer at the buyer's expense?

The commission. Under what circumstances will a commission be paid: only upon the sale of the property or upon any transfer of interest created by the broker? Will it be a percentage or a flat fee? When will it be paid? Will it be paid directly by the seller or by the party handling the closing?

The termination of the contract. Under what circumstances will the contract terminate? Can the seller arbitrarily refuse to sell or cooperate with the listing broker?

The broker protection clause. Under what circumstances will the broker still be entitled to a commission, and how long will such a clause remain in effect after the listing expires?

Warranties by the owner. Is the property suitable for its intended purpose? Does it comply with the appropriate zoning and building codes? Will it be transferred to the buyer in essentially the same condition as it was originally presented, considering repairs or alterations to be made as provided for in a purchase contract? Are there any known defects?

Indemnification ("hold harmless") wording. Do the seller and the broker agree to hold each other harmless for incorrect information supplied by one to the other, regardless of whether such inaccuracies were intentional or unintentional?

Nondiscrimination ("equal opportunity") wording. Does the seller understand that the property must be shown and offered without respect to the race, color, creed or religious preference, national origin, sex, sexual orientation, age, handicap or source of income of the prospective buyer? Refer to federal, state and local fair housing laws for protected classes.

Antitrust wording. Does the contract indicate that all commissions are negotiable between the seller and the broker and that they are not set by any regulatory agency, trade association or other industry organization?

The signatures of the parties. All parties identified in the contract must sign it, including all individuals who have a legal interest in the property.

The date the contract is signed. This date may differ from the date the contract actually becomes effective, particularly if a salesperson is taking the listing and must subsequently have his or her broker sign the contract to accept employment under its terms.

Anyone taking a listing should use *only* the appropriate documents as provided by the broker. Most brokers are conscientious enough to utilize only documents that have been carefully drafted or reviewed by an attorney so that their construction and legal language comply with the appropriate federal, state and local laws. Such contracts should also give consideration to local customs, such as closing dates and the proration of income and expenses, with which most real estate attorneys would be familiar.

●   ●   ●   ●   ●   ●   ●

KEY TERMS

competitive market analysis (CMA)   multiple-listing service
exclusive-agency listing   net listing
exclusive-right-to-sell listing   open listing
market value   option listing

SUMMARY

To acquire an inventory of property to sell, brokers must obtain listings. Types of listings include exclusive-right-to-sell, exclusive-agency and open listings.

With an exclusive-right-to-sell listing the seller employs only one broker and must pay that broker a commission regardless of whether it is the broker or the seller who finds a buyer—provided the buyer is found within the listing period.

Under an exclusive-agency listing the broker is given the exclusive right to represent the seller, but the seller can avoid paying the broker a commission by selling the property to someone not procured by the broker.

With an open listing the broker must find a buyer before the property is sold by the seller or another broker to obtain a commission.

A multiple-listing provision may appear in an exclusive-right-to-sell or an exclusive-agency listing. It gives the broker the additional authority and obligation to distribute the listing to other members of the broker's multiple-listing organization. A net listing, which is outlawed in some states and considered unethical in most areas, is based on the net price the seller will receive if the property is sold. The broker is free to offer the property for sale at the highest available price and will receive as commission any amount over and above the seller's stipulated net. An option listing, which also must be handled with caution, gives the broker the option to purchase the listed property.

A listing agreement may be terminated for the same reasons as any other agency relationship.

When listing a property for sale, the seller is concerned about the selling price and the net amount that will be received from the sale. A competitive market analysis is a comparison of the prices of recently sold properties that are similar to the seller's property. The CMA or a formal appraisal report can be used to help the seller determine a reasonable listing price. The amount the seller will net from the sale is calculated by subtracting the broker's commission and any other expenses that the seller incurs from the selling price.

A wide variety of listing contract forms may be used, depending on the customs and laws in an area. Typically they are pre-printed forms that include such information as the type of listing agreement, the broker's authority and responsibility under the listing, listing price, duration of the listing, information about the property, terms for the payment of commission (including antitrust concerns and encumbrances) and the buyer's possession and nondiscrimination laws. Detailed information about the property may be included in the listing contract or on a separate property data sheet. Disclosure of the broker's law of agency relationship and discussion of the broker's agency policies has become the focus of laws in many states. The seller may also be expected to comply with mandatory disclosure of property conditions.

Questions

1. A listing taken by a real estate salesperson belongs to the
   a. broker.
   b. seller.
   c. salesperson.
   d. salesperson and broker equally.

2. Which of the following is a similarity between an exclusive-agency listing and an exclusive-right-to-sell listing?
   a. Under both types of listings the seller retains the right to sell the real estate without the broker's help and without paying the broker a commission.
   b. Under both the seller authorizes only one particular salesperson to show the property.
   c. Both give the responsibility of representing the seller to one broker only.
   d. Both are open listings.

3. All of the following would terminate a listing *except* the
   a. expiration of the contract.
   b. death or incapacity of the broker.
   c. nonpayment of the commission by the seller.
   d. destruction of the improvements on the property.

4. The seller has listed his property under an exclusive-agency listing with the broker. If the seller sells his property himself during the term of the listing without using the broker's services, he will owe the broker
   a. no commission.
   b. the full commission.
   c. a partial commission.
   d. only reimbursement for the broker's costs.

5. A broker sold a residence for $88,000 and received $6,160 as her commission in accordance to the terms of the listing. What percentage of the sales price was the broker's commission?
   a. 6 percent
   b. 6.5 percent
   c. 7 percent
   d. 7.5 percent

6. A seller's residence is listed with a broker, and the seller stipulates that she wants to receive $85,000 from the sale but the broker can sell the property for as much as possible and keep the difference as the commission. The broker agrees. This type of listing is a(n)
   a. exclusive-right-to-sell listing.
   b. exclusive-agency listing.
   c. open listing.
   d. net listing.

7. All of the following provisions are usually found in a listing agreement *except* the
   a. rate of commission.
   b. monthly utility bill.
   c. price the seller wants.
   d. contract expiration date.

8. The listed price for a property should be based on
   a. the net to the seller.
   b. the appraised value.
   c. what the seller chooses.
   d. the maximum of a range of values.

9. A listing contract
   a. is an employment contract for the personal and professional services of the broker.
   b. obligates the seller to convey the property if the broker procures a ready, willing and able buyer.
   c. obligates the broker to work diligently for both the seller and the buyer.
   d. automatically requires the payment of a commission while the broker protection clause is in effect.

10. A seller hired broker N under the terms of an open listing. While that listing was still in effect, the seller—without informing broker N—hired broker F under an exclusive-right-to-sell listing for the same property. If broker N produces a buyer for the property whose offer the seller accepts, then the seller must pay a
    a. full commission only to broker N.
    b. full commission only to broker F.
    c. full commission to both broker N and broker F.
    d. half commission to both broker N and broker F.

11. Seller G listed her residence with broker D. Broker D brought an offer at full price and terms of the listing from buyers who are ready, willing and able to pay cash for the property. However, seller G changed her mind and rejected the buyers' offer. In this situation seller G
    a. must sell her property.
    b. owes a commission to broker D.
    c. is liable to the buyers for specific performance.
    d. is liable to the buyers for compensatory damages.

12. Which of the following is a similarity between an open listing and an exclusive-agency listing?
    a. Under both the seller avoids paying the broker a commission if the seller sells the property to someone the broker did not procure.
    b. Both grant a commission to any broker who procures a buyer for the seller's property.
    c. Under both the broker earns a commission regardless of who sells the property as long as it is sold within the listing period.
    d. Both grant an exclusive right to sell to whatever broker procures a buyer for the seller's property.

13. The parties to the listing contract are the
    a. seller and the buyer.
    b. seller and the broker.
    c. seller and the salesperson.
    d. broker and the salesperson.

14. A competitive market analysis
    a. is the same as an appraisal.
    b. can help the seller price the property.
    c. by law must be completed for each listing taken.
    d. should not be retained in the property's listing file.

15. A property was listed with a broker who belonged to a multiple-listing service and was sold by another member broker for $53,500. The total commission was six percent of the sales price. The selling broker received 60 percent of the commission, and the listing broker received the balance. What was the listing broker's commission?
    a. $1,284   c. $1,926
    b. $1,464   d. $2,142

6 Interests in Real Estate

As discussed in Chapter 2, the rights of real estate ownership are extensive. However, not all of the many different interests in real estate that can be acquired convey the entire bundle of legal rights to the owner. Licensees must take great care to ensure that prospective buyers understand exactly what interest a seller wishes to transfer.

Ownership of real estate is not absolute and does not confer absolute power. Even the most complete ownership that the law allows is limited by public and private restrictions intended to ensure that one owner's use or enjoyment of the ownership does not interfere with another's or with the general welfare. Licensees should have a working knowledge of the restrictions that might limit current or future owners. A zoning ordinance that will not allow a doctor's office to coexist with a residence, a condo association bylaw prohibiting resale without board approval or an easement allowing the neighbors to use the private beach may not only burden today's purchaser but may also deter a future buyer.

This chapter puts the various interests in real estate in perspective: what rights they confer and how use of the ownership may be limited.

GOVERNMENT POWERS

Individual ownership rights are subject to certain powers, or rights, held by federal, state and local governments. These limitations on the ownership of real estate are imposed for the general welfare of the community and, therefore, supersede the rights or interests of the individual. Government powers include the following.

Police Power

States have the power to enact legislation to preserve order, protect the public health and safety and promote the general welfare. That authority is known as the states' **police power**. The authority is passed on to municipalities and counties through legislation called *enabling acts*.

What is identified as being in the public interest will, of course, vary widely from area to area. Generally, however, a state's police power is used to enact environmental protection laws, zoning ordinances, building codes and regulations governing the use, occupancy, size, location and construction of real estate. The laws must be uniform and nondiscriminatory so as not to be an advantage or disadvantage to any one particular owner or owners. The community's needs and desires can be reflected in these laws. If, for example, a city deems growth to be desirable, it will exercise its police powers so that the local laws encourage purchase and improvement of land. If an area wishes to retain its current character, it may enact laws that discourage construction and expansion of population. See Chapter 19 for more information on police power.

Eminent Domain

Eminent domain is the right of the government to acquire privately owned real estate for public use. **Condemnation** is the process, either by judicial or administrative proceedings, by which the government exercises this right. The proposed use must be for the public good, just compensation must be paid to the owner and the rights of the property owner must be protected by due process of law. Public use has been defined very broadly by the courts to include not only public facilities but also property that is no longer fit and must be closed or destroyed.

Generally the states delegate their power of eminent domain to quasi-public bodies and publicly held companies responsible for various facets of public service. A public housing authority might take privately owned land to build low-income housing on it; the state's land-clearance commission or redevelopment authority could use the power of eminent domain to make way for urban renewal. If there were no other feasible way to do so, a railway, utility company or state highway department might acquire farmland to extend a railroad track, build a highway or bring electricity to a remote new development—again, as long as that purpose contributes to the public good.

Ideally the public agency and the owner of the property in question reach agreement through direct negotiation, and the government purchases the property for a price viewed as fair by the owner. In some cases the owner even dedicates the property to the government as a site for a school, park, library or other use the owner deems worthy. When the owner's consent cannot be obtained, however, the government agency can initiate condemnation to acquire the property. Considering that no private real property is exempt from the power of eminent domain, its potential impact on property owners is significant.

Taxation

Taxation is a charge on real estate to raise funds to meet the public needs of a government. See Chapter 9 for more information on real estate taxes.

Escheat

Although escheat is not actually a limitation on ownership, it is an avenue by which the state can acquire privately owned real or personal property. State laws provide for ownership to transfer, or **escheat,** to the state when an owner dies leaving no heirs and no will designating the disposition of the real estate. In some states real property will escheat to the county where the land is located rather than to the state. Escheat is intended to prevent property from being ownerless.

ESTATES IN LAND   An **estate in land** defines an owner's degree, quantity, nature and extent of interest in real property. Many different types of estates exist, but it is important to understand that not all *interests* in real estate are *estates*. To be an estate in land an interest must allow possession (either now or in the future) and must be measurable by duration. Lesser interests such as easements (discussed later in this chapter), which allow use but not possession, are not estates. The various estates and interests in real estate are illustrated in Figure 6.1.

Historically, estates in land have been classified as freehold estates and leasehold estates. According to English common law, freehold estates were real estate, while leasehold (less-than-freehold) estates were merely contracts and thus personal property. Both then and now, the two types of estates are distinguished primarily by their duration.

Freehold estates last for an *indeterminable length of time,* such as for a lifetime or forever. These include fee simple, also called an indefeasible fee, defeasible fee and life estates. The first two of these estates continue for an indefinite period and can be passed along to the heirs of the owner. The life estate is based on the lifetime of a person and ends when that individual dies.

Leasehold estates last for a *fixed period of time.* They include estates for years and estates from period to period. Estates at will and estates at sufferance are also leaseholds, though by their operation they are not generally viewed as being for fixed terms. Leaseholds are discussed in the chapter on leases.

Fee Simple Estate   An estate in **fee simple** is the maximum estate possible. It is the *highest quality of interest in real estate recognized by law.* The holder is entitled to all rights incident to the property. Because this estate is of unlimited duration, it is said to run forever. Upon the death of its owner it passes to the owner's heirs or as provided by will. A fee simple estate is also referred as an *estate of inheritance.*

Fee simple absolute. An estate in **fee simple absolute** is limited only by controls imposed by public and private restrictions. In common usage, the terms *fee* and *fee simple* are used interchangeably with *fee simple absolute.*

Fee simple defeasible. A **fee simple defeasible** (or *defeasible fee*) estate is a qualified estate, subject to the occurrence or nonoccurrence of a specified event. There are two types of defeasible estates. A fee simple estate may be qualified by a *condition subsequent.* This dictates some action or activity that the new owner must not perform. The former owner retains a *right of reentry,* so that if the condition is broken, the former owner can retake possession of the property. A grant of land "on the condition that" there be no consumption of alcohol on the premises is a fee simple on condition subsequent. If alcohol is consumed on the property, the former owner has the right to reacquire full ownership, but it will be necessary for the grantor (or the grantor's heirs or successors) to go to court to assert that right. Conditions in a deed are different from restrictions or covenants because of the grantor's right to reclaim ownership, a right that does not exist under private restrictions.

A fee simple estate may be qualified by a *special limitation.* The estate ends *automatically* upon failure to comply with the limitation. The former owner (or the former owner's heirs or successors) retains a *possibility of reverter* and reac-

Figure 6.1
Estates and Interests
in Real Estate

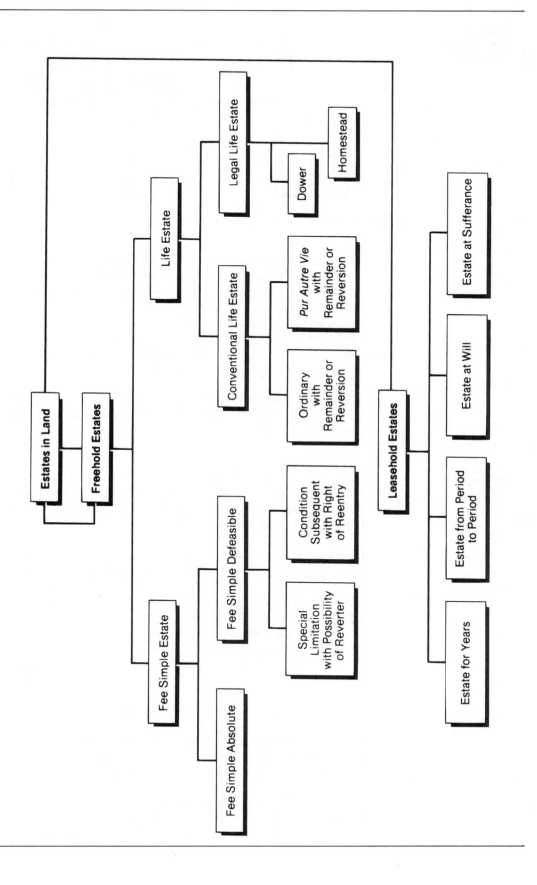

**Figure 6.2
Conventional
Life Estate**

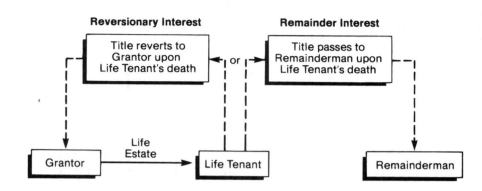

quires full ownership, with no need to reenter the land. A fee simple with a special limitation is also called a **fee simple determinable** because it may end automatically. The language used to distinguish a special limitation—the words "so long as" or "while" or "during"—is the key to the creation of this estate. For example, a grant of land from an owner to her church "so long as" the land is used only for religious purposes is a fee simple with a special limitation. If the church uses the land for a nonreligious purpose, title reverts back to the previous owner or her heirs or successors.

The *right of entry* and *possibility of reverter* may never take effect. If they do, it will only be sometime in the future. Therefore, both of these rights are considered *future interests*.

Life Estate

A **life estate** is a freehold estate that is limited in *duration to the life of the owner or the life of some other designated person or persons.* Unlike other freehold estates, a life estate is not inheritable. It will pass to future owners according to the provisions of the life estate.

Conventional life estate. A *conventional life estate* is created by the intentional act of the owner either by deed when the ownership is transferred or by a will. The estate is conveyed to an individual known as the *life tenant.* The life tenant has full enjoyment of the ownership for the duration of the individual's life. Upon the death of the life tenant, the estate ends and the ownership will pass to another designated individual or return to the previous owner. For example, A, who has a fee simple estate in Blackacre, conveys a life estate to P for P's lifetime. P is the life tenant. Upon P's death the life estate terminates. (See Figure 6.2.)

A life estate can also be based on the lifetime of another person. This is known as an *estate pur autre vie* (for the life of another). In this case, A conveys a life estate in Blackacre to P as the life tenant for the duration of the life of D. P is still the life tenant, but the measuring life is D's. Upon D's death, the life estate ends. Although a life estate is not considered an estate of inheritance, a life estate pur autre vie provides for inheritance by the life tenant's heirs only until the death of the person against whose life the estate is measured. In the example, if P died while D is still alive, P's heirs could be the owners of the life estate. When D dies the estate ends for the heirs. Life estates pur autre vie are usually

**Figure 6.3
Pur Autre Vie
Life Estate**

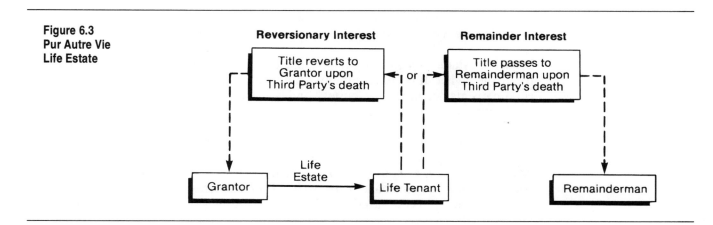

created in favor of someone who is physically or mentally incapacitated in the hope of providing an incentive for someone else to care for them. (See Figure 6.3).

A life tenant is entitled the rights of ownership (not to be confused with the interest of a tenant as a leasee). The life tenant can enjoy possession and the ordinary use and profits arising from the ownership, just as if the individual was a fee owner. The ownership may be sold, mortgaged or leased.

The ownership rights for a life tenant are not absolute, however. The life tenant may not injure the property, such as by destroying a building or allowing it to deteriorate. This injury is known in legal terms as *waste*. Those who will eventually own the property could seek an injunction against the life tenant or sue for damages. Because the ownership will terminate upon the death of the person against whose life the estate is measured, a purchaser, leasee or lender can be impacted. The life tenant can sell, lease or mortgage only the interest that he or she has, that is ownership for a lifetime. Because the interest is less desirable than a fee simple estate, the life tenant's rights are somewhat limited in practice.

Remainder and reversion. The fee simple owner who creates a conventional life estate must plan for its future ownership. When the life estate ends, it is replaced by a fee simple estate. The future owners of the fee simple estate may be designated in one of two ways:

1. **Remainder interest:** The creator of the life estate may name a *remainderman* as the person to whom the property will pass when the life estate ends. In the example, when A conveys Blackacre to P for P's lifetime, at the time the life estate is created, A can designate R to be the remainderman. While P is still alive, R owns a *remainder* interest which is a nonpossessory estate. This is a *future interest* in the fee simple estate. Upon P's death, R becomes the fee simple owner with all of the rights associated with that estate.

2. **Reversionary interest:** The creator of the life estate may choose not to name a remainderman and recapture the ownership when the life estate ends. In this case, A conveys Blackacre to P for P's lifetime. Upon P's death, the ownership reverts to A. A has a *reversionary* interest which is also a nonpossessory estate. A has a *future interest* in the ownership and reclaims the fee simple estate when

P dies. If A dies before P, the ownership reverts to A's heirs or individuals specified in A's will when P dies.

Legal life estate. A *legal life estate* is one created by statute rather than voluntarily by the owner. It becomes effective automatically, by operation of law, when certain events occur. Dower, curtesy and homestead are the forms of legal life estate currently used in some states.

This "marital life estate" arises from the common law concept of *dower and curtesy,* which provided the nonowning spouse with a means of support after the death of the owning spouse. *Dower* is the life estate that a wife has in the real estate of her deceased husband. *Curtesy* is a similar interest that a husband has in the real estate of his deceased wife. Dower and curtesy provide that the nonowning spouse has a right to a one-half or one-third interest in the real estate for the rest of his or her life, even if the owning spouse wills the estate to others. Because a nonowning spouse might claim an interest in the future even where one may not exist, both spouses may have to sign the proper documents when real estate is conveyed. The signature of the nonowning spouse would be needed to release any potential common law interests in the property being transferred.

Most separate property states have abolished the common law concepts of dower and curtesy in favor of the Uniform Probate Code, which gives the surviving spouse a right to an elective share upon the death of the other spouse. Community property states never used dower and curtesy.

A **homestead** is a legal life estate in real estate occupied as the family home. In effect the home (or part of it) is protected from creditors during the occupant's lifetime. In states that have homestead exemption laws, a portion of the area or value of the property occupied as the family home is exempt from certain judgments for debts not secured by the property, such as charge accounts or personal loans. The homestead is not protected from real estate taxes levied against the property or a mortgage for the purchase or cost of improvements.

In some states all that is required to establish a homestead is for the head of a family (sometimes a single person) to own or lease the premises occupied by the family as a residence. In others the family must file a notice as required by statute. A family can have only one homestead at any one time.

How does the exemption actually work? Though the entire homestead is protected from being sold in a few states, usually the homestead merely reserves a certain amount of money for the family in the event of a court sale. Upon such a sale, any debts secured by the home such as a mortgage, unpaid taxes or mechanics' liens—which are exceptions to homestead protection—will first be paid from the proceeds. Then the family will receive the amount reserved by the homestead exemption. Whatever remains will be applied to the family's unsecured debts.

Suppose Blackacre is T's homestead and her state's homestead exemption is $25,000. At a court-ordered sale the property is purchased for $60,000. First T's remaining $15,000 mortgage balance is paid; then T receives $25,000. The remaining $20,000 is then applied to T's unsecured debts.

Figure 6.4
Encumbrances

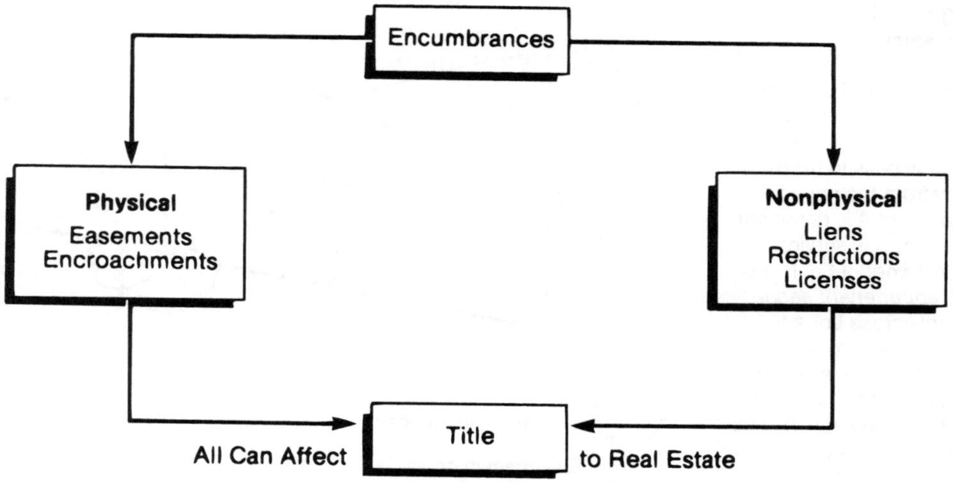

```
                              ┌──────────────┐
                              │ Encumbrances │
                    ┌─────────┴──────────────┴─────────┐
                    ↓                                   ↓
          ┌──────────────────┐              ┌──────────────────┐
          │    Physical      │              │   Nonphysical    │
          │   Easements      │              │      Liens       │
          │  Encroachments   │              │   Restrictions   │
          └──────────────────┘              │    Licenses      │
                    │                        └──────────────────┘
                    │          ┌──────────┐            │
                    └─────────→│  Title   │←───────────┘
                  All Can Affect └──────────┘ to Real Estate
```

Of course no sale would be ordered in the first place if the court could determine that nothing would be left over from the proceeds for the creditors. Say Blackacre could not be expected to bring more than $40,000; the priority of the mortgage lien (see Chapter 9) and homestead exemption would make a sale pointless.

ENCUMBRANCES

An **encumbrance** is a claim, charge or liability that attaches to and is binding on real estate. Simply put, it is *anything* that affects title to real estate as a right or interest held by someone other than the fee owner of the property. An encumbrance may lessen the value or obstruct the use of the property, but it does not necessarily prevent a transfer of title.

Encumbrances may be divided into two general classifications: liens that are usually monetary charges and encumbrances that affect the physical condition of the property, such as restrictions, easements, and encroachments. (See Figure 6.4.)

Liens

A **lien** *is a charge against property that provides security for a debt or obligation of the property owner.* If the obligation is not repaid, the lienholder, or creditor, has the right to have it paid out of the debtor's property, usually from the proceeds of a court-ordered sale. Real estate taxes, mortgages and trust deeds, judgments and mechanics' liens (for people who have furnished labor or materials in the construction or repair of real estate) all represent possible liens against an owner's real estate. Liens are discussed in detail in Chapter 9.

Restrictions

Deed restrictions, also referred to as *covenants, conditions* and *restrictions* (CC&Rs) are private agreements that affect the use of land. They can be imposed by an owner of real estate and included in the seller's deed to the buyer. Typically restrictive covenants are imposed by a developer or subdivider to maintain specific standards in a subdivision, and they are listed in the original

Figure 6.5
Easements

The owner of Lot A has an *appurtenant ease-ment* across Lot B to gain access to his prop-erty from the paved road. Lot A is dominant, and Lot B is servient. The owner of Lot B has an *appurtenant ease-ment* across Lot A to gain access to the beach. In this situation Lot B is dominant and Lot A is servient. The util-ity company has an *ease-ment in gross* across both parcels of land for its power lines.

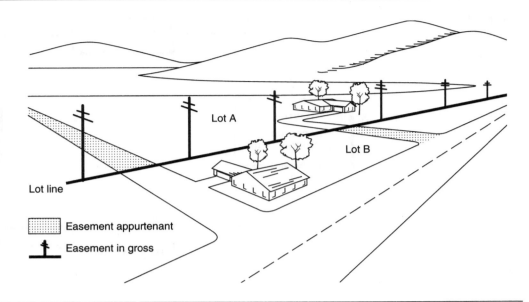

development plans for the subdivision filed in the public record. Deed restric-tions are discussed further in Chapter 19.

Easements

*An **easement** is the right to use the land of another for a particular purpose.* An easement may exist in any portion of the real estate, including the airspace above a parcel, or represented by a right-of-way across the land.

Appurtenant easement. An *appurtenant easement* is annexed to the ownership of one parcel and allows this owner the use of a neighbor's land. For such an easement to exist there must be two adjacent parcels of land owned by two dif-ferent parties. The parcel over which the easement runs is known as the *servient tenement;* the neighboring parcel that benefits is known as the *dominant tene-ment.*

For example, A and B own properties in a lake resort community, but only A's prop-erty borders the lake. A may grant B an easement across A's property to give B ac-cess to the beach (see Figure 6.5). A's property is the servient tenement, and B's property is the dominant tenement. Conversely, B may grant A an easement across B's property so that A can have access to the road. In this situation B's property is the servient tenement and A's property is the dominant tenement.

An appurtenant easement is part of the dominant tenement, and if the dominant tenement is conveyed to another party, the easement transfers with the title. This type of easement is said to *run with the land.* It is an encumbrance on property, and unless the holder of the dominant tenement somehow releases that right, it will transfer with the deed of the dominant tenement forever.

Party wall easements. A **party wall** can be an exterior wall of a building that strad-dles the boundary line between two lots, with half of the wall on each lot, or it can be a commonly shared partition wall between two properties. Each lot owner owns the half of the wall on his or her lot, and each has an appurtenant easement in the other half of the wall. A written party wall agreement must be used to create the easement rights. Expenses to build and maintain the wall are usually shared. A *party driveway* shared by and partly on the land of adjoining owners must also be created by written agreement, specifying responsibility for expenses.

The owner of Lot A has an *appurtenant easement* across Lot B to gain access to his property from the paved road. Lot A is dominant, and Lot B is servient. The owner of Lot B has an *appurtenant easement* across Lot A to gain access to the beach. In this situation Lot B is dominant and Lot A is servient. The utility company has an *easement in gross* across both parcels of land for its power lines.

Easement in gross.   An *individual interest* in or right to use the land of another is an **easement in gross.** Examples of easements in gross are the easement right a railroad has in its right-of-way or the right-of-way for a pipeline or high-tension power line (utility easements). Commercial easements in gross may be assigned or conveyed and may be inherited. However, personal easements in gross usually are not assignable and terminate upon the death of the easement owner. Easements in gross are often confused with the similar personal right of license, discussed later in this chapter.

Easement by necessity.   An appurtenant easement that arises when an owner sells part of his or her land that has no access to a street or public way except over the seller's remaining land is an **easement by necessity.** An easement by necessity arises because all owners have rights of ingress to and egress from their land—they cannot be landlocked.

Easement by prescription.   When the claimant has made use of another's land for a certain period of time as defined by state law, an **easement by prescription** or *prescriptive easement* may be acquired. The prescriptive period may be from 10 to 21 years. The claimant's use must have been continuous, exclusive and without the owner's approval. The use must be visible, open and notorious, so that the owner could readily learn of it.

The concept of *tacking* provides that successive periods of continuous occupation by different parties may be tacked, or combined, to reach the prescriptive period to successfully establish a claim for a prescriptive easement. To tack on one person's possession to that of another, the parties must have been successors in interest, such as an ancestor and his or her heir, landlord and tenant, or seller and buyer.

Easement by condemnation.   An **easement by condemnation** is acquired for a public purpose, such as a power line or sewage treatment facility, through the right of eminent domain. The owner of the servient tenement must be compensated for any loss in property value.

Creating an easement.   Easements are commonly created by written agreement between the parties establishing the easement right. They also may be created by the grantor in a deed of conveyance either *reserving* an easement over the sold land or *granting* the new owner an easement over the grantor's remaining land; by longtime *usage*, as in an easement by prescription; by necessity; and by *implication,* that is, the situation or the parties' actions may imply that they intend to create an easement. The creation of an easement involves two separate parties, one of whom is the owner of the land over which the easement runs. It is impossible for the owner of a parcel of property to have an easement over his or her own land.

Terminating an easement. Easements may be ended

- when the purpose for which the easement was created no longer exists;
- when the owner of either the dominant or the servient tenement becomes the owner of both and the properties are merged under one legal description (termination by merger);
- by release of the right of easement to the owner of the servient tenement;
- by abandonment of the easement (the intention of the parties is the determining factor);
- by nonuse of a prescriptive easement;
- by adverse possession by the owner of the servient tenement;
- by destruction of the servient tenement, as in the demolition of a party wall;
- by lawsuit (an *action to quiet title*) against someone claiming an easement; or
- by excessive use, as when a residential use is converted to commercial purposes.

Note that an easement may not *automatically* terminate for these reasons. Certain legal steps may be required.

License

A personal privilege to enter the land of another for a specific purpose is a **license.** A license differs from an easement in that *it can be terminated or canceled by the licensor* (the person who granted the license). If a right to use another's property is given orally or informally, it will generally be considered to be a license rather than a personal easement in gross. A license ends upon the death of either party or the sale of the land by the licensor. Examples are permission to park in a neighbor's driveway and the privileges that a theater or a sports event ticket conveys.

Encroachments

An **encroachment** occurs when a building (or some portion of it) or a fence or driveway *illegally extends beyond the land of its owner or beyond the legal building lines*. It is usually disclosed by either a physical inspection of the property or a spot survey. A spot survey shows the location of all improvements located on a property and whether they extend over the lot or building lines. If a building encroaches on neighboring land, the neighbor may be able to either recover damages or secure removal of the portion of the building that encroaches. Encroachments of long standing (for the states' prescriptive period) may give rise to easements by prescription.

IN PRACTICE. . .

Because an undisclosed encroachment could make a title unmarketable, an encroachment should be noted in a listing agreement and the sales contract. Encroachments are not disclosed by the usual title evidence provided in a real estate sale unless a survey is submitted while the title examination is being made.

**Figure 6.6
Riparian
Rights**

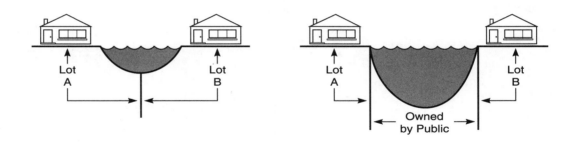

WATER RIGHTS

Whether the water will be used for agricultural, recreational or other purposes, waterfront real estate has always been desirable. Therefore each state has strict laws governing the ownership and use of water and the adjacent land. The laws vary among the states, but much depends on climatic and topographical conditions. Where water is plentiful, many states rely on the simple parameters set by the common law doctrines of riparian and littoral rights. Where water is scarce, however, the state controls all but limited domestic use of water according to the doctrine of prior appropriation.

Riparian Rights

Many states subscribe to the common law doctrine of **riparian rights.** These rights are granted to owners of land along the course of a river, stream or lake. These owners have the unrestricted right to use the water, provided the use does not interrupt or alter the flow of the water or contaminate the water. In addition, an owner of land that borders a nonnavigable waterway owns the land under the water to the exact center of the waterway. Land adjoining navigable rivers is usually owned to the water's edge, with the state holding title to the submerged land (see Figure 6.6). Navigable waters are considered public highways in which the public has an easement or right to travel. The laws governing and defining riparian rights differ from state to state.

Littoral Rights

Closely related to riparian rights are the **littoral rights** of owners whose land borders on large, navigable lakes, seas and oceans. Owners with littoral rights enjoy unrestricted use of available waters but own the land adjacent to the water only up to the mean ("average") high-water mark (see Figure 6.7). All land below this point is owned by the government.

Riparian and littoral rights are appurtenant (attached) to the land and cannot be retained when the property is sold. The right to use the water belongs to whoever owns the bordering land and cannot be retained by a former owner after the land is sold.

The quantity of land ownership can be affected by the natural action of the water. An owner is entitled to all land created through **accretion**—increases in the land resulting from the deposit of soil by the water's action. (Such deposits are called *alluvion* or *alluvium.*) If water recedes, new land is acquired by *reliction.*

Figure 6.7
Littoral Rights

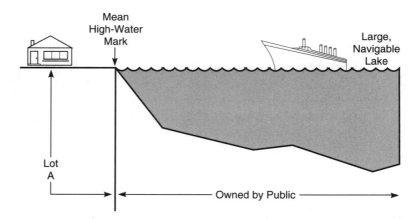

Conversely, an owner may lose land through *erosion,* the gradual and imperceptible wearing away of the land caused by flowing water (or other natural forces). This contrasts with **avulsion,** the sudden removal of soil by an act of nature.

Doctrine of Prior Appropriation

In states where water is scarce the ownership and use of water are often determined by the doctrine of **prior appropriation.** Under this doctrine *the right to use any water, with the exception of limited domestic use, is controlled by the state rather than by the landowner adjacent to the water.*

To secure water rights a person must show a beneficial use for the water, such as crop irrigation, and obtain a permit from the proper state department. Although statutes governing prior appropriation vary from state to state, the priority of water rights is usually determined by the oldest recorded permit date.

Once granted, water rights may be perfected through the legal processes prescribed by the individual state. When the water right is perfected, it generally becomes attached to the land of the person holding the permit. The permit holder may sell such a water right to another party.

Issuance of a water permit does not grant access to the water source. All access rights-of-way over the land of another (easements) must be obtained from the property owner.

● ● ● ● ● ● ●

KEY TERMS

accretion
avulsion
appurtenant easement
condemnation
deed restrictions
easement
easement by condemnation
easement by necessity
easement by prescription
easement in gross
eminent domain
encroachment
encumbrance
escheat
estate in land
fee simple
fee simple absolute

fee simple defeasible
fee simple determinable
freehold estate
future interest
homestead
leasehold estate
license
lien
life estate
littoral rights
party wall
police power
prior appropriation
remainder
reversion
riparian rights
taxation

SUMMARY

An individual's ownership rights are subject to the powers held by government. These powers include the police power, by which states can enact legislation such as environmental protection laws and zoning ordinances. The government may also acquire privately owned land for public use through the power of eminent domain. Real estate taxes are imposed to raise government funds. When a property becomes ownerless, ownership of the property may transfer, or escheat, to the state.

An estate is the degree, quantity, nature and extent of interest a person holds in land. Freehold estates are estates of indeterminate length. Less-than-freehold estates are called leasehold estates, and they involve tenants.

A freehold estate may be a fee simple estate or a life estate. A fee simple estate can be absolute or defeasible upon the happening of some event. A conventional life estate is created by the owner of a fee estate; a legal life estate is created by law. Legal life estates include curtesy, dower and homestead.

Encumbrances against real estate can be liens, deed restrictions, easements, licenses or encroachments.

An easement is the right acquired by one person to use another's real estate. Easements are classified as interests in real estate but are not estates in land. Appurtenant easements involve two separately owned tracts. The tract benefited is known as the dominant tenement; the tract that is subject to the easement is called the servient tenement. An easement in gross is a personal right, such as that granted to utility companies to maintain poles, wires and pipelines.

Easements may be created by agreement, express grant or reservation in a deed, necessity, prescription or condemnation. They can be terminated when the purpose of the easement no longer exists, by merger of both interests, with an express intention to extinguish the easement by release or by abandonment of the easement.

A license is permission to enter another's property for a specific purpose. A license is usually created orally, is temporary and can be revoked.

An encroachment is an unauthorized use of another's real estate.

Ownership of land encompasses not only the land itself but also the right to use the water on or adjacent to it. Many states subscribe to the common law doctrine of riparian rights, which gives the owner of land adjacent to a nonnavigable stream ownership of the stream to its midpoint. Littoral rights are held by owners of land bordering large lakes and oceans and include rights to the water and ownership of the land up to the mean high-water mark. In states where water is scarce water use is often decided by the doctrine of prior appropriation. Under prior appropriation water belongs to the state and it is allocated to users who have obtained permits.

Questions

1. The right of a government body to take ownership of real estate for public use is called
   a. escheat.
   b. eminent domain.
   c. condemnation.
   d. police power.

2. A purchaser of real estate learned that his ownership rights will continue forever and that no other person claims to be the owner or has any ownership control over the property. This person owns a
   a. fee simple interest.
   b. life estate.
   c. determinable fee estate.
   d. fee simple on condition.

3. J owned the fee simple title to a vacant lot adjacent to a hospital and was persuaded to make a gift of the lot. She wanted to have some control over its use, so her attorney prepared her deed to convey ownership of the lot to the hospital "so long as it is used for hospital purposes." After completion of the gift the hospital will own a
   a. fee simple absolute estate.
   b. license.
   c. fee simple determinable.
   d. leasehold estate.

4. After D had purchased his house and moved in, he discovered that his neighbor regularly used D's driveway to reach a garage located on the neighbor's property. D's attorney explained that ownership of the neighbor's real estate includes an easement over the driveway. D's property is properly called
   a. the dominant tenement.
   b. a freehold.
   c. a leasehold.
   d. the servient tenement.

5. A *license* is an example of a(n)
   a. easement.   c. encumbrance.
   b. encroachment. d. restriction.

6. Which one of the following best describes a life estate?
   a. An estate conveyed to A for the life of Z
   b. An estate held by lease
   c. An estate without condition
   d. A fee simple estate

7. When a homeowner who is entitled by state law to a homestead exemption is sued by his or her creditors, the creditors
   a. can have the court sell the home and apply the full proceeds of sale to the debts.
   b. have no right to have the debtor's home sold.
   c. can force the debtor to sell the home to pay them.
   d. can request a court sale and apply the sale proceeds, in excess of the statutory exemption and secured debts, to the unsecured debts.

8. If the owner of real estate does not take action against a trespasser before the statutory period has passed, the trespasser may acquire
   a. an easement by necessity.
   b. a license.
   c. an easement by implication of law.
   d. a prescriptive easement.

9. Many states determine water use by allocating water to users who hold recorded beneficial-use permits. This type of water use privilege is called
   a. riparian rights.
   b. littoral rights.
   c. the doctrine of prior appropriation.
   d. the doctrine of highest and best use.

10. All of the following are powers of the government *except*

    a. condemnation.   c. eminent domain.
    b. police power.   d. taxation.

11. Property deeded to a school "for educational purposes only" conveys a

    a. fee simple absolute.
    b. fee simple determinable.
    c. leasehold interest.
    d. fee simple on condition subsequent.

12. T has the legal right to pass over the land owned by his neighbor. This is a(n)

    a. estate in land.   c. policy power.
    b. easement.   d. encroachment.

13. All of the following are legal life estates *except*

    a. leasehold.   c. homestead.
    b. curtesy.   d. dower.

14. A father conveys ownership of his residence to his daughter but reserves for himself a life estate in the residence. The interest the daughter owns during her father's lifetime is

    a. pur autre vie.   c. a reversion.
    b. a remainder.   d. a leasehold.

15. K has fenced his property. The fence extends one foot over his lot line onto the property of a neighbor, M. The fence is an example of a(n)

    a. license.
    b. encroachment.
    c. easement by necessity.
    d. easement by prescription.

16. A homeowner may be allowed certain protection from judgments of creditors as a result of his state's

    a. littoral rights.   c. homestead rights.
    b. curtesy rights.   d. dower rights.

17. K has permission from X to hunt on X's property during dove season. K has

    a. an easement by necessity.
    b. an easement by condemnation.
    c. riparian rights.
    d. a license.

18. Encumbrances on real estate

    a. include easements, encroachments and licenses.
    b. make it impossible to sell the encumbered property.
    c. must all be removed before the title can be transferred.
    d. are of no monetary value to those who own them.

19. A tenant in an apartment holds a(n)

    a. easement.
    b. license.
    c. freehold interest.
    d. leasehold interest.

7

How Ownership Is Held

FORMS OF OWNERSHIP

Chapter 6 described the various interests in land that an owner can hold. This information is important to real estate licensees because they must know exactly what sellers wish to convey and buyers wish to acquire in every transaction. Licensees also need to understand how real property may be held in their community. Although questions about forms of ownership should be referred to an attorney, brokers and salespeople must understand the fundamental types of ownership so that they will know *who must sign listing contracts, acceptances of offers to purchase and deeds.* They also must understand *what form of ownership the purchaser desires and what choices are possible when more than one individual will take title.*

Although the forms of ownership available in a specific area are controlled by state law, three basic forms exist: A fee simple estate may be held in **severalty**, where title is held by one individual. (The term *individual* means, for the purposes of this chapter, both a natural person and a legal person, such as a corporation.) Title may also be held in **co-ownership**—by two or more individuals. Finally, title can be held in **trust**, where a third individual holds it for the benefit of another.

OWNERSHIP IN SEVERALTY

When title to real estate is *vested in*—presently owned by—one individual that individual owns the property *in severalty*. The term comes from the fact that this *sole* owner is "severed" or "cut off" from other owners. The severalty owner has sole rights to the ownership and sole discretion over the transfer of the ownership. When either a husband or wife owns property in severalty, state law may affect how ownership is held. In states that have dower or curtesy rights, the nonowning spouse may have to sign documents to release these rights. Where homeowners are protected by the homestead exemption, the nonowning spouse must sign to release that right. A nonowning spouse who is a minor will also have to sign. In other states only the owner's signature is needed.

CO-OWNERSHIP

When title to one parcel of real estate is vested in two or more individuals, those parties are called *co-owners,* or *concurrent owners.* The forms of co-ownership most commonly recognized by the various states, each with unique legal characteristics, are tenancy in common, joint tenancy, tenancy by the entirety, community property and partnership property.

Tenancy in Common

A parcel of real estate may be owned by two or more people as **tenants in common.** Each tenant holds an *undivided fractional interest* in the property. A tenant in common may hold, say, a one-half or one-third interest in a property. The physical property, however, is not divided into a specific half or third. It is the *ownership* interest and not the property that is divided. The co-owners have *unity of possession*, that is they are entitled to possession of the whole property. The deed creating a tenancy in common may or may not state the fractional interest held by each co-owner. If no fractions are stated, the tenants are presumed to hold equal shares. For example, if five people hold title, each would own an undivided one-fifth interest.

Because the co-owners do own separate interests, each can sell, convey, mortgage or transfer his or her interest without consent of the other co-owners. However, no individual tenant may transfer the ownership of the entire property. Upon the death of a co-owner that tenant's undivided interest passes to his or her heirs or devisees according to the will (see Figure 7.1).

When two or more people acquire title to real estate and the deed does not stipulate the tenancy, by operation of law, the new owners usually acquire title as tenants in common. But if the deed is made to a husband and wife with no further explanation, this assumption may not apply. In some states a deed made to a husband and wife creates a tenancy by the entirety; in others, community property; and in at least one state, a joint tenancy.

Joint Tenancy

Most states recognize some form of **joint tenancy** in property owned by two or more people. The feature that distinguishes a joint tenancy from a tenancy in common is *unity of ownership*. Title is held as though all owners collectively constitute one unit. The death of one of the joint tenants does not destroy the ownership unit; it only reduces by one the number of people who make up the unit. This occurs because of the **right of survivorship.** The joint tenancy continues until there is only one owner, who then holds title in severalty. The right of survivorship applies to the co-owners of the joint tenancy, not to their heirs. As each successive joint tenant dies, the surviving joint tenant(s) acquire(s) the interest of the deceased joint tenant. The last survivor takes title in severalty and then has all of the rights of sole ownership, including the right to have the property pass to his or her heirs. (See Figure 7.2.)

IN PRACTICE. . .	*The form under which title is to be taken, particularly by a married couple should always be discussed with an attorney. Joint tenacy should not be used as a substitute for a will.*

Creating joint tenancies. A joint tenancy can be created only by the intentional act of conveying a deed or giving the property by will (known as a devise). It cannot be implied or created by operation of law. The deed must specifically state the parties' intention to create a joint tenancy, and the parties must be

**Figure 7.1
Tenancy in
Common**

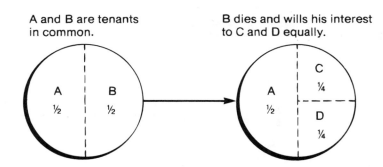

explicitly identified as joint tenants. Typical wording in a deed creating a joint tenancy would be "to A and B as joint tenants and not as tenants in common." Some states, however, have abolished the right of survivorship as the distinguishing characteristic of joint tenancy. In these states only when the deed explicitly indicates the intention to create the right of survivorship does that right exist. In these cases appropriate wording might be "to A and B and to the survivor of them, his or her heirs and assigns, as joint tenants."

Four "unities" are required to create a joint tenancy:

1. Unity of *possession*—all joint tenants holding an undivided right to possession

2. Unity of *interest*—all joint tenants holding equal ownership interests

3. Unity of *time*—all joint tenants acquiring their interests at the same time

4. Unity of *title*—all joint tenants acquiring their interests by the same document.

The four unities (PITT) are present when title is acquired by *one deed, executed and delivered at one time and conveying equal interests to all of the parties, who hold undivided possession of the property as joint tenants.*

Because the unities must be satisfied, many states require the use of an intermediary when a sole owner wishes to create a joint tenancy between himself or herself and others. The owner conveys the property to a nominee, or straw man, who then conveys it back, naming all the parties as joint tenants in the deed. Thus all joint tenants have acquired title at the same time by one deed.

Some states, however, have eliminated this "legal fiction" and allow the sole owner to execute a deed to himself or herself and others "as joint tenants and not as tenants in common" and thereby create a valid joint tenancy.

Terminating joint tenancies. A joint tenancy is destroyed when any one of the four unities of joint tenancy is terminated. A joint tenant is free to convey his or her interest in the jointly held property, but doing so will destroy the unity of interest. The new owner cannot become a joint tenant. Rights of other joint tenants, however, will be unaffected. For example, if *A, B* and *C* hold title as joint tenants and *A* conveys her interest to *D,* then *D* will own a fractional interest as a tenant in common with *B* and *C,* who will continue to own their undivided interest as joint tenants (see Figure 7.3). The tenant in common may be presumed to have a one-third interest unless otherwise stated.

**Figure 7.2
Joint Tenancy
with Right of
Survivorship**

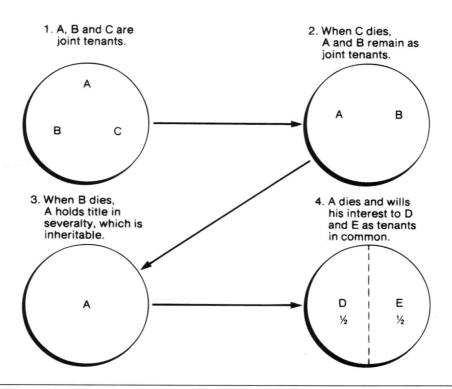

1. A, B and C are
   joint tenants.

2. When C dies,
   A and B remain as
   joint tenants.

3. When B dies,
   A holds title in
   severalty, which is
   inheritable.

4. A dies and wills
   his interest to D
   and E as tenants
   in common.

**Termination of
Co-Ownership by
Partition Suit**

Cotenants who wish to terminate their co-ownership may file an action in court to **partition** of land. Partition is a legal way to dissolve the relationship when the parties do not voluntarily agree to its termination. If the court determines that the land cannot be divided physically into parts, it will order the real estate sold. The court will then divide the proceeds of the sale among the co-owners according to their fractional interests.

**Ownership by
Married Couples**

Tenancy by the entirety. Some states allow husbands and wives to use a special form of co-ownership called **tenancy by the entirety.** Each spouse has an equal, undivided interest in the property. The term entirety refers to the fact the owners are considered one indivisible unit because early common law viewed a married couple as one legal person. A husband and wife who are tenants by the entirety have rights of survivorship. During their lives they can convey title *only by a deed signed by both parties.* One party cannot convey a one-half interest, and generally there is no right to partition. Upon the death of one spouse the surviving spouse automatically becomes sole owner. Married couples often take title to property as tenants by the entirety so that the surviving spouse can enjoy the benefits of ownership without waiting for the conclusion of probate proceedings.

Those who want a tenancy by the entirety in a state that allows it should consult an attorney about the requirements to create this form of ownership. Under common law a grant to husband and wife created a tenancy by the entirety even when no form of ownership was specified in the deed. Some states, however,

**Figure 7.3
Combination of
Tenancies**

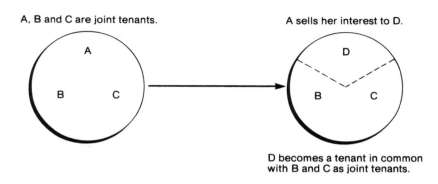

A, B and C are joint tenants.

A sells her interest to D.

D becomes a tenant in common
with B and C as joint tenants.

require that the intention to create a tenancy by the entirety be specifically stated. If it is not stated in the deed, a tenancy in common can result.

A tenancy by the entirety may be terminated by the death of either spouse which leaves the survivor as owner in severalty. It can be ended by divorce which leaves the parties as tenants in common. Both spouses can agree to end it. If the court has rendered a judgment against the husband and wife as joint debtors, the tenancy is dissolved so that the property can be sold to pay the judgment.

Community property rights. The concept of community property originated in Spanish law rather than English common law. Community property laws are based on the idea that a husband and wife, rather than merging into one entity, are equal partners in the marriage. Any property acquired during a marriage is considered to be obtained by mutual effort. The community property laws of the states vary widely. Essentially they recognize two kinds of property. **Separate property** is owned solely by either spouse before the marriage or acquired by gift or inheritance during the marriage. It includes any property purchased with separate funds during the marriage. Any income earned from a person's separate property generally remains part of his or her separate property. Separate property can be mortgaged or conveyed by the owning spouse without the signature of the nonowning spouse.

Community property consists of all other property, real and personal, acquired by either spouse during the marriage. Any conveyance or encumbrance of community property requires the signatures of *both* spouses. Upon the death of one spouse the survivor automatically owns one-half of the community property. The other half is distributed according to the decedent's will. If the decedent died without a will, the other half is inherited by the surviving spouse or by the decedent's other heirs, depending on state law. Community property does *not* automatically provide survivorship as joint tenancy does.

**Examples of
Co-Ownership**

To clarify the concepts of co-ownership, here are some examples of co-ownership arrangements:

- A deed conveys title to A and B. The intention of the parties is not stated, so ownership as tenants in common is created in most cases. If A dies, her one-half interest will pass to her heirs or devisees.

- A deed conveying title one-third to C and two-thirds to D creates a tenancy in common, with each owner having the fractional interest specified.

- A deed to H and W as husband and wife creates a tenancy by the entirety, community property or other interests between the husband and wife as provided by state law.

- A conveyance of real estate to two people (not husband and wife) by such wording as "to Y and Z, as joint tenants and not as tenants in common" may create a joint tenancy. In some states additional language is required such as "right of survivorship" or "to the survivor and his or her heirs and assigns" to guarantee that upon the death of Y the title to the property passes to Z.

TRUSTS

A trust is a vehicle by which an individual can transfer ownership of property to another individual to hold or manage for the benefit of yet another person. Perhaps a grandfather wishes to ensure the college education of his granddaughter, so he transfers the oilfield he owns to the grandchild's mother. He instructs the mother to use its income to pay for the grandchild's college tuition. In this case the grandfather is the *trustor*—the individual who creates the trust and who originally owned the property. The granddaughter is the *beneficiary*, the person who reaps the benefits of the trust. The mother is the *trustee*, the party who holds legal title to the property and is entrusted with carrying out the instructions regarding the benefit the granddaughter is to receive. The trustee is a *fiduciary,* who acts in confidence or trust and has a special legal relationship with the beneficiary. (See Figure 7.4.)

This example is, of course, oversimplified. Trusts can be created for myriad reasons—to prevent an heir from using bequeathed property unwisely, to provide funds for a specific anticipated need when that need arises, to preserve the anonymity of a purchaser of real estate, to enable a group to invest in property that individually they could not afford, to give a trustor tax benefits, etc. The legal and tax implications are complex and vary widely from state to state, so attorneys and tax experts should always be consulted on the subject of trusts.

Personal property can be held in trust, and most states allow real estate to be held in trust as well. Depending on the type of trust and its purpose, the trustor, trustee and beneficiary can all be either people or legal entities, such as corporations. Trustees often are corporations set up for this specific purpose called *trust companies.* The trustee has only as much power and authority as the trustor gives through a trust agreement, will or deed in trust.

Real estate can be owned under living or testamentary trusts and land trusts. It can also be held by investors in a *real estate investment trust (REIT),* discussed in Chapter 22.

Living and Testamentary Trusts

Property owners may provide for their own financial care and/or that of their families by establishing a trust. Such trusts may be created by agreement during a property owner's lifetime (living) or established by will after his or her death (testamentary).

The trustor conveys real or personal property to a trustee (usually a corporate trustee) with the understanding that the trustee will assume certain duties. Those duties may include the care and investment of the trust assets to produce an income. After payment of operating expenses and trustee's fees, the income is paid to or used for the benefit of the beneficiary. The trust may continue for the lifetime of the beneficiary, or the assets can be distributed when the beneficiary reaches a predetermined age or when other conditions of the trust agreement are met.

Land Trusts

A few states permit the creation of land trusts, in which real estate is the only asset. As in all trusts, the title to the property is conveyed to a trustee and the beneficial interest belongs to the beneficiary. In the case of land trusts, however, the beneficiary is usually also the trustor. While the beneficial interest is *personal property,* the beneficiary retains management and control of the real property and has the right of possession and the right to any income or proceeds from its sale.

One of the distinguishing characteristics of a land trust is that the *public records usually do not name the beneficiary.* A land trust may be used for secrecy when assembling separate parcels. There are other benefits as well. A beneficial interest can be transferred by assignment, making the formalities of a deed unnecessary. The property can be pledged as security for a loan without having a mortgage recorded. Real property is subject to the laws of the state in which it is located. But since the beneficiary's interest is personal, it will pass at the beneficiary's death under the laws of the state in which the beneficiary resided. If the deceased owned property in several states, additional probate costs and inheritance taxes can thus be avoided.

Usually only individuals create land trusts, but corporations as well as individuals can be beneficiaries. A land trust ordinarily continues for a definite term, such as 20 years. If the beneficiary does not extend the trust term when it expires, the trustee is usually obligated to sell the real estate and return the net proceeds to the beneficiary.

IN PRACTICE. . .

Licensees should exercise caution in using the term trust deed. It can be used to mean both a deed in trust (which relates to the creation of a living, testamentary or land trust) and a deed of trust (which is a financing document similar to a mortgage). Because these documents are not interchangeable, using an inprecise term can cause misunderstanding.

OWNERSHIP OF REAL ESTATE BY BUSINESS ORGANIZATIONS

A business organization is an entity that exists independently of its members. Ownership by a business organization makes it possible for many people to hold an interest in the same parcel of real estate. Investors may be organized to finance a real estate project in various ways. Some provide for the real estate to be owned by the entity; others provide for direct ownership by the investors.

Partnerships

An association of two or more persons who carry on a business for profit as co-owners is a **partnership.** In a **general partnership** all partners may participate to some extent in the operation and management of the business and share full liability for business losses and obligations. A **limited partnership** consists of

**Figure 7.4
Trust
Ownership**

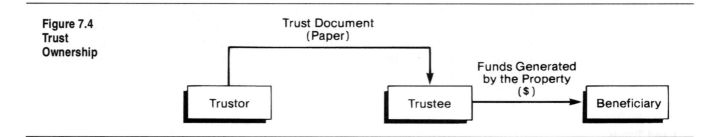

one or more general partners as well as limited partners. The business is run by the general partner or partners. The limited partners are not legally permitted to participate, and each can be held liable for business losses only to the extent of his or her investment. The limited partnership is a popular method of organizing investors because it permits investors with small amounts of capital to participate in large real estate projects.

Under common law a partnership is not a legal entity and cannot own real estate. Title must be held by the partners as individuals in a tenancy in common or joint tenancy. Most states, however, have adopted the *Uniform Partnership Act,* under which realty may be held in the partnership name, and the *Uniform Limited Partnership Act,* which establishes the legality of the limited partnership entity and provides that realty may be held in the partnership name. Profits and losses are passed through the partnership to the individual partners, whose individual tax situations determine the tax consequences.

General partnerships are dissolved and must be reorganized if one partner dies, withdraws or goes bankrupt. In a limited partnership the agreement creating the partnership may provide for the continuation of the organization upon the death or withdrawal of one of the partners.

Corporations

A **corporation** is a nonnatural person, or legal entity, created under the authority of the laws of the state from which it receives its charter. Because the corporation is a legal entity, it can own real estate in *severalty*. A corporation is managed and operated by its *board of directors*. The charter sets forth the powers of the corporation, including its right to buy and sell real estate after passage of a resolution to that effect by its board of directors. Some corporations are permitted to purchase real estate for any purpose; others limit such purchases to land that is needed to fulfill the entity's corporate purpose.

As a legal entity a corporation exists in perpetuity until it is formally dissolved. The death of one of the officers or directors does not affect title to property owned by the corporation.

Individuals participate, or invest, in a corporation by purchasing stock. Because stock is *personal property,* stockholders do not have a direct ownership interest in real estate owned by a corporation. Each stockholder's liability for the corporation's losses is usually limited to the amount of his or her investment.

One of the main disadvantages of corporate ownership of income property is that the profits are subject to double taxation. As a legal entity a corporation must file an income tax return and pay tax on its profits. The portion of the remaining profits distributed to stockholders as dividends is taxed again as part of the stockholders' individual incomes. An alternative that provides the benefit of a corporation as a legal entity but avoids the double taxation is known as an *S Corporation*. Only the shares of the profits that are passed to the stockholder are taxed. The profits of the corporation are not taxed.

Syndicates

Generally speaking, a **syndicate** is a *joining together of two or more people or firms to make and operate a real estate investment.* A syndicate is not in itself a legal entity; however, it may be organized into a number of ownership forms, including co-ownership (tenancy in common, joint tenancy), partnership, trust or corporation. A *joint venture* is a form of partnership in which two or more people or firms carry out a *single business project.* Joint ventures are characterized by a time limitation resulting from the fact that the joint venturers do not intend to establish a permanent relationship. These organizations are discussed further in Chapter 22.

COOPERATIVES, CONDOMINIUMS AND TIME-SHARES

As the nation's population grew, the population concentrated in large urban areas. This led to multiple-unit housing—high-rise apartment buildings in the central city and low-rise apartment complexes in adjoining suburbs that were occupied by tenants under the traditional rental system. But the urge to "own a part of the land," together with certain tax advantages that accrue to such ownership, led to the *cooperative* and *condominium* forms of ownership.

Cooperative Ownership

In the usual **cooperative**, a corporation that holds title to the land and building offers shares of stock to a prospective tenant. The price the corporation sets for each apartment becomes the price of the stock. The purchaser becomes a shareholder in the corporation by virtue of stock ownership and receives a proprietary ("owner's") lease to the apartment for the life of the corporation. The cooperative tenant/owners do not own real estate as is the case in a condominium, because stock is *personal property.*

Operation and management. The shareholders control the property and its operation. They elect officers and directors, as provided for in the corporation bylaws, who are responsible for directing the affairs of the corporation and its real estate operation. They may engage the services of a professional property manager to assist them. The bylaws also provide for tenant use of the property and the method by which the shares in the corporation may be transferred and any approval of prospective shareholders by the board of directors that may be required. In some cooperatives a tenant/owner must sell the stock back to the corporation at the original purchase price so that the corporation will realize any profits when the shares are resold. Individual shareholders are obligated to abide by the bylaws established by the corporation.

The corporation incurs costs in the operation and maintenance of the entire parcel, including the common property as well as the individual apartments. These costs include real estate taxes and any mortgage payments that the corporation may have. The corporation also budgets funds for such expenses as insurance, utilities, repairs and maintenance, janitorial and other services, replacement of equipment and reserves for capital expenditures. Funds for the budget are assessed to the individual shareholders, generally in the form of monthly fees similar to those charged by a homeowners' association in a condominium.

Unlike in a condominium association, which has the authority to impose a lien on the title owned by one who defaulted on maintenance payments, the burden of any defaulted payment in a cooperative falls on the remaining shareholders. Each shareholder is affected by the financial ability of the others. For this reason approval of prospective tenant/owners by the board of directors frequently involves financial evaluation. If the corporation is unable to make mortgage and tax payments because of shareholder defaults, the property might be sold by court order in a foreclosure suit. This would destroy the interests of all tenant/shareholders, including those who have paid their assessments.

Advantages. Cooperative ownership, despite its risks, has become more desirable in recent years for several reasons. Lending institutions view the shares of stock, although personal property, as acceptable collateral for financing, which was not always the case. The availability of financing expands the transferability of shares beyond "cash buyers." As a tenant/owner, rather than a tenant who pays rent to a landlord, the shareholder has some control over the property and realizes some income-tax advantage from the payment of property tax. Owners also enjoy freedom from maintenance.

IN PRACTICE. . .	*The laws in some states may prohibit real estate licensees from listing or selling cooperative interests because the owners own only personal property. Brokers who participate in these transactions may need a securities license that is appropriate for the type of cooperative interest involved.*

Condominium Ownership

The **condominium** form of ownership has become increasingly popular in the United States. Condominium laws, often called *horizontal property acts,* have been enacted in every state. Under these laws the owner of each unit holds a *fee simple title* to the unit. The individual unit owners also own a specified share of the undivided interest in the remainder of the building and land. These are known as the **common elements** (see Figure 7.5). The individual unit owners own these common elements as *tenants in common.* State law usually provides, however, that unit owners do not have the right to partition that other tenants in common have.

Architectural style. The condominium form of ownership can exist in a variety of architectural styles, ranging from single free-standing units and town house structures to high-rise buildings. The common elements include such items as the land, walls, hallways, elevators, stairways and roof. In some instances lawns and recreational facilities such as swimming pools, clubhouses, tennis courts and golf courses may also be considered common elements. The condominium form of ownership is also used for commercial property, office buildings and multiuse buildings that contain offices and retail shops as well as residential units.

Creation of a condominium. According to the provisions of the Uniform Condominium Act, which has been adopted in many states, a condominium is created and established when the owner of an existing building or the developer of unimproved property executes and records a *Declaration of Condominium*. The declaration includes a legal description of the condominium units and the common elements (including *limited* common elements—those that serve only one particular unit). The recording generally must also include a copy of the condominium's bylaws, drafted to govern the operation of the owners' association; a survey of the property; and an architect's drawings of the buildings, illustrating both the vertical and horizontal boundaries of each unit. It may also include restrictive covenants controlling the use of the rights of ownership.

Ownership. Once the property is established as a condominium, each unit becomes a separate parcel of real estate that is *owned in fee simple and may be held by one or more people in any type of ownership or tenancy recognized by state law. It can be mortgaged like any other parcel of real estate.* A condominium unit can usually be sold or transferred to whomever the owner chooses, unless the condominium association provides for a "first right of refusal." In this case the owner must first offer the unit at the same price to the other owners in the condominium or the association before accepting an offer to purchase from the public.

Real estate taxes are assessed and collected on each unit as an individual property. Default in the payment of taxes or a mortgage loan by one unit owner may result in a foreclosure sale of that owner's unit but does not affect the ownership of the other unit owners.

Operation and administration. The condominium property generally is administered by an association of unit owners according to the bylaws set forth in the declaration. The association may be governed by a board of directors or other official entity, manage the property on its own or engage a professional property manager to perform this function.

Acting through its board of directors or other officers, the association must enforce any rules it adopts regarding the operation and use of the property. The association is responsible for the maintenance, repair, cleaning and sanitation of the common elements and structural portions of the property. It must also maintain fire and extended-coverage insurance as well as liability insurance for those portions of the property.

Expenses incurred in fulfilling the association's responsibilities are paid by the unit owners in the form of assessments collected by the owners' association. These fees are assessed to each unit owner and are due monthly, quarterly, semiannually or annually, depending on the provisions of the bylaws. If the assessments are not paid, the association usually may seek a court-ordered judgment to have the property sold to cover the outstanding amount.

Time-Shared Ownership

Time-sharing permits multiple purchasers to buy interests in real estate—usually in a resort property—with each purchaser receiving the right to use the facilities for a certain period of time. A *time-share estate* includes a real property interest in condominium ownership, a *time-share use* is a right by contract under which the developer owns the real estate.

A time-share *estate* is a fee simple interest. The owner's occupancy and use of the property is limited to the contractual period purchased; for example, during

**Figure 7.5
Condominium
Ownership**

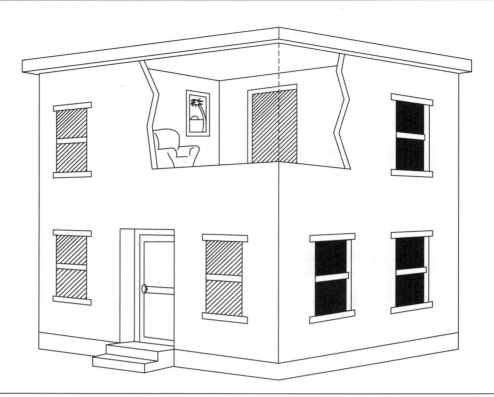

the 17th complete week, Sunday through Saturday, of each calendar year. The owner is assessed for maintenance and common area expenses based on the ratio of the ownership period to the total number of ownership periods in the property. Time-share estates theoretically never end because of the real property interest. However, the physical life of the improvements is limited and must be looked at carefully when considering such a purchase.

The principal difference between a time-share estate and a time-share use lies in the interest transferred to an owner by the developer of the project. A time-share *use* consists of the right to occupy and use the facilities for a certain number of years—30 years is a common period. At the end of the time any rights in the property held by the owner terminate. In effect the developer has sold only a right of occupancy and use to the owner, not a fee simple interest.

Some time-sharing programs specify certain months or weeks of the year during which the owner can use the property. Others provide a rotation system under which the owner can occupy the unit during different times of the year in different years. Some include a "swapping" privilege for transferring the ownership period to another property to provide some variety for the owner. Time-shared properties typically are used for 50 weeks each year, with the remaining two weeks reserved for the maintenance of the improvements.

Membership camping is similar to a time-share use in that the owner has the right to use the facilities of the developer. There is usually an open range area available with minimal improvements (such as camper/trailer hook-ups and restrooms). Normally the owner is not limited to a specific time for use of the property; use is limited only by weather and access.

IN PRACTICE...	*The laws governing the development and sale of time-share units are generally complex and vary substantially from state to state. In many states time-share properties are now subject to subdivision requirements. Familiarity with such provisions of real estate statutes helps brokers minimize problems when dealing with such specialized properties.*

● ● ● ● ● ● ●

KEY TERMS

common elements
co-ownership
community property
condominium
cooperative
corporation
general partnership
joint tenancy
limited partnership
partition

partnership
right of survivorship
separate property
severalty
syndicate
tenancy by the entirety
tenancy in common
time-sharing
trust

SUMMARY

Sole ownership, or ownership in severalty, means that title is held by one natural person or legal entity. Under co-ownership title can be held concurrently by more than one person in several ways.

Under tenancy in common each party holds a separate title but shares possession with other tenants. Individual owners may sell their interests. Upon death a tenant in common's interest passes to the tenant's heirs or according to a will. There are no special requirements for creating this interest. When two or more parties hold title to real estate, they will hold title as tenants in common unless another intention is expressed. Joint tenancy indicates two or more owners with the right of survivorship. The intention of the parties to establish a joint tenancy with right of survivorship must be stated clearly. The four unities of possession, interest, time and title must be present.

Tenancy by the entirety, in those states where it is recognized, is actually a joint tenancy between husband and wife. It gives the husband and wife the right of survivorship in all lands acquired by them during marriage. During their lives both must sign the deed for any title to pass to a purchaser. Community property rights exist only in certain states and pertain only to land owned by husband and wife. Usually the property acquired by combined efforts during the marriage is community property and one-half is owned by each spouse. Properties acquired by a spouse before the marriage and through inheritance or gifts during the marriage are termed separate property.

Real estate ownership may also be held in trust. To create a trust, the trustor conveys title to the property to a trustee, who owns and manages the property.

Various types of business organizations may own real estate. A corporation is a legal entity and can hold title to real estate in severalty. While a partnership is technically not a legal entity, the Uniform Partnership Act and the Uniform Limited Partnership Act, adopted by most states, recognizes a partnership as an entity that enables it to own property in the partnership's name. A syndicate is an association of two or more people or firms to make an investment in real estate. Many syndicates are joint ventures and are organized for only a single project. A syndicate may be organized as a co-ownership trust, corporation or partnership.

Cooperative ownership indicates title in one entity (corporation or trust) that must pay taxes, mortgage interest and principal, and all operating expenses. Reimbursement comes from shareholders through monthly assessments. Shareholders have proprietary, long-term leases entitling them to occupy their apartments. Under condominium ownership each owner/occupant holds fee simple title to a unit plus a share of the common elements. Each unit owner receives an individual tax bill and may mortgage the unit. Expenses for operating the building are collected by an owners' association through monthly assessments. Time-sharing enables multiple purchasers to own an estate or use interest in real estate, with the right to use it for a part of each year.

Questions

1. The four unities of possession, interest, time and title are associated with which of the following?
   a. Tenancy by the entirety
   b. Severalty ownership
   c. Tenants in common
   d. Joint tenancy

2. A parcel of property was purchased by K and Z. The deed they received from the seller at the closing conveyed the property "to K and Z" without further explanation. K and Z most likely took title as
   a. joint tenants.
   b. tenants in common.
   c. tenants by the entirety.
   d. community property owners.

3. M, B and F are joint tenants with rights of survivorship in a tract of land. F conveys her interest to V. Which of the following statements is true?
   a. M and B are joint tenants.
   b. M, B and V are joint tenants.
   c. M, B and V are tenants in common.
   d. V now has severalty ownership.

4. Individual ownership of an individual unit and common ownership of the common area best describes
   a. a cooperative.
   b. a condominium.
   c. a time-share.
   d. membership camping.

5. In a trust the person in whom the title is vested is the
   a. trustor.
   b. trustee.
   c. beneficiary.
   d. straw man.

6. D and S are getting married. Under the laws of their state any real property that either owns at the time of the marriage will remain separate property. And any real property acquired by either during the marriage, except by gift or inheritance, will belong to both of them equally. This form of ownership is called
   a. a partnership.
   b. joint tenancy.
   c. tenancy by the entirety.
   d. community property.

7. E, J and Q were concurrent owners of a parcel of real estate. J died, and his interest passed according to his will to become part of his estate. J was a
   a. joint tenant.
   b. tenant in common.
   c. tenant by the entirety.
   d. severalty owner.

8. A legal arrangement under which the title to real property is held to protect the interests of a beneficiary is a
   a. trust.
   b. corporation.
   c. limited partnership.
   d. general partnership.

9. A condominium is created when
   a. the construction of the improvements is completed.
   b. the owner files a declaration in the public record.
   c. the condominium owners' association is established.
   d. all of the unit owners file their documents in the public record.

10. Ownership that allows possession for only a specific time each year is a
    a. cooperative.   c. time-share.
    b. condominium.   d. trust.

11. A corporation may own real estate in all of the following manners *except* in
    a. trust.   c. partnership.
    b. severalty.   d. joint tenancy.

12. All of the following are forms of concurrent ownership *except*
    a. tenancy by the entirety.
    b. community property.
    c. tenancy in common.
    d. severalty.

13. The right of survivorship is associated with
    a. severalty ownership.
    b. community property.
    c. tenancy in common.
    d. joint tenancy.

14. All of the following involve a fee simple interest *except*
    a. a condominium.
    b. a time-share use.
    c. a tenancy by the entirety.
    d. a tenancy in common.

15. If property is held by two or more owners as tenants in common, the interest of a deceased cotenant will pass to the
    a. surviving owner or owners.
    b. heirs of the deceased.
    c. state by the law of escheat.
    d. trust under which the property was owned.

16. Which of the following best evidences the ownership of a cooperative?
    a. A tax bill for the individual unit
    b. The existence of a reverter clause
    c. A shareholder stock certificate
    d. A right of first refusal

17. A proprietary lease is characteristic of the ownership of a
    a. condominium unit.
    b. cooperative unit.
    c. time-share estate.
    d. membership camping interest.

18. Which of the following statements applies to both joint tenancy and tenancy by the entirety?
    a. There is no right to file a partition suit.
    b. The survivor becomes a severalty owner.
    c. A deed signed by one owner will convey a fractional interest.
    d. A deed will not convey any interest unless signed by both spouses.

19. T owns a fee simple interest in Unit 9 and 5 percent of the common elements. T owns a
    a. membership camping interest.
    b. time-share estate.
    c. cooperative unit.
    d. condominium unit.

20. If property is held by two or more owners as joint tenants, the interest of a deceased cotenant will be passed to the
    a. surviving owner or owners.
    b. heirs of the deceased.
    c. state under the law of escheat.
    d. trust under which the property was owned.

8 Legal Descriptions

DESCRIBING LAND

In everyday life we often refer to real estate by its street address, such as "1234 Main Street." While that information is usually adequate for the average person to find the designated house, it is not precise enough to be used on documents, such as sales contracts, deeds, mortgages and trust deeds. The courts have stated that a description is legally sufficient for such documents if a competent surveyor can locate the parcel using it. However, *locate* in this context means to define the exact boundaries of the property. The street address 1234 Main Street would not tell a surveyor how large the property is or where it begins and ends. Therefore several systems of identification have been developed to produce a **legal description.**

Typically ownership of a parcel of property has been transferred many times. The legal description used in the documents for each transfer should be identical to the one used in prior transfers. This practice can minimize or prevent legal problems.

METHODS OF DESCRIBING REAL ESTATE

The methods used to describe real estate are metes and bounds, rectangular (government) survey and lot and block (recorded plat). Although each method can be used independently, the methods may be combined in some situations. Figure 8.1 shows the types of legal descriptions historically used in the United States.

Metes-and-Bounds Method

A **metes-and-bounds description,** the earliest type of legal description, uses the boundaries and measurements of the parcel in question. The description starts at a designated place on the parcel called the **point of beginning (POB)** and proceeds around the boundaries referring to linear measurements and directions. A metes-and-bounds description always ends at the POB so that the tract being described is completely enclosed.

Monuments are fixed objects used to establish real estate boundaries. Natural objects such as stones, large trees, lakes and streams, as well as man-made objects like streets, highways and markers placed by surveyors, are commonly used as monuments. Measurements often include the words "more or less"; the

**Figure 8.1
Public Land Survey
Systems of the United
States**

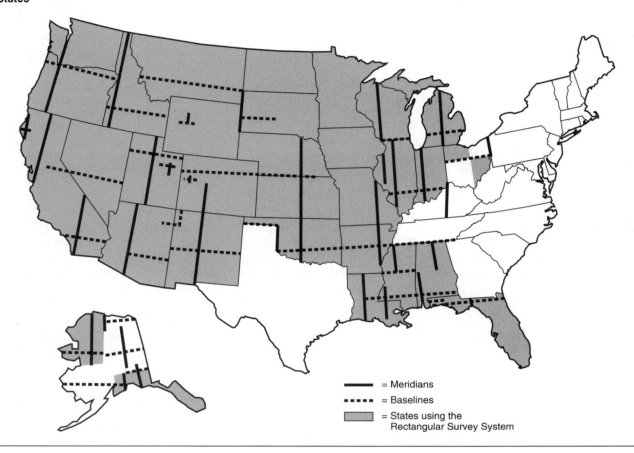

= Meridians

= Baselines

= States using the
Rectangular Survey System

location of the monuments is more important than the distance stated in the wording. The actual distance between monuments takes precedence over linear measurements set forth in the description if the two measurements differ.

An example of a metes-and-bounds description of a parcel of land (pictured in Figure 8.2) follows:

A tract of land located in Red Skull, Boone County, Virginia, described as follows: Beginning at the intersection of the east line of Jones Road and the south line of Skull Drive; then east along the south line of Skull Drive 200 feet; then south 15° east 216.5 feet, more or less, to the center thread of Red Skull Creek then northwesterly along the center line of said creek to its intersection with the east line of Jones Road; then north 105 feet, more or less, along the east line of Jones Road to the point of beginning.

When used to describe property within a town or city, a metes-and-bounds description may begin as follows:

**Figure 8.2
Metes-and-
Bounds Tract**

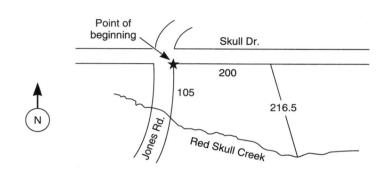

Beginning at a point on the southerly side of Kent Street, 100 feet easterly from the corner formed by the intersection of the southerly side of Kent Street and the easterly side of Broadway; then . . . .

In this description the POB is given by reference to the corner intersection. *Again, the description must close by returning to the POB.*

Metes-and-bounds descriptions can be complex and should be handled with extreme care. When they include detailed compass directions or concave and convex lines, they can be difficult to understand. Natural deterioration or destruction (usually by vandalism) of the monuments in a description can make boundaries difficult to identify. And in some parts of the country the colloquialisms and slang that they contain have made some very early metes-and-bounds descriptions colorful but incomprehensible to people not familiar with that area. In such situations the advice of a surveyor should be obtained. Computer programs are available that convert the data of the compass directions and dimensions to a drawing that verifies that the description closes to the POB.

**Rectangular
(Government)
Survey System**

The **rectangular survey system,** sometimes called the *government survey system,* was established by Congress in 1785, soon after the federal government was organized. The system was developed as a standard method of describing all lands conveyed to or acquired by the federal government, including the extensive area of the Northwest Territory.

The rectangular survey system is based on two sets of intersecting lines: principal meridians and base lines. The **principal meridians** run north and south, and the **base lines** run east and west. Both are located by reference to degrees of longitude and latitude. Each principal meridian has a name or number and is crossed by a base line. These lines are pictured in Figure 8.1. Each principal meridian and its corresponding base line are used to survey a definite area of land, indicated on the map by boundary lines.

Each principal meridian affects or controls *only* the specific area of land shown by the boundaries in Figure 8.1. No parcel of land is described by reference to more than one principal meridian, and the meridian used may not necessarily be the nearest one.

Figure 8.3
Township Lines

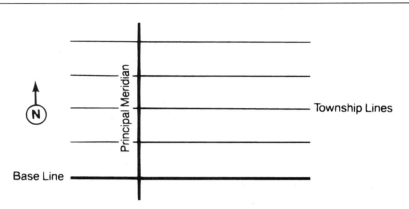

Further divisions—township lines, ranges, section lines and quarter-section lines—are used in the same way as monuments in the metes-and-bounds method.

Townships. Lines running east and west, parallel with the base line and six miles apart, are referred to as **township strips,** and they form *strips* of land (or **tiers**) called **townships** (see Figure 8.3). These tiers of townships are designated by consecutive numbers north or south of the base line. For instance, the strip of land between 6 and 12 miles north of a base line is Township 2 North.

Ranges. The land on either side of a principal meridian is divided into *six-mile-wide strips* by lines that run north and south, parallel to the meridian. These north–south strips of land are called **range strips** (see Figure 8.4). They are designated by consecutive numbers east or west of the principal meridian. For example, Range 3 East would be a strip of land between 12 and 18 miles east of its principal meridian.

The township squares formed by the intersecting township and range lines are the basic units of the rectangular survey system (see Figure 8.5). Theoretically townships are 6 miles square and contain 36 square miles (23,040 acres). Note that *although a township square is part of a township strip, the two terms do not refer to the same thing.* In this discussion the word *township* used by itself refers to the township square.

Each township is given a legal description by using the designation of the township strip in which the township is located, the designation of the range strip and the name or number of the principal meridian for that area. For example, in Figure 8.5, the township marked X is described as Township 3 North, Range 4 East of the Principal Meridian. That township is the third strip, or tier, north of the base line. This strip (or tier) designates the township number and direction. The township is also located in the fourth range strip (those running north and south) east of the Principal Meridian. Finally, reference is made to the Principal Meridian because the land being described is within the boundary of land surveyed from that meridian. This description is abbreviated as *T3N, R4E Principal Meridian.*

Sections. Each township contains 36 **sections,** each one square mile, or *640 acres.* Sections are numbered 1 through 36, as shown in Figure 8.6. Section 1 is always in the northeast, or upper right-hand, corner. By law each section

Figure 8.4
Range Lines

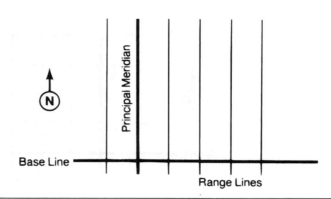

number 16 was set aside for school purposes and is referred to as a *school section.* The sale or rental proceeds from this land were originally available for township school use, and the schoolhouse was usually located in this section so that it would be centrally located for all of the students in the township.

Sections (see Figure 8.7, page 112) are divided into *halves* (320 acres), *quarters* (160 acres) and halves and quarters of those divisions. The southeast quarter of a section, which is a 160-acre tract, is abbreviated SE¼. The SE¼ of SE¼ of SE¼ of Section 1 would be a 10-acre square in the lower right-hand corner of Section 1. Sometimes this description is written without the word *of* because a comma means *of:* SE¼, SE¼, SE¼ Section 1. It is possible to combine portions of a section, such as NE¼ of SW¼ and N½ of NW¼ of SE¼ of Section 1, which could also be written NE¼, SW¼; N½, NW¼, SE¼ of Section 1. A semicolon means *and.* Notice that because of the word *and* in this description the area is 60 acres.

Correction lines. Due to the curvature of the earth, the convergence of the range lines, which run north and south, must be compensated for. All range lines continually approach each other and, if extended northward, would eventually meet at the North Pole. An accurate survey of a township would show its north line to be about 50 feet shorter than its south line. In the case of the fourth township north of the base line the difference is four times as great, or about 200 feet. The rectangular survey system compensates for the resulting shortages with **correction lines** (see Figure 8.8, page 113). Every fourth township line both north and south of the base line is designated a correction line, and on each correction line the range lines are measured to the full distance of six miles apart. Guide meridians run north and south at 24-mile intervals from the principal meridian. A **government check** is the area bounded by two guide meridians and two correction lines, approximately 24 miles square. Because of the curvature of the earth and the crude instruments used in early days, in practice few townships are exactly six-mile squares or contain exactly 36 square miles.

Because most townships do not contain exactly 36 square miles, surveyors follow well-established rules in adjusting such errors. These rules provide that any overage or shortage in a township be adjusted in those sections adjacent to its north and west boundaries (Sections 1, 2, 3, 4, 5, 6, 7, 18, 19, 30 and 31). These are called *fractional sections* (discussed in the following paragraph). All other sections are exactly one square mile and are known as *standard sections.* These

**Figure 8.5
Townships in the
Rectangular Survey
System**

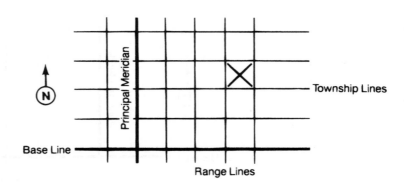

provisions for making corrections explain some of the variations in township and section acreage under the rectangular survey system of legal description.

Fractional sections and government lots. Undersized or oversized sections are classified as **fractional sections** and may occur for a number of reasons. For example, part of a section may be submerged in water. In some areas the rectangular survey was made by separate crews and may have resulted in gaps less than a section wide being left when the surveys met. Other errors may have resulted from the physical difficulties encountered in the actual survey.

Areas smaller than full quarter-sections were numbered and designated as **government lots** by government surveyors. An overage or shortage was corrected whenever possible by placing the government lots in the north or west portions of the fractional sections. For example, a government lot might be described as Government Lot 2 in the northwest quarter of fractional section 18, Township 2 North, Range 4 East of the Salt Lake Meridian.

**Figure 8.6
Sections in a
Township**

```
              N
        6  5  4  3  2  1
        7  8  9 10 11 12
       18 17 (16)15 14 13
    W  19 20 21 22 23 24   E
       30 29 28 27 26 25
       31 32 33 34 35 36
              S
```

> **IN PRACTICE...**
>
> *When reading a government survey description of land, read from right to left, starting at the end and working backward to the beginning, to determine the location and size of the property. For example, consider the following description:*
>
> *The S½ of the NW¼ of the SE¼ of Section II, Township 8 North, Range 6 West of the Fourth Principal Meridian.*
>
> *To locate this tract of land from this citation alone, first search for the Fourth Principal Meridian on a map of the United States. Then, on a regional map, find the township in which the property is located by counting six range strips west of the Fourth Principal Meridian and eight townships north of its corresponding base line. After locating Section II you would divide the section into quarters, the SE¼ into quarters and then the NW¼ of that into halves. The S½ of that NW¼ contains the property in question.*
>
> *In computing the size of this tract of land, first determine that the SE¼ of the section contains 160 acres (640 acres divided by 4). The NW¼ of that quarter-section contains 40 acres (160 acres divided by 4), and the S½ of that quarter-section—the property in question—contains 20 acres (40 acres divided by 2).*
>
> *In general, if a rectangular survey description does not use the conjunction* and *or a semicolon (indicating various parcels are combined), the longer the description, the smaller the tract of land it describes.*

Metes-and-bounds descriptions within the rectangular survey system. Land in states using the rectangular survey system may also require a metes-and-bounds description. This usually occurs in describing an irregular tract, a tract too small to be described by quarter-sections or a tract that does not follow either the lot or block lines of a recorded subdivision or section, quarter-section or other fractional section lines. An example of a combined metes-and-bounds and rectangular survey system description is as follows (see Figure 8.9, page 114):

> That part of the northwest quarter of Section 12, Township 10 North, Range 7 West of the Third Principal Meridian, bounded by a line described as follows: Commencing at the southeast corner of the northwest quarter of said Section 12 then north 500 feet; then west parallel with the south line of said section 1,000 feet; then south parallel with the east line of said section 500 feet to the south line of said northwest quarter; then east along said south line to the point of beginning.

Lot-and-Block System

The third method of legal description is the **lot-and-block** (recorded plat) system. This system uses *lot-and-block numbers* referred to in a **plat map** filed in the public records of the county where the land is located.

Initially a large parcel of land is described either by metes and bounds or by rectangular survey. Once this large parcel is surveyed, it is broken down into smaller parcels, so the lot-and-block legal description is always based on a refer-

Figure 8.7
A Section

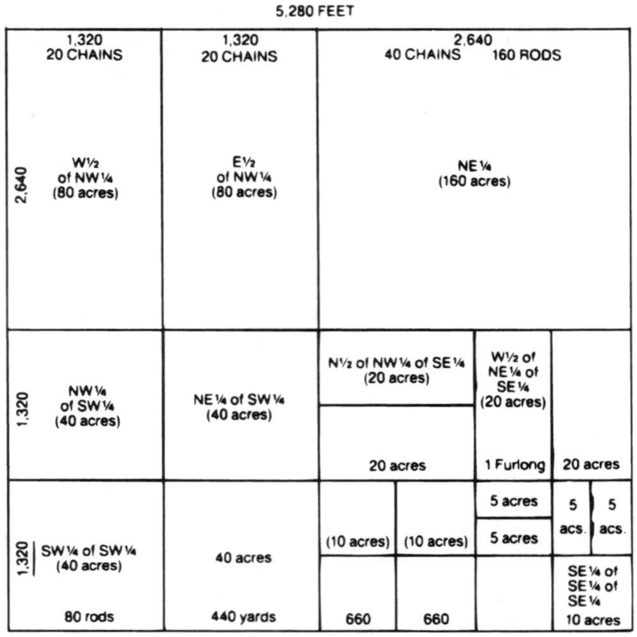

5,280 FEET

1,320 20 CHAINS	1,320 20 CHAINS	2,640 40 CHAINS 160 RODS		
W½ of NW¼ (80 acres) *(2,640)*	E½ of NW¼ (80 acres)	NE¼ (160 acres)		
NW¼ of SW¼ (40 acres) *(1,320)*	NE¼ of SW¼ (40 acres)	N½ of NW¼ of SE¼ (20 acres)	W½ of NE¼ of SE¼ (20 acres)	
		20 acres	1 Furlong 20 acres	
SW¼ of SW¼ (40 acres) *(1,320)*	40 acres	(10 acres) (10 acres)	5 acres / 5 acres	5 acs. / 5 acs.
80 rods	440 yards	660 660		SE¼ of SE¼ of SE¼ 10 acres

ence to a prior metes-and-bounds or rectangular survey description. For each parcel described under the lot-and-block system the lot refers to the numerical designation of any particular parcel and the block refers to the name of the subdivision under which the map is recorded. The block reference is drawn from the early 1900s, when a city block was the most common type of subdivided property.

The lot-and-block system starts with the preparation of a *survey plat* by a licensed surveyor or an engineer as illustrated in Figure 8.10. On this plat the land is divided into numbered or lettered lots and blocks, and streets or access roads for public use are indicated. Lot sizes and street details must be indicated completely and must comply with all local ordinances and requirements. When properly signed and approved, the subdivision plat is recorded in the county in which the land is located; it thereby becomes part of the legal description. In describing a lot from a recorded subdivision plat, the lot and block number, name or number of the subdivision plat and name of the county and state are used. For example:

Lot 71, Happy Valley Estates 2, located in a portion of the southeast quarter of Section 23, Township 7 North, Range 4 East of the Seward Principal Meridian in _____ County, _____ [state].

Anyone wishing to locate this parcel would start with the map of the Seward Principal Meridian to locate the township and range reference; then consult the township map of Township 7 North, Range 4 East; then the section map of Section 23; then the quarter-section map of the southeast quarter, which would refer to the plat map for the subdivision known as the second unit (second parcel subdivided) under the name of Happy Valley Estates.

**Figure 8.8
Correction Lines and
Guide Meridians**

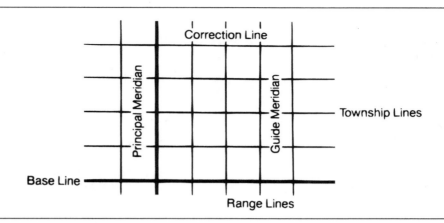

Some subdivided lands are further divided by a later resubdivision. For example, if one developer (in this example, "Western View") purchased a large parcel from a second developer ("Homewood") and resubdivided this into different-sized parcels, the resulting legal description might be as follows:

Lot 4, Western View Resubdivision of the Homewood Subdivision, located in a portion of west half of Section 19, Township 10 North, Range 13 East of the Black Hills Principal Meridian, _____ County, _____ [state].

The lot-and-block system is now used to some degree in all states. Some states have passed plat acts that specify the smallest parcel that may be sold without a subdivision plat map being prepared, approved and recorded. For example, in some states the minimum size is five acres; in others it is one acre.

PREPARATION AND USE OF A SURVEY

Legal descriptions should not be changed, altered or combined without adequate information from a competent authority, such as a surveyor or title attorney. Legal descriptions should always include the name of the county and state in which the land is located because meridians often relate to more than one state and occasionally relate to two base lines. For example, the description "the southwest quarter of Section 10, Township 4 North, Range 1 West of the Fourth Principal Meridian" could refer to land in either Illinois or Wisconsin.

A licensed surveyor is trained and authorized to locate a given parcel of land and determine its legal description. The surveyor does this by preparing a *survey,* which sets forth the legal description of the property, and a *survey sketch,* which shows the location and dimensions of the parcel. When a survey also shows the location, size and shape of buildings located on the lot, it is referred to as a *spot survey.* Surveys are required in many real estate transactions, such as when conveying a portion of a given tract of land, conveying real estate as security for a mortgage loan, showing the location of new construction, locating roads and highways, determining the legal description of the land on which a particular building is located and determining if there are any encroachments.

**Figure 8.9
Metes and Bounds
with Rectangular
Survey**

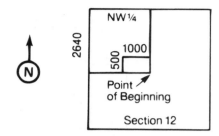

"Section 12, TN10, R7W, Third Principal
Meridian"

IN PRACTICE... | *Because legal descriptions, once recorded, affect title to real estate, they should be prepared only by a surveyor. Real estate licensees who attempt to draft legal descriptions create potential risks for themselves and their clients and customers. Further, legal descriptions should be copied with care. An incorrectly worded legal description in a sales contract may obligate the seller to convey or the buyer to purchase more or less land than intended. Title problems can arise for the buyer who seeks to convey the property at a future date. Even if the contract can be corrected by the parties involved before the sale is closed, the licensee runs the risk of losing a commission and may be held liable for damages suffered by an injured party because of an improperly worded legal description.*

**MEASURING
ELEVATIONS**

Surveyors must properly and accurately mark the survey points they have established using *monuments* and *benchmarks*.

Monuments are traditionally used to mark only surface measurements between points. A monument is any item used to mark a corner or an angle in a survey. It could be a marker set in concrete, a piece of steel reinforcing bar ("rebar") or pipe driven into the soil or simply a wooden stake placed in the dirt. Their accuracy can be suspect because they are subject to the whims of nature and vandals. Therefore, surveyors rely most heavily on benchmarks to mark their work accurately and permanently.

Benchmarks (see Figure 8.11) are permanent reference points that have been established throughout the United States. They are usually embossed brass markers set into solid concrete or asphalt bases. While used to some degree for surface measurements, their principal reference use is for marking datums.

A **datum** *is a point, line or surface from which elevations are measured or indicated.* For the purpose of the United States Geological Survey (USGS), *datum* is defined as the mean sea level at New York Harbor. It is of special significance to surveyors in determining the height of structures, establishing the grades of streets and similar situations.

**Figure 8.10
Subdivision
Plat Map**

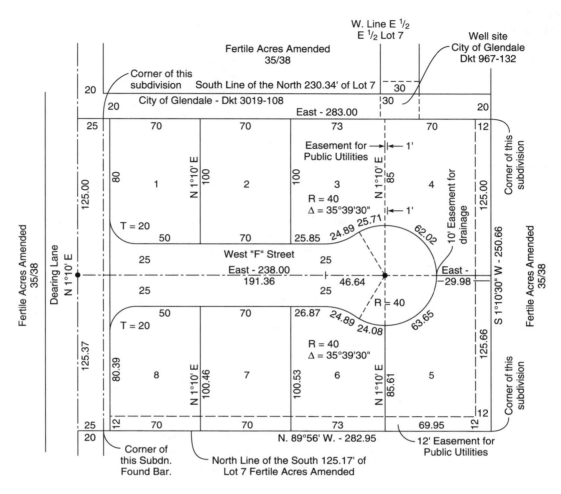

All large cities have established a local official datum that is used in place of the USGS datum. For instance, the official datum for Chicago is known as the *Chicago City Datum* and is a horizontal plane below the surface of the city. This plane was established in 1847 as corresponding to the low-water level of Lake Michigan in that year and is considered to be at zero elevation.

Cities with local datums also have designated local benchmarks, which are given official status when assigned a permanent identifying number. Local benchmarks simplify surveyors' work because measurements may be based on them rather than on the basic benchmark, which may be miles away. A surveyor's measurement of elevation based on the USGS datum will differ from one computed according to a local datum. A surveyor can always translate an elevation based on a local datum to the elevation based on the USGS.

Air Rights

Just as surface rights must be surveyed and specifically identified, so must air rights and subsurface rights. The owner of a parcel of land may subdivide the air above his or her land into **air lots.** Air lots are composed of airspace within specific boundaries located over a parcel of land. This type of description is

Figure 8.11
Benchmark

found in titles to tall buildings located in air rights, generally over railroad tracks. Similarly a surveyor, in preparing a subdivision plat for condominium use, describes each condominium unit by reference to the elevation of the floors and ceilings on a vertical plane above the city datum.

The condominium laws passed in all states (see Chapter 7) require that a registered land surveyor prepare a plat map showing the elevations of floor and ceiling surfaces and the vertical boundaries of each condominium unit with reference to an official datum. Typically a separate plat will be prepared for each floor in the condominium building.

The following is an example of the legal description of a condominium apartment unit that includes a fractional share of the common elements of the building and land:

UNIT_____ as delineated on survey of the following described parcel of real estate (hereinafter referred to as Development Parcel): The north 99 feet of the west ½ of Block 4 (except that part, if any, taken and used for street), in Sutton's Division Number 5 in the east ½ of the southeast ¼ of Section 24, Township 3 South, Range 68 West of the Sixth Principal Meridian, in Denver County, Colorado, which survey is attached as Exhibit A to Declaration made by Colorado National Bank as Trustee under Trust No. 1250, recorded in the Recorder's Office of Denver County, Colorado, as Document No. 475637; together with an undivided _____% interest in said Development Parcel (excepting from said Development Parcel all the property and space comprising all the units thereof as defined and set forth in said Declaration and Survey).

Table 8.1
Units of Land
Measurement

Unit	Measurement
mile	5,280 feet; 1,760 yards; 320 rods
rod	16.5 feet; 5.50 yards
sq. mile	640 acres (5,280 × 5,280 = 27,878,400 ÷ 43,560)
acre	43,560 sq. feet; 160 sq. rods
sq. yard	9 sq. feet
sq. foot	144 sq. inches
chain	66 feet; 4 rods; 160 links

MATH CONCEPT Land Acquisition Costs	To calculate the cost of purchasing land you must calculate using the same unit in which the cost is given. Costs quoted per square foot must be multiplied by the proper number of square feet, costs quoted per acre must be multiplied by the proper number of acres and so on.

To calculate the cost of a parcel of land of 3 acres at $1.10 per square foot, convert the acreage to square feet before multiplying

43,560 square feet per acre × 3 acres = 130,680 square feet
130,680 square feet × $1.10 per square foot = $143,748

To calculate the cost of a parcel of land of 17,500 square feet at $60,000 per acre, convert the cost per acre into the cost per square foot before multiplying by the number of square feet in the parcel:

$60,000 per acre ÷ 43,560 square feet per acre = $1.38 (rounded) per square foot;
17,500 square feet × $1.38 per square foot = $24,150

Subsurface Rights

Subsurface rights can be legally described in the same manner as air rights. However, they are measured *below* the datum rather than above it. Subsurface rights are used not only for coal mining, petroleum drilling and utility line location but also for multistory condominiums—both residential and commercial—that have several floors below ground level. In urban areas this type of land planning affords a practical solution to the problem of imposing skylines, and in extreme climates it can reduce utility bills.

LAND UNITS AND MEASUREMENTS

It is important to understand land units and measurements because they are an integral part of legal descriptions. Some commonly used measurements are listed in Table 8.1. Remember that a *section* of land is one square mile and contains 640 acres; a *quarter-section* contains 160 acres; a *quarter of a quarter-section* contains 40 acres. A *circle* contains 360 degrees; a *quarter-segment* of a circle contains 90 degrees; a *half-segment* of a circle contains 180 degrees. One *degree* (1°) can be subdivided into 60 minutes (60′), each of which contains 60 seconds (60″). One-and-a-half degrees would be written 1°30′0″.

●   ●   ●   ●   ●   ●   ●

KEY TERMS

air lot   monument
base line   plat map
benchmark   point of beginning (POB)
correction line   principal meridian
datum   range strip
fractional section   rectangular (government) survey system
government check   section
government lot   tier
legal description   township
lot-and-block (recorded plat) system   township strip
metes-and-bounds description

SUMMARY

A legal description is a precise method of identifying a parcel of land. There are three methods of legal description: metes and bounds, rectangular (government) survey system and lot-and-block (plat map) system. A property's description should always be the same as the one used in previous documents.

A metes-and-bounds description uses direction and distance measurement to establish precise boundaries for a parcel. Monuments are fixed objects used to establish boundaries. Their actual location takes precedence over the written linear measurement in a document. When property is being described by metes and bounds, the description must always enclose a tract of land; the boundary line must end at the point at which it started, the point of beginning of land.

The rectangular (government) survey system is used in 30 states. It involves surveys based on 35 principal meridians. Under this system each principal meridian and its corresponding base line are specifically located. Any particular parcel of land is surveyed from only one principal meridian and its base line.

East and west lines parallel with the base line form six-mile-wide strips called township strips or tiers. North and south lines parallel with the principal meridian form range strips. The resulting squares are 36 square miles in area and are called townships. Townships are designated by their township and range numbers and their principal meridian—for example, Township 3 North, Range 4 East of the _____ Meridian. Townships are divided into 36 sections of one square mile each.

When a tract is irregular or its boundaries do not coincide with a section, regular fractions of a section or a boundary of a lot or block in a subdivision, a surveyor can prepare a combination rectangular survey and metes-and-bounds description.

Land in every state can be subdivided into lots and blocks by means of a plat map. An approved plat of survey showing the division into blocks, giving the size, location and designation of lots and specifying the location and size of streets to be dedicated for public use is filed for record in the recorder's office of the county in which the land is located. A subdivision plat will give the legal description of a building site in a town or city by lot, block and subdivision in a section, township and range of a principal meridian in a county and state.

Air lots, condominium descriptions and other measurements of vertical elevations may be computed from the United States Geological Survey datum, which is the mean sea level in New York Harbor. Most large cities have established local survey datums for surveying within the area. The elevations from these datums are further supplemented by reference points, called benchmarks, placed at fixed intervals from the datums.

Questions

1. What is the proper description of the following shaded area?

   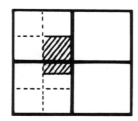

   a. SW¼ of the NE¼ and the N½ of the SE¼
      of the SW¼
   b. N½ of the NE¼ of the SW¼ and the SE¼
      of the NW¼
   c. SW¼ of the SE¼ of the NW¼ and the
      N½ of the NE¼ of the SW¼
   d. S½ of the SW¼ of the NE¼ and the NE¼
      of the NW¼ of the SE¼

2. When surveying land, a surveyor refers to
   the principal meridian that is

   a. nearest the land being surveyed.
   b. in the same state as the land being
      surveyed.
   c. not more than 40 townships or 15 ranges
      distant from the land being surveyed.
   d. within the rectangular survey system
      area in which the land being surveyed is
      located.

3. The N½ of the SW¼ of a section contains

   a. 40 acres.   c. 160 acres.
   b. 20 acres.   d. 80 acres.

4. In describing real estate, the system that
   uses feet, degrees and natural markers as
   monuments is

   a. rectangular survey.
   b. metes and bounds.
   c. government survey.
   d. lot and block.

Questions 5 through 8 refer to the following
illustration of a whole township and parts of
the adjacent townships:

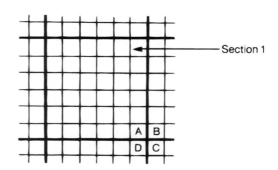

5. The section marked *A* is which of the following?

   a. School section   c. Section 31
   b. Section 36   d. Government lot

6. Which of the following is Section 6?

   a. D   c. B
   b. C   d. A

7. The section directly below C is

   a. Section 12.   c. Section 30.
   b. Section 25.   d. Section 7.

8. Which of the following is Section D?

   a. Section 36   c. Section 1
   b. Section 31   d. Section 6

9. Which of these shaded areas depicts the NE¼ of the SE¼ of the SW¼?

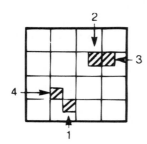

   a. Area 1   c. Area 3
   b. Area 2   d. Area 4

10. An acre contains
    a. 160 square feet.
    b. 43,560 square feet.
    c. 640 square feet.
    d. 360 degrees.

11. How many acres are there in the tract described as "Beginning at the NW corner of the SW¼, then south along the west line to the SW corner of the section, then east along the south line of the section 2,640 feet, more or less, to the SE corner of the said SW¼, then in a straight line to the POB"?
    a. 100 acres   c. 90 acres
    b. 160 acres   d. 80 acres

12. The proper description of the shaded township area in this illustration is

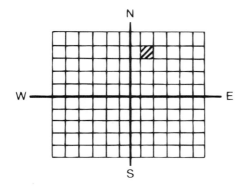

    a. T4N R2W.   c. T4N R2E.
    b. T2W R4N.   d. T2E R4N.

13. If a farm described as "the NW¼ of the SE¼ of Section 10, Township 2 North, Range 3 West of the 6th. P.M." sold for $1,500 an acre, what would the sales price be?
    a. $30,000   c. $45,000
    b. $15,000   d. $60,000

14. The legal description "the northwest ¼ of the southwest ¼ of Section 6, Township 4 North, Range 7 West" is defective because there is no reference to
    a. lot numbers.
    b. boundary lines.
    c. a principal meridian.
    d. a record of survey.

15. To keep the principal meridian and range lines as near six miles apart as possible, a correction known as a *government check* is made every
    a. one square mile.
    b. three square miles.
    c. six square miles.
    d. 24 square miles.

16. Fractional sections in the rectangular survey system that are less than a quarter-section in area are known as
    a. fractional parcels.
    b. government lots.
    c. hiatus.
    d. fractional townships.

17. A woman purchased 4.5 acres of land for which she paid $78,400. An adjoining owner wants to purchase a strip of her land measuring 150 feet by 100 feet. What should this strip cost the adjoining owner if the woman sells it for the same price she originally paid for it?
    a. $3,000   c. $7,800
    b. $6,000   d. $9,400

18. How many acres are contained in the parcel defined as "Beginning at the NE corner of the SW¼ of Section 23; then one mile, more or less, in a northerly direction to the NW corner of the SE¼ of Section 14; then one mile, more or less, in a southeasterly direction to the NW corner of the SE¼ of Section 24; then one mile, more or less, in a westerly direction to the point of beginning"?

a. 160
b. 320
c. 640
d. 1,280

19. A property contained ten acres. How many 50-foot by 100-foot lots could be subdivided from the property if 26,000 square feet were dedicated for roads?

a. 80
b. 81
c. 82
d. 83

20. A parcel of land is 400 feet by 640 feet. The parcel is cut in half diagonally by a stream. How many acres are there in each half of the parcel?

a. 2.75
b. 2.94
c. 5.51
d. 5.88

21. What is the shortest distance between Section 4 and Section 32 in the same township?

a. 3 miles
b. 4 miles
c. 5 miles
d. 6 miles

22. A man owns the NW¼ and the SW¼ of Section 17, and his neighbor owns the NE¼ and the SE¼ of Section 18. If they agree that each will install one-half of a common fence, how many rods of fence will each install?

a. 0
b. 160
c. 320
d. 440

23. The section due west of Section 18, Township 5 North, Range 8 West, is

a. Section 19, T5N, R8W.
b. Section 17, T5N, R8W.
c. Section 13, T5N, R9W.
d. Section 12, T5N, R7W.

24. An owner is considering building a patio in her backyard. The 60-foot by 15-foot by 4-inch slab would cost $78.40 per cubic yard of concrete, and the finishing would cost $.38 per square foot. The total cost would be

a. $875.33.
b. $1,045.33.
c. $1,182.13.
d. $1,213.11.

25. In any township the section designated as the school section is Section

a. 1.
b. 16.
c. 25.
d. 36.

26. The least acceptable method for identifying real property is

a. rectangular survey.
b. metes and bounds.
c. street address.
d. lot and block.

9

Real Estate Taxes and Other Liens

LIENS

A **lien** is the charge or claim against the property of another that provides security for a debt. It is an encumbrance that represents an interest in the ownership; it does not constitute ownership in the property. The interest gives the lienholder the right to force the sale or confiscate the property if the owner defaults on the debt. Generally, a lienholder must institute a legal action to force sale of the property to collect the debt or acquire title. Liens distinguish themselves from other encumbrances because, although they attach the property, they do so because of a debt. For this reason, all liens are viewed as encumbrances, but not all encumbrances are liens.

Liens can be categorized on several levels (see Figure 9.1). They are classified according to how they are created: a lien can be voluntary or involuntary. A **voluntary lien** is created intentionally by the debtor's action, such as when someone takes out a mortgage loan. An **involuntary lien** is created by law and can be either statutory or equitable. A **statutory lien** is created by statute. A real estate tax lien, for example, is an involuntary, statutory lien; it is created by statute without any action by the property owner. An **equitable lien** arises out of common law and may be created by a court based on the concept of "fairness." A court-ordered judgment requiring payment of the balance on a delinquent charge account would be an involuntary, equitable lien on the debtor's real estate.

Liens are also classified according to the property they affect. **General liens** affect all the property of a debtor, both real and personal. They include judgments, estate and inheritance taxes, debts of a decedent, corporation franchise taxes and Internal Revenue Service taxes. There is a difference, however, between a lien on real and a lien on personal property: A lien attaches to real property when it is filed. In contrast, the lien does not attach to personal property until the personal property is seized. **Specific liens** are secured by specific property and affect only that particular property. Specific liens on real estate include mechanics' liens, mortgage liens, tax liens and liens for special assessments and utilities. (Specific liens can also secure personal property, such as when a lien is placed on a car to secure payment of a car loan.)

Figure 9.1
Types of Liens

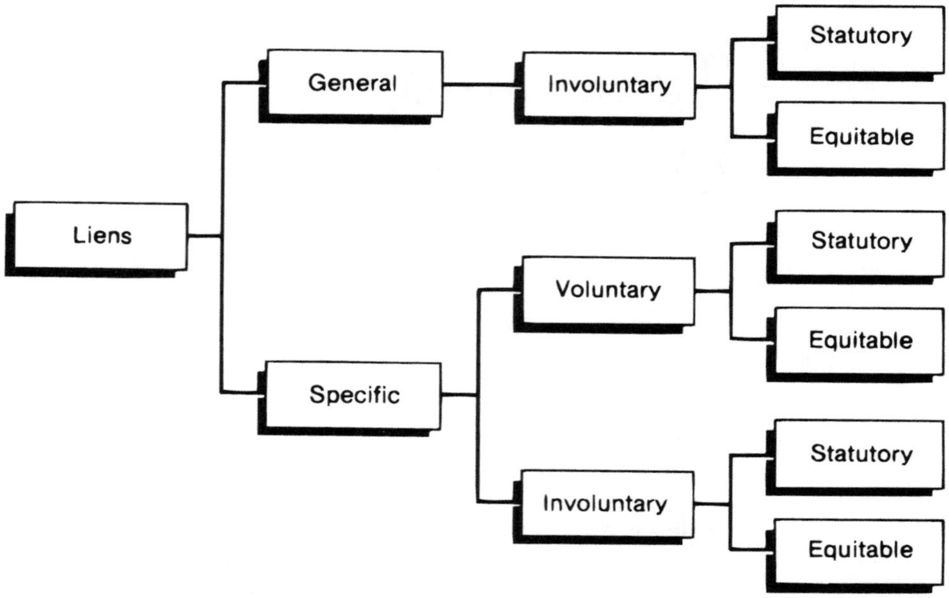

Effects of Liens on Title

The existence of a lien does not prevent the property owner from conveying title to someone else. The lien could very well reduce the value of the real estate, however, because the seller could find it difficult to locate a buyer willing to take on the risk of such a burdened property. Although a purchaser will not be obligated to pay the debt of a specific lien on the real estate—which attaches to that property, not to the property owner—the new owner could lose the property if the creditors take court action to enforce payment. Once properly established, liens *run with the land* and will bind all successive owners until the liens are cleared. Therefore future resales could also be jeopardized if the debt is not satisfied.

Priority of liens. *Priority of liens* establishes the order of claim against the property. Liens take priority from the *date of recording* in the public records of the county where the property is located.

There are notable exceptions to this rule. Real estate taxes and special assessments generally take priority over all other liens. This means that if the property goes through a court sale to satisfy unpaid debts or obligations, outstanding real estate taxes and special assessments will be paid from the proceeds *first.* The remainder of the proceeds will be used to pay other outstanding liens in the order of their priority. Mechanics' liens, will take priority as provided by state law but never take priority over tax and special assessment liens.

For example, if the courts ordered a parcel of land sold to satisfy a judgment lien entered in the public record on February 7, 1991, subject to a first mortgage lien recorded January 22, 1988, and to this year's unpaid real estate taxes, the proceeds of the sale would be distributed in the following order:

1. To the taxing bodies for this year's real estate taxes

2. To the mortgage lender for the entire amount of the mortgage loan outstanding as of the date of the sale

3. To the creditor named in the judgment lien (if any proceeds remain after paying the first two items)

4. To the foreclosed-on landowner (if any proceeds remain after paying the first three items)

Subordination agreements are written agreements between lienholders to change the priority of mortgage, judgment and other liens under certain circumstances. Priority and recording of liens will be discussed further in Chapter 12.

REAL ESTATE TAX LIENS

As discussed in Chapter 6, the ownership of real estate is subject to certain government powers. One of these is the right of state and local governments to impose **tax liens** for the support of their functions. Because the location of real estate is permanently fixed, the government can levy taxes with a high degree of certainty that the taxes will be collected. The annual taxes levied on real estate usually have priority over previously recorded liens, so they may be enforced by a court-ordered sale.

There are two types of real estate taxes. Both are levied against specific parcels of property and automatically become liens on those properties.

General Tax (Ad Valorem Tax)

The general real estate tax, or **ad valorem tax,** is made up of the taxes levied on real estate by various governmental agencies and municipalities. These include states, counties, cities, towns and villages. Other taxing bodies are school districts (including local elementary and high schools, junior colleges and community colleges), drainage districts, water districts and sanitary districts. Municipal authorities operating recreational preserves such as forest preserves and parks are also authorized by the legislatures of the various states to levy real estate taxes.

General real estate taxes are levied for the *general operation* of the governmental agency authorized to impose the levy. These taxes are known as *ad valorem* (Latin for "according to value") *taxes* because the amount of the tax is based on the *value of the property being taxed.* Ad valorem taxes are specific, involuntary, statutory liens.

Exemptions from general taxes. Under most state laws certain real estate is exempt from real estate taxation. For example, property owned by cities, various municipal organizations (such as schools, parks and playgrounds), the state and federal governments, religious organizations, hospitals or educational institutions is tax-exempt. The property must be used for tax-exempt purposes.

Many state laws also allow special exemptions to reduce real estate tax bills for certain property owners or land uses. Homeowners and senior citizens are frequently granted set reductions in the assessed values of their homes. Some states offer real estate tax reductions to attract industries, and many states offer tax reductions for agricultural land.

Assessment. Real estate is valued, or assessed, for tax purposes by county or township assessors or appraisers. The land is usually assessed separately from the buildings or other improvements. Some states require assessments to be a certain percentage of market value. State laws may provide for property to be reassessed periodically.

Property owners who claim that errors were made in determining the assessed value of their property may present their objections, usually to a local board of appeal or board of review. Protests or appeals regarding tax assessments may ultimately be taken to court.

Equalization. In some jurisdictions, when it is necessary to correct general inequalities in statewide tax assessments, uniformity may be achieved by use of an **equalization factor.** Such a factor may be provided for use in counties or districts where the assessments are to be raised or lowered. The assessed value of each property is multiplied by the equalization factor, and the tax rate is then applied to the equalized assessment. For example, the assessments in one county are determined to be 20 percent lower than the average assessments throughout the rest of the state. This underassessment can be corrected by requiring the application of an equalization factor of 120 percent to each assessment in that county. Thus a parcel of land assessed for tax purposes at $98,000 would be taxed on an equalized value of $117,600 ($98,000 × 1.20 = $117,600).

Tax rates. The process of arriving at a real estate tax rate begins with the *adoption of a budget* by each taxing district. Each budget covers the financial requirements of the taxing body for the coming fiscal year, which may be the January to December calendar year or some other 12-month period designated by statute. The budget must include an estimate of all expenditures for the year and indicate the amount of income expected from all fees, revenue sharing and other sources. The net amount remaining to be raised from real estate taxes is then determined from these figures.

The next step is *appropriation,* the action taken by each taxing body that authorizes the expenditure of funds and provides for the sources of such monies. Appropriation generally involves the adoption of an ordinance or the passage of a law setting forth the specifics of the proposed taxation.

The amount to be raised from the general real estate tax is then imposed on property owners through a *tax levy,* the formal action taken to impose the tax, by a vote of the taxing district's governing body.

The *tax rate* for each individual taxing body is computed separately. To arrive at a tax rate the total monies needed for the coming fiscal year are divided by the total assessments of all real estate located within the jurisdiction of the taxing body. For example, a taxing district's budget indicates that $300,000 must be raised from real estate tax revenues, and the assessment roll (assessor's record) of all taxable real estate within this district equals $10,000,000. The tax rate is computed thus:

$$\$300,000 \div \$10,000,000 = .03, \text{ or } 3\%$$

The *tax rate* may be stated in a number of different ways. In many areas it is expressed in mills. A **mill** is *1/1,000 of a dollar, or $.001.* The tax rate may be expressed as a mill ratio, in dollars per hundred or in dollars per thousand. The tax rate computed in the preceding example could be expressed as

30 mills

or

$3 per $100 of assessed value

or

$30 per $1,000 of assessed value

Tax bills. A property owner's tax bill is computed by applying the tax rate to the assessed valuation of the property. For example, on property assessed for tax purposes at $90,000, at a tax rate of 3 percent, or 30 mills, the tax will be $2,700 ($90,000 × .030 = $2,700). If an equalization factor is used, the computation with an equalization factor of 120 percent will be

$$\$\,90,000 \times 1.20 = \$108,000$$

$$\$108,000 \times .030 = \$\,3,240 \text{ tax}$$

Generally one tax bill that incorporates all real estate taxes levied by the various taxing districts is prepared for each property. In some areas, however, separate bills are prepared by each taxing body. Sometimes the real estate taxing bodies may operate on different budget years so that the taxpayer receives separate bills for various taxes at different times during the year.

Due dates for tax payments are usually set by statute. Taxes may be payable in two installments (semiannually), four installments (quarterly) or 12 installments (monthly). In some areas taxes become due at the beginning of the current tax year and must be paid in advance (1993 taxes paid at the beginning of 1993). In others they are payable during the year after the taxes are levied (1993 taxes paid throughout 1993). And in still others a partial payment is due in the year of the tax with the balance due in the following year (1993 taxes payable during 1993 and 1994). Knowledge of local tax payment schedules is critical in computing the real estate taxes owed when a property is sold.

Some states offer discounts to encourage prompt payment of real estate taxes. Penalties in the form of monthly interest charges are added to all taxes that are not paid when due. The due date may also be called the *penalty date*.

Enforcement of tax liens. To be enforceable real estate taxes must be valid, which means they must be levied properly, used for a legal purpose and applied equitably to all affected property. Real estate taxes that have remained delinquent for the period of time specified by state law can be collected by the tax collecting officer through either tax foreclosure (similar to mortgage foreclosure) or **tax sale.** While there are substantial differences in the methods and details of the various states' tax sale procedures, the results are the same.

Tax sales are usually held according to a published notice after a court has rendered a judgment for the tax and penalties and ordered that the property be sold. Because a specific amount of delinquent tax and penalty must be collected, the purchaser at a tax sale must pay at least this amount. A defaulted taxpayer may have the right of **redemption** (the right to buy back the real estate), so in some areas the bidding at a tax sale is based on the interest rate the defaulted taxpayer would have to pay to redeem the property. That is, the person bidding the lowest redemption interest rate (the one most beneficial for the taxpayer) becomes the successful bidder; that interest rate theoretically would be the easiest for the taxpayer to meet and thus redeem the property. A *certificate of sale* is usually given to the successful bidder when he or she pays the delinquent tax amount.

Generally the delinquent taxpayer can redeem the property at any time before the tax sale by paying the delinquent taxes plus interest and charges (any court costs or attorney's fees); this is known as an *equitable right of redemption.* Some state laws also grant a period of redemption *after the tax sale* during which the defaulted owner or creditors of the defaulted owner may redeem the property by paying the amount paid at the tax sale plus interest and charges (including any taxes levied since the sale); this is known as the *statutory right of redemption.* (The right of redemption is discussed further in Chapter 14.) If the property is not redeemed within the statutory period, the certificate holder can apply for a *tax deed.* The quality of the title conveyed by a tax deed varies from state to state.

In some states tax-delinquent land is sold or conveyed to the state or a taxing authority. At the expiration of the redemption period title to such land is sold at auction to the highest bidder(s). The tax deed issued to the purchasers is regarded as conveying good title, because it is considered a conveyance by the state of state-owned land. In some jurisdictions tax-delinquent land that is not sold at a tax sale due to lack of buyers is forfeited to the state. The state may then either use the land for its own purposes or sell it later.

Special Assessments (Improvement Taxes)

Special assessments, the second category of real estate taxes, are special taxes levied on real estate for public improvements to that real estate. Property owners in the area of the improvements are required to pay for them because their properties benefit directly from the improvements. The installation of paved streets, curbs, gutters, sidewalks, storm sewers and street lighting increases the values of the affected properties, so the owners are, in effect, merely reimbursing the levying authority for that increase. However, dollar-for-dollar increases in value are rarely the result.

Special assessments are always specific and statutory, but they can be either involuntary or voluntary liens. Improvements initiated by a public agency create involuntary liens. However, when property owners petition the local government to install a public improvement for which the owners agree to pay, the assessment lien is voluntary.

Whether the lien is voluntary or involuntary, typically each property in the improvement district will be charged a prorated share of the total amount of the assessment, either on a fractional basis (four houses may equally share the cost of one streetlight) or on a cost-per-front-foot basis (wider lots will incur a greater cost than narrower lots for street paving and curb and sidewalk installation).

Special assessments are usually due in equal annual installments over a period of five to ten years, with the first installment usually due during the year following the public authority's approval of the assessment. The first bill will include one year's interest on the property owner's share of the entire assessment; subsequent bills will include one year's interest on the unpaid balance. Property owners have the right to prepay any or all installments to avoid future interest charges.

Today strict subdivision regulations have almost eliminated the concept of special assessments in some parts of the country. Most items for which assessments have traditionally been levied are now required to be installed as part of a subdivision's approval.

OTHER LIENS ON REAL PROPERTY

In addition to real estate tax and special assessment liens, the following types of liens may also be charged against real property.

Mortgage Liens and Deed of Trust Liens

In general a **mortgage lien** or a deed of trust lien is a voluntary lien on real estate given to a lender by a borrower as security for a real estate loan. It becomes a lien on real property when the lender records the documents in the office of the proper official of the county where the property is located. Lenders generally require a preferred lien, referred to as a *first mortgage lien,* meaning that no other liens against the property aside from real estate taxes would take priority over mortgage lien. (Mortgages and deeds of trust are discussed in detail in Chapter 14.)

Mechanics' Liens

The purpose of the **mechanic's lien** is to *give security to those who perform labor or furnish material to improve real property.* A mechanic's lien is a specific, involuntary lien and is available to contractors, subcontractors, architects, equipment lessors, surveyors, laborers and others. This type of lien is filed when the owner has not fully paid for the work or when the general contractor has been paid but has not paid the subcontractors or suppliers of materials. However, statutes in some states prohibit subcontractors from placing liens directly on certain types of property, such as owner-occupied residences.

To be entitled to a mechanic's lien the person who did the work must have had a contract (express or implied) with the owner or the owner's authorized representative. If improvements that were not ordered by the property owner have commenced, the property owner should execute a document called a *notice of nonresponsibility* to relieve himself or herself from possible mechanics' liens. By posting this notice in some conspicuous place on the property and recording a verified copy of it in the public record, the owner gives notice that he or she will not be responsible for the work done.

A person claiming a mechanic's lien must file a notice of lien in the public record of the county where the property is located within a certain period of time after the work has been completed. According to state law, priority of a mechanics' lien may be established as of the date the construction began or materials were first furnished, the date the work was completed, the date the individual subcontractor's work was either commenced or completed, the date the contract was signed or work ordered or the date a notice of the lien was recorded, filed, posted or served. In some states mechanics' liens may be given priority over previously recorded liens such as mortgages.

In most states, while a mechanic's lien takes priority from the time it attaches, a claimant's notice of lien will not be filed in the public records until some time after that. A prospective purchaser of property that has been recently constructed, altered or repaired should therefore be cautious about possible unrecorded mechanics' liens against the property.

Judgments

A **judgment** is a *decree issued by a court.* When the decree provides for the awarding of money and sets forth the amount owed by the debtor to the creditor, the judgment is referred to as a *money judgment.*

A judgment is a *general, involuntary, equitable lien on both real and personal property* owned by the debtor. A judgment differs from a mortgage in that a specific parcel of real estate was not given as security at the time that the debtor-creditor relationship was created. Because a lien usually covers only property located within the county in which the judgment is issued, a notice of the lien must be filed in any county to which a creditor wishes to extend the lien coverage. To enforce a judgment the creditor must obtain from the court a *writ of execution* directing the sheriff to levy upon and sell as much of the debtor's property as is necessary to pay the debt and the expenses of the sale. A judgment does not become a lien against the personal property of a debtor until the creditor orders the sheriff to levy on the property and the levy is actually made.

A judgment lien's priority is established by one or a combination of the following (as provided by state law): the date the judgment was entered by the court, the date the judgment was filed for record in the recorder's office or the date a writ of execution was issued. When property is sold to satisfy a debt, the debtor should demand a legal document known as a *satisfaction of judgment,* or *satisfaction piece,* which should be filed with either the clerk of the court or, in some states, the recorder of deeds so that the record will be cleared of the judgment.

Attachments. To prevent a debtor from conveying title to previously unsecured real estate (realty that is not mortgaged or similarly encumbered) while a court suit is being decided, a creditor may seek a writ of **attachment.** By this writ the court retains custody of the property until the suit is concluded. The creditor must first post a surety bond or deposit with the court sufficient to cover any possible loss or damage to the debtor while the court has custody of the property, in case the judgment is not awarded to the creditor.

Lis pendens. Generally there is a considerable time lag between the filing of a lawsuit and the rendering of a judgment. When any suit is filed that affects title to a specific parcel of real estate (such as a foreclosure suit), a notice known as a **lis pendens** (Latin for "litigation pending") is recorded. A lis pendens is not a lien but rather a *notice of a possible future lien.* Recording of the lis pendens gives notice to all interested parties, such as prospective purchasers and lenders, and establishes a priority for the later lien, which is dated back to the date the lis pendens was recorded.

Estate and Inheritance Tax Liens

Federal **estate taxes** and state **inheritance taxes** (as well as the debts of decedents) are *general, statutory, involuntary liens* that encumber a deceased person's real and personal property. These are normally paid or cleared in probate court proceedings. Probate and issues of inheritance are discussed in Chapter 11.

Table 9.1 Real Estate–Related Liens		General	Specific	Voluntary		Involuntary
	General Real Estate Tax (Ad Valorem Tax) Lien		xx			xx
	Special Assessment (Improvement Tax) Lien		xx	xx	or	xx
	Mortgage Lien		xx	xx		
	Deed of Trust Lien		xx	xx		
	Mechanic's Lien		xx			xx
	Judgment Lien	xx				xx
	Estate Tax Lien	xx				xx
	Inheritance Tax Lien	xx				xx
	Debts of a Decedent	xx				xx
	Municipal Utilities Lien		xx			xx
	Bail Bond Lien		xx	xx		
	Corporation Franchise Tax Lien	xx				xx
	Income Tax Lien	xx				xx

Liens for Municipal Utilities

Municipalities are generally given the right to a *specific, equitable, involuntary lien* on the property of an owner who refuses to pay bills for water or other municipal utility service.

Bail Bond Lien

A real estate owner charged with a crime for which he or she must face trial may choose to put up real estate instead of cash as surety for bail. The execution and recording of such a bail bond creates a *specific, statutory, voluntary lien* against the owner's real estate. This lien is enforceable by the sheriff or other court officer if the accused person does not appear in court as required.

Corporation Franchise Tax Lien

State governments generally levy a corporation franchise tax on corporations as a condition of allowing them to do business in the state. Such a tax is a *general, statutory, involuntary lien* on all property, real and personal, owned by the corporation.

IRS Tax Lien

An Internal Revenue Service (IRS) tax lien results from a person's failure to pay any portion of IRS taxes, such as income and withholding taxes. A federal tax lien is a *general, statutory, involuntary lien* on all real and personal property held by the delinquent taxpayer. Its priority, however, is based on the date of filing or recording; it does not supersede previously recorded liens.

A summary of the real estate-related liens discussed in this chapter appears in Table 9.1.

●   ●   ●   ●   ●   ●   ●

KEY TERMS

ad valorem tax   mechanic's lien
attachment   mill
equalization factor   mortgage lien
equitable lien   redemption
estate taxes   special assignment
general lien   specific lien
inheritance taxes   statutory lien
involuntary lien   subordination agreement
judgment   tax lien
lien   tax sale
lis pendens   voluntary lien

SUMMARY

Liens are claims of creditors or taxing authorities against the real and personal property of a debtor. A lien is a type of encumbrance. Liens are either general, covering all real and personal property of a debtor/owner, or specific, covering only identified property. They are also either voluntary (arising from an action of the debtor) or involuntary—created by statute (statutory) or based on the concept of fairness (equitable).

With the exception of real estate tax liens and mechanics' liens, the priority of liens is generally determined by the order in which they are placed in the public record of the county in which the property is located.

Real estate taxes are levied annually by local taxing authorities and are generally given priority over other liens. Payments are required before stated dates, after which penalties accrue. An owner may lose title to property for nonpayment of taxes, because such tax-delinquent property can be sold at a tax sale. Some states allow a time period during which a defaulted owner can redeem his or her real estate from a tax sale.

Special assessments are levied to allocate the cost of public improvements to the specific parcels of real estate that benefit from them. Assessments are usually payable annually over a five- or ten-year period, together with interest due on the balance of the assessment.

Mortgage liens and deeds of trust liens are voluntary, specific liens given to lenders to secure payment for real estate loans.

Mechanics' liens protect general contractors, subcontractors and material suppliers whose work enhances the value of real estate.

A judgment is a court decree obtained by a creditor, usually for a monetary award from a debtor. A judgment lien can be enforced by court issuance of a writ of execution and sale by the sheriff to pay the judgment amount and costs.

Attachment is a means of preventing a defendant from conveying property before completion of a suit in which a judgment is sought.

Lis pendens is a recorded notice of a lawsuit that is pending in court and may result in a judgment that will affect title to a parcel of real estate.

Federal estate taxes and state inheritance taxes are general liens against a deceased owner's property.

Liens for water charges or other municipal utilities and bail bond liens are specific liens, while corporation franchise tax liens are general liens against a corporation's assets.

Internal Revenue Service tax liens are general liens against the property of a person who is delinquent in payment of IRS taxes.

Questions

1. Which of the following best refers to the type of lien that affects all real and personal property of a debtor?
   a. Specific lien
   b. Voluntary lien
   c. Involuntary lien
   d. General lien

2. *Priority of liens* refers to which of the following?
   a. The order in which a debtor assumes responsibility for payment of obligations
   b. The order in which liens will be paid if property is sold to satisfy a debt
   c. The dates liens are filed for record
   d. The fact that specific liens have greater priority than general liens

3. A lien on real estate made to secure payment for specific municipal improvements is which of the following?
   a. Mechanic's lien
   b. Special assessment
   c. Ad valorem
   d. Utility lien

4. Which of the following is classified as a general lien?
   a. Mechanic's lien
   b. Bail bond lien
   c. Judgment
   d. Real estate taxes

5. Which of the following liens would usually be given highest priority?
   a. A mortgage dated last year
   b. Real estate tax
   c. A mechanic's lien for work started before the mortgage was made
   d. A judgment rendered yesterday

6. A specific parcel of real estate has a market value of $80,000 and is assessed for tax purposes at 25 percent of market value. The tax rate for the county in which the property is located is 30 mills. The tax bill will be
   a. $50.
   b. $60.
   c. $600.
   d. $700.

7. Which of the following is used to distribute the cost of public services among real estate owners?
   a. Personal property tax
   b. Sales tax
   c. Real property tax
   d. Special assessment

8. A mechanic's lien claim arises when a contractor has performed work or provided material to improve a parcel of real estate on the owner's order and the work has not been paid for. Such a contractor has a right to
   a. tear out his or her work.
   b. record a notice of the lien.
   c. record a notice of the lien and file a court suit within the time required by state law.
   d. have personal property of the owner sold to satisfy the lien.

9. What is the annual real estate tax on a property that is valued at $135,000 and assessed for tax purposes at $47,250 with an equalization factor of 125 percent, when the tax rate is 25 mills?
   a. $1,418
   b. $1,477
   c. $945
   d. $1,181

10. Which of the following is a voluntary, specific lien?
    a. IRS tax lien
    b. Mechanic's lien
    c. Mortgage lien
    d. Seller's lien

11. A seller sold a buyer a parcel of real estate. Title has passed, but to date the buyer has not paid the purchase price in full as originally agreed on. If the seller does not receive payment, which of the following would she be entitled to enforce?

    a. Attachment
    b. Buyer's lien
    c. Lis pendens
    d. Judgment

12. A general contractor is going to sue a homeowner for nonpayment; the suit will be filed in two weeks. The contractor just learned that the homeowner has listed the property for sale with a real estate broker. In this situation, which of the following will be used by the contractor and his attorneys to protect his interest?

    a. Seller's lien
    b. Buyer's lien
    c. Assessment
    d. Attachment

13. Special assessment liens

    a. are general liens.
    b. are paid on a monthly basis.
    c. take priority over mechanics' liens.
    d. cannot be prepaid in full without penalty.

14. Which of the following is a lien on real estate?

    a. An easement running with the land
    b. An unpaid mortgage loan
    c. A license
    d. An encroachment

15. Both a mortgage lien and a judgment lien

    a. must be entered by the court.
    b. involve a debtor-creditor relationship.
    c. are general liens.
    d. are involuntary liens.

16. A mechanic's lien would be available to all of the following *except* a

    a. subcontractor.
    b. contractor.
    c. surveyor.
    d. broker.

17. The right of a defaulted taxpayer to recover his or her property prior to its sale for unpaid taxes is the

    a. statutory right of reinstatement.
    b. equitable right of appeal.
    c. statutory right of assessment.
    d. equitable right of redemption.

18. Which of the following is a specific, involuntary lien?

    a. A real estate tax lien
    b. An income tax lien
    c. An estate tax lien
    d. A judgment lien

19. Taxes levied for the operation of the government are called

    a. assessment taxes.
    b. ad valorem taxes.
    c. special taxes.
    d. improvement taxes.

20. All of the following probably would be exempt from real estate taxes *except*

    a. a medical research facility.
    b. a public golf course.
    c. a community church.
    d. an apartment building.

10 Real Estate Contracts

CONTRACT LAW

Brokers and salespeople use many types of contracts and agreements to carry out their responsibilities to sellers, buyers and the general public. The general body of law that governs such agreements is known as *contract law*. A **contract** can be defined as a voluntary agreement or promise between legally competent parties to perform or refrain from performing some legal act, supported by legal consideration. Essentially, a contract is an enforceable promise.

Depending on the situation and the nature or language of the agreement, a contract may be categorized in several ways.

Express and Implied Contracts

A contract may be express or implied depending on how it is created. An **express contract** exists when the parties state the terms and show their intentions in words. An express contract may be either oral or written. The majority of real estate contracts are express contracts, having been reduced to writing. Under the **Statute of Frauds** certain types of contracts must be in writing to be enforceable (to force performance) in a court of law. In an **implied contract** the agreement of the parties is demonstrated by their acts and conduct. The restaurant patron who orders a meal has implied a promise to pay for the food.

Bilateral and Unilateral Contracts

Contracts also may be classified as either bilateral or unilateral. In a **bilateral contract** both parties promise to do something; one promise is given in exchange for another. "I will do this, *and* you will do that." "Okay." A real estate sales contract is a bilateral contract because the seller promises to sell a parcel of real estate and convey title to the property to the buyer, who promises to pay a certain sum of money for the property.

A **unilateral contract,** however, is a one-sided agreement. One party makes a promise to induce a second party to do something. The second party is not legally obligated to act; however, if the second party does comply, the first party is obligated to keep the promise. "I will do this *if* you will do that." For example, a law enforcement agency might offer a monetary payment to anyone who can aid in the capture of a criminal. Only if someone *does* aid in the capture is the reward paid. An option, which will be discussed later, is another example of a unilateral contract.

Executed and Executory Contracts

A contract may be classified as either executed or executory, depending on whether the agreement is performed. An **executed contract** is one in which all parties have fulfilled their promises and thus performed the contract. This usage is not to be confused with the use of *execute,* which refers to the signing of a contract. An **executory contract** exists when an act remains to be performed by one or both parties in the future. A sales contract is an executory contract from the time it is signed until closing, at which time it is said to be executed.

Validity of Contracts

A contract can be described as valid, void, voidable or unenforceable (see Table 10.1), depending on the circumstances.

A contract is **valid** when it meets all the essential elements that make it legally sufficient to be enforceable.

A contract is **void** when it has no legal force or effect because it does not have all the essential elements of a contract. One of the requirements for a valid contract is that it be for a legal purpose; thus, a contract that violates a law is void.

A contract that is **voidable** appears on the surface to be valid but may be rescinded or disaffirmed by one or both parties based on some legal principle. For example, a contract must be entered into by legally competent parties. A contract with a minor is usually voidable, because legal age to contract is normally 18. Generally, a minor is permitted to disaffirm a real estate contract at any time while under age and for a certain period of time after reaching majority age. A voidable contract will be considered by the courts to be a valid contract if the party who has the option to disaffirm the agreement does not do so within a period of time prescribed by state law.

A contract that is **unenforceable** also seems on the surface to be valid; however, neither party can sue the other to force performance. For example, an oral agreement for the sale of a parcel of real estate is unenforceable. This means that if either the buyer or the seller does not comply with the terms of an oral agreement of sale, the other party will be unable to sue to force the defaulting party to perform. There is a distinction between a suit to force performance and a suit for damages, which is permissible in an oral agreement. Unenforceable contracts are said to be "valid as between the parties," because once the agreement is fully executed and both parties are satisfied, neither has reason to initiate a lawsuit to force performance.

Elements Essential to a Valid Contract

A contract must meet certain minimum requirements to be considered legally valid. The following are the basic essential elements.

Offer and acceptance. There must be an offer by one party, the *offeror,* that is accepted by the other, the *offeree.* This requirement, also called *mutual assent,* means that there must be a "meeting of the minds." Courts look to the objective intent of the parties to determine if they intended to enter into a binding agreement. In cases where the Statute of Frauds applies, the offer and acceptance

Table 10.1 Legal Effects of Contracts	Classification of Contract	Legal Effect	Example
	Valid	Binding and enforceable on both parties	Agreement complying with essentials of a valid contract
	Void	No legal effect	Contract for an illegal purpose
	Voidable	Valid, but may be disaffirmed by one party	Contract with a minor
	Unenforceable	Valid between the parties, but neither may force performance	Certain oral agreements

must be in writing. The wording of the contract must express all the agreed upon terms and must be clearly understood by the parties.

An **offer** is a promise made by one party with the request for something in exchange for that promise. The offer is made with the intention that the offeror will be bound to the terms if the offer is accepted. The terms of the offer must be definite and specific and must be communicated to the offeree.

An **acceptance** is the promise by the offeree to be bound by the *exact* terms proposed by the offeror. The acceptance must be communicated to the offeror. Proposing any deviation from the terms of the offer constitutes a rejection of the original offer and becomes a new offer. This is known as a **counteroffer** that must be communicated to the original offering party. The counteroffer must be accepted for a contract to exist.

Besides being terminated by a counteroffer, an offer may be terminated by the offeree's outright rejection of it. The offeree may fail to accept the offer within the prescribed period of time stipulated in the offer. Also the offeror may revoke the offer at any time prior to receipt of the acceptance. This *revocation* must be communicated directly to the offeree by the offeror. The offer is also revoked if the offeree learns of the revocation and observes the offeror act in a manner that indicates that the offer no longer exists.

Consideration. The contract must be based on consideration. **Consideration** is something of legal value offered by one party and accepted by another as an inducement to act or to refrain from some act. There must be a definite statement of consideration in a contract to evidence that something of value was given in exchange for the promise made. Consideration is referred to as that which is "good or valuable" between the parties. The courts do not inquire into the adequacy of consideration. A promise that has been bargained for and exchanged is legally sufficient to satisfy the requirement for consideration as long as there has been no undue influence or fraud.

Legally competent parties. All parties to the contract must have *legal capacity.* That is, they must be of legal age and have sufficient mental capacity to understand the nature or consequences of their actions in the contract. In most states 18 is the age of contractual capacity. As previously discussed, a minor may disaffirm a contract, which would result in the contract's not being enforceable. A contract by a party who has been judged insane is void, and it may be void*able* once the individual is judged capable to contract. Mental capacity is not the same as medical sanity. A valid contract must not contemplate a purpose that is illegal or against public policy. Parties cannot mutually agree to acts that are contrary to law.

A contract may comply with all of these basic requirements but be either void or voidable because of circumstances that violate *reality of consent*. A contract must be entered into as the free and voluntary act of each party. Each party must be able to make a prudent and knowledgeable decision without undue influence. A mistake, misrepresentation, fraud, undue influence or duress deprives a person of that ability. If these detriments are present, the contract is voidable by the injured party, who could sue for breach, using lack of voluntary assent as a defense.

Performance of a Contract

Each party has certain rights and duties to fulfill. The question of *when* a contract must be performed is an important factor. Many contracts call for a specific time at or by which the agreed-upon acts must be completely performed. In addition, many contracts provide that **time is of the essence.** This means that the contract must be performed within the time limit specified, and any party who does not perform on time will be liable for breach of contract.

When a contract does not specify a date for performance, the acts it requires should be performed within a reasonable time. The interpretation of what constitutes a reasonable time will depend upon the situation. Generally, if the act can be done immediately, such as a payment of money, it should be performed immediately, unless the parties agree otherwise. Courts have sometimes declared contracts to be invalid because they did not contain a time or date for performance.

Assignment and Novation

After a contract has been signed, one party may want to withdraw without actually terminating the agreement. This may be accomplished through either an assignment or a novation.

Assignment is a transfer of rights and/or duties under a contract. Generally rights may be assigned to a third party, the assignee, unless the contract forbids it. Obligations may also be assigned (delegated), but the original obligor, the assignor, remains primarily liable for them, unless specifically released from this responsibility. A party to a contract might elect to assign the contract obligations in lieu of defaulting or performing on a contract that is no longer in the party's best interest. Many contracts include a clause that either permits or forbids assignment.

A contract may also be performed by **novation,** the substitution of a new contract. The new agreement may be between the same parties, or a new party may be substituted for either (this is *novation of the parties*). The parties' intent must be to discharge the old obligation. For example, when a real estate purchaser assumes the seller's existing mortgage loan, the lender may choose to release the seller and substitute the buyer as the party primarily liable for the mortgage debt.

Discharge of Contracts

The contract is discharged upon termination of the agreement. The most desirable case is when a contract is terminated because of complete performance, with all terms carried out.

A contract also may be terminated because it is breached (broken) by the default of one of the parties. A **breach of contract** is a violation of any of the terms or conditions of a contract without legal excuse. For example, a seller breaches a sales contract by not delivering title to the buyer under the conditions stated in the agreement. The breaching or defaulting party assumes certain burdens, and the nondefaulting party has certain remedies.

If the *seller defaults* in a real estate agreement of sale, the buyer has three alternatives:

1. The buyer may *rescind* (known as the *right of rescission), or cancel, the contract.* Rescission returns the parties to their position prior to the contract. The buyer has the right to a return of the earnest money deposited on the contract.

2. The buyer may file a court suit, known as a **suit for specific performance,** to force the seller to perform the contract (that is, convey the property by delivery of deed).

3. The buyer may *sue the seller for compensatory damages.* A suit for damages is seldom used in this instance, however, because in most cases the buyer would have difficulty proving the extent of damages.

If the *buyer defaults,* the seller may pursue one of four contractual remedies:

1. The seller may *declare the contract forfeited.* The right to forfeit is usually provided in the terms of the contract, and the seller is usually entitled to retain the earnest money and all payments received from the buyer as *liquidated damages.*

2. The seller may *rescind the contract,* that is, cancel or terminate the contract as if it had never been made. This action requires that the seller return all payments the buyer has made.

3. The seller may *sue for the purchase price.* This remedy requires that the seller offer, or tender, a valid deed to the buyer to show the seller's compliance with the contract terms.

4. The seller may *sue for compensatory damages.*

Statute of limitations. The law of every state limits the time within which parties to a contract may bring legal suit to enforce their rights. The *statute of limitations* varies for different legal actions, and any rights not enforced within the applicable time period are lost.

Contracts may also be discharged or terminated when any of the following occur:

- *Partial performance* of the terms, along with a written acceptance by the person for whom acts have not been done or to whom money has not been paid

- *Substantial performance,* in which one party has substantially performed on the contract but does not complete all the details exactly as the contract requires (Such performance may be sufficient to force payment, with certain adjustments for any damages suffered by the other party.)

- *Impossibility of performance,* in which an act required by the contract cannot be legally accomplished

- *Mutual agreement* of the parties to cancel

- *Operation of law,* such as in the voiding of a contract by a minor, as a result of fraud, the expiration of the statute of limitations or because a contract was altered without the written consent of all parties involved

CONTRACTS USED IN THE REAL ESTATE BUSINESS

The written agreements most commonly used by brokers and salespeople are listing agreements, real estate sales contracts, option agreements, contracts for deed, leases and escrow agreements.

Broker's Authority To Prepare Documents

In many states specific guidelines have been drawn, whether by state real estate officials, court decision or statute, regarding the authority of real estate licensees to prepare contracts for their clients and customers. A licensed real estate broker is not authorized to practice law, for example, to prepare legal documents such as deeds and mortgages. A broker or salesperson may, however, be permitted to fill in the blanks on certain approved preprinted documents (such as sales contracts and leases), provided the licensee does not charge a separate fee for completing such forms.

Contract forms. *Printed forms* are used for all kinds of contracts because most transactions are basically similar in nature. The use of printed forms raises three problems: what to *fill in the blanks,* what printed matter is not applicable to a particular sale and is to be *ruled out* by drawing lines through the unwanted words and what additional clauses or agreements (called *riders or addenda*) are to be *added.* All changes and additions are usually initialed in the margin or on the rider by both parties when a contract is signed.

IN PRACTICE. . .

It is essential that both parties to a contract understand exactly what they are agreeing to. Poorly drafted documents, especially those containing extensive legal language, may be subject to various interpretations and lead to litigation. The parties to a real estate transaction should be advised to have sales contracts and other legal documents examined by their lawyers before signing, to ensure that the agreements accurately reflect their intentions. When preprinted forms do not sufficiently cover special provisions in a transaction, the parties should be encouraged to have an attorney draft a contract that properly covers such provisions.

To gain familiarity with the forms used in a local area, students should ask brokers or real estate companies for copies of their sales contract, listing agreement and other forms. Title or abstract companies and some banks and savings and loan associations are other sources, or they may be purchased at local office supply and stationery stores.

Listing Agreements

Listing agreements are contracts that establish the rights and obligations of the broker as agent and of the buyer or seller as principal. Refer to Chapter 5 for a complete discussion of listing agreements.

Some states suggest or require the use of specific forms of listing contracts. Oral listing contracts for a period of less than one year are recognized in some states, while in others only written listing contracts are recognized.

IN PRACTICE. . .	*If there is any ambiguity in a contract, the courts generally will interpret the agreement against the party who prepared it. For example, a broker usually prepares a listing agreement. If there is any doubt as to whether a listing agreement is an exclusive agency or an exclusive right to sell, a court will probably construe it to be an exclusive agency, ruling against the broker who prepared the document.*

Sales Contracts

A real estate sales contract sets forth all details of the agreement between a buyer and a seller for the purchase and sale of a parcel of real estate. Depending on the area, this agreement may be known as an *offer to purchase, a contract of purchase and sale, a purchase agreement, an earnest money agreement, a deposit receipt* or by some other term.

Whatever the contract is called, when it has been prepared and signed by the purchaser it is an offer to purchase the subject real estate. If the document is accepted and signed by the seller, it becomes, or "ripens into," a contract of sale.

The contract of sale is the most important document in the sale of real estate because it establishes the legal rights and obligations of the buyer and seller. In effect, it dictates the contents of the deed.

Details that are frequently included in addition to the essential elements of a contract are the price, terms, legal description of the land, kind and condition of the title, form of deed the seller will deliver, kind of title evidence required, who will provide title evidence and how defects in the title, if any, are to be eliminated. The contract must state all the terms and conditions of the agreement and spell out all contingencies (discussed later in the chapter).

The following pages discuss some of the typical other issues that arise as an offer to purchase ripens into a contract of sale.

Offer. A broker lists an owner's real estate for sale at the price and conditions set by the owner. When a prospective buyer is found, an offer to purchase is drawn up, signed by the prospective buyer and presented by the broker to the seller (see Figure 10.1). This is an *offer.*

Earnest money deposits. It is customary, but not essential, for a purchaser to provide a deposit, usually in the form of a check, when making an offer to purchase real estate. This is commonly referred to as an **earnest money deposit.** *It gives evidence of the buyer's intention to carry out the terms of the contract.* It is given to the broker, and the sales contract typically provides that the broker will hold the deposit for the parties. In some areas it is common practice for deposits to be held in escrow by the seller's attorney. If the offer is not accepted, the earnest money deposit is returned to the would-be buyer immediately.

**Figure 10.1
Offer and
Acceptance**

The amount of the deposit is a matter to be agreed on by the parties. Under the terms of most listing agreements a real estate broker is required to accept a reasonable amount as earnest money. Generally the deposit should be sufficient to discourage the buyer from defaulting, compensate the seller for taking the property off the market and cover any expenses the seller might incur if the buyer defaults. A purchase offer with no earnest money, however, is valid. Most contracts provide that the deposit becomes the seller's property as liquidated damages if the buyer defaults. The seller might also claim further damages.

Earnest money held by a broker must be held in a special *trust,* or *escrow, account.* This money cannot be *commingled,* or mixed, with a broker's personal funds. A broker may not use such funds for personal use; this illegal act is known as *conversion.* A broker need not open a special escrow account for each earnest money deposit received but may deposit all such funds in one account. A broker should maintain full, complete and accurate records of all earnest money deposits. This uncertain distribution of earnest money deposits makes it absolutely necessary that the funds be properly protected pending a final decision on their disbursement.

Binder. In a few localities it is customary to prepare a shorter document, known as a *binder,* for the purchaser to sign. This document states the essential terms of the purchaser's offer and acknowledges receipt of the deposit. It also provides that the parties agree to have a more formal and complete contract of sale drawn up by an attorney upon the seller's acceptance and signing of the binder. A binder receipt might be used in a situation where the details of the transaction are too complex for the standard sales contract form.

Counteroffer. As discussed earlier, any attempt by the seller to change the terms proposed by the buyer creates a *counteroffer.* The original offer ceases because the seller has rejected it. The buyer can accept the seller's counteroffer or can reject it and, if desired, make another counteroffer. Any change in the last offer made results in a counteroffer until one party finally agrees to the other party's last offer and both parties sign the final contract (see Figure 10.2).

An offer or counteroffer *may be revoked at any time before it has been accepted,* even if the person making the offer or counteroffer agreed to keep the offer open for a set period of time.

**Figure 10.2
Counteroffer and
Acceptance**

Acceptance. If the seller agrees to the original offer or a later counteroffer *exactly as it was made* and signs the contract, the offer has been *accepted* and the contract is *formed.* The broker then must advise the buyer of the seller's acceptance, obtain lawyers' approval if the contract calls for it and deliver a duplicate original of the contract to each party.

An offer is not considered accepted until the person making the offer has been *notified of the other party's acceptance.* When the parties are communicating through an agent or at a distance, questions may arise regarding whether an acceptance, a rejection or a counteroffer has effectively occurred. Currently the use of telephones and electronics communication devices is popular. A signed agreement that is "faxed" would constitute adequate communication. The real estate broker or salesperson must transmit all offers, acceptances or other responses as soon as possible to avoid questions of proper communication.

Equitable title. When buyers sign a contract to purchase real estate, they do not receive title to the land; title transfers only upon delivery and acceptance of a deed. However, after both buyer and seller have executed a sales contract, the buyer acquires an interest in the land known as **equitable title.** Rights of a holder of equitable title vary from state to state. Equitable title may give the buyer an insurable interest in the property. If the parties decide not to go through with the purchase and sale, the buyer may be required to give the seller a quitclaim deed to release the equitable interest in the land. (Quitclaim deeds are discussed in Chapter 11.)

Destruction of premises. In many states, once the sales contract is signed by both parties but before the deed is delivered (and unless the contract provides otherwise), the buyer must bear the loss of any damage to or destruction of the property by fire or other casualty because the buyer has equitable title. Through laws and court decisions, however, a growing number of states have placed the risk of any such loss on the seller. Many of these states have adopted the *Uniform Vendor and Purchaser Risk Act,* which specifically provides that the seller bears any loss that occurs before the title passes or the buyer takes possession.

Liquidated damages. **Liquidated damages** are an amount of money, agreed to in advance by buyer and seller, that will serve as compensation if one party does not live up to the contract. If a sales contract specifies that the earnest money deposit is to serve as liquidated damages in case of default by the buyer, the seller will be entitled to keep the deposit if the buyer refuses to perform for no good reason. The seller who does choose to keep the deposit as liquidated damages may not sue for any further damages.

Parts of a sales contract. All real estate sales contracts can be divided into a number of general parts. Although each form of contract will contain these divisions, their location within a particular contract may vary (Figure 10.3 provides an example of a real estate sales contract). The information generally required will include at least the following items:

- The identification of the purchaser and the statement of the purchaser's obligation to purchase the property, including an indication of how the purchaser intends to take title to the property

- The legal or adequate description of the property and, if appropriate, the street address

- The identification of the seller and the statement of the type of deed the seller agrees to give, including the covenants, conditions and restrictions to which the deed will be subject

- The statement of the purchase price and how the purchaser intends to pay for the property, including earnest money deposits, additional cash from the purchaser and the conditions of any mortgage financing the purchaser intends to obtain or assume

- The provision for the closing of the transaction and the transfer of possession of the property to the purchaser

- The provision for title evidence (abstract and legal opinion, certificate of title, Torrens certificate, title insurance policy)

- The provision for the proration of (adjustment for) real estate taxes, hazard insurance, rents, fuel, and the like

- The provision for the completion of the contract should the property be damaged or destroyed between the signing of the contract and the closing of the transaction

- The provision for remedies available should either party default on the contract (including liquidated damages, the right to sue, etc.)

- The provision for any contingencies (such as delays in obtaining or inability to obtain financing, inability of the purchaser to sell a previously owned property, inability of the seller to acquire another desired property, inability of the seller to clear the title, etc.)

- The dated signatures of all parties (the signature of a witness is not essential to a valid contract). In some states the seller's nonowning spouse may also be required to sign to release potential marital or homestead rights. An agent may sign for a principal when proper authority, such as a power of attorney, has been granted. When sellers are co-owners all must sign if the entire ownership is being transferred.

Additional provisions. Among the more common inclusions in many sales contracts are

- the identification of any personal property to be left with the premises for the purchaser (such as major appliances, lawn and garden equipment);

- the identification of any real property to be removed by the seller prior to the closing (such as storage sheds);

- the transfer of any applicable warranties on items such as heating and cooling systems, built-in appliances, etc.;

- the identification of any leased equipment that must be transferred to the purchaser or returned to the lessor (such as security systems, cable television boxes, water softeners);

- the appointment of a closing or settlement agent;

- the closing or settlement instructions;

- the transfer of any impound or escrow account funds;

- the transfer of the hazard insurance policy or the issuance of a new one;

- the transfer or payment of any outstanding special assessments;

- the provision by either party for a homeowner warranty program;

- the purchaser's need to secure a specific type of loan;

- the provision that the contract can be voided by the purchaser if the property is appraised for less than the contracted sales price;

- the purchaser's right to a satisfactory structural engineering report, pest/insect infestation report or habitability report within a specified few days;

- the purchaser's right to inspect the property shortly before the closing or settlement (often called the *walk-through*);

- the purchaser's right to have a family member or an attorney approve the contract within a specified few days;

- the agreement as to what documents will be provided by each party and when and where they will be delivered; and

- the purchaser's right to sell a presently owned home before purchasing the next residence under this contract.

Contingencies. **Contingencies** create additional conditions that must be satisfied before a sales contract is fully enforceable. They specify the actions that are necessary to satisfy the contingency, the time frame within which these actions are to be performed and, if any costs are involved, who is responsible for paying them. The most common one is a mortgage contingency, which protects the buyer's earnest money until a lender has committed the mortgage loan funds. A common practice in some areas is to make a sales contract contingent on the buyer obtaining inspections of the real estate being purchased. Inspections may include those for wood-boring insects, structural and mechanical systems, sewage facilities and radon or other toxic materials. A purchaser who has another house to sell may make the sales contract contingent on the sale of the buyer's current home. This protects the buyer from being legally bound to the purchase before being assured that the existing home is sold. The seller may insist on an escape clause that would allow the seller to continue to solicit additional buyers. The original buyer retains the right, if an offer that is more favorable to the seller comes forth, to either eliminate the contingency or to void the contract.

Disclosures. As discussed in previous chapters many states have enacted mandatory disclosure laws to enable consumers to make informed decisions. Without regard to statutory requirements, many brokers have instituted procedures for making disclosures and recommending the use of technical experts to ensure

**Figure 10.3
Real Estate
Sales Contract**

**RESIDENTIAL
REAL ESTATE PURCHASE CONTRACT AND RECEIPT FOR DEPOSIT**

THE PRINTED PORTION OF THIS CONTRACT HAS BEEN APPROVED BY THE ARIZONA ASSOCIATION OF REALTORS®. THIS IS INTENDED TO BE A BINDING CONTRACT. NO REPRESENTATION IS MADE AS TO THE LEGAL VALIDITY OR ADEQUACY OF ANY PROVISION OR THE TAX CONSEQUENCES THEREOF. IF YOU DESIRE LEGAL OR TAX ADVICE, CONSULT YOUR ATTORNEY OR TAX ADVISOR.

RECEIPT

1. **Received From:** _____ ("Buyer")
2. **Title:** Buyer will take title as: ☐ **Determined before Close of Escrow**   ☐ **Community Property**   ☐ **Joint Tenants with Right of Survivorship**
   ☐ **Sole and Separate Property**   ☐ **Tenants in Common**   ☐ **Other:**

3. **Earnest Money Deposit:** Earnest money shall be held by Broker named in Line 7 until offer is accepted, subject to prior sale. Upon acceptance, Broker is
4. authorized to deposit the earnest money with the escrow company to which the check is payable. If the check is payable to Broker, Broker may deposit in
5. Broker's trust account or endorse the check without recourse and deposit it with a duly licensed escrow company. All earnest money is subject to collection
6. and is considered to be part of the purchase price for the Premises described below.

   a. Amount of Deposit $ _____   **b.** Form of Earnest Money: ☐ Personal Check ☐ Other: _____   **c.** Deposited With: ☐ Broker's Trust Account ☐ Escrow Company: _____

7. **Received By:** _____
                           Firm Name   Agent's Signature   Mo/Da/Yr

OFFER

8. **Property Description & Offer:** Buyer agrees to purchase the real property and all fixtures and improvements thereon and appurtenances incident thereto,
9. plus personal property described below (collectively the "Premises")

10. **Property Address:** _____   Assessor's#: _____
11. **City:** _____   **County:** _____   **AZ, Zip Code:** _____
12. **Legal Description:** _____

13. **Fixtures and Personal Property:** All existing storage sheds; heating and cooling equipment; built-in appliances; light fixtures; ceiling fans; window and
14. door screens; sun screens; storm windows and doors; towel, curtain and drapery rods; draperies and other window coverings; attached carpeting; attached
15. fireplace equipment; pool and spa equipment (including any mechanical or other cleaning systems); garage door openers and controls; and attached TV
16. antennas, excluding satellite dishes, shall be left upon and included with the Premises.

17. **Additional Personal Property Included:** _____
18. **Fixtures and Leased Equipment NOT Included:** _____
19. **Terms and Conditions Include:** ☐ Government Financing Addendum ☐ Financing Addendum ☐ Addendum: _____   ☐ None

20. $ _____ **Full purchase price,** payable as follows:
21. $ _____ Earnest deposit as indicated above.
22. $ _____
23. $ _____
24. _____
25. _____
26. _____
27. _____
28. **Assumption of Existing Loans:** The balance of any encumbrance being assumed is approximate. Any difference shall be reflected in the
29. ☐ Cash down payment   ☐ Seller Carryback   ☐ Other: _____ Buyer shall reimburse Seller for any impounds transferred to Buyer.
30. **Close of Escrow:** Seller and Buyer will comply with all terms and conditions of this Contract and close escrow on or before: _____
31. Seller and Buyer hereby agree that close of escrow shall be defined as recordation of the documents. If escrow does not close by such date, this Contract
32. is subject to cancellation as provided on lines 147-154.
33. **Possession:** Possession shall be delivered to Buyer at ☐ Close of Escrow   ☐ Other: _____
34. **Assessments:** The amount of any assessment which is a lien as of the close of escrow shall be ☐ Paid in Full by Seller   ☐ Prorated and Assumed by Buyer
35. Any assessment that becomes a lien after close of escrow is the Buyer's responsibility.
36. **Proration and Costs:** Taxes, homeowner association fees, and irrigation fees, and if assumed, insurance premiums, interest on assessments and interest
37. on encumbrances shall be prorated as of ☐ Close of Escrow   ☐ Other: _____

**Figure 10.3
(continued)**

38. **Home Protection Plan:** A home protection plan will be obtained for the Premises at close of escrow ☐ Yes ☐ No   The plan will be obtained at the
39. expense of the ☐ Seller ☐ Buyer   Name of Plan:_____   Type of Plan or Maximum Cost:
40. **Fire and Extended Insurance Coverage:** | ☐ A new policy to be issued | ☐ Existing policy to be assumed | ☐ Determined in escrow |
41. **Escrow Instructions:** | ☐ Separate escrow instructions will be executed | ☐ This Contract will be used as escrow instructions |
42. The escrow company shall be:
43. **Time for Acceptance:** This offer must be accepted by Seller on or before_____. Written acceptance of this Contract
44. given to the Broker named on Line 7 of this Contract shall be notice to Buyer.
45. COMMISSIONS PAYABLE FOR THE SALE, LEASING OR MANAGEMENT OF PROPERTY ARE NOT SET BY ANY BOARD OR ASSOCIATION OF
46. REALTORS® OR MULTIPLE LISTING SERVICE OR IN ANY MANNER OTHER THAN BETWEEN THE BROKER AND CLIENT.
47. **Terms on Reverse:** THE TERMS AND CONDITIONS ON THE REVERSE SIDE HEREOF ARE INCORPORATED HEREIN BY REFERENCE.
48. **Agency Confirmation:** Unless otherwise disclosed in writing, Buyer and Seller understand and agree that Brokers represent the Seller only, and have a
49. duty to treat fairly all parties to the transaction.
50. The undersigned agree to purchase the Premises on the terms and conditions herein stated and acknowledge receipt of a copy hereof.
51. _____   _____
    (Buyer's Signature)   Mo/Da/Yr   (Buyer's Signature)   Mo/Da/Yr
52. _____
    Street   City   State   Zip

ACCEPTANCE

53. Seller agrees to sell the Premises as stated herein and for services rendered, agrees to pay a brokerage fee as follows:
54. _____ to _____ ("Broker named in Line 7")
55. _____ to _____ ("Listing Broker")
56. Seller instructs escrow company to pay such fee to Brokers in cash as a condition to closing and, to the extent necessary, irrevocably assigns Seller's
57. proceeds to Brokers at close of escrow. If completion of the sale is prevented by default of Seller, or with the consent of Seller, the entire brokerage fee
58. shall be paid directly by Seller. If the earnest deposit is forfeited for any reason, Seller shall pay a brokerage fee equal to one-half of the earnest deposit,
59. provided such payment shall not exceed the full amount of the brokerage fee. Nothing in this paragraph shall be construed as limiting applicable provisions
60. of law or any listing agreement relating to when commissions are earned or payable. UPON ACCEPTANCE OF THIS CONTRACT, SELLER HEREBY
61. WAIVES HIS RIGHT TO RECEIVE ANY SUBSEQUENT OFFER TO PURCHASE THE PREMISES UNTIL AFTER FORFEITURE BY BUYER OR OTHER
62. CANCELLATION OF THIS CONTRACT.
63. **Seller Receipt of Copy:** The undersigned acknowledge receipt of a copy hereof and grant permission to Broker in Line 7 to deliver a copy to Buyer.
64. ☐ **Counter Offer** is attached, which is incorporated herein by reference. If there is a conflict between this Contract and the Counter Offer, the provisions of
65. the Counter Offer shall be controlling. (NOTE: If this box is checked, Seller must sign both Contract and Counter Offer.)
66. _____   _____
    (Seller's Signature)   Mo/Da/Yr   (Seller's Signature)   Mo/Da/Yr
67. _____   _____
    (Print Name of Seller)   (Print Name of Seller)
68. _____
    Street   City   State   Zip

For Broker Use Only | Brokerage File/Log No._____ Manager's Initials_____ Broker's Initials_____ Date_____

°Arizona Association of REALTORS® 1990 **This Form Available Through Your Local Board of REALTORS®**   FORM RREPCRD 4/90

Figure 10.3 (continued)

69. **Time of Essence:** Time is of the essence.

70. **Permission:** Buyer and Seller grant Brokers permission to advise the public of the sale upon execution of this Contract, and Brokers may disclose
71. price and terms herein after close of escrow.

72. **Entire Agreement:** This Contract, any attached exhibits and any addenda or supplements signed by the parties, shall constitute the entire agreement
73. between Seller and Buyer, and shall supersede any other written or oral agreement between Seller and Buyer. This Contract can be modified only by
74. a writing signed by Seller and Buyer. A fully executed facsimile copy of the entire agreement shall be treated as an original Contract.

75. **Title and Title Insurance:** Seller hereby instructs the escrow company to obtain and distribute to Buyer a preliminary title report together with
76. complete and legible copies of all documents which will remain as exceptions to Buyer's policy of title insurance. Title to the real property described
77. in Lines 8-12 of this Contract shall be conveyed by a general warranty deed. Title to the personal property described in Lines 13-17 of this Contract
78. shall be transferred free and clear of any liens or encumbrances. Seller shall furnish to Buyer, at Seller's expense, a Standard Owner's Title
79. Insurance Policy in the full amount of the purchase price issued by a title insurance company, showing good and marketable title to the real property
80. vested in Buyer free from defects and encumbrances except as follows: (1) liens and other matters described in this Contract, (2) building, use and
81. other restrictive covenants of record, (3) claims, title or rights to water (4) zoning regulations, (5) easements and rights-of-way for roadways,
82. canals, laterals, ditches and public utilities, (6) taxes, paving, irrigation and other assessments not delinquent as of the close of escrow, (7) rights of
83. tenants in possession, if any. (8) rights and minerals reserved in patents or otherwise by any entity, (9) printed exceptions contained in the Standard
84. Owner's Title Insurance Policy. If title to the real property otherwise is defective at the time set for close of escrow, Buyer may elect, as Buyer's sole
85. option, either to accept title subject to defects which are not cured or to cancel this Contract whereupon all money paid by Buyer pursuant to this
86. Contract shall be returned to Buyer. Buyer shall furnish to Seller, at Buyer's expense, a Standard Loan Policy in the full amount of any loan carried
87. back by Seller and secured by the real property described in Lines 8-12 of this Contract. Such Standard Loan Policy shall show that Seller's lien has
88. the priority agreed to by the parties. If applicable Seller agrees to complete, sign and deliver to escrow company a certificate indicating whether
89. Seller is a foreign person or non-resident alien pursuant to the Foreign Investment in Real Property Tax Act. (FIRPTA)

90. **Documents and Escrow:** (1) If Seller and Buyer elect to execute escrow instructions to fulfill the terms hereof, they shall deliver the same to escrow
91. company within 15 days of the acceptance of this Contract. (2) All documents necessary to close this transaction shall be executed promptly by
92. Seller and Buyer in the standard form used by escrow company. Seller and Buyer hereby instruct escrow company to modify such documents to the
93. extent necessary to be consistent with the Contract. (3) If any conflict exists between this Contract and any escrow instructions executed pursuant
94. hereto, the provisions of this Contract shall be controlling. (4) All closing and escrow costs shall be allocated between Seller and Buyer in accordance
95. with local custom and applicable laws and regulations. (5) Escrow company is hereby instructed to send to Brokers copies of all notices and
96. communications directed to Seller or Buyer and shall provide to such Brokers access to escrowed materials and information about the escrow upon
97. request. (6) Any documents necessary to close the escrow may be signed in counterparts, each of which shall be effective as an original upon
98. execution and all of which together shall constitute one and the same instrument.

99. **Default and Remedies:** If Buyer defaults in any respect on any material obligations under this Contract, Seller may elect to be released from the
100. obligation to sell the Premises to Buyer. Seller may proceed against Buyer upon any claim or remedy which he may have, in law or equity, or
101. because it would be difficult to fix actual damages in case of Buyer's default, the amount of the earnest deposit may be deemed a reasonable
102. estimate of the damages; and Seller may, at his option retain the earnest deposit, subject to the brokerage fee as provided herein, as his sole right to
103. damages. If Buyer or Seller files suit against the other to enforce any provision of this Contract or for damages sustained by its breach, all
104. parties prevailing in such action, on trial and appeal, shall receive their reasonable attorneys' fees and costs as awarded by the court. In
105. addition, both Seller and Buyer agree to indemnify and hold harmless all Brokers against all costs and expenses, which any Broker may incur or
106. sustain in connection with any lawsuit arising from this Contract and will pay the same on demand unless the court shall grant judgment in such
107. action against the party to be indemnified. Costs shall include, without limitation: attorneys' fees, expert witness fees, fees paid to investigators and
108. court costs.

109. **Warranties:** Except as otherwise provided in this Contract, Seller warrants and shall maintain and repair the Premises so that, at the earlier of
110. possession or the close of escrow: (1) the Premises shall be in substantially the same condition as on the effective date of this Contract, (2) the roof
111. has no known leaks, (3) all heating, cooling, mechanical, plumbing and electrical systems and built-in appliances will be in working condition, (4) if the
112. Premises has a swimming pool and/or spa, the motors, filter systems, cleaning systems, and heaters, if so equipped, will be in working condition.
113. The Seller grants Buyer or Buyer's representative reasonable access to enter and inspect the Premises for the purpose of satisfying Buyer that the
114. items warranted by Seller are in working condition. Buyer shall keep the Premises free and clear of any liens; indemnify and hold Seller and Brokers
115. harmless from all liability, claims, demands and costs; and repair all damages to the Premises caused by said inspection. At the earlier of
116. possession or close of escrow, Buyer acknowledges that all warranties concerning the Premises have been satisfied or extinguished. Any personal
117. property included herein shall be transferred IN AS IS CONDITION AND SELLER MAKES NO WARRANTY of any kind, express or implied (including,
118. without limitation, ANY WARRANTY OF MERCHANTABILITY). Brokers are hereby relieved of any and all liability and responsibility from everything
119. stated in this paragraph and the following paragraph.

120. **Warranties That Survive Closing:** Prior to the close of escrow, Seller warrants that, payment in full will have been made for all labor, professional
121. services, materials, machinery, fixtures or tools furnished within the 120 days immediately preceding the close of escrow in connection with the
122. construction, alteration or repair of any structure on or improvement to the Premises. Seller warrants that the information in the current listing
123. agreement, if any, regarding connection to a public sewer system, septic tank or other sanitation system is correct to the best of his knowledge.
124. Seller warrants that he has disclosed to Buyer and Brokers all material latent defects concerning the Premises that are known to Seller. Seller further
125. warrants that he has disclosed to all parties any information, excluding opinions of value, that he possesses which materially and adversely affects the
126. consideration to be paid by Buyer.

127. **Representations and Releases:** By signing this Contract, Buyer represents that he has or will have prior to close of escrow conducted all
128. independent investigations desired by Buyer of any and all matters concerning this purchase and by closing accepts the Premises. Seller and Buyer
129. hereby release all Brokers from all responsibility and liability regarding the condition, square footage, lot lines or boundaries, value, rent rolls,
130. compliance with building codes or other governmental regulations, or other material matters relating to the Premises; and neither Seller, Buyer, nor
131. any Broker shall be bound by any understanding, agreement, promise or representation, express or implied, not specified herein.

132. **Wood Infestation Report:** Seller will, at his expense, place in escrow a wood infestation report by a qualified licensed pest control operator, which,
133. when considered in its entirety, indicates that all residences and buildings attached to the Premises are free from evidence of current infestation and
134. damage from wood-destroying pests or organisms. Seller agrees to pay up to one percent of the purchase price for the treatment and repair of the
135. damage caused by infestation and correct any conditions conducive to infestation. If such costs exceed one percent of the purchase price: (1)
136. Buyer may elect to cancel this Contract unless Seller agrees in writing to pay such costs, or (2) Seller may elect to cancel this contract unless Buyer
137. agrees in writing to either accept the Premises or to pay such costs in excess of one percent that the Seller has agreed to pay.

138. **Recommendations:** If any Broker recommends a builder, contractor, or other person or entity to Seller or Buyer for any purpose, such
139. recommendation will be independently investigated and evaluated by Seller or Buyer, who hereby acknowledge that any decision to enter into any
140. contractual arrangements with any such person or entity recommended by any Broker will be based solely upon such independent investigation and
141. evaluation. Seller and Buyer understand that said contractual arrangement may result in a commission or fee to Broker.

142. **Risk of Loss:** If there is any loss or damage to the Premises between the date hereof and the close of escrow, by reason of fire, vandalism, flood,
143. earthquake or act of God, the risk of loss shall be on the Seller, provided, however, that if the cost of repairing such loss or damage would exceed
144. ten percent of the purchase price. (1) Buyer may elect to cancel this Contract unless Seller agrees in writing to pay the cost of repairing all such loss
145. or damage, or (2) Seller may elect to cancel this Contract unless Buyer agrees in writing to accept the Premises and to pay the cost of repair in
146. excess of ten percent of the purchase price that the Seller has agreed to pay.

147. **Cancellation:** Any party who wishes to cancel this Contract because of any breach by another party, or because escrow fails to close by the agreed
148. date, and who is not himself in breach of this Contract, except as occasioned by a breach by the other party, may cancel this Contract by delivering a
149. notice to either the breaching party or to the escrow company stating the nature of the breach and that this Contract shall be cancelled unless the
150. breach is cured within 13 days following the delivery of the notice. If this notice is delivered to the escrow company, it shall contain the address of
151. the party in breach. Any notice delivered to any party must be delivered to the Brokers and the escrow company. Within three days after receipt of
152. such notice, the escrow company shall send the notice by United States Mail to the party in breach at the address contained in the notice. No further
153. notice shall be required. In the event that the breach is not cured within 13 days following the delivery of the notice to the party in breach or to the
154. escrow company, this Contract shall be cancelled.

155. **Brokers' Rights:** If any Broker hires an attorney to enforce the collection of the commission payable pursuant to this Contract, and is successful in
156. collecting some or all of such commission, Seller agrees to pay such Broker's costs including, but not limited to: attorneys' fees, expert witness fees,
157. fees paid to investigators, and court costs. The parties agree that any monies deposited in the trust account of the Broker named in line 7 pursuant
158. to this Contract may earn interest, and that the Broker shall be entitled to all of the interest from said interest-bearing trust account as additional
159. compensation. The Seller and the Buyer acknowledge that the Brokers are third-party beneficiaries of this Contract.

160. **FHA or VA:** If applicable, the current language prescribed by FHA or VA pertaining to the value of the Premises shall be incorporated in this
161. Contract by reference as if set forth in full herein, and Seller and Buyer agree to execute any appropriate FHA or VA supplements to this Contract.
162. Buyer is entitled to a return of the earnest deposit if, after a diligent and good faith effort, Buyer does not qualify for a VA or FHA Loan. Buyer
163. acknowledges that prepaid items paid separately from earnest money are not refundable.

164. **Buyer's Loan:** If Buyer is seeking a new loan or an assumption of an existing loan that requires qualification in connection with this transaction.
165. Buyer agrees to file a substantially complete loan application within five business days after the acceptance of this Contract and to promptly supply all
166. documentation required by the lender.

167. **Severability:** If a court of competent jurisdiction makes a final determination that any term or provision of this Contract is invalid or unenforceable, all
168. other terms and provisions shall remain in full force and effect, and the invalid or unenforceable term or provision shall be deemed replaced by a term
169. or provision that is valid and enforceable and comes closest to expressing the intention of the invalid term or provision.

170. **Construction of Language:** The language of this Contract shall be construed according to its fair meaning and not strictly for or against either party.
171. Words used in the masculine, feminine or neuter shall apply to either gender or the neuter, as appropriate. All singular and plural words shall be
172. interpreted to refer to the number consistent with circumstances and context.

This form is available for use by the entire real estate industry. The use of this form is not intended to identify the user as a REALTOR. REALTOR is a registered collective membership mark which may be used only by real estate licensees who are members of the NATIONAL ASSOCIATION OF REALTORS and who subscribe to its Code of Ethics

Arizona Association of REALTORS 1990 **This Form Available Through Your Local Board of REALTORS**   FORM RREPCRD 4/90 that purchasers have accurate information about the real estate. Disclosure of property conditions may be part of a sales contract. Disclosure of the broker's agency relationship may also be included; it is required in some states.

Option Contracts

An **option** is a *contract by which an* optionor *(generally an owner) gives an* optionee *(a prospective purchaser or lessee) the right to buy or lease the owner's property at a fixed price within a stated period of time.* The optionee pays a fee (the agreed-on consideration) for this option right and assumes no other obligation until he or she decides, within the specified time, to exercise the option right (to buy or lease the property) or allow the option right to expire. The owner may be bound to sell; the optionee is not bound to buy. An option is enforceable by only one party—the optionee.

For example, for a consideration of a specified amount of money, a present owner (optionor) agrees to give an optionee an irrevocable right to buy real estate at a certain price for a limited period of time. At the time the option is signed by the parties, the owner does not sell nor does the optionee buy. They merely agree that the optionee will have the right to buy and the owner will be obligated to sell *if* the optionee decides to exercise his or her right of option. Options must contain all the terms and provisions required for a valid contract.

The option agreement, which is a unilateral contract, requires the optionor to act only after the optionee gives notice that he or she elects to execute the option and buy. If the option is not exercised within the time specified, then the optioner's obligation and the optionee's right expire, unless the contract provides for a renewal. The optionee cannot recover the consideration paid for the option right. The contract may state whether the money paid for the option is to be applied to the purchase price of the real estate if the option is exercised.

A common application of an option is a lease that includes an option for the tenant to purchase the property. Options on commercial real estate are frequently made dependent on the fulfillment of specific conditions, such as obtaining a zoning change or a building permit. The optionee is usually obligated to exercise the option if the conditions are met. Similar terms could also be included in a sales contract.

Land Contracts

A real estate sale can be made under a **land contract,** sometimes called a *contract for deed,* an **installment contract** or *articles of agreement for warranty deed.* Under a typical land contract the seller, also known as the *vendor,* retains legal title while the buyer, known as the *vendee,* takes possession and gets an equitable title to the property. The buyer agrees to give the seller a down payment and pay regular monthly installments of principal and interest over a number of years. The buyer also agrees to pay real estate taxes, insurance premiums, repairs and upkeep on the property. Although the buyer obtains possession when the contract is signed by both parties, *the seller is not obligated to execute and deliver a deed to the buyer until the terms of the contract have been satisfied.* This frequently occurs when the buyer has made a sufficient number of payments to obtain a mortgage loan and pay off the balance due on the contract.

Real estate is occasionally sold with the new buyer assuming an existing land contract from the original buyer/vendee. Generally the seller/vendor must approve the new purchaser.

IN PRACTICE. . .	Legislatures and courts have not looked favorably on the harsh provisions of some real estate installment contracts. A seller and buyer contemplating such a sale should first consult an attorney to make sure that the agreement meets all legal requirements and address the individual concerns of the parties.

●   ●   ●   ●   ●   ●   ●

KEY TERMS

assignment	land contract
bilateral contract	liquidated damages
breach of contract	novation
consideration	offer and acceptance
contingency	option
contract	suit for specific performance
counteroffer	statute of frauds
earnest money deposit	time is of the essence
equitable title	unenforceable contract
executed contract	unilateral contract
executory contract	valid
express contract	void
intallment contract	voidable
implied contract	

SUMMARY

A contract is defined as a legally enforceable promise or set of promises that must be performed and, if a breach occurs, for which the law provides a remedy.

Contracts may be classified according to whether the parties' intentions are express or are implied by their actions. They may also be classified as bilateral, when both parties have obligated themselves to act, or unilateral, when one party is obligated to perform only if the other party acts. In addition, contracts may be classified according to their legal enforceability as either valid, void, voidable or unenforceable.

Many contracts specify a time for performance. In any case all contracts must be performed within a reasonable time. An executed contract is one that has been fully performed. An executory contract is one in which some act remains to be performed.

The essentials of a valid contract are legally competent parties, offer and acceptance, legality of object and consideration. A valid real estate contract must include a description of the property, and it should be in writing and signed by all parties to be enforceable in court.

In many types of contracts either of the parties may transfer his or her rights and obligations under the agreement by assignment of the contract or novation (substitution of a new contract).

Contracts usually provide that the seller has the right to declare a sale canceled if the buyer defaults. If either party has suffered a loss because of the other's default, he or she may sue for damages to cover the loss. If one party insists on completing the transaction, he or she may sue the defaulter for specific performance of the terms of the contract; a court can order the other party to comply with the agreement.

Contracts frequently used in the real estate business include listing agreements, sales contracts, options, land contracts (installment contracts) and leases.

A real estate sales contract binds a buyer and a seller to a definite transaction as described in detail in the contract. The buyer is bound to purchase the property for the amount stated in the agreement. The seller is bound to deliver title, free from liens and encumbrances (except those identified in the contract).

Under an option agreement the optionee purchases from the optionor, for a limited time period, the exclusive right to purchase or lease the optionor's property. A land contract, or installment contract, is a sales/financing agreement under which a buyer purchases a seller's real estate on time. The buyer takes possession of and responsibility for the property but does not receive the deed immediately.

Questions

1. A legally enforceable agreement under which two parties agree to do something for each other is known as a(n)

   a. escrow agreement.
   b. legal promise.
   c. valid contract.
   d. option agreement.

2. D drives into a filling station and tops off her gas tank. She is obligated to pay for the fuel through what kind of contract?

   a. Express   c. Oral
   b. Implied   d. Voidable

3. A contract is said to be *bilateral* if

   a. one of the parties is a minor.
   b. the contract has yet to be fully performed.
   c. only one party to the agreement is bound to act.
   d. all parties to the contract are bound to act.

4. During the period of time after a real estate sales contract is signed but before title actually passes, the status of the contract is

   a. voidable.   c. unilateral.
   b. executory.   d. implied.

5. A contract for the sale of real estate that does not state the consideration to be paid for the property and is not signed by the parties is considered to be

   a. voidable.   c. void
   b. executory.   d. enforceable.

6. A suit for specific performance of a real estate contract asks for

   a. money damages.
   b. a new contract.
   c. a deficiency judgment.
   d. the conveyance of the property.

7. If a real estate sales contract does not state that time is of the essence and the stipulated date of transfer comes and goes without a closing, the contract is

   a. binding for only 30 more days.
   b. novated.
   c. still valid.
   d. automatically void.

8. In filling out a sales contract someone crossed out several words and inserted others. To eliminate future controversy as to whether the changes were made before or after the contract was signed, the usual procedure is to

   a. write a letter to each party listing the changes.
   b. have each party write a letter to the other approving the changes.
   c. redraw the entire contract.
   d. have both parties initial or sign in the margin near each change.

9. A real estate purchaser is said to have *equitable title* when

   a. the sales contract is signed by both buyer and seller.
   b. the transaction is closed.
   c. escrow is opened.
   d. a contract for deed is paid off.

10. The sales contract says J will purchase only if his wife flies up and approves the sale by the following Saturday. Mrs. J's approval is a

    a. contingency.   c. warranty.
    b. reservation.   d. consideration.

11. When the buyer promises to purchase only if he can sell his own present home, the seller gains some protection from a(n)

    a. escrow.   c. equitable title.
    b. option.   d. contingency.

12. An option to purchase binds
    a. the buyer only.
    b. the seller only.
    c. neither buyer nor seller.
    d. both buyer and seller.

13. Which of the following best describes a land contract, or installment contract?
    a. A contract to buy land only
    b. A mortgage on land
    c. A means of conveying title immediately while the purchaser pays for the property in installments
    d. A method of selling real estate whereby the purchaser pays in regular installments while the seller retains legal title

14. The purchaser of real estate under an installment contract
    a. generally pays no interest charge.
    b. receives title immediately.
    c. is not required to pay property taxes for the duration of the contract.
    d. is called a vendee.

15. Under the statute of frauds all contracts for the sale of real estate must be
    a. originated by a real estate broker.
    b. on preprinted forms.
    c. in writing to be enforceable.
    d. accompanied by earnest money deposits.

16. The Fs offer in writing to purchase a house for $120,000, including its draperies, with the offer to expire on Saturday at noon. The Ws reply in writing on Thursday, accepting the $120,000 offer but excluding the draperies. On Friday, while the Fs are considering this counteroffer, the Ws decide to accept the original offer, draperies included, and state that in writing. At this point the Fs
    a. must buy the house and have the right to insist on the draperies.
    b. are not bound to buy and can forget the whole situation.
    c. must buy the house but are not entitled to the draperies.
    d. must buy the house and can deduct the value of the draperies from the $120,000.

17. A buyer makes an offer to purchase certain property listed with a broker and leaves a deposit with the broker to show good faith. The broker should
    a. immediately apply the deposit to the listing expenses.
    b. put the deposit in an account as provided by state law.
    c. give the deposit to the seller when the offer is presented.
    d. put the deposit in her checking account.

18. T has a contract to buy property but would rather let his friend M buy it instead. If the contract allows, M can take over T's obligation by the process known as
    a. assignment.
    b. substantial performance.
    c. subordination.
    d. mutual consent.

19. A broker has found a buyer for a seller's home. The buyer has indicated in writing his willingness to buy the property for $1,000 less than the asking price and has deposited $5,000 earnest money with the broker. The seller is out of town for the weekend, and the broker has been unable to inform him of the signed document. At this point the buyer has signed a(n)
    a. voidable contract.
    b. offer.
    c. executory agreement.
    d. implied contract.

11 Transfer of Title

TITLE

The term *title* has two functions. **Title** to real estate means the right to or ownership of the land; it represents the bundle of rights the owner possesses. Title also serves as *evidence* of ownership; it represents the facts that, if proven, would enable a person to recover or retain ownership or possession of a parcel of real estate.

Real estate may be transferred *voluntarily* by sale or gift or *involuntarily* by operation of law. It may be transferred while the owner is living or by will or descent after the owner has died.

VOLUNTARY ALIENATION

Voluntary alienation is the legal term for the voluntary transfer of title. The owner may voluntarily transfer title by either making a gift or selling the property. To transfer during one's lifetime, the owner must use some form of deed of conveyance.

A **deed** is a *written instrument by which an owner of real estate intentionally conveys the owner's right, title or interest in a parcel of real estate to another.* The statute of frauds requires all deeds to be in writing. The owner who is transferring the title is referred to as the **grantor,** and the one who is acquiring title is called the **grantee.** A deed is executed (signed) by the grantor.

Requirements for a Valid Deed

Although the formal requirements vary, most states require the following for a valid deed (see Figure 11.1):

- A *grantor* who has the legal capacity to execute (sign) the deed
- A *grantee* named with reasonable certainty to be identified
- A recital of *consideration*
- A *granting clause* (words of conveyance)
- A *habendum clause* (to define ownership taken by the grantee)
- Designation of any *limitations* on the conveyance of a full fee simple estate

- An accurate *legal description* of the property conveyed

- *Exceptions and reservations,* if any, affecting the title ("subject to" clauses)

- The *signature of the grantor,* sometimes with a seal, witness and/or acknowledgment

- *Delivery* of the deed and *acceptance* by the grantee to pass title

Grantor. A grantor must be of lawful age, usually at least 18 years old. As for most other documents, a deed executed by a *minor* (one who has not reached majority, or lawful age) is considered voidable (see Chapter 10).

A grantor also must be of sound mind. Generally any grantor who can understand the action will be viewed as mentally capable of executing a valid deed. A deed executed by someone who was mentally impaired at the time will be voidable but not void. If, however, the grantor has been judged legally incompetent, the deed will be void. Real estate owned by one who is legally incompetent can be conveyed only with the authority of a court.

In some states a grantor's spouse is required to sign any deed of conveyance so as to waive any marital and/or homestead rights. This requirement varies according to state law and the manner in which the title to real estate is held, as discussed in Chapters 6 and 7.

The grantor's name must be spelled correctly and consistently throughout the deed. If the grantor's name has been changed since the title was acquired, such as when a woman changes her name by marriage, both names should be shown as, for example, "Mary Smith, formerly Mary Jones."

Grantee. To be valid a deed must name a grantee and do so in such a way that the grantee is readily identifiable.

Consideration. Deeds should contain a clause acknowledging the grantor's receipt of consideration. Generally, the amount of consideration is stated in dollars. When a deed conveys real estate as a gift to a relative, "love and affection" may be sufficient consideration. In most states, however, it is customary to recite a *nominal* consideration, such as "$10 and other good and valuable consideration."

Granting clause (words of conveyance). A deed must state, in the **granting clause,** the grantor's intention to convey the property. Depending on the type of deed and the obligations agreed to by the grantor, the wording generally is either "convey and warrant," "grant," "grant, bargain and sell" or "remise, release and quitclaim." Deeds that convey the grantor's entire fee simple interest usually contain wording such as "to Jacqueline Smith and to her heirs and assigns forever." If the grantor is conveying less than his or her complete interest, such as a life estate, the wording must indicate this limitation; for example, "to Jacqueline Smith for the duration of her natural life."

If more than one grantee is involved, the granting clause should specify their rights in the property. The clause might state, for example, that the grantees will take title as joint tenants or tenants in common. This is especially important when specific wording is necessary to create a joint tenancy.

Habendum clause. When it is necessary to define or explain the ownership to be enjoyed by the grantee, a **habendum clause** follows the granting clause. The habendum clause begins with the words "to have and to hold." Its provisions must agree with those set forth in the granting clause. For example, when conveying a time-share interest or an interest less than fee simple absolute, the habendum clause specifies the rights that the owner is entitled to as well as how they are limited (time-frame, prohibited activity, etc.).

Legal description of real estate. To be valid a deed must contain an accurate legal description of the real estate conveyed. Land is considered adequately described if a competent surveyor can locate the property using the description.

Exceptions and reservations. A deed should specifically note any encumbrances, reservations or limitations that affect the title being conveyed, such as restrictions and easements that run with the land. In addition to existing encumbrances, a grantor may reserve some right in the land for his or her own use (an easement, for instance). A grantor may also place certain restrictions on a grantee's use of the property. For example, a developer may restrict the number of houses that may be built on a one-acre lot in a subdivision. Such private restrictions must be stated in the deed or contained in a previously recorded document (such as the subdivider's master deed) that is expressly cited in the deed. Many of these deed restrictions have time limits, often including renewal clauses.

Signature of grantor. To be valid a deed must be signed by *all grantors* named in the deed. As discussed previously, in some states the nonowning spouse must also sign the deed to release marital or other rights. Some states also require witnesses to the grantor's signature. Most states permit an attorney-in-fact to sign for a grantor. The attorney must be acting under a *power of attorney,* the specific written authority to execute and sign one or more legal instruments for another person. Usually the power of attorney must be recorded in the county where the property is located. Because the power of attorney terminates upon the death of the person granting such authority, adequate evidence must be submitted that the grantor was alive at the time the attorney-in-fact signed the deed.

In some states it is still necessary for a seal or the word *seal* to be written or printed after an individual grantor's signature. The corporate seal may be required by corporations.

Acknowledgment. An **acknowledgment** is a formal declaration that a person who is signing a written document does so *voluntarily* and that the person's *signature is genuine.* The declaration is made before a *notary public* or an authorized public officer, such as a judge, justice of the peace, court or county clerk or one of certain officers in the military as prescribed by state law. An acknowledgment usually states that the person signing the deed or other document is known to the officer or has produced sufficient identification to prevent a forgery. The form of acknowledgment required by the state where the property is located should be used even if the party signing is a resident of another ("foreign") state.

Although an acknowledgment is not essential to the *validity* of the deed unless state statutes require it, a deed that is not acknowledged is not a completely sat-

**Figure 11.1
Requirements for
a Valid Deed**

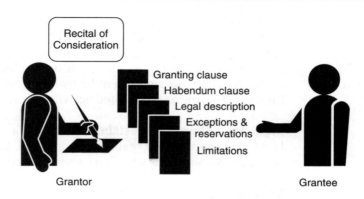

isfactory instrument. In most states an unacknowledged deed is not eligible for recording.

Delivery and acceptance. A title is not considered transferred until actual *delivery* of the deed by the grantor and either actual or implied *acceptance* by the grantee. The grantor may deliver the deed either to the grantee personally or to a third party, commonly known as an escrow agent (discussed in Chapter 23), for ultimate delivery to the grantee upon the fulfillment of certain requirements. *Title is said to "pass" when a deed is delivered.* The effective date of the transfer of title from the grantor and to the grantee is the date of delivery of the deed itself. When a deed is delivered in escrow, the date of delivery generally "relates back" to the date that it was deposited with the escrow agent. (However, under the Torrens system, as discussed in Chapter 12, title does not pass until the deed has been examined and accepted for registration).

**Execution of
Corporate Deeds**

The laws affecting corporations' rights to convey real estate vary from state to state. Some basic rules must be followed:

- A corporation can convey real estate only by authority granted in its *bylaws* or upon a proper resolution passed by its *board of directors*. If all or a substantial portion of a corporation's real estate is being conveyed, usually a resolution authorizing the sale must be secured from the *stockholders*.

- Deeds to real estate can be signed *only by an authorized officer*.

Rules pertaining to religious corporations and not-for-profit corporations vary widely. Because the legal requirements must be followed explicitly, it is advisable to consult an attorney for all corporate conveyances.

Types of Deeds

The deed can take several forms, depending on the extent of the grantor's pledges to the grantee (see Figure 11.2). Regardless of whatever guarantees the deed offers to the grantee, however, the grantee will want additional assurance that the grantor does indeed have the right to offer what the deed conveys. To obtain this protection grantees seek evidence of title, discussed in Chapter 12.

Figure 11.2
Sample Deeds

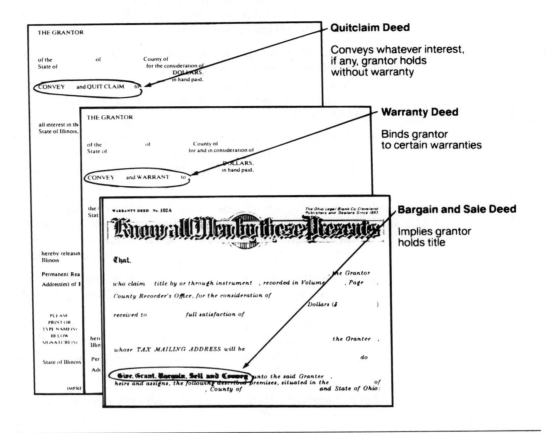

The most common deed forms are the

- general warranty deed,

- special warranty deed,

- bargain and sale deed,

- quitclaim deed,

- deed in trust,

- trustee's deed,

- reconveyance deed, and

- deed executed pursuant to a court order.

General warranty deed. A **general warranty deed** provides the grantee with the *greatest protection* of any deed. It is called a *general warranty deed* because the grantor is legally bound by certain covenants or warranties. In most states the warranties are implied by the use of certain words specified in the state statutes. In other localities the grantor's warranties are expressly written into the deed itself. Each state law should be examined, but some of the specific words include "convey and warrant," "warrant generally" and, in some states, "grant, bargain and sell." The basic warranties are:

1. *Covenant of seisin:* The grantor warrants that he or she is the owner of the property and has the right to convey title to it. The grantee may recover damages up to the full purchase price if this covenant is broken.

2. *Covenant against encumbrances:* The grantor warrants that the property is free from liens or encumbrances except those specifically stated in the deed. Encumbrances generally include mortgages, mechanics' liens and easements. If this covenant is breached, the grantee may sue for expenses to remove the encumbrance(s).

3. *Covenant of quiet enjoyment:* The grantor guarantees that the grantee's title will be good against third parties who might bring court actions to establish superior title to the property. If the grantee's title is found to be inferior, the grantor is liable for damages.

4. *Covenant of further assurance:* The grantor promises to obtain and deliver any instrument needed to make the title good. For example, if the grantor's spouse has failed to sign away dower rights, the grantor must deliver a quitclaim deed (discussed later) executed by the spouse to clear the title.

5. *Covenant of warranty forever:* The grantor guarantees to compensate the grantee for the loss sustained if the title fails at any time in the future.

These covenants in a general warranty deed are not limited to matters that occurred during the time the grantor owned the property; they extend back to its origins. The grantor defends the title against himself *and against all others as predecessors in title.*

Special warranty deed. A **special warranty deed** warrants that *the grantor received title* and that *the property was not encumbered during the time the grantor held title,* except as noted in the deed. The grantor defends the title against himself. The granting clause generally contains the words "remise, release, alienate and convey." The grantor may include additional warranties, but they must be specifically stated in the deed. In areas where a special warranty deed is more commonly used, the purchase of title insurance is viewed as providing adequate protection to the grantee in lieu of a general warranty deed.

A special warranty deed may be used by fiduciaries, such as trustees, executors and corporations, and sometimes by grantors who have acquired title at a tax sale. A fiduciary has no authority to warrant against acts of its predecessors in title. Fiduciaries may hold title for a limited time without having a personal interest in the proceeds.

Bargain and sale deed. A **bargain and sale deed** contains no express warranties against encumbrances; however, it does *imply* that the grantor holds title and possession of the property. The words in the granting clause are usually "grant and release" or "grant, bargain and sell." Because the warranty is not specifically stated, the grantee has little legal recourse if defects later appear in the title. In some areas this deed is used in foreclosures and tax sales. The buyer should purchase title insurance for protection.

A covenant against encumbrances initiated by the grantor may be added to a standard bargain and sale deed to create a *bargain and sale deed with covenant against the grantor's acts.* This deed is roughly equivalent to a special warranty deed. Warranties used in general warranty deeds may be inserted into a bargain and sale deed to give the grantee similar protection.

Quitclaim deed. A **quitclaim deed** provides the grantee with the least protection. It carries no covenants or warranties and generally conveys only whatever interest the grantor may have when the deed is delivered. If the grantor has no interest the grantee will acquire nothing. Nor will the grantee acquire any right of warranty claim against the grantor. A quitclaim deed can convey title as effectively as a warranty deed if the grantor has good title when he or she delivers the deed, but it provides none of the guarantees that a warranty deed does. Through a quitclaim deed, the grantor only "remises, releases and quitclaims" his or her interest in the property to the grantee.

Usually, a quitclaim deed is the only type of deed that may be used to convey less than a fee simple estate because it conveys only the grantor's right, title or interest. For example, it might convey an easement or it might reconvey equitable title back to a seller.

A quitclaim deed is also frequently used to cure a defect, called a *cloud on the title*. For example, if the name of the grantee is misspelled on a warranty deed filed in the public record, a quitclaim deed with the correct spelling may be executed to the grantee to perfect the title.

A quitclaim deed is also used when a grantor allegedly has *inherited* property but is not certain that the decedent's title was valid. A warranty deed in such an instance could carry with it obligations of warranty, while a quitclaim deed would convey only the grantor's interest.

Deed in trust. A **deed in trust** is the means by which a trustor conveys real estate to a *trustee* for the benefit of a *beneficiary*. The real estate is held by the trustee to fulfill the purpose of the trust.

Trustee's deed. A deed executed in turn by a trustee is a **trustee's deed.** It is used when a trustee named in a will, trust agreement or trust deed conveys the trust real estate to anyone other than the trustor. The trustee's deed sets forth the fact that the trustee is executing the instrument in accordance with the powers and authority granted by the trust instrument.

Reconveyance deed. A **reconveyance deed** is used by a trustee under a deed of trust (a financing document) to return title to the trustor. For example, when a loan secured by a deed of trust has been fully paid, the beneficiary notifies the trustee, who then reconveys the property to the trustor. As with any document of title, a reconveyance deed should be recorded to prevent future title problems.

Deed executed pursuant to court order. This classification covers such deed forms as executors' (or administrators') deeds, masters' deeds, sheriffs' deeds and many others. These statutory deed forms are used to convey title to property that is transferred by court order or by will. The forms of such deeds must conform to the laws of the state where the property is located.

One characteristic of such instruments is that the *full consideration* is usually stated in the deed. Instead of $10 and other valuable consideration, the deed would list the actual sales price.

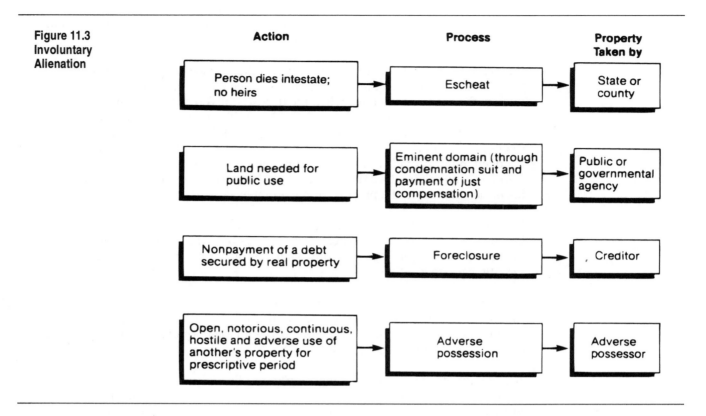

**Figure 11.3
Involuntary
Alienation**

Action	Process	Property Taken by
Person dies intestate; no heirs	Escheat	State or county
Land needed for public use	Eminent domain (through condemnation suit and payment of just compensation)	Public or governmental agency
Nonpayment of a debt secured by real property	Foreclosure	Creditor
Open, notorious, continuous, hostile and adverse use of another's property for prescriptive period	Adverse possession	Adverse possessor

**Transfer Tax
Stamps**

Most states have enacted laws providing for a tax, usually referred to as the state **transfer tax,** on conveyances of real estate. In these states the tax is usually payable when the deed is recorded, through the purchase of *stamps* (sometimes called *documentary stamps*) from the recorder of the county in which the deed is recorded. The stamps are then affixed to deeds and conveyances before the document can be recorded.

The transfer tax can be paid by the seller, buyer or split between them, depending on local custom or agreement in the sales contract. The *tax rate* varies from state to state; an example is 1% of the taxable consideration.

In many states a *transfer declaration form (or transfer statement or affidavit of real property value)* must be signed by both the buyer and the seller or their agents. This form states the full sales price of the property; its legal description; the type of improvement and the address, date and type of deed. The form also must specify when a transfer is being made between relatives or in accordance with a court order.

Certain deeds may be *exempted* from the tax, such as gifts of real estate; deeds not made in connection with a sale (such as a change in the form of co-ownership); conveyances to, from or between governmental bodies; deeds by charitable, religious or educational institutions; deeds securing debts or releasing property as security for a debt; partitions; tax deeds; deeds pursuant to mergers of corporations; and deeds from subsidiary to parent corporations for cancellations of stock.

INVOLUNTARY ALIENATION

Title to property can be transferred without the owner's consent (see Figure 11.3) by **involuntary alienation.** Such transfers are usually carried out by operation of law, such as by condemnation or the sale of property to satisfy delinquent tax or mortgage liens. When a person dies intestate and leaves no heirs, the title to the real estate passes to the state by the state's power of escheat.

As described in Chapter 6, federal, state and local governments, school boards, some government agencies and certain public and quasi-public corporations and utilities (railroads and gas and electric companies) have the right of *eminent domain.* Under this right private property may be taken for public use through *condemnation.* Eminent domain may be exercised only when the use is for the benefit of the public, an equitable amount of compensation is paid to the owner and the rights of the property owner are protected by due process of law. Recent court decisions have affirmed the right of property owners to be compensated when certain actions by the government have been determined to deprive landowners of their private property rights granted under the U.S. Constitution.

Land may also be transferred without an owner's consent to satisfy debts incurred by the owner. In such cases the property is sold and the proceeds of the sale are applied to pay off the debt. As discussed in Chapter 6, debts that could be foreclosed include mortgage loans, real estate taxes, mechanics' liens and general judgments against the property owner.

In addition to the involuntary transfer of land by legal processes, land may be transferred by natural forces. As discussed in Chapter 6, owners of land bordering on rivers, lakes and other bodies of water may acquire additional land through the process of *accretion,* the slow accumulation of soil, rock or other matter deposited by the movement of water on an owner's property. The opposite of accretion is *erosion,* the gradual wearing away of land by the action of water and wind. In addition, property may be lost through *avulsion,* the sudden tearing away of land by such natural means as earthquakes or tidal waves.

Adverse possession is another means of involuntary transfer. An owner who does not use or inspect the land for a number of years may lose title to someone who makes some claim to the land, takes possession and, most important, uses the land. The law recognizes that the use of land is an important function of its ownership. Usually the possession by the claimant must be open, notorious, continuous (uninterrupted for the number of years set by state law—as long as 20 years in some states), hostile and adverse to the true owner's possession. Through the principle of *tacking,* successive periods of different adverse possession by different adverse possessors can be combined, enabling a person who is not in possession for the entire required time to establish a claim. To claim title the adverse possessor normally files an action in court to receive undisputed title. A claimant who does not receive title may acquire an easement by prescription (see Chapter 6). Because the right of adverse possession is statutory, and state requirements must be followed carefully, the parties to a transaction that might involve adverse possession should seek legal counsel.

**Figure 11.4
Requirements
for a Valid
Will**

```
┌─────────────────────────────┐
│            WILL             │
│                             │
│  1. Legal Age               │
│  2. Sound Mind              │
│  3. Proper Wording          │
│  4. No Undue Influence      │
│  5. Witnesses               │
│                             │
└─────────────────────────────┘
```

TRANSFER OF A DECEASED PERSON'S PROPERTY

A person who dies **testate** has prepared a will indicating the way the property will be disposed of after the person's death. In contrast, when a person dies **intestate** (without a will), the real estate and personal property pass to the decedent's heirs according to the *statute of descent and distribution.* In effect, the state makes a will for such decedents.

Legally, when a person dies, title to the real estate immediately passes either to the heirs by descent or to the persons named in the will. Before these individuals can take possession of the property, however, the estate must be probated and all claims against it must be satisfied.

Transfer of Title by Will

A **will** is an instrument made by an owner to convey title to property after the owner's death. Because a will takes effect only after death, until that time, any property covered by the will can be conveyed by the owner and thus be removed from the owner's estate. The gift of real property by will is known as a **devise,** and a person who receives property by will is known as a *devisee.*

A will differs from a deed in that a deed conveys a present interest in real estate during the lifetime of the grantor, while a will conveys no interest in the property until after the death of the testator. To be valid a deed *must* be delivered during the lifetime of the grantor. The parties named in a will have no rights or interests as long as the party who has made the will is alive; they acquire interest or title only after the owner's death. For title to pass to the devisees, state laws require that upon the death of a testator the will must be filed with the court and *probated.*

A will cannot supersede the state laws of dower and curtesy, which were enacted to protect the inheritance rights of the surviving spouse. In a case where a will does not provide a spouse with the minimum statutory inheritance, the surviving spouse may demand it from the estate.

Legal requirements for making a will. Because a will must be valid and admitted to probate to effectively convey title to real estate, it should be executed and prepared in accordance with the laws of the state where the real estate is located. A **testator** must have legal capacity to make a will (see Figure 11.4). Usually a person must be of *legal age* and of *sound mind.* There are, however, no rigid tests to determine the capacity to make a will. Generally the courts hold that to make a valid will the testator must have sufficient mental capacity to understand the nature and extent of the property owned, the identity of natural heirs and that at the testator's death the property will go to those named in the will. The drawing of a will must be a voluntary act, free of any undue influence by other people.

In most states a written will must be signed by its testator before two or more witnesses who must also sign the document. The witnesses should not be individuals who are named as devisees in the will.

The testator may alter the will. A modification of, an amendment of or an addition to a previously executed will is set forth in a separate document called a *codicil.*

A *holographic will* is one that is in the testator's handwriting and, depending on state laws, need not be further witnessed or acknowledged. A *nuncupative will* is one that is given orally by a testator. Certain states do not permit the use of holographic and/or nuncupative wills to convey title to property.

Transfer of Title by Descent

By law the title to real estate and personal property of a person who dies intestate passes to the decedent's heirs. Under the statute of descent and distribution the primary **heirs** of the deceased are the spouse and close blood relatives, such as children, parents, brothers, sisters, aunts, uncles and, in some cases, first and second cousins. The right to inherit under laws of descent varies from state to state, and intestate property is distributed according to the laws of the state in which the property is located.

Probate Proceedings

Probate is the formal judicial process to prove or confirm the validity of a will (if there is one) and to determine the assets of the deceased person (the decedent) and the persons to whom the assets will pass. The purpose of probate is to see that the assets are distributed correctly. They must be properly accounted for and the debts of the decedent and taxes on the estate must be satisfied prior to the distribution of the assets. The laws of each state govern the probate proceedings and the functions of the individuals who are appointed to administer the decedent's affairs. Assets that are distributed through probate are those which do not otherwise distribute themselves because of the way they are titled, such as in joint tenancy or tenancy by the entirety. Probate proceedings take place in the county in which the decedent resided. If the decedent owned real estate in another county, probate would occur in that county as well.

When an individual dies *testate,* probate is necessary to prove the validity of the will before the assets can be distributed. The person who has possession of the will, normally the individual designated as *executor* or *executrix* in the will, presents it for filing with the court. The court is responsible for determining that the will meets the statutory requirements for its form and execution and, in the event there is a codicil or several wills, how these documents should be probated. There are normally criminal sanctions for concealing or destroying a will to prevent wrongdoing by relatives who would otherwise receive more under the laws of descent and distribution. The court must rule on a challenge if a will is contested. Once the will is upheld, the assets can be distributed according to its provisions. Probate courts will distribute assets according to statute only when no other reasonable alternative exists.

When a person dies *intestate,* the court determines who inherits the assets by reviewing proof from relatives of the decedent and their entitlement under the statute of descent and distribution in its state. Once the heirs are determined, the court will appoint an *administrator* or *personal representative* (in lieu of an executor who would have been named in a will) to administer the affairs of the estate.

The administrator, executor or executrix has the authority to see that the assets of the estate are appraised and satisfy all debts owed by the decedent. The estate representative is also responsible for paying federal estate taxes and state inheritance taxes. Once all obligations have been satisfied, the representative distributes the remaining assets of the estate according to the person's will or the state's law of descent.

IN PRACTICE... | *A broker entering into a listing agreement with the executor or administrator of an estate in probate should be aware that the amount of commission will be fixed by the court and that the commission is payable only from the proceeds of the sale. The broker will not be able to collect a commission unless the court approves the sale.*

KEY TERMS

acknowledgment
adverse possession
bargain and sale deed
deed
deed in trust
devise
general warranty deed
grantee
granting clause
grantor
habendum clause
heir
intestate

involuntary alienation
probate
quitclaim deed
reconveyance deed
special warranty deed
testate
testator
title
transfer tax
trustee's deed
voluntary alienation
will

SUMMARY

Title to real estate is the right to and evidence of ownership of the land. It may be transferred by voluntary alienation, involuntary alienation, will and descent.

The voluntary transfer of an owner's title is made by a deed, executed (signed) by the owner as grantor to the purchaser or donee as grantee.

Among the most common requirements for a valid deed are a grantor with legal capacity to contract, a readily identifiable grantee, a granting clause, a legal description of the property, a recital of consideration, exceptions and reservations on the title and the signature of the grantor. In addition, the deed should be acknowledged before a notary public or other officer to provide evidence that the signature is genuine and to allow recording. Title to the property passes when the grantor delivers a deed to the grantee and it is accepted. The obligation of a grantor is determined by the form of the deed. The words of conveyance in the granting clause are important in determining the form of deed.

A general warranty deed provides the greatest protection of any deed by binding the grantor to certain covenants or warranties. A special warranty deed warrants only that the real estate is not encumbered except as stated in the deed. A bargain and sale deed carries with it no warranties but implies that the grantor holds title to the property. A quitclaim deed carries with it no warranties whatsoever and conveys only the interest, if any, the grantor possesses in the property.

An owner's title may be transferred without his or her permission by a court action, such as a foreclosure or judgment sale, a tax sale, condemnation under the right of eminent domain, adverse possession or escheat. Land may also be transferred by the natural forces of water and wind, which either increase property by accretion or decrease it through erosion or avulsion.

The real estate of an owner who makes a valid will (who dies testate) passes to the devisees through the probating of the will. The title of an owner who dies without a will (intestate) passes according to the provisions of the law of descent and distribution of the state in which the real estate is located.

Questions

•   •   •   •   •   •   •

1. The basic requirements for a valid conveyance are governed by
   a. state law.   c. national law.
   b. local custom.   d. law of descent.

2. It is essential that every deed be signed by
   the
   a. grantor.   c. grantor and grantee.
   b. grantee.   d. devisee.

3. H, age 15, recently inherited many parcels
   of real estate from his late father and has decided to sell one of them to pay inheritance
   taxes. If H entered into a deed conveying
   his interest in the property to a purchaser,
   such a conveyance would be
   a. valid.   c. invalid.
   b. void.   d. voidable.

4. An instrument authorizing one person to act
   for another is called a(n)
   a. power of attorney.
   b. release deed.
   c. quitclaim deed.
   d. acknowledgment.

5. The grantee receives greatest protection
   with what type of deed?
   a. Quitclaim
   b. Warranty
   c. Bargain and sale with covenant
   d. Executor's

6. The type of deed used in conveying title can
   be identified by examining the
   a. grantor's name.
   b. grantee's name.
   c. granting clause.
   d. acknowledgement.

7. Which of the following best describes the
   covenant of quiet enjoyment?
   a. The grantor promises to obtain and
      deliver any instrument needed to make
      the title good.
   b. The grantor guarantees that if the title
      fails in the future he or she will
      compensate the grantee.
   c. The grantor warrants that he or she is
      the owner and has the right to convey
      title to it.
   d. The grantor assures that the title will be
      good against the title claims of third par-
      ties.

8. Which of the following types of deeds
   would be most likely to recite the full, actual consideration paid for the property?
   a. Gift deed
   b. Trustee's deed
   c. Deed in trust
   d. Deed executed pursuant to court order

9. Which of the following types of deeds
   merely implies but does not specifically
   warrant that the grantor holds good title to
   the property?
   a. Special warranty deed
   b. Bargain and sale deed
   c. Quitclaim deed
   d. Trustee's deed

10. Title to property transfers at the moment a
    deed is
    a. signed.
    b. acknowledged.
    c. delivered and accepted.
    d. recorded.

11. Consideration in a deed refers to
    a. gentle handling of the document.
    b. something of value given by each party.
    c. the habendum clause.
    d. the payment of transfer tax stamps.

12. A declaration before a notary or other official providing evidence that a signature is genuine is an
    a. affidavit.
    b. acknowledgment.
    c. affirmation.
    d. estoppel.

13. R executes a deed to P as grantee, has it acknowledged and receives payment from the buyer. R holds the deed, however, and arranges to meet P the next morning at the courthouse to deliver the deed to her. In this situation at this time
    a. P owns the property because she has paid for it.
    b. title to the property will not officially pass until P has been given the deed the next morning.
    c. title to the property will not pass until P has received the deed and recorded it the next morning.
    d. P will own the property when she has signed the deed the next morning.

14. Title to real estate may be transferred during a person's lifetime by
    a. devise.
    b. descent.
    c. involuntary alienation.
    d. escheat.

15. F bought acreage in a distant county, never went to see the acreage and did not use the ground. H moved his mobile home onto the land, had a water well drilled and lived there for 22 years. H may become the owner of the land if he has complied with the state law regarding
    a. requirements for a valid conveyance.
    b. adverse possession.
    c. avulsion.
    d. voluntary alienation.

16. Which of the following is *not* one of the ways in which title to real estate may be transferred by involuntary alienation?
    a. Eminent domain
    b. Escheat
    c. Erosion
    d. Seisin

17. The acquisition of land through deposit of soil sand washed up by water is called
    a. accretion.   c. erosion.
    b. avulsion.   d. condemnation.

18. A house sells for $89,500; the buyer pays $50,000 cash and gives the seller a mortgage for the balance. At a rate of 1%, what is the amount of state transfer tax that must be paid on this transaction?
    a. $895   c. $8,950
    b. $3,950   d. $17,900

19. A person who has died leaving a valid will is called a(n)
    a. devisee.   c. legatee.
    b. testator.   d. intestate.

20. Title to real estate can be transferred at death by which of the following documents?
    a. Warranty deed
    b. Special warranty deed
    c. Trustee's deed
    d. Will

21. J, a bachelor, died owning real estate that he devised by his will to his niece, K. In essence at what point does title pass to his niece?
    a. Immediately upon J's death
    b. After his will has been probated
    c. After K has paid all inheritance taxes
    d. When K executes a new deed to the property

22. An owner of real estate who was adjudged legally incompetent made a will during his stay at a nursing home. He later died and was survived by a wife and three children. His real estate will pass
    a. to his wife.
    b. to the heirs mentioned in his will.
    c. according to the state laws of descent.
    d. to the state.

12 Title Records

PUBLIC RECORDS

Public records are maintained to make readily available a wide variety of information about each parcel of real estate. These records are crucial in establishing official ownership, give notice of encumbrances and establish priority of liens, thereby protecting the interests of real estate owners, taxing bodies, creditors and the general public. The real estate recording system includes written documents that affect title such as deeds, mortgages, contracts for sale, options and assignments. There are also public records regarding taxes, judgments, probate and marriage that will have a bearing on the title. The recorder of deeds, county clerk, county treasurer, city clerk and collector and clerks of various courts maintain these records.

Because the records are open to the public, anyone interested in a particular property can review the records to learn about the documents, claims and other interests that affect its ownership. A prospective purchaser, for example, needs to be sure that the seller can convey title to the property as well as what liens and other encumbrances exist. By examining the public records before settlement, the purchaser can ascertain that he or she will receive good title and that any debts that are secured by liens will be properly accounted for at the settlement.

Recording

Recording is the act of placing documents in public record. The specific rules are set forth in each state's recording acts. The details vary, but all recording acts provide that all written documents affecting any estate, right, title or interest in land *must be recorded in the county where the land is located* to serve as public notice. Everyone interested in the title to a parcel of property can discover the various interests of all other parties. From a practical point of view the recording acts generally give legal priority to those interests that are recorded first.

To be *eligible for recording* a document must be drawn and executed as stipulated in the recording acts of the state in which the real estate is located. Many states require that the names be typed below the signatures and that the document be acknowledged before a notary public or other officer. In a few states the document must also be witnessed. A number of states require that the name of the person who prepared the document appear on it.

Notice

Anyone who has an interest in a parcel of real estate can take certain steps, called giving *notice,* to provide information that makes that interest known to anyone who inquires. **Constructive notice** is the legal presumption that information is available and by diligent inquiry an individual can obtain it. Properly recording documents in public record or the physical possession of a property serves as constructive notice to the world of an individual's rights or interest. Because the information is readily available, prospective purchasers or mortgage lenders are responsible for discovering the interests that any others may have in the real estate.

In contrast, **actual notice** means the person has been given the information and actually knows it. (See Figure 12.1.) An individual who has searched the public records and inspected the property has actual notice, *direct knowledge,* of the information. If an individual can be proved to have *actual knowledge* of information concerning a parcel of real estate, he or she cannot use a lack of *constructive notice,* such as an unrecorded deed or an owner who is not in possession, to justify a claim.

Priority. Many complicated situations can arise that affect the priority of rights in a parcel of real estate. For example, a purchaser may receive a deed and take possession of the property but not record the deed. By taking possession, the purchaser gives constructive notice of an interest in the land. His or her rights would be considered superior to the rights of a subsequent purchaser who accepted a deed from the original owner at a later date and recorded the deed but did not inspect the property to determine whether someone was in possession. How the courts rule in any situation depends, of course, on the specific facts of the case. These are strictly legal questions that should be referred to the parties' attorneys.

Unrecorded Documents

Deeds that are not recorded cannot serve constructive notice of their existence and raise the issues previously mentioned about their impact on future owners and parties in possession. There also are certain types of liens that are not recorded. Real estate taxes and special assessments are direct liens on specific parcels of real estate and need not be recorded. Other liens that are not recorded include inheritance taxes and franchise taxes. These are placed by statutory authority against all real estate owned either by a decedent at the time of death or by a corporation at the time the franchise tax became a lien.

Notice of these liens must be gained from sources other than the recorder's office. Evidence of the payment of real estate taxes, special assessments, municipal utilities and other taxes can be gathered from paid tax receipts and letters from municipalities to provide information about the likelihood of a title being encumbered by these "off the record" liens.

Chain of Title

Chain of title is the recorded history of all of the matters that affect the title to a specific parcel of real property. These include ownership, encumbrances and liens. Beginning from the original source, ownership subsequently passes to many individuals. Each owner is linked to the next so that a "chain" is formed. An unbroken chain of title can be traced through linking conveyances from the present owner back to its origin.

Figure 12.1
Notice

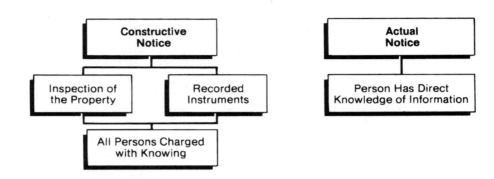

If ownership cannot be traced through an unbroken chain, it is said that there is a *gap* in the chain. In these cases there is a cloud on the title and it will be necessary to establish ownership by a court action called a **suit to quiet title.** A suit might be required, for example, when a grantor acquired title under one name and conveyed it under another or because of a forged deed in the chain, after which no subsequent grantee acquired legal title. All possible claimants will be allowed to present evidence during a court proceeding, and then the court's judgment will be filed. Often the simple procedure of obtaining any relevant quitclaim deeds (discussed in Chapter 11) will be used to establish ownership.

Title Search and Abstract of Title

A **title search** is an examination of all of the public records to determine what, if any, defects exist in the chain of title. The records of the conveyances of ownership are examined beginning with the present owner. The title is traced back to its origin or 40 to 60 years, depending on local custom. The time beyond which the title must be searched is limited in states that have adopted The Marketable Title Act. This law extinguishes certain interests and cures certain defects arising prior to the "root of the title"—the conveyance that establishes the source of the chain of title. Normally the root is considered to be 40 years or more. Therefore it is necessary to only search from the current owner to the root.

Other public records are examined to identify wills, judicial proceedings and other encumbrances that affect the title to a specific parcel of real estate. Most notably these include a variety of taxes, any special assessments and other liens that are on record.

Normally a title search is not ordered until after the major contingencies in a sales contract have been cleared, such as after a loan commitment has been secured to satisfy a mortgage contingency. A lender will generally order a title search, at the borrower's expense, to assure itself that there will be no liens superior to its mortgage lien before it forwards the money for the loan.

An **abstract of title** is a summary report of the items about a property that can be found in public record. The person preparing this report, called an *abstractor,* searches all of the public records and then summarizes the various instruments and proceedings that affect the title throughout its history. The report lists the instruments in chronological order of recording, beginning with the original grant or root, together with a statement of all recorded liens and encumbrances and their current status. A list of all of the public records that were examined is included as well. The abstract of title is a condensed history of those items that can be found in public records. It will not reveal such items as encroachments or forgeries or any interests or conveyances that have not been recorded.

Marketable Title

Under the terms of the typical real estate sales contract, the seller is required to deliver **marketable title** to the buyer at the closing. To be marketable, a title must

- disclose no serious defects and not depend on doubtful questions of law or fact to prove its validity.

- not expose a purchaser to the hazard of litigation or threaten the quiet enjoyment of the property.

- convince a reasonably well-informed and prudent person, acting on business principles and willful knowledge of the facts and their legal significance, that he or she could, in turn, sell or mortgage the property.

Although a title that does not meet these requirements may still be transferred, it contains *certain defects that may limit or restrict its ownership.* A buyer cannot be forced to accept a conveyance that is materially different from the one bargained for in the sales contract. Questions of marketable title must be raised by a buyer prior to acceptance of the deed. Once a buyer has accepted a deed with unmarketable title, the only available legal recourse is to sue the seller under the covenants of warranty (if any) contained in the deed.

It is customary in some states for a preliminary title search to be conducted after an offer to purchase is accepted. In fact, there may be a contingency in the sales contract that gives the buyer the right to review and approve the title report before proceeding with the purchase of the property. A preliminary title report can also benefit a seller. It may reveal items that are unknown to the seller, thereby giving the seller an opportunity to cure a problem before closing.

EVIDENCE OF TITLE

Evidence of title is proof of ownership. A deed by itself is not considered sufficient evidence of ownership. Although it conveys the interest of the grantor, even a warranty deed contains no proof of the condition of the grantor's title at the time it is conveyed. The grantee needs some assurance that, in fact, he or she is acquiring ownership and that the title is marketable. The most common examples of title are a certificate of title, title insurance and a Torrens certificate.

Certificate of Title

A **certificate of title** is a statement of opinion of the title's status as of the date it is issued. The certificate is not a guarantee of ownership. Rather it certifies the condition of the title based on an examination of the public records, that is the title search. The certificate may be prepared by a title company, licensed abstractor or an attorney. An owner, mortgage lender or buyer may request the certificate.

Although a certificate of title is used as evidence of ownership, it is not perfect. Based on the public records, it may appear that no other interests in the ownership or claims exist. However, unrecorded liens or rights of parties in possession cannot be discovered. Nor can hidden defects such as forged documents, incorrect marital information, transfers by incompetent parties or minors or fraud be detected. A certificate offers no defense against these defects because they are unknown. The person who prepares the certificate is only liable for negligence in preparing the certificate and only to the extent of his or her personal effects or those of the preparer's employer.

An abstract and **attorney's opinion of title** is used in some areas as evidence of title. It is an opinion of the status of the title based on a review of the abstract. Similar to a certificate of title, the opinion of title does not protect against defects that cannot be discovered from the public records. A growing practice today is for buyers to purchase title insurance because it defends the title from these defects.

Title Insurance

Title insurance is a contract under which the policyholder is protected from losses arising from defects in the title. A title insurance company will determine if the title is insurable based on a review of the public records. If so, a policy will be issued. Unlike other insurance policies that insure against future losses, title insurance protects the insured from an occurrence before the policy is issued. Title insurance is considered to be the best defense of title because the company will defend any lawsuit that is based on an insurable defect and pay claims if the title proves to be defective.

Exactly which defects the title company will defend depends on the type of policy it issues. (See Table 12.1) A *standard coverage policy* normally insures the title as it is known to exist from the public records plus such hidden defects as forged documents, conveyances by incompetent grantors, incorrect marital statements and improperly delivered deeds. *Extended coverage* as provided by an *American Land Title Association policy* includes the protections of a standard policy plus defects that may be discovered by inspection of the property, such as rights of parties in possession, examination of a survey and certain unrecorded liens.

Title insurance, however, will not protect against all defects. Obviously a title company will not insure a bad title or defects that can be found in a title search. The policy generally names certain uninsurable losses or *exclusions* such as zoning ordinances, restrictive covenants, easements, certain water rights and current taxes and special assessments.

There are different types of policies depending on who is named as the insured. An *owner's policy* is issued for the benefit of the owner and his or her heirs or devisees. A *lender's policy* is issued for the benefit of the mortgagee. The amount of the coverage is commensurate with the amount of the mortgage loan and coverage decreases as the loan balance is reduced. Because only the lender's interest is insured, it is advisable for the owner to obtain a policy as well. There are also *leasehold* policies to insure a lessee's interests and *certificate of sale* policies for purchasers in a court sale.

Upon completion of the examination, the title company usually issues what may be called a *preliminary report of title* or a *commitment* to issue a title policy. This describes the policy that will be issued and includes

- the name of the insured party

Table 12.1 Owner's Title Insurance Policy	Standard Coverage	Extended Coverage	Not Covered by Either Policy
	1. Defects found in public records	Standard coverage plus defects discoverable through:	1. Defects and liens listed in policy
	2. Forged documents	1. Property inspection including unrecorded rights of persons in possession	2. Defects known to buyer
	3. Incompetent grantors		3. Changes in land use brought about by zoning ordinances
	4. Incorrect marital statements	2. Examination of survey	
	5. Improperly delivered deeds	3. Unrecorded liens not known of by policyholder	

- the legal description of the real estate
- the estate or interest covered
- conditions and stipulations under which the policy is issued and
- a schedule of all exceptions, including such items as encumbrances and defects found in the public records and unrecorded defects of which the policyholder has knowledge, depending on the type of policy.

The *premium* for the policy is paid once for the life of the policy. The maximum loss for which the company may be liable cannot exceed the face amount of the policy (unless the amount of coverage has been extended by use of an *inflation rider*). When a title company makes a payment to settle a claim covered by a policy, the company acquires by the right of *subrogation* to all the remedies and rights of the insured party against anyone responsible for the settled claim.

The Torrens System

The **Torrens system** is a legal registration system used to verify ownership and encumbrances. Registration in the Torrens system provides evidence of title without the need for an additional search of the public records. Under the Torrens system a written application to register a title to real estate is made with the clerk of the court of the county in which the real estate is located. If the applicant proves that he or she is the owner, the court enters an order to register the real estate, and the *registrar of titles* is further directed to issue a certificate of title. At any time the Torrens original certificate of title in the registrar's office reveals the owner of the land and all mortgages, judgments and similar liens. It does not reveal federal or state taxes and some other items. The Torrens system of registration is the title itself; a person acquires title only when it is registered.

UNIFORM COMMERCIAL CODE

The **Uniform Commercial Code (UCC)** is a commercial law statute that has been adopted, wholly or in part, in all states to govern personal property transactions. The UCC does not apply to real estate; it governs the documents when personal property is used as security for a loan.

For a lender to create a security interest in personal property, including personal property that will become fixtures, the code requires the borrower to sign a **security agreement.** It must contain a complete description of the items against which the lien applies. A short notice of this agreement, called a **financing statement** or UCC-1, which includes the identification of any real estate involved in those cases where the personalty is made part of the real estate, must be filed. The recording of the financing statement constitutes notice to subsequent purchasers and lenders of the security interest in personal property and fixtures on the real estate. Many lenders require the signing of a security agreement and filing of a financing statement when the real estate includes chattels or readily removable fixtures.

•   •   •   •   •   •   •

KEY TERMS

abstract of title   priority
actual notice   recording
attorney's opinion of title   security agreement
certificate of title   suit to quiet title
chain of title   title insurance
constructive notice   title search
evidence of title   Torrens system
financing statement   Uniform Commercial Code
marketable title

SUMMARY

The purpose of the recording acts is to give legal, public and constructive notice to the world of parties' interests in real estate. The recording provisions have been adopted to create system and order in the transfer of real estate. Without them, it would be virtually impossible to transfer real estate from one party to another. The interests and rights of the various parties in a particular parcel of land must be recorded so that such rights will be legally effective against third parties who do not have knowledge or notice of the rights.

Possession of real estate is generally interpreted as constructive notice of the rights of the person in possession. Actual notice is knowledge acquired directly and personally.

Title evidence shows whether or not a seller is conveying marketable title. A deed of conveyance is evidence that a grantor has conveyed his or her interest in land, but it is not evidence of the kind or condition of the title. Marketable title is generally one that is so free from significant defects that the purchaser can be assured against having to defend the title.

There are four forms of providing title evidence commonly used throughout the United States: abstract and attorney's opinion of title, certificate of title, Torrens certificate and title insurance policy. Each form reveals the history of a title. Each must be later dated, or continued or reissued, to cover a more recent date.

Under the Uniform Commercial Code the filing of a financing statement gives notice to purchasers and mortgagees of the security interests in personal property and fixtures on the specific parcel of real estate.

Questions

1. Public records may be inspected by
   a. anyone.
   b. attorneys and abstractors only.
   c. attorneys, abstractors and real estate licensees only.
   d. anyone who obtains a court order under the Freedom of Information Act.

2. Which of the following statements best explains why instruments affecting real estate are recorded?
   a. Recording gives constructive notice to the world of the rights and interests in a particular parcel of real estate.
   b. The law requires that such instruments be recorded.
   c. The instruments must be recorded to comply with the terms of the statute of frauds.
   d. Recording proves the execution of the instrument.

3. A purchaser went to the county building to check the recorder's records. She found that the seller was the grantee in the last recorded deed and that no mortgage was on record against the property. The purchaser may assume which of the following?
   a. All taxes are paid and no judgments are outstanding.
   b. The seller has good title.
   c. The seller did not mortgage the property.
   d. No one else is occupying the property.

4. The date and time a document was recorded establish which of the following?
   a. Priority of liens or title
   b. Chain of title
   c. Subrogation
   d. Marketable title

5. P bought L's house, received a deed and moved into the residence but neglected to record the document. One week later L died, and his heirs in another city, unaware that the property had been sold, conveyed title to M, who recorded the deed. Who owns the property?
   a. P   c. L's heirs
   b. M   d. Both P and M

6. If a property has encumbrances, it
   a. cannot be sold.
   b. can be sold only if title insurance is provided.
   c. cannot have a deed recorded without a survey.
   d. can be sold if a buyer agrees to take it subject to the encumbrances.

7. Which of the following is *not* acceptable proof of ownership?
   a. A Torrens certificate
   b. A title insurance policy
   c. An abstract and attorney's opinion
   d. A deed signed by the last seller

8. *Chain of title* refers to which of the following?
   a. A summary or history of all documents and legal proceedings affecting a specific parcel of land
   b. A series of links measuring 7.92 inches each
   c. An instrument or a document that protects the insured parties (subject to specific exceptions) against defects in the examination of the record and hidden risks such as forgeries, undisclosed heirs, errors in the public records and so forth
   d. The succession of conveyances from some starting point whereby the present owner derives title

9. Proof of the kind of estate and all liens against an interest in a parcel of real estate can usually be found through
   a. a recorded deed.
   b. a court suit for specific performance.
   c. one of the four evidences of title.
   d. a foreclosure suit.

10. The person who prepares an abstract of title for a parcel of real estate
    a. writes a brief history of the title after inspecting the county records for documents affecting the title.
    b. insures the condition of the title.
    c. inspects the property.
    d. issues a certificate of title.

11. S is frantic because she cannot find her deed and now wants to sell the property. She
    a. may need a suit to quiet title.
    b. will have to buy title insurance.
    c. does not need the deed to sell if it was recorded.
    d. should execute a replacement deed to herself.

12. Mortgagee title policies protect which parties against loss?
    a. Buyers   c. Lenders
    b. Sellers   d. Buyers and lenders

13. When a title examination is completed, the title insurance company notifies the parties in writing of the condition of the title. This notification is referred to as
    a. a chain of title.
    b. a preliminary report of commitment for title insurance.
    c. a Torrens certificate.
    d. an abstract.

14. When a claim is settled by a title insurance company, the company acquires all rights and claims of the insured against any other person who is responsible for the loss. This is called
    a. escrow.   c. subordination.
    b. abstract or title.   d. subrogation.

15. A title insurance policy with standard coverage generally covers all but which of the following?
    a. Forged documents
    b. Incorrect marital statements
    c. Unrecorded rights of parties in possession
    d. Incompetent grantors

16. The documents referred to as *title evidence* include
    a. title insurance.
    b. warranty deeds.
    c. security agreements.
    d. abstract of title.

17. To give notice of a security interest in personal property items, a lienholder must file which of the following?
    a. A security agreement
    b. A financing statement
    c. A chattel agreement
    d. A quitclaim deed

13 Real Estate License Laws

All states, the District of Columbia and all Canadian provinces license and regulate the activities of real estate brokers and salespeople. Certain details of the laws vary from state to state, but the main provisions of many state laws are similar. In addition, uniform policies and standards in the fields of license law administration and enforcement are promoted by an organization of state license law officials known as NARELLO—the National Association of Real Estate License Law Officials.

PURPOSE OF LICENSE LAWS

The real estate license laws have been enacted to protect the public interest by establishing certain requirements for licensure and defining licensed activities and acceptable standards of conduct and practice for licensees. Although licensees may see these laws as those which regulate the real estate industry, their purpose is to serve the public interest by ensuring that the rights of purchasers, sellers, tenants and owners are protected from unscrupulous practices. The laws are not meant to prevent licensees from conducting their businesses successfully. They are designed to ensure that the customers and clients are not disadvantaged by these business practices. Laws cannot legislate morality; they can, however, establish minimum levels of competency and standards of practice and prescribe disciplinary actions that can be taken against violators.

Each state and province has a licensing authority—a commission, department, division, board or agency—for real estate brokers and salespersons. (In this chapter the term *commission* will be used to mean any such licensing authority.) This authority has the power to issue licenses, make real estate information available to licensees and the public and enforce the statutory real estate law.

Each commission has also adopted a set of administrative **rules and regulations** that further define the statutory law, provide for its administration and set operating guidelines for its licensees. These rules and regulations have the same force and effect as the law. Both the law and the rules are usually enforced through the *denial, suspension* or *revocation of licenses* and other disciplinary actions, although civil and criminal court actions can be brought against violators in some serious cases. Throughout this chapter the discussion of license law includes many typical provisions of commission rules and regulations.

**Who Must Be
Licensed**

Generally the state license laws stipulate that a person must be licensed as a real estate broker if he or she, *for another and for compensation or the intent to collect compensation*

- lists real property;

- sells it;

- rents or leases it;

- manages it;

- exchanges it;

- negotiates with or aids a person in obtaining for purchase, lease or acquisition an interest in real estate;

- deals in real estate options;

- offers to perform or negotiate one of these activities; or

- represents that he or she engages in any of these activities.

In some states a person who performs these activities with regard to business opportunities must also be licensed as a real estate broker.

The specific provisions vary from state to state, and many states cite additional activities that require a license. In some states, for example, a person who, *for others and for a fee,* auctions real estate, negotiates a mortgage loan, deals in cemetery lots, time-shares or campgrounds may be required to have a broker's license. It is important to identify the specific requirements for your state.

Any person who performs any of the previously listed activities while employed by or associated with a real estate broker must be licensed as a real estate salesperson. In addition, some states have a special name or issue a special license for an individual who has qualified as a real estate broker and passed the broker's exam but is currently acting as a salesperson associated with and responsible to another licensed broker. Such a person may be known as an *associate broker.* A broker is authorized to operate his or her own real estate business; anyone licensed with a broker can operate only in the name of and under the supervision of that broker.

Exceptions

The real estate license laws *generally do not apply* to

- a person or firm that deals in his, her or its own property (owners) when this is not the person's or firm's principal vocation;

- a person acting under a power of attorney; (The power of attorney cannot be used to circumvent the requirements for licensure.)

- a salaried employee of a property owner who acts on behalf of the property owner, when dealing in real estate is not the owner's principal vocation;

- an attorney-at-law performing regular duties as part of a legal practice;

- a receiver, trustee, guardian, administrator, executor or other person acting under court order;

- an auctioneer performing regular duties (although, as mentioned, such person must be licensed in some states); or

- a public official or employee performing regular duties of employment.

LICENSING PROCEDURE

While specific requirements for licensing vary, all states require applicants to be of legal age. In addition, applicants must not have had a real estate license or any other professional license revoked within a certain period of time in any state. They must not have been convicted of a serious crime within a certain period of time. Some states also require fingerprint cards, FBI clearance or other criminal background check or personal references. A broker applicant usually will be required to have a minimum amount of experience as a salesperson.

Educational Requirements

Many states require applicants to complete a certain number of hours of real estate education before they can obtain a license. These requirements vary from state to state, but generally broker applicants are required to complete more hours of classroom time than salesperson applicants. In addition, a number of states now require licensees to complete *continuing education* courses to qualify for license renewal.

Examinations

All states require license applicants to pass a written real estate examination prior to licensing. The length of the exam, test procedures and minimum passing grade vary, but generally the broker's exam is more inclusive and longer than the salesperson's exam. The states also vary in their regulations regarding retests and appeals for applicants who have failed the exams.

Licensing of Nonresidents

Some state licensing authorities have reciprocity agreements with the commissions of certain other states. Generally reciprocity agreements are made between states with similar licensing requirements or adjoining states. These agreements allow out-of-state brokers who meet certain requirements to operate within the state. In some cases the out-of-state brokers must take the local state real estate licensing exam; in other states they do not. In addition, most states require nonresident brokers to file an irrevocable consent agreement or power of attorney with the state licensing agency. This document states that suits and actions may be brought against the out-of-state broker within the state in which the agreement is filed and that the outcome of such suits will be valid and binding.

Licensing of Corporations and Partnerships

In most cases a real estate brokerage may be established as a corporation if at least one officer of the corporation is a licensed real estate broker. All members of a partnership may be required to be brokers. Some states require that all officers or partners who are not participating in the business be registered as inactive brokers. The license laws usually prohibit officers or partners from being registered as real estate salespersons.

REAL ESTATE RECOVERY FUND

Many states have instituted a special **real estate recovery fund** from which members of the general public may collect if they have suffered financial loss as a result of certain actions by a licensee. The fund is usually maintained by part of the fees that licensees must pay. Generally people who seek reimbursement from the fund can do so after they have filed a court suit and obtained judgment against the licensee. An aggrieved individual who cannot collect the judgment from the licensee in any other way can apply for payment from the recovery fund. The broker's or salesperson's license is usually suspended until the recovery fund is reimbursed with interest.

GENERAL OPERATION OF A REAL ESTATE BUSINESS

License laws regulate many of the everyday operations of real estate brokers and salespeople. Generally every resident real estate broker must maintain a definite place of business within the state and may operate one or more **branch offices.** The operation of the main office, branch offices, management responsibilities and procedures for changing office locations are frequently defined. The licenses of salespeople depend on that of their broker. Termination, suspension or revocation of the broker's license means that all activities of salespeople must cease.

In all transactions brokers must keep detailed accounting records and retain copies of the documents used for a specified period of time. In addition, many license laws include specific provisions regarding the contents of contracts and other documents used in transactions.

Escrow Accounts

Each broker must maintain either a special trust account for the deposit of funds belonging to clients and customers or use a neutral escrow depository for this purpose. One of the areas most frequent violations of the licensing laws is the mishandling of escrow funds. Most laws define very precisely the procedures for depositing, withdrawing and accounting for these monies and stipulate how interest earned on the funds, if any, is to be handled. Trust accounts are established to ensure that funds which belong to others are protected and accounted for separately from the broker's general operating account. Brokers are not permitted to use these funds or *commingle* them with the broker's business or personal funds. In some states, it is permissible for the broker to deposit a small amount of the broker's own money in the escrow account to cover service charges assessed by a banking institution. Licensees should also be aware of procedures for handling escrow monies in co-brokerage transactions. In some states, there may be separate requirements for handling rental management accounts.

Prohibited Acts

There is a wide variety of practices that the license laws prohibit and for which the licensee can be subjected to disciplinary action. Individuals can also be disciplined for unlicensed activity. Licensees should be aware of the prohibited practices in their states and the disciplinary actions that the licensing authority can take against them.

Licensing laws address procedures for soliciting business, advertising services and listings and the use of "for sale" and "for rent" signs. Any misleading or fraudulent advertising and blind ads (those that do not disclose that a property is being advertised by a real estate broker) are prohibited. Advertising by a salesperson must identify the broker with whom the individual is affiliated.

Laws normally also address misrepresentation, making false promises to influence a transaction, conflict of interest, listing and selling real estate owned by a licensee, the manner in which commissions and fees are to be charged and to whom they may be paid and other activities that demonstrate dishonesty, bad faith, untrustworthiness or incompetency.

SUSPENSION OR REVOCATION OF A REAL ESTATE LICENSE

Most state license laws detail the various violations of the license law and other reasons for which a real estate license may be suspended or revoked. Students should study the rules for their own state.

●   ●   ●   ●   ●   ●   ●

KEY TERMS

branch office   real estate recovery fund   rules and regulations

SUMMARY

The real estate license laws were enacted by the states and Canadian provinces to protect the public from unscrupulous practices of licensees, and to prescribe certain licensing requirements and standards of practices in the real estate profession.

Each state stipulates who must be licensed and who is exempt from licensing, sets forth certain operating standards to which brokers and salespersons must adhere and creates certain licensing procedures and requirements.

Note that the laws of each state are different. Students must know their own state license law and should obtain a copy. The analysis form that takes the place of questions in this chapter will help students determine and learn the requirements of their state law. It can be used as a study device while students read through their state law and state supplement (where available) or as a testing device after they study the license law. (Be sure to check your answers against the provisions of the law.)

Remember, all licensees will be operating and working under their state real estate license law and must know it well.

ANALYSIS FORM: REAL ESTATE BROKER'S AND SALESPERSON'S LAW

State or province of _____

Instructions: After studying your state law, answer the questions and fill in the Salesperson's Law information. If the question or point does not apply in your state, indicate this fact by some statement such as *no, none, not required* or *does not apply.* If you complete this form carefully, the information will be valuable when you prepare for your state license examination.

1. When was your state law originally passed? _____
2. Has it been amended? _____ If so, when was the last amendment passed? _____
3. What are the requirements for licensure in your state?

	For Broker's License	For Salesperson's License
Minimum age	_____	_____
Apprenticeship	_____	_____
Education	_____	_____
Examination	_____	_____
Bond	_____	_____
Number and type of recommendations	_____	_____
Photograph	_____	_____
Fingerprints	_____	_____

4. Copy exactly the definition of a *broker* as given by your law. Know this definition and be able to list the activities that it includes.

_____
_____
_____

5. Copy exactly the definition of a *salesperson* as given by your law. Learn this definition.

_____
_____
_____

6. What persons or groups are *exempt* from licensure in your state?

_____
_____
_____

7. What fees are required in your state?

	For Broker	For Salesperson
Original license application fee	_____	_____
Examination fee	_____	_____
Periodic renewal fee	_____	_____
Recovery fund fee (if separate)	_____	_____

8. For what period is the license issued? _____   _____

On what date does it expire? _____   _____

What continuing education is
required for renewal? _____   _____

9. The following are some of the reasons a state may discipline a licensee, refuse to issue a license or revoke or suspend a license. Place a check mark in front of the reasons given in your state law. Cross out the reasons that do not apply and add the reasons that are not listed here. When you have compiled your list, memorize it.

_____   Filing or recording any papers to cloud title as claim for commission

_____   Making false affidavits or committing perjury in any court proceeding

_____   Pursuing a continued and flagrant course of misrepresentation

_____   Making false promises through salespeople, advertising and the like

_____   Acting for more than one party without approval of all parties (dual agency)

_____   Failing to remit or account for funds belonging to others

_____   Misleading by false advertising or advertising without the broker's name

_____   Procuring a license by fraud, such as by filing a fraudulent application

_____   Willfully disregarding or violating provisions of the licensing law or the commission rules and regulations

_____   Paying a commission to any unlicensed person in violation of the law

_____   Representing a broker other than one's employing broker

_____   Being convicted of embezzlement, fraud and similar crimes or state or federal felonies

_____   Placing signs on property without proper authorization from the client

_____   Demonstrating negligence in one's capacity as a real estate licensee

_____   Not clearly explaining to a principal the duration of an exclusive listing agreement

_____   Engaging in conduct that constitutes bad faith or improper, incompetent, fraudulent or dishonest dealing

_____   Employing unlicensed salespeople

_____   Accepting a commission in violation of the licensing law

_____   Operating an office or branch office from an unregistered location

_____   Commingling funds or property of a principal with a broker's personal funds

_____   Failing to deposit the money of others in an escrow or trust account

_____   Other: _____

10. What penalties are provided in your state law for operating without a license?

	Individuals		Corporations	
	1st Offense	2nd Offense	1st Offense	2nd Offense
Fine	_____	_____	_____	_____
Imprisonment	_____	_____	_____	_____

Are other penalties or fines provided and, if so, for what offenses?

_____

11. What is the name of the state agency that is responsible for administering the real estate law in your state?

_____

12. If there is a real estate commission or advisory committee, how many members does it have? Are they appointed or elected? What is their term of office?

_____

13. What are the requirements for a broker's maintaining an office and a sign?

14. What provisions and requirements are made for the discharge or termination of a real estate salesperson by a broker?

_____

15. List the main requirements for issuance of a license to a nonresident broker.

16. Does your state have a real estate recovery fund?

_____

17. How long must a broker retain records of a real estate transaction in his or her office?

_____

14 Real Estate Financing: Principles

MORTGAGE LAW

American courts of equity have always considered a mortgage a voluntary lien on real estate. That is, a person who borrows money to buy a piece of property willingly gives the lender the right to take that property if the borrower fails to repay the loan. The borrower, or **mortgagor,** pledges the land to the lender, or **mortgagee,** as *security* for the debt. Exactly what the mortgagor must give the mortgagee in making that pledge, however, varies from state to state.

In **title theory** states the mortgagor actually gives *legal title* to the mortgagee and retains *equitable title*. Legal title is returned to the mortgagor only upon full payment of the debt (or performance of some other obligation). In theory the lender actually owns the property until the debt is paid, meanwhile allowing the borrower all the usual rights of ownership such as possession and use. In effect, because the lender actually holds legal title, the lender has the right to possession of the real estate and rents from the mortgaged property immediately upon default by the mortgagor.

In **lien theory** states the mortgagor retains both legal and equitable title, and the mortgagee merely has a lien on the property as security for the mortgage debt. The mortgage is simply collateral for the loan. If the mortgagor defaults, the mortgagee must foreclose (generally through court action) to obtain legal title. The property is offered for sale, and the funds from the sale are used to pay all or part of the remaining debt. Some states protect the borrower by allowing the defaulting mortgagor to redeem the property during a certain period after the sale. A borrower who fails to redeem the property during that time loses the property irrevocably.

A number of states have adopted an *intermediate theory* that is based on the principles of title theory but requires the mortgagee to foreclose to obtain legal title. *In reality the differences between the parties' rights in a lien theory state and those in a title theory state are more technical than actual.*

SECURITY AND DEBT

Generally any interest in real estate that may be sold may be pledged as security for a debt. The basic principle of the property law, that a person cannot convey greater rights in property than he or she actually has, applies equally to the right to mortgage. So the owner of a fee simple estate can mortgage the fee, and the owner of a leasehold or subleasehold can mortgage that leasehold interest. For example, a large retail corporation renting space in a shopping center may mortgage its leasehold interest to finance some remodeling work.

The owner of a condominium unit can mortgage the fee interest in the condominium apartment. Although the owner of a cooperative interest holds a personal property interest, it is becoming more acceptable as collateral to lenders in many areas.

Mortgage Loan Instruments

There are two parts to a mortgage loan—the debt itself and the security for the debt. When a property is to be mortgaged, the owner must execute (sign) two separate instruments:

1. The **note,** or *financing instrument,* is the personal promise to repay a debt according to agreed-on terms. The note exposes all of the borrower's assets to claims by creditors. The mortgagor executes one or more promissory notes to total the amount of the debt.
2. The **mortgage,** or *security instrument,* creates the lien on the property. The mortgage exposes the real estate to claim by the creditor and is the document on which the lender would sue for foreclosure.

Hypothecation is the term used to describe the pledging of property as security for payment of a loan without surrendering possession of the property. A pledge of security—a mortgage or deed of trust—cannot be legally effective unless there is a debt to secure. Both a note and mortgage are executed to create a secured loan.

Deeds of trust. In some areas of the country and in certain situations, lenders prefer to use a three-party instrument known as a **deed of trust,** or trust deed, rather than a mortgage document. A trust deed conveys "naked title" or "bare legal title" (title without the right of possession) to the real estate as security for the loan to a third party, called the *trustee.* The trustee then holds title on behalf of the lender, known as the **beneficiary,** who is the legal owner and holder of the note. The wording of the conveyance sets forth actions that the trustee may take if the borrower, the *trustor,* defaults under any of the deed of trust terms. (See Figure 14.1 for a comparison of mortgages and deeds of trust.) In states where deeds of trust are generally preferred, foreclosure procedures for default are usually simpler and faster than for mortgage loans.

Usually the lender chooses the trustee and reserves the right to substitute trustees in the event of death or dismissal. State law usually dictates who may serve as trustee. Although the deed of trust is particularly popular in certain states, it is used all over the country. For example, in the financing of a commercial or industrial real estate venture that involves a large loan and several lenders, the borrower generally executes a single deed of trust to secure as many notes as are necessary.

PROVISIONS OF THE NOTE

In general a promissory note executed by a borrower (known as the *maker* or *payor*) states the amount of the debt, the time and method of payment and the rate of interest. If a note is used with a mortgage, it names the lender (mortgagee) the payee; if it is used with a deed of trust, the note may be made payable to the bearer. The note may also refer to or repeat several of the clauses that appear in the mortgage

**Figure 14.1
Mortgages and
Deeds of Trust**

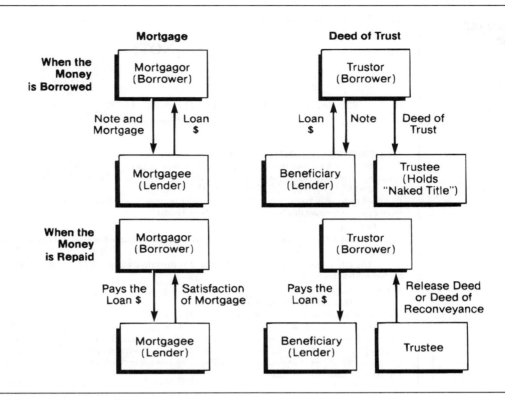

document or deed of trust. The note, like the mortgage or deed of trust, should be signed by all parties who have an interest in the property. In states where dower and curtesy are in effect or where homestead or community property is involved, both spouses may have an interest in the property and both should sign the note.

Figure 14.2 is an example of a note commonly used with a mortgage. It is one of the standard forms used by lenders who may want to sell the loan to the Federal Home Loan Mortgage Corporation (FHLMC) or the Federal National Mortgage Association (FNMA). FHLMC and FNMA are discussed in Chapter 15.

A note is a **negotiable instrument** like checks or bank drafts. The holder, the payee, may transfer the right to receive payment to a third party, either by signing the instrument over (assigning it) to the third party or, in some cases, by merely delivering the instrument to the third party.

Interest

A charge for the use of money is called **interest.** Interest may be due either at the end of each payment period (known as payment *in arrears*) or at the beginning of each payment period (payment *in advance*). Whether interest is charged in arrears or in advance is specified in the note. In practice the distinction becomes important if the property is sold before the debt is repaid in full, as will become evident in Chapter 23.

Usury. To protect consumers from unscrupulous lenders who charge unreasonably high rates, many states have enacted laws limiting the interest rate that

**Figure 14.2
Note**

NOTE

.... April 12 ...., 19 ..93..   .... Chicago ...., ... Illinois ....
                                                                              [City]   [State]
.... 222 Kelly Street, Chicago, Illinois 60601 ....
                                                      [Property Address]

1. BORROWER'S PROMISE TO PAY

In return for a loan that I have received, I promise to pay U.S. $..79,000.00................ (this amount is called "principal"), plus interest, to the order of the Lender. The Lender is ..First City Savings and Loan....... .... Association of Chicago, Illinois .... I understand that the Lender may transfer this Note. The Lender or anyone who takes this Note by transfer and who is entitled to receive payments under this Note is called the "Note Holder."

2. INTEREST

Interest will be charged on unpaid principal until the full amount of principal has been paid. I will pay interest at a yearly rate of ....9.5......%.

The interest rate required by this Section 2 is the rate I will pay both before and after any default described in Section 6(B) of this Note.

3. PAYMENTS

(A) **Time and Place of Payments**

I will pay principal and interest by making payments every month.

I will make my monthly payments on the ......1st... day of each month beginning on ...May 1........................., 19..93.... I will make these payments every month until I have paid all of the principal and interest and any other charges described below that I may owe under this Note. My monthly payments will be applied to interest before principal. If, on ....April 1, 2023 ...., I still owe amounts under this Note, I will pay those amounts in full on that date, which is called the "maturity date."

I will make my monthly payments at ....130 North LaSalle Street, Chicago, Illinois........ .... or at a different place if required by the Note Holder.

(B) **Amount of Monthly Payments**

My monthly payment will be in the amount of U.S. $..664.29............................

4. BORROWER'S RIGHT TO PREPAY

I have the right to make payments of principal at any time before they are due. A payment of principal only is known as a "prepayment." When I make a prepayment, I will tell the Note Holder in writing that I am doing so.

I may make a full prepayment or partial prepayments without paying any prepayment charge. The Note Holder will use all of my prepayments to reduce the amount of principal that I owe under this Note. If I make a partial

**Figure 14.2
(continued)**

prepayment, there will be no changes in the due date or in the amount of my monthly payment unless the Note Holder agrees in writing to those changes.

5. LOAN CHARGES

If a law, which applies to this loan and which sets maximum loan charges, is finally interpreted so that the interest or other loan charges collected or to be collected in connection with this loan exceed the permitted limits, then: (i) any such loan charge shall be reduced by the amount necessary to reduce the charge to the permitted limit; and (ii) any sums already collected from me which exceeded permitted limits will be refunded to me. The Note Holder may choose to make this refund by reducing the principal I owe under this Note or by making a direct payment to me. If a refund reduces principal, the reduction will be treated as a partial prepayment.

6. BORROWER'S FAILURE TO PAY AS REQUIRED

(A) Late Charge for Overdue Payments

If the Note Holder has not received the full amount of any monthly payment by the end of .....fifteen.... calendar days after the date it is due, I will pay a late charge to the Note Holder. The amount of the charge will be ....5..% of my overdue payment of principal and interest. I will pay this late charge promptly but only once on each late payment.

(B) Default

If I do not pay the full amount of each monthly payment on the date it is due, I will be in default.

(C) Notice of Default

If I am in default, the Note Holder may send me a written notice telling me that if I do not pay the overdue amount by a certain date, the Note Holder may require me to pay immediately the full amount of principal which has not been paid and all the interest that I owe on that amount. That date must be at least 30 days after the date on which the notice is delivered or mailed to me.

(D) No Waiver By Note Holder

Even if, at a time when I am in default, the Note Holder does not require me to pay immediately in full as described above, the Note Holder will still have the right to do so if I am in default at a later time.

(E) Payment of Note Holder's Costs and Expenses

If the Note Holder has required me to pay immediately in full as described above, the Note Holder will have the right to be paid back by me for all of its costs and expenses in enforcing this Note to the extent not prohibited by applicable law. Those expenses include, for example, reasonable attorneys' fees.

7. GIVING OF NOTICES

Unless applicable law requires a different method, any notice that must be given to me under this Note will be given by delivering it or by mailing it by first class mail to me at the Property Address above or at a different address if I give the Note Holder a notice of my different address.

Any notice that must be given to the Note Holder under this Note will be given by mailing it by first class mail to the Note Holder at the address stated in Section 3(A) above or at a different address if I am given a notice of that different address.

MULTISTATE FIXED RATE NOTE—Single Family—**FNMA/FHLMC UNIFORM INSTRUMENT**   Form 3200 12/83 may be charged on loans. In some states the legal maximum rate is a fixed amount. In others it is a *floating interest rate,* which is adjusted up or down at specific intervals based on a certain economic standard, such as the prime lending rate or the rate of return on government bonds.

Whichever approach is taken, charging interest in excess of the maximum rate is called **usury,** and lenders are penalized for making usurious loans. In some states a lender who makes a usurious loan will be permitted to collect the borrowed money, but only at the legal rate of interest. In other states a usurious lender may lose the right to collect any interest or may lose the entire amount of the loan in addition to the interest.

There is, however, a broad exemption from these state usury laws created by federal law. Residential first mortgage loans made after March 31, 1980, by federally chartered institutions or insured or guaranteed by a federal agency are exempt from state interest limitations. Included in the definition of residential loans are those to buy manufactured housing (mobile homes) and to buy stock in a cooperative. In effect the federal act limits state usury laws to private lenders.

Discount points. The rate of interest that a lender charges for a mortgage loan might be less than the yield (true rate of return) required by an investor who would purchase that loan. For this reason the lender charges **discount points** to make up the difference between the mortgage interest rate and the required investor yield. The number of points charged varies, depending both on the difference between the interest rate and the required yield and on the average time the lender expects the loan to be outstanding. Lenders calculate that it takes an average of eight discount points to increase the yield one percent depending on the length of the loan. A good rule of thumb is that one discount point will increase the lender's yield ⅛ of one percent on a 30-year loan. Discount points can be charged on FHA-insured, VA-guaranteed and conventional loans.

One discount point equals 1 percent of the loan amount and is charged as prepaid interest at the closing. For example, three discount points charged on a $100,000 loan would be $3,000 ($100,000 × 3%). In this situation the lender would actually fund $97,000 (the $100,000 principal amount of the loan minus the $3,000 discount), but $100,000 would have to be repaid by the borrower, thereby increasing the investor's yield (a $97,000 loan receiving interest calculated on $100,000).

Loan origination fee. When a mortgage loan is originated, a **loan origination fee,** or transfer fee, is charged by most lenders for generating the loan. Loan origination fees are not prepaid interest; they are an expense that must be paid to the lender. The typical fee is 1 percent of the loan amount regardless of any discount points that might also be charged.

Prepayment

When a loan is paid in installments over a long term, the total interest paid by the borrower can be larger than the principal amount of the loan. If the borrower repays the loan before the end of the term, the lender will collect less interest. For this reason, some mortgage and deed of trust notes contain a *prepayment clause.* This clause requires the borrower to pay a **prepayment penalty** against the unearned portion of the interest for any payments made ahead of schedule.

MATH CONCEPT Discount Points and Investor Yield

As a general rule it takes 8 discount points to change the interest rate 1% on a 30-year loan. From the standpoint of the borrower 1 discount point equals 1% of the loan amount.

To calculate the dollar value of 4 discount points (.04 as a decimal) on a $95,000 loan, multiply the loan amount by the number of points:

$$\$95,000 \times 4\% = \$95,000 \times .04 = \$3,800 \text{ discount}$$

To calculate the net amount of a $75,000 loan after a 3-point discount is taken, multiply the loan amount by 100% minus the discount;

$$\$75,000 \times (100\% - 3\%) = \$75,000 \times 97\% = \$75,000 \times .97 = \$72,750$$

Or deduct the dollar amount of the discount from the loan:

$$\$75,000 - (\$75,000 \times 3\%) = \$75,000 - \$2,250 = \$72,750$$

From the standpoint of the investor 1 discount point received increases the yield on the loan by ⅛%. Two points would increase the yield by ¼%, 4 discount points by ½%, 6 points by ¾% and 8 points by 1%.

For example, if a loan carried an interest rate of 9½% and a discount of 6 points, the yield to the investor would be calculated as follows:

$$6 \text{ discount points} = \tfrac{3}{4}\% \text{ increase in yield;}$$
$$9\tfrac{1}{2}\% \text{ interest per the contract} + \tfrac{3}{4}\% \text{ increase from the discount} =$$
$$10\tfrac{1}{4}\% \text{ yield to the investor}$$

If an investor requires a 10½% yield on a loan with a 10⅛% interest rate, the number of discount points needed would be calculated as follows:

$$10\tfrac{1}{2}\% = 10\tfrac{4}{8}\%; \ 10\tfrac{4}{8}\% \text{ required yield} - 10\tfrac{1}{8}\% \text{ interest rate} =$$
$$\tfrac{3}{8}\% \text{ difference; } \tfrac{3}{8}\% = 3 \text{ discount points needed}$$

The premium charged may run from 1 percent of the balance due at the time of prepayment to all interest due for the first ten years of the loan. Some lenders allow the borrower to pay off 20 percent of the original loan in any one year without paying a premium, but if the loan is paid off in full the borrower may be charged a percentage of the principal paid in excess of that allowance. Some states either limit or do not permit a lender to charge a penalty on prepaid residential mortgage or deed of trust loans. Lenders are also prohibited from charging prepayment penalties on mortgage loans insured or guaranteed by the federal government. Other states allow a lender to charge a prepayment penalty *only* if the loan is paid off with funds borrowed from another source.

PROVISIONS OF THE MORTGAGE DOCUMENT OR DEED OF TRUST

The mortgage document or deed of trust refers to the terms of the note and clearly establishes that the property is security for the debt. It identifies the lender and borrower and includes an accurate legal description of the property. It should be signed by all parties who have an interest in the real estate. Common provisions follow.

Duties of the Mortgagor or Trustor

The borrower is required to fulfill many obligations. These usually include the following:

- Payment of the debt in accordance with the terms of the note

- Payment of all real estate taxes on the property given as security

- Maintenance of adequate insurance to protect the lender if the property is destroyed or damaged by fire, windstorm or other hazard

- Maintenance of the property in good repair at all times

- Lender authorization before making any major alterations on the property

Failure to meet any of these obligations—most frequently failure to meet monthly installments—can result in a borrower's default. The loan documents may, however, provide for a grace period (30 days, for example) during which the borrower can meet the obligation and cure the default. If the borrower does not do so, the lender has the right to foreclose the mortgage or deed of trust and collect on the note.

Provisions for Default

The mortgage or deed of trust typically includes an **acceleration clause** to assist the lender in foreclosure. If a borrower defaults, the lender has the right to accelerate the maturity of the debt, that is to declare the *entire* debt due and payable *immediately.* Without the acceleration clause the lender would have to sue the borrower every time a payment was overdue.

Other clauses in a mortgage or deed of trust enable the lender to take care of the property in the event of the borrower's negligence or default. If the borrower does not pay taxes or insurance premiums or make necessary repairs on the property, the lender may step in and do so to protect the security (the real estate). Any money advanced by the lender to cure such defaults is either added to the unpaid debt or declared immediately due from the borrower.

Assignment of the Mortgage

When a note is sold to a third party, the mortgagee will endorse the note to the third party and also execute an *assignment of mortgage* or an *assignment of deed of trust.* The assignee becomes the new owner of the debt and security instrument. Upon payment in full, or satisfaction of the debt, the assignee is required to execute the satisfaction, or release, of the security instrument as discussed in the following section.

Release of the Mortgage Lien

When all mortgage loan payments have been made and the note has been paid in full, the mortgagor wants the public record to show that the debt has been paid and that the mortgagee is divested of all rights conveyed under the mortgage. By the provisions of the **defeasance clause** in the typical mortgage document the mortgagee is required to execute a **satisfaction** of mortgage, also known as a *release of mortgage* or *mortgage discharge* when the note has been fully paid. This document returns to the mortgagor all interest in the real estate that was conveyed to the mortgagee by the original recorded mortgage document. Entering this release in the public record shows that the mortgage lien has been removed from the property.

If a mortgage has been assigned by a recorded assignment, the release must be executed by the assignee/mortgagee.

When a real estate loan secured by a deed of trust has been completely repaid, the beneficiary requests in writing that the trustee convey the property back to the grantor. The trustee then executes and delivers a **release deed,** sometimes called a *deed of reconveyance,* to the trustor conveying the same rights and powers that the trustee was given under the trust deed. The release deed should be acknowledged and recorded in the public records of the county where the property is located.

Tax and Insurance Reserves

Many lenders require borrowers to provide a reserve fund, called an *impound* or *trust* or *escrow account,* to meet future real estate taxes and property insurance premiums. When the mortgage or deed of trust loan is made, the borrower starts the reserve by depositing funds to cover the amount of unpaid real estate taxes. If a new insurance policy has just been purchased, the insurance premium reserve will be started with the deposit of one-twelfth of the annual tax and insurance premium liability. Thereafter the borrower's monthly loan payments will include principal, interest and tax and insurance reserves (PITI). RESPA, the federal Real Estate Settlement Procedures Act (discussed in Chapter 23), limits the total amount of reserves that may be required by a lender.

Assignment of Rents

The borrower may provide for rents to be assigned to the lender upon the borrower's default. The assignment may be included in the mortgage or deed of trust or made as a separate document. In either case language should clearly indicate that the borrower intends to assign the rents and not merely to pledge them as security for the loan. In title theory states the lender is, in most cases, automatically entitled to any rents if the borrower defaults.

Buying Subject to or Assuming a Seller's Mortgage or Deed of Trust

When a person purchases real estate that has an outstanding mortgage or deed of trust on it the buyer may take the property *subject to* the mortgage or may *assume* it and agree to pay the debt. This technical distinction becomes important if the buyer defaults and the mortgage or deed of trust is foreclosed.

When the property is sold *subject to* the mortgage, the courts frequently rule that the buyer is not personally obligated to pay the debt in full. The buyer has taken title to the real estate knowing that he or she must make payments on the existing loan. Upon default the lender will foreclose and the property will be sold by court order to pay the debt. If the sale does not pay off the entire debt, the purchaser is not liable for the difference, though the original seller might be.

In contrast, a buyer who purchases the property and *assumes and agrees to pay* the seller's debt becomes personally obligated for the payment of the *entire debt.* If the mortgage is foreclosed and the court sale does not bring enough money to pay the debt in full, a deficiency judgment against the assumer and the original borrower (unless the borrower has been released) may be obtained for the unpaid balance of the note.

Before a conventional mortgage may be assumed, most lending institutions require the assumer to qualify financially and charge a transfer fee to cover the costs of changing its records. This charge is customarily borne by the purchaser.

Alienation clause. The lender may want to prevent a future purchaser of the property from being able to assume that loan, particularly at its old rate of interest. For this reason some lenders include an **alienation clause** (also known as a *resale clause, due-on-sale clause* or *call clause*) in the note. An alienation clause provides that upon the sale of the property the lender can either declare the entire debt due immediately or permit the buyer to assume the loan at current market interest rates.

Recording Mortgages and Deeds of Trust

The mortgage document or deed of trust must be recorded in the recorder's office of the county in which the real estate is located. Recording gives constructive notice to the world of the borrower's obligations and establishes the lien's priority. If the property is registered in the Torrens system, notice of the lien must be entered on the original Torrens certificate on file.

First and Second Mortgages or Deeds of Trust

Priority of mortgages and other liens normally is determined by the order in which they were recorded. A mortgage or deed of trust on land that has no prior mortgage lien on it is a *first mortgage* or *first deed of trust.* When the owner later executes another loan for additional funds, the new loan becomes a *second mortgage or deed of trust,* or a *junior lien,* when recorded. The second lien is subject to the first lien; the first has prior claim to the value of the land pledged as security. Because second loans represent a greater risk to the lender, they are usually issued at higher interest rates.

The priority of mortgage or deed of trust liens may be changed by a *subordination agreement,* in which the first lender subordinates his or her lien to that of the second lender. To be valid such an agreement must be signed by both lenders.

PROVISIONS OF LAND CONTRACTS (INSTALLMENT CONTRACTS OR CONTRACTS FOR DEED)

As discussed in Chapter 10, real estate can be purchased under *land contract,* also known as a *contract for deed* or an *installment contract.* Real estate is often sold on contract when mortgage financing is unavailable or too expensive or when the purchaser does not have a sufficient down payment to cover the difference between a mortgage or deed of trust loan and the selling price of the real estate.

Under a land contract the buyer, called the *vendee,* agrees to make a down payment and a monthly loan payment that includes interest and principal (and possibly real estate tax and insurance impounds). The seller, called the *vendor,* retains legal title to the property during the contract term, and the buyer is granted equitable title (see Chapter 10) and possession. At the end of the loan term the seller delivers clear title. The land contract usually includes a provision that if the buyer defaults, the seller can evict the buyer and retain any money paid by the buyer, which is construed to be rent. Many states now offer some legal protection to a defaulting buyer under a land contract.

FORECLOSURE

When a borrower defaults on the payments or fails to fulfill any of the other obligations set forth in the mortgage or deed of trust, the lender's rights can be enforced through foreclosure. **Foreclosure** is a legal procedure whereby the property pledged as security in the mortgage document or deed of trust is sold to satisfy the debt. The foreclosure procedure brings the rights of the parties and all junior lienholders to a conclusion. It passes title in the subject property to either the person holding the mortgage document or deed of trust or to a third party who purchases the realty at a *foreclosure sale*. The property is sold *free of the foreclosing mortgage and all junior liens.*

Methods of Foreclosure

There are three general types of foreclosure proceedings—judicial, nonjudicial and strict foreclosure. The specific provisions of these vary from state to state.

Judicial foreclosure. Judicial foreclosure allows the property pledged as security to be sold by court order after the mortgagee has given sufficient public notice. Upon a borrower's default the lender may *accelerate* the due date of all remaining monthly payments. The lender's attorney can then file a suit to foreclose the lien. After presentation of the facts in court the property is ordered sold. A public sale is advertised and held, and the real estate is sold to the highest bidder.

Nonjudicial foreclosure. Other states allow nonjudicial foreclosure procedures to be used when the security instrument contains a *power-of-sale clause*. No court action is required. In those states that recognize deed of trust loans, the trustee is generally given the power of sale. Some states allow a similar power of sale to be used with a mortgage loan.

To institute a nonjudicial foreclosure the trustee (or mortgagee) must record a notice of default at the county recorder's office within a designated time period to give notice to the public of the intended auction. This official notice is generally accompanied by advertisements published in local newspapers that state the total amount due and the date of the public sale. The purpose of this notice is to publicize the sale. After selling the property the trustee (or mortgagee) may be required to file a copy of a notice of sale or an affidavit of foreclosure.

Strict foreclosure. Although the judicial and nonjudicial foreclosure procedures are the prevalent practices today, in some states it is still possible for a lender to acquire the mortgaged property through a strict foreclosure process. After appropriate notice has been given to the delinquent borrower and the proper papers have been prepared and recorded, the court establishes a specific time period during which the balance of the defaulted debt must be paid in full. If this is not done, the court usually awards full legal title to the lender. No sale takes place.

Deed in Lieu of Foreclosure

As an alternative to foreclosure, the lender can accept a **deed in lieu of foreclosure** from the borrower. This is sometimes known as a *friendly foreclosure,* for it is carried out by agreement rather than by civil action. The major disadvantage of this manner of default settlement is that the mortgagee takes the real estate subject to all junior liens; foreclosure eliminates all such liens. Also, by

**Figure 14.3
Redemption**

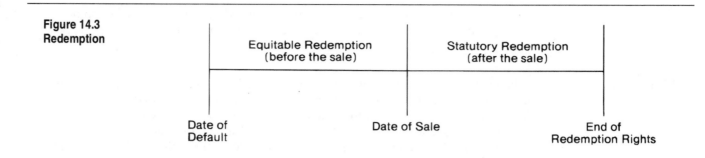

| Equitable Redemption (before the sale) | Statutory Redemption (after the sale) |

Date of
Default

Date of Sale

End of
Redemption Rights

accepting a deed in lieu of foreclosure the lender usually loses any rights pertaining to FHA insurance, VA guarantees or private mortgage insurance.

Redemption

Most states give defaulting borrowers a chance to redeem their property (see Chapter 9). Historically the right of redemption is inherited from the old common law proceedings in which the court sale ended the **equitable right of redemption.** Carried over to statutory law, this concept provides that if, after default but *before the foreclosure sale,* the borrower or any other person who has an interest in the real estate (such as another creditor) pays the lender the amount currently due, plus costs, the debt will be reinstated. In some cases the person who redeems may be required to repay the accelerated loan in full. If some person other than the mortgagor or trustor redeems the real estate, the borrower becomes responsible to that person for the amount of the redemption.

Certain states also allow defaulted borrowers a period in which to redeem their real estate *after the sale.* During this period the borrower has a **statutory right of redemption** (which may be as long as one year). The court may appoint a receiver to take charge of the property, collect rents, pay operating expenses and so forth. The mortgagor or trustor who can raise the necessary funds to redeem the property within the statutory period pays the redemption money to the court. Because the debt was paid from the proceeds of the sale, the borrower then can take possession free and clear of the former defaulted loan. Redemption is illustrated in Figure 14.3.

**Deed to
Purchaser
at Sale**

If redemption is not made or if state law does not provide for a redemption period, the successful bidder at the sale receives a deed to the real estate. A sheriff or master-in-chancery executes this deed to the purchaser to *convey whatever title the borrower had.* The deed contains no warranties. Title passes as is, but free of the former defaulted debt, however.

**Deficiency
Judgment**

If the foreclosure sale does not produce a sufficient sales price to pay the loan balance in full after deducting expenses and accrued unpaid interest, the mortgagee may be entitled to a *personal judgment* against the borrower for the unpaid balance. Such a judgment is called a **deficiency judgment.** It may also be obtained against any endorsers or guarantors of the note and any owners of the mortgaged property who assumed the debt by written agreement. If there are any surplus proceeds from the foreclosure sale after the debt, all other liens (such as second mortgage, mechanic's lien), expenses and interest are deducted, these proceeds are paid to the borrower.

●   ●   ●   ●   ●   ●   ●

KEY TERMS

acceleration clause
alienation clause
beneficiary
deed in lieu of foreclosure
deed of trust
defeasance clause
deficiency judgment
discount point
equitable right of redemption
foreclosure
hypothecation
interest
lien theory

loan origination fee
mortgage
mortgagee
mortgagor
negotiable instrument
prepayment penalty
note
release deed
satisfaction
statutory right of redemption
title theory
usury

SUMMARY

Some states recognize the lender as the owner of mortgaged property; these are known as title theory states. Others recognize the borrower as the owner of mortgaged property and are known as lien theory states. A few intermediary states recognize modified versions of these theories.

Mortgage and deed of trust loans provide the principal sources of financing for real estate operations. Mortgage loans involve a borrower, called the mortgagor, and a lender, the mortgagee. Deed of trust loans involve a third party, called the trustee, in addition to the borrower (the trustor) and the lender (the beneficiary).

After a lending institution has received, investigated and approved a loan application, it issues a commitment to make the mortgage loan. The borrower is required to execute a note agreeing to repay the debt and a mortgage or deed of trust placing a lien on the real estate to secure the note. The security instrument is recorded to give notice to the world of the lender's interest.

The mortgage document or deed of trust secures the debt and sets forth the obligations of the borrower and the rights of the lender. Full payment of the note by its terms entitles the borrower to a satisfaction, or release, which is recorded to clear the lien from the public records. Default by the borrower may result in acceleration of payments, a foreclosure sale and, after the redemption period (if provided by state law), loss of title.

Questions

1. A charge of three discount points on a $120,000 loan is
   a. $450.
   b. $116,400.
   c. $4,500.
   d. $3,600.

2. The person who obtains a real estate loan by signing a note and a mortgage is called the
   a. mortgagor.
   b. beneficiary.
   c. mortgagee.
   d. vendor.

3. The borrower under a deed of trust is known as the
   a. trustor.
   b. trustee.
   c. beneficiary.
   d. vendee.

4. Which of the following is true about a second mortgage?
   a. It has priority over a first mortgage.
   b. It cannot be used as a security instrument.
   c. It is not negotiable.
   d. It usually has a higher interest rate than a first mortgage.

5. All of the following would be true for the vendee in a contract for deed *except* that the vendee
   a. is responsible for the real estate taxes on the property.
   b. must pay interest and principal.
   c. obtains possession at closing.
   d. obtains actual title at closing.

6. Laws that limit the amount of interest that can be charged to the borrower are called
   a. Truth-in-Lending laws.
   b. usury laws.
   c. the statute of frauds.
   d. RESPA.

7. After the foreclosure sale a borrower who has defaulted on a loan seeks to pay off the debt plus any accrued interest and costs under the right of
   a. equitable redemption.
   b. defeasance.
   c. usury.
   d. statutory redemption.

8. The clause in a note that gives the lender the right to have all future installments become due upon default is the
   a. escalation clause.
   b. defeasance clause.
   c. alienation clause.
   d. acceleration clause.

9. What document is given to the mortgagor when the mortgage debt is completely repaid?
   a. Satisfaction of mortgage
   b. Defeasance certificate
   c. Deed of trust
   d. Mortgage estoppel

10. Under a typical land contract, when does the vendor give the deed to the vendee?
    a. When the contract is fulfilled
    b. At the closing
    c. When the contract for deed is approved by the parties
    d. After the first year's real estate taxes are paid

11. If a borrower must pay $2,700 for points on a $90,000 loan, how many points is the lender charging for this loan?
    a. Two
    b. Three
    c. Five
    d. Six

12. At the closing of a transaction involving an installment contract the vendor would *not*
    a. provide financing for the vendee.
    b. still be liable for any senior financing.
    c. retain actual title.
    d. retain possession of the property.

13. Which of the following allows a mortgagee to proceed to a foreclosure sale without having to go to court first?
    a. Waiver of redemption right
    b. Power of sale
    c. Alienation clause
    d. Hypothecation

14. Pledging property for a loan without giving up possession is best described as
    a. hypothecation. c. alienation.
    b. defeasance.   d. novation.

15. Discount points on a mortgage are computed as a percentage of the
    a. selling price.
    b. amount borrowed.
    c. closing costs.
    d. down payment.

15

Real Estate Financing: Practice

FINANCING TECHNIQUES

Fluctuating economic conditions and a complex and dynamic real estate market have produced a rapidly evolving mortgage market as well. With few real estate transactions consummated without financing, one of the greatest challenges faced by today's real estate licensees is to maintain a working knowledge of the myriad financing techniques now available. By altering the terms of the basic mortgage or deed of trust and note, a borrower and a lender can tailor financing instruments to suit the type of transaction and the financial needs of both parties. Having an overview of current financing techniques and sources of financing can help salespeople direct buyers to the mortgage loan that will help them reach their real estate goals.

Note that, while the payment plans described in the following sections are commonly referred to as "mortgages," they are actually *loans* that are secured by either a mortgage or a deed of trust.

STRAIGHT LOANS

A borrower may choose a *straight payment plan,* which calls for periodic payments of interest followed by the payment of the principal *in full at the end of the loan term.* This is known as a **straight,** or *term,* **loan.** For example, on a loan of $100,000 at 12 percent interest per year, with payments due monthly, a borrower would pay $1,000 each month. At the end of the term of the loan, the last payment would be the final interest payment of $1,000 plus the $100,000 principal loan amount. Prior to the 1930s the straight loan was the only form of mortgage loan available. It was payable after a relatively short term, such as three to five years. The high rate of foreclosure of such loans during the Depression years prompted the use of more manageable amortized loans. Today straight loans are generally used for home improvement loans and second mortgages rather than for residential first mortgage loans.

AMORTIZED LOANS

Most mortgage and deed of trust loans are **amortized loans.** Regular payments are made over a term of perhaps 15 to 30 years, and each payment is applied first to the interest owed with the balance being applied to the principal amount.

MATH CONCEPT
Interest and Principal Credited from Amortized Payments

A lender charges a borrower a certain percentage of the principal as interest for each year the debt is outstanding. The amount of interest due on any one installment payment date is calculated by computing the total yearly interest, based on the unpaid balance, and dividing that figure by the number of payments made each year. For example, if the current outstanding loan balance is $50,000 with interest at the rate of 10 percent per annum and constant monthly payments of $439, the interest and principal due on the next payment would be computed as shown:

$50,000.00
×   0.10
$ 5,000.00   annual interest
$ 439.00   monthly payment
−   416.67   month's interest
$ 22.33   month's principal

$416.666   month's interest
12)$5,000.00

(round to $416.67)

At the end of the term the full amount of the principal and all interest due will be reduced to zero. Such loans are also called *direct reduction loans.* Most amortized mortgage and deed of trust loans are paid in monthly installments; some, however, are payable quarterly or semiannually.

Different payment plans tend alternately to gain and lose favor with lenders and borrowers as the cost and availability of mortgage money fluctuate. The most frequently used plan is the *fully amortized loan,* also called a *level payment* loan. The mortgagor pays a *constant amount,* usually monthly. The lender credits each payment first to the interest due and then to the principal amount of the loan. Thus, while each payment is the same, the portion applied to repayment of the principal grows and the interest due declines as the unpaid balance of the loan is reduced (see Figure 15.1). The loan can be amortized more rapidly, unless prohibited by a lock-in clause in the note, by paying additional amounts that are applied directly to the principal. The result is that less interest is paid because the loan is paid off before the end of its term.

The amount of the constant payment is determined from a prepared mortgage payment book or a mortgage factor chart (see Table 15.1). The mortgage factor chart indicates the amount of monthly payment per $1,000 of loan, depending on the term and interest rate. The factor is multiplied by the number of thousands (and fractions thereof) of the amount being borrowed.

In addition to fully amortized, fixed-interest/fixed-payment loans, the following payment programs have evolved. (See Figure 15.2.)

Adjustable-Rate Mortgages (ARMs)

Adjustable-rate mortgages (ARMs) are generally originated at one rate of interest, with the rate fluctuating up or down during the loan term based on some economic indicator. Because the interest rate may change, so may the mortgagor's loan repayments. Details of how and when the interest rate will change are included in the note. Common components of an ARM include the following.

**Table 15.1
Mortgage Factor
Chart**

EQUAL MONTHLY PAYMENT TO AMORTIZE A LOAN OF $1,000

Term Rate	10 Years	15 Years	20 Years	25 Years	30 Years
4	10.13	7.40	6.06	5.28	4.78
4 1/8	10.19	7.46	6.13	5.35	4.85
4 1/4	10.25	7.53	6.20	5.42	4.92
4 3/8	10.31	7.59	6.26	5.49	5.00
4 1/2	10.37	7.65	6.33	5.56	5.07
4 5/8	10.43	7.72	6.40	5.63	5.15
4 3/4	10.49	7.78	6.47	5.71	5.22
4 7/8	10.55	7.85	6.54	5.78	5.30
5	10.61	7.91	6.60	5.85	5.37
5 1/8	10.67	7.98	6.67	5.92	5.45
5 1/4	10.73	8.04	6.74	6.00	5.53
5 3/8	10.80	8.11	6.81	6.07	5.60
5 1/2	10.86	8.18	6.88	6.15	5.68
5 5/8	10.92	8.24	6.95	6.22	5.76
5 3/4	10.98	8.31	7.03	6.30	5.84
5 7/8	11.04	8.38	7.10	6.37	5.92
6	11.10	8.44	7.16	6.44	6.00
6 1/8	11.16	8.51	7.24	6.52	6.08
6 1/4	11.23	8.57	7.31	6.60	6.16
6 3/8	11.29	8.64	7.38	6.67	6.24
6 1/2	11.35	8.71	7.46	6.75	6.32
6 5/8	11.42	8.78	7.53	6.83	6.40
6 3/4	11.48	8.85	7.60	6.91	6.49
6 7/8	11.55	8.92	7.68	6.99	6.57
7	11.61	8.98	7.75	7.06	6.65
7 1/8	11.68	9.06	7.83	7.15	6.74
7 1/4	11.74	9.12	7.90	7.22	6.82
7 3/8	11.81	9.20	7.98	7.31	6.91
7 1/2	11.87	9.27	8.05	7.38	6.99
7 5/8	11.94	9.34	8.13	7.47	7.08
7 3/4	12.00	9.41	8.20	7.55	7.16
7 7/8	12.07	9.48	8.29	7.64	7.25
8	12.14	9.56	8.37	7.72	7.34
8 1/8	12.20	9.63	8.45	7.81	7.43
8 1/4	12.27	9.71	8.53	7.89	7.52
8 3/8	12.34	9.78	8.60	7.97	7.61
8 1/2	12.40	9.85	8.68	8.06	7.69
8 5/8	12.47	9.93	8.76	8.14	7.78
8 3/4	12.54	10.00	8.84	8.23	7.87
8 7/8	12.61	10.07	8.92	8.31	7.96
9	12.67	10.15	9.00	8.40	8.05
9 1/8	12.74	10.22	9.08	8.48	8.14
9 1/4	12.81	10.30	9.16	8.57	8.23
9 3/8	12.88	10.37	9.24	8.66	8.32
9 1/2	12.94	10.45	9.33	8.74	8.41
9 5/8	13.01	10.52	9.41	8.83	8.50
9 3/4	13.08	10.60	9.49	8.92	8.60
9 7/8	13.15	10.67	9.57	9.00	8.69
10	13.22	10.75	9.66	9.09	8.78
10 1/8	13.29	10.83	9.74	9.18	8.87
10 1/4	13.36	10.90	9.82	9.27	8.97
10 3/8	13.43	10.98	9.90	9.36	9.06
10 1/2	13.50	11.06	9.99	9.45	9.15
10 5/8	13.57	11.14	10.07	9.54	9.25
10 3/4	13.64	11.21	10.16	9.63	9.34

**Figure 15.1
Level-Payment
Amortized Loan**

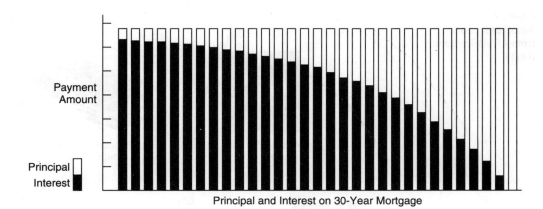

Payment
Amount

Principal
Interest

Principal and Interest on 30-Year Mortgage

- The interest rate is tied to the movement of an *index,* such as the cost-of-funds index for federally chartered lenders. Most indexes are tied to U.S. Treasury securities.

- Usually the interest rate is the index rate plus a premium, called the *margin,* which is the lender's cost of doing business, such as profits and costs. For example, the loan rate may be 2 percent over the U.S. Treasury bill rate.

- *Rate caps* limit the amount the interest rate may change. Most ARMs have both periodic rate caps, which limit the amount the rate may increase at any one time, and aggregate rate caps, which limit the amount the rate may increase over the entire life of the loan.

- The mortgagor is protected from unaffordable individual payments by the *payment cap,* which sets a maximum amount for payments. With a payment cap, however, a rate increase could result in negative amortization—an increase in the loan balance.

- The *adjustment period* establishes how often the rate may be changed. Common adjustment periods are monthly, quarterly and annually.

- Lenders may offer a *conversion option*, which enables the mortgagor to convert from an adjustable-rate to a fixed-rate loan at certain intervals during the loan. The option will stipulate the terms and conditions for the conversion.

**Graduated-
Payment
Mortgage (GPM)**

A *flexible-payment plan,* such as a **graduated-payment mortgage,** allows a mortgagor to make lower monthly payments for the first few years of the loan (typically the first five years) and larger payments for the remainder of the term. Often it is used when the mortgagor's income is expected to increase in several years. This type of loan may enable first-time buyers and buyers in times of high interest rates to purchase real estate. However, the monthly payments may be less than the interest due, resulting in negative amortization. As each payment is made, the unpaid interest is added to the principal balance, resulting in an increasing loan balance for the first few years. GPMs are fixed-rate loans.

**Figure 15.2
Amortized Loans
from ARMs Through
RAMs**

Adjustable-rate
mortgage

Graduated-payment
mortgage

Shared-appreciation
mortgage

Reverse-annuity mortgage

Growing-equity mortgage

**Balloon Payment
Loan**

When the periodic payments are not large enough to fully amortize the loan by the time the final payment is due, the final payment is larger than the others. This is called a **balloon payment.** It is a *partially amortized loan.* For example, a loan made for $80,000 at 11½ percent interest may be computed on a 30-year amortization schedule but paid over a 20-year term with a final balloon payment due at the end of the 20th year. In this case each monthly payment would be $792.24 (the amount taken from a 30-year amortization schedule), with a final balloon payment of $56,340 (the amount of principal still owed after 20 years). It is frequently assumed that if the payments are made promptly the lender will extend the balloon payment for another limited term. The lender, however, is not legally obligated to grant this extension and can require payment in full when the note is due.

**Growing-Equity
Mortgage (GEM)**

The **growing-equity mortgage,** or *rapid-payoff mortgage,* uses a fixed interest rate, but payments of principal are increased according to an index or a schedule. The total payment thus increases, but the borrower's income is expected to keep pace, and the loan is paid off more quickly.

**Shared-
Appreciation
Mortgage (SAM)**

A shared-appreciation mortgage is one in which the lender originates a mortgage or deed of trust loan at a favorable interest rate, usually several points below the current rate, in return for a guaranteed share of any gain the borrower will realize when the property is eventually sold. This type of loan was originally made to developers of large real estate projects, but in times of expensive mortgage money it has appeared in the residential financing market. The specific details of the shared-appreciation agreement are set forth in the mortgage or deed of trust and note documents.

Reverse-Annuity Mortgage (RAM)

A reverse-annuity mortgage is one in which regular monthly payments are made *to the borrower,* based on the equity the homeowner has invested in the property given as security for the loan. This loan allows senior citizens on fixed incomes to realize the equity buildup in their homes without having to sell. The borrower is charged a fixed rate of interest, and the loan is eventually paid from the sale of the property or from the borrower's estate upon his or her death.

LOAN PROGRAMS

Mortgage loans are generally classified based on their **loan-to-value ratio,** that is, the ratio of debt to value of the property. Value is the sale price or the appraisal value, which is lower. The lower the ratio of debt to value means a higher down payment by the borrower. For the lender, the higher down payment means a more secure loan, minimizing the lender's risk.

Conventional Loans

Conventional loans are viewed as the most secure loans because the loan-to-value ratio is lowest. Usually the ratio is 80 percent of the value of the property or lower; the borrower makes a down payment of 20 percent or more. The security for the loan is provided solely by the mortgage. The payment of the debt rests on the ability of the borrower to pay. In making these loans the lender relies primarily on its appraisal of the security (the real estate) and information from credit reports that indicate the reliability of the prospective borrower. No additional insurance or guarantee on the loan is necessary to protect the lender's interest.

Lenders can set criteria by which the borrower and the collateral will be evaluated to qualify for the loan. However, in recent years the secondary mortgage (which will be discussed in detail later) has had a significant impact on the borrower qualifications, standards for the collateral and documentation procedures that the lenders follow. For loans to be salable to the Federal National Mortgage Association and the Federal Home Loan Mortgage Corporation, they must meet their requirements. Lenders can still be flexible in their lending decisions but would have to retain loans that are unsalable in the secondary market.

Private Mortgage Insurance

One way borrowers can obtain mortgage loans with a lower down payment is under **private mortgage insurance** programs. Because the loan-to-value ratio is higher than for other conventional loans, up to 95 percent of the appraised value of the property, the lender requires additional security to minimize its risk. The lender purchases insurance from a private mortgage insurance company as additional security to insure the lender against borrower default.

The insurance protects a certain percentage of the loan, usually 20 to 25 percent, against borrower default. Normally the borrower is charged a fee for this insurance coverage at closing plus additional monthly fees while the insurance is in force. Because only a portion of the loan is insured, once the loan is repaid to a certain level, the lender may terminate the coverage. Practices for termination vary from lender to lender.

FHA-Insured Loans

The FHA, which operates under the Department of Housing and Urban Development (HUD), neither builds homes nor lends money itself. The common term **FHA loan** refers to a loan that is not made by the agency but *insured* by it.

These loans must be made by approved FHA lending institutions. FHA-insured loans provide another alternative for borrowers who have only a low down payment. These are normally high loan-to-value ratio loans. The FHA insurance provides security to the lender in addition to the real estate. As with private mortgage insurance, FHA insures the lender against loss from a borrower's default.

The most popular FHA program is Title II, Section 203(b), which applies to loans on one- to four-family residences. Although interest rates on these loans are not fixed by the FHA, the rates are generally lower because the protection of the FHA mortgage insurance makes them a lower risk to the lender. Certain technical requirements must be met before the FHA will issue the insurance. Three of these requirements are

1. In addition to paying interest, the borrower is charged a premium for the FHA insurance. The amount of the upfront premium is paid at closing by the borrower or someone else, or it may be added to the loan amount. An annual premium may also be charged. Insurance premiums vary for new loans, refinancing and condominiums.

2. The FHA regulations set standards for type and construction of buildings, quality of neighborhood and credit requirements for borrowers. Regulations also set standards for condominium complexes and the ratio of owner-occupants to renters that must be met for a loan on a condominium unit to be financed through the FHA insurance programs.

3. The mortgaged real estate must be appraised by an *approved FHA appraiser.* The loan amount insured generally cannot exceed 97 percent on the first $25,000 of appraised value or purchase price, whichever is less; 95 percent up to $125,000; and 90 percent of the remainder (including the allowable amount for closing costs). If the purchase price exceeds the FHA-appraised value, the buyer may pay the difference in cash as part of the down payment. In addition, the FHA has set maximum loan amounts for various regions of the country.

Contact your local FHA office or mortgage lender for loan amounts in your area and specific loan requirements, which change from time to time.

Prepayment privileges. A borrower may repay a FHA-insured loan on a one- to four-family residence without penalty. The borrower must give the lender written notice of intention to exercise this privilege at least 30 days before the anticipated prepayment; otherwise the lender has the option of charging up to 30 days' interest.

Assumption rules. The assumption rules for FHA-insured loans vary, depending on the date that the loan was originated.

- FHA loans originated prior to December 1986 generally have no restrictions on their assumption.

- For FHA loans originated since December 1, 1986, a creditworthiness review of the prospective assumer is required. If the original loan was for the purchase of a principal residence, this review is required during the first 12 months of the loan's existence. If the original loan was for the purchase of an investment property, the review is required during the first 24 months of the loan.

- For FHA loans originated December 15, 1989, and thereafter, no assumptions are permitted without complete buyer qualification. Also there are no longer any investor loans; all FHA loans made under the 203(b) program will be for owner-occupied properties only.

Discount points. The lender of an FHA-insured loan can charge discount points in addition to a 1 percent loan origination fee. The payment of points is a matter of negotiation between the seller and the buyer. However, if the seller pays more than 6 percent of the costs normally paid by the buyer (such as discount points, the loan origination fee, the mortgage insurance premium, buydown fees, prepaid items and impound or escrow amounts), the lender treats such payments as sales concessions. It is assumed that the sales price may be inflated because of these payments, which would result in the price being reduced for loan purposes.

Other FHA loan programs. In addition to loans made under Title II, Section 203(b), FHA loans are also granted under the following programs:

- Title I: Home improvement loans are covered under this title.

- Title II, Section 246: Loans made to purchase condominiums are covered under this program, which in most respects is similar to the basic 203(b) program.

- Title II, Section 245: This title covers five basic graduated-payment loan plans, which vary the rate of monthly payment increases and the number of years over which the payments increase.

- Title II, Section 251: Adjustable-rate loans are allowed under this program. The interest rate cannot increase more than 1 percent per year or more than 5 percent from the initial rate.

VA-Guaranteed Loans

Under the Servicemen's Readjustment Act of 1944 and subsequent federal legislation, the Department of Veterans Affairs is authorized to guarantee loans to purchase or construct homes for eligible veterans. These are individuals who were honorably discharged from eligible service: at least *90 days* of active service for veterans of World War II, the Korean War and/or the Vietnam conflict; at least *181 days* of active service during the time periods between these wars until September 7, 1980 (enlisted), or October 16, 1981 (officer); or *two full years* for service beginning after September 7, 1980 (enlisted), or October 16, 1981 (officer). Individuals who have completed 6 years in the Reserves or National Guard and who do not otherwise meet the eligibility requirements can obtain VA loans. However, they pay higher funding fees than veterans.

VA loans assist veterans in financing the purchase of homes with little or no down payment at comparatively low interest rates. The VA also guarantees loans to purchase mobile homes and plots on which to place them. The VA issues rules and regulations from time to time, setting forth the qualifications, limitations and conditions under which a loan may be guaranteed. (Table 15.2 is a comparison of FHA and VA loan programs.)

As with the FHA loan, the term **VA loan** is something of a misnomer. The VA does not normally lend money, except in certain situations where financing is not reasonably available, such as in isolated rural areas. A veteran obtains a loan

Table 15.2 Comparison of FHA and VA Loan Programs	Federal Housing Administration	Department of Veterans Affairs
	1. Financing is available to veterans and nonveterans alike	1. Financing available only to those who meet eligibility requirements and certain unremarried widows and widowers
	2. Financing programs for owner-occupied only	2. VA financing limited to owner-occupied residential (one- to four-family) dwellings—must sign occupancy certificate
	3. Requires a larger down payment than VA	3. Does not normally require down payment, though lender may require small down payment
	4. FHA valuation sets the maximum loan FHA will insure but does not limit the sales price	4. With regard to home loans, the VA loan may not exceed the appraised value of the home
	5. No prepayment penalty	5. No prepayment penalty
	6. Insures the loan by way of mutual mortgage insurance; mortgage insurance; mortgage insurance premiums (MIP) paid by borrower	6. Guarantees up to a maximum of $46,000, for loans up to $184,000
	7. Discount points can be charged, payable by either seller or buyer or split between them	7. Discount points can be charged and are payable by either seller, buyer or split between them
	8. Borrower is subject to 1 percent loan origination fee (can be paid by seller)	8. Borrower pays 1 percent loan origination fee to the lender
	9. FHA loan assumption rules vary, depending on the date of loan origination	9. VA loan can be assumed by nonveteran; assumption rules vary, depending on date of loan origination
		10. Borrower pays a VA funding fee that varies depending on the amount of down payment and eligibility status.

from a VA-approved lending institution; the VA partially guarantees loans made by these institutions. The term *VA loan* does not refer to a loan that is made by the agency but one that is guaranteed by it. This is normally a high loan-to-value ratio loan, as well. The guarantee provided by the VA provides the lending institution with additional security in place of insurance. The lender would receive the amount of the guarantee from the VA if a foreclosure sale did not bring enough to cover the outstanding loan balance.

Maximum loan terms are 30 years for one- to four-family dwellings and 40 years for farms. Interest rates are negotiable between the lender and borrower. The VA will guarantee fixed-rate and adjustable-rate loans. Residential property purchased with a VA loan must be owner-occupied. The VA also requires that the real estate to be mortgaged meet certain requirements.

Since the interest rate on VA loans is usually lower than the rate on conventional loans, the lender will charge points to make up the difference. Points are payable by a veteran, the seller or split between them. However, they cannot be included in the loan amount. Lenders are also permitted to charge reasonable closing costs plus a loan origination fee that may not exceed 1 percent of the loan amount. A VA funding fee to be paid either at closing or included in the loan amount will also be charged. The rate of funding fees also varies depending on the amount of the down payment and whether the loan is to finance the purchase of an existing home, new construction or for refinancing.

There is no VA limit on the amount of the loan a veteran can obtain; this is determined by the lender. The VA does, however, limit the amount of loan that it will guarantee. For loans of $45,000 or less, 50 percent of the loan is guaranteed. For loans above this amount up to $144,000, 40 percent of the loan is guaranteed up to a maximum of $36,000 (but not less than $22,500). For loans of more than $144,000 for the purchase or construction of a home or farm residence or for the purchase of a residential condominium unit, the lesser of $46,000 or 25 percent of the loan is guaranteed. These calculations are subject to the amount of guarantee remaining in the veteran's entitlement, depending on the amounts and effective dates of entitlement established by the VA.

To determine what portion of a mortgage loan the VA will guarantee, a veteran must apply for a *certificate of eligibility*. This certificate does not mean that the veteran will automatically receive a mortgage. It merely establishes the maximum guarantee entitlement of the veteran. For individuals with full eligibility, no down payment would be required for loans up to $184,000.

The VA also will issue a *certificate of reasonable value* (CRV) for the property being purchased, stating its current market value based on a VA-approved appraisal. The CRV places a ceiling on the amount of a VA loan allowed for the property. No down payment will be required if the purchase price does not exceed the amount cited in the CRV; if the purchase price is greater, the veteran must pay the difference in cash.

Assumption of rules. VA loans made prior to March 1, 1988 remain freely assumable, but an assumption processing fee will be charged. All loans made on or after that date require approval of the buyer and an assumption agreement. The original veteran/borrower, however, remains personally liable for the repayment of the loan unless the VA approves a *release of liability*. The release of liability will be issued by the VA if the buyer assumes all of the veteran's liabilities on the loan and the VA or the lender approves the buyer and the assumption agreement. A ½ percent funding fee will be required (½ percent of the loan balance). A release would also be possible if another veteran used his or her own entitlement in assuming the loan. Any release of liability issued by the VA does not release the veteran's liability from the lender. This must be obtained separately from the lender.

Prepayment privileges. As with an FHA loan, the borrower under a VA loan can prepay the debt at any time without penalty.

Contact your local VA office or mortgage lender for specific requirements for VA loans. The programs change from time to time.

OTHER FINANCING TECHNIQUES

A variety of other financing techniques have been created to fulfill specific purposes, meet certain needs of borrowers and fit different types of collateral. The following loans, which do not fit strictly into the categories previously described, are among the most common.

Purchase-Money Mortgages

A **purchase-money mortgage** is a note and mortgage created at the time of purchase to facilitate the sale. The term is used in two ways—to refer to any security instrument originating at the time of sale or, most often, to refer to the instrument *given by the purchaser to a seller who "takes back" a note for part or all of the purchase price.* The mortgage may be a first or a junior lien, depending on whether prior mortgage liens exist.

Package Loans

A **package loan** includes not only the real estate but also *all personal property and appliances installed on the premises.* In recent years this kind of loan has been used extensively in some parts of the country to finance furnished condominium units. Such loans usually include furniture, drapes, carpets, the kitchen range, refrigerator, dishwasher, garbage disposal unit, washer and dryer, food freezer and other appliances as part of the real estate in the sales price of the home.

Blanket Loans

A **blanket loan** covers *more than one parcel or lot.* It is usually used to finance subdivision developments, though it can be used to finance the purchase of improved properties or to consolidate loans as well. Blanket loans usually include a provision known as a *partial release clause,* so that the borrower may obtain the release of any one lot or parcel from the lien by repaying a certain amount of the loan. The lender issues a partial release for each parcel released from the mortgage lien; this release form includes a provision that the lien will continue to cover all other unreleased lots.

Wraparound Loans

A **wraparound loan** enables a borrower with an existing mortgage or deed of trust loan to obtain additional financing from a second lender without paying off the first loan. *The second lender gives the borrower a new, increased loan at a higher interest rate and assumes payment of the existing loan.* The total amount of the new loan includes the existing loan as well as the additional funds needed by the borrower. The borrower makes payments to the new lender on the larger loan. The new lender makes the payments on the original loan out of the borrower's payments.

A wraparound mortgage can be used as a method of refinancing real property or financing the purchase of real property when an existing mortgage cannot be prepaid. It also is used to finance the sale of real estate when the buyer wishes to invest a minimum amount of initial cash for the sale. A wraparound loan is possible only if the original loan permits such a refinancing. An acceleration and alienation or due-on-sale clause in the original loan documents may prevent a sale under these terms. The buyer executes a wraparound mortgage to the seller, who will collect payments on the new loan and continue to make payments on the old loan. To protect themselves in the case of the seller's default on the old loan, buyers should require a protective clause in the document granting the right to make payments directly to the original lender.

Open-End Loans

An **open-end loan** secures a *note* executed by the borrower to the lender as well as any future *advances* of funds made by the lender to the borrower. The interest rate on the initial amount borrowed is fixed, but interest on future advances may be charged at the market rate then in effect. Often a less costly alternative to a home improvement loan, this financing technique allows the borrower to "open" the mortgage or deed of trust to increase the debt to its original amount, or the amount stated in the note, after the debt has been reduced by payments over a period of time. The mortgage usually states the maximum amount that can be secured, the terms and conditions under which the loan can be opened and the provisions for repayment.

Construction Loans

A **construction loan** is made to *finance the construction of improvements* on real estate such as homes, apartments and office buildings. The lender commits to the full amount of the loan but disburses the funds in payments during construction. Those payments, also known as *draws,* are made to the general contractor or the owner for that part of the construction work that has been completed since the previous payment. Before each payment, the lender inspects the work. The general contractor must provide the lender with adequate waivers of lien that release all mechanics' lien rights for the work covered by the payment.

This kind of loan generally bears a higher-than-market interest rate because of the risks assumed by the lender. These risks include the inadequate releasing of mechanics' liens, possible delays in completing the construction or the financial failure of the contractor or subcontractors. This type of financing is generally *short-term* or *interim financing.* The borrower pays interest only, periodically, on the monies that have been disbursed to that payment date. The borrower is expected to arrange for a permanent loan, also known as an *end loan* or *take-out loan,* that will repay or "take out" the construction financing lender when the work is completed.

Sale and Leaseback

Sale-and-leaseback arrangements are used to finance large commercial or industrial properties. The land and building, usually used by the seller for business purposes, are sold to an investor, such as an insurance company. The real estate is then leased back by the buyer (the investor) to the seller, who continues to conduct business on the property as a tenant. The buyer becomes the lessor, and the original owner becomes the lessee. This enables a business firm with money invested in the real estate to free that money so it can be used as working capital.

Sale-and-leaseback arrangements involve complicated legal procedures, and their success is usually related to the effects the transaction has on the firm's tax situation. Legal and tax experts should be involved in this type of transaction.

Buydowns

A **buydown** is a way of temporarily lowering the initial interest rate on a mortgage or deed of trust loan. Perhaps a home builder wishes to stimulate sales by offering a lower-than-market rate. Or a particular buyer is having trouble qualifying for a loan at the prevailing rates, and some relatives or the sellers want to help the buyer qualify. By donating in advance or "prepaying" some of the interest to the lender on the borrower's behalf, one can "buy down" the original interest rate for a period of time. Typical buydown arrangements reduce the interest rate by 1 to 3 percent over the first one to three years of the loan term.

Home Equity Loans

Home equity loans are a source of funds for homeowners who wish to finance the purchase of expensive items, consolidate existing installment loans on credit card debt or pay for medical, education, home improvement or other expenses. Use of this type of financing has increased in recent years, partly because interest on consumer loans is no longer deductible under IRS rules. Home equity loans are secured by the borrower's residence, and the interest charged is deductible up to a loan limit of $100,000.

A home equity loan can be taken out as a fixed loan amount or as an equity line of credit. With the home equity line of credit, the lender extends a line of credit that the borrowers can use whenever they want. The borrowers can receive their money by a check sent to them, deposits made in a checking or savings account, or a book of drafts the borrowers can use up to their credit limit.

Using the equity buildup in the home to finance purchases is an alternative to refinancing. The original mortgage loan remains in place; the home equity loan is junior to that lien. If the homeowner refinances, the original mortgage loan is paid off and replaced by a new loan. The homeowner must compare the costs for a new mortgage loan, interest rates, total monthly payments and income tax consequences to decide which alternative is best.

SOURCES OF REAL ESTATE FINANCING— THE PRIMARY MORTGAGE MARKET

The **primary mortgage market** is comprised of the lenders who originate the loans, making money available directly to the borrowers. From the borrower's point of view the loan is a means of financing an expenditure; from a lender's point of view the loan is an investment. The investment must generate sufficient income to be attractive to the lender. Income on the loan is realized from finance charges collected at closing (loan origination fees and discount points) and recurring income (the interest collected during the term of the loan). An increasing number of lenders look at the income generated from the fees charged in originating loans as their primary investment objective. Once the loans are made, they are sold to investors, thereby generating funds with which to originate additional loans. The *secondary mortgage market* (as will be discussed later) is a source of investors.

In addition to the income directly related to the loan, some lenders derive income from *servicing loans* for other mortgage lenders or the investors who have purchased the loans. Servicing involves duties such as collecting payments, (including insurance and taxes), accounting, bookkeeping, preparing insurance and tax records and processing payments of taxes and insurance and following up on loan payment and delinquency. Rather than administer their own loan portfolios, some loan originators will enter into a servicing agreement with other lenders or entities whose business it is to act as mortgage loan correspondents to provide the service. The terms of the servicing agreement will stipulate the responsibilities and fees for the service.

Savings and Loan Associations

Savings and loan associations are active participants in the home loan mortgage market, specializing in long-term residential loans. A savings and loan earns money by paying less for the funds it receives than it charges for the loans it makes. Loan income includes more than interest, however—there are loan origination, loan assumption and other fees.

Traditionally savings and loan associations have the most flexible mortgage lending procedures of all the lending institutions, and they are generally local in scope. In addition, they participate in FHA-insured and VA-guaranteed loans, though only to a limited extent.

All savings and loan associations must be chartered, either by the federal government or by the states in which they are located. The **Financial Institutions Reform, Recovery and Enforcement Act of 1989 (FIRREA),** enacted in response to the savings and loan association crisis of the 1980s, was intended to ensure the continued viability of the savings and loan industry. FIRREA restructured the thrift regulatory system as well as the insurance system that protects its depositors. The **Federal Deposit Insurance Corporation (FDIC)** now manages the insurance funds for both savings and loan associations and commercial banks. Savings and loan deposits are insured through the **Savings Association Insurance Fund (SAIF),** and bank deposits are insured through the **Bank Insurance Fund (BIF).**

FIRREA also created the **Office of Thrift Supervision (OTS)** to monitor and regulate the savings and loan industry and the **Resolution Trust Corporation (RTC)** to assume the management of insolvent savings and loan institutions and liquidate the assets of failed institutions.

Because of their performance record of the 1980s, savings and loans are now subject to stricter capital requirements as well as new housing loan requirements. Effective July 1, 1991, savings and loan associations are required to maintain 70 percent of their loan portfolios in housing-related loans, such as residential mortgage loans, residential construction loans and home equity loans.

Mutual Savings Banks

These institutions, which operate as do savings and loan associations, are located primarily in the northeastern United States. They issue no stock and are mutually owned by their investors. Although mutual savings banks do offer limited checking account privileges, they are primarily savings institutions and are highly active in the mortgage market, investing in loans secured by income property as well as residential real estate. In addition, because mutual savings banks usually seek low-risk loan investments, they often prefer to originate FHA-insured or VA-guaranteed loans.

Commercial Banks

Commercial banks are an important source of real estate financing. Though historically they were interested primarily in short-term loans such as construction, home improvement and mobile-home loans, these institutions are increasingly more active in conventional mortgage lending. Commercial banks also play a significant role in issuing VA and FHA loans. Like the savings and loan associations, banks must be chartered by the state or federal government.

Insurance Companies

Insurance companies amass large sums of money from the premiums paid by their policyholders. While a certain portion of this money is held in reserve to satisfy claims and cover operating expenses, much of it is invested in profit-earning enterprises, such as long-term real estate loans.

Most insurance companies like to invest their money in large, long-term loans that finance commercial and industrial properties. They also invest in residential mortgage and deed of trust loans by purchasing large blocks of FHA-insured and VA-guaranteed loans from the Federal National Mortgage Association and other agencies that warehouse such loans for resale in the secondary mortgage market (discussed later in this chapter).

Many insurance companies seek additional safety on their investments by insisting on equity positions (known as *equity kickers*) in the projects they finance. The company acquires an equity position by becoming a partner with, for example, the project developer or subdivider as a condition of making a loan. This is called *participation financing*.

Mortgage Banking Companies

Mortgage banking companies originate mortgage loans with money belonging to insurance companies, pension funds and individuals and with funds of their own. They make real estate loans with the intention of later selling them to investors and receiving a fee for servicing the loans. Mortgage banking companies often are involved in all types of real estate loan activities and often serve as intermediaries between investors and borrowers. They are not mortgage brokers.

Mortgage banking companies are generally organized as stock companies. As a source of real estate financing, they are subject to fewer lending restrictions than commercial banks or savings and loans.

Credit Unions

Credit unions are cooperative organizations in which members place money in savings accounts. Most credit unions used to make only short-term consumer and home improvement loans, but recently they have been branching out to originating longer-term first and second mortgage and deed of trust loans.

Mortgage Brokers

Mortgage brokers are not lenders but act as intermediaries in bringing borrowers and lenders together. They locate potential borrowers, process preliminary loan applications and submit the applications to lenders for final approval. Frequently they work with or for mortgage banking companies in these activities. They do not service loans once they are made. Mortgage brokers may also be real estate brokers who offer these financing services in addition to their regular brokerage activities. Many state governments are adding separate licensure requirements for mortgage brokers to regulate these activities.

Pension Funds

Pension funds have begun to participate actively in financing real estate projects. Most of the real estate activity for pension funds is handled through mortgage bankers and mortgage brokers.

Investment Group Financing

Large real estate projects, such as high-rise apartment buildings, office complexes and shopping centers, are often financed as a joint venture through group financing arrangements such as syndicates, limited partnerships and real estate investment trusts. These complex investment agreements are discussed in Chapter 22.

IN PRACTICE. . .	*Because interest rates and loan terms change frequently, licensees should check with local sources of real estate financing regularly to learn of specific loan rates and terms. Licensees can better serve customers—and thus more effectively sell clients' properties—when they can knowledgeably refer buyers to local lenders offering the most favorable terms.*

GOVERNMENT INFLUENCE IN MORTGAGE LENDING

The federal government influences mortgage lending through the Federal Reserve System and various federal agencies such as the Farmer's Home Administration. It also deals in the secondary mortgage market through the Government National Mortgage Association, the Federal Home Loan Mortgage Corporation and the Federal National Mortgage Association.

Federal Reserve System

The role of the **Federal Reserve System** (also known as "the Fed") is to maintain sound credit conditions, help counteract inflationary and deflationary trends and create a favorable economic climate. The Federal Reserve System divides the country into 12 federal reserve districts, each served by a federal reserve bank. All nationally chartered banks must join the Federal Reserve and purchase stock in its district reserve banks.

The Federal Reserve regulates the flow of money and interest rates in the marketplace indirectly, through its member banks, by controlling their *reserve requirements* and *discount rates*.

Reserve requirements. The Federal Reserve requires each member bank to keep a certain amount of its assets on hand as reserve funds unavailable for loans or any other use. This requirement was intended primarily to protect customer deposits, but, more important, it provides a means of manipulating the flow of cash in the money market.

By increasing its reserve requirements the Federal Reserve in effect limits the amount of money that member banks can use to make loans, causing interest rates to rise. In this manner the government can slow down an overactive economy by limiting the number of loans that would have been directed toward major purchases of goods and services. The opposite is also true: by decreasing the reserve requirements the Federal Reserve can allow more loans to be made, thus increasing the amount of money circulated in the marketplace and causing interest rates to drop.

Discount rates. Federal Reserve member banks are permitted to borrow money from the district reserve banks to expand their lending operations. The interest rate that the district banks charge for the use of this money is called the *discount rate*. This rate is the basis on which the banks determine the percentage rate of interest that they, in turn, charge their loan customers. Theoretically, when the Federal Reserve discount rate is high, bank interest rates are high; therefore fewer loans will be made and less money will circulate in the marketplace. Conversely, a lower discount rate results in lower interest rates, more bank loans and more money in circulation.

Government Influence in the Secondary Market

In addition to the primary mortgage market, where loans are originated, there is the **secondary mortgage market,** where loans are bought and sold only after they have been funded. A lender sometimes sells loans to raise immediate funds when it needs more money to meet the mortgage demands in its area. Secondary market activity is especially desirable when money is in short supply, because it provides a great stimulant to the housing construction market as well as to the mortgage market.

When a loan has been sold, the original lender may continue to collect the payments from the borrower. The lender then passes the payments along to the investor who has purchased the loan and charges the investor a fee for servicing the loan.

Warehousing agencies purchase a number of mortgage loans, assemble them into packages of loans and sell securities that represent shares in these pooled mortgages to investors. Loans are eligible for sale to the secondary market only when the collateral, borrower and documentation meet certain requirements to provide a degree of safety for the investors. The major warehousing agencies are discussed in the following paragraphs.

Federal National Mortgage Association. The **Federal National Mortgage Association (FNMA, "Fannie Mae"),** is a quasi-governmental agency organized as a privately owned corporation that issues its own common stock and provides a secondary market for mortgage loans—conventional as well as FHA and VA loans. FNMA will buy a *block* or *pool* of mortgages from a lender in exchange for *mortgage-backed securities* that the lender may keep or sell. FNMA guarantees payment of all interest and principal to the holder of the securities.

Mortgage banking firms are generally actively involved with FNMA, originating loans and selling them to FNMA while retaining the servicing functions.

Government National Mortgage Association. The **Government National Mortgage Association (GNMA, "Ginnie Mae")** exists as a corporation without capital stock and is a division of HUD. GNMA is designed to administer special assistance programs and work with FNMA in secondary market activities. Fannie Mae and Ginnie Mae can join forces in times of tight money and high interest rates through their tandem plan. Basically the *tandem plan* provides that FNMA can purchase high-risk, low-yield (usually FHA) loans at full market rates, with GNMA guaranteeing payment and absorbing the difference between the low yield and current market prices.

Ginnie Mae also guarantees investment securities issued by private offerors (such as banks, mortgage companies and savings and loan associations) and backed by pools of FHA and VA mortgage loans. The *Ginnie Mae pass-through certificate* is a security interest in a pool of mortgages that provides for a monthly "pass-through" of principal and interest payments directly to the certificate holder. Such certificates are guaranteed by Ginnie Mae.

Federal Home Loan Mortgage Corporation. The **Federal Home Loan Mortgage Corporation (FHLMC, "Freddie Mac"),** provides a secondary market for mortgage loans, primarily conventional loans. Freddie Mac has the authority to purchase mortgages, pool them and sell bonds in the open market with the mortgages as security. Note, however, that FHLMC does not guarantee payment of Freddie Mac mortgages.

Many lenders use the standardized forms and follow the guidelines issued by Fannie Mae and Freddie Mac; the use of FNMA/FHLMC forms is mandatory for lenders who wish to sell mortgages in the agencies' secondary mortgage market. The standardized documents include loan applications, credit reports and appraisal forms.

Farmer's Home Administration

The **Farmer's Home Administration (FmHA)** is a federal agency of the Department of Agriculture. FmHA offers programs to help purchase or operate family farms. It also provides loans to help purchase or improve single-family homes in rural areas (generally areas with a population of fewer than 10,000). Loans are made to low- and moderate-income families, and the interest rate charged can be as low as 1 percent, depending on the borrower's income.

FmHA loan programs fall into two categories: guaranteed loans, made and serviced by a private lender and guaranteed for a specific percentage by the FmHA, and loans made directly by the FmHA.

FINANCING LEGISLATION

The federal government regulates the lending practices of mortgage lenders through the Truth-in-Lending Act, the Equal Credit Opportunity Act and the Real Estate Settlement Procedures Act.

Truth-in-Lending Act and Regulation Z

Regulation Z, which was promulgated pursuant to the *Truth-in-Lending Act,* requires credit institutions to inform borrowers of the true cost of obtaining credit so that the borrower can compare the costs of various lenders and avoid the uninformed use of credit. Regulation Z applies when credit is extended to individuals for personal, family or household uses and the amount of credit is $25,000 or less. Regardless of the amount, Regulation Z always applies when a credit transaction is secured by a residence. The regulation does not apply to business or commercial loans or to agricultural loans of more than $25,000.

The regulation requires that the consumer be fully informed of all finance charges, as well as the true annual interest rate, before a transaction is consummated. The finance charges must include any loan fees, finders' fees, service charges and points as well as interest. In the case of a mortgage loan made to finance the purchase of a dwelling the lender must compute and disclose the *annual percentage rate (APR)* but does not have to indicate the total interest payable during the term of the loan. Also, the lender does not have to include as part of the finance charge actual costs such as title fees, legal fees, appraisal fees, credit reports, survey fees and closing expenses.

Creditor. A *creditor,* for purposes of Regulation Z, is a person who extends consumer credit more than 25 times a year or more than 5 times a year if the transaction involves a dwelling as security. The credit must be subject to a finance charge or payable in more than four installments by written agreement.

Three-day right of rescission. In the case of most consumer credit transactions covered by Regulation Z the borrower has 3 days in which to rescind the transaction by merely notifying the lender. This right of rescission does not apply to residential purchase money or first mortgage or deed of trust loans. In an emergency the right to rescind may be waived in writing to prevent a delay in funding.

Advertising. Regulation Z provides strict regulation of real estate advertisements that include mortgage financing terms. General phrases like "liberal terms available" may be used, but if details are given they must comply with this act. By the provisions of the Act the APR—which is calculated based on all charges rather than the interest rate alone—*must be stated*.

Specific credit terms, such as down payment, monthly payment, dollar amount of the finance charge or term of the loan, may not be advertised unless the following information is set forth as well: cash price; required down payment; number, amounts and due dates of all payments; and annual percentage rate. The total of all payments to be made over the term of the mortgage must also be specified unless the advertised credit refers to a first mortgage or deed of trust to finance acquisition of a dwelling.

Penalties. Regulation Z provides penalties for noncompliance. The penalty for violation of an administrative order enforcing Regulation Z is $10,000 for each day the violation continues. A fine of up to $10,000 may be imposed for engaging in an unfair or deceptive practice. In addition, a creditor may be liable to a consumer for twice the amount of the finance charge, for a minimum of $100 and a maximum of $1,000, plus court costs, attorney's fees and any actual damages. Willful violation is a misdemeanor punishable by a fine of up to $5,000 or one year's imprisonment or both.

Federal Equal Credit Opportunity Act

The federal **Equal Credit Opportunity Act** (ECOA), in effect since 1975, prohibits lenders and others who grant or arrange credit to consumers from discriminating against credit applicants on the basis of race, color, religion, national origin, sex, marital status, age (provided the applicant is of legal age) or dependence on public assistance. In addition, lenders and other creditors must inform all rejected credit applicants, in writing, within 30 days, of the principal reasons for denial or termination of credit.

Real Estate Settlement Procedures Act

The federal Real Estate Settlement Procedures Act (RESPA) was created to ensure that the buyer and seller in a residential real estate transaction involving a new first mortgage loan have knowledge of all settlement costs. This important federal law is discussed in detail in Chapter 23.

• • • • • • •

KEY TERMS

adjustable-rate mortgage (ARM)
amortized loan
balloon payment
Bank Insurance Fund (BIF)
blanket loan
buydown
construction loan
conventional loan
Equal Credit Opportunity Act
Farmer's Home Administration
  (FmHA)
Federal Deposit Insurance Corporation
  (FDIC)
Federal Home Loan Mortgage
  Corporation (FHLMC "Freddie
  Mac")
Federal National Mortgage
Association (FNMA "Fannie Mae")
Federal Reserve System
FHA loan
Financial Institutions Reform
  Recovery and Enforcement Act of
  1989 (FIRREA)
Government National Mortgage
Association (GNMA "Ginnie Mae")

graduated-payment mortgage (GPM)
growing-equity mortgage (GEM)
home equity loan
loan to value ratio
Office of Thrift Supervision (OTS)
open-end loan
package loan
primary mortgage market
package loan
primary mortgage market
private mortgage insurance
  (PMI)
purchase-money mortgage
  (PMM)
Regulation Z
Resolution Trust Corporation (RTC)
reverse-annuity mortgage (RAM)
sale and leaseback
Savings Association Insurance Fund
  (SAIF)
shared-appreciation mortgage (SAM)
straight loan
Truth-in-Lending Act
VA loan
wraparound loan

SUMMARY

Types of loans include fully amortized and straight loans as well as adjustable-rate mortgages, graduated-payment mortgages, growing-equity mortgages, balloon-payment mortgages, shared-appreciation mortgages and reverse-annuity mortgages.

There are many types of mortgage and deed of trust loan programs, including conventional loans and those insured by the FHA or private mortgage insurance companies or guaranteed by the VA. FHA and VA loans must meet certain requirements for the borrower to obtain the benefits of government backing, which induces the lender to lend its funds. The interest rates for these loans may be lower than those charged for conventional loans. Lenders may also charge points.

Other types of real estate financing include seller-financed purchase-money mortgages or deeds of trust, blanket mortgages, package mortgages, wraparound mortgages, open-end mortgages, construction loans, sale-and-leaseback agreements and home equity loans.

The federal government affects real estate financing money and interest rates through the Federal Reserve Board's discount rate and reserve requirements; it also participates in the secondary mortgage market. The secondary market is generally composed of the investors who ultimately purchase and hold the loans as investments. These include insurance companies, investment funds and pension plans. Fannie Mae (Federal National Mortgage Association), Ginnie Mae

(Government National Mortgage Association) and Freddie Mac (Federal Home Loan Mortgage Corporation) take an active role in creating a secondary market by regularly purchasing mortgage and deed of trust loans from originators and retaining, or warehousing, them until investment purchasers are available.

Regulation Z, implementing the federal Truth-in-Lending Act, requires lenders to inform prospective borrowers who use their homes as security for credit of all finance charges involved in such a loan. Severe penalties are provided for noncompliance. The federal Equal Credit Opportunity Act prohibits creditors from discriminating against credit applicants on the basis of race, color, religion, national origin, sex, marital status, age or dependence on public assistance. The Real Estate Settlement Procedures Act requires lenders to inform both buyers and sellers in advance of all fees and charges required for the settlement or closing of a residential real estate transaction.

Questions

1. The buyers are purchasing a lakefront summer home in a new resort development. They have obtained a deed of trust loan that covers the purchase price of the residence, including furnishings and appliances. This kind of financing is called
   a. a wraparound deed of trust.
   b. a package deed of trust.
   c. a blanket deed of trust.
   d. an unconventional deed of trust.

2. The buyers purchased a residence for $95,000. They made a down payment of $15,000 and agreed to assume the seller's existing mortgage, which had a current balance of $23,000. The buyers financed the remaining $57,000 of the purchase price by executing a mortgage and note to the seller. This type of loan, by which the seller becomes the mortgagee, is called a
   a. wraparound mortgage.
   b. package mortgage.
   c. balloon note.
   d. purchase-money mortgage.

3. Which of the following is *not* a participant in the secondary market?
   a. FNMA   c. RESPA
   b. GNMA   d. FHLMC

4. F continues to live in the home she purchased 30 years ago, but she now receives monthly checks thanks to her
   a. shared-appreciation mortgage.
   b. adjustable-rate mortgage.
   c. reverse-annuity mortgage.
   d. overriding deed of trust.

5. If buyers were seeking a mortgage on a single-family house, they would *least* likely obtain the mortgage from a
   a. mutual savings bank.
   b. life insurance company.
   c. credit union.
   d. commercial bank.

6. Which of the following institutions does *not* deal with conventional loans?
   a. FHLMC   c. FIRREA
   b. FNMA   d. GNMA

7. A purchaser obtains a fixed-rate loan to finance a home. Which of the following characteristics is true of this type of loan?
   a. The amount of interest to be paid is predetermined.
   b. The loan cannot be sold in the secondary market.
   c. The monthly payment amount will fluctuate each month.
   d. The interest rate change may be based on an index.

8. All of the following statements are true regarding mutual savings banks *except*
   a. they combine some of the characteristics of both banks and S&Ls.
   b. they are very prevalent in the eastern part of the country.
   c. they compete aggressively for savings deposits.
   d. they are primary lenders for real estate loans.

9. In theory, when the Federal Reserve Board raises its discount rate, all of the following will happen *except*

   a. interest rates will rise.
   b. interest rates will fall.
   c. mortgage money will become scarce.
   d. less money will circulate in the market-place.

10. In a loan that requires periodic payments that do not fully amortize the loan balance by the final payment, what term best describes the final payment?

    a. Adjustment payment
    b. Acceleration payment
    c. Balloon payment
    d. Variable payment

11. A developer received a loan that covers five parcels of real estate and provides for the release of the mortgage lien on each parcel when certain payments are made on the loan. This type of loan arrangement is called a

    a. purchase-money loan.
    b. blanket loan.
    c. package loan.
    d. wraparound loan.

12. Funds for Federal Housing Administration (FHA) loans are usually provided by

    a. the Federal Housing Administration (FHA).
    b. the Federal Reserve.
    c. qualified lenders.
    d. the seller.

13. Under the provisions of the Truth-in-Lending Act (Regulation Z) the annual percentage rate (APR) of a finance charge includes all of the following components *except*

    a. discount points.
    b. broker's commission.
    c. loan origination fee.
    d. loan interest rate.

14. An annual insurance fee of ¼ percent on the unpaid balance would most likely be used with which of the following types of mortgages?

    a. A privately insured conventional loan
    b. An FHA-insured loan
    c. A VA-guaranteed loan
    d. A purchase-money mortgage

15. A home is purchased using a fixed-rate, fully amortized mortgage loan. Which of the following is true regarding this mortgage?

    a. A balloon payment will be made at the end of the loan.
    b. Each payment amount is the same.
    c. Each payment reduces the principal by the same amount.
    d. The principal amount in each payment is greater than the interest amount.

16. Which of the following *best* defines the secondary market?

    a. Lenders who deal exclusively in second mortgages
    b. Where loans are bought and sold after they have been originated
    c. The major lender of residential mortgages and deeds of trust
    d. The major lender of FHA and VA loans

17. A borrower obtains a mortgage loan to make repairs on her home. The loan is not insured or guaranteed by a government agency, and the mortgage document secures the amount of the loan as well as any future funds advanced to the borrower by the lender. This borrower has obtained a(n)

    a. wraparound mortgage.
    b. conventional loan.
    c. open-end loan.
    d. growing-equity mortgage.

18. A graduated-payment mortgage

    a. allows for smaller payments to be made in the early years of the loan.
    b. allows for the debt's interest rate to increase or decrease from time to time, depending on certain economic factors.
    c. is also called a growing-equity mortgage.
    d. must be insured by the Federal Housing Administration.

19. With a fully amortized mortgage or deed of trust loan
    a. interest may be charged in arrears, meaning at the end of each period for which interest is due.
    b. the interest portion of each payment remains the same throughout the entire term of the loan.
    c. interest only is paid each period.
    d. a portion of the principal will be owed after the last payment is made.

20. Freddie Mac
    a. mortgages are guaranteed by the full faith and credit of the federal government.
    b. buys and pools blocks of conventional mortgages, selling bonds with such mortgages as security.
    c. can act in tandem with GNMA to provide special assistance in times of tight money.
    d. buys and sells VA and FHA mortgages.

21. The federal Equal Credit Opportunity Act prohibits lenders from discriminating against potential borrowers on the basis of all of the following *except*
    a. race.
    b. sex.
    c. source of income.
    d. amount of income.

22. A borrower obtains a $76,000 mortgage loan at 10½ percent interest. If the monthly payments of $695.21 are credited first to interest and then to principal, what will the balance of the principal be after the borrower makes the first payment?
    a. $75,335.00
    b. $75,943.33
    c. $75,969.79
    d. $75,304.79

16 Leases

LEASING REAL ESTATE

A **lease** is a contract between an owner of real estate (the **lessor**) and a tenant (the **lessee**) that transfers the rights to exclusive possession and use of the owner's property to the tenant for a specified period of time. This agreement sets forth the length of time the contract is to run, the amount the lessee is to pay for the use of the property and other rights and obligations of the parties.

In effect the lease agreement is a combination of a conveyance of an interest in the real estate and a contract to pay rent and assume other obligations. The lessor grants the lessee the right to occupy the real estate and use it for purposes stated in the lease. In return the landlord receives payment for the use of the premises and retains a **reversionary right** to possession after the lease term has expired. The lessor's interest is called a *leased fee estate plus reversionary right.*

The statute of frauds in most states requires lease agreements to be in writing to be enforceable if they are for more than one year or leases for one year or less that cannot be performed within one year of their making. Generally verbal leases for one year or less that can be performed within a year of their making are enforceable. Written leases should be signed by both lessor and lessee.

IN PRACTICE. . .

Even though a particular lease may be enforceable if agreed to orally, such as a lease for one year commencing the day of agreement, it is always better practice to put lease agreements in writing and to have the writing signed by all parties to the agreement. The lease document should be as inclusive as possible.

LEASEHOLD ESTATES

As mentioned in Chapter 6, the tenant's right to possess the real estate for the term of the lease is called a **leasehold** (less-than-freehold) **estate.** A leasehold is generally considered personal property. When the tenant assumes many of the landowner's obligations under a lease for life or for more than 99 years, certain states give the tenant some of the benefits and privileges of ownership.

Table 16.1 Leasehold Estates	Type of Estate	Distinguishing Characteristic
	Estate for years	For a definite period of time
	Estate from period to period	For a definite period initially, but continues indefinitely until terminated
	Estate at will	For an indefinite period of time
	Estate at sufferance	Without landlord's consent

As there are several types of freehold (ownership) estates (covered in Chapter 6), there are also various leasehold estates (see Table 16.1).

Estate for Years

An **estate (tenancy) for years** is a leasehold estate that continues for a *definite period of time,* whether for years, months, weeks or even days. An estate for years (sometimes referred to as an *estate for term*) always has specific starting and ending dates. When that period expires, the lessee is required to vacate the premises and surrender possession to the lessor. No notice is required to terminate the lease because the lease agreement states a specific expiration date. If both parties agree, the lease for years may be terminated prior to the expiration date. Otherwise neither party may terminate without showing that the lease agreement has been breached. Any extension of the tenancy requires the negotiation of a new contract, unless the original agreement provides for the conversion to a periodic tenancy. As is characteristic of all leases, a tenancy for years gives the lessee the right to occupy and use the leased property according to the terms and covenants contained in the lease agreement.

Estate from Period to Period

An **estate from period to period,** or *periodic tenancy,* is created when the landlord and tenant enter into an agreement *for an indefinite time without a specific expiration date.* These tenancies are created *initially to run for a definite amount of time*—for instance, month to month, week to week, or year to year—*but continue indefinitely until proper notice of termination is given.* Rent is payable at definite intervals. The tenancies are characterized by continuity because they are automatically renewable under the original terms of the agreement for similar succeeding periods until one of the parties gives notice to terminate. In effect, the payment and acceptance of rent extends the lease for another period. A **month-to-month tenancy** is, for example, created when a tenant takes possession with no definite termination date and pays rent on a monthly basis. Periodic tenancy is commonly used in residential leases.

An estate from period to period also might be created when a tenant with an estate for years remains in possession, or holds over, after the expiration of the lease term. If no new lease agreement has been made, a **holdover tenancy** is created. The landlord may evict the tenant or treat the holdover tenant as a periodic tenancy. The landlord's acceptance of rent usually is considered conclusive proof of acquiescence to the periodic tenancy. The courts customarily rule that a tenant who holds over can do so for a term equal to the term of the original lease, provided the period is for one year or less. For example, a tenant with a lease for six months would be entitled to a new six-month tenancy. However, if the original lease were for five years, the holdover tenancy could not exceed one year. Some leases stipulate that in the absence of a renewal agreement, a tenant who holds over does so as a month-to-month tenant. In a few states a holdover tenancy is considered a tenancy at will (discussed below).

To *terminate* a periodic estate either the landlord or the tenant must give *proper notice.* The form of the notice and the time at which it must be given are usually defined in state statutes. Normally to terminate an estate from week to week, one week's notice is required; to terminate an estate from month to month, one or two months' notice is required. For an estate from year to year the requirements vary widely—usually a minimum of two months' and a maximum of six months' notice.

Estate at Will

An **estate** (tenancy) **at will** gives the tenant the right to possess with the *consent of the landlord* for a term of unspecified or uncertain duration. The term of an estate at will is indefinite until it is terminated by either party giving proper notice. No definite initial period is specified, as is the case in a periodic tenancy. An estate at will is automatically terminated by the death of either the landlord or the tenant. It may be created by express agreement or by operation of law and during its existence, the tenant has all the rights and obligations of a lessor-lessee relationship, including payment of rent at regular intervals.

As a practical matter, tenancy at will is rarely used in a written agreement and is viewed skeptically by the courts. Most likely it will be interpreted as a periodic tenancy—the period being defined by the interval of rental payments.

Estate at Sufferance

An **estate** (tenancy) **at sufferance** arises when a tenant who was lawfully in possession of real property continues in possession of the premises *without the consent of the landlord* after the rights have expired. This estate can arise when a tenant for years *fails to surrender* possession at the expiration of the lease. A tenancy at sufferance can occur *by operation of law* when a borrower continues in possession after the foreclosure sale and expiration of the redemption period.

STANDARD LEASE PROVISIONS

Most states require no special wording to establish the landlord-tenant relationship. The lease may be written, oral or implied, depending on the circumstances and the requirements of the statute of frauds. The law of the state where the real estate is located must be followed to assure the validity of the lease. Figure 16.1 is an example of a typical lease.

Once a valid lease has been executed, the lessor, as the owner of the real estate, is usually bound by the implied *covenant* of *quiet enjoyment.* That is, the lessor guarantees that the lessee may take possession of the leased premises and that the landlord will not interfere in the tenant's possession or use of the property. The lease may, however, allow the landlord to reenter, with the tenant's permission, to do maintenance, repairs or for other stated purposes.

The requirements for a valid lease are essentially the same as those for any other contract as discussed in Chapter 10.

- *Offer and acceptance.* The parties must reach a mutual agreement on all the terms of the contract.

**Figure 16.1
Sample Lease**

GENERAL LEASE
COMMERCIAL OR RESIDENTIAL

THIS LEASE, made and entered into this _____ day of _____, 19_____, by and between

_____ the lessor, and

_____ _____ , the lessee.

WITNESSETH: That the lessor, in consideration of the covenants of said lease hereinafter set forth, does by these presents lease to said lessee, under the terms and conditions set forth, the premises described as follows: _____

_____

_____

1. TERMS
That the term of said lease is for a period of _____ years, commencing on the _____ day of _____ 19_____

and ending on the _____ day of _____, 19_____.

2. RENTS
That the total rents for said lease shall be the sum of $_____, payable in _____ installments of $_____

each, plus any excise, privilege or sales taxes levied by a political subdivision, for an additional sum of $_____ per _____

Total rents and applicable taxes, if any, equal the sum of $_____ per _____

3. SECURITY DEPOSIT
Lessee has paid, upon the execution hereof, the amount of $_____, as security for the performance of the terms and conditions of this lease, which said sums shall be returned to lessee at the termination of this lease if the obligations of this lease have been fully discharged

4. USE OF PREMISES
The premises described above are leased to lessee for the sole purpose of _____
_____ And lessee agrees that the premises will be used only for such activity, complying fully with all applicable laws, ordinances or regulations regarding the use of the leased premises, including all sanitary and health regulations.

5. INSURANCE
a) Lessee shall obtain and continue in force during the term of this lease, a policy or policies of Insurance covering: (1) Loss or damages by fire or other perils to the appliances, contents, equipment, fixtures, furniture, interior motif or decor, and/or stock in trade, (2) Injury or death to any person or persons including lessee, (3) Vandalism, and/or malicious mischief.

b) Lessor shall obtain and continue in force during the term of this lease, a policy or policies of Insurance covering loss or damages to the premises by fire or other perils in the amount of the full replacement value thereof.

c) Lessee agrees to provide lessor with a memorandum copy of all Insurance Policies so obtained under this lease, and additionally name lessor as an additional assured party.

6. REPAIRS
a) Lessor agrees to make all necessary repairs to the exterior walls, doors, windows, roof and/or any other exterior features of the premises including air conditioning, heating and lighting equipment.

b) Lessee agrees to make all necessary repairs to the interior portions of the premises including any extraordinary damages to the electrical or plumbing facilities.

7. ALTERATIONS OR IMPROVEMENTS
Lessee may make improvements or other alterations in the interior of the leased premises at his (her) (its) own expense, provided, however, that prior to commencing any such work, lessee shall first obtain written consent from lessor. Such improvements or alterations shall remain the property of the **lessor** at the termination of this lease.

8. SERVICES/UTILITIES
Lessor agrees to provide the following utilities or other services to lessee, to wit: _____
_____

9. ASSIGNMENT/SUBLETTING
Lessee agrees that he (she) (it) will not assign or sublet in whole or part any portion of the leased premises without the prior written consent of lessor, which said consent will not be unreasonably withheld. Lessor may sell, transfer, or assign all or any part of his (her) (its) interest in the premises without the consent of the lessee.

10. INJURY OR LOSS
Lessor shall not be responsible or liable for any loss, theft, or damage to property or injury to, or death of, Lessee or any person on or about the leased premises, and Lessee agrees to indemnify, defend and hold Lessor harmless therefrom.

11. ENTRY OF LANDLORD
Lessor reserves the right to enter upon the leased premises at reasonable times for the purpose of inspecting the premises, and reserves the right, during the last two months of the term of the lease, to show the premises at reasonable times to prospective tenants, providing lessee has not tendered a written intent to Lessor of renewing said lease, or an intention to negotiate a new lease for the premises.

12. RENEWAL OF LEASE
Lessor agrees to entertain an intention by Lessee to renew this lease at its expiration thereof, provided the same is made at least ninety (90) days prior to the expiration of this lease. Such renewal shall be accomplished either by an addendum to this lease or the execution of a new lease upon such terms and conditions as may be required by Lessor

©1986, ALPHA ENTERPRISES OF ARIZONA — P.O. Box 26326 — Tucson, AZ 85726   FORM 101

**Figure 16.1
(continued)**

13. BREACH

a) The failure of either party to fully perform under any or all of the terms and conditions of this lease shall constitute a Breach of this lease, entitling the offended party to take any and all such action provided by law, including, but not limited to, one or more of the following: (1) Lock the doors to the leased premises, (2) Retain or take possession of any property on the premises pursuant to Lessor's Landlord Lien, (3) Enter the premises and remove all persons and property therefrom, (4) Declare the lease at an end and terminated, (5) Sue for the full balance due under the lease, and any damages sustained by Lessor.

b) Any breach alleged under this lease, shall be occasioned by a ten (10) day written notice of the same to the defaulting party. If at the end of such ten (10) days as provided in said notice, the defaulting party has not cured the breach, the offending party may take any and all such action provided by law, including an additional amount for Attorney's fees and cost.

14. SURRENDER OF PREMISES

Lessee shall, upon the expiration of the term of the Lease, or upon an earlier termination hereof, quit and surrender the premises in good order or condition and repair, reasonable wear and tear and acts of God excepted.

15. SIGNS/DECALS/POSTERS

Lessee agrees that he (she) (it) will not place, affix, or otherwise install any decals, posters, signs or other advertising, artistic, commemorative or communicative illustrations without the written consent of Lessor. If consent is so given, any such installations shall be at Lessee's expense.

16. SAVINGS CLAUSE

If any term or provision of this Lease or any application thereof shall be declared or held to be invalid or unenforceable, then the remaining terms and provisions of this Lease shall not be affected thereby.

17. OTHER CONDITIONS

_____

_____

_____

18. NOTICES

a) Any notices or demands to be given hereunder shall be given to Lessor at _____

_____

b) The person or firm authorized to manage this property is _____

_____

IN WITNESS WHEREOF, the parties have hereunto set their hands, or caused this Lease to be executed by their authorized agent this _____ day of

_____, 19_____.

_____   _____
            LESSEE   LESSOR

_____   _____
            LESSEE   LESSOR

A copy of the foregoing Lease was received by Lessee/Authorized Agent this _____ day of _____, 19_____.

                                              _____
                                                          LESSEE

- *Consideration.* All leases, being contracts, must be supported by valid consideration. *Rent* is the normal consideration given for the right to occupy the leased premises; however, the payment of rent is not essential as long as consideration was granted in creation of the lease itself (sometimes, this consideration is labor performed on the property). Because a lease is a contract, it is not subject to subsequent changes in the rent or other terms unless these changes are in writing and executed in the same manner as the original lease.

- *Capacity to contract.* The parties must have the legal capacity to contract.

- *Legal objectives.* The objectives of the lease must be legal.

The leased premises should be clearly described. The legal description of the real estate should be used if the lease covers land, such as a ground lease. If the lease is for a part of a building, such as office space or an apartment, the space itself or the apartment designation should be described specifically. If supplemental space is to be included, the lease should clearly identify it.

Use of Premises

A lessor may restrict a lessee's use of the premises through provisions included in the lease. Such restrictions are most important in leases for stores or commercial space. For example, a lease may provide that the leased premises are to be used only as a real estate office *and for no other purpose.* In the absence of such limitations a lessee may use the premises for any *lawful* purpose.

Term of Lease

The term of a lease is the period for which the lease will run. It should be stated precisely, including the beginning and ending date together with a statement of the total period of the lease: for example, "for a term of 30 years beginning June 1, 1993, and ending May 31, 2023." Perpetual leases for an inordinate amount of time or an indefinite term will be ruled invalid unless the language of the lease and the surrounding circumstances clearly indicate that the parties intend such a term. Some states, in fact, prohibit leases that run for more than 99 years.

Security Deposit

Most leases require the tenant to provide some form of **security deposit** to be held by the landlord during the lease term. If the tenant defaults on payment of rent or destroys the premises, the lessor may keep all or part of the deposit to compensate for the loss. Some state laws set maximum amounts for security deposits and specify how they must be handled. Some prohibit security deposits from being used for both nonpayment of rent and property damage. Some require that lessees receive annual interest on their security deposits.

Other safeguards against nonpayment of rent may include an advance rental payment, contracting for a lien on the tenant's property or requiring the tenant to have a third person guarantee payment.

IN PRACTICE. . . | *A lease should specify whether a payment is a security deposit or an advance rental. If it is a security deposit, the tenant is usually not entitled to apply it to the final month's rent. If it is an advance rental, the landlord must treat it as income for tax purposes.*

LEGAL PRINCIPLES OF LEASES

Possession of leased premises is considered constructive notice to the world of the lessee's leasehold interests, and anyone who inspects the property receives actual notice. For these reasons recording a lease is usually considered unnecessary. However, most states do allow leases to be recorded in the county where the property is located, and leases of three years or longer often are recorded. Some states *require* long-term leases to be recorded, especially when the lessee intends to mortgage the leasehold interest.

In some states only a *memorandum of lease* is filed. This gives notice of the interest but does not disclose the terms of the lease. The only required information is the names of the parties and a description of the property.

Possession of Leased Premises

As noted earlier, leases carry the implied covenant that the landlord will give the tenant enjoyment (possession) of the premises. If the premises are occupied by a holdover tenant or adverse claimant at the beginning of the new lease period, in most states the landlord must bring whatever action is necessary to recover actual possession and bear the expense of this action. In a few states, however, the landlord is bound only to give the tenant the right of possession; it is the tenant who must bring any court action necessary to secure actual possession.

Improvements

Neither the landlord nor the tenant is required to make any improvements to the leased property. In the absence of an agreement to the contrary, the tenant may make improvements with the landlord's permission. Any such alterations generally become the property of the landlord; that is, they become fixtures. However, as discussed in Chapter 2, the lease may give a tenant the right to install trade fixtures. It is customary to allow the tenant to remove the trade fixtures before the lease expires, provided the tenant restores the premises to their previous condition.

Maintenance of Premises

Historically a landlord was not obligated to make any repairs to leased premises. However, many states now require a residential lessor to maintain dwelling units in a habitable condition and to make any necessary repairs to common areas, such as hallways, stairs or elevators, and to safety features, such as fire sprinklers and smoke alarms. The tenant does not have to make any repairs, but must return the premises in the same condition they were received, with allowances for ordinary wear and tear.

Assignment and Subleasing

Assignment and subleasing are permitted whenever the lease does not prohibit it. A tenant who transfers all of his or her leasehold interests *assigns* the lease. One who transfers less than all of the leasehold interests by leasing them to a new tenant **subleases** (see Figure 16.2).

In most cases the sublease or assignment of a lease does not relieve the original lessee of the obligation to make rental payments unless the landlord agrees to waive such liability. Most leases prohibit the lessee from assigning or subletting without the lessor's consent. The lessor thus retains control over the occupancy of the leased premises but must not unreasonably withhold consent. The sublessor's (original lessee's) interest in the real estate is known as a *sandwich lease*.

**Figure 16.2
Assignment versus
subletting**

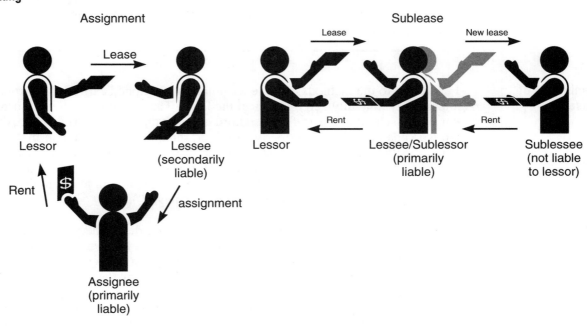

Assignment

Lessor — Lease → Lessee (secondarily liable)

Rent ↑ $ ↗ assignment

Assignee (primarily liable)

Sublease

Lessor — Lease → Lessee/Sublessor (primarily liable) — New lease → Sublessee (not liable to lessor)

← Rent ← Rent

Options

A lease may contain an *option* that grants the lessee the privilege of *renewing* the lease. The lessee must, however, give *notice* before a specific date of the intention to exercise the option. Some leases grant the lessee the *option to purchase* the leased premises. This option normally allows the tenant the right to purchase the property at a predetermined price within a certain time period, possibly the lease term. Although it is not required, the owner may give the tenant credit toward the purchase price for some of the rent paid. The lease agreement is a primary contract over the option to purchase. Option contracts were discussed in Chapter 10.

Destruction of Premises

In leases involving *agricultural land* the courts have held that when the improvements are damaged or destroyed, even if not the tenant's fault, the tenant is not relieved from the obligation to pay rent to the end of the term. This ruling has been extended in most states to include *ground leases* on which the tenant has constructed a building. In many instances it also includes leases that give possession of an entire building to the tenant, in which case the tenant is leasing the land on which that building is located as well.

A tenant who is leasing only a part of the building, such as office or commercial space or an apartment, is *not* required to continue to pay rent upon destruction of the leased premises. In some states, if the property was destroyed as a result of the landlord's negligence, the tenant can recover damages from the landlord.

IN PRACTICE. . .	*All of these general statements concerning destruction of leased premises are controlled largely by the terms of the lease. Printed lease forms and all carefully prepared leases usually include a provision covering destruction of the premises. Great care must be exercised in reading the entire lease document before signing it.*

Termination of Lease

In addition to the methods of lease termination mentioned earlier, the parties to a lease may mutually agree to cancel the lease. The tenant may offer to surrender the leasehold interest; if the landlord accepts, the lease is terminated. A tenant who abandons leased property, however, remains liable for the terms of the lease—including the rent. The terms of the lease will usually indicate whether the landlord is obligated to try to rerent the space. If the landlord intends to sue for unpaid rent, however, most states will require an attempt to rerent the premises to limit the amount owed (to "mitigate damages").

The lease *does not terminate* if the parties to a lease die or the property is sold. There are two exceptions: a lease from the owner of a life estate ends upon the death of that person, and the death of either party terminates a tenancy at will. Otherwise the heirs of a deceased landlord are bound by the terms of existing valid leases. *In addition, if a landlord conveys leased real estate, the new landlord takes the property subject to the rights of the tenants.* A lease agreement may, however, require a new landlord, after taking title, to give some period of notice to the tenant to terminate an existing lease. This is commonly known as a *sale clause.* Because the new owner has taken title subject to the rights of the tenant, the sale clause enables the new landlord to claim possession and/or negotiate new leases under his or her own terms and conditions.

A tenancy may be terminated by operation of law, as in a bankruptcy or condemnation proceeding.

Breach of Lease

When a tenant breaches any lease provision, the landlord may sue the tenant to obtain a judgment to cover past due rent, damages to the premises or other defaults. Likewise, when a landlord breaches any lease provision, the tenant is entitled to certain remedies.

Suit for possession—actual eviction. When a tenant breaches a lease or improperly retains possession of leased premises, the landlord may regain possession through a **suit for possession.** This process is known as **actual eviction.** The law requires the landlord to serve *notice* on the tenant before commencing the suit. Most lease terms require at least a ten-day notice in the case of *default,* but in many states only a five-day notice must be given when it is a default in payment of rent. When a court issues a judgment for possession to a landlord, the tenant must leave peaceably and take all belongings. Otherwise the landlord can have the judgment enforced by a *bailiff* or other court officer, who will *forcibly remove* the tenant and the tenant's possessions. The landlord then has the right to reenter and regain possession of the property.

Until such a judgment is issued, the landlord must be careful not to harass the tenant in any manner, such as by locking the tenant out of the property, impounding the tenant's possessions or disconnecting utility service (such as electricity and natural gas) making the property unusable.

Tenants' remedies—constructive eviction. If a landlord breaches any clause of a lease agreement, the tenant has the right to sue, claiming a judgment for damages against the landlord. If an action or omission on the landlord's part results in the leased premises becoming unusable for the purpose stated in the lease, the tenant may have the right to abandon the premises. This action, called **constructive eviction,** terminates the lease agreement if the tenant can prove that the premises have become unusable because of the conscious neglect of the landlord. To claim constructive eviction *the tenant must leave the premises* while the conditions that made the premises uninhabitable exist.

For example, a lease requires the landlord to furnish heat; because of the landlord's failure to repair a defective heating plant, the heat is not provided. If this results in the leased premises becoming uninhabitable, the tenant may abandon them. Some leases provide that accidental failure to furnish heat that is not the landlord's fault is not grounds for constructive eviction.

Pro-Tenant Legislation

For the most part leases are drawn up primarily for the benefit of the landlord. However, recent consumer awareness has fostered the belief that a valid lease depends on both parties' fulfillment of certain obligations. To provide laws outlining such obligations several states have adopted some variation of the *Uniform Residential Landlord and Tenant Act.* This model law addresses such issues as the landlord's right of entry and maintenance of premises, the tenant's protection against retaliation by the landlord for complaints and the disclosure of the property owners' names and addresses to the tenants. The act further sets down specific remedies available to both the landlord and the tenant if a breach of the lease agreement occurs.

The federal Tenants' Eviction Procedures Act of 1976 establishes standardized eviction procedures for people living in *government-subsidized housing.* It requires the landlord to have a valid reason for evicting the tenant and to give the tenant proper notice of eviction. This act does not supersede state laws; however, it does provide recourse for tenants in states that have no such laws. The act applies only to multiunit residential buildings owned or subsidized by the Department of Housing and Urban Development and to buildings that have government-backed mortgages.

CIVIL RIGHTS LAWS

The fair housing laws affect landlords and tenants just as they do sellers and purchasers. All persons must have access to housing of their choice without any differentiation in the terms and conditions because of their race, color, religion, national origin, sex, handicap or familial status. State and local municipalities may have their own fair housing laws that add protected classes such as age and sexual orientation. Withholding an apartment that is available for rent, segregating certain persons in separate sections of an apartment complex or parts of a building and charging different amounts for rent or security deposits to persons in the protected classes are examples of violations of the law. The fair housing laws are discussed in greater detail in Chapter 21.

Table 16.2 Types of Leases	Type of Lease	Lessee	Lessor
	Gross lease	Pays basic rent	Pays property charges (taxes, repairs, insurance, etc.)
	Net lease	Pays basic rent plus all or most property charges	May pay some property charges
	Percentage lease (commercial industrial)	Pays basic rent plus percent of gross sales (may pay property costs)	

It is important that landlords realize that changes in the laws stemming from the federal Fair Housing Amendments Act of 1988 significantly alter past practices, particularly as they affect individuals with disabilities and families with children. Persons with disabilities must be afforded the opportunity to make alterations that enable them to enjoy the property. They are entitled to have access to the same services as other persons. Families with children have, in the past, had difficulty finding suitable rentals because many landlords refused to accept children. Under the laws today, if a landlord has determined, for example, that an apartment is suitable for two people, then the apartment must be available to any two people—two adults or one adult and one child. The landlord cannot charge a different amount of rent or security deposit because one of the tenants is a child. While landlords have historically argued that children are noisy or destructive, a better question is "Aren't some adults noisy or destructive?" The fair housing laws require that the same tenant criteria be applied to families with children as well as to adults.

The Americans with Disabilities Act (ADA, discussed in greater detail in Chapter 17) also impacts leasing practices. A property in which public services and goods are provided must be free of architectural barriers or provide accommodations so that individuals with disabilities can patronize those businesses or access the services. Landlords of nonresidential properties should be familiar with the requirements of the ADA. They are responsible for ensuring that their buildings comply with the law.

TYPES OF LEASES

The manner in which rent is determined indicates the type of lease that exists (see Table 16.2).

In a **gross lease** the tenant pays a *fixed rental,* and the landlord pays all taxes, insurance, repairs, utilities and the like connected with the property (usually called *property charges or operating expenses*).

Net Lease

In a **net lease** the *tenant pays all or some of the property charges* in addition to the rent. The monthly rental is net income for the landlord after operating costs have been paid. Leases for entire commercial or industrial buildings and the land on which they are located, ground leases and long-term leases are usually net leases.

MATH CONCEPT
Calculating Percentage Lease Rents

Percentage leases usually call for a minimum monthly rent plus a percentage of gross sales income over a stated annual amount. For example, a lease might require minimum rent of $1,300 per month plus 5 percent of the business's sales over $160,000. On an annual sales volume of $250,000, the annual rent would be calculated as follows:

$$\$1,300 \text{ per month} \times 12 \text{ months} = \$15,600$$

$$\$250,000 - \$160,000 = \$90,000; \$90,000 \times .05 \ (5\%) = \$4,500$$

$$\$15,600 \text{ base rent} + \$4,500 \text{ percentage rent} = \$20,100 \text{ total rent}$$

In a *triple net lease,* or *net-net-net lease,* the tenant pays all operating and other expenses, such as taxes, insurance, assessments, maintenance utilities and other charges, in addition to periodic rent.

Percentage Lease

Either a gross lease or a net lease may be a **percentage lease.** The rent is based on a *percentage of the gross income* received by the tenant doing business on the leased property. This type of lease is usually used for retail businesses.

Under a percentage lease the lessee pays a minimum fixed rental fee plus a percentage of that portion of the tenant's business income that exceeds a stated minimum. The percentage charged varies widely with the nature of the business, the location of the property and general economic conditions. It is negotiable between landlord and tenant. A tenant's bargaining power is determined by the volume of the business.

Other Lease Types

Variable leases. Several types of leases allow for increases in the rental charge during the lease period. One of the more common is the *graduated lease,* which provides for increases in rent at set future dates in specified amounts. Another is the *index lease,* which allows rent to be increased or decreased periodically based on changes in the consumer price index or some other index agreed to by the landlord and tenant.

Ground lease. When a landowner leases unimproved land to a tenant who agrees to *erect a building* on the land, the lease is usually referred to as a **ground lease.** Ground leases usually involve separate ownership of land and building. These leases must be for a long enough term to make the transaction desirable to the tenant investing in the building. Ground leases are generally *net leases* that require the lessee to pay rent on the ground as well as real estate taxes, insurance, upkeep and repairs. Such leases often run for terms of 50 years or longer, and a lease for 99 years is not impossible.

Oil and gas leases. When oil companies lease land to explore for oil and gas, a special lease agreement must be negotiated. Usually the landowner receives a cash payment for executing the lease. If no well is drilled within the period stated in the lease, the lease expires; however, most oil and gas leases permit the oil company to continue its rights for another year by paying another flat rental fee. Such rentals may be paid annually until a well is produced. If oil and/or gas is found, the landowner usually receives one-eighth of its value as a royalty. In this case the lease will continue for as long as oil or gas is obtained in significant quantities.

A **lease purchase** is used when a tenant who wants to purchase the property but is unable to do so still needs the use of the leased facility. Perhaps the tenant is currently unable to obtain favorable financing or obtain clear title. Or maybe the tax consequences of a current purchase would be unfavorable. Here the purchase agreement is the primary consideration and the lease is secondary.

Agricultural landowners often lease their land to tenant farmers, who provide the labor to produce and bring in the crop. The owner can be paid by the tenant in one of two ways: as an agreed-on rental amount in cash in advance (**cash rents**) or as a percentage of the profits from the sale of the crop when it is sold (**sharecropping**).

●   ●   ●   ●   ●   ●   ●

KEY TERMS

actual eviction   lessee
cash rent   lease purchase
constructive eviction   leasehold estate
estate at sufferance   month-to-month tenancy
estate at will   net lease
estate for years   percentage lease
estate from period to period   reversionary right
gross leases   security deposit
ground lease   sharecropping
holdover tenancy   sublease
lease   suit for possession
lessor

SUMMARY

A lease is an agreement that grants one person the right to use the property of another in return for consideration.

A leasehold estate that runs for a specific length of time creates an estate for years; one that runs for an indefinite period creates an estate from period to period (year to year, month to month). An estate at will runs as long as the landlord permits, and an estate at sufferance is possession without the consent of the landlord. A leasehold estate is classified as personal property.

The requirements of a valid lease include offer and acceptance, consideration, capacity to contract and legal objectives. In addition, state statutes of frauds generally require that any lease that will not be completed within one year of the date of its making must be in writing to be enforceable in court. Most leases also include clauses relating to rights and obligations of the landlord and tenant such as the use of the premises, subletting, judgments, maintenance of the premises and termination of the lease period.

Leases may be terminated by the expiration of the lease period, the mutual agreement of the parties or a breach of the lease by either landlord or tenant. In most cases neither the death of the tenant nor the landlord's sale of the rental property terminates a lease.

If the tenant defaults on any of the lease provisions, the landlord may sue for a money judgment or for actual eviction. If the premises have become uninhabitable due to the landlord's negligence or failure to correct within a reasonable time, the tenant may have the remedy of constructive eviction, that is, the right to abandon the premises and refuse to pay rent until the premises are repaired.

The fair housing laws protect the rights of tenants. Besides prohibiting discrimination on the basis of race, color, religion, national origin and sex, the laws address the rights of individuals with disabilities and families with children.

The Americans with Disabilities Act provides for access to goods and services by people with disabilities.

There are several basic types of leases, including net leases, gross leases and percentage leases. These leases are classified according to the method used in determining the rental rate of the property.

Questions

1. A ground lease is usually
   a. short-term.
   b. for 100 years or longer.
   c. long-term.
   d. a gross lease.

2. A percentage lease is a lease that provides for a
   a. rental of a percentage of the value of a building.
   b. definite periodic rent not exceeding a stated percentage.
   c. definite minimum monthly rent plus a percentage of the tenant's gross receipts in excess of a certain amount.
   d. graduated amount due monthly and not exceeding a stated percentage.

3. If several tenants moved out of a rented store building because the building collapsed
   a. this would be an actual eviction.
   b. the tenants would be liable for the rent until the expiration date of their leases.
   c. the landlord would have to provide substitute space.
   d. this would be a constructive eviction.

4. The tenant's written five-year lease with monthly rental payments expired last month, but the tenant has remained in possession and the landlord has accepted his most recent rent payment without comment. At this point
   a. the tenant is a holdover tenant.
   b. the tenant's lease has been renewed for another five years.
   c. the tenant's lease has been renewed for another month.
   d. the tenant is a tenant at sufferance.

5. A lease for two years must be in writing because
   a. either party may forget the terms.
   b. the tenant must sign the agreement to pay rent.
   c. the statute of frauds requires it.
   d. it is the customary procedure to protect the tenant.

6. A tenant who transfers the entire remaining term of the lease to a third party is
   a. a sublessor.
   b. assigning the lease.
   c. automatically relieved of any further obligation under it.
   d. giving the third party a sandwich lease.

7. A tenant's lease has expired. The tenant has neither vacated nor negotiated a renewal lease, and the landlord has declared that she does not want the tenant to remain in the building. The tenancy is called a(n)
   a. estate for years.
   b. periodic estate.
   c. estate at will.
   d. estate at sufferance.

8. A tenant has a lease that will expire in two weeks. At that time he will move into larger quarters on the other side of town. To terminate this agreement
   a. the tenant must give his landlord prior notice.
   b. the landlord must give the tenant prior notice.
   c. nothing needs to be done—the agreement will terminate automatically.
   d. the agreement will terminate only after both parties renegotiate the original agreement.

9. When a tenant holds possession of a land-lord's property without a current lease agreement and without the landlord's approval

    a. the tenant is maintaining a gross lease.
    b. the landlord can file suit for possession.
    c. the tenant has no obligation to pay rent.
    d. the landlord may be subject to a constructive eviction.

10. Under the terms of a residential lease the landlord is required to maintain the water heater. If a tenant is unable to get hot water because of a faulty water heater that the landlord has failed to repair, all of the following remedies would be available to the tenant *except* that the tenant can

    a. sue the landlord for damages.
    b. sue the landlord for back rent.
    c. abandon the premises under constructive eviction.
    d. terminate the lease agreement.

11. The leasehold interest that automatically renews itself at each expiration is the

    a. tenancy for years.
    b. tenancy from period to period.
    c. tenancy at will.
    d. tenancy at sufferance.

12. K has leased space in her shopping center to B for B's dress store. However, B's business fails and she sublets the space to D. If D does not make her rental payments when they are due

    a. K will have recourse against B only.
    b. K will have recourse against D only.
    c. K will have recourse against both B and D.
    d. D will have recourse against B.

13. Which of the following would most likely terminate a lease?

    a. The destruction of the property
    b. The sale of the property
    c. The failure of the tenant to pay the rent
    d. Constructive eviction

14. Which of the following best describes a *net* lease?

    a. An agreement in which the tenant pays a fixed rent and the landlord pays all taxes, insurance, and so forth, on the property
    b. A lease in which the tenant pays rent in addition to some or all operating expenses
    c. A lease in which the tenant pays the landlord a percentage of the monthly income derived from the property
    d. An agreement granting an individual a leasehold interest in fishing rights for shoreline properties

15. A holdover tenancy can also be referred to as

    a. tenancy for years.
    b. periodic tenancy.
    c. tenancy at will.
    d. tenancy at sufferance.

16. A lease calls for a minimum rent of $1,200 per month plus 4 percent of the annual gross business over $150,000. If the total rent paid at the end of one year was $19,200, how much business did the tenant do during the year?

    a. $159,800   c. $270,000
    b. $25,200   d. $169,200

Part Two

PRINCIPLES

17 Property Management

The use of professional property managers for both residential and commercial properties has expanded in recent years as the size of buildings has increased; and construction, maintenance and repair have become more complex. There is also a growing trend toward absentee ownership by individual investors and investment groups. Today many brokerage firms maintain separate departments staffed by carefully selected, well-trained people. Corporate and institutional owners of real estate have also established property management departments. However, many real estate investors still manage their own property and thus must acquire the knowledge and skills of a property manager.

In most states property managers serving the public for a fee must be licensed real estate brokers. In others, property managers must be licensed specifically as property managers.

THE PROPERTY MANAGER

The real estate specialty of property management involves the leasing, managing, marketing and overall maintenance of real estate owned by others. The **property manager** is responsible for the fiscal management (financial affairs), the physical management (structure and grounds) and the administrative management (files and records) for each property being managed. The property manager strives to maintain the investment and income for the owner. The objectives are to merchandise the property and control expenses to maximize income and to maintain and modernize the physical property to preserve and enhance the owner's capital investment. Securing suitable tenants, collecting rents, caring for the physical premises, budgeting and controlling expenses, hiring and supervising employees, keeping proper accounts and making periodic reports to the owner are among the specific tasks of a property manager.

The property manager may be a licensee in a real estate firm or property management company that manages properties for a number of owners under management agreements (discussed later). The property manager has an agency relationship with the owner, which involves greater authority and discretion over the management decisions than an employee would. A property manager or the owner may employ individual building managers to supervise the daily operations of a building. In some case these individuals may be residents of the building.

Securing Management Business

Corporate owners, apartments and condominiums, homeowners' associations, investment syndicates, trusts and absentee owners are possible sources of management business. In securing business from any of these sources, word of mouth is often the property manager's best advertising. A manager who consistently demonstrates the ability to increase property income over previous levels should have little difficulty finding new business.

Before contracting to manage any property, however, the professional property manager should be certain that the building owner has realistic income expectations and is willing to spend money on necessary maintenance. Attempting to meet impossible owner demands by dubious methods can endanger the manager's reputation and prove detrimental to obtaining future business.

The Management Agreement

The first step in taking over the management of any property is to enter into a **management agreement** with the owner (see Figure 17.1). This agreement creates an agency relationship between the owner and the property manager. The property manager usually is considered to be a *general agent,* whereas a real estate broker in a listing agreement is usually considered to be a special agent. As agent, the property manager is charged with the fiduciary responsibilities of care, obedience, accounting, loyalty and disclosure (see Chapter 4). After entering into an agreement with a property owner, a manager handles the property as the owner would. In all activities the manager's first responsibility is to *realize the highest return on the property that is consistent with the owner's instructions.*

The management agreement should be in writing and should cover the following points:

- *Description* of the property
- *Time period* the agreement will cover
- *Definition of management's responsibilities:* All of the manager's duties should be stated in the contract; exceptions should be noted.
- *Statement of owner's purpose:* This statement should indicate what the owner desires the manager to accomplish with the property. One owner may wish to maximize net income and therefore instruct the manager to cut expenses and minimize reinvestment. Another owner may want to increase the capital value of the investment, in which case the manager should initiate a program for improving the property's physical condition.
- *Extent of manager's authority:* This provision should state what authority the manager is to have in matters such as hiring, firing and supervising employees; fixing rental rates for space; making expenditures and authorizing repairs within the limits established previously with the owner. (Repairs that exceed a certain expense limit may require the owner's written approval.)

MATH CONCEPT Rental Commissions	Residential commissions are usually based on the annualized rent from a property. For example, if an apartment unit rents for $475 per month and the commission payable is 8%, the commission will be calculated as follows:

$475 per month × 12 months = $5,700; $5,700 × .08 (8%) = $456

- *Reporting:* Agreement should be reached on the frequency and detail of the manager's periodic reports on operations and financial position. These reports serve as a means for the owner to monitor the manager's work and as a basis for both the owner and the manager to assess trends that can be used in shaping future management policy.

- *Management fee:* The fee can be based on a percentage of gross or net income, a commission on new rentals, a fixed fee or a combination. Management fees are subject to the same antitrust considerations as sales commissions. They cannot be standardized in the marketplace because that would be viewed as price fixing. The fee must be negotiated between the agent and the principal.

- *Allocation of costs:* The agreement should state which of the property manager's expenses, such as office rent, office help, telephone, advertising, association fees and social security, will be paid by the manager and which will be charged to the property's expenses and paid by the owner.

MANAGEMENT FUNCTIONS

A property manager must live up to both the letter and the spirit of the management agreement. The owner must be kept well informed on all matters of policy as well as on the financial condition and the operation of the property.

Budgeting Expenses

Before attempting to rent any property, a property manager should develop an operating budget based on anticipated revenues and expenses and reflecting the long-term goals of the owner. In preparing a budget a manager should begin by allocating money for continuous, fixed expenses such as employees' salaries, real estate taxes, property taxes and insurance premiums. Although budgets should be as accurate an estimate of cost as possible, adjustments may sometimes be necessary, especially in the case of new properties.

Next the manager should establish a cash reserve fund for variable expenses such as repairs, decorating and supplies. The amount allocated for the reserve fund can be computed from the previous yearly costs of the variable expenses.

Capital expenditures. If an owner and a property manager decide that modernization or renovation of the property will enhance its value, the manager should budget money to cover the costs of remodeling. The property manager should be thoroughly familiar with the *principle of contribution* (discussed in Chapter 18) or seek expert advice when estimating any increase in value expected by an improvement. In the case of large-scale construction the expenses charged against the property's income should be spread over several years.

**Figure 17.1
Sample Agreement
to Manage
Real Estate**

AGREEMENT TO MANAGE REAL ESTATE

Between _____, Owner

and

_____, Manager

THIS AGREEMENT dated as of the _____ day of _____,

19____, by and between _____, as

principal (hereinafter collectively referred to as "Owner"), and _____,

a Corporation chartered in the State of _____, hereinafter referred to as

"Manager," as agent, shall be in effect for a period of _____ from date.

WITNESSETH

WHEREAS, Owner owns the tracts of real estate legally described in "Exhibit A" attached hereto and made a part hereof; and

WHEREAS, Owner desires to appoint Manager as Owner's agent to handle, manage and control the real estate described in said "Exhibit A," and also such other real estate as may be added to said "Exhibit A" from time to time by mutual agreement of the parties, hereinafter collectively called "THE PROPERTIES" in accordance with the terms and conditions hereinafter set out.

NOW THEREFORE, in consideration of the premises and the mutual promises and covenants herein contained, Owner and Manager agree as follows:

ARTICLE I

Powers and Duties of the Manager

1.01   Owner hereby appoints Manager as Owner's agent to handle, manage and control THE PROPERTIES and expressly authorizes and empowers Manager as follows:

(a) To advertise THE PROPERTIES for lease and to execute leases covering THE PROPERTIES, or any part thereof, for such rent and upon such terms and conditions as Manager may deem wise and proper, PROVIDED, HOWEVER, that Manager shall not enter into a lease for a period longer than five (5) years from the beginning date of such lease without Owner's written consent.

(b) To collect the rents and revenues from THE PROPERTIES.

(c) To maintain and keep THE PROPERTIES in a reasonable state of repair and to expend such part of the rents and revenues from THE PROPERTIES, which it collects, as may be necessary in so doing; PROVIDED, HOWEVER, Manager shall not spend more than $_____ in repairing any one tract of real estate (or the improvements thereon) constituting THE PROPERTIES during any 12-month period unless and until first receiving the written consent of Owner to do so.

Source: Floyd M. Baird, Tulsa, Oklahoma

Figure 17.1 (continued)

(d) To keep the improvements of THE PROPERTIES insured against the hazards normally covered by fire and extended-coverage insurance policies and rental income insurance and public liability insurance policies in such amounts as Manager may determine to be adequate to protect the interest of Owner.

(e) To pay ad valorem taxes and improvement assessments against THE PROPERTIES before same become delinquent.

(f) To maintain out of the rents and revenues collected from THE PROPERTIES such reserves as Manager may deem wise and proper.

(g) To employ such attorneys, agents, contractors and workmen as Manager may deem wise and proper in connection with the handling, managing and control of THE PROPERTIES.

(h) To adjust and compromise any claim that may be asserted with respect to THE PROPERTIES and/or which may arise in connection with the management of THE PROPERTIES and to give binding releases in connection therewith.

(i) Generally, to handle, manage and control THE PROPERTIES and to execute such agreements, contracts or other documents or do such other acts or things as Manager, from time to time, may deem wise and proper to carry out the duties stated in this Agreement.

1.02   Manager shall keep proper books of account of this agency, which said books shall be open to inspection by Owner during the regular business hours of the Manager. Manager need not maintain segregated bank accounts relating to THE PROPERTIES, but the books and records shall reflect at all times the rents and revenues received and the disbursements made as to each tract of real estate comprising THE PROPERTIES. Accounts shall be kept in compliance with all applicable state laws. At such periodic intervals as Owner shall request, but not more frequently than monthly, Manager shall furnish to Owner a statement showing the rents and revenues received, the disbursements made and the other transactions had with respect to THE PROPERTIES for the period indicated by Owner.

1.03   Manager may continue to hold THE PROPERTIES to be handled, managed and controlled in accordance with the terms and conditions of this Agreement without liability or depreciation or loss, and the liability of Manager shall be limited to reasonable diligence in exercising the powers and authorities herein granted.

1.04   Manager is not authorized by this Agreement either to make any capital improvements on THE PROPERTIES or to sell any of the real estate constituting a part of THE PROPERTIES. Manager is not authorized to create any mortgages, liens or encumbrances against any of the real estate constituting a part of THE PROPERTIES, unless and until first instructed in writing by Owner to do so.

1.05   Owner agrees that Manager shall be under no duty to undertake any action, other than as herein specified, with respect to the handling, managing and controlling of THE PROPERTIES, unless and until specifically agreed to in writing by Manager.

1.06   Owner agrees that Manager shall have a lien against THE PROPERTIES to secure the payment of Manager's compensation and any advances Manager may make from other funds.

1.07   Owner's objectives in the management of this property are:_____

_____

_____

_____

_____

_____

Manager shall manage the properties accordingly.

**Figure 17.1
(continued)**

ARTICLE II

Rights Reserved by the Parties

2.01   This Agreement may be altered, amended or modified at any time by a written mutual agreement signed by Owner and Manager.

2.02   This Agreement may be terminated by either Owner or Manager giving to the other at least _____ days written notice of intention to terminate this Agreement on a certain date specified in such notice; PROVIDED, HOWEVER, the termination of this Agreement shall not affect the right of Manager to receive leasing commissions or fees which have accrued on the date specified in such notice and have not been paid.

ARTICLE III

Manager's Compensation and Right of Reimbursement

3.01   For service hereunder, Manager shall be entitled to receive and retain such compensation as is fair, reasonable and customary at the time such services are performed. Owner and Manager, however, may from time to time mutually agree in writing as to the amount of compensation that Manager may receive for services hereunder. Owner agrees to pay to Manager upon demand any fee for services rendered by Manager and/or out-of-pocket expenses incurred by Manager in the handling and managing of THE PROPERTIES where Manager does not have available funds from the rents and revenues from THE PROPERTIES from which to be reimbursed.

3.02   Owner promises and agrees to indemnify Manager and hold Manager harmless from and against any and all losses and liabilities incurred by Manager as a result of any action in good faith taken or not taken by Manager pursuant to the terms and conditions of this Agreement. The promise and agreement of Owner contained in this paragraph 3.02 shall survive any termination of this Agreement as to any such action taken or not taken by Manager prior to the receipt of Manager of written notice of such termination.

ARTICLE IV

Miscellaneous

4.01   This Agreement shall be binding upon and shall inure to the benefit of Owner and Manager and their respective heirs, executors, administrators, successors and assigns.

4.02   All notices authorized or required between the parties or required by any provisions of this Lease or by law shall be in writing and must be received by the parties or delivered by receipted means to the notification address of the receiving party, as set forth below, or to such other address as the parties may direct by notice given as herein provided. The effective date of any notice given hereunder shall be the date on which such notice is received or delivered as above set forth.

NOTIFICATION ADDRESSES

Owner	Manager
_____	_____
_____	_____
_____	_____

Figure 17.1
(continued)

ARTICLE V

Special Terms and Conditions

(Here insert any special provisions relating to this particular relationship and/or properties.)

ARTICLE VI

Distribution of Income

6.01   Manager shall distribute the "net income," as that term is hereinafter defined, derived from the handling, managing and controlling of THE PROPERTIES to Owner in accordance with the written instructions of Owner at such interval, not more frequently than monthly, as Owner may state in said written instructions. "Net income," as used in this paragraph, means gross rents and revenues derived from THE PROPERTIES after deducting proper expenses and amounts requisite for maintenance of authorized reserves.

IN WITNESS WHEREOF, Owner and Manager have executed this Agreement, as of the date first above written.

OWNER: _____

MANAGER:_____

_____

ATTEST:

_____ By:_____
        Assistant Secretary   President

Owner Contact:_____
                              Name   Telephone

Manager Contact:_____
                              Name   Telephone

"EXHIBIT A"

List of Owner's Properties to be Managed by Manager

(Normally this Agreement is not acknowledged. In event the parties desire that it be notarized, attach acknowledgments for both parties.)

The cost of equipment to be installed in a modernization or renovation must be evaluated over its entire useful life. This is called **life cycle costing.** This term simply means that both the *initial* and the *operating* costs of equipment over its expected life must be measured to compare the total cost of one type of equipment with that of another.

Renting the Property

Effective rental of the property is essential to the success of a property manager. However, the role of the manager in managing a property should not be confused with that of a broker acting as a leasing agent and solely concerned with renting space. The property manager may use the services of a leasing agent, but that agent does not undertake the full responsibility of maintenance and management of the property.

Setting rental rates. In establishing rental rates a basic concern must be that, in the long term, the income covers the fixed charges and operating expenses and also provides a fair return on the investment. The property manager must also consider the prevailing rates in comparable buildings and the current vacancy level in the property to be rented. In the short term, rental rates are influenced primarily by supply and demand. Following a detailed survey of the competitive space available in the neighborhood, the manager should note sales prices and adjust for differences between neighboring properties and the property being managed. Annual rent adjustments are usually warranted.

Rental rates for residential space are usually stated in monthly amounts for a unit. Office and commercial space rentals, in contrast, are usually stated according to either the annual or the monthly rate per square foot.

If the vacancy level is high, the manager should attempt to determine why. *A high level of vacancy does not necessarily indicate that rents are too high;* instead the problem may be inept management or defects in the property. The manager should attempt to identify and correct the problems first, rather than immediately lower rents. Conversely, *while a high percentage of occupancy may appear to indicate an effective rental program, it could also mean that rental rates are too low.* Whenever the occupancy level of an apartment house or office building exceeds 95 percent, serious consideration should be given to raising rents.

Selecting Tenants. Generally the highest rents can be secured when tenants are satisfied. While a broker may sell a property and then have no further dealings with the purchaser, a building manager's success depends greatly on retaining sound, long-term relationships. The first and most important step is selection of tenants. The manager should be sure that the premises are suitable for the tenant's needs. The manager should ascertain that the *size of the space* meets the tenant's requirements and that the tenant will be able to pay for the space. A *commercial tenant's business should be compatible* with the building and the other tenants. If the tenant is likely to expand in the future, *expansion space should be available.*

The property manager must be sure to comply with all federal, state and local fair housing laws in the selection of tenants (see Chapters 16 and 21).

Collecting rents. The best way to minimize problems with rent collection is, again, to *carefully select* tenants. The desire for a high occupancy level should not override good judgment. A property manager should accept only those tenants who can be expected to meet their financial obligations to the property owner. The manager should investigate financial references given by the prospect, check with local credit bureaus and, when possible, interview the prospective tenant's former landlord.

The terms of rental payment should be spelled out in detail in the lease agreement, including the time and place of payment, provisions and penalties for late payment and provisions for cancellation and damages in case of nonpayment. The property manager should establish a *firm and consistent collection plan* with a sufficient system of notices and records. In cases of delinquency, every attempt must be made to collect rent without resorting to legal action. For those cases in which legal action is required, a property manager must be prepared to initiate and follow through with the necessary steps in conjunction with the property owner's or management firm's legal counsel.

Maintaining Good Relations with Tenants

The ultimate success of a property manager will depend greatly on the ability to maintain good relations with tenants. Dissatisfied tenants eventually vacate the property, and a high tenant turnover means greater expense for the owner for advertising, redecorating and uncollected rents. The increased attention being given to landlord-tenant relationships by legal and judicial systems has added to the importance of this issue.

An effective property manager will establish a good communication system with tenants, use intangible as well as tangible benefits to keep tenants satisfied, ensure that maintenance and service requests are attended to promptly and enforce all lease terms and building rules. A good manager is tactful and decisive and will act to the benefit of both owner and occupants. The property manager must be able to handle residents who do not pay their rent on time or who break building regulations and breed dissatisfaction among other tenants. Careful record keeping will show whether rent is being remitted promptly and in the proper amount. Records of all lease renewal dates should be kept so that the manager can anticipate expiration and retain good tenants who might otherwise move when their leases end.

Maintaining the Property

One of the most important functions of a property manager is the supervision of property maintenance. A manager must learn to balance the services provided with their costs so as to satisfy the tenants' needs while minimizing operating expenses.

Efficient property maintenance demands accurate assessment of the needs of the building and the number and kinds of personnel that will meet these needs. Staffing and scheduling requirements will vary with the type, size and geographic location of the property, so owner and manager usually agree in advance on maintenance objectives for the property. In some cases the most viable plan may be to operate with a low rental schedule and minimal expenditures for services and maintenance. Another property may be more lucrative if kept in top condition and operated with all possible tenant services, because it can then command premium rental rates.

A primary maintenance objective is to *protect the physical integrity of the property over the long term.* For example, preserving the property by repainting the exterior or replacing the heating system will help to keep the building functional and decrease routine maintenance costs. Keeping the property in good condition involves preventive maintenance, repair or corrective maintenance, routine maintenance and construction.

Preventive maintenance includes regularly scheduled activities, such as regular painting and periodic lubrication of gears and motors, that will preserve the long-range value and physical integrity of the building. Most authorities agree this is the most critical but most neglected maintenance responsibility. Failure to do preventive maintenance invariably leads to greater expense in other areas of maintenance.

Repair or corrective maintenance involves the actual repairs that keep the building's equipment, utilities and amenities functioning as contracted for by the tenants. Repairing a boiler, fixing a leaky faucet and repairing a broken air-conditioning unit are acts of repair maintenance.

A property manager must also *supervise the routine cleaning and repair* of the building, including day-to-day duties such as cleaning common areas, doing minor carpentry and plumbing and providing regularly scheduled upkeep of heating, air-conditioning and landscaping.

Last is new or renovative *construction.* Especially when dealing with commercial or industrial space, a property manager will be called on to make **tenant improvements**—alterations to the interior of the building to meet the functional demands of the tenant. These alterations range from repainting to completely gutting the interior and redesigning the space. Tenant improvements are especially important when renting new buildings, because the interior is usually left incomplete so that it can be adapted to the needs of the individual tenants. It must be clarified which improvements are to be considered as trade fixtures (personal property belonging to the tenant) and which belong to the owner of the real estate.

Supervision of modernization or renovation of buildings that have become functionally obsolete and thus unsuited to today's building needs is also important. (See Chapter 18 for a definition of *functional obsolescence.*) The renovation of a building often increases the building's marketability and thus its potential income.

Hiring employees versus contracting for services. One of the major decisions a property manager faces is whether to contract for maintenance services from an outside firm or hire on-site employees to perform such tasks. This decision should be based on a number of factors, including size of the building, complexity of tenants' requirements and availability of suitable labor.

Handling Environmental Concerns

With the proliferation of federal and state laws and increasing local regulation, environmental concerns have become a major responsibility of the property manager. These concerns will require an increasing amount of management time and attention in the future. While property managers are not expected to be experts in all of the disciplines necessary to operate a modern building, they are expected to be knowledgeable in many diverse subjects, most of which are technical in nature. Environmental concerns are one such subject.

The property manager must be able to respond to a variety of environmental problems. He or she may manage structures containing asbestos or radon or be called on to arrange an environmental audit of a property. The manager must see that any hazardous wastes produced by the manager's employer or tenants are properly disposed of. Even the normally nonhazardous waste of an office building must be controlled to avoid violation of laws requiring segregation of types of wastes. The property manager may have to provide recycling facilities and see that tenants sort their trash properly.

Complying with the ADA

The passage of the *Americans with Disabilities Act (ADA)* in 1990 has a significant impact on the responsibilities of the property manager. Title I of the Act prohibits discrimination against qualified job applicants and employees who have a disability. The property manager, as an employer, should be familiar with ADA to ensure that interview and selection procedures are not discriminatory. Employers are required also to make *reasonable accommodations* that enable an individual with a disability to perform essential job functions. Such accommodations include making the work site accessible, restructuring a job, perhaps by providing part-time or modified work schedules, and modifying equipment that is used on the job. Although the employment provisions of ADA will not apply to all property managers, any employer with 15 or more employees must comply with the law by July 26, 1994.

Property managers must be very familiar with Title III of ADA which addresses the requirements for buildings in which business establishments are located and public services are provided. This section of the law prohibits discrimination against people with disabilities by ensuring access to the facilities and enjoyment of services in a full and equal manner. The property manager will typically be responsible for procuring an audit of an existing building to determine if it meets the accessibility requirements of ADA and preparing and executing a plan for restructuring or retrofitting a building that is not in compliance. Experts who are versed in ADA and architectural design for individuals with disabilities may be consulted for audits and advice on achieving accessibility.

Existing barriers must be removed and accommodations must be provided when this can be accomplished in a *readily achievable* manner that is easy to do at a low cost. Examples are ramping a small stoop or removing an obstacle from an otherwise accessible entrance, lowering telephones, adding raised letters and Braille markings on elevator buttons and installing auditory signals in elevators. Alternative methods can be used to provide accommodations if extensive restructuring or burdensome expense make retrofitting impractical. Examples are installing a cup dispenser at a water fountain that is too high for an individual in a wheel chair or providing assistance to retrieve merchandise from an inaccessible location. Newly constructed buildings (to be occupied after January 26, 1993) and alterations must meet stricter accessibility requirements because it is less costly to incorporate accessible design into new construction than to retrofit an existing structure.

RISK MANAGEMENT   Because enormous monetary losses can result from certain occurrences, one of the most critical areas of responsibility for a property manager is **risk management.** Risk management involves answering the question "What will happen if something goes wrong?" The perils of any risk must be evaluated in terms of options. In considering the possibility of a loss, the property manager must decide whether it is better to

- *avoid it,* by removing the source of risk, such as a swimming pool;

- *control it,* by installing sprinklers, fire doors, security devices and other preventive measures;

- *transfer it,* by taking out an insurance policy; or

- *retain it,* to a certain extent, by insuring with a large *deductible* (loss not covered by the insurer).

Security of Tenants   The physical safety of tenants in the leased premises has become an important issue for property managers and owners. Recent court decisions in several parts of the country have held landlords and their agents responsible for physical harm that was inflicted on tenants by intruders. These decisions have prompted property managers and owners to evaluate measures to protect tenants from unauthorized entry to building complexes and to secure individual apartments from intruders.

Types of Insurance   Utilizing insurance is one of the major ways to protect against losses. Many types of insurance are available. A competent, reliable insurance agent familiar with the problems that typically arise with the type of property involved should be selected to survey the property and make recommendations. Additional insurance surveys should be obtained if any questions remain. Final decisions, however, must be made by the property owner. Some of the common types of coverage available to income property owners and managers are:

- *Fire and hazard.* Fire insurance policies provide coverage against direct loss or damage to property from a fire on the premises. Standard fire coverage can be extended to cover hazards such as windstorm, hail, smoke damage or civil insurrection.

- *Consequential loss, use and occupancy.* Consequential loss insurance, which can include rent loss, covers the loss of revenue to a business that occurs if the business's property cannot be used.

- *Contents and personal property.* Some insurance covers building contents and personal property during periods when they are not actually located on the business premises.

- *Liability.* Public liability insurance covers the risks an owner assumes when the public enters the building. Claims paid under this coverage are used for medical expenses by a person injured in the building as a result of the landlord's negligence. Claims for medical or hospital payments for injuries sustained by building employees hurt in the course of their employment are covered by state laws known as **workers' compensation acts.** These laws require a building owner who is an employer to obtain a workers' compensation policy from a private insurance company.

- *Casualty.* Casualty insurance policies include coverage against theft, burglary, vandalism, machinery damage and health and accident insurance. Casualty policies are usually written on specific risks, such as theft, rather than being all-inclusive.

- *Surety bonds.* **Surety bonds** cover an owner against financial losses resulting from an employee's criminal acts or negligence while performing assigned duties.

Today many insurance companies offer **multiperil policies** for apartment and business buildings. These policies offer the property manager an insurance package that includes standard types of commercial coverage such as fire, hazard, public liability and casualty.

Claims

When a claim is made under a policy insuring a building or other physical object, there are two possible methods of determining the amount of the claim. One is the *depreciated* actual or cash value of the damaged property, and the other is current replacement cost. When purchasing insurance, a manager must assess whether the property should be insured at full replacement cost or at a depreciated cost. As with the homeowners' policies discussed in Chapter 3, commercial policies include *coinsurance clauses* that require the insured to carry fire coverage, usually in an amount equal to 80 percent of the building's replacement value.

THE MANAGEMENT PROFESSION

Most metropolitan areas have local associations of building and property owners and managers that are affiliates of regional and national associations. The Institute of Real Estate Management was founded in 1933 and is one of the affiliates of the National Association of REALTORS®. The institute awards the designation of Certified Property Manager (CPM) to persons who have met certain requirements. The Building Owners and Managers Association International (BOMA International) is a federation of local associations of owners and managers, primarily of office buildings. Training courses leading to the designation Real Property Administrator (RPA), Systems Maintenance Administrator (SMA) and Facilities Management Administrator (FMA) are offered by the Building Owners and Managers Institute International (BOMI International), an independent institute affiliated with BOMA. In addition, there are many specialized professional organizations for apartment managers, community association managers, shopping center managers and others.

●   ●   ●   ●   ●   ●   ●

KEY TERMS

life cycle costing
management agreement
multiperil policies
property manager

risk management
surety bond
tenant improvements
workers' compensation acts

SUMMARY

Property management is a specialized service provided to owners of income-producing properties in which the managerial function may be delegated to an individual or a firm with particular expertise in the field. The manager, as agent of the owner, becomes the administrator of the project and assumes the executive functions required for the care and operation of the property.

A management agreement establishing the agency relationship between owner and manager must be prepared carefully to define and authorize the manager's duties and responsibilities.

Projected expenses, combined with the manager's analysis of the condition of the building and the rent patterns in the neighborhood, will form the basis on which rental rates for the property are determined. Once a rent schedule is established, the property manager is responsible for soliciting tenants whose needs are suited to the available space and who are financially capable of meeting the proposed rents. The manager is generally obligated to collect rents, maintain the building, hire necessary employees, pay taxes for the building and deal with tenant problems.

Maintenance includes safeguarding the physical integrity of the property and performing routine cleaning and repairs as well as making tenant improvements—adapting the interior space and overall design of the property to suit the tenants' needs and meet the demands of the market.

In addition, the manager is expected to secure adequate insurance coverage for the premises. The basic types of coverage applicable to commercial structures include fire and hazard insurance on the property and fixtures, consequential loss, use and occupancy insurance to protect the owner against revenue losses and casualty insurance to provide coverage against losses such as theft, vandalism and destruction of machinery. The manager should also secure public liability insurance to insure the owner against claims made by people injured on the premises and workers' compensation policies to cover the claims of employees injured on the job.

This growing real estate specialty is supported by many regional and national organizations that help property managers maintain high professional standards.

Questions

1. Which of the following types of insurance coverage insures the property owner against the claims of employees injured while on the job?
   a. Consequential loss
   b. Workers' compensation
   c. Casualty
   d. Surety bond

2. Apartment rental rates are usually expressed
   a. in monthly amounts.
   b. on a per-room basis.
   c. in square feet per month.
   d. in square feet per year.

3. From a management point of view, apartment building occupancy that reaches as high as 98 percent would tend to indicate that
   a. the building is poorly managed.
   b. the building has reached its maximum potential.
   c. the building is a desirable place to live.
   d. rents should be raised.

4. A guest slips on an icy apartment building stair and is hospitalized. A claim against the building owner for medical expenses may be paid under which of the following policies held by the owner?
   a. Workers' compensation
   b. Casualty
   c. Liability
   d. Fire and hazard

5. Which of the following should *not* be a consideration in selecting a tenant?
   a. The size of the space versus the tenant's requirements
   b. The tenant's ability to pay
   c. The racial and ethnic background of the tenant
   d. The compatibility of the tenant's business with other tenants' businesses

6. When a property manager chooses an insurance policy with a $500 deductible, the risk management technique being employed is
   a. avoiding risk.   c. controlling risk.
   b. retaining risk.   d. transferring risk.

7. Tenant improvements are
   a. fixtures.
   b. adaptations of space to suit tenants' needs.
   c. removable by the tenant.
   d. paid for by the landlord.

8. In preparing a budget, the property manager should set up for variable expenses
   a. a control account.
   b. a floating allocation.
   c. a cash reserve fund.
   d. an asset account.

9. Rents should be determined by
   a. rates prevailing in the area.
   b. the local apartment owners' association.
   c. HUD.
   d. a tenants' union.

10. What type of insurance covers a landlord against loss of rent if an occupied building is burned to the ground?
    a. Fire and hazard
    b. Liability
    c. Consequential loss, use and occupancy
    d. Casualty

11. Property manager J hires W as the full-time maintenance person for one of the buildings she manages. While repairing a faucet in one of the apartments, W steals a television set. J could protect the owner against this type of loss by purchasing
    a. liability insurance.
    b. workers' compensation insurance.
    c. a surety bond.
    d. casualty insurance.

12. Which of the following might indicate rents are too low?
    a. A poorly maintained building
    b. Many "for lease" signs in the area
    c. High building occupancy
    d. High vacancy level

13. Repairing a boiler is classified as which type of maintenance?
    a. Preventive   c. Routine
    b. Corrective   d. Construction

18 Real Estate Appraisal

APPRAISING

Formal appraisal reports are relied on by mortgage lenders, investors, public utilities, governmental agencies, businesses and individuals. Home mortgage lenders, for instance, need to know a property's market value to be sure that the amount of the loan is based on an accurate valuation of the collateral.

An **appraisal** is a supportable estimate or opinion of value. The appraiser is an independent third party required to provide an *unbiased* estimate of value. Appraising is a professional service performed for a fee based on the amount of time and effort needed to accomplish the task.

Regulation of Appraisal Activities

The crucial role of appraisals was underscored by the consequences of the surge into unwise investments following the enactment of the Depository Institutions Deregulation and Monetary Control Act of 1980. Many of these investment decisions were based on faulty appraisals, which resulted in improperly valued collateral. That in turn resulted in the collapse of many savings and loan associations. To stabilize the S&Ls and protect their depositors from unwise or risky practices, Congress passed the Financial Institutions Reform, Recovery and Enforcement Act (FIRREA) of 1989, whose provisions included the first attempt at compulsory appraiser regulation.

Title XI of FIRREA was enacted to ensure that federal financial and public policy interests in real estate-related transactions are protected. It requires that real estate appraisals used in connection with federally related transactions be performed by competent individuals whose professional conduct is subject to effective supervision. Previously only a few states required appraisers to have even a real estate license. In recent years a few states have offered voluntary certification procedures to appraisers and/or established criteria for what could be called a "certified" appraisal.

Each state adopts its own law, which must conform to the federal requirements for governing standards for appraisals and licensure of appraisers. The law must follow the minimum criteria for certification of real estate appraisers established by the Appraiser Qualifications Board of the Appraisal Foundation and set the standards for appraisals by following the "Uniform Standards of Professional Appraisal Practice,'' which were established by the Appraisal Standards Board of the Foundation. The Appraisal Foundation is a national body composed of representatives of the major appraisal and related organizations.

As of January 1, 1993, all appraisals for federally related transactions must be performed by state-certified appraisers. A *federally related transaction* is any real estate-related financial transaction in which a federal financial institution, a regulatory agency or the Resolution Trust Corporation engages. This includes transactions involving the sale, lease, purchase, investment or exchange of real property and the financing, refinancing or the use of real property as security for a loan or investment, including mortgage-backed securities.

Competitive Market Analysis

Not all estimates of value are made by professional appraisers. As discussed in Chapter 5, a salesperson often must help a seller arrive at a listing price or a buyer determine an offering price for property without the aid of a formal appraisal report. In these cases the salesperson prepares a report compiled from research of the marketplace, primarily similar properties that have been sold, known as a *competitive market analysis* (CMA). The salesperson must be knowledgeable about the fundamentals of valuation to compile the market data. The competitive market analysis is not as comprehensive or technical as an appraisal and may be biased by a salesperson's anticipated agency relationship. A competitive market analysis should *not* be represented as an appraisal.

VALUE

Value is an abstract word with many definitions. In a broad sense **value** may be defined as the monetary worth arising from the ownership of a desired object. In the marketplace value is the power of a good or service to command other goods or services in exchange. The value of an object to an individual owner, based on its usefulness to that owner, may differ from the value of that object to other individuals in the marketplace. In terms of real estate appraisal, value may be described as the *present worth of future benefits arising from the ownership of real property.*

To have value in the real estate market, a property must have the following characteristics:

- *Demand:* the need or desire for possession or ownership backed by the financial means to satisfy that need

- *Utility:* the capacity to satisfy human needs and desires

- *Scarcity:* a finite supply

- *Transferability:* the relative ease with which ownership rights are transferred from one person to another

Market Value

A given parcel of real estate may have many different kinds of value at the same time, such as market value (used to estimate selling price), assessed value (used for property taxes), insured value, book value, mortgage value, salvage value, condemnation value and depreciated value. Generally the goal of an appraiser is to estimate market value. The **market value** of real estate is *the most probable price that a property should bring in a competitive and open market under all* *conditions requisite to a fair sale, given that the buyer and seller are each acting prudently and knowledgeably and assuming the price is not affected by undue stimulus.* The following conditions are essential to market value:

- The *most probable* price is not the average or highest price.

- The buyer and seller must be unrelated and acting without *undue pressure.*

- Both buyer and seller must be *well informed* as to the property's use and potential, including its assets and defects.

- A *reasonable time* must be allowed for exposure in the open market.

- Payment must be made in cash or its equivalent.

- The price must represent a normal consideration for the property sold, unaffected by special financing amounts and/or terms, services, fees, costs or credits incurred in the market transaction.

Market value versus market price. Market value is an opinion of value based on an analysis of data, which may include not only an analysis of comparable sales but also an analysis of potential income and expenses and replacement costs (less depreciation). *Market price,* on the other hand, is what a property *actually* sells for—its sales price. Theoretically the market price should be the same as the market value. Market price can be taken as accurate evidence of current market value, however, only if the conditions essential to market value exist. There are circumstances under which a property may be sold below market value, such as when the seller is forced to sell quickly or when a sale is arranged between relatives.

Market value versus cost. There is an important distinction between market value and *cost.* One of the most common misconceptions about valuing property is that cost represents market value. Cost and market value *may* be equal and often are when the improvements on a property are new. But more often, cost does not equal market value. For example, two homes are identical in every respect, except that one is located on a street with heavy traffic and the other is on a quiet, residential street. The value of the former may be less than that of the latter, although the cost of each may be exactly the same. A homeowner may install a swimming pool for a cost of $15,000, however, the cost of the improvement may not add $15,000 to the value of the property.

Basic Principles of Value

A number of economic principles can affect the value of real estate. The most important are defined in the text that follows.

Anticipation. The principle of **anticipation** says that value is created by the expectation that certain benefits will be realized in the future. Value can increase or decrease in anticipation of some future benefit or detriment affecting the property. For example, the value of a house may be affected if there are rumors that an adjacent property may be converted to commercial use in the near future.

Change. The cause and effect of social and economic forces keep property values in transition. No physical or economic condition remains constant. Real estate is subject to natural phenomena such as tornadoes, fires and routine wear and tear of the elements. The real estate business is also subject to the demands of its market, as is any business. An appraiser must be knowledgeable about the past and perhaps predictable effects of natural phenomena and the behavior of the marketplace.

Competition. **Competition** is the interaction of supply and demand. Excess profits tend to attract competition. For example, the success of a retail store may cause investors to open similar stores in the area. This tends to mean less profit for all stores concerned, unless the purchasing power in the area increases substantially.

Conformity. The principle of **conformity** says that value is created when the components of the property are in harmony with the surroundings. Maximum value is realized if the use of land conforms to existing neighborhood standards. In single-family residential neighborhoods, for example, buildings should be similar in design, construction, size and age.

Contribution. The principle of **contribution** says that the value of any component of a property is measured by the amount it contributes to the value of the whole or the amount its absence detracts from the value of the whole. For example, the cost of installing an air-conditioning system and remodeling an older office building may be greater than is justified by any increase in market value (a function of expected net increase) that may result from the improvement to the property.

Highest and best use. The most profitable single use to which the property may be adapted or the use that is likely to be in demand in the reasonably near future is the property's **highest and best use.** The use must be legally permitted, financially feasible, physically possible and maximally productive. The highest and best use of a site can change with social, political and economic forces. Highest and best use is noted in every appraisal but may also be the object of a more extensive analysis. For example, a highest-and-best-use study may show that a parking lot in a busy downtown area does not maximize the productivity of the land to the degree that a building would.

Increasing and diminishing returns. The addition of more improvements to land and structures will increase value only to a certain point, that being the point of the asset's maximum value. Beyond that point additional improvements will no longer effect the property's value. As long as money spent on improvements produces an increase in income or value, the *law of increasing returns* is applicable. At the point where additional improvements will not produce a proportionate increase in income or value, the *law of diminishing returns* applies.

Plottage. The principle of **plottage** holds that merging or consolidating adjacent lots held by separate landowners into one larger lot may produce a higher total land value than the sum of the values of the two sites valued separately. For example, two adjacent lots valued at $35,000 each might be valued at $90,000 if consolidated into one larger lot under a single use. The process of merging the two lots under one owner is known as **assemblage.**

Regression and progression. The principle that between dissimilar properties, the worth of the better-quality property is adversely affected by the presence of the lesser-quality property is known as **regression.** Thus, in a neighborhood of modest homes, a structure that is larger, better maintained and/or more luxurious would tend to be valued in the same range as the others. Conversely, the principle of **progression** states that the worth of a lesser property tends to increase if it is located among better properties.

Substitution. The principle of **substitution** says that the maximum value of a property tends to be set by the cost of purchasing an equally desirable and valuable substitute property.

Supply and demand. The principle of **supply and demand** says that the value of a property depends on the number of properties available in the marketplace and their respective prices and the number of prospective purchasers and the price they are willing to pay. For example, the last lot to be sold in a residential area where the demand for homes is high will probably be worth more than the first lot sold in that area.

THE THREE APPROACHES TO VALUE

To arrive at an accurate estimate of value appraisers traditionally use three basic valuation techniques: the sales comparison approach, the cost approach and the income approach. Each method serves as a check against the others and narrows the range within which the final estimate of value will fall. Each method is generally considered most reliable for specific types of property.

The Sales Comparison Approach

In the **sales comparison approach** an estimate of value is obtained by comparing the subject property (the property under appraisal) with recently sold comparable properties (properties similar to the subject). Because no two parcels of real estate are exactly alike, each comparable property must be analyzed for differences and similarities between it and the subject property. The sales prices of the comparables must be adjusted for any dissimilarities. The principal factors for which adjustments must be made include:

- *Property rights:* An adjustment must be made in cases when less than the full legal bundle of rights is involved, such as land leases, ground rents and life estates.

- *Financing concessions:* The financing terms must be considered, including adjustments for differences such as mortgage loan terms and owner financing.

- *Conditions of sale:* Adjustments must be made for motivational factors that would affect the sale, such as foreclosure, a sale between family members or some nonmonetary incentive.

- *Date of sale:* An adjustment must be made if economic changes occur between the date of sale of the comparable property and the date of the appraisal.

- *Location:* An adjustment may be necessary to compensate for locational differences. For example, similar properties might differ in price from neighborhood to neighborhood or even between locations within the same neighborhood.

- *Physical features and amenities:* Physical features that may cause adjustments include age of building, size of lot, landscaping, construction, number of rooms, square feet of living space, interior and exterior condition, presence or absence of a garage, fireplace or air conditioner, and so forth.

Table 18.1
Sales Comparison
Approach to Value

	Subject Property	Comparables				
		A	B	C	D	E
Sales price		$118,000	$112,000	$121,000	$116,500	$110,000
Financing concessions	none	none	none	none	none	none
Date of sale		current	current	current	current	current
Location	good	same	poorer +6,500	same	same	same
Age	6 years	same	same	same	same	same
Size of lot	60′ × 135′	same	same	larger –5,000	same	larger –5,000
Landscaping	good	same	same	same	same	same
Construction	brick	same	same	same	same	same
Style	ranch	same	same	same	same	same
No. of rooms	6	same	same	same	same	same
No. of bedrooms	3	same	same	same	same	same
No. of baths	1½	same	same	same	same	same
Sq. ft. of living space	1,500	same	same	same	same	same
Other space (basement)	full basement	same	same	same	same	same
Condition—exterior	average	better –1,500	poorer +1,000	better –1,500	same	poorer +2,000
Condition—interior	good	same	same	better –500	same	same
Garage	2-car attached	same	same	same	same	none +5,000
Other improvements	none	none	none	none	none	none
Net Adjustments		–1,500	+7,500	–7,000	-0-	+2,000
Adjusted Value		$116,500	$119,500	$114,000	$116,500	$112,000

Note: Because the value range of the properties in the comparison chart (excluding comparable B) is close, and comparable D required no adjustment, an appraiser would conclude that the indicated market value of the subject is $116,500.

After a careful analysis of the differences between the comparable properties and the subject property, the appraiser must *adjust the comparables* to reflect the market's reaction to the differences. Following the principle of contribution, the value of an amenity or the impact of date of sale, location or terms of a sale are assigned by the market. The appraiser *estimates either dollar or percentage adjustments* that reflect the value of these differences.

The value of a feature that is present in the subject but not in the comparable property is *added* to the sale price of the comparable. This presumes that, all other conditions being equal, a property having a feature not present in the comparable property (such as a fireplace or wet bar) would tend to have a higher market value solely because of this feature. (The feature need not be a physical amenity; it may be a locational or aesthetic feature.) Likewise, the value of a feature that is present in the comparable but not the subject property is *subtracted*. The adjusted sales prices of the comparables represent the probable range of value of the subject property. From this range, a single market value estimate can be selected.

The sales comparison approach is essential in almost every appraisal of real estate. It is considered the most reliable of the three approaches in appraising residential property, where the intangible benefits may be difficult to measure otherwise. Most appraisals include a minimum of three comparable sales reflective of the subject property. Some appraisal forms require the inclusion of currently listed properties that are similar to the subject to indicate the current market competition. An example of the sales comparison approach is shown in Table 18.1

The Cost Approach

The **cost approach** to value is based on the principle of substitution. The cost approach consists of these steps:

1. Estimate the value of the land as if it were vacant and available to be put to its highest and best use.

2. Estimate the current cost of constructing buildings and site improvements.

3. Estimate the amount of accrued depreciation of the building resulting from physical deterioration, functional obsolescence and/or external depreciation.

4. Deduct accrued depreciation from the estimated construction cost of new building(s) and site improvements.

5. Add the estimated land value to the depreciated cost of the building(s) and site improvements to arrive at the total property value.

Land value (step 1) is usually estimated by using the sales comparison approach; that is, the location and site improvements (such as the presence of utilities and sewer lines) of the subject property are compared with those of similar nearby sites, and adjustments are made for significant differences.

There are two ways to look at the construction cost of a building for appraisal purposes (step 2): reproduction cost and replacement cost. **Reproduction cost** is the construction cost at current prices of an *exact duplicate* of the subject improvement, including both the benefits and the drawbacks of the property. **Replacement cost** is the construction cost at current prices of improvements with utility or function similar to the subject property but not necessarily an exact duplicate. Replacement cost is more frequently used in appraising older structures because it eliminates obsolete features and takes advantage of current construction materials and techniques.

An example of the cost approach to value is shown in Table 18.2.

Determining reproduction or replacement cost. An appraiser using the cost approach computes the reproduction or replacement cost of a building using one of the following four methods:

1. **Square-foot method:** The cost per square foot of a recently built comparable structure is multiplied by the number of square feet (using exterior dimensions) in the subject building. This is the most common and easiest method of cost estimation. The example in Table 18.2. uses the square-foot method, which is also referred to as the *comparison method*. For some properties the cost per *cubic foot* of a recently built comparable structure is multiplied by the number of cubic feet in the subject structure.

Table 18.2 Cost Approach to Value	**Land Valuation:** Size 60′ × 135′ @ $450 per front foot			= $27,000
	Plus site improvements: driveway, walks, landscaping, etc.			= 8,000
	Total Land Valuation			$35,000
	Building Valuation: Replacement Cost			
	1,500 sq. ft. @ $65 per sq. ft. =			
		$97,500		
	Less Depreciation:			
	Physical depreciation			
	curable			
	(items of deferred maintenance)			
	exterior painting	$4,000		
	incurable (structural deterioration)	9,750		
	Functional obsolescence	2,000		
	External depreciation	-0-		
	Total Depreciation		−15,750	
	Depreciated Value of Building			$ 81,750
	Indicated Value by Cost Approach			$116,750

2. **Unit-in-place method:** In the unit-in-place method the replacement cost of a structure is estimated based on the construction cost per unit of measure of individual building components, including material, labor, overhead and builder's profit. Most components are measured in square feet, although items such as plumbing fixtures are estimated by cost. The sum of the components is the cost of the new structure.

3. **Quantity-survey method:** The quantity and quality of all materials (such as lumber, brick and plaster) and the labor are estimated on a unit cost basis. These factors are added to indirect costs (building permit, survey, payroll, taxes, builder's profit) to arrive at the total replacement cost of the structure. Because it is so detailed and time-consuming, this method is usually used only in appraising historical properties.

4. **Index method:** A factor representing the percentage increase of construction costs up to the present time is applied to the original cost of the subject property. Because it fails to take into account individual property variables, this method is useful only as a check of the estimate reached by one of the other methods.

Depreciation. In a real estate appraisal **depreciation** is a loss in value due to any cause; it refers to any condition that adversely affects the value of an improvement to real property. Land does not depreciate—it retains its value indefinitely, except in such rare cases as downzoned urban parcels, improperly developed land or misused farmland. Depreciation is considered to be curable or incurable, depending on the contribution of the expenditure to the value of the property. For appraisal purposes (as opposed to depreciation for tax purposes, which is discussed in Chapter 22), depreciation is divided into three classes according to its cause.

1. **Physical deterioration**—*curable:* an item in need of repair, such as painting (deferred maintenance), that is economically feasible and would result in an increase in appraised value equal to or exceeding the cost.

   Physical deterioration—incurable: a defect caused by physical wear and tear if its correction would not be economically feasible or contribute a comparable value to the building. A major repair, such as replacement of weatherworn siding, may not warrant the financial investment.

2. **Functional obsolescence**—*curable:* outmoded or unacceptable physical or design features that are no longer considered desirable by purchasers but could be replaced or redesigned at a cost that would be offset by the anticipated increase in ultimate value. Outmoded fixtures, such as plumbing, are usually easily replaced. Room function may be redefined at no cost if the basic room layout allows for it. A bedroom adjacent to a kitchen, for example, may be converted to a family room.

   Functional obsolescence—incurable: currently undesirable physical or design features that could not be easily remedied because the cost of effecting a cure would be greater than its resulting increase in value. An office building that cannot be air-conditioned, for example, suffers from incurable functional obsolescence if the cost outweighs its contribution to the value.

3. **External obsolescence**—*incurable* only: caused by negative factors not on the subject property, such as environmental, social or economic forces. This type of depreciation usually cannot be considered curable because the loss in value cannot be affected by expenditures to the property. Proximity to a nuisance, such as a polluting factory or a deteriorating neighborhood, would be unchangeable factors that could not be cured by the owner of the subject property.

In determining a property's depreciation, most appraisers use the *breakdown method,* in which depreciation is broken down into all three classes, with separate estimates for curable and incurable factors in each class. Depreciation, however, is difficult to measure; and the older the building, the more difficult it is to estimate. The easiest but least precise way to determine depreciation is the **straight-line method,** also called the *economic age-life method.* Depreciation is assumed to occur at an even rate over a structure's **economic life,** the period during which it is expected to remain useful for its original intended purpose. The property's cost is divided by the number of years of its expected economic life to derive the amount of annual depreciation.

For example, a $120,000 property may have a land value of $30,000 and an improvement value of $90,000. If the improvements are expected to last 60 years, the annual straight-line depreciation would be $1,500 ($90,000 divided by 60 years). Such depreciation can be calculated as an annual dollar amount or as a percentage of the property's replacement cost.

Much of the functional obsolescence and all of the external depreciation can be evaluated only by considering the actions of buyers in the marketplace.

The cost approach is most helpful in the appraisal of special-purpose buildings such as schools, churches and public buildings. Such properties are difficult to appraise using other methods, because there are seldom many local sales to use as comparables, and the properties do not ordinarily generate income.

The Income Approach

The **income approach** to value is based on the present value of the rights to future income. It assumes that the income derived from a property will, to a large extent, control the value of that property. The income approach is used for valuation of income-producing properties—apartment buildings, office buildings, shopping centers, and the like. In estimating value using the income approach, an appraiser must take the following steps:

1. Estimate annual *potential gross income.* An estimate of economic rental income must be made based on market studies. Current rental income may not reflect the current market rental rates, especially in the cases of short-term leases or leases about to terminate. Potential income includes other income to the property from such sources as vending machines, parking fees and laundry machines.

2. Deduct an appropriate allowance for vacancy and rent loss, based on the appraiser's experience, and arrive at *effective gross income.*

3. Deduct the annual *operating expenses,* enumerated in Table 18.3, from the effective gross income to arrive at the annual *net operating income* (NOI). Management costs are always included, even if the current owner manages the property. Mortgage payments (principal and interest) are *debt service* and not considered operating expenses.

4. Estimate the price a typical investor would pay for the income produced by this particular type and class of property. This is done by estimating the rate of return (or yield) that an investor will demand for the investment of capital in this type of building. This rate of return is called the **capitalization** (or "cap") **rate** and is determined by comparing the relationship of net operating income to the sales prices of similar properties that have sold in the current market. For example, a comparable property that is producing an annual net income of $15,000 is sold for $187,500. The capitalization rate is $15,000 divided by $187,500, or 8 percent. If other comparable properties sold at prices that yielded substantially the same rate, it may be concluded that 8 percent is the rate that the appraiser should apply to the subject property.

5. Apply the capitalization rate to the property's annual net operating income to arrive at the estimate of the property's value.

With the appropriate capitalization rate and the projected annual net operating income, the appraiser can obtain an indication of value by the income approach in the following manner:

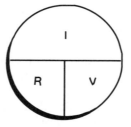

Net Operating Income ÷ Capitalization Rate = Value

Example: $18,000 income ÷ 9% cap rate = $200,000 value or

$18,000 income ÷ 8% cap rate = $225,000 value

Table 18.3
Income
Capitalization
Approach to Value

Potential Gross Annual Income		
Market Rent		$60,000
Income from other sources		
(vending machines and pay phones)		+600
		$60,600
Less vacancy and collection losses (estimated) @ 4%		−2,424
Effective Gross Income		$58,176
Expenses:		
Real estate taxes	$9,000	
Insurance	1,000	
Heat	2,800	
Maintenance	6,400	
Utilities, electricity, water, gas	800	
Repairs	1,200	
Decorating	1,400	
Replacement of equipment	800	
Legal and accounting	600	
Management	3,000	
Total Expenses		$27,000
Annual Net Operating Income		$31,176

Capitalization Rate = 10%

Capitalization of annual net income: $\dfrac{\$31,176}{.10}$

Indicated Value by Income Approach = $311,760

Note the inverse relationship between the rate and value. As the rate goes down, the value increases.

This formula and its variations are important in dealing with income property.

$$\frac{\text{Income}}{\text{Rate}} = \text{Value} \qquad \frac{\text{Income}}{\text{Value}} = \text{Rate} \qquad \text{Value} \times \text{Rate} = \text{Income}$$

A very simplified version of the computations used in applying the income approach is illustrated in Table 18.3.

IN PRACTICE. . .

The most difficult step in the income approach to value is determining the appropriate capitalization rate for the property. This rate must be selected to accurately reflect the recapture of the original investment over the building's economic life, give the owner an acceptable rate of return on investment and provide for the repayment of borrowed capital. Note that an income property that carries with it a great deal of risk as an investment generally requires a higher rate of return than a property considered a safe investment.

Gross rent or income multipliers. Certain properties, such as single-family homes or two-unit buildings, are not purchased primarily for income. As a substitute for a more elaborate income capitalization analysis, the **gross rent multiplier** (GRM) and **gross income multiplier** (GIM) are often used in the appraisal process. Each relates the sales price of a property to its rental income.

Because single-family residences usually produce only a rental income, the gross rent multiplier is used. This relates the sales price to *monthly* rental income. However, commercial and industrial properties generate income from many other sources (rent, concessions, escalator clause income and so forth), and they are valued using their *annual* income from all sources.

The formulas are as follows:

$$\frac{\text{Sales Price}}{\text{Gross Income}} = \frac{\text{Gross Income Multiplier}}{\text{(GIM)}}$$

or

$$\frac{\text{Sales Price}}{\text{Gross Rent}} = \frac{\text{Gross Rent Multiplier}}{\text{(GRM)}}$$

For example, if a home recently sold for $82,000 and its monthly rental income was $650, the GRM for the property would be computed thus:

$$\frac{\$82,000}{\$650} = 126.2 \text{ GRM}$$

To establish an accurate GRM, an appraiser must have recent sales and rental data from at least four properties that are similar to the subject property. The resulting GRM can then be applied to the estimated fair market rental of the subject property to arrive at its market value. The formula would then be

$$\text{Rental Income} \times \text{GRM} = \text{Estimated Market Value}$$

Table 18.4 shows some examples of GRM comparisons.

IN PRACTICE. . .

Much skill is required to use multipliers accurately, because there is no fixed multiplier for all areas or all types of properties and the data for each comparable must be carefully scrutinized. Therefore, many appraisers view the technique simply as a quick, informal way to check the validity of a property value obtained by one of the other appraisal methods.

Reconciliation

When the three approaches to value are applied to the same property, they will normally produce three separate indications of value. **Reconciliation** is the art of analyzing and effectively weighing the findings from the three approaches.

Although each approach may serve as an independent guide to value, whenever possible all three approaches should be used as a check on the final estimate of value. The process of reconciliation is more complicated than simply taking the

Table 18.4	Comparable No.	Sales Price	Monthly Rent	GRM
Gross Rent	1	$93,600	$650	144
Multiplier	2	78,500	450	174
	3	95,500	675	141
		82,000	565	145
	Subject	?	625	?

Note: Based on an analysis of these comparisons, a GRM of 145 seems reasonable for homes in this area. In the opinion of an appraiser, then, the estimated value of the subject property would be $625 × 145, or $90,625.

average of the three derived value estimates. An average implies that the data and logic applied in each of the approaches are equally valid and reliable and should therefore be given equal weight. In fact, however, certain approaches are more valid and reliable with some kinds of properties than with others.

For example, in appraising a home the income approach is rarely valid, and the cost approach is of limited value unless the home is relatively new; therefore, the sales comparison approach is usually given greatest weight in valuing single-family residences. In the appraisal of income or investment property, the income approach would normally be given the greatest weight. In the appraisal of churches, libraries, museums, schools and other special-use properties where there is little or no income or sales revenue, the cost approach would usually be assigned the greatest weight. From this analysis, or reconciliation, a single estimate of market value is produced.

THE APPRAISAL PROCESS

Although appraising is not an exact or precise science, the key to an accurate appraisal lies in the methodical collection of data. The appraisal process is an orderly set of procedures used to collect and analyze data to arrive at an ultimate value conclusion. The data are divided into two basic classes:

1. *General data,* covering the nation, region, city and neighborhood. Of particular importance is the neighborhood, where an appraiser finds the physical, economic, social and political influences that directly affect the value and potential of the subject property.

2. *Specific data,* covering details of the subject property as well as comparative data relating to costs, sales and income and expenses of properties similar to and competitive with the subject property.

Figure 18.1 outlines the steps an appraiser takes in carrying out an appraisal assignment. The numbers in the following list correspond to the numbers on the flowchart.

1. *State the problem.* The kind of value to be estimated must be specified and the valuation approach(es) most valid and reliable for the kind of property under appraisal must be selected.

2. *List the data needed and the sources.* Based on the approach(es) the appraiser will be using, the types of data needed and the sources to be consulted are listed.

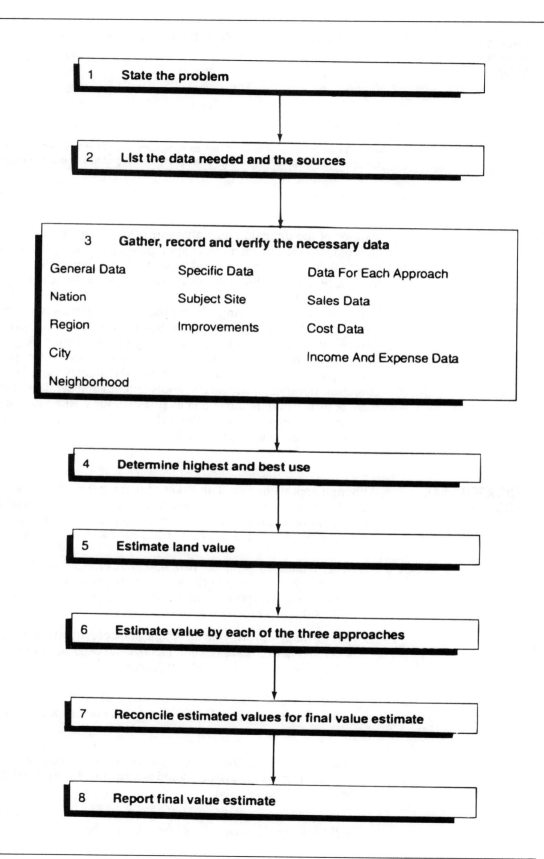

Figure 18.1
The Appraisal
Process

Figure 18.1
The Appraisal
Process

1   State the problem

2   List the data needed and the sources

3   Gather, record and verify the necessary data

General Data	Specific Data	Data For Each Approach
Nation	Subject Site	Sales Data
Region	Improvements	Cost Data
City		Income And Expense Data
Neighborhood		

4   Determine highest and best use

5   Estimate land value

6   Estimate value by each of the three approaches

7   Reconcile estimated values for final value estimate

8   Report final value estimate

3. *Gather, record and verify the necessary data.* Detailed information concerning the economic, political and social conditions of the region and/or city and comments on the effects of these data on the subject property must be obtained. Specific data about the subject site and improvements must be collected and verified.

   Depending on the approach(es) used, comparative information relating to sales, income and expenses, and construction costs of comparable properties must be collected. All data should be verified, usually by checking the same information against two different sources. In the case of sales data, one source should be a person directly involved in the transaction.

4. *Determine highest and best use.* The appraiser analyzes market forces such as competition and current versus potential uses to determine the reasonableness of the property's present use in terms of its profitability.

5. *Estimate land value:* The features and sales prices of comparable sites are compared with the subject to determine the value of the land alone.

6. *Estimate value by each of the three approaches.* The sales comparison, cost and income approaches are used to estimate the value of the subject property.

7. *Reconcile estimated values for final value estimate.* The appraiser reconciles the findings of the three approaches and forms an opinion of the value estimate of the property.

8. *Report final value estimate.* After the three approaches have been reconciled and an opinion of value has been reached, the appraiser prepares a formal written report for the client. The statement may be a completed *form,* a *letter* or a lengthy written *narrative.* It should contain

   a. the estimate of value and the date to which it applies;

   b. the purpose for which the appraisal was made;

   c. a description of the neighborhood and the subject property;

   d. factual data covering costs, sales and income, and expenses of similar, recently sold properties;

   e. an analysis and interpretation of the data collected;

   f. a presentation of one or more of the three approaches to value in enough detail to support the appraiser's final value conclusion;

   g. any qualifying conditions;

   h. supportive material, such as charts, maps, photographs, floor plans, leases and contracts; and

   i. the certification, qualifications and signature of the appraiser.

Figure 18.2 is the *Uniform Residential Appraisal Report* form required by many government agencies. Even in a brief report, detailed descriptions of the neighborhood and property being appraised are required.

**Figure 18.2
Uniform Residential
Appraisal Report**

Property Description   **UNIFORM RESIDENTIAL APPRAISAL REPORT**   File No. ___

SUBJECT

Property Address		City		State	Zip Code
Legal Description				County	

Assessor's Parcel No. _____ Tax Year ____ R.E. Taxes $ ____ Special Assessments $ ____

Borrower _____ Current Owner _____ Occupant [ ] Owner [ ] Tenant [ ] Vacant

Property rights appraised [ ] Fee Simple [ ] Leasehold Project Type [ ] PUD [ ] Condominium (HUD/VA only) HOA$ ____ /Mo.

Neighborhood or Project Name _____ Map Reference _____ Census Tract _____

Sales Price $ ____ Date of Sale ____ Description and $ amount of loan charges/concessions to be paid by seller ____

Lender/Client _____ Address _____

Appraiser _____ Address _____

NEIGHBORHOOD

Location	[ ] Urban	[ ] Suburban	[ ] Rural	**Predominant occupancy**	**Single family housing** PRICE $ (000) / AGE (yrs)	**Present land use %**	**Land use change**
Built up	[ ] Over 75%	[ ] 25-75%	[ ] Under 25%			One family ____	[ ] Not likely [ ] Likely
Growth rate	[ ] Rapid	[ ] Stable	[ ] Slow	[ ] Owner	Low ____	2-4 family ____	[ ] In process
Property values	[ ] Increasing	[ ] Stable	[ ] Declining	[ ] Tenant	High ____	Multi-family ____	To: ____
Demand/supply	[ ] Shortage	[ ] In balance	[ ] Over supply	[ ] Vacant (0-5%)	Predominant ____	Commercial ____	
Marketing time	[ ] Under 3 mos.	[ ] 3-6 mos.	[ ] Over 6 mos.	[ ] Vacant (over 5%)		( )	

Note: Race and the racial composition of the neighborhood are not appraisal factors.

Neighborhood boundaries and characteristics: ____

Factors that affect the marketability of the properties in the neighborhood (proximity to employment and amenities, employment stability, appeal to market, etc.): ____

Market conditions in the subject neighborhood (including support for the above conclusions related to the trend of property values, demand/supply, and marketing time - - such as data on competitive properties for sale in the neighborhood, description of the prevalence of sales and financing concessions, etc.): ____

PUD

Project Information for PUDs (If applicable) - - Is the developer/builder in control of the Home Owners' Association (HOA)? [ ] Yes [ ] No

Approximate total number of units in the subject project ____. Approximate total number of units for sale in the subject project ____.

Describe common elements and recreational facilities: ____

SITE

Dimensions ____

Site area ____ Corner Lot [ ] Yes [ ] No

Specific zoning classification and description ____

Zoning compliance [ ] Legal [ ] Legal nonconforming (Grandfathered use) [ ] Illegal [ ] No zoning

Highest & best use as improved [ ] Present use [ ] Other use (explain)

Utilities	Public	Other	Off-site Improvements	Type	Public	Private
Electricity			Street			
Gas			Curb/gutter			
Water			Sidewalk			
Sanitary sewer			Street lights			
Storm sewer			Alley			

Topography ____
Size ____
Shape ____
Drainage ____
View ____
Landscaping ____
Driveway Surface ____
Apparent easements ____
FEMA Special Flood Hazard Area [ ] Yes [ ] No
FEMA Zone ____ Map Date ____
FEMA Map No. ____

Comments (apparent adverse easements, encroachments, special assessments, slide areas, illegal or legal nonconforming zoning use, etc.): ____

DESCRIPTION OF IMPROVEMENTS

GENERAL DESCRIPTION	EXTERIOR DESCRIPTION	FOUNDATION	BASEMENT	INSULATION
No. of Units ____	Foundation ____	Slab ____	Area Sq. Ft. ____	Roof [ ]
No. of Stories ____	Exterior Walls ____	Crawl Space ____	% Finished ____	Ceiling [ ]
Type (Det./Att.) ____	Roof Surface ____	Basement ____	Ceiling ____	Walls [ ]
Design (Style) ____	Gutters & Dwnspts. ____	Sump Pump ____	Walls ____	Floor [ ]
Existing/Proposed ____	Window Type ____	Dampness ____	Floor ____	None [ ]
Age (Yrs.) ____	Storm/Screens ____	Settlement ____	Outside Entry ____	Unknown [ ]
Effective Age (Yrs.) ____	Manufactured House ____	Infestation ____		

ROOMS	Foyer	Living	Dining	Kitchen	Den	Family Rm.	Rec. Rm.	Bedrooms	# Baths	Laundry	Other	Area Sq. Ft.
Basement												
Level 1												
Level 2												

Finished area **above** grade contains: ____ Rooms; ____ Bedroom(s); ____ Bath(s); ____ Square Feet of Gross Living Area

INTERIOR	Materials/Condition	HEATING	KITCHEN EQUIP.	ATTIC	AMENITIES	CAR STORAGE:
Floors		Type ____	Refrigerator [ ]	None [ ]	Fireplace(s) # ____	None [ ]
Walls		Fuel ____	Range/Oven [ ]	Stairs [ ]	Patio ____	Garage ____ # of cars
Trim/Finish		Condition ____	Disposal [ ]	Drop Stair [ ]	Deck ____	Attached ____
Bath Floor		COOLING	Dishwasher [ ]	Scuttle [ ]	Porch ____	Detached ____
Bath Wainscot		Central ____	Fan/Hood [ ]	Floor [ ]	Fence ____	Built-In ____
Doors		Other ____	Microwave [ ]	Heated [ ]	Pool ____	Carport ____
		Condition ____	Washer/Dryer [ ]	Finished [ ]		Driveway ____

COMMENTS

Additional features (special energy efficient items, etc.): ____

Condition of the improvements, depreciation (physical, functional, and external), repairs needed, quality of construction, remodeling/additions, etc.: ____

Adverse environmental conditions (such as, but not limited to, hazardous wastes, toxic substances, etc.) present in the improvements, on the site, or in the immediate vicinity of the subject property: ____

Freddie Mac Form 70   6-93   10 CH   PAGE 1 OF 2   Fannie Mae Form 1004   6-93

Figure 18.2 (continued)

Valuation Section

UNIFORM RESIDENTIAL APPRAISAL REPORT   File No.

COST APPROACH

ESTIMATED SITE VALUE. = $ _____
ESTIMATED REPRODUCTION COST-NEW OF IMPROVEMENTS:
Dwelling _____ Sq. Ft @ $ _____ = $ _____
_____ Sq. Ft @ $ _____ = _____
_____ = _____
Garage/Carport _____ Sq. Ft @ $ _____ = _____
Total Estimated Cost-New . . . . = $ _____
Less   Physical | Functional | External
Depreciation _____ = $ _____
Depreciated Value of Improvements . . . . = $ _____
"As-is" Value of Site Improvements . . . . = $ _____
INDICATED VALUE BY COST APPROACH. . . . . = $ _____

Comments on Cost Approach (such as. source of cost estimate, site value, square foot calculation and. for HUD. VA and FmHA. the estimated remaining economic life of the property): _____
_____
_____
_____
_____
_____
_____
_____

ITEM	SUBJECT	COMPARABLE NO. 1		COMPARABLE NO. 2		COMPARABLE NO. 3	
Address							
Proximity to Subject							
Sales Price	$		$		$		$
Price/Gross Liv. Area	$ ☑	$ ☑		$ ☑		$ ☑	
Data and/or Verification Sources							
VALUE ADJUSTMENTS	DESCRIPTION	DESCRIPTION	+ (−) $ Adjustment	DESCRIPTION	+ (−) $ Adjustment	DESCRIPTION	+ (−) $ Adjustment
Sales or Financing Concessions							
Date of Sale/Time							
Location							
Leasehold/Fee Simple							
Site							
View							
Design and Appeal							
Quality of Construction							
Age							
Condition							
Above Grade	Total Bdrms Baths	Total Bdrms Baths		Total Bdrms Baths		Total Bdrms Baths	
Room Count							
Gross Living Area	Sq. Ft.	Sq. Ft.		Sq. Ft.		Sq. Ft.	
Basement & Finished Rooms Below Grade							
Functional Utility							
Heating/Cooling							
Energy Efficient Items							
Garage/Carport							
Porch, Patio, Deck, Fireplace(s), etc.							
Fence, Pool, etc.							
Net Adj. (total)		+ ☐ − ☐	$	+ ☐ − ☐	$	+ ☐ − ☐	$
Adjusted Sales Price of Comparable			$		$		$

(left margin vertical label: SALES COMPARISON ANALYSIS)

Comments on Sales Comparison (including the subject property's compatibility to the neighborhood, etc.): _____
_____
_____
_____
_____

ITEM	SUBJECT	COMPARABLE NO. 1	COMPARABLE NO. 2	COMPARABLE NO. 3
Date, Price and Data Source for prior sales within year of appraisal				

Analysis of any current agreement of sale, option, or listing of the subject property and analysis of any prior sales of subject and comparables within one year of the date of appraisal:
_____
_____

INDICATED VALUE BY SALES COMPARISON APPROACH . . . . $ _____
INDICATED VALUE BY INCOME APPROACH (If Applicable) Estimated Market Rent $_____ /Mo. x Gross Rent Multiplier _____ = $ _____

This appraisal is made ☐ "as is" ☐ subject to the repairs, alterations, inspections, or conditions listed below ☐ subject to completion per plans and specifications.
Conditions of Appraisal: _____
_____

Final Reconciliation: _____
_____

(left margin vertical label: RECONCILIATION)

The purpose of this appraisal is to estimate the market value of the real property that is the subject of this report, based on the above conditions and the certification, contingent and limiting conditions. and market value definition that are stated in the attached Freddie Mac Form 439/Fannie Mae Form 1004B (Revised _____).
I (WE) ESTIMATE THE MARKET VALUE, AS DEFINED, OF THE REAL PROPERTY THAT IS THE SUBJECT OF THIS REPORT, AS OF _____
(WHICH IS THE DATE OF INSPECTION AND THE EFFECTIVE DATE OF THIS REPORT) TO BE $ _____ .
APPRAISER: SUPERVISORY APPRAISER (ONLY IF REQUIRED):

Signature _____   Signature _____   ☐ Did ☐ Did Not
Name _____   Name _____   Inspect Property
Date Report Signed _____   Date Report Signed _____
State Certification # _____   State   State Certification # _____   State
Or State License # _____   State   Or State License # _____   State

Freddie Mac Form 70 6-93   10 CH   PAGE 2 OF 2   Fannie Mae Form 1004 6-93

U.S. Forms, Inc. 1-800-225-9583   USF# 00110

IN PRACTICE...	*The role of an appraiser is not to determine value but to develop a supportable and objective report about the value of the subject property. The appraiser relies on experience and expertise in valuation theories to evaluate market data. The appraiser does not create numbers or "pick them from the air." It is not what the appraiser thinks the property is worth but what the market indicates the value is that the appraiser can verify. This is important to remember, particularly when dealing with a property owner who may, understandably, lack the necessary objectivity to see the property realistically. The possible lack of objectivity can complicate the salesperson's ability to list a property within the most probable range of market value as well.*

KEY TERMS

anticipation	index method
appraisal	market value
assemblage	physical deterioration
capitalization rate	plottage
change	progression
competition	quantity-survey method
conformity	reconciliation
contribution	regression
cost approach	replacement cost
depreciation	reproduction cost
economic life	sales comparison approach
external depreciation	square-foot method
functional obsolescence	straight-line method
gross income multiplier	substitution
gross rent multiplier	supply and demand
highest and best use	unit-in-place method
income approach	value

SUMMARY

To appraise real estate means to estimate its value. Although there are many types of value, the most common objective of an appraisal is to estimate market value—the most probable sale price of a property. Basic to appraising are certain underlying economic principles, such as highest and best use, substitution, supply and demand, conformity, anticipation, increasing and diminishing returns, regression, progression, plottage, contribution, competition and change.

Appraisals are concerned with values, prices and costs; it is vital to understand the distinctions among the terms. Value is an estimate of future benefits, cost represents a measure of past expenditures and price reflects the actual amount of money paid for a property.

A professional appraiser analyzes a property through three approaches to value. In the sales comparison approach the value of the subject property is compared with the values of others like it that have sold recently. Because no two properties are exactly alike, adjustments must be made to account for any differences.

With the cost approach an appraiser calculates the cost of building a similar structure on a similar site. The appraiser then subtracts depreciation (losses in value), which reflects the differences between new properties of this type and the present condition of the subject property. The income approach is an analysis based on the relationship between the rate of return that an investor requires and the net income that a property produces.

An informal version of the income approach, called the gross rent multiplier (GRM), may be used to estimate the value of single-family residential properties that are not usually rented but could be. The GRM is computed by dividing the sales price of a property by its gross monthly rent. For commercial or industrial property a gross income multiplier (GIM), based on annual income from all sources, may be used.

Normally the application of the three approaches will result in three different estimates of value. In the process of reconciliation, the validity and reliability of each approach are weighed objectively to arrive at the single best and most supportable estimate of value.

Questions

1. Which of the following makes use of a rate of investment return?
   a. Sales comparison approach
   b. Cost approach
   c. Income approach
   d. Gross income multiplier method

2. The elements of value include which of the following?
   a. Competition   c. Anticipation
   b. Scarcity   d. Balance

3. The principle of value that states that two adjacent parcels of land combined into one larger parcel could have a greater value than the two parcels valued separately is called
   a. substitution.   c. regression.
   b. plottage.   d. progression.

4. The amount of money a property commands in the marketplace is its
   a. intrinsic value.
   b. market value.
   c. capitalization rate.
   d. gross-income multiplier.

5. H has his "dream house" constructed for $100,000 in an area where most newly constructed houses are not as well equipped as his and typically sell for only $80,000. The value of H's house is likely to be affected by the principle of
   a. progression.   c. change.
   b. assemblage.   d. regression.

6. In Question 5 the owners of the lesser-valued houses in H's immediate area may be affected by the principle of
   a. progression.
   b. increasing returns.
   c. competition.
   d. regression.

7. Accrued depreciation for appraisal purposes is not caused by which of the following?
   a. Functional obsolescence
   b. Physical deterioration
   c. External obsolescence
   d. Accelerated depreciation

8. *Reconciliation* refers to which of the following?
   a. Loss of value due to any cause
   b. Separating the value of the land from the total value of the property to compute depreciation
   c. Analyzing the results obtained by the different approaches to value to determine a final estimate of value
   d. The process by which an appraiser determines the highest and best use for a parcel of land

9. One method an appraiser can use to determine a building's reproduction cost involves the estimated cost of the materials needed to build the structure, plus labor and indirect costs. This is called the
   a. square-foot method.
   b. quantity-survey method.
   c. cubic-foot method.
   d. unit-in-place method.

10. If a property's annual net income is $24,000 and it is valued at $300,000, what is its capitalization rate?
   a. 12.5 percent   c. 15 percent
   b. 10.5 percent   d. 8 percent

11. Certain figures must be determined by an appraiser before value can be computed by the income approach. Which one of the following is *not* required for this process?

    a. Annual net operating income
    b. Capitalization rate
    c. Accrued depreciation
    d. Annual gross income

12. The income approach would be given the most weight in the valuation of a

    a. single-family residence.
    b. library.
    c. strip shopping center.
    d. school.

13. The market value of a parcel of real estate is

    a. an estimate of its future benefits.
    b. the amount of money paid for the property.
    c. an estimate of the most probable price it should bring.
    d. its value without improvements.

14. Capitalization is the process by which annual net operating income is used to

    a. determine cost.
    b. estimate value.
    c. establish depreciation.
    d. determine potential tax value.

15. From the reproduction or replacement cost of a building the appraiser deducts depreciation, which represents

    a. the remaining economic life of the building.
    b. remodeling costs to increase rentals.
    c. loss of value due to any cause.
    d. costs to modernize the building.

16. In the sales comparison approach to value the probable sales price of a building may be estimated by

    a. capitalizing net operating income.
    b. considering sales of similar properties.
    c. deducting accrued depreciation.
    d. determining construction cost.

17. Which of the following factors would *not* be important in comparing properties under the sales comparison approach to value?

    a. Differences in dates of sale
    b. Differences in financing terms
    c. Differences in appearance and condition
    d. Differences in original cost

18. In the income approach to value

    a. the reproduction or replacement cost of the building must be computed.
    b. the capitalization rate must be estimated.
    c. depreciation must be determined.
    d. sales of similar properties must be considered.

19. In the cost approach to value it is necessary to

    a. determine a dollar value for depreciation.
    b. estimate future expenses and operating costs.
    c. check sales prices of recently sold homes in the area.
    d. reconcile differing value estimates.

20. The appraised value of a residence with four bedrooms and one bathroom would probably be reduced because of

    a. external obsolescence.
    b. functional obsolescence.
    c. physical deterioration—curable.
    d. physical deterioration—incurable.

21. A factor representing the percentage increase in construction costs over time is used in the

    a. square-foot method.
    b. quantity-survey method.
    c. unit-in-place method.
    d. index method.

19 Control of Land Use

LAND-USE CONTROLS

Broad though they may be, the rights of real estate ownership are not absolute. Chapter 6 defined the parameters within which owners of real property interests may exercise their rights. This chapter delves into the subject of land-use controls from a more detailed, logistical standpoint. Land use is controlled and regulated through public and private restrictions and public ownership of land by federal, state and local governments.

PUBLIC CONTROLS

As stated in Chapter 6, the police power of the states is the inherent authority to create regulations needed to protect the public health, safety and welfare. The states in turn delegate to counties and local municipalities the authority to enact ordinances in keeping with general laws. The largely urban population and the increasing demands placed on finite natural resources have made it necessary for cities, towns and villages to increase their limitations on the private use of real estate. There are now controls over noise, air and water pollution as well as population density.

Privately owned real estate is regulated through

- land-use planning
- zoning ordinances
- subdivision regulations
- building codes and
- environmental protection legislation.

The Comprehensive Plan

Local governments establish development goals by formulating a **comprehensive plan**, also referred to as a *master plan*. Municipalities and counties develop plans to ensure that social and economic needs are balanced against environmental and aesthetic concerns. The plan includes the objectives of the municipality for its future development and the strategies and timing for its implementation. Municipalities are authorized to establish a comprehensive plan, zoning ordinances and subdivision regulations to govern land use within their jurisdictions. The comprehensive plan usually includes the following basic elements:

- *Land use,* including that which may be proposed for residence, industry, business, agriculture, traffic and transit facilities, utilities, community facilities, parks and recreation, floodplains and areas of special hazards

- *Housing needs* of present and anticipated future residents, which may include rehabilitation in declining neighborhoods and accommodation of new housing in different dwelling types for households of all income levels

- *Movement of people and goods,* which may include highways and public transit, parking facilities, pedestrian and bikeway systems

- *Community facilities and utilities,* which may include education, libraries, hospitals, recreation, fire and police, water resources, sewerage and waste treatment and disposal, storm drainage and flood management

- *Energy conservation* to reduce energy consumption and promote utilization of renewable energy sources

The preparation of a comprehensive plan involves surveys, studies and analyses of housing, demographic and economic characteristics and trends. The natural characteristics of land and the interrelationship of different kinds of land use affect the plan. The municipality's planning activities may be coordinated with other government bodies to achieve orderly growth and development.

Zoning

Zoning ordinances are local laws that implement the comprehensive plan and regulate and control the use of land and structures within designated land use districts. Zoning affects such things as use of the land, lot sizes, types of structures, building heights, setbacks (the minimum distance away from streets or sidewalks that structures may be built), density (the ratio of land area to structure area or population) and protection of natural resources. Ordinances cannot be static; they must remain flexible to meet the ever-changing needs of society.

There are no nationwide or statewide zoning ordinances. Rather, zoning powers are conferred on municipal governments by state **enabling acts.** State and federal governments may, however, regulate land use through special legislation, such as scenic easement and coastal management and environmental laws.

Zoning ordinances have traditionally divided land use into residential, commercial, industrial and agricultural classifications. These land-use areas are further divided into subclasses. For example, residential areas may be subdivided to provide for detached single-family dwellings, semi-detached structures containing not more than four dwelling units, walk-up apartments, high-rise apartments, and so forth.

In this era of increasing urbanization, growing demand for housing of all types and designs, and need for innovative residential and nonresidential development to encourage more efficient use of land and public services, municipalities are adopting ordinances for subdivisions and *Planned Residential Developments.* Some municipalities also use **buffer zones,** such as landscaped parks and playgrounds, to provide transitional use near the boundaries of districts to screen residential from nonresidential areas. Certain types of zoning are used in some areas that focus on special kinds of land use objectives. These include

- *Bulk zoning* to control density and avoid overcrowding by imposing restrictions such as setbacks, building heights and percentage of open area

- *Aesthetic zoning* to specify certain types of architecture for new buildings

- *Incentive zoning* to ensure that certain kinds of uses are incorporated into developments such as requiring the street floor of an office building to be used for retail establishments

Adoption of zoning ordinances. Today almost all cities with populations in excess of 10,000 have enacted comprehensive zoning ordinances governing the utilization of land located *within corporate limits*. Many states also have enacted legislation that provides that the use of land located *within one to three miles* of an incorporated area must receive the approval and consent of the incorporated area, even if the property is not adjacent to the village, town or city.

Zoning is an often-controversial issue that is impacted by questions of constitutional law. The very preamble of the U.S. Constitution provides for the promotion of the general welfare, but the Fourteenth Amendment prevents the states from depriving "any person of life, liberty, or property, without due process of law." Therein lies the dilemma faced by local governments' zoning bodies: How do they enact zoning ordinances that protect public safety and welfare without violating the constitutional rights of property owners and other individuals?

Any land-use legislation that is destructive, unreasonable, arbitrary or confiscatory usually will be considered void. Further, zoning ordinances must not violate the various provisions of the constitution of the state in which the real estate is located. Tests commonly applied in determining the validity of ordinances require that

- the power be exercised in a reasonable manner;

- the provisions be clear and specific;

- the ordinance be free from discrimination;

- the ordinance promotes public health, safety and general welfare under the police power concept; and

- the ordinance applies to all property in a similar manner.

When land is taken for public use by the government's power of eminent domain, the owner must receive compensation. When *downzoning* occurs in an area—for instance, when land zoned for residential construction is rezoned for conservation or recreational purposes—the government ordinarily is not responsible for compensating property owners for any resulting loss of value. However, if the courts find that a "taking" has occurred, then the downzoning will be ruled to be an unconstitutional attempt to use eminent domain without providing fair compensation to the property owner.

Zoning laws are generally enforced by requiring that zoning permits must be obtained before property owners can begin development. A permit will not be issued unless a proposed development conforms to the permitted zoning, among other requirements. Zoning permits are usually required before a building permit can be issued.

Zoning hearing board. Zoning hearing boards (or zoning boards of appeal) have been established in most communities for the specific purpose of hearing complaints about the effects of zoning ordinances on specific parcels of property. Petitions for variances in or exceptions to the zoning law may be presented to the appeal board.

Nonconforming use. In the enforcement of a zoning ordinance, a frequent problem is the situation in which a lot or improvement does not conform to the zoning use because it was erected prior to the enactment or amendment of the zoning ordinance. Such a **nonconforming use** may be allowed to continue legally as long as it complies with the regulations governing nonconformities in the local ordinance or until the improvements are destroyed or torn down or the current use is abandoned. If the nonconforming use is allowed to continue indefinitely, it is considered to be "grandfathered in" to the new zoning.

Variances and conditional-use permits. Each time a plan or zoning ordinance is enacted, some owners are inconvenienced and want to change the use of a property. Generally these owners may appeal for either a conditional-use permit or a variance to allow a use that does not meet zoning requirements.

A **conditional-use permit** is usually granted to a property owner to allow a special use of property that is defined as an allowable conditional use within that district, such as a church in a residential district. For each use there are standards that must be met. A **variance** may be sought to provide relief if zoning regulations create a physical hardship for the development of a specific property. For example, if an owner's lot is level next to a road but slopes steeply 30 feet away from the road, the zoning board may be willing to allow a variance so the owner can build closer to the road than the setback allows.

Property owners can seek a change in the zoning classification of a parcel of real estate by obtaining an *amendment* to the district map or a zoning ordinance for that area. The proposed amendment must be brought before a public hearing on the matter and approved by the governing body of the community.

Subdivision and Land Development Ordinances

Most communities have adopted *subdivision and land development ordinances* as part of their comprehensive plan. An ordinance will include provisions for submitting and processing subdivision plats, including the charging of fees and review of plats and surveys that are submitted for approval. (See Chapter 20). A major advantage of subdivision ordinances is that they encourage flexibility, economy and ingenuity in the use of land. The layout and arrangement of a subdivision or land development usually provide for

- location, grading, alignment, surfacing and widths of streets and walkways;
- location and design of curbs, gutters, streetlights and water and sewage facilities;
- easements or rights-of-way for drainage and utilities;
- minimum setback lines and lot sizes;

Figure 19.1
Environmental
Protection
Legislation

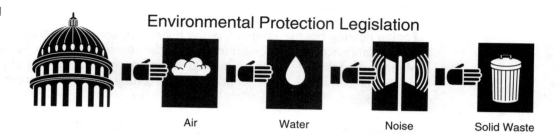

Environmental Protection Legislation

Air   Water   Noise   Solid Waste

- renewable energy systems and energy-conserving building design; and
- areas to be reserved or dedicated for public use, such as parks or recreation facilities.

Building Codes

Most municipalities have enacted ordinances to *specify construction standards* that must be met when repairing or erecting buildings. These are called **building codes,** and they set the requirements for kinds of materials and standards of workmanship, sanitary equipment, electrical wiring, fire prevention standards and the like.

Most communities require a property owner who wishes to build a structure or alter or repair an existing building to obtain a **building permit.** Through the permit requirement, municipal officials are made aware of new construction or alterations and can verify compliance with building codes and zoning ordinances by examining the plans and inspecting the work. Once the completed structure has been inspected and found satisfactory, the municipal inspector issues a *certificate of occupancy* or *occupancy permit.*

If the construction of a building or an alteration violates a deed restriction (discussed later in the chapter), the issuance of a building permit will *not* cure this violation. A building permit is merely evidence of the applicant's compliance with municipal regulations.

Environmental Protection Legislation

Federal and state legislators, as well as some cities and counties, have passed a number of environmental protection laws in an attempt to respond to the growing public concern over the improvement and preservation of America's natural resources.

The various states have responded to the environmental issue by passing a variety of localized environmental protection laws regarding all forms of pollution—air, water, noise and solid waste. For example, many states have enacted laws that prevent builders or private individuals from constructing septic tanks or other effluence-disposal systems in certain areas, particularly where public bodies of water—streams, lakes and rivers—are affected.

See the appendix for additional information about environmental issues and hazardous substances.

IN PRACTICE. . .	*The subject of planning, zoning and restriction of the use of real estate is extremely technical, and the interpretation of the law is not always clear. Questions concerning any of these subjects in relation to real estate transactions should be referred to legal counsel. Further there can be costs for various permits that the landowner should be aware of.*

PRIVATE LAND-USE CONTROLS

Certain restrictions to *control and maintain the desirable quality and character of a property or subdivision* may be created. These restrictions are separate from, and in addition to, the land-use controls exercised by the government. **Deed restrictions** are originated at the time ownership is conveyed by the owner, limiting the use of the property. **Restrictive covenants** can be included in the subdivision plat or set forth in a separate recorded instrument.

There is a distinction between restrictions on the right to *sell* and restrictions on the right to *use.* In general, a deed conveying a fee simple estate may not restrict the right of subsequent owners to sell, mortgage or convey it. Such restrictions attempt to limit the basic right of the *free alienation (transfer) of property;* the courts consider them against public policy and therefore unenforceable.

Restrictive covenants set standards for all the parcels within a defined subdivision. They usually govern the type of building that individual owners can erect as well as how they can use the land, the type of construction, height of structures, setbacks and square footage. The deed conveying a particular lot in the subdivision will refer to the plat or declaration of restrictions, thus limiting the title conveyed and binding all grantees.

These covenants are usually considered valid if they are reasonable restraints and are for the benefit of all property owners in the subdivision. If, however, the terms of the restrictions are too broad, they will be construed as preventing the free transfer of property. If they are "repugnant" to the estate granted, they probably will not be enforceable. If any restrictive covenant or condition is considered unenforceable by a court, the estate will then stand free from the invalid covenant or condition.

Private land use controls may be more restrictive of an owner's use than the local zoning ordinances. The more restrictive of the two takes precedence. Restrictions may have a *time limitation,* for example, "effective for a period of 25 years from this date." After that time, they become inoperative or, in the case of covenants, may be extended by agreement of the majority of the owners.

Private restrictions can be enforced in court when one lot owner applies to the court for an *injunction* to prevent a neighboring lot owner from violating the recorded restrictions. If granted, the court injunction will direct the violator to stop or remove the violation. The court retains the power to punish the violator for failure to obey the court order. If adjoining lot owners stand idly by while a violation is being committed, they can *lose the right* to an injunction by their inaction. The court might claim their right was lost through *laches,* that is, loss of a right through undue delay or failure to assert it.

DIRECT PUBLIC OWNERSHIP

Over the years the government's general policy has been to encourage private ownership of land. It is necessary, however, for a certain amount of land to be owned by the government for such uses as municipal buildings, state legislative houses, schools and military stations. Such direct public ownership is a means of land control.

There are other examples of necessary public ownership. Urban renewal efforts, especially government-owned housing, are one way that public ownership serves the public interest. Publicly owned streets and highways serve a necessary function that benefits the entire population. In addition, public land is often used for recreational purposes such as national and state parks and forest preserves which at the same time help to conserve our natural resources.

At present, the federal government owns approximately 775 million acres of land, nearly one-third of the total area of the United States. At times the federal government has held title to as much as 80 percent of the nation's total land area.

KEY TERMS

buffer zone
building code
building permit
comprehensive plan
conditional-use permit
deed restriction

enabling acts
nonconforming use
restrictive covenants
variance
zoning ordinances

SUMMARY

The control of land use is exercised through public controls, private (or nongovernment) controls and direct public ownership of land.

Through power conferred by state enabling acts, local governments exercise public controls based on the states' police powers to protect the public health, safety and welfare.

Comprehensive plans set forth the development goals and objectives for the community. Zoning ordinances carrying out the provisions of the plan control the use of land and structures within designated land-use districts. Zoning enforcement problems involve zoning hearing boards, conditional-use permits, variances and exceptions, as well as nonconforming uses. Subdivision and land development regulations are adopted to maintain control of the development of expanding community areas so that growth will be harmonious with community standards.

Building codes specify standards for construction, plumbing, sewers, electrical wiring and equipment.

In addition to land-use control on the local level the state and federal governments have occasionally intervened when necessary to preserve natural resources through environmental legislation.

Private land-use controls are exercised by owners through deed restrictions and restrictive covenants. These private restrictions may be enforced by obtaining a court injunction to stop a violator.

Public ownership is a means of land-use control that provides land for such public benefits as parks, highways, schools and municipal buildings.

Questions

1. A provision in a subdivision declaration used to force the grantee to live up to the terms under which he or she holds title to the land is a
   a. restrictive covenant.
   b. reverter.
   c. laches.
   d. conditional-use clause.

2. A landowner, who wants to use property in a manner that is prohibited by a local zoning ordinance but would be of benefit to the community, can apply for which of the following?
   a. Variance
   b. Downzoning
   c. Occupancy permit
   d. Dezoning

3. Public land-use controls include all of the following *except*
   a. subdivision regulations.
   b. deed restrictions.
   c. environmental protection laws.
   d. comprehensive plan specifications.

4. The police power allows regulation of all of the following *except*
   a. the number of buildings.
   b. the size of buildings.
   c. building ownership.
   d. building occupancy.

5. The purpose of a building permit is to
   a. override a deed restriction.
   b. maintain municipal control over the volume of building.
   c. provide evidence of compliance with municipal regulations.
   d. show compliance with deed restrictions.

6. The grantor of a deed may place effective restrictions on
   a. the right to sell the land.
   b. the use of the land.
   c. who the next purchaser will be.
   d. who may occupy the property.

7. Zoning powers are conferred on municipal governments
   a. by state enabling acts.
   b. through police power.
   c. by eminent domain.
   d. through escheat.

8. Zoning hearing boards are established to hear complaints about
   a. restrictive covenants.
   b. the effects of a zoning ordinance.
   c. building codes.
   d. the effects of public ownership.

9. A new zoning code is enacted. A building that is permitted to continue in its former use even though that use does not conform to a new zoning ordinance is an example of
   a. a nonconforming use.
   b. a variance.
   c. a special use.
   d. inverse condemnation.

10. To determine whether or not a location can be put to future use as a retail store one would examine the
    a. building code.
    b. list of permitted nonconforming uses.
    c. housing code.
    d. zoning code.

11. Which of the following would probably *not* be included in a list of deed restrictions?

    a. Types of buildings that may be constructed
    b. Allowable ethnic origins of purchasers
    c. Activities that are not to be conducted at the site
    d. Minimum size of buildings to be constructed

12. A restriction in a seller's deed may be enforced by which of the following?

    a. Court injunction
    b. Zoning board of appeal
    c. City building commission
    d. State legislature

20

Property Development and Subdivision

As cities grow, additional land is required for their expansion. Land in large tracts must receive special attention before it can be successfully converted into sites for homes, stores or other uses. Competent subdividers and land developers are required for new areas to develop soundly. A **subdivider** buys undeveloped acreage and divides it into smaller lots for sale to individuals or developers or for the subdivider's own use. A **developer** (who may also be a subdivider) improves the land, constructs homes or other buildings on the lots and sells them. Developing is generally a much more extensive activity than subdividing.

**Regulation of
Land
Development**

There is *no uniform planning and land development legislation that affects the entire country.* Laws governing subdividing and land planning are controlled by the state and local governing bodies where the land is located. Rules and regulations developed by government agencies have, however, provided certain minimum standards that serve as guides. Local regulations reflect customs and local climate, health and hazard conditions. Many local governments have established standards that are higher than the minimum standards.

Before the actual subdividing can begin, the subdivider/developer must go through the process of land planning. The resulting land development plan must comply with the municipality's *comprehensive plan* (see Chapter 19). Although comprehensive plans and zoning ordinances are not necessarily inflexible, a land development plan that relies on alterations often will require long, expensive and frequently complicated hearings to get the needed authorizations.

From the land development and subdivision plans the subdivider/developer must then draw plats—detailed maps that illustrate not only geographic boundaries of the individual lots but also blocks, sections, streets, public easements and monuments in the prospective subdivision. A plat may also include engineering data and restrictive covenants. The plats must be approved by the municipality before they can be recorded.

Approval is usually obtained in two stages. *Preliminary approval* will be granted on the basis of the plats, often after a public hearing has been held so that the community is involved in the process. *Final approval* is normally conditioned on the subdivider/developer providing some form of financial security or bonding to guarantee completion of certain improvements required by the municipality. The installation of these improvements such as streets, curbs, gutters, fire hydrants, water mains and sanitary and storm sewers involves a major financial commitment from the subdivider/developer.

Providing an adequate supply of water and environmentally sound sewage disposal are major considerations in the development of land. Ordinances frequently require that water be supplied by a certificated public utility unless the individual lots within a subdivision can be properly served by private wells. Sewage disposal that does not pollute streams, rivers and underground water supplies is another major concern. Many states regulate the planning of community and individual sewerage systems. These regulations may not permit septic systems where the soil's absorption or drainage capacity, as determined by a *percolation test,* precludes their use. With the growing emphasis on environmental concerns, a developer may be required to submit an *environmental impact report* with the application for subdivision approval.

With increasing development there is a corresponding demand for municipal capital improvements. Municipalities must develop revenue sources to provide adequate transportation routes via municipal highways, roads and streets to accommodate increased traffic flow. Although the developer is responsible for installation of streets within a subdivision (an "on-site" improvement), the municipality is responsible for these "off-site" improvements. Some states have authorized the local governing body to establish a program to collect *impact fees* at the time of approval of a new subdivision or development for funding these off-site public transportation improvements.

SUBDIVISION

The process of **subdivision** normally involves three distinct stages of development: the initial planning stage, the final planning stage and the disposition, or start-up.

During the *initial planning stage* the subdivider seeks out raw land in a suitable area. Once the land is located, the property is analyzed for its highest and best use, and preliminary subdivision plans are drawn up accordingly. Close contact between the subdivider and local planning and zoning officials is initiated. If the project requires zoning variances, negotiations begin. The subdivider also locates financial backers and initiates marketing strategies.

The *final planning stage* is basically a follow-up of the initial stage. Final plans are prepared, approval is sought from local officials, permanent financing is obtained, the land is purchased, final budgets are prepared and marketing programs are designed.

The *disposition,* or *start-up,* carries the subdividing process to a conclusion. Subdivision plans are recorded with local officials. Once the plat is filed, all areas that have been accepted by the municipality for streets or parks and recreation are considered to be *dedicated,* which is the transfer of privately owned land to the public that is accepted to be used for public purposes. Streets, sewers and utilities are installed. Buildings, open parks and recreational areas are constructed and landscaped if they are part of the subdivision plan. Marketing programs are then initiated, and title to the individual parcels of subdivided land is transferred as the lots are sold.

Subdivision Plans

In plotting out a subdivision according to local planning and zoning controls a subdivider usually determines the size as well as the location of the individual lots. The size of the lots, both in front footage and in depth, together with the total amount of square footage is generally regulated by local ordinances and must be considered carefully. Frequently ordinances regulate both the minimum and the maximum size of a lot.

The land itself must be studied, usually in cooperation with a surveyor, so that the subdivision can be laid out considering natural drainage and land contours. A subdivider should provide for *utility easements* as well as easements for water and sewer mains.

Most subdivisions are laid out by use of *lots and blocks.* An area of land is designated as a block, and the area making up this block is divided into lots.

Although subdividers customarily designate areas reserved for schools, parks and future church sites, this is usually not considered good practice. Once a subdivision has been recorded, the purchasers of the lots have a vested interest in those areas reserved for schools, parks and churches. If for any reason in the future any such purpose is not appropriate, it will become difficult for the developer to abandon the original plan and use that property for residential purposes. To get around this situation many developers designate such areas as *out-lot A, out-lot B* and so forth. Such a designation does not vest any rights in these out-lots in the purchasers of the homesites. If one of these areas is to be used for church purposes, it can be so conveyed and so used. If, on the other hand, the out-lot is not to be used for such a purpose, it can be resubdivided into residential properties without the burden of securing the consent of the lot owners in the area.

Subdivision plat. The subdivider's completed plat of subdivision must contain all necessary approvals of public officials and must be recorded in the county where the land is located.

Because the plat will be the basis for future conveyances, the subdivided land should be measured carefully, with all lot sizes and streets noted by the surveyor and entered accurately on the document. Survey monuments should be established, and measurements should be made from these monuments, with the location of all lots carefully marked.

Covenants and restrictions. Restrictive covenants or deed restrictions are originated and recorded by a subdivider as a means of *controlling and maintaining the desirable quality and character of the subdivision.* These restrictions can be included in the subdivision plat, or they may be set forth in a separate recorded instrument, commonly referred to as a *declaration of restrictions.*

Subdivision Density

Zoning ordinances control land use. Such controls often include minimum lot sizes and population density requirements for subdivisions and land developments. For example, a typical zoning restriction may set the minimum lot area on which a subdivider can build a single-family housing unit at 10,000 square

**Figure 20.1
Street Patterns**

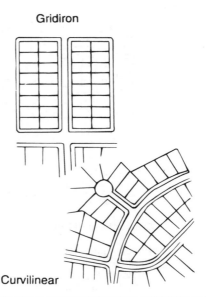

Gridiron

Curvilinear

feet. This means that the subdivider will be able to build four houses per acre. Many zoning authorities now establish special density zoning standards for certain subdivisions. **Density zoning** ordinances restrict the *average maximum number of houses per acre* that may be built within a particular subdivision. If the area is density zoned at an average maximum of four houses per acre, for example, by *clustering* building lots the developer is free to achieve an open effect. Regardless of lot size or the number of units, the subdivider will be consistent with the ordinance as long as the average number of units in the development remains at or below the maximum density. This average is called *gross density.*

Street patterns. By varying street patterns and clustering housing units a subdivider can dramatically increase the amount of open and/or recreational space in a development. Two of these patterns are illustrated in Figure 20.1.

The gridiron pattern evolved out of the government rectangular survey system. Featuring large lots, wide streets and limited-use service alleys, the system works reasonably well up to a point. An overabundance of grid-patterned streets often results in monotonous neighborhoods, with all lots facing busy streets. In addition, sidewalks are usually adjacent to the streets, and the system provides for little or no open space.

The curvilinear system integrates major arteries of travel with smaller secondary and cul-de-sac streets carrying minor traffic. In addition, small parks are often provided at intersections.

Clustering for open space. By slightly reducing lot sizes and **clustering** them around varying street patterns a developer can house as many people in the same area as could be done using traditional subdividing plans but with substantially increased tracts of open space.

For example, compare the two illustrations in Figure 20.2. The first is a plan for a conventionally designed subdivision containing 368 housing units. It uses

**Figure 20.2
Clustered
Subdivision
Plan**

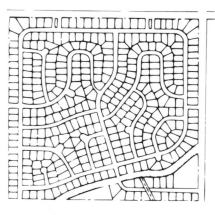
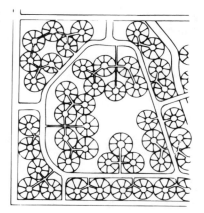

Conventional Plan

12,500-square-foot lots
368 housing units
1.6 acres of parkland
23,200 linear feet of street

Cluster Plan

7,500-square-foot lots
366 housing units
23.5 acres of parkland
17,700 linear feet of street

23,200 linear feet of street and leaves only 1.6 acres open for park areas. Contrast this with the second subdivision pictured. Both subdivisions are equal in size and terrain. But when lots are reduced in size and clustered around limited-access cul-de-sac streets, the number of housing units remains nearly the same (366), with less street area (17,700 linear feet) and drastically increased open space (23.5 acres). In addition, with modern building designs this clustered plan could be modified to accommodate 550 patio homes or 1,100 town houses.

**Interstate Land
Sales Full
Disclosure Act**

To protect consumers from "overenthusiastic sales promotions" in interstate land sales Congress passed the **Interstate Land Sales Full Disclosure Act.** The purpose of the act is to require disclosure of complete and accurate information about the property *before* prospective buyers decide to buy. The law requires those engaged in the *interstate* sale or leasing of 100 or more lots to file a *statement of record* and *register* the details of the land with HUD.

The seller is also required to furnish prospective buyers a **property report** containing all essential information about the property, such as distance over paved roads to nearby communities, number of homes currently occupied, soil conditions affecting foundations and septic systems, type of title a buyer will receive and existence of liens. The property report must be given to a prospective purchaser at least three business days before any sales contract is signed. Although the developer is not required to register a development with HUD that is less than 100 lots, the requirement to furnish property information applies to any development that exceeds 25 lots.

Any contract to purchase a lot covered by this act may be revoked at the purchaser's option until midnight of the seventh day following the signing of the contract. If a contract is signed for the purchase of a lot covered by the act and a property report is not given to the purchaser, an action to revoke the contract may be brought by the purchaser within two years.

If the seller misrepresents the property in any sales promotion, a buyer induced by such a promotion is entitled to sue the seller for civil damages. Failure to comply with the law may also subject a seller to criminal penalties of fines and imprisonment.

**State
Subdivided-Land
Sales Laws**

Many state legislatures have enacted their own subdivided-land sales laws. Some affect only the sale of land located outside the state to state residents, while others affect sales of land located both inside and outside the state. Generally these state land sales laws tend to be stricter and more detailed than the federal law. Students should be aware of the laws in their states and how they compare with federal law.

●   ●   ●   ●   ●   ●   ●

KEY TERMS

clustering   property report
density zoning   subdivider
developer   subdivision
Interstate Land Sales Full
    Disclosure Act

SUMMARY

A subdivider buys undeveloped acreage, divides it into smaller parcels and develops it or sells it. A developer builds homes on the lots and sells them, through the developer's own sales organization or through local real estate brokerage firms. City planners and land developers, working together, plan whole communities that are later incorporated into cities, towns or villages.

Land development must comply with the master plans adopted by counties, cities, villages or towns. This may entail approval of land-use plans by local planning committees or commissioners.

The process of subdivision includes dividing the tract of land into lots and blocks and providing for utility easements, as well as laying out street patterns and widths. A subdivider must generally record a completed plat of subdivision, with all necessary approvals of public officials, in the county where the land is located. Subdividers usually place restrictions on the use of all lots in a subdivision as a general plan for the benefit of all lot owners.

By varying street patterns and housing density and clustering housing units a subdivider can dramatically increase the amount of open and recreational space within a development.

Subdivided land sales are regulated on the federal level by the Interstate Land Sales Full Disclosure Act. This law requires developers engaged in interstate land sales or the leasing of 100 or more units to register the details of the land with HUD. At least three business days before any sales contract is signed, developers must also provide prospective purchasers with a property report containing all essential information about the property in any development that exceeds 25 lots. Subdivided land sales may also be regulated by states' laws.

Questions

1. To control and maintain the quality and character of a subdivision a developer will establish which of the following?
   a. Easements
   b. Restrictive covenants
   c. Buffer zones
   d. Building codes

2. An owner of a large tract of land who, after adequate study of all facts, legally divides the land into lots of suitable size and location for the construction of residences, is known as a(n)
   a. subdivider.   c. land planner.
   b. developer   d. urban planner.

3. A map illustrating the sizes and locations of streets and lots in a subdivision is called a
   a. gridiron pattern.
   b. survey.
   c. plat of subdivision.
   d. property report.

4. *Gross density* refers to which of the following?
   a. The maximum number of residents that may, by law, occupy a subdivision
   b. The average maximum number of houses per acre that may, by law, be built in a subdivision
   c. The maximum-size lot that may, by law, be built in a subdivision
   d. The minimum number of houses that may, by law, be built in a subdivision

5. The type of street pattern that is based on the rectangular survey system is called the
   a. block plan.
   b. gridiron system.
   c. rectangular streets plan.
   d. cul-de-sac system.

6. Legal restrictions established by a recorded deed or subdivision plat, if permitted by public policy and not in violation of constitutional or statutory rights, are enforceable through
   a. zoning ordinances.
   b. court injunctions.
   c. covenants.
   d. laches.

7. Soil absorption and drainage are measured by a
   a. land survey.
   b. plat of subdivision.
   c. density test.
   d. percolation test.

8. All of the following items are usually designated on the plat for a new subdivision *except*
   a. easements for sewer and water mains.
   b. land to be used for streets, schools and civic facilities.
   c. numbered lots and blocks.
   d. prices of residential and commercial lots.

9. A street pattern featuring housing units grouped into large cul-de-sac blocks is generally called a
   a. cluster plan.
   b. curvilinear system.
   c. rectangular street system.
   d. gridiron system.

10. A subdivider can increase the amount of open and/or recreational space in a development by

    a. varying street patterns.
    b. meeting local housing standards.
    c. scattering housing units.
    d. ignoring the zoning codes.

11. To protect the public from fraudulent interstate land sales a developer involved in interstate land sales of 25 or more lots must

    a. provide each purchaser with a report of the details of the land.
    b. pay the prospective buyer's expenses to see the property involved.
    c. provide preferential financing.
    d. include deed restrictions.

21 Fair Housing and Ethical Practices

EQUAL OPPORTUNITY IN HOUSING

Civil rights laws that affect real estate have been enacted to create a marketplace in which all persons of similar financial means have a similar range of choices in the purchase, rental or financing of real property. The goal is to create an open, unbiased housing market in which every person has the opportunity to live where he or she chooses. Owners, real estate licensees, apartment management companies, real estate organizations, lending agencies, builders and developers must all take a part in creating this single housing market. Federal, state and local fair housing or equal opportunity laws affect every phase of a real estate transaction, from listing to closing.

The U.S. Congress and the Supreme Court have labored to create a legal framework that preserves the rights granted to all citizens under the Constitution. Discrimination in this nation has a long history, dating back to the beginning of slavery. While the passage of laws establishes a code for public conduct, centuries of discriminatory practices result in attitudes and stereotypes that are not easily changed by laws. Real estate licensees cannot allow their own prejudices or those of property owners or prospective property seekers to affect compliance with the fair housing laws.

Potential licensees must have a thorough knowledge of the fair housing laws to avoid illegal practices. Illegal activity is not limited to racial discrimination; amendments to the fair housing laws have expanded the number of protected classes. *Failure to comply with fair housing laws is not only a criminal act but also grounds for disciplinary action against the licensee.* State laws may be stricter than the federal requirements. Individual states may name the same protected classes as the federal laws and may protect additional classes as well. It is imperative that licensees learn all pertinent federal and state regulations.

Federal Laws

The efforts of the federal government to guarantee equal housing opportunities to all U.S. citizens began more than 100 years ago with the passage of the **Civil Rights Act of 1866.** This law, an outgrowth of the Thirteenth Amendment to the Constitution, which abolished slavery, prohibits any type of discrimination based on race: "All citizens of the United States shall have the same right in every state and territory as is enjoyed by white citizens thereof to inherit, purchase, lease, sell, hold, and convey real and personal property."

In 1896 the U.S. Supreme Court established the "separate but equal" doctrine, which provided that separate but equal accommodations for the races were not in conflict with the Constitution. However, this segregated the races, creating classes among citizens. Although accommodations were separate, they were rarely equal. Patterns of segregation were perpetuated by zoning ordinances and restrictive covenants. The FHA, in administering its mortgage insurance programs, encouraged practices that maintained segregated housing patterns. Not until 1948 did the U.S. Supreme Court decide that racially restrictive covenants violated rights granted under the Constitution and were, therefore, unenforceable. In 1950 the federal government prohibited insuring mortgages on property encumbered by racially restrictive covenants.

It was not until the civil rights efforts of the 1960s that discriminatory conduct in housing was singled out for specific legislation. In 1962 President John Kennedy issued an executive order that guaranteed nondiscrimination in housing that is financed by FHA and VA loans. The Civil Rights Act of 1964 prohibited discrimination in any housing program that receives whole or partial federal funding. However, both of these efforts had limited impact on discriminatory housing practices, particularly because a relatively small percentage of housing was affected by these programs. Finally, in 1968, Title VIII of the Civil Rights Act prohibited specific practices in housing.

Fair Housing Act

Title VIII of the Civil Rights Act of 1968 prohibited discrimination in housing based on race, color, religion and national origin. In 1974 the Housing and Community Development Act added sex. In 1988 the Fair Housing Amendments Act added handicap and familial status as protected classes. Today the **Fair Housing Act,** as it is known, prohibits discrimination on the basis of *race, color, religion, sex, handicap, familial status and national origin.* The Act also prohibits discrimination against individuals because of their *association* with persons in the protected classes. This law is administered by the **Department of Housing and Urban Development (HUD),** which has promulgated rules and regulations that further interpret the practices defined by the law.

The regulations define housing as a "dwelling," being any building or portion thereof (including a single-family house, condominium, cooperative or mobile home) designed for occupancy as a residence by one or more families. This also includes vacant land for sale or lease for the location or construction of these structures. Relating to persons in the *protected classes,* it shall be unlawful to

- refuse to sell, rent or negotiate with any person or otherwise make a dwelling unavailable;
- differentiate in terms, conditions or services for the purpose of discriminating;
- practice discrimination through any statement or advertisement that indicates any preference, limitation or discrimination;
- represent that a property is not available when in fact it is available for sale or rent;

- make a profit by inducing owners to sell or rent because of the prospective entry into the neighborhood of persons in the protected classes;

- alter the terms or conditions for a loan for the purchase, construction, improvement or repair of a dwelling as a means of discrimination; or

- deny membership or limit the participation in any real estate organization as a means of discriminating.

In addition to these general provisions of the law, HUD has issued rules and regulations that define specific procedures that affect practices in the real estate industry, mortgage lending and advertising.

Familial status. The most recent amendment to the Fair Housing Act included familial status as a protected class. Congress intended that this would assist families with children to find suitable housing that previously was unavailable, particularly in rentals. *Familial status* is defined as one or more individuals who have not reached the age of 18 being domiciled with a parent or another person who has or is seeking legal custody. It also includes a person who is pregnant. Unless a property meets the standards for exemption as "housing for older persons" all properties must be made available under the same terms and conditions as are available to all other persons. Including families with children as a protected class requires property owners and licensees to change their standards for occupancy and their advertising and marketing practices. It is no longer legal to advertise "adults only" or to make other similar references. The number of persons permitted to reside in a property (the occupancy standards) cannot be restrictive with the intent or effect of eliminating families with children.

Handicap. *Handicap* is defined as a physical or mental impairment or having a history of such impairment that substantially limits one or more of a person's major life activities. It does *not* include the current illegal use of or addiction to a controlled substance. However, an individual in an addiction recovery program is protected. Individuals who have AIDS *are* protected by the fair housing laws under the handicap classification.

It is unlawful to discriminate against prospective buyers or tenants because of a handicap. There must be services or facilities that will afford them the opportunity to use and enjoy the dwelling. Discrimination includes refusing to permit the person with the handicap to make reasonable modifications, at his or her own expense, of the existing premises that may be necessary for full enjoyment. In the case of a rental, the landlord can require, if it is reasonable to do so, that the person restore the interior of the premises to its previous condition if these modifications would make the property undesirable to the general population.

The law does not prohibit restricting occupancy exclusively to persons with a handicap in dwellings that are designed specifically for their accommodation.

For new construction of certain multifamily properties, a number of accessibility and usability requirements must be met under federal law. Access is specified for public and common-use portions of the buildings and adaptive and accessible design for the interior of the dwelling units. Some states have their own laws as well.

**Figure 21.1
Fair Housing
and Ethical
Practices**

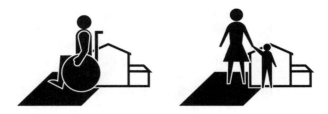

**Exemptions to
the Fair
Housing Act**

The federal Fair Housing Act provides for certain exemptions. It is, however, important to know in what situations they apply. There are *no* exemptions involving race *or* in transactions involving a real estate licensee.

- The sale or rental of a single-family home is exempted when the home is owned by an individual who does not own more than three such homes at one time, a broker or salesperson is *not* used and discriminatory advertising is not used. Only one such sale by an owner not living in the dwelling at the time of the transaction or not the most recent occupant is exempt from the law within any 24-month period.

- The rental of rooms or units is exempted in an owner-occupied one- to four-family dwelling.

- Dwelling units owned by religious organizations may be restricted to people of the same religion if membership in the organization is not restricted on the basis of race, color, national origin, handicap or familial status.

- A private club that is not open to the public may restrict the rental or occupancy of lodgings that it owns to its members as long as the lodgings are not operated commercially. The private club may not discriminate in its requirements for membership.

Housing for older persons. While the Fair Housing Act protects families with children, certain properties can be restricted for occupancy by the elderly. Housing occupied (or intended to be occupied) solely by persons age 62 or older or housing occupied (or intended to be occupied) by at least one person 55 years of age or older per unit is exempt from the familial status protection. In determining if property meets the "55 or older" exemption, there must be significant facilities and services to meet the physical and social needs of older persons, and at least 80 percent of the units must be occupied by an individual 55 years of age or older. There also must be published policies and procedures that demonstrate the intent to provide housing for these individuals.

Other provisions. The Fair Housing Act does not require that housing be made available to individuals whose tenancy would constitute a direct threat to the health or safety of other individuals or that would result in substantial physical damage to the property of others. Nor are individuals who have been *convicted* of the illegal manufacture or distribution of a controlled substance protected under this law.

Jones v. Mayer. In 1968 the Supreme Court heard the case of *Jones v. Alfred H. Mayer Company,* 392 U.S. 409 (1968). In its decision the Court upheld the Civil Rights Act of 1866, which "prohibits all racial discrimination, private or public, in the sale and rental of property." This decision is important because, although the federal law exempts individual homeowners and certain groups, the 1866 law *prohibits all racial discrimination without exception.* An aggrieved person may seek remedy for racial discrimination under the 1866 law. *Where race is involved, no exceptions apply.*

In 1987 the U.S. Supreme Court further defined *race* to include more than non-white persons. In the decision of two cases the court used ancestral and ethnic characteristics, including certain physical, cultural or linguistic characteristics that are commonly shared by a national origin group, to expand the definition of race. These rulings are significant because discrimination on the basis of race, as it is now defined, affords due process of complaints under the provisions of the Civil Rights Act of 1866.

Equal Housing Opportunity Poster

The Fair Housing Act instituted the use of an equal housing opportunity poster. This poster, which is available from HUD and illustrated in Figure 21.2, features the equal housing opportunity slogan, an equal housing statement pledging adherence to the Fair Housing Act and support of affirmative marketing and advertising programs and the equal housing opportunity logo (shown in Figure 21.3). The use of the equal housing logo and slogan in advertising is discussed in HUD's regulations.

When HUD investigates a broker for discriminatory practices, it may consider failure to prominently display the poster in the broker's place of business as prima facie evidence of discrimination.

Equal Credit Opportunity Act

The federal **Equal Credit Opportunity Act (ECOA)** prohibits discrimination based on race, color, religion, national origin, sex, marital status or age (if the applicant has reached the age of contractual capacity) in the granting of credit. Note the dissimilarity in the protected classes between the Fair Housing Act and the ECOA in which marital status and age are included. As in the Fair Housing Act, ECOA requires that credit applications be considered only on the basis of income, net worth, job stability and credit rating.

Americans with Disabilities Act

The **Americans with Disability Act (ADA)** was signed into law in 1990 by President Bush. Although it is not a housing or credit law, it does impact real estate licensees because it addresses the rights of individuals with disabilities in employment and public accommodations. Congress acknowledged that individuals with disabilities have been excluded from employment opportunities and confronted by architectural, transportation and communication barriers and purposeful unequal treatment in society. Although Congress passed the Rehabilitation Act in 1973, its focus was to prohibit discrimination in federally funded programs. ADA has been called the most comprehensive civil rights legislation since the 1960s as it intends to enable individuals with disabilities to become part of the economic and social mainstream of society.

As discussed in Chapter 17, Title I of ADA provides for the employment of qualified job applicants regardless of their disability. As of July 26, 1994 any employer with 15 or more employees must adopt nondiscriminatory employment procedures and make reasonable accommodations to enable an individual

Figure 21.2
Equal Housing
Opportunity
Poster

U.S.. Department of Housing and Urban Development

EQUAL HOUSING
OPPORTUNITY

We Do Business in Accordance With the Federal Fair Housing Law

(The Fair Housing Amendments Act of 1988)

It is Illegal to Discriminate Against Any Person Because of Race, Color, Religion, Sex, Handicap, Familial Status, or National Origin

- In the sale or rental of housing or residential lots
- In advertising the sale or rental of housing
- In the financing of housing

- In the provision of real estate brokerage services
- In the appraisal of housing
- Blockbusting is also illegal

Anyone who feels he or she has been discriminated against may file a complaint of housing discrimination:

   1-800-424-8590 (Toll Free)
   1-800-424-8529 (TDD)

U.S. Department of Housing and
Urban Development
Assistant Secretary for Fair Housing and
Equal Opportunity
Washington, D.C. 20410

Previous editions are obsolete   form HUD-928.1 (3-89)

**Figure 21.3
Equal Housing
Opportunity
Symbol**

**EQUAL HOUSING
OPPORTUNITY**

with a disability to perform essential job functions. By complying with this law, brokers can demonstrate in their employment practices support for equal opportunity, the principles they support also in housing.

Title III of ADA provides for accessibility to goods and services by individuals with disabilities. While the federal civil rights laws have traditionally been viewed in the real estate industry as housing-related, the practices of licensees who deal with nonresidential property are significantly impacted by ADA. Because people with disabilities have the right to full and equal access to businesses and public services under ADA, building owners and managers must ensure that obstacles restricting those rights are eliminated. Comprehensive guidance for making public facilities accessible is provided in the law. To protect property owners from incurring burdensome expense to extensively retrofit an existing building, *reasonably achievable accommodations* are recommended that will accomplish the purpose of providing access to the facility and services. New construction, including remodeling, must meet higher standards, being *readily accessible and usable,* because it costs less to incorporate accessible features in the design than to retrofit. Though the law intends to provide for people with disabilities, many of the accessible design features and accommodations are desirable for all.

**FAIR HOUSING
PRACTICES**

It is important for licensees to know the classes of individuals whose rights are protected under these laws and the practices that are prohibited. For the civil rights laws to accomplish their goals of eliminating discrimination, they must be applied in daily practice. In the following section the topics are selected for discussion because they are either clearly illegal or provide insight into the specific situations that confront real estate licensees.

Blockbusting

Blockbusting is the unlawful activity of inducing or attempting to induce a person to sell or rent a dwelling by making representations regarding the entry or prospective entry into the neighborhood of a person in one of the protected classes. Any action, including uninvited solicitations, that conveys the message that a neighborhood is undergoing changes and encourages the property owner to sell or rent will be considered blockbusting. Asserting that the entry of certain persons will have undesirable consequences such as a lowering of property values, an increase in criminal or antisocial behavior or a decline in the quality of schools to encourage a sale or rental is also illegal. A critical element in blockbusting, according to HUD's regulations, is that profit is a motive for engaging in this activity. A property owner may be intimidated into selling the property at a depressed price to the blockbuster, who in turn sells the property to another person at a higher price. Another term for this activity is *panic selling*. To avoid accusations of blockbusting, licensees should use good judgment when choosing locations and methods for soliciting listings.

Steering

Steering is the channeling of homeseekers to or away from particular neighborhoods, thereby limiting their choices. This practice makes certain homes unavailable, which is contrary to the fair housing laws. Steering may be done either to preserve the homogeneity of a neighborhood or to change its character intentionally. Many cases of steering are subtle, motivated by *assumptions or perceptions* about a home seeker's desires or preferences for a neighborhood or assumptions about financial ability. Assumptions are dangerous—they are often *wrong*.

The salesperson's role is to qualify the prospective home seeker *objectively* to identify housing requirements and determine financial ability. The salesperson then makes recommendations based on the individual's needs and finances. It is the prospective home seeker who selects the neighborhoods or specific properties to be viewed. The licensee cannot *assume* that a prospective home seeker expects to be directed to certain neighborhoods or properties. Steering anyone is illegal.

Intent and Effect

If the owner or real estate licensee *purposely* sets different sales or rental prices or different down payment or security deposit requirements to "chill the interest" of certain individuals or establishes policies to segregate families with children in certain parts of a housing complex, for example, the *intention* to illegally discriminate is obvious. However, owners and licensees must scrutinize their policies and procedures to determine if, even without intent, they have the *effect* of discriminating. Whenever such practices *result* in unequal treatment of individuals in the protected classes, they are regarded as being discriminatory. This is known as the *effects test,* which is used by compliance agencies to determine if an individual has been discriminated against. Certain policies and procedures may have been adopted to serve other business purposes unrelated to discriminating against persons in the protected classes. But if they affect those individuals differently from others, the policies and procedures are discriminatory. This effect is known as *disparate impact.*

Advertising

Any printed or published advertisement of property for sale or rent cannot include language that indicates a preference or limitation, regardless of how subtle the choice of words. (See Figure 21.4.) HUD's regulations cite examples that are considered discriminatory: "adult building, Jewish home, restricted, private, integrated, traditional." References to a property's location can also imply discriminatory preference or limitation, such as its relation to landmarks that are associated with a nationality or religion. References to a parish or a synagogue or to a club or school used exclusively by one sex are also examples. Pictorial rep-

**Figure 21.4
Advertising**

FOR RENT: 2 Bedroom Apt. in adult
building within walking distance of the
synagogue. $500 per month plus utilities.
New carpeting. No pets allowed.
Fireplace, eat-in kitchen, lots of storage
space. Prefer quiet nonsmoker.
Call 555-3490.

FOR RENT: 2 Bedroom Apt. $500 per
month plus utilities. New carpeting. No
pets allowed. Fireplace, eat-in kitchen,
lots of storage space. Prefer quiet nonsmoker. Call 555-3490.

resentations using human models as residents or customers that depict one segment of the population while not including others in the protected classes are discriminatory. The media used for promoting property or real estate services cannot target one population to the exclusion of others. The selective use of media, whether by language or geography, for example, may have discriminatory impact. Consult HUD's regulations for a full discussion of advertising procedures.

Appraising

Those who prepare appraisals or any statements of valuation, whether they are formal or informal, oral or written (including a comparative market analysis), may consider any factors that affect value. However, race, color, religion, national origin, sex, handicap and familial status are *not* factors that may be taken into consideration.

Redlining

The practice of refusing to make mortgage loans or issue insurance policies in specific areas for reasons other than the economic qualifications of the applicants is known as **redlining.** This practice, which often contributes to the deterioration of older, transitional neighborhoods, was frequently based on racial grounds rather than on any real objections to the applicant. The federal Fair Housing Act prohibits discrimination in mortgage lending and covers not only the actions of primary lenders but also activities in the secondary mortgage market. A lending institution, however, can refuse a loan solely on *sound* economic grounds.

In an effort to counteract redlining, the federal government passed the *Home Mortgage Disclosure Act* in 1975. This act requires all institutional mortgage lenders with assets in excess of $10 million and one or more offices in a given geographic area to make annual reports by census tracts of all mortgage loans the institution makes or purchases. This law enables the government to detect lending or insuring patterns that might constitute redlining.

ENFORCEMENT OF THE FAIR HOUSING ACT

The federal Fair Housing Act is administered by the Office of Fair Housing and Equal Opportunity (OFHEO) under the direction of the Secretary of HUD. Any aggrieved person who believes illegal discrimination has occurred may file a complaint with HUD within one year of the alleged act. HUD may also initiate its own complaint. Complaints may be reported to the Office of Fair Housing and Equal Opportunity, Dept. of Housing and Urban Development, Washington, DC 20410, or to the Office of Fair Housing and Equal Opportunity c/o the nearest HUD regional office.

Upon receipt of a complaint HUD will initiate an investigation and, within 100 days of the filing of the complaint, either determine that reasonable cause exists to bring a charge that illegal discrimination has occurred or dismiss the complaint. During this investigation period HUD can attempt to resolve the dispute informally through conciliation. *Conciliation* is the process initiated to resolve the complaint by obtaining assurance that the person against whom the complaint was filed (the respondent) will remedy any violation of the rights of the aggrieved party and take action that will ensure the elimination or prevention of discriminatory practices in the future. These agreements can be enforced through civil action if necessary.

If a charge of discrimination is issued the aggrieved person has the right to seek relief through administrative proceedings before an administrative law judge (ALJ). The ALJ has the authority to award actual damages to the aggrieved person or persons and, if it is believed the public interest will be served, to impose penalties as well. The penalties range from up to $10,000 for the first offense to $25,000 for a second violation within five years and $50,000 for further violations within seven years. The ALJ also has the authority to issue an injunction to order the offender to either do something—rent to the complaining party, for example—or refrain from doing something.

The parties may elect civil (judicial) action in federal court at any time within two years of the discriminatory act. For cases heard in federal court, unlimited punitive damages can be awarded in addition to actual damages. The court can also issue injunctions. As noted in Chapter 4, errors and omissions insurance carried by licensees normally does not pay on violations of the fair housing laws.

Whenever the attorney general has reasonable cause to believe that any person or group is engaged in a pattern or practice of resistance to the full enjoyment of any of the rights granted by the federal fair housing laws, the attorney general may file a civil action in any federal district court. Civil penalties may result in an amount not to exceed $50,000 for a first violation and an amount not to exceed $100,000 for second and subsequent violations.

Complaints brought under the Civil Rights Act of 1866 are taken directly to a federal court. The only time limit for action is the state's statute of limitation for *torts,* that is, injuries one individual inflicts on another.

State and Local Enforcement Agencies

Whenever a state or municipality has a fair housing law that has been ruled *substantially equivalent* to the federal law, all complaints that are filed with HUD are referred to and handled by the local enforcement agency responsible for those laws. To be considered substantially equivalent, the local law and its related regulations must contain prohibitions comparable to those in the federal law. In addition, the state or locality must show that its local enforcement agency is taking sufficient affirmative action in processing and investigating complaints and in finding remedies for discriminatory practices.

Some municipalities have ordinances that deal with discriminatory housing practices. Real estate licensees should be familiar with any local laws.

**Figure 21.5
Implications for
Salespeople**

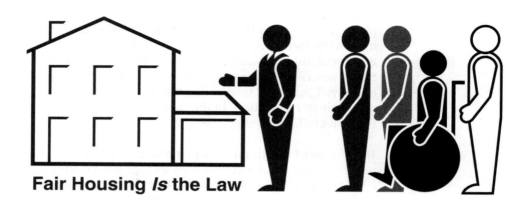

Fair Housing *Is* the Law

**Threats or Acts
of Violence**

The federal Fair Housing Act of 1968 contains criminal provisions protecting the rights of those who seek the benefits of the open housing law as well as owners, brokers or salespeople who aid or encourage the enjoyment of open housing rights. Unlawful actions involving threats, coercion and intimidation are punishable by civil action. In such cases the victim should report the incident immediately to the local police and to the nearest office of the Federal Bureau of Investigation.

**IMPLICATIONS FOR
BROKERS AND
SALESPEOPLE**

An enormous responsibility for effecting and maintaining an open housing market falls on the real estate industry. Brokers and salespeople promote themselves as the real estate experts in the community. With this visibility comes the *social* as well as the *legal* responsibility for ensuring that the civil rights of all persons are protected. The community has the right to expect the real estate industry to do its part in overcoming illegal discrimination. The reputation of the industry cannot afford *any* appearance that its licensees are not committed to the principles of fair housing. Licensees and the industry must be publicly conspicuous in their equal opportunity efforts. Establishing relationships with community and fair housing groups to discuss common concerns and develop programs to address problems is constructive activity.

Fair housing *is* the law. (See Figure 21.5.) The consequences for anyone who violates the law are serious and potentially very expensive. That the offense was unintentional is no defense. Although there are overt acts of discrimination, many are very subtle. Licensees must scrutinize their practices and be careful not to fall victim to clients or customers who expect to discriminate.

Complaints may be filed by anyone who even *suspects* that illegal discrimination has occurred. The enforcement agency is responsible for uncovering the facts during an investigation to determine whether grounds for the complaint exist. *The complainant does not have to prove guilty knowledge or specific intent.* Licensees should be scrupulous in their conduct to avoid a complaint being filed. An investigation can be time consuming and expensive even if the complaint is unfounded.

It is essential that the broker establish office policies and procedures that ensure compliance with the laws. A *standardized inventory* of properties available for sale or rent will ensure that all persons who inquire about availability will be offered a uniform listing of properties. *Consistent practices* for qualifying prospective purchasers and tenants, showing properties, following the progress of a transaction and presenting offers ensure equal treatment for everyone. Establishing *verifiable and measurable criteria* that can be justified for prudent business decisions is essential for qualifying all tenant applicants equally. *Written documentation* of applications, conversations, showings and follow-up contacts are essential evidence to defend against a complaint. A major pitfall for licensees is failing to communicate with all parties. The complexities of a real estate transaction are commonplace to a licensee, but they can be a confusing maze for a client or customer. Actions can be misinterpreted if they are not completely explained.

All parties deserve the same standard of service, that is, "equal treatment," within their property requirements, financial ability and experience in the marketplace. A good test is to answer the question "Are we doing this for everyone?" If an act is not performed consistently or if an act affects some individuals differently from others, it could be construed as discriminatory.

The prejudices and stereotypes individuals have can surface in a real estate transaction and can result in discriminatory behavior. Even innocent actions may be viewed later as prejudicial. For instance, a seller asks the nationality of a prospective purchaser. The licensee must consider the *effect* his or her response will have on the transaction. If the seller refuses to negotiate or decides to pursue a different course of negotiations based on the response, the question of discrimination could arise. A licensee cannot control effect and must be aware of how actions could be construed.

HUD requires that its fair housing posters be displayed in any place of business where real estate is offered for sale or rent. Following HUD's advertising procedures and using the fair housing slogan and logo keep the public aware of the broker's commitment to equal opportunity. The public must know that it is the broker's policy, for example, not to offer any information on the racial, ethnic or religious composition of a neighborhood or place restrictions on listing, showing or providing information on the availability of homes.

Fair housing is *good business*. It maximizes the number of properties available for sale and rent to the maximum of potential purchasers and tenants.

PROFESSIONAL ETHICS

Professional conduct involves more than just complying with the laws of the industry. In real estate the licensing laws set forth activities that are illegal and therefore prohibited. Licensees may be performing legally yet not be performing ethically. **Ethics** is a system of *moral* principles, rules and standards of conduct. The ethical system of a profession establishes conduct that *exceeds* legal compliance. These moral principles establish standards for integrity and competence in dealing with the consumers of an industry's services, as well as a code of conduct between professionals of that industry.

The basic rule of professional ethics is to *above all do no harm*. A course of action may appear to be justified because it is not illegal. However, if it causes

Figure 21.6
REALTORS®
Code of Ethics

Code of Ethics and Standards of Practice

of the
NATIONAL ASSOCIATION OF REALTORS®
Effective January 1, 1993

Where the word REALTORS® is used in this Code and Preamble, it shall be deemed to include REALTOR-ASSOCIATE®s.

While the Code of Ethics establishes obligations that may be higher than those mandated by law, in any instance where the Code of Ethics and the law conflict, the obligations of the law must take precedence.

Preamble ...

Under all is the land. Upon its wise utilization and widely allocated ownership depend the survival and growth of free institutions and of our civilization. REALTORS® should recognize that the interests of the nation and its citizens require the highest and best use of the land and the widest distribution of land ownership. They require the creation of adequate housing, the building of functioning cities, the development of productive industries and farms, and the preservation of a healthful environment.

Such interests impose obligations beyond those of ordinary commerce. They impose grave social responsibility and a patriotic duty to which REALTORS® should dedicate themselves, and for which they should be diligent in preparing themselves. REALTORS®, therefore, are zealous to maintain and improve the standards of their calling and share with their fellow REALTORS® a common responsibility for its integrity and honor. The term REALTOR® has come to connote competency, fairness, and high integrity resulting from adherence to a lofty ideal of moral conduct in business relations. No inducement of profit and no instruction from clients ever can justify departure from this ideal.

In the interpretation of this obligation, REALTORS® can take no safer guide than that which has been handed down through the centuries, embodied in the Golden Rule, "Whatsoever ye would that others should do to you, do ye even so to them."

Accepting this standard as their own, REALTORS® pledge to observe its spirit in all of their activities and to conduct their business in accordance with the tenets set forth below.

Articles 1 through 5 are aspirational and establish ideals REALTORS® should strive to attain.

ARTICLE 1

In justice to those who place their interests in a real estate professional's care, REALTORS® should endeavor to become and remain informed on matters affecting real estate in their community, the state, and nation. (Amended 11/92)

ARTICLE 2

In the interest of promoting cooperation and enhancing their professional image, REALTORS® are encouraged to refrain from un-

solicited criticism of other real estate practitioners and, if an opinion is sought about another real estate practitioner, their business or their business practices, any opinion should be offered in an objective, professional manner. (Amended 11/92)

ARTICLE 3

REALTORS® should endeavor to eliminate in their communities any practices which could be damaging to the public or bring discredit to the real estate profession. REALTORS® should assist the governmental agency charged with regulating the practices of brokers and sales licensees in their states. (Amended 11/87)

ARTICLE 4

To prevent dissension and misunderstanding and to assure better service to the owner, REALTORS® should urge the exclusive listing of property unless contrary to the best interest of the owner. (Amended 11/87)

ARTICLE 5

In the best interests of society, of their associates, and their own businesses, REALTORS® should willingly share with other REALTORS® the lessons of their experience and study for the benefit of the public, and should be loyal to the Board of REALTORS® of their community and active in its work.

Articles 6 through 23 establish specific obligations. Failure to observe these requirements subject REALTORS® to disciplinary action.

ARTICLE 6

REALTORS® shall seek no unfair advantage over other REALTORS® and shall conduct their business so as to avoid controversies with other REALTORS®. (Amended 11/87)

• Standard of Practice 6-1

REALTORS® shall not misrepresent the availability of access to show or inspect a listed property. (Cross-reference Article 22.) (Amended 11/87)

• Standard of Practice 6-2

Article 6 is not intended to prohibit otherwise ethical, aggressive or innovative business practices. "Controversies", as used in Article 6, does not relate to disputes over commissions or divisions of commissions. (Adopted 4/92)

ARTICLE 7

When representing a buyer, seller, landlord, tenant, or other client as an agent, REALTORS® pledge themselves to protect and promote the interests of their client. This obligation of absolute fidelity to the client's interests is primary, but it does not relieve REALTORS® of their obligation to treat all parties honestly. When serving a buyer, seller, landlord, tenant or other party in a non-agency capacity, REALTORS® remain obligated to treat all parties honestly. (Amended 11/92)

• Standard of Practice 7-1(a)

REALTORS® shall submit offers and counter-offers as quickly as possible. (Adopted 11/92)

 NATIONAL ASSOCIATION OF REALTORS®

REALTOR®   *The Voice for Real Estate®*

**Figure 21.6
(continued)**

- **Standard of Practice 7-1(b)**
  When acting as listing brokers, REALTORS® shall continue to submit to the seller/landlord all offers and counter-offers until closing or execution of a lease unless the seller/landlord has waived this obligation in writing. REALTORS® shall not be obligated to continue to market the property after an offer has been accepted by the seller/landlord. REALTORS® shall recommend that sellers/landlords obtain the advice of legal counsel prior to acceptance of a subsequent offer except where the acceptance is contingent on the termination of the pre-existing purchase contract or lease. (Cross-reference Article 17.) (Amended 11/92)

- **Standard of Practice 7-1(c)**
  REALTORS® acting as agents of buyers/tenants shall submit to buyers/tenants all offers and counter-offers until acceptance but have no obligation to continue to show properties to their clients after an offer has been accepted unless otherwise agreed in writing. REALTORS® acting as agents of buyers/tenants shall recommend that buyers/tenants obtain the advice of legal counsel if there is a question as to whether a pre-existing contract has been terminated. (Adopted 11/92)

- **Standard of Practice 7-2**
  REALTORS®, when seeking to become a buyer/tenant representative, shall not mislead buyers or tenants as to savings or other benefits that might be realized through use of the REALTOR®'s services. (Amended 11/92)

- **Standard of Practice 7-3**
  REALTORS®, in attempting to secure a listing, shall not deliberately mislead the owner as to market value

- **Standard of Practice 7-4**
  (Refer to Standard of Practice 22-1, which also relates to Article 7, Code of Ethics.)

- **Standard of Practice 7-5**
  (Refer to Standard of Practice 22-2, which also relates to Article 7, Code of Ethics.)

- **Standard of Practice 7-6**
  REALTORS®, when acting as principals in a real estate transaction, remain obligated by the duties imposed by the Code of Ethics. (Amended 11/92)

- **Standard of Practice 7-7**
  REALTORS® may represent the seller/landlord and buyer/tenant in the same transaction only after full disclosure to and with informed consent of both parties. (Cross-reference Article 9) (Adopted 11/92)

- **Standard of Practice 7-8**
  The obligation of REALTORS® to preserve confidential information provided by their clients continues after the termination of the agency relationship. REALTORS® shall not knowingly, during or following the termination of a professional relationship with their client:
  1) reveal confidential information of the client; or
  2) use confidential information of the client to the disadvantage of the client; or
  3) use confidential information of the client for the REALTORS®' advantage or the advantage of a third party unless the client consents after full disclosure unless:
     a) required by court order; or
     b) it is the intention of the client to commit a crime and the information is necessary to prevent the crime; or
     c) necessary to defend the REALTOR® or the REALTOR®'s

employees or associates against an accusation of wrongful conduct. (Cross-reference Article 9) (Adopted 11/92)

ARTICLE 8
In a transaction, REALTORS® shall not accept compensation from more than one party, even if permitted by law, without disclosure to all parties and the informed consent of the REALTOR®'s client or clients. (Amended 11/92)

ARTICLE 9
REALTORS® shall avoid exaggeration, misrepresentation, or concealment of pertinent facts relating to the property or the transaction. REALTORS® shall not, however, be obligated to discover latent defects in the property, to advise on matters outside the scope of their real estate license, or to disclose facts which are confidential under the scope of agency duties owed to their clients. (Amended 11/92)

- **Standard of Practice 9-1**
  REALTORS® shall not be parties to the naming of a false consideration in any document, unless it be the naming of an obviously nominal consideration.

- **Standard of Practice 9-2**
  (Refer to Standard of Practice 21-3, which also relates to Article 9, Code of Ethics.)

- **Standard of Practice 9-3**
  (Refer to Standard of Practice 7-3, which also relates to Article 9, Code of Ethics.)

- **Standard of Practice 9-4**
  REALTORS® shall not offer a service described as "free of charge" when the rendering of a service is contingent on the obtaining of a benefit such as a listing or commission.

- **Standard of Practice 9-5**
  REALTORS® shall, with respect to the subagency of another REALTOR®, timely communicate any change of compensation for subagency services to the other REALTOR® prior to the time such REALTOR® produces a prospective buyer who has signed an offer to purchase the property for which the subagency has been offered through MLS or otherwise by the listing agency.

- **Standard of Practice 9-6**
  REALTORS® shall disclose their REALTOR® status and contemplated personal interest, if any, when seeking information from another REALTOR® concerning real property. (Cross-reference to Article 12) (Amended 11/92)

- **Standard of Practice 9-7**
  The offering of premiums, prizes, merchandise discounts or other inducements to list, sell, purchase, or lease is not, in itself, unethical even if receipt of the benefit is contingent on listing, purchasing, or leasing through the REALTOR® making the offer. However, REALTORS® must exercise care and candor in any such advertising or other public or private representations so that any party interested in receiving or otherwise benefiting from the REALTOR®'s offer will have clear, thorough, advance understanding of all the terms and conditions of the offer. The offering of any inducements to do business is subject to the limitations and restrictions of state law and the ethical obligations established by Article 9, as interpreted by any applicable Standard of Practice. (Amended 11/92)

- **Standard of Practice 9-8**
  REALTORS® shall be obligated to discover and disclose adverse factors reasonably apparent to someone with expertise in only

Figure 21.6
(continued)

those areas required by their real estate licensing authority. Article 9 does not impose upon the REALTOR® the obligation of expertise in other professional or technical disciplines. (Cross-reference Article 11.) (Amended 11/86)

• Standard of Practice 9-9

REALTORS®, acting as listing brokers, have an affirmative obligation to disclose the existence of dual or variable rate commission arrangements (i.e., listings where one amount of commission is payable if the listing broker's firm is the procuring cause of sale and a different amount of commission is payable if the sale results through the efforts of the seller or a cooperating broker). The listing broker shall, as soon as practical, disclose the existence of such arrangements to potential cooperating brokers and shall, in response to inquiries from cooperating brokers, disclose the differential that would result in a cooperative transaction or in a sale that results through the efforts of the seller. (Amended 11/91)

• Standard of Practice 9-10(a)

When entering into listing contracts, REALTORS® must advise sellers/landlords of:

1) the REALTOR®'s general company policies regarding cooperation with subagents, buyer/tenant agents, or both;
2) the fact that buyer/tenant agents, even if compensated by the listing broker, or by the seller/landlord will represent the interests of buyers/tenants; and
3) any potential for the listing broker to act as a disclosed dual agent, e.g. buyer/tenant agent. (Adopted 11/92)

• Standard of Practice 9-10(b)

When entering into contracts to represent buyers/tenants, REALTORS® must advise potential clients of:

1) the REALTOR®'s general company policies regarding cooperation with other firms; and
2) any potential for the buyer/tenant representative to act as a disclosed dual agent, e.g. listing broker, subagent, landlord's agent, etc. (Adopted 11/92)

• Standard of Practice 9-11

Factors defined as "non-material" by law or regulation or which are expressly referenced in law or regulation as not being subject to disclosure are considered not "pertinent" for purposes of Article 9. (Adopted 11/92)

ARTICLE 10

REALTORS® shall not deny equal professional services to any person for reasons of race, color, religion, sex, handicap, familial status, or national origin. REALTORS® shall not be parties to any plan or agreement to discriminate against a person or persons on the basis of race, color, religion, sex, handicap, familial status, or national origin. (Amended 11/89)

ARTICLE 11

REALTORS® are expected to provide a level of competent service in keeping with the standards of practice in those fields in which the REALTOR® customarily engages.

REALTORS® shall not undertake to provide specialized professional services concerning a type of property or service that is outside their field of competence unless they engage the assistance of one who is competent on such types of property or service, or unless the facts are fully disclosed to the client. Any persons engaged to provide such assistance shall be so identified to the client and their contribution to the assignment should be set forth.

REALTORS® shall refer to the Standards of Practice of the National Association as to the degree of competence that a client has a right to expect the REALTOR® to possess, taking into consideration the complexity of the problem, the availability of expert assistance, and the opportunities for experience available to the REALTOR®

• Standard of Practice 11-1

Whenever REALTORS® submit an oral or written opinion of the value of real property for a fee, their opinion shall be supported by a memorandum in the file or an appraisal report, either of which shall include as a minimum the following:

1. Limiting conditions
2. Any existing or contemplated interest
3. Defined value
4. Date applicable
5. The estate appraised
6. A description of the property
7. The basis of the reasoning including applicable market data and/or capitalization computation

This report or memorandum shall be available to the Professional Standards Committee for a period of at least two years (beginning subsequent to final determination of the court if the appraisal is involved in litigation) to ensure compliance with Article 11 of the Code of Ethics of the NATIONAL ASSOCIATION OF REALTORS®.

• Standard of Practice 11-2

REALTORS® shall not undertake to make an appraisal when their employment or fee is contingent upon the amount of appraisal.

• Standard of Practice 11-3

REALTORS® engaged in real estate securities and syndications transactions are engaged in an activity subject to regulations beyond those governing real estate transactions generally, and therefore have the affirmative obligation to be informed of applicable federal and state laws, and rules and regulations regarding these types of transactions.

ARTICLE 12

REALTORS® shall not undertake to provide professional services concerning a property or its value where they have a present or contemplated interest unless such interest is specifically disclosed to all affected parties.

• Standard of Practice 12-1

(Refer to Standards of Practice 9-4 and 16-1, which also relate to Article 12, Code of Ethics.) (Amended 5/84)

ARTICLE 13

REALTORS® shall not acquire an interest in or buy or present offers from themselves, any member of their immediate families, their firms or any member thereof, or any entities in which they have any ownership interest, any real property without making their true position known to the owner or the owner's agent. In selling property they own, or in which they have any interest, REALTORS® shall reveal their ownership or interest in writing to the purchaser or the purchaser's representative. (Amended 11/90)

• Standard of Practice 13-1

For the protection of all parties, the disclosures required by Article 13 shall be in writing and provided by REALTORS® prior to the signing of any contract. (Adopted 2/86)

ARTICLE 14

In the event of a controversy between REALTORS® associated with different firms, arising out of their relationship as REALTORS®, the REALTORS® shall submit the dispute to arbitration in accordance with the regulations of their Board or Boards rather than litigate the matter.

Figure 21.6 (continued)

In the event clients of REALTORS® wish to arbitrate contractual disputes arising out of real estate transactions, REALTORS® shall arbitrate those disputes in accordance with the regulations of their Board, provided the clients agree to be bound by the decision. (Amended 11/92)

- **Standard of Practice 14-1**

  The filing of litigation and refusal to withdraw from it by REALTORS® in an arbitrable matter constitutes a refusal to arbitrate. (Adopted 2/86)

- **Standard of Practice 14-2**

  Article 14 does not require REALTORS® to arbitrate in those circumstances when all parties to the dispute advise the Board in writing that they choose not to arbitrate before the Board. (Amended 11/92)

ARTICLE 15

If charged with unethical practice or asked to present evidence or to cooperate in any other way, in any disciplinary proceeding or investigation, REALTORS® shall place all pertinent facts before the proper tribunals of the Member Board or affiliated institute, society, or council in which membership is held and shall take no action to disrupt or obstruct such processes. (Amended 11/89)

- **Standard of Practice 15-1**

  REALTORS® shall not be subject to disciplinary proceedings in more than one Board of REALTORS® with respect to alleged violations of the Code of Ethics relating to the same transaction.

- **Standard of Practice 15-2**

  REALTORS® shall not make any unauthorized disclosure or dissemination of the allegations, findings, or decision developed in connection with an ethics hearing or appeal or in connection with an arbitration hearing or procedural review. (Amended 11/91)

- **Standard of Practice 15-3**

  REALTORS® shall not obstruct the Board's investigative or disciplinary proceedings by instituting or threatening to institute actions for libel, slander or defamation against any party to a professional standards proceeding or their witnesses. (Adopted 11/87)

- **Standard of Practice 15-4**

  REALTORS® shall not intentionally impede the Board's investigative or disciplinary proceedings by filing multiple ethics complaints based on the same event or transaction. (Adopted 11/88)

ARTICLE 16

When acting as agents, REALTORS® shall not accept any commission, rebate, or profit on expenditures made for their principal, without the principal's knowledge and consent. (Amended 11/91)

- **Standard of Practice 16-1**

  REALTORS® shall not recommend or suggest to a client or a customer the use of services of another organization or business entity in which they have a direct interest without disclosing such interest at the time of the recommendation or suggestion. (Amended 5/88)

- **Standard of Practice 16-2**

  When acting as agents or subagents, REALTORS® shall disclose to a client or customer if there is any financial benefit or fee the REALTOR® or the REALTOR®'s firm may receive as a direct result of having recommended real estate products or services (e.g., homeowner's insurance, warranty programs, mortgage financing, title insurance, etc.) other than real estate referral fees. (Adopted 5/88)

ARTICLE 17

REALTORS® shall not engage in activities that constitute the unauthorized practice of law and shall recommend that legal counsel be obtained when the interest of any party to the transaction requires it.

ARTICLE 18

REALTORS® shall keep in a special account in an appropriate financial institution, separated from their own funds, monies coming into their possession in trust for other persons, such as escrows, trust funds, clients' monies, and other like items.

ARTICLE 19

REALTORS® shall be careful at all times to present a true picture in their advertising and representations to the public. REALTORS® shall also ensure that their professional status (e.g., broker, appraiser, property manager, etc.) or status as REALTORS® is clearly identifiable in any such advertising. (Amended 11/92)

- **Standard of Practice 19-1**

  REALTORS® shall not offer for sale/lease or advertise property without authority. When acting as listing brokers or as subagents, REALTORS® shall not quote a price different from that agreed upon with the seller/landlord. (Amended 11/92)

- **Standard of Practice 19-2**

  (Refer to Standard of Practice 9-4, which also relates to Article 19, Code of Ethics.)

- **Standard of Practice 19-3**

  REALTORS®, when advertising unlisted real property for sale/lease in which they have an ownership interest, shall disclose their status as both owners/landlords and as REALTORS® or real estate licensees. (Amended 11/92)

- **Standard of Practice 19-4**

  REALTORS® shall not advertise nor permit any person employed by or affiliated with them to advertise listed property without disclosing the name of the firm. (Adopted 11/86)

- **Standard of Practice 19-5**

  Only REALTORS® as listing brokers, may claim to have "sold" the property, even when the sale resulted through the cooperative efforts of another broker. However, after transactions have closed, listing brokers may not prohibit successful cooperating brokers from advertising their "cooperation," "participation," or "assistance" in the transaction, or from making similar representations.

  Only listing brokers are entitled to use the term "sold" on signs, in advertisements, and in other public representations. (Amended 11/89)

ARTICLE 20

REALTORS®, for the protection of all parties, shall see that financial obligations and commitments regarding real estate transactions are in writing, expressing the exact agreement of the parties. A copy of each agreement shall be furnished to each party upon their signing such agreement.

- **Standard of Practice 20-1**

  At the time of signing or initialing, REALTORS® shall furnish to each party a copy of any document signed or initialed. (Adopted 5/86)

- **Standard of Practice 20-2**

  For the protection of all parties, REALTORS® shall use reasonable care to ensure that documents pertaining to the purchase, sale, or lease of real estate are kept current through the use of written extensions or amendments. (Amended 11/92)

**Figure 21.6
(continued)**

ARTICLE 21

REALTORS℠ shall not engage in any practice or take any action inconsistent with the agency of other REALTORS®.

- **Standard of Practice 21-1**

  Signs giving notice of property for sale, rent, lease, or exchange shall not be placed on property without consent of the seller/landlord. (Amended 11/92)

- **Standard of Practice 21-2**

  REALTORS® acting as subagents or as buyer/tenant agents, shall not attempt to extend a listing broker's offer of cooperation and/or compensation to other brokers without the consent of the listing broker. (Amended 11/92)

- **Standard of Practice 21-3**

  REALTORS® shall not solicit a listing which is currently listed exclusively with another broker. However, if the listing broker, when asked by the REALTOR®, refuses to disclose the expiration date and nature of such listing; i.e., an exclusive right to sell, an exclusive agency, open listing, or other form of contractual agreement between the listing broker and the client, the REALTOR® may contact the owner to secure such information and may discuss the terms upon which the REALTOR® might take a future listing or, alternatively, may take a listing to become effective upon expiration of any existing exclusive listing. (Amended 11/86)

- **Standard of Practice 21-4**

  REALTORS® shall not use information obtained by them from the listing broker, through offers to cooperate received through Multiple Listing Services or other sources authorized by the listing broker, for the purpose of creating a referral prospect to a third broker, or for creating a buyer/tenant prospect unless such use is authorized by the listing broker. (Amended 11/92)

- **Standard of Practice 21-5**

  The fact that an agency agreement has been entered into with a REALTOR® shall not preclude or inhibit any other REALTOR® from entering into a similar agreement after the expiration of the prior agreement. (Amended 11/92)

- **Standard of Practice 21-6**

  The fact that a client has retained a REALTOR® as an agent in one or more past transactions does not preclude other REALTORS® from seeking such former client's future business. (Amended 11/92)

- **Standard of Practice 21-7**

  REALTORS® shall be free to list property which is "open listed" at any time, but shall not knowingly obligate the seller to pay more than one commission except with the seller's knowledgeable consent. (Cross-reference Article 7.) (Amended 5/88)

- **Standard of Practice 21-8**

  When REALTORS® are contacted by the client of another REALTOR® regarding the creation of an agency relationship to provide the same type of service, and REALTORS® have not directly or indirectly initiated such discussions, they may discuss the terms upon which they might enter into a future agency agreement or, alternatively, may enter into an agency agreement which becomes effective upon expiration of any existing exclusive agreement. (Amended 11/92)

- **Standard of Practice 21-9**

  In cooperative transactions REALTORS® shall compensate cooperating REALTORS® (principal brokers) and shall not compen-sate nor offer to compensate, directly or indirectly, any of the sales licensees employed by or affiliated with other REALTORS® without the prior express knowledge and consent of the cooperating broker.

- **Standard of Practice 21-10**

  Article 21 does not preclude REALTORS® from making general announcements to prospective clients describing their services and the terms of their availability even though some recipients may have entered into agency agreements with another REALTOR®. A general telephone canvass, general mailing or distribution addressed to all prospective clients in a given geographical area or in a given profession, business, club, or organization, or other classification or group is deemed "general" for purposes of this standard.

  Article 21 is intended to recognize as unethical two basic types of solicitations:

  First, telephone or personal solicitations of property owners who have been identified by a real estate sign, multiple listing compilation, or other information service as having exclusively listed their property with another REALTOR®; and

  Second, mail or other forms of written solicitations of prospective clients whose properties are exclusively listed with another REALTOR® when such solicitations are not part of a general mailing but are directed specifically to property owners identified through compilations of current listings, "for sale" or "for rent" signs, or other sources of information required by Article 22 and Multiple Listing Service rules to be made available to other REALTORS® under offers of subagency or cooperation. (Amended 11/92)

- **Standard of Practice 21-11**

  REALTORS®, prior to entering into an agency agreement, have an affirmative obligation to make reasonable efforts to determine whether the client is subject to a current, valid exclusive agreement to provide the same type of real estate service. (Amended 11/92)

- **Standard of Practice 21-12**

  REALTORS®, acting as agents of buyers or tenants, shall disclose that relationship to the seller/landlord's agent at first contact and shall provide written confirmation of that disclosure to the seller/landlord's agent not later than execution of a purchase agreement or lease. (Cross-reference Article 7.) (Amended 11/92)

- **Standard of Practice 21-13**

  On unlisted property, REALTORS® acting as buyer/tenant agents shall disclose that relationship to the seller/landlord at first contact for that client and shall provide written confirmation of such disclosure to the seller/landlord not later than execution of any purchase or lease agreement.

  REALTORS® shall make any request for anticipated compensation from the seller/landlord at first contact. (Cross-reference Article 7.) (Amended 11/92)

- **Standard of Practice 21-14**

  REALTORS®, acting as agents of sellers/landlords or as subagents of listing brokers, shall disclose that relationship to buyers/tenants as soon as practicable and shall provide written confirmation of such disclosure to buyers/tenants not later than execution of any purchase or lease agreement. (Amended 11/92)

- **Standard of Practice 21-15**

  Article 21 does not preclude REALTORS® from contacting the client of another broker for the purpose of offering to provide, or entering into a contract to provide, a different type of real estate

Figure 21.6 (continued)

service unrelated to the type of service currently being provided (e.g., property management as opposed to brokerage). However, information received through a Multiple Listing Service or any other offer of cooperation may not be used to target clients of other REALTORS® to whom such offers to provide services may be made. (Amended 11/92)

- ### Standard of Practice 21-16

REALTORS®, acting as subagents or buyer/tenant agents, shall not use the terms of an offer to purchase/lease to attempt to modify the listing broker's offer of compensation to subagents or buyer's agents nor make the submission of an executed offer to purchase/lease contingent on the listing broker's agreement to modify the offer of compensation. (Amended 11/92)

- ### Standard of Practice 21-17

Where property is listed on an open listing basis, REALTORS® acting as buyer/tenant agents may deal directly with the seller/landlord. (Adopted 11/92)

- ### Standard of Practice 21-18

All dealings concerning property exclusively listed, or with buyer/tenants who are exclusively represented shall be carried on with the client's agent, and not with the client, except with the consent of the client's agent. (Adopted 11/92)

ARTICLE 22

REALTORS® shall cooperate with other brokers except when cooperation is not in the client's best interest. (Amended 11/92)

- ### Standard of Practice 22-1

It is the obligation of subagents to promptly disclose all pertinent facts to the principal's agent prior to as well as after a purchase or lease agreement is executed. (Cross-reference to Article 9) (Amended 11/92)

- ### Standard of Practice 22-2

REALTORS® shall submit offers and counter-offers, in an objective manner. (Amended 11/92)

- ### Standard of Practice 22-3

REALTORS® shall disclose the existence of an accepted offer to any broker seeking cooperation. (Adopted 5/86)

- ### Standard of Practice 22-4

REALTORS®, acting as exclusive agents of sellers, establish the terms and conditions of offers to cooperate. Unless expressly indicated in offers to cooperate made through MLS or otherwise, a cooperating broker may not assume that the offer of cooperation includes an offer of compensation. Entitlement to compensation in a cooperative transaction must be agreed upon between a listing and cooperating broker prior to the time an offer to purchase the property is produced. (Adopted 11/88)

ARTICLE 23

REALTORS® shall not knowingly or recklessly make false or misleading statements about competitors, their businesses, or their business practices. (Amended 11/91)

The Code of Ethics was adopted in 1913. Amended at the Annual Convention in 1924, 1928, 1950, 1951, 1952, 1955, 1956, 1961, 1962, 1974, 1982, 1986, 1987, 1989, 1990, 1991, and 1992.

EXPLANATORY NOTES (Amended 11/88)

The reader should be aware of the following policies which have been approved by the Board of Directors of the National Association:

In filing a charge of an alleged violation of the Code of Ethics by a REALTOR®, the charge shall read as an alleged violation of one or more Articles of the Code. A Standard of Practice may only be cited in support of the charge.

The Standards of Practice are not an integral part of the Code but rather serve to clarify the ethical obligations imposed by the various Articles. The Standards of Practice supplement, and do not substitute for, the Case Interpretations in *Interpretations of the Code of Ethics.*

Modifications to existing Standards of Practice and additional new Standards of Practice are approved from time to time. The reader is cautioned to ensure that the most recent publications are utilized.

Articles 1 through 5 are aspirational and establish ideals that a REALTOR® should strive to attain. Recognizing their subjective nature, these Articles shall not be used as the bases for charges of alleged unethical conduct or as the bases for disciplinary action.

NATIONAL ASSOCIATION OF REALTORS®
430 North Michigan Avenue
Chicago, Illinois 60611

harm to the client, the customer, the public or other licensees, it violates the rule of ethical behavior.

Code of Ethics

One way that many organizations address ethics among their members or in their respective businesses is by adopting codes of professional conduct. A **Code of Ethics** is a written system of standards for ethical conduct. These codes contain statements that are designed to advise, guide and regulate job behavior. They usually include references to topics such as conflict of interest, compliance with the law, commitment to protecting the public good and maintaining a high standard of business conduct. To be effective a code of ethics must be specific by dictating rules that either prohibit or demand certain behavior rather than being purely aspirational and must provide for sanctions for violators so that they are enforced.

The real estate business is only as good as its reputation; reputations are built on fair dealings with the public. There are organizations within the real estate industry that have established codes of ethics for their members. These codes are expected to increase the level of professional conduct of their subscribers, thereby enhancing their reputation. A high standard of ethics is needed in the principal-agent relationship to ensure that the agent performs his or her fiduciary duties in the best interests of the principal.

The National Association of REALTORS® (NAR), the largest trade association in the country, adopted a Code of Ethics for its members in 1913. REALTORS® are expected to subscribe to this strict code of conduct. Not all licensees are REALTORS® , only those who are members of NAR. NAR has established procedures for professional standards committees at the local, state and national levels of the organization to administer compliance. Interpretations of the Code are known as Standards of Practice. The Code of Ethics has proved helpful because it contains practical applications of business ethics. Many other professional organizations in the industry have codes of ethics as well. The REALTORS® Code of Ethics and Standards of Practice are provided in Figure 21.6 as an example.

●   ●   ●   ●   ●   ●   ●   ●

KEY TERMS

blockbusting
Civil Rights Act of 1866
Code of ethics
Department of Housing and Urban
   Development (HUD)

Ethics
Equal Credit Opportunity Act (ECOA)
Fair Housing Act
redlining
steering

SUMMARY

The federal regulations regarding equal opportunity in housing are contained principally in two laws. The Civil Rights Act of 1866 prohibits all racial discrimination, and the Fair Housing Act (Title VIII of the Civil Rights Act of 1968), as amended, prohibits discrimination on the basis of race, color, religion, sex, handicap, familial status or national origin in the sale, rental or financing of residential property. Discriminatory actions include refusing to deal with an individual or a specific group, changing any terms of a real estate or loan transaction, changing the services offered for any individual or group, making statements or advertisements that indicate discriminatory restrictions, or otherwise attempting to make a dwelling unavailable to any person or group because of race, color, religion, sex, handicap, familial status or national origin. The law also prohibits steering, blockbusting and redlining.

Complaints under the Fair Housing Act may be reported to and investigated by the Department of Housing and Urban Development (HUD). Such complaints may also be taken directly to a U.S. district court. In states and localities that have enacted fair housing legislation that is "substantially equivalent to the federal law," complaints are handled by state and local agencies and state courts. Complaints under the Civil Rights Act of 1866 must be taken to a federal court.

A real estate business is only as good as its reputation. Real estate licensees can maintain good reputations by demonstrating good business ability and adhering to an ethical standard of business practices. Many licensees subscribe to a code of ethics as members of professional real estate organizations. The Code of Ethics of the National Association of REALTORS® is reprinted in this chapter. Its provisions suggest an excellent set of standards for all licensees to follow.

Questions

1. Which of the following acts is permitted under the federal Fair Housing Act?

   a. Advertising property for sale only to a special group
   b. Altering the terms of a loan for a member of a minority group
   c. Refusing to sell a home to an individual because of a poor credit history
   d. Telling an individual that an apartment has been rented when in fact it has not

2. Complaints relating to the Civil Rights Act of 1866

   a. must be taken directly to a federal court.
   b. are no longer reviewed in the courts.
   c. are handled by HUD.
   d. are handled by state enforcement agencies.

3. The Civil Rights Act of 1866 is unique because it

   a. has been broadened to protect the aged.
   b. adds welfare recipients as a protected class.
   c. contains "choose your neighbor" provisions.
   d. provides no exceptions to racial discrimination.

4. "I hear they're moving in; there goes the neighborhood. Better sell to me today!" is an example of

   a. steering.   c. redlining.
   b. blockbusting.   d. testing.

5. The act of channeling home seekers to a particular area either to maintain or to change the character of a neighborhood is

   a. blockbusting.
   b. redlining.
   c. steering.
   d. permitted under the Fair Housing Act of 1968.

6. A lender's refusal to lend money to potential homeowners attempting to purchase property located in predominantly black neighborhoods is known as

   a. redlining.   c. steering.
   b. blockbusting.   d. qualifying.

7. Which of the following would *not* be permitted under the federal Fair Housing Act?

   a. The Harvard Club in New York will rent rooms only to graduates of Harvard who belong to the club.
   b. The owner of a 20-unit apartment building rents to women only.
   c. A Catholic convent refuses to furnish housing for a Jewish man.
   d. An owner refuses to rent the other side of her duplex home to families with children.

8. Under the federal law families with children may be refused rental or purchase in buildings where occupancy is reserved exclusively for those aged at least

   a. 40.   c. 62.
   b. 60.   d. 65.

9. Guiding prospective buyers to a particular area because the agent feels they belong there may lead to

   a. blockbusting.   c. steering.
   b. redlining.   d. bird-dogging.

10. A black real estate broker's practice of offering a special discount to black clients is

    a. satisfactory.
    b. illegal.
    c. legal but ill advised.
    d. not important.

11. Under the Supreme Court decision in the case of *Jones v. Alfred H. Mayer Company*
    a. racial discrimination is prohibited by any party in the sale or rental of real estate.
    b. sales by individual residential homeowners are exempted provided the owner does not employ a broker.
    c. laws against discrimination apply only to federally related transactions.
    d. persons with handicaps are a protected class.

12. After the broker takes a sale listing of a residence, the owner specifies that he will not sell his home to a black person. The broker should *not*
    a. show the property to anyone who is interested, including blacks.
    b. explain to the owner that this violates federal law and he cannot do it.
    c. abide by the principal's directions.
    d. put the listing in the multilist.

13. The fine for a first violation of the federal Fair Housing Act could be as much as
    a. $500.   c. $5,000.
    b. $1,000.   d. $10,000.

14. A single man with two small children has been told by a real estate salesperson that homes for sale in a condominium complex are available only to married couples with no children. Which of the following is true?
    a. Single parent families can be disruptive because there could be less supervision of the children.
    b. Condominium complexes are exempt from the fair housing laws and can therefore restrict children.
    c. The man should file a complaint alleging discrimination on the basis of familial status.
    d. Restrictive covenants in a condominium would take precedence over the fair housing laws.

15. The following ad appeared in the newspaper: "For sale: 4 BR brick home; Redwood School District; Excellent Elm Street location; next door to St. John's Church and right on the bus line. Move-in condition; priced to sell." Which of the following is true?
    a. The ad is descriptive of the property for sale and is very appropriate.
    b. The fair housing laws do not apply to newspaper advertising.
    c. The ad should state that the property is available to families with children.
    d. The ad should not mention St. John's Church.

22

Introduction to Real Estate Investment

INVESTING IN REAL ESTATE

For many reasons real estate has remained a popular investment in the United States. Even though the fluctuating economy has increased risk or lowered returns, the investment market has devised innovative investment vehicles and strategies that make investing in real estate attractive. These developments only make it more important for real estate licensees to have an elementary and up-to-date knowledge of real estate investment so they can serve a variety of customer needs. Even the average home buyer will want assurance that a residential purchase is a good investment. This does not mean that licensees should act as investment counselors. They should always *refer investors to a competent tax accountant, attorney or investment specialist* who can give expert advice on the investor's specific interest.

Advantages of Real Estate Investment

In recent years real estate values have fluctuated widely in various regions of the country, resulting in some investments not producing a return greater than the inflation rate or serving as an "inflation hedge." Yet many real estate investments have shown an above-average *rate of return,* generally higher than the prevailing interest rate charged by mortgage lenders. Theoretically this means that an investor can use the *leverage* of borrowed money to finance a real estate purchase and feel relatively sure that, if held long enough, the asset will yield more money than it cost to finance the purchase.

Real estate investors also receive certain tax benefits. Both leveraging and taxes are discussed in full later in this chapter.

Disadvantages of Real Estate Investment

Unlike stocks and bonds, *real estate is not highly liquid* over a short period of time. This means that an investor cannot usually sell real estate quickly without taking some sort of loss. An investor in listed stocks need only call a stockbroker to liquidate such assets quickly when funds are needed. In contrast, even though a real estate investor may be able to raise a limited amount of cash by refinancing the property, the investor may have to sell at a substantially lower price than desired to facilitate a quick sale.

In addition, *it is difficult to invest in real estate without some expert advice.* Investment decisions must be based on a careful study of all the facts, reinforced by a thorough knowledge of real estate and the manner in which it is affected by the marketplace.

Rarely can a real estate investor sit idly by and watch his or her money grow. *Management decisions must be made.* For example, can the investor effectively manage the property personally, or would it be preferable to hire a professional property manager? How much rent should be charged? How should repairs and tenant grievances be handled? "Sweat equity" (physical improvements accomplished by the investor personally) may be required to make the asset profitable. Many good investments fail because of poor management.

Finally, and most important, *a high degree of risk* can be involved in real estate investment. There is always the possibility that an investor's property will decrease in value during the period it is held or that it will not generate an income sufficient to make it profitable.

THE INVESTMENT

The most prevalent form of real estate investment is *direct ownership*. Both individuals and corporations may own real estate directly and manage it for appreciation or cash flow (income). Property held for **appreciation** is generally expected to increase in value and to show a profit when sold at some future date. Income property is just that—property held for current income as well as a potential profit upon its sale.

Appreciation

Real estate is an avenue of investment open to those interested in holding property *primarily* for appreciation.

Two main factors affect appreciation: inflation and intrinsic value. **Inflation** is defined as the *increase in the amount of money in circulation, which results in a decline in its value coupled with a rise in wholesale and retail prices.* The **intrinsic value** of real estate is the result of a person's individual choices and preferences for a given geographical area, based on the features and amenities that the area has to offer. For example, property located in a well-kept suburb near business and shopping areas would have a greater intrinsic value to most people than similar property in a more isolated location. As a rule, the greater the intrinsic value, the more money a property can command upon its sale.

Unimproved land. Quite often investors speculate in purchases of either agricultural (farm) land or undeveloped (raw) land located in what is expected to be a major path of growth. In these cases, however, the property's intrinsic value and potential for appreciation are not easy to determine. Indeed this type of investment carries with it many inherent risks. How fast will the area develop? Will it grow sufficiently for the investor to make a good profit? Will the expected growth even occur? More important, will the profits eventually realized from the property be great enough to offset the costs (such as property taxes) of holding the land? Because these questions often cannot be answered with certainty, lending institutions are often reluctant to lend money for the purchase of raw land.

In addition, the income tax laws do not allow the depreciation (cost recovery) of land. Finally, such land may not be liquid (salable) at certain times under certain circumstances, because few people are willing to purchase raw or agricultural land on short notice. Despite all the risks, land has historically been a good inflation hedge if held for a long term. It can also be a source of income to offset some of the holding costs. For example, agricultural land can be leased out for crops, timber production or grazing.

Investment in land ultimately is best left to experts, and even they frequently make bad land investment decisions.

Income

The wisest initial investment for a person who wishes to buy and personally manage real estate may be the purchase of rental income property.

Cash flow. The object of directing funds into income property is to generate spendable income, usually called *cash flow*. The **cash flow** is the total amount of money remaining after all expenditures have been paid, including taxes, operating costs and mortgage payments. The cash flow produced by any given parcel of real estate is determined by at least three factors: amount of rent received, operating expenses and method of debt repayment.

Generally the amount of *rent* (income) that a property may command depends on a number of factors, including location, physical appearance and amenities. If the cash flow from rents is not enough to cover all expenses, a *negative cash flow* will result.

To keep cash flow high an investor should attempt to *keep operating expenses reasonably low.* Such operating expenses include general maintenance of the building, repairs, utilities, taxes and tenant services (switchboard facilities, security systems and so forth).

IN PRACTICE...

With many of the tax advantages of real estate investment being reduced or withdrawn by Congress, licensees should advise investors to analyze each proposed purchase carefully with an accountant. It is more important than ever to be sure an investment will "carry itself by covering its own expenses." Where negative cash flow is anticipated, the investor's own tax bracket may be the deciding factor. (Income tax calculations are usually figured at the investor's marginal tax rate, that rate at which his or her top dollar of income is taxed.)

An investor often stands to make more money by investing borrowed money, usually obtained through a mortgage loan or deed of trust loan. *Low mortgage payments* spread over a long period of time result in a higher cash flow because they allow the investor to retain more income each month; conversely, higher mortgage payments would contribute to a lower cash flow.

Investment opportunities. Traditional income-producing property investments include apartment and office buildings, hotels, motels, shopping centers and industrial properties. Investors have historically found well-located, one- to four-family dwellings to be favorable investments. However, in recent years many communities have seen severe overbuilding of office space and shopping centers, with high vacancy rates.

LEVERAGE

Leverage is the use of *borrowed money to finance an investment.* As a rule an investor can receive a maximum return from the initial investment (the down payment and closing and other costs) by making a small down payment, paying a low interest rate and spreading mortgage payments over as long a period as possible.

The effect of leveraging is to provide, upon the sale of the asset, a return that reflects the effect of market forces on the entire amount of the original purchase price but is measured against only the actual cash invested. For example, if an investor spends $100,000 for rental property and makes a $20,000 down payment, then sells that property five years later for $125,000, the return over five years is $25,000. Disregarding ownership expenses, the return is not 25 percent ($25,000 compared to $100,000), but 125 percent of the original amount invested ($25,000 compared to $20,000).

Risks are directly proportionate to leverage. A high degree of leverage gives the investor and lender a high degree of risk because of the high ratio of borrowed money to the value of the real estate. Lower leverage results in a lower risk. When values drop in an area or vacancy rates rise, the highly leveraged investor may be unable to pay even the financing costs of the property.

Equity buildup. Equity buildup is that portion of the payment directed toward the principal rather than the interest, *plus* any gain in property value due to appreciation. In a sense equity buildup is like money in the bank to the investor. Although this accumulated equity is not realized as cash unless the property is sold or refinanced, the equity interest may be sold, exchanged or mortgaged (refinanced) to be used as leverage for other investments.

Pyramiding through refinancing. By holding and refinancing using equity and appreciation buildup rather than selling or exchanging already-owned properties, an investor can increase his or her holdings without investing any additional capital. Through this practice, known as **pyramiding,** an investor who started out with a small initial cash down payment could end up owning heavily mortgaged properties worth hundreds of thousands or millions of dollars. With sufficient cash flow to cover all costs the income derived from such assets could pay off the various mortgage debts and produce a handsome profit.

TAX BENEFITS

One of the main reasons real estate investments were popular and profitable in the past is that tax laws allowed investors to use losses generated by such investments to shelter income from other sources. Although laws have changed and some tax advantages of owning investment real estate are altered periodically by Congress, with professional tax advice the investor can still make a wise real estate purchase.

Capital Gains

The tax law no longer favors long-term investments by reducing taxable gain (profit) on their sale or exchange. Capital gain is defined as the difference between the adjusted basis of property and its net selling price. At various times tax law has excluded a portion of capital gains from income tax, in percentages ranging from 0 to 50 percent.

Basis. A property's cost basis will determine the amount of gain to be taxed. The **basis** of the property is the investor's initial cost of the real estate. The investor adds to the basis the cost of any physical improvements subsequently made to the property and subtracts from the basis the amount of any depreciation claimed as a tax deduction (explained later) to derive the property's adjusted basis. When the property is sold by the investor, the amount by which the sales price exceeds the property's **adjusted basis** is the capital gain.

For example, an investor purchased a single-family dwelling for use as a rental property. The purchase price was $45,000. The investor is now selling the property for $100,000. Shortly before the sale date the investor made $3,000 worth of capital improvements to the home. Depreciation of $10,000 on the property improvements has been taken during the term of the investor's ownership. The investor will pay a broker's commission of seven percent of the sales price and will also pay closing costs of $600. The investor's capital gain is computed as follows:

Selling price:		$100,000
Less:		
7% commission	$7,000	
closing costs	+ 600	
	$7,600	–7,600
Net sales price:		$ 92,400
Basis:		
original cost	$45,000	
improvements	+ 3,000	
	$48,000	
Less:		
depreciation	–10,000	
Adjusted basis:	$38,000	–38,000
Total capital gain:		$ 54,400

Again, current law will specify what percentage of capital gains is taxable as income. To determine the taxable amount the investor multiplies the total capital gain by the current percentage (in decimal form).

Exchanges

Real estate investors can defer taxation of *capital gains* by making a property **exchange.** Even if property has appreciated greatly since its initial purchase, it may be exchanged for other property and the property owner will incur tax liability on the sale only if additional capital or property is also received. Note, however, that *the tax is deferred, not eliminated.* Whenever the investor sells the property, the capital gain will be taxed.

To qualify as a tax-deferred exchange, the properties involved must be of *like kind*—for example, real estate for real estate of equal value. Any additional capital or personal property included with the transaction to even out the value of the exchange is considered **boot,** and the party receiving it is taxed at the time of the exchange. The value of the boot is added to the basis of the property with which it is given. Tax-deferred exchanges are governed by strict federal requirements, and competent guidance from a tax professional is essential.

For example, investor A owns an apartment building with an adjusted basis of $225,000 and a market value of $375,000. Investor A exchanges the building plus $75,000 cash for another apartment building having a market value of $450,000. That building, owned by investor B, has an adjusted basis of $175,000. A's basis in the new building will be $300,000 (the $225,000 basis of the building exchanged plus the $75,000 cash boot paid), and A has no tax liability on the exchange. B must pay tax on the $75,000 boot received and has a basis of $175,000 (the same as the previous building) in the building now owned.

Depreciation (Cost Recovery)

Depreciation, or **cost recovery,** allows an investor to recover the cost of an income-producing asset by way of tax deductions over the period of the asset's useful life. While investors rarely purchase property without expecting it to appreciate over time, the view of the tax laws is that all physical structures will deteriorate and hence lose value over time. Cost recovery deductions may be taken only on personal property and improvements to land and only if they are used in a trade or business or for the production of income. Thus a cost recovery deduction cannot be claimed on an individual's personal residence, and *land cannot be depreciated*—technically it never wears out or becomes obsolete.

If depreciation is taken periodically in equal amounts over an asset's useful life, the method used is called *straight-line depreciation.* For certain property purchased before 1987 it was also possible to have used an *accelerated cost recovery system (ACRS)* to claim greater deductions in the early years of ownership, gradually reducing the amount deducted in each year of the useful life.

For residential rental property placed in service as of January 1, 1987, the recovery period is set at 27.5 years and for nonresidential property, placed in service after May 12, 1993, at 31.5 years, using *only* the straight-line depreciation method.

Deductions and TRA '86

In addition to tax deductions for depreciation, investors may be able to deduct losses from their real estate investments. The tax laws are very complex, particularly as a result of TRA '86. The amount of loss that may be deducted depends on whether an investor actively participates in the day-to-day management of the rental property or makes management decisions, the amount of the loss and the source of the income against which the loss is to be deducted. Investors who do not actively participate in the management or operation of the real estate are considered passive investors, which prevents them from using a loss to offset active income (that generates from active participation in real estate management, wages or income from stocks, bonds and the like). The tax code cites specific rules for active and passive income and losses and may be subject to changes in the law.

Certain tax credits, a direct reduction in the tax due rather than a deduction from income before tax is computed, are allowed for renovation of older buildings, low-income housing projects and historic property. These credits encourage the revitalization of older properties and creating low-income housing. The tax laws are complex, as well.

Real estate must be analyzed in conjunction with other investments and the individual's overall investment goals and objectives. The income tax consequences will have a significant bearing on an investor's decisions. Competent tax advice should be sought to carefully evaluate the ramifications of an investment decision.

Installment Sales

A taxpayer who sells real property and receives payment on an installment basis pays tax only on the profit portion of each payment received. Interest received is taxable as ordinary income. Many complex laws apply to installment sales, and a competent tax advisor should be consulted.

REAL ESTATE INVESTMENT SYNDICATES

A real estate investment **syndicate** is a form of business venture in which a group of people pool their resources to own and/or develop a particular piece of property. In this manner people with only modest capital can invest in large-scale operations such as high-rise apartment buildings and shopping centers. A certain amount of profit is realized from rents collected on the investment, but the main return usually comes when the syndicate sells the property.

Syndicate participation can take many different legal forms, from tenancy in common and joint tenancy to various kinds of partnerships, corporations and trusts. *Private syndication,* which generally involves a small group of closely associated or widely experienced investors, is distinguished from *public syndication,* which generally involves a much larger group of investors who may or may not be knowledgeable about real estate as an investment. Any pooling of individuals' funds raises questions of registration of securities under federal securities laws and state securities laws, commonly referred to as *blue-sky laws.*

To protect members of the public who are not sophisticated investors but may be solicited to participate, securities laws include provisions that control and regulate the offering and sale of securities. Real estate securities must be registered with state officials and the federal Securities and Exchange Commission (SEC) when they meet the defined conditions of a public offering. The number of prospects solicited, the total number of investors, the financial background and sophistication of the investors and the value or price per unit of investment are pertinent facts. Salespeople of real estate securities may be required to obtain special licenses and state registration.

Forms of Syndicates

A general partnership is organized so that *all members of the group share equally in the managerial decisions, profits and losses involved with the investment.* A certain member (or members) of the syndicate is designated to act as trustee for the group, holds title to the property and maintains it in the syndicate's name.

Under a limited partnership agreement *one party* (or parties), usually a developer or real estate broker, *organizes, operates and is responsible for the entire syndicate.* This person is called the *general partner.* The other members of the partnership are merely investors; they have no voice in the organization and direction of the operation. These *passive investors are called limited partners.*

The limited partners share in the profits and compensate the general partner out of such profits. The limited partners stand to lose only as much as they invest—nothing more. The general partner(s) is (are) totally responsible for any excess losses incurred by the investment. The sale of a limited partnership interest involves the sale of an *investment security* as defined by the SEC. Therefore such sales are subject to state and federal laws concerning the sale of securities. Unless exempt, the securities must be registered with the federal Securities and Exchange Commission and the appropriate state authorities.

REAL ESTATE INVESTMENT TRUSTS

By directing their funds into **real estate investment trusts (REITs)** real estate investors can take advantage of the same tax benefits as mutual fund investors. A real estate investment trust does not have to pay corporate income tax as long as 95 percent of its income is distributed to its shareholders and certain other conditions are met. To qualify as a REIT at least 75 percent of the trust's income must come from real estate. Investors purchase certificates in the trust, which, in turn, invests in real estate or mortgages (or both.) Profits are distributed to investors.

REAL ESTATE MORTGAGE INVESTMENT CONDUITS

The Tax Reform Act created a new tax entity that may issue multiple classes of investor interests (securities) backed by a pool of mortgages. The **real estate mortgage investment conduit (REMIC)** has complex qualification, transfer and liquidation rules. Qualifications include the asset test (substantially all assets after a start-up period must consist of qualified mortgages and permitted investments) and the requirement that investors' interests consist of one or more classes of regular interests and a single class of residual interests. Holders of regular interests receive interest or similar payments based on either a fixed rate or a variable rate. Holders of residual interests receive distributions (if any) on a pro-rata basis.

•   •   •   •   •   •   •

KEY TERMS

adjusted basis	inflation
appreciation	intrinsic value
basis	leverage
boot	pyramiding
cash flow	real estate investment trust (REIT)
cost recovery	real estate mortgage investment conduit
depreciation	(REMIC)
exchange	syndicate

SUMMARY

Traditionally real estate investment has offered an above-average rate of return while acting as an effective inflation hedge and allowing an investor to make use of other people's money through leverage. There may also be tax advantages to owning real estate. However, real estate is not a highly liquid investment and often carries with it a high degree of risk. Also, it is difficult to invest in real estate without expert advice, and a certain amount of involvement is usually required to establish and maintain the investment.

Investment property held for appreciation purposes is generally expected to increase in value to a point where its selling price is enough to cover holding costs and show a profit as well. The two main factors affecting appreciation are inflation and the property's present and future intrinsic value. Real estate held for income purposes is generally expected to generate a steady flow of income, called cash flow, and to show a profit upon its sale.

An investor hoping to use maximum leverage in financing an investment should make a small down payment, pay low interest rates and spread mortgage payments over as long a period as possible. By holding and refinancing properties, known as pyramiding, an investor may substantially increase investment holdings without contributing additional capital. The highly leveraged investor has correspondingly high risk.

By exchanging one property for another with an equal or greater selling value an investor can defer paying tax on the gain realized until a sale is made. A total tax deferment is possible only if the investor receives no cash or other incentive to even out the exchange. If received. such cash or property is called boot and is taxed.

Depreciation (cost recovery) is a concept that allows an investor to recover in tax deductions the basis of an asset over the period of its useful life. Only costs of improvements to land may be recovered, not costs for the land itself. The Tax Reform Act of 1986 greatly limited the potential for investment losses to shelter other income. But tax credits are still allowed for projects involving low income housing and older buildings.

An investor may defer federal income taxes on a gain realized from the sale of an investment property through an installment sale of property.

Individuals may also invest in real estate through an investment syndicate; these generally include general and limited partnerships. Other forms of real estate investment are the real estate investment trust (REIT) and the real estate mortgage investment conduit (REMIC).

The real estate broker and salesperson should be familiar with the rudimentary tax implications of real property ownership but should refer clients to competent tax advisers for answers to specific questions.

Questions

1. The advantages of real estate investment include
   a. the illiquidity of the investment.
   b. the need for expert advice.
   c. the fact that the investment can be an inflation hedge.
   d. the degree of risk involved.

2. Vacant land can be a good investment because
   a. it must appreciate enough to cover expenses.
   b. it can have intrinsic value.
   c. bank financing is easily arranged.
   d. it may not be depreciated.

3. The increase of money in circulation, resulting in a sharp rise in prices and an equally sharp decline in the value of money, is called
   a. appreciation.   c. negative cash flow.
   b. inflation.   d. recapture.

4. A small multifamily property generates $50,000 in rental income with expenses of $45,000 annually, including $35,000 in debt service. The property appreciates about $25,000 a year. On this property the cash flow is
   a. $5,000.   c. $25,000.
   b. $15,000.   d. $35,000.

5. Leverage involves the use of
   a. cost recovery.
   b. borrowed money.
   c. government subsidies.
   d. alternative taxes.

6. A property's equity represents its current value less
   a. depreciation.
   b. mortgage indebtedness.
   c. physical improvements.
   d. selling costs and depreciation.

7. An investor's marginal tax rate is the
   a. total tax bill divided by net taxable income.
   b. extra tax if he has too many tax shelters.
   c. top applicable income tax bracket.
   d. percentage taxable on an installment sale.

8. The primary source of tax shelter in real estate investments comes from the accounting concept known as
   a. recapture.
   b. boot.
   c. net operating income.
   d. depreciation.

9. For tax purposes the initial cost of an investment property plus the cost of any subsequent improvements to the property, less depreciation, represents the investment's
   a. adjusted basis.   c. basis.
   b. capital gains.   d. salvage value.

10. The money left in an investor's pocket after expenses, including debt service, have been paid is known as
    a. net operating income.
    b. gross income.
    c. cash flow.
    d. internal rate of return.

11. An investment syndicate in which all members share equally in the managerial decisions, profits and losses involved in the venture is an example of a

    a. real estate investment trust.
    b. limited partnership.
    c. real estate mortgage trust.
    d. general partnership.

12. Shareholders in a real estate investment trust generally

    a. receive most of the trust's income each year.
    b. take an active part in management.
    c. find it difficult to sell their shares.
    d. realize their main profit through sales of property.

13. In an installment sale of one's own home taxable gain is received and may be reported as income by the seller

    a. in the year the sale is initiated.
    b. in the year the final installment payment is made.
    c. in each year that installment payments are received.
    d. at any one time during the period installment payments are received.

14. A separate license or registration may be required for the sale of

    a. all investment property.
    b. real estate securities.
    c. installment property.
    d. boot.

15. A new tax entity that issues securities backed by a pool of mortgages is a

    a. REIT.   c. TRA.
    b. REMIC.   d. general partnership.

23 Closing the Real Estate Transaction

CLOSING PRACTICES

Closing is the consummation of the real estate transaction, the time when the title to the real estate is transferred in exchange for payment of the purchase price. It is known by many other names, including *settlement* and *transfer* (of title). In the Northeast, where the parties to the transaction sit around a single table and exchange a bewildering variety of documents, the process is known as *passing papers.* ("We passed papers on the new house Wednesday morning.") In the West, where buyer and seller may never meet and paperwork is handled by an escrow agent, the process is known as *closing escrow.* ("We're going to close escrow on the place next week.") Whether the closing occurs face-to-face or through escrow, the main concerns are that the buyer receives the marketable title, the seller receives the purchase price and certain other items be adjusted properly between the two.

Though real estate licensees do not always conduct the proceedings at a closing, they usually attend and therefore should be thoroughly familiar with the process and the procedures involved in preparing the closing statement, which includes the expenses and prorations of costs to close the transaction. It is also in the brokers' interest that transactions in which they have been instrumental be finalized successfully and smoothly.

Face-to-Face Closing

A face-to-face closing of a real estate transaction involves two issues: fulfilling the promises made in the sales contract, closing the buyer's loan and the mortgage lender's dispersing the loan funds. The preceding chapters have discussed the various steps that lead to this point. A sales contract is the blueprint for the completion of the transaction. Before documents and funds are exchanged, the parties should assure themselves that the various stipulations of the contract have been met.

The buyer will want to be sure that the seller is delivering title and that the property is in the promised condition. This involves inspecting the title evidence, the deed the seller will give, any documents representing the removal of undesired liens and encumbrances, the survey, the termite and any other inspection reports and any leases if there are tenants on the premises. The seller will want to be sure that the buyer has obtained the necessary financing and has sufficient funds to complete the sale. Both parties will want to inspect the closing statement to make sure that all monies involved in the transaction have been accounted for properly. The parties may be accompanied by their attorneys.

When the parties are satisfied that everything is in order, the exchange is made and all pertinent documents are then recorded in the correct order to avoid creating a defect in the title. For example, if the seller is paying off an existing loan and the buyer is obtaining a new loan, the seller's satisfaction of mortgage must be recorded before the seller's deed to the buyer is recorded. The buyer's new mortgage or deed of trust must then be recorded after the deed, because the buyers cannot pledge the property as security for the loan until they own it.

The closing represents the culmination of the service the broker's firm provides. Licensees should assist in preclosing arrangements as part of this final service. In some states they are required to advise the parties of their expenses when they sign the sales contract by estimating the approximate amounts the buyer will need and the seller will actually receive at the closing. The sale that the broker has negotiated is completed once the closing takes place. The broker's commission (and thus the salesperson's commission) is generally paid out of the proceeds at the closing.

Conducting closings. Face-to-face closings may be held at a number of locations, including the office of the title company, the lending institution, one of the parties' attorneys, the broker, the county recorder or the escrow company. Those attending a closing may include

- the buyer;
- the seller;
- the real estate salesperson or broker (from the selling and/or listing office[s]);
- the attorney(s) for the seller and/or buyer;
- the representatives and/or attorneys for lending institutions involved with the buyer's new mortgage loan, the buyer's assumption of the seller's existing loan or the seller's payoff of an existing loan; and
- the representative of the title insurance company.

Closing agent or closing officer. One person usually conducts the proceedings at a closing and calculates the official settlement, or division of income and expenses, between the parties. In some areas real estate brokers preside; in others the closing agent is the buyer's or seller's attorney, a representative of the lender or the representative of a title company. Some title companies and law firms employ paralegal assistants who conduct closings for their firms. Before closing, the title insurance or title certificate, surveys, property insurance policy and other items must be ordered and reviewed; arrangements must be made with the parties for the time and place of closing; and closing statements and other documents must be prepared.

Closing in Escrow

Although there are a few states where transactions are never closed in escrow, escrow closings are used to some extent in most states, especially in the West.

An **escrow** is a method of closing in which a disinterested third party is authorized to act as escrow agent and to coordinate the closing activities. The escrow agent may also be called the *escrow holder.* The escrow agent may be an attorney, a title company, a trust company, an escrow company or the escrow department of a lending institution. While real estate firms do offer escrow services, a broker cannot be a disinterested party in a transaction from which he or she expects to collect a commission. Because the escrow agent is placed in a position of great trust, many states have laws regulating escrow agents and limiting who may serve in this capacity.

Escrow procedure. When a transaction will be closed in escrow, the buyer and seller execute escrow instructions to the escrow agent after the sales contract is signed. The buyer or seller selects an escrow agent; some states have laws dictating that the buyer select the escrow agent and the time and place of closing. Once the contract is signed, the broker turns over the earnest money to the escrow agent, who deposits it in a special trust, or escrow, account.

Buyer and seller deposit all pertinent documents and other items with the escrow agent before the specified date of closing. The seller will usually deposit

- the *deed* conveying the property to the buyer;
- title *evidence* (abstract and attorney's opinion, certificate of title, title insurance or Torrens certificate);
- existing hazard *insurance* policies;
- a letter or mortgage reduction certificate from the lender stating the exact principal remaining if the buyer is assuming the seller's loan;
- *affidavits of title* (if required);
- a reduction certificate (payoff statement) if the seller's loan is to be paid off; and
- other instruments or documents necessary to clear the title or to complete the transaction.

The buyer will deposit

- the balance of the *cash needed* to complete the purchase usually in the form of a certified check;
- loan documents if the buyer is securing a new loan;
- proof of hazard insurance, including, where required, flood insurance; and
- other necessary documents.

The escrow agent has the authority to examine the title evidence. When marketable title is shown in the name of the buyer and all other conditions of the escrow agreement have been met, the agent is authorized to disburse the purchase price—minus all charges and expenses—to the seller and record the deed and mortgage or deed of trust (if a new loan has been obtained by the purchaser).

If the escrow agent's examination of the title discloses liens, the escrow instructions usually provide that a portion of the purchase price can be withheld from the seller and used to pay such liens as are necessary to clear the title so the transaction can be closed.

If the seller cannot clear the title, or if for any reason the sale cannot be consummated and the buyer will not accept the title as is, then the escrow instructions usually provide that the parties be returned to their former status as if no sale had occurred. To accomplish this the escrow agent reconveys title to the seller and restores all purchase money to the buyer. Because the escrow depends on specific conditions being met before the transfer binds the parties, the courts have held that the parties can be reinstated to their former status.

IRS Reporting Requirements

Every real estate transaction must be reported to the IRS by the closing agent on a form 1099-S. Information includes the sales price, the amount of property tax reimbursement credited to the seller and the seller's social security number. If the closing agent does not notify the IRS, the responsibility for filing the form falls on the mortgage lender, although the brokers or the parties to the transaction ultimately could be held liable.

Broker's Role at Closing

Depending on local practice, the broker's role at closing can vary from simply collecting the commission to conducting the proceedings. As discussed earlier in the text, a real estate broker is not authorized to give legal advice or otherwise engage in the practice of law. In some areas of the country this means that a broker's job is essentially finished when the sales contract is signed; at that point the attorneys take over. Even so, a broker's service generally continues after the contract is signed. The broker makes sure all the details are taken care of so that the closing can proceed smoothly by making arrangements for title evidence, surveys, appraisals, inspections or repairs for wood-boring insects, structural conditions, water supplies, sewage facilities or toxic substances. Licensees should avoid *recommending* sources for any inspections or testing services because of the potential liability created in the event the buyer is injured by a provider's service.

Lender's Interest in Closing

Whether a buyer is obtaining new financing or assuming the seller's existing loan, the lender wants to protect its security interest in the property—to make sure that the buyer is getting good, marketable title and that tax and insurance payments are maintained so that there will be no liens with greater priority than the mortgage lien and the insurance will be paid up if the property is damaged or destroyed. For this reason the lender will generally require a title insurance policy; a fire and hazard insurance policy, with receipt for the premium; additional information, such as a survey, a termite or other inspection report or a certificate of occupancy (for newly constructed buildings); establishment of a reserve, or escrow, account for tax and insurance payments; and possibly representation by its own attorney at the closing.

RESPA Requirements

The federal **Real Estate Settlement Procedures Act (RESPA)** was enacted *to eliminate "kickbacks" and other referral fees that tend to unnecessarily increase the costs of settlement and to provide consumers with greater and more timely information on the nature and costs of settlement.* RESPA requirements apply when the purchase is financed by a federally related mortgage loan. Federally related loans include those made by banks, savings and loan associations or other lenders whose deposits are insured by federal agencies; loans insured by the FHA or guaranteed by the VA; loans administered by the U.S. Department of Housing and Urban Development; or loans intended to be sold by the lender to Fannie Mae, Ginnie Mae or Freddie Mac. RESPA is administered by HUD.

RESPA regulations apply to first and second lien residential mortgage loans made to finance the purchase or refinance, either for investment or occupancy, of one-family to four-family homes, cooperatives and condominiums. A transaction financed solely by a purchase-money mortgage taken back by the seller, an installment contract (contract for deed) or the buyer's assumption of the seller's existing loan are not covered by RESPA unless the terms of the assumed loan are modified or the lender charges more than $50 for the assumption.

Disclosure requirements. Lenders and settlement agents have certain *disclosure* obligations at the time of loan application and loan closing.

- *Special information booklet:* Lenders must provide a copy of the HUD booklet *Settlement Costs and You* to every person from whom they receive or for whom they prepare a loan application (except for refinancing). The booklet must be given at the time the application is received or within three days thereafter. It provides the borrower with general information about settlement (closing) costs and explains the various provisions of RESPA, including a line-by-line discussion of the Uniform Settlement Statement. Prospective licensees should review a copy of the booklet to be familiar with its contents.

- *Good-faith estimate of settlement costs:* No later than three business days after the receipt of the loan application, the lender must provide to all borrowers a good-faith estimate of the settlement costs the borrower is likely to incur. This estimate may be a specific figure or a range of costs based on comparable past transactions in the area. In addition, if the lender requires use of a particular attorney or title company to conduct the closing, the lender must state whether it has any business relationship with that firm and must estimate the charges for this service.

- *Uniform Settlement Statement (HUD Form 1):* RESPA requires that a special HUD form be completed to itemize all charges to be paid by the borrower and seller in connection with settlement. The **Uniform Settlement Statement** includes all charges that will be collected at closing, whether required by the lender or a third party. Items paid by the borrower and seller outside closing, not required by the lender, are not included on HUD-1. Charges required by the lender that are paid for before closing are indicated as "paid outside of closing" (POC). RESPA prohibits lenders from requiring borrowers to deposit amounts in escrow accounts for taxes and insurance that exceed certain limits, thus preventing the lender from taking advantage of the borrower. *Sellers* are also prohibited from requiring, as a condition of the sale, that the buyer purchase title insurance from a particular company. A copy of the HUD-1 form is illustrated in Figure 23.1.

The settlement statement must be made available for inspection by the borrower *at or before* settlement. Borrowers have the right to inspect the completed HUD-1, to the extent that the figures are available, *one business day before the closing.* Under the Act sellers are not entitled to this privilege.

Lenders must retain these statements for five years after the date of closing. If the loan or its servicing is sold, the new owner or servicer must retain the statements for the balance of the five-year period. The Uniform Settlement Statement may be altered to allow for local custom, and certain lines may be deleted if they do not apply in the area.

Kickbacks and referral fees. RESPA *prohibits the payment of kickbacks, or unearned fees* incident to or as part of a real estate settlement service. It prohibits referral fees *when no services are actually rendered.* The *payment* or *receipt* of a fee, kickback or anything of value for referrals for settlement services includes activities such as making mortgage loans, title searches, title insurance, services rendered by attorneys, surveys, credit reports or appraisals.

The publication of rules that implement RESPA in 1992 clarified certain practices that will enable the real estate industry and affiliated businesses to provide services that will enhance the home buying process. *Computerized loan origination (CLO) systems* enable a real estate broker to call up a menu of mortgage loan products from the broker's office to help a buyer select and originate a loan. This "one stop shopping" service can enable the broker to begin the loan application process and in some cases prequalify the borrower electronically. The system may offer the products of a single lender or multiple lenders, though the broker must disclose the existence of other competitive loan products that are not part of the CLO system. The broker may charge whatever fee the broker determines is fair for the service. The *borrower must pay the fee,* not the mortgage broker or lender, though it may be financed. The RESPA regulations clarified that these services and fee arrangements are permissible provided proper disclosures are made, fees are charged for actual services rendered and the mortgage broker or lender does not pay a referral fee for the loan.

Real estate firms, title insurance companies, mortgage brokerage firms, and even pest control companies, may be affiliated with one another. These business arrangements have become increasingly common in various parts of the country in recent years. However, there has been considerable concern about how these arrangements affect the consumer, particularly if the consumer is unaware of the relationship among the various firms with whom the consumer is doing business or if the consumer is coerced in some way to use the services of an affiliated business. The RESPA regulations have clarified that these *controlled business arrangements,* where affiliated firms offer different settlement services, are permitted provided (1) *the relationship between the firms is disclosed in writing to consumers,* (2) *consumers are free to obtain the service elsewhere and* (3) *that fees are not exchanged among the affiliated companies simply for the referral of business.* A controlled business arrangement exists when an individual or firm has more than a 1 percent ownership interest in a company to which the individual or firm regularly refers business.

Brokers are advised to seek legal counsel or advice from HUD regarding the details of these recent rules. Fee splitting or referral fees between cooperating brokers or members of multiple-listing services, brokerage referral arrangements and the division of a commission between a broker and the broker's salespeople are not prohibited under RESPA.

THE TITLE PROCEDURES

As discussed earlier, the buyer and the buyer's lender want to assure themselves that the seller's property and title comply with the requirements of the sales contract at settlement. The contract usually includes time limitations for the parties to obtain and present title evidence and remove any objections to the title. A contract that includes the provision "time is of the essence" expresses the agreement of the parties that all *time limitations are to be met exactly as stated.*

The seller is usually required to produce a current *abstract* or *title commitment* from the title insurance company. When an abstract of title is used, the purchaser's attorney examines it and issues an opinion of title. This opinion, like the title commitment, sets forth the status of the seller's title, showing liens, encumbrances, easements, conditions or restrictions that appear on the record and to which the seller's title is subject.

On the date when the sale is actually completed (the date of delivery of the deed), the buyer has a title commitment or an abstract that was issued several days or weeks before the closing. For this reason there are usually two searches of the public records. The first shows the status of the seller's title on the date of the first search, which the seller usually pays for. The second search, known as a "bring down," is made after the closing and generally paid for by the purchaser.

As part of this later search the seller may be required to execute an *affidavit of title.* This is a sworn statement in which the seller assures the title insurance company (and the buyer) that since the date of the title examination there have been no judgments, bankruptcies or divorces involving the seller, no unrecorded deeds or contracts made, no repairs or improvements that have not been paid for and no defects in the title that the seller knows of. The seller also assures that he or she is in possession of the premises. This form is required in some areas by the title insurance company before it will issue an owner's policy, particularly an extended coverage policy, to the buyer. Through this affidavit the title insurance company obtains the right to sue the seller if his or her statements in the affidavit prove incorrect.

In some areas where real estate sales transactions are customarily closed through an escrow, the escrow instructions usually provide for an extended coverage policy to be issued to the buyer as of the date of closing. In these cases there is no need for the seller to execute an affidavit of title.

Checking the Premises

It is important for the buyer to inspect the property to determine the interests of any parties in possession or other interests that cannot be determined from inspecting the public records. Shortly before the closing takes place the buyer will usually make a *final inspection* of the property (often called the *walk-through*) with the broker. Through this inspection the buyer can make sure that necessary repairs have been made, that the property has been well maintained (both inside and outside), that all fixtures are in place and that there has been no unauthorized removal or alteration of any part of the improvements.

A *survey* is frequently required so that the purchaser will know the location and size of the property. The contract will specify who is to pay for this. It is usual for the survey to "spot" the location of all buildings, driveways, fences and other improvements located primarily on the premises being purchased, as well as any such improvements located on adjoining property that may encroach on the premises being bought. The survey also sets out, in full, any existing easements and encroachments.

**Releasing
Existing Liens**

When the purchaser is paying cash or is obtaining a new loan to purchase the property, the seller's existing loan is paid in full and satisfied on record. The exact amount required to pay the existing loan is provided in a current *payoff statement* from the lender effective the date of closing. This payoff statement sets forth the unpaid amount of principal, interest due through the date of payment, the fee for issuing the certificate of satisfaction or release deed, credits (if any) for tax and insurance reserves and penalties that may be due because the loan is being paid before its maturity. The same procedure would be followed for any other liens that must be released before the buyer takes title.

For transactions in which the buyer assumes the seller's existing mortgage loan, the buyer will want to know the exact balance of the loan as of the closing date. In some areas it is customary for the buyer to obtain a *mortgage reduction certificate* from the lender, which certifies the amount owed on the mortgage loan, the interest rate and the last interest payment made.

**PREPARATION
OF CLOSING
STATEMENTS**

A typical real estate transaction involves expenses for both parties in addition to the purchase price. These include items prepaid by the seller for which he or she must be reimbursed (such as prepaid taxes) and items of expense the seller has incurred but the buyer will be billed for (such as mortgage interest paid in arrears). The financial responsibility for these items must be prorated (or divided) between the buyer and the seller. All expense and prorated items are accounted for on the settlement statement, to determine the cash required by the buyer and the net proceeds to the seller.

**How the Closing
Statement Works**

The completion of a **closing statement** involves an accounting of the parties' debits and credits. A **debit** is a charge, an amount that the party being debited owes and must pay at the closing. A **credit** is an amount entered in a person's favor—either an amount that has already been paid, an amount being reimbursed or an amount the buyer promises to pay in the form of a loan.

To determine the amount the buyer needs at the closing, the buyer's debits are totaled—any expenses and prorated amounts for items prepaid by the seller are added to the purchase price. Then the buyer's credits are totaled. These include the earnest money (already paid), the balance of the loan the buyer is obtaining or assuming and the seller's share of any prorated items that the buyer will pay in the future. Finally the total of the buyer's credits is subtracted from the total amount the buyer owes (debits) to arrive at the actual amount of cash the buyer must bring to the closing. Usually the buyer brings a cashier's or a certified check.

A similar procedure is followed to determine how much money the seller will actually receive. The seller's debits and credits are each totaled. The credits include the purchase price plus the buyer's share of any prorated items that the seller has prepaid. The seller's debits include expenses, the seller's share of prorated items to be paid later by the buyer and the balance of any mortgage loan or other lien that the seller is paying off. Finally the total of the seller's charges is subtracted from the total credits to arrive at the amount the seller will receive.

Broker's commission. The responsibility for paying the broker's commission will have been determined by previous agreement. If the broker is the agent for the seller (as in a listing agreement), the seller will be responsible for paying the commission. If there is an agency agreement between a broker and the buyer, or if two agents are involved, one for the seller and one for the buyer, the commission may be apportioned as an expense between both parties or according to some other arrangement agreed to prior to the sales contract.

Attorney's fees. If either of the parties' attorneys will be paid from the closing proceeds, that party will be charged with the expense in the closing statement. This expense may include fees for the preparation or review of documents or for representing the parties at settlement.

Recording expenses. The charges for recording different types of documents vary widely. These charges are established by law and are based on the number of pages included in the instrument.

The *seller* usually pays for recording charges (filing fees) necessary to clear all defects and furnish the purchaser with a marketable title in accordance with the contract. Items customarily charged to the seller include the recording of release deeds or satisfaction of mortgages, quitclaim deeds, affidavits and satisfaction of mechanic's lien claims. The *purchaser* pays for recording charges incidental to the actual transfer of title. Usually such items include recording the deed that conveys title to the purchaser and a mortgage or deed of trust executed by the purchaser.

Transfer tax. Most states require some form of transfer tax, conveyance fee or tax stamps on real estate conveyances. This expense is most often borne by the seller, although customs vary. In addition, many cities and local municipalities charge transfer taxes. The responsibility for these charges will be paid according to local practice.

Title expenses. The responsibility for title expenses varies according to local custom. In most areas the seller is required to furnish evidence of good title and pay for the title search. If the buyer's attorney inspects the evidence or if the buyer purchases title insurance policies, the buyer is charged for these expenses. There may also be expenses for lien letters and the certification letters as evidence that there are no pending liens that have not been recorded.

Loan fees. When the purchaser is securing a new loan to finance the purchase, the lender will ordinarily charge a loan origination fee of 1 percent of the loan. The fee is usually paid by the purchaser at the time the transaction is closed. The lender may also charge discount points. If the buyer is assuming the seller's existing financing, there may be an assumption fee. Also, under the terms of some mortgage loans the seller may be required to pay a prepayment charge or penalty for paying off the mortgage loan in advance of its due date.

Tax reserves and insurance reserves (escrow or impound accounts). Most mortgage lenders require that borrowers provide a reserve fund or escrow account to pay future real estate taxes and insurance premiums. The borrower starts the account at closing by depositing funds to cover at least the amount of unpaid real estate taxes from the date of lien to the end of the current month. (The buyer receives a credit from the seller at closing for any unpaid taxes.) Thereafter, the borrower is normally required to pay an amount equal to one month's portion of the estimated taxes. The borrower is responsible for maintaining adequate fire or hazard insurance as a condition of the mortgage loan. Generally the first year's premium is paid in full at closing. An amount equal to one month's premium is paid thereafter. The borrower's monthly loan payment includes the principal and interest on the loan plus one-twelfth of the estimated taxes and insurance (PITI). The taxes and insurance are held by the lender in the escrow or impound account until the bills are due.

Appraisal fees. Either the seller or the purchaser pays the appraisal fees, depending on who orders the appraisal. When the buyer obtains a mortgage, it is customary for the lender to require an appraisal, which the buyer pays for.

Survey fees. The purchaser who obtains new mortgage financing customarily pays the survey fees. In some cases the sales contract may require the seller to furnish a survey.

Additional fees. An FHA borrower owes a lump sum for payment of the mortgage insurance premium (MIP) if it is not being financed as part of the loan. A VA mortgagor pays a funding fee directly to the VA at closing. If a conventional loan carries private mortgage insurance, the buyer prepays one year's insurance premium at closing.

Prorations

Most closings involve the division of financial responsibility between the buyer and seller for such items as loan interest, taxes, rents, fuel and utility bills. These allowances are called **prorations.** Prorations are necessary to ensure that expenses are divided fairly between the seller and the buyer. For example, the seller may owe current taxes that have not been billed; the buyer would want this settled at the closing. Where taxes must be paid in advance, the seller would be entitled to a rebate at the closing. If the buyer assumes the seller's existing mortgage or deed of trust, the seller usually owes the buyer an allowance for accrued interest through the date of closing.

Accrued items are items to be prorated (such as water bills and interest on an assumed mortgage) that are owed by the seller but will later be paid by the buyer. The seller therefore pays for these items by giving the buyer credit for them at closing.

Prepaid items are items to be prorated—such as fuel oil in a tank—that have been prepaid by the seller but not fully earned (not fully used up). They are therefore credits to the seller.

General rules for prorating. The rules or customs governing the computation of prorations for the closing of a real estate sale vary widely from state to state. In many states the real estate boards and the bar association have established closing rules and procedures. These rules and procedures may apply to closings for the entire state or they may merely affect closings within a given city, town or county.

Here are some general guidelines for preparing the closing statement:

- In most states the seller owns the property on the day of closing, and prorations or apportionments are usually made *to and including the day of closing.* In a few states, however, it is provided specifically that the buyer owns the property on the closing date and that adjustments shall be made as of the day preceding the day on which title is closed.

- Mortgage interest, general real estate taxes, water taxes, insurance premiums and similar expenses are usually computed by using *360 days in a year and 30 days in a month.* However, the rules in some areas provide for computing prorations on the basis of the *actual number of days* in the calendar month of closing. The agreement of sale should specify which method is to be used.

- Accrued or prepaid *general real estate taxes* are usually prorated at the closing. When the amount of the current real estate tax cannot be determined definitely, the proration is usually based on the last obtainable tax bill.

- *Special assessments* for municipal improvements such as sewers, water mains or streets are usually paid in annual installments over several years. The municipality usually charges the property owner annual interest on the outstanding balance of future installments. In a sales transaction the seller normally pays the current installment and the buyer assumes all future installments. *The special assessment installment is not generally prorated at the closing;* some buyers, however, insist that the seller allow them a credit for the seller's share of the interest to the closing date. The agreement of sale may address the manner in which special assessments are to be handled at settlement.

- *Rents* are usually adjusted on the basis of the *actual* number of days in the month of closing. It is customary for the seller to receive the rents for the day of closing and to pay all expenses for that day. If any rents for the current month are uncollected when the sale is closed, the buyer will often agree by a separate letter to collect the rents if possible and remit the pro rata share to the seller.

- *Security deposits* made by tenants to cover the last month's rent of the lease or to cover the cost of repairing damage caused by the tenant are generally transferred by the seller to the buyer.

Real estate taxes. Proration of real estate taxes will vary widely, depending on how the taxes are paid in the area where the real estate is located. In some states real estate taxes are paid *in advance:* if the tax year runs from January 1 to December 31, taxes for the coming year are due on January 1. In that case the seller, who has prepaid a year's taxes, should be reimbursed for the portion of the year remaining after the buyer takes ownership of the tax-paid-up property. In other areas taxes are paid *in arrears,* on December 31 for the year just ended. In that case the buyer should be credited by the seller for the time the seller was occupying the property. Sometimes taxes are due during the tax year, partly in arrears and partly in advance; sometimes they are payable in installments. To compound the confusion city, state, school and other property taxes may start their tax years in different months. Whatever the case may be in a particular transaction, the licensee should understand how the taxes are to be prorated.

Mortgage loan interest. On almost every mortgage loan the interest is paid *in arrears,* so buyers and sellers must understand that the mortgage payment due on

June 1, for example, includes interest due for the month of May. Thus the buyer who assumes a mortgage on May 31 and makes the June payment will be paying for the time the seller occupied the property and should be credited with a month's interest. On the other hand, the buyer who places a new mortgage loan on May 31 may be pleasantly surprised to hear that he or she will not need to make a mortgage payment until a month later.

Accounting for Credits and Charges

The items that must be accounted for in the closing statement fall into two general categories: prorations or other amounts due to either the buyer or seller (credit to) and paid for by the other party (debit to) and expenses or items paid by the seller or buyer (debit only). In the following lists the items marked by an asterisk (*) are not prorated; they are entered in full as listed.

Items credited to the buyer and debited to the seller. These items include

- the buyer's earnest money*;
- the principal amount of a new mortgage loan or unpaid principal balance of an outstanding mortgage loan being assumed by the buyer*;
- interest on an existing assumed mortgage not yet paid (accrued);
- the unearned portion of current rent collected in advance;
- tenants' security deposits*;
- a purchase-money mortgage*; and
- unpaid water and other utility bills.

The *buyer's earnest money,* while credited to the buyer, *is not usually debited to the seller.* The buyer receives a credit because he or she has already paid that amount toward the purchase price. Under the usual sales contract the money is held by the broker or attorney until the settlement, when it will be included as part of the total amount due the seller. If the seller is paying off an existing loan and the buyer is obtaining a new one, these two items are accounted for with a debit only to the seller for the amount of the payoff and a credit only to the buyer for the amount of the new loan.

Items credited to the seller and debited to the buyer. These items include

- the sales price*;
- any fuel oil on hand, usually figured at current market price (prepaid);
- an insurance and tax reserve (if any) when an outstanding mortgage loan is being assumed by buyer (prepaid);
- a refund to the seller of prepaid water charge and similar expenses; and
- any portion of general real estate tax paid in advance.

Accounting for expenses. Expenses paid out of the closing proceeds are debited only to the party making the payment. Occasionally an expense item—such as an escrow fee, a settlement fee or a transfer tax—may be shared by the buyer and the seller, and each party will be debited for the share of the expense.

THE ARITHMETIC OF PRORATING

Accurate prorating involves four considerations: what the item being prorated is; whether it is an accrued item that requires the determination of an earned amount; whether it is a prepaid item that requires the unearned amount—a refund to the seller—to be determined; and what arithmetic processes must be used. The information contained in the previous sections will assist in answering the first three questions.

The computation of a proration involves identifying a yearly charge for the item to be prorated, then dividing by 12 to determine a monthly charge for the item. Usually it is also necessary to identify a daily charge for the item by dividing the monthly charge by the number of days in the month. These smaller portions are then multiplied by the number of months and/or days in the prorated time period to determine the accrued or unearned amount that will be figured in the settlement.

Using this general principle, there are two methods of calculating prorations:

1. The yearly charge is divided by a *360-day year* (commonly called a *banking year*), or 12 months of 30 days each.

2. The yearly charge is divided by *365* (366 in a leap year) to determine the daily charge. Then the actual number of days in the proration period is determined, and this number is multiplied by the daily charge.

The final proration figure will vary slightly, depending on which computation method is used. The final figure will also vary according to the number of decimal places to which the division is carried. *All of the computations in this chapter are computed by carrying the division to three decimal places.* The third decimal place is rounded off to cents only after the final proration figure is determined.

Accrued Items

When the real estate tax is levied for the calendar year and is payable during that year or in the following year, the accrued portion is for the period from January 1 to the date of closing (or to the day before the closing in states where the sale date is excluded). If the current tax bill has not yet been issued, the parties must agree on an estimated amount based on the previous year's bill and any known changes in assessment or tax levy for the current year.

For example, assume a sale is to be closed on September 17, current real estate taxes of $1,200 are to be prorated accordingly and a 360-day year is being used. The accrued period, then, is eight months and 17 days. First determine the prorated cost of the real estate tax per month and day:

$$\frac{\$100}{12)\$1,200} \text{ per month} \qquad \frac{\$3.333}{30)\$100.000} \text{ per day}$$

months   days

Next, multiply these figures by the accrued period and add the totals to determine the prorated real estate tax:

$100	$ 3.333	$800.000
× 8 months	× 17 days	+ 56.661
$800	$56.661	$856.661

Thus the accrued real estate tax for 3 months, 17 days is $856.66 (rounded off to two decimal places after the final computation). This amount represents the seller's accrued earned tax; it will be *a credit to the buyer* and a *debit to the seller on the closing statement.*

To compute this proration using the actual number of days in the accrued period, the following method is used: The accrued period from January 1 to September 17 runs 260 days (January, 31 days plus February's 28 days, and so on). A tax bill of $1,200 ÷ 365 days = $3.288 per day. $3.288 × 260 days = $854.880, or $854.88.

While these examples show proration as of the date of settlement, the agreement of sale may require otherwise. One possibility is the case in which the buyer's and seller's possession date does not coincide with the settlement date. The parties may elect to prorate according to the date of possession.

IN PRACTICE...	*On state licensing examinations, tax prorations are usually based on a 30-day month (360-day year) unless specified otherwise in the problem. This may differ with local customs regarding tax prorations. Many title insurance companies provide proration charts that detail tax factors for each day in the year. To determine a tax proration using one of these charts, you would multiply the factor given for the closing date by the annual real estate tax.*

Prepaid Items

A tax proration could be a prepaid item. Because real estate tax may be paid in the early part of the year, tax prorations calculated for closings taking place later in the year must reflect the fact that the seller has already paid the tax. For example, in the preceding problem, suppose that the taxes had been paid. The buyer, then, would have to reimburse the seller; the proration would be *credited to the seller* and *debited to the buyer.*

In figuring the tax proration, it is necessary to ascertain the number of future days, months and years for which the taxes have been paid. The formula commonly used for this purpose is as follows:

	Years	**Months**	**Days**
Taxes paid to (Dec. 31, end of tax year)	1993	12	31
Date of closing (Sept. 17, 1993)	1993	9	17
Period for which tax must be paid		3	14

With this formula we can find the amount the buyer will reimburse the seller for the *unearned* portion of the real estate tax. The prepaid period, as determined using the formula for prepaid items, is 3 months, 14 days. Three months at $100 per month equals $300, and 14 days at $3.333 per day = $46.662. Add this up to determine that the proration is $346.662, or $346.66 *credited to the seller* and *debited to the buyer*.

Another example of a prepaid item is a water bill. Assume that the water is billed in advance by the city without using a meter. The six months' billing is $60 for the period ending October 31. The sale is to be closed on August 3. Because the water bill is paid to October 31, the prepaid time must be computed. Using a 30-day basis, the time period is the 27 days left in August plus two full months: $60 ÷ 6 = $10 per month. For one day, divide $10 by 30, which equals $0.333 per day. The prepaid period is two months, 27 days, so:

$$27 \text{ days} \quad \times \$0.333 = \$\ 8.991$$
$$\underline{2 \text{ months} \times \$10.00 = \$20.00}$$
$$\$28.991 \text{ or } \$28.99$$

This is a prepaid item; it is *credited to the seller* and *debited to the buyer on the closing statement*.

To figure this on the basis of the actual days in the month of closing, the following process would be used:

$10 per month ÷ 31 days in August	= $0.323 per day
August 4 through August 31	= 28 days
28 days × $0.323	= $9.044
2 months × $10	= $20.00
$9.044 + $20.00	= $29.044 or $29.04

SAMPLE CLOSING STATEMENT

As stated previously, there are many possible formats for settlement computations. The remaining portion of this chapter illustrates a sample transaction using the HUD Uniform Settlement Statement in Figure 23.1. Because customs differ in various parts of the country, the way certain expenses are charged in some locations may be different from the illustration.

Uniform Settlement Statement

Basic information of offer and sale. John and Joanne Iuro listed their home at 3045 North Racine Avenue in Riverdale, Illinois, with the Open Door Real Estate Company. The listing price was $118,500, and possession could be given within two weeks after all parties had signed the contract. Under the terms of the listing agreement the sellers agreed to pay the broker a commission of 6 percent of the sales price.

On May 18 the Open Door Real Estate Company submitted a contract offer to the Iuros from Brook Redemann, a bachelor, presently residing at 22 King Court, Riverdale. Redemann offered $115,000, with earnest money/down payment of $23,000 and the remaining $92,000 of the purchase price to be obtained through a new conventional loan. No private mortgage insurance will be necessary because the loan-to-value ratio will not exceed 80 percent. The Iuros signed the contract on May 29. Closing was set for June 15 at the office of the Open Door Real Estate Company, 720 Main Street, Riverdale.

The unpaid balance of the Iuros' mortgage as of June 1, 19— will be $57,700. Payments are $680 per month with interest at 11 percent per annum on the unpaid balance.

The sellers submitted evidence of title in the form of a title insurance binder at a cost of $10. The title insurance policy paid by the seller at the time of closing cost an additional $540, including $395 for lender's coverage and $145 for homeowner's coverage. Recording charges of $20 were paid for the recording of two instruments to clear defects in the sellers' title, and state transfer tax in the amount of $115 ($.50 per $500 of sales price or fraction thereof) were affixed to the deed. In addition, the sellers must pay an attorney's fee of $400 for preparation of the deed and for legal representation; this amount will be paid from the closing proceeds.

The buyer must pay an attorney's fee of $300 for examination of the title evidence and legal representation, as well as $10 to record the deed. These amounts will also be paid from the closing proceeds.

Real estate taxes in Riverdale are paid in arrears. Taxes for this year, estimated at last year's figure of $1,725, have not been paid. According to the contract, prorations are to be made on the basis of 30 days in a month.

Computing the prorations and charges. Following are illustrations of the various steps in computing the prorations and other amounts to be included in the settlement thus far.

1. *Closing date:* June 15

2. *Commission:* 6% × $115,000 (sales price) = $6,900

3. *Seller's mortgage interest:*
   11% × $57,700 (principal due after June 1 payment) = $6,347 interest per year
   $6,347 ÷ 360 days = $17.631 interest per day
   15 days of accrued interest to be paid by the seller
   15 × $17.631 = $264.465, or $264.47 interest owed by the seller
   $57,700 + $264.465 = $57,964.47 payoff of seller's mortgage

4. *Real estate taxes* (estimated at $1,725):
   $1,725.00 ÷ 12 months = $143.75 per month
   $ 143.75 ÷ 30 days = $ 4.792 per day
   The earned period is from January 1 to and including June 15 and equals 5 months, 15 days:
   $143.75 × 5 months = $718.750
   $ 4.792 × 15 days   = $ 71.880
                             $790.630, or $790.63 seller owes buyer

5. *Transfer tax* ($.50 per $500 of consideration or fraction thereof):
   $115,000 ÷ $500 = $230
   $230 × $.50 = $115.00 transfer tax owed by seller

The sellers' loan payoff is $57,964.47, and they must pay an additional $10 to record the mortgage release as well as $85 for a pest inspection. The buyer's new loan is from Thrift Federal Savings, 1100 Fountain Plaza, Riverdale, in the amount of $92,000 at 10 percent interest. In connection with this loan he will be

**Figure 23.1
RESPA Uniform
Settlement
Statement**

A. SETTLEMENT STATEMENT U.S. DEPARTMENT OF HOUSING AND URBAN DEVELOPMENT
HUD-1 Rev. 3/86

OMB NO. 2502-0265 (Exp. 12-31-86)

B. TYPE OF LOAN

| 1. ☐ FHA | 2. ☐ FmHA | 3. ☒ CONV. UNINS. | 6. File Number | 7. Loan Number | 8. Mortgage Insurance Claim Case Number |
| 4. ☐ VA | 5. ☐ CONV. INS. | | | | |

C. NOTE: *This form is furnished to give you a statement of actual settlement costs. Amounts paid to and by the settlement agent are shown. Items marked "(p.o.c.)" were paid outside the closing; they are shown here for informational purposes and are not included in the totals.*

D. NAME AND ADDRESS OF BORROWER:	E. NAME AND ADDRESS OF SELLER:	F. NAME AND ADDRESS OF LENDER:
Brook Redemann 22 King Court Riverdale, Illinois	John and Joanne Iuro 3045 North Racine Avenue Riverdale, Illinois	Thrift Federal Savings 1100 Fountain Plaza Riverdale, Illinois

G. PROPERTY LOCATION: 3045 North Racine Avenue Riverdale, Illinois	H. SETTLEMENT AGENT: Open Door Real Estate Company PLACE OF SETTLEMENT: Open Door Real Estate Company 720 Main Street, Riverdale, Illinois	I. SETTLEMENT DATE: June 15,

J. SUMMARY OF BORROWER'S TRANSACTION		K. SUMMARY OF SELLER'S TRANSACTION	
100. GROSS AMOUNT DUE FROM BORROWER:		**400. GROSS AMOUNT DUE TO SELLER:**	
101. Contract sales price	$115,000.00	401. Contract sales price	$115,000.00
102. Personal property		402. Personal property	
103. Settlement charges to borrower (line 1400)	5,075.84	403.	
104.		404.	
105.		405.	
Adjustments for items paid by seller in advance		*Adjustments for items paid by seller in advance*	
106. City/town taxes to		406. City/town taxes to	
107. County taxes to		407. County taxes to	
108. Assessments to		408. Assessments to	
109.		409.	
110.		410.	
111.		411.	
112.		412.	
120. GROSS AMOUNT DUE FROM BORROWER	$120,075.84	**420. GROSS AMOUNT DUE TO SELLER**	$115,000.00
200. AMOUNTS PAID BY OR IN BEHALF OF BORROWER:		**500. REDUCTIONS IN AMOUNT DUE TO SELLER:**	
201. Deposit or earnest money	23,000.00	501. Excess deposit (see instructions)	
202. Principal amount of new loan(s)	92,000.00	502. Settlement charges to seller (line 1400)	8,080.00
203. Existing loan(s) taken subject to		503. Existing loan(s) taken subject to	
204.		504. Payoff of first mortgage loan	57,964.47
205.		505. Payoff of second mortgage loan	
206.		506.	
207.		507.	
208.		508.	
209.		509.	
Adjustments for items unpaid by seller		*Adjustments for items unpaid by seller*	
210. City/town taxes to		510. City/town taxes to	
211. County taxes 1/1 to 6/15/	790.63	511. County taxes 1/1 to 6/15/	790.63
212. Assessments to		512. Assessments to	
213.		513.	
214.		514.	
215.		515.	
216.		516.	
217.		517.	
218.		518.	
219.		519.	
220. TOTAL PAID BY/FOR BORROWER	$115,790.63	**520. TOTAL REDUCTION AMOUNT DUE SELLER**	$66,835.10
300. CASH AT SETTLEMENT FROM/TO BORROWER		**600. CASH AT SETTLEMENT TO/FROM SELLER**	
301. Gross amount due from borrower (line 120)	120,075.84	601. Gross amount due to seller (line 420)	115,000.00
302. Less amounts paid by/for borrower (line 220)	(115,790.63)	602. Less reductions in amount due seller (line 520)	(66,835.10)
303. CASH (☐ FROM) (☐ TO) BORROWER	$ 4,285.21	**603. CASH (☐ TO) (☐ FROM) SELLER**	$ 48,164.90

I have carefully reviewed the HUD-1 Settlement Statement and to the best of my knowledge and belief, it is a true and accurate statement of all receipts and disbursements made on my account or by me in this transaction. I further certify that I have received a copy of the HUD-1 Settlement Statement.

Borrower _____   Seller _____

Borrower _____   Seller _____

The HUD-1 Settlement Statement which I have prepared is a true and accurate account of this transaction. I have caused or will cause the funds to be disbursed in accordance with this statement.

Settlement Agent _____   Date _____

Warning: It is a crime to knowingly make false statements to the United States on this or any other similar form. Penalties upon conviction can include a fine and imprisonment. For details see: Title 18 U.S. Code Section 1001 and Section 1010.

2128 (6-86) 41b

Figure 23.1 (continued)

— 2 —

L. SETTLEMENT CHARGES

	PAID FROM BORROWER'S FUNDS AT SETTLEMENT	PAID FROM SELLER'S FUNDS AT SETTLEMENT
700. TOTAL SALES/BROKER'S COMMISSION based on price $ 115,000 @ 6 % = $6,900.00		
Division of Commission (line 700) as follows:		
701. $ to		
702. $ to		
703. Commission paid at Settlement		$6,900.00
704.		
800. ITEMS PAYABLE IN CONNECTION WITH LOAN		
801. Loan Origination Fee %	$ 920.00	
802. Loan Discount 2 %	$1,840.00	
803. Appraisal Fee $125.00 to Swift Appraisal	POC	
804. Credit Report $ 60.00 to ACME Credit Bureau	POC	
805. Lender's Inspection Fee		
806. Mortgage Insurance Application Fee to		
807. Assumption Fee		
808. Application Fee		
809. Wholesale Interest Differential Fee		
810. Underwriting Fee		
811. Buydown Fee		
812. Commitment Fee		
813.		
814. Messenger Service		
815. Shortfall		
816.		
817.		
818.		
819.		
900. ITEMS REQUIRED BY LENDER TO BE PAID IN ADVANCE		
901. Interest from 6/16/ to 6/30/ @ $ 25.556 /day	383.34	
902. Mortgage Insurance Premium for months to		
903. Hazard Insurance Premium for 1 years to Hite Insurance Co.	345.00	
904. One-Time FHA Insurance Premium		
905. VA Funding Fee		
906.		
907.		
1000. RESERVES DEPOSITED WITH LENDER		
1001. Hazard insurance 3 months @ $ 28.75 per month	86.25	
1002. Mortgage insurance months @ $ per month		
1003. City property taxes months @ $ per month		
1004. County property taxes 7 months @ $ 143.75 per month	1,006.25	
1005. Annual assessments months @ $ per month		
1006. months @ $ per month		
1007. months @ $ per month		
1008. months @ $ per month		
1100. TITLE CHARGES		
1101. Settlement or closing fee to		
1102. Abstract or title search to		
1103. Title examination to		
1104. Title insurance binder to		10.00
1105. Document preparation to		
1106. Notary fees to		
1107. Attorney's fees to	300.00	400.00
(includes above items numbers;)		
1108. Title insurance to		540.00
(includes above items numbers;)		
1109. Lender's coverage $ 395.00		
1110. Owner's coverage $ 145.00		
1111. Tax Service Contract Fee to		
1112. Amortization Schedule to		
1113.		
1114.		
1115.		
1116.		
1200. GOVERNMENT RECORDING AND TRANSFER CHARGES		
1201. Recording Fees: Deed $ 10.00 ; Mortgage $ 10.00 ; Releases $ 10.00	20.00	10.00
1202. City/county tax/stamps: Deed $; Mortgage $		
1203. State tax/Stamps: Deed $ 115.00 ; Mortgage $		115.00
1204. Record two documents to clear title		20.00
1205.		
1300. ADDITIONAL SETTLEMENT CHARGES		
1301. Survey to	175.00	
1302. Pest inspection to		85.00
1303.		
1304.		
1305.		
1400. TOTAL SETTLEMENT CHARGES (enter on lines 103, Section J and 502, Section K)	$5,075.84	$8,080.00

2128 (6-88) 41b Reverse

HUD-1 Rev. 5/76

charged $125 to have the property appraised by Swift Appraisal and $60 for a credit report from the Acme Credit Bureau. (Because appraisal and credit reports are performed prior to loan approval, they are paid at the time of loan application, whether or not the transaction eventually closes. These items will be noted as POC—paid outside closing—on the settlement statement.) In addition, buyer Redemann will pay for interest on his loan for the remainder of the month of closing—15 days at $25.556 per day, or $383.34. His first full payment (including July's interest) will be due August 1. He must deposit $1,006.25, or 7/12 of the anticipated county real estate tax (of $1,725) into a tax reserve account. A one-year hazard insurance premium at $3 per $1,000 of appraised value ($115,000 ÷ 1,000 × 3 = $345) is paid in advance to Hite Insurance Company. An insurance reserve to cover the premium for three months is deposited with the lender. Redemann will have to pay an additional $10 to record the mortgage and $175 for a survey. He will also pay a loan origination fee of $920 and two discount points.

The Uniform Settlement Statement is divided into 12 sections. The most important information is included in Sections J, K and L. The borrower's and seller's summaries (J and K) are very similar. In Section J, the summary of the borrower's transaction, the buyer/borrower's debits are listed in lines 100 through 112 and totaled on line 120 (gross amount due from borrower). The total of the settlement costs itemized in Section L of the statement is entered on line 103 as one of the buyer's charges. The buyer's credits are listed on lines 201 through 219 and totaled on line 220 (total paid by/for borrower). Then the buyer's credits are subtracted from the charges to arrive at the cash due from the borrower to close (line 303).

In Section K, the summary of the seller's transaction, the seller's credits are entered on lines 400 through 412 and totaled on line 420 (gross amount due to seller). The seller's debits are entered on lines 501 through 519 and totaled on line 520 (total reduction amount due seller). The total of the seller's settlement charges is on line 502. Then the debits are subtracted from the credits to arrive at the cash due to the sellers to close (line 603).

Section L is a summary of all the settlement charges for the transaction; the buyer's expenses are listed in one column and the sellers' expenses in the other. If an attorney's fee is listed as a lump sum in line 1107, the settlement should list by line number the services that were included in that total fee.

●   ●   ●   ●   ●   ●   ●

KEY TERMS

accrued items
closing statement
credit
debit
escrow
prepaid items

prorations
Real Estate Settlement Procedures
  Act (RESPA)
Uniform Settlement Statement
  (HUD-I)

SUMMARY

Closing a real estate sale involves both title procedures and financial matters. The real estate salesperson or broker is often present at the closing to see that the sale is actually concluded and to account for the earnest money deposit.

Closings must be reported to the IRS on form 1099-S.

The federal Real Estate Settlement Procedures Act (RESPA) requires disclosure of all settlement costs when a residential real estate purchase is financed by a federally related mortgage loan. RESPA requires lenders to use a Uniform Settlement Statement to detail the financial particulars of a transaction.

The actual amount to be paid by the buyer at the closing is computed by preparation of a closing, or settlement, statement. This lists the sales price, earnest money deposit and all adjustments and prorations due between buyer and seller. The purpose of this statement is to determine the net amount due the seller at closing. The buyer reimburses the seller for prepaid items like unused taxes or fuel oil. The seller credits the buyer for bills the seller owes that will be paid by the buyer (accrued items), such as unpaid water bills.

Questions

1. Which of the following is true of real estate closings in most states?
   a. Closings are generally conducted by real estate salespeople.
   b. The buyer usually receives the rents for the day of closing.
   c. The buyer must reimburse the seller for any title evidence provided by the seller.
   d. The seller usually pays the expenses for the day of closing.

2. All encumbrances and liens shown on the report of title, other than those waived or agreed to by the purchaser and listed in the contract, must be removed so that the title can be delivered free and clear. The removal of such encumbrances is the duty of the
   a. buyer.   c. broker.
   b. seller.   d. title company.

3. Legal title always passes from the seller to the buyer
   a. on the date of execution of the deed.
   b. when the closing statement has been signed.
   c. when the deed is placed in escrow.
   d. when the deed is delivered.

4. Which of the following would a lender generally require to be produced at the closing?
   a. Title insurance policy
   b. Market value appraisal
   c. Application
   d. Credit report

5. When a transaction is to be closed in escrow, the seller generally deposits all but which of the following items with the escrow agent before the closing date?
   a. Deed to the property
   b. Title evidence
   c. Estoppel certificate
   d. Cash needed to complete the purchase

6. The RESPA Uniform Settlement Statement must be used to illustrate all settlement charges for
   a. every real estate transaction.
   b. transactions financed by VA and FHA loans only.
   c. residential transactions financed by federally related mortgage loans.
   d. all transactions involving commercial property.

7. A mortgage reduction certificate is executed by a(n)
   a. abstract company.
   b. attorney.
   c. lending institution.
   d. grantor.

8. The principal amount of the purchaser's new mortgage loan is a
   a. credit to the seller.
   b. credit to the buyer.
   c. debit to the seller.
   d. debit to the buyer.

9. The earnest money left on deposit with the broker is a
   a. credit to the seller.
   b. credit to the buyer.
   c. debit to the seller.
   d. debit to the buyer.

10. The annual real estate taxes amount to
    $1,800 and have been paid in advance for
    the calendar year. If closing is set for June
    15, which of the following is true?
    a. Credit seller $825; debit buyer $975.
    b. Credit seller $1,800; debit buyer $825.
    c. Credit buyer $975; debit seller $975.
    d. Credit seller $975; debit buyer $975.

11. The seller collected rent of $400, payable in
    advance, from the attic tenant on August 1.
    At the closing on August 15 the
    a. seller owes the buyer $400.
    b. buyer owes the seller $400.
    c. seller owes the buyer $200.
    d. buyer owes the seller $200.

12. Security deposits should be listed on a clos-
    ing statement as a credit to the
    a. buyer.   c. lender.
    b. seller.   d. broker.

13. A building was bought for $85,000, with 10
    percent down and a loan for the balance. If
    the lender charged the buyer two discount
    points, how much cash did the buyer need
    to come up with?
    a. $10,200   c. $8,500
    b. $10,030   d. $1,700

14. A buyer of a $50,000 home has paid $2,000
    as earnest money and has a loan commit-
    ment for 70 percent of the purchase price.
    How much more cash does the buyer need
    to complete the transaction?
    a. $10,000   c. $15,000
    b. $13,000   d. $35,000

15. At the closing the broker's commission will
    usually be shown as
    a. credit to the seller.
    b. credit to the buyer.
    c. debit to the seller.
    d. debit to the buyer.

16. At the closing the seller's attorney gave
    credit to the buyer for certain accrued
    items. These items were
    a. bills relating to the property that have
       already been paid by the seller.
    b. bills relating to the property that will
       have to be paid by the buyer.
    c. all of the seller's real estate bills.
    d. all of the buyer's real estate bills.

17. The Real Estate Settlement Procedures Act
    applies to the activities of
    a. brokers selling commercial and office
       buildings.
    b. security salespersons selling limited
       partnerships.
    c. Ginnie Mae or Fannie Mae when
       purchasing mortgages.
    d. lenders financing the purchase of a bor-
       rower's residence.

18. The purpose of RESPA (Real Estate Settle-
    ment Procedures Act) is to
    a. make sure buyers do not borrow more
       than they can repay.
    b. make real estate brokers more
       responsive to buyers' needs.
    c. help buyers know how much money is
       required.
    d. see that buyers and sellers know all set-
       tlement costs.

Real Estate Mathematics Review

Success in real estate math requires good, comprehensive reading skills, some simple math skills and knowledge of certain basic facts.

Most real estate math consists of fairly simple calculations, those we learn in elementary school. Math is a part of our everyday life, and yet when the word *math* is used in the context of a course or an exam, some experience a degree of anxiety. Learn to overcome anxiety or that panicky feeling by preparing yourself through practice and study.

Read the question carefully to ascertain what is being asked. *Analyze* or take apart the question. Sort the facts or information necessary to arrive at the answer. Determine the *procedure* or method necessary to calculate the answer. *Calculate* the answer. *Check* your answer to see if you have answered the question. *Look* at the answer to see if it makes sense, is reasonable and "looks right."

When using a calculator, check the calculator window to be sure the numbers you are entering are registering. Note important calculations on your scrap paper to make it easier to check your work. One of the more common errors when using a calculator is in the placement of the decimal. If the answer to a question should be $110.25, it is not $11.02 or $11,025 or $110,250. On an exam you may be given a choice of answers that are all possible if you were to use the facts in different ways or if you misplaced the decimal.

To find the answer to many questions, you must learn some basic facts and terminology.

Calculating square area or cubic volume is fairly simple. Mistakes can be made when dealing with feet and yards, and the means of measuring must be converted to one single form of measurement. If the answer is to be in yards, do not answer in feet or inches. Be cautious when converting units of measurement. For example, to convert a cubic yard to cubic feet, you must multiply by 27, *not* by 9 (cubic = $3 \times 3 \times 3 = 27$).

OUTLINE OF
ESSENTIAL
CONCEPTS

I.   Important definitions
All definitions offered pertain solely to the use of words in real estate mathematics.

A. Annual: Yearly, of or pertaining to a year.

B. Biannual: Twice a year; also semiannual.

C. Biennial: Every two years.

D. Calculate: To figure, compute or find out by adding, subtracting, multiplying or dividing.

E. Capitalization rate (cap rate): Income divided by value, used to calculate the rate of return on an investment.

F. Cubic measure: A system of measuring volume in cubic units. Cubic units have three dimensions: height (or depth), length and width. Think in terms of a cube.

G. Distractor: A factor in test questions that draws attention from the true question and answer. Distractors may confuse the test taker.

H. Dimension: measurement of length, width, height or thickness; size; extent.

I.   Fact: A truth or reality to be used in calculating. Examples: height, amount, time, percent, interest, sales price, commission, etc.

J.   Fraction: One or more of the parts of a whole. Ten is 10% of 100; $^{10}/_{100}$; 100 being the whole number, 10 being the part. 10 = 10% of 100.

K. Front foot: A standard one-foot-wide measurement of the width of a parcel of land applied at the frontage on its *main* street line. A front foot extends to the depth of the parcel.

L.   Income: What comes in from property or an investment; receipts, revenue, proceeds, profit.

M. Interest: Money paid for the use of money, usually calculated as a percentage.

N. Linear measure (also *lineal measure*): A measurement made on a line.

O. Mill: Expressing a tax rate—$^1/_{10}$ of one cent; .001. Mill rate is a tax rate expressed as so many mills on each dollar ($1.00) of assessed value.

P. Percentage: Rate or proportion of each hundred; part of each hundred. Allowance, commission, discount, rate of interest figured by percent (%).

Q. Principal: The sum of money on which interest is paid; money or property from which income is received.

R. Quarterly: Four times per year.

S. Rate: Quantity, amount or degree measured in proportion to something else; price. Rate is often expressed as a percentage.

T. Square measure: A system of measurement of area in square units. Square units have two dimensions and can be thought of as flat space, such as seeing a circle or a square on a piece of paper.

U. Tax: Money paid for the support of the government.

V. Time: A prescribed or allotted term or period, a specific measured time, such as four days, two months, 2½ years, etc.

II. Measurements

A. Linear

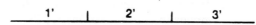

Linear is a measurement made on a line. One linear yard is three feet in dimension.

B. Square

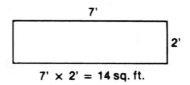

7' × 2' = 14 sq. ft.

Square is a flat two-dimensional entity. A square yard is a square with sides of three feet each, or 3' × 3' = 9 sq. ft. = 1 sq. yd.

C. Cubic

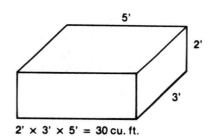

2' × 3' × 5' = 30 cu. ft.

Cubic is a three-dimensional volume measurement. A cubic yard is a cube with height, width and depth of three feet each: 3' × 3' × 3' = 27 cu. ft.; 27 cu. ft. = 1 cu. yd.

III. Units of measure

A. 12" (inches) = 1' (foot)

B. 1 mile = 5,280 feet

C. 1 acre = 43,560 sq. ft.

D. 1 rod = 16½ feet

E. 1 mile = 320 rods

IV. Conversions

A. To convert square feet to square inches, multiply the number of square feet by 144. (sq. ft. × 144 = sq. in.)

B. To convert square inches to square feet, divide the number of square inches by 144. (sq. in. ÷ 144 = sq. ft.)

C. To convert square yards to square feet, multiply the number of square yards by 9. (sq. yd. × 9 = sq. ft.)

D. To convert square feet to square yards, divide the number of square feet by 9. (sq. ft. ÷ 9 = sq. yd.)

E. To convert square yards to square inches, multiply the number of sq. yds. by 1,296. (sq. yd. × 1,296 = sq. in.)

F. To convert square inches to square yards, divide the number of square inches by 1,296. (sq. in. ÷ 1,296 = sq. yd.)

G. To convert square feet to acres, divide the number of square feet by 43,560. (sq. ft. ÷ 43,560 = acres)

H. To convert cubic feet to cubic yards, divide the number of cubic feet by 27. (cu. ft. ÷ 27 = cu. yd.)

V. Fractions

A. $\dfrac{\text{Numerator} = \text{\# parts of a fraction}}{\text{Denominator} = \text{\# parts in whole}}$

B. Proper fraction = part of a whole (less than one). Example: ½

C. Improper fraction = more than part of whole. Example: ³⁄₂

D. Mixed number = whole number + fraction. Example: 1½

E. Converting fractions: Improper fraction to mixed number (³⁄₂ to 1½); mixed number to improper fraction—Multiply whole number by the denominator, add the numerator, place same over the denominator.

F. Multiplying fractions:

$\dfrac{\text{Multiply numerators}}{\text{Multiply denominators}}$ Reduce simple fraction

$$\frac{3}{20} \times \frac{5}{6} = \frac{15}{120} = \frac{3}{24} = \frac{1}{8}$$

G. Dividing fractions:
Invert fraction you are dividing by, then proceed by multiplying.

$$\frac{5}{8} \div \frac{2}{3} = \frac{5}{8} \times \frac{3}{2} = \frac{15}{16}$$

VI. Percentages

A. Percent (%) means per hundred or per hundred parts. 25% = ¼ or 25 parts of 100 parts

B. Converting % to simple fractions:

$$20\% = \frac{20}{100} = \frac{1}{5}$$

C. Converting % to decimals: Drop % sign and move decimal two places to the left: 10% = .10; 1% = .01. Each decimal place to the right of a decimal point = ¹⁄₁₀ or a tenth of a number.

D. Adding or subtracting decimals: line up decimal points.

E. Multiplying decimals: move back the decimal points in answer.

$$\begin{array}{r} .25 \\ \times\ .03 \\ \hline .0075 \end{array}$$

F. Dividing decimals: move over the decimal points.

$$\begin{array}{r} .12 \\ 3)\overline{\,.36} \end{array} \qquad\qquad \begin{array}{r} 30 \\ .5)\overline{\,15.0} \end{array}$$

G. Dividing by % (percent):

$$100 \div 5\% = 100 \div \frac{5}{100} = 100 \div \frac{1}{20} = 100 \times \frac{20}{1} = 2{,}000 \ or$$

$$\frac{100}{5\%} = \frac{100}{.05} = \frac{10{,}000}{5} = 2{,}000$$

VII. Capitalization rate (cap rate) calculations:

$$\text{Cap Rate} = \frac{\text{Income}}{\text{Value}} \qquad R = \frac{I}{V} \ or \ V = \frac{I}{R}$$

VIII. Computing area and volume

A. Index

		a	=	area	cu.	=	cubic
		b	=	base	ft.	=	feet
interchangeable	{	d	=	depth	in.	=	inches
		h	=	height	sq.	=	square
		l	=	length	symbols: ′ =		feet
		v	=	volume	″	=	inches
		w	=	width	×	=	multiply

B. Parallelogram: A quadrilateral having its opposite sides parallel

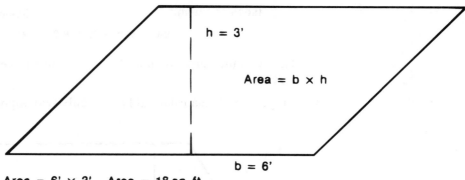

Area = 6' × 3'   Area = 18 sq. ft.

The altitude (height) of a parallelogram or trapezoid is a perpendicular distance between the parallel sides.

C. Computing volume: Volume is a cubic measurement.

$$\text{Volume} = l \times w \times h \text{ (d)}$$

$6' \times 3' \times 2' = 36$ cu. ft.

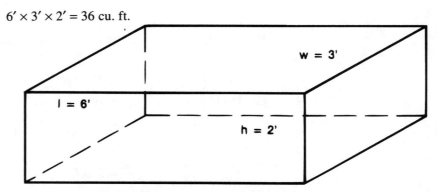

1 cu. ft. = 1,728 cu. in. or (12″ × 12″ × 12″ = 1,728 cu. in.)
1 yd. = 3 ft.   **1 cu. yd. = 27 cu. ft. (3′ × 3′ × 3′)**

D. Triangle: A three-sided polygon

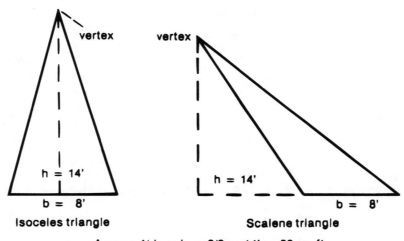

Area = ½b × h, or 8/2 × 14′ = 56 sq. ft.

Height is the perpendicular distance from any vertex to the opposite side.

E. Trapezoid: A quadrilateral having only two opposite sides parallel

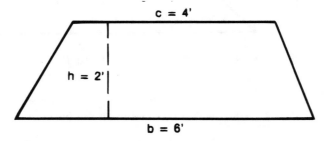

Area = h × ½(b + c) or Area = 2′ × ½(6′ + 4′) or 10 sq. ft.

F.   Irregular polygons: Various shapes for calculating purposes
     Areas 1 and 3 are triangles; area 2 is a trapezoid.

     To determine the area, divide the irregular shape into parts, then add
     up the areas to determine the whole area.

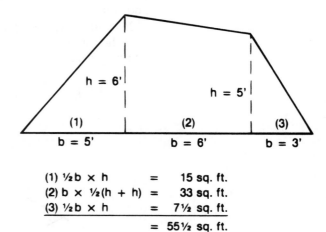

(1) ½b × h =	**15 sq. ft.**
(2) b × ½(h + h) =	**33 sq. ft.**
(3) ½b × h =	**7½ sq. ft.**
=	**55½ sq. ft.**

G.   Sample area and volume problems

     1.   A couple wishes to purchase an air conditioner for their bedroom.
          To determine what unit to buy, they need to know the cubic vol-
          ume. $12' \times 10' \times 8' = 960$ cu. ft. Compute the volume in cu. yds.
          $960 \div 27 = 35.56$ cu. yds. or 35½ cu. yds.

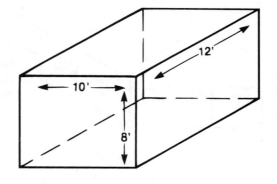

2. The Greenes' insurance company needs to know how many square
    feet of living space they have in their new house.

    Family room: 26′ − 14′ = 12′w
       12′w × 15′1 = 180 sq. ft.
    1st floor: 24′ × 48′ = 1,152 sq. ft.
    2nd floor:
       26′ × 48′ = 1,248 sq. ft.
    Add the three
       living areas:

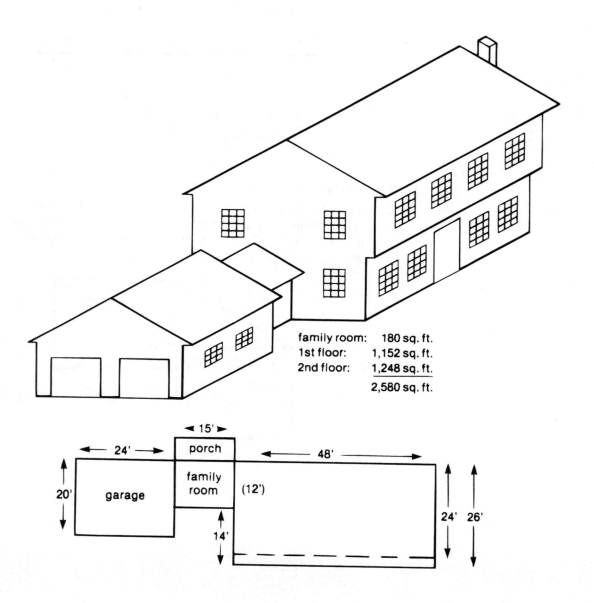

family room: 180 sq. ft.
1st floor: 1,152 sq. ft.
2nd floor: 1,248 sq. ft.
              2,580 sq. ft.

Questions

•   •   •   •   •   •   •

1. The broker of Happy Valley Realty recently sold a home for $79,500. The broker charged the seller a 6½ percent commission and will pay 30 percent of that amount to the listing salesperson and 25 percent to the selling salesperson. What amount of commission will the listing salesperson receive from the sale?

   a. $5,167.50   c. $3,617.25
   b. $1,550.25   d. $1,291.87

2. A buyer signed an agreement to purchase a condominium apartment. The contract stipulated that the seller replace the damaged bedroom carpet. The buyer has chosen carpet that costs $16.95 per square yard plus $2.50 per square yard for installation. If the bedroom dimensions are as illustrated, how much will the seller have to pay for the job?

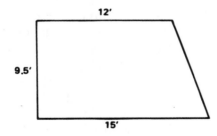

   a. $241.54   c. $277.16
   b. $189.20   d. $2,494.46

3. H, O, R and M decided to pool their savings and purchase a small apartment building for $125,000. If H invested $30,000 and O and R each contributed $35,000, what percentage of ownership was left for M?

   a. 20 percent   c. 28 percent
   b. 24 percent   d. 30 percent

4. A father is curious to know how much money his son and daughter-in-law still owe on their mortgage loan. The father knows that the interest portion of their last monthly payment was $391.42. If they are paying interest at the rate of 11½ percent, what was the outstanding balance of their loan before that last payment was made?

   a. $43,713.00   c. $36,427.50
   b. $40,843.83   d. $34,284.70

5. A home was purchased a year ago for $98,500. Property in the neighborhood is said to be increasing in value at a rate of 5 percent annually. If this is true, what is the current market value of the real estate?

   a. $103,425   c. $104,410
   b. $93,575   d. $93,809

6. A home is valued at $95,000. Property in the area is assessed at 60 percent of its value, and the local tax rate is $2.85 per $100. What is the amount of the annual taxes?

   a. $2,451   c. $135.38
   b. $1,470.60   d. $1,624.50

7. The owners are planning to construct a patio in their backyard. An illustration of the surface area to be paved appears here. If the cement is to be poured as a six-inch slab, how many cubic feet of cement will be poured into this patio?

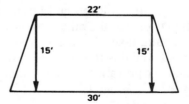

   a. 660 cubic feet   c. 330 cubic feet
   b. 450 cubic feet   d. 195 cubic feet

8. A salesperson receives a monthly salary of $1,000 plus 3 percent commission on all of his listings that sell and 2.5 percent on all of his sales. None of the listings that the salesperson took sold last month, but he received $4,175 in salary and commission. What was the value of the property that he sold?

   a. $147,000   c. $122,500
   b. $127,000   d. $105,833

9. Because the residence has proved difficult to sell, a salesperson suggests it might sell faster if the owners enclose a portion of the backyard with a privacy fence. If the area to be enclosed is as illustrated, how much will the fence cost at $6.95 per linear foot?

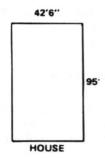

42'6"

95'

HOUSE

   a. $1,911.25   c. $1,615.88
   b. $450,000   d. $955.63

10. Twelve apartments in the Overton Arms are leased for a total monthly rental of $4,500. If this figure represents an 8 percent annual return on the owner's investment, what was the original cost of the property?

   a. $675,000   c. $54,000
   b. $450,000   d. $56,250

   For questions 11–16 regarding closing statement prorations, base your calculations on a 30-day month. Carry all computations to three decimal places until the final solution.

11. A sale is to be closed on March 15. Real estate taxes for the current year have not been paid; taxes for last year amounted to $1,340. What is the amount of the real estate tax proration to be credited to the buyer?

   a. $1,060.84   c. $223.33
   b. $279.16   d. $1,116.60

12. The buyers are assuming an outstanding mortgage, which had an unpaid balance of $58,200 after the last payment on August 1. Interest at 12 percent per annum is paid in arrears each month; the sale is to be closed on August 11. What is the amount of mortgage interest proration to be debited the seller at the closing?

   a. $698.40   c. $368.60
   b. $582.00   d. $213.40

13. In a sale of residential property real estate taxes for the current year amounted to $975 and have already been paid by the seller. The sale is to be closed on October 26; what is the amount of real estate tax proration to be credited the seller?

   a. $173.33   c. $798.96
   b. $162.50   d. $83.96

14. The buyer is assuming the seller's mortgage. The unpaid balance after the most recent payment (September 1) was $61,550. Interest is paid in arrears each month at 13 percent per annum. The sale is to be closed on September 22. What is the amount of mortgage interest proration to be credited to the buyer at the closing?

   a. $666.97   c. $177.82
   b. $488.97   d. $689.01

15. A 100-acre farm is divided into house lots. The streets require one-eighth of the whole farm, and there are 140 lots. How many square feet are in each lot?

   a. 35,004   c. 27,225
   b. 31,114   d. 43,560

16. The commission on a sale was $14,100, which was 6 percent of the sales price. What was the sales price?

   a. $235,000   c. $846,000
   b. $154,255.31   d. $234,500

17. Compute the square feet of living space in this house:

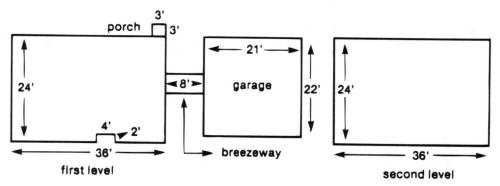

first level   second level

    a. 1,728 sq. ft.   c. 1,720 sq. ft.
    b. 1,752 sq. ft.   d. 1,761 sq. ft.

18. Find the cubic yards in a bedroom measuring 9′ high, 12′ long and 12′ wide.

    a. 144 cu. yds.   c. 48 cu. yds.
    b. 108 cu. yds.   d. 1,296 cu. yds.

19. An estate, listed on multiple listing with a commission to the selling broker of 3½%, sold for the full price of $2,250,000. What was the commission to the selling broker?

    a. $78,750   c. $77,875
    b. $7,875   d. $78,890

20. With the incentive plan of increased commissions based on increased earnings for the firm, salesperson J now earns 65% of the office retention on her sales. She sold a property for $325,000 which was listed with her own office with a real estate fee of 6½%. What was J's share of the fee?

    a. $73,937.50   c. $7,393.75
    b. $37,312.50   d. $13,731.25

21. If a lot is 65,340 sq. ft., how many acres are there?

    a. two   c. ¾
    b. 1½   d. 2½

22. If taxes on a property are $5,800 based on an assessed value of $145,000, what is the millage?

    a. 40 mills   c. 0.04 mills
    b. .40 mills   d. 4 mills

23. A couple wishes to list their house with you at a price that will net them $260,000 after your 7% real estate fee is paid. What will you suggest as a *minimum* listing price?

    a. $278,200   c. $279,600
    b. $275,500   d. $269,500

24. A couple wishes to purchase a house with an annual tax payment of $4,200. Their combined annual income is $82,000 and the bank offers a mortgage, amortizing at 11.30 per month per thousand. The bank requires that the monthly mortgage payment, including taxes and insurance cannot exceed 28% of the combined annual gross income. What mortgage can this couple qualify for?

    a. $191,313   c. $138,348
    b. $158,313   d. $169,300

25. A property sells for $875,000 with an annual return of 11%. What is the annual income on the property?

    a. $96,250.00   c. $87,500.00
    b. $79,545.45   d. $95,545.45

26. Another property sells for $275,000 with an annual income of $28,875. What rate of return will she receive on this investment?

    a. 10¼%   c. 10½%
    b. 11%   d. 9¾%

27. A factory building is said to contain 41,130
    sq. ft. Express this space in square yards.
    a. 13,710 sq. yds.   c. 4,750 sq. yds.
    b. 4,570 sq. yds.   d. 10,282½ sq. yds.

28. An entrance hall is measured to be 40″ wide
    and 72″ long. How many sq. ft. are in the
    hall?
    a. 19   c. 28
    b. 20   d. 9⅓

Sample Examinations

The following sample exams contain the type of questions examinees might find on their licensing examinations. These questions are meant to provide prospective licensees with additional practice in preparing for the examination. Note that proration calculations are based on a 30-day month unless otherwise stated.

SAMPLE EXAMINATION ONE

1. Which of the following is a lien on real estate?
   a. A recorded easement
   b. A recorded mortgage
   c. An encroachment
   d. A deed restriction

2. A contract agreed to under duress is
   a. voidable.   c. discharged.
   b. breached.   d. void.

3. A broker receives a check for earnest money from a buyer and deposits the money in an escrow or trust account to protect herself from the charge of
   a. commingling.
   b. novation.
   c. lost or stolen funds.
   d. embezzlement.

4. A mortgage loan that requires monthly payments of $875.70 for 20 years and a final payment of $24,095 is known as a(n)
   a. wraparound loan.
   b. accelerated loan.
   c. balloon loan.
   d. variable loan.

5. The borrower computed the interest he was charged for the previous month on his $60,000 loan balance as $412.50. What is his interest rate?
   a. 7.5 percent   c. 8.25 percent
   b. 7.75 percent   d. 8.5 percent

6. A loan originated by a bank may be sold in which of the following?
   a. Primary market
   b. Secondary market
   c. Mortgage market
   d. Investor market

7. The deed that contains five covenants is the
   a. warranty deed.   c. grant deed.
   b. quitclaim deed.   d. deed in trust.

8. Steering is
   a. leading prospective homeowners to or away from certain areas.
   b. refusing to make loans to persons residing in certain areas.
   c. a requirement to join a multiple-listing service.
   d. a practice of illegally setting commission rates.

9. H grants a life estate to her grandson and stipulates that upon the grandson's death the title to the property will pass to her son-in-law. This second estate is known as an
   a. estate in remainder.
   b. estate in reversion.
   c. estate at sufferance.
   d. estate for years.

10. Under joint tenancy
    a. a maximum of two people can own the real estate.
    b. the fractional interests can be different.
    c. additional owners can be added later.
    d. there is normally right of survivorship.

11. A real estate salesperson may
    a. write checks from his or her trust account.
    b. advertise the property in his or her own name.
    c. collect a commission directly from the principal.
    d. act under the supervision of the employing broker.

12. The states in which the lender is the owner of mortgaged real estate are known as
    a. title theory states.
    b. lien theory states.
    c. statutory share states.
    d. strict forfeiture states.

13. What is a tenancy for years?
    a. A tenancy with the consent of the landlord
    b. A tenancy that expires on a specific date
    c. A tenancy created by the death of the owner
    d. A tenancy created by a testator

14. A residence with outmoded plumbing is suffering from
    a. functional obsolescence.
    b. curable physical deterioration.
    c. incurable physical deterioration.
    d. external obsolescence.

15. K built a structure that has six stories. Several years later an ordinance was passed in that area banning any building six stories or higher. This instance represents
    a. a nonconforming use.
    b. a situation in which the structure would have to be demolished.
    c. a conditional use.
    d. a violation of the zoning laws.

16. Assuming that the listing broker and the selling broker in a transaction split their commission equally, what was the sales price of the property if the commission rate was 6.5 percent and the listing broker received $2,593.50?
    a. $39,900   c. $79,800
    b. $56,200   d. $88,400

17. According to the statute of frauds in most states, an oral lease for five years is
    a. a long-term lease.
    b. renewable.
    c. illegal.
    d. unenforceable.

18. A mortgage lender intends to lend money at $9\frac{3}{4}$ percent on a 30-year loan. If the lender intends to yield $10\frac{3}{8}$ percent, how many discount points must be charged on this loan?
    a. Eight   c. Four
    b. Five   d. One-half

19. The market value of a parcel of land
    a. is an estimate of the present worth of future benefits.
    b. represents a measure of past expenditures.
    c. is what the seller wants for the property.
    d. is the same as the market price.

20. Police powers include all of the following *except*

    a. zoning.
    b. deed restrictions.
    c. building codes.
    d. subdivision regulations.

21. The seller wants to net $65,000 from the sale of his house after paying the broker's fee of 6 percent. His gross sales price will be

    a. $69,149.   c. $61,321.
    b. $68,900.   d. $61,100.

22. An acre contains

    a. 360 degrees.   c. 160 square yards.
    b. 36 sections.   d. 43,560 square feet.

23. W is purchasing a condominium unit in a subdivision and obtaining financing from a local savings and loan association. In this situation, which of the following best describes W?

    a. Vendor   c. Grantor
    b. Mortgagor   d. Lessor

24. The current value of a property is $40,000. The property is assessed at 40 percent of its current value for real estate tax purposes, with an equalization factor of 1.5 applied to the assessed value. If the tax rate is $4 per $100 of assessed valuation, what is the amount of tax due on the property?

    a. $640   c. $1,600
    b. $960   d. $2,400

25. A building was sold for $60,000 with the purchaser putting 10 percent down and obtaining a loan for the balance. The lending institution charged a 1 percent loan origination fee. What was the total cash used for the purchase?

    a. $540   c. $6,540
    b. $6,000   d. $6,600

26. After a snowstorm a property owner offers to pay $10 to anyone who will shovel his driveway. This is an example of

    a. an implied contract.
    b. an executed contract.
    c. a bilateral contract.
    d. a unilateral contract.

27. Capitalization rates are

    a. determined by the gross rent multiplier.
    b. the rates of return a property will produce.
    c. a mathematical value determined by the sales price.
    d. determined by the amount of depreciation in the property.

28. An eligible veteran made an offer of $50,000 to purchase a home to be financed with a VA-guaranteed loan. Four weeks after the offer was accepted a certificate of reasonable value (CRV) for $47,800 was issued for the property. In this case the veteran may

    a. withdraw from the sale with a 1 percent penalty.
    b. purchase the property with a $2,200 down payment.
    c. not withdraw from the sale.
    d. withdraw from the sale upon payment of $2,200.

29. If a house was sold for $40,000 and the buyer obtained an FHA-insured mortgage loan for $38,500, how much money would be paid in discount points if the lender charged four points?

    a. $1,600   c. $1,500
    b. $1,540   d. $385

30. The commission rate is 7¾ percent on a sale of $50,000. What is the dollar amount of the commission?

    a. $3,500   c. $4,085
    b. $3,875   d. $4,585

31. All of the following will terminate an offer *except*

    a. revocation of the offer before its acceptance.
    b. the death of the offeror before acceptance.
    c. a counteroffer by the offeree.
    d. an offer from a third party.

32. G is purchasing a home under a land contract. Until the contract is paid in full, G has

    a. legal title to the premises.
    b. no interest in the property.
    c. a legal life estate in the premises.
    d. equitable title in the property.

33. F and K enter into an agreement wherein K will mow F's lawn every week during the summer. Shortly thereafter K decides to go into a different business. V would like to assume K's duties mowing F's lawn. F agrees and enters into a new contract with V. F and K tear up their original agreement. This is known as

    a. assignment.   c. substitution.
    b. novation.   d. rescission.

34. G borrowed $4,000 from a private lender using the services of a mortgage broker. After deducting the loan costs, G received $3,747. What is the face amount of the note?

    a. $3,747   c. $4,253
    b. $4,000   d. $7,747

35. An offer to purchase real estate becomes a contract when it is signed by which of the following?

    a. Buyer
    b. Buyer and seller
    c. Seller
    d. Seller and broker

36. A borrower has just made the final payment on his mortgage loan to his bank. Regardless of this fact, the lender will still hold a lien on the mortgaged property until which of the following is recorded?

    a. A satisfaction of the mortgage document
    b. A reconveyance of the mortgage document
    c. A novation of the mortgage document
    d. An estoppel of the mortgage document

37. If the annual net income from a commercial property is $22,000 and the capitalization rate is 8 percent, what is the value of the property using the income approach?

    a. $275,000   c. $183,000
    b. $200,000   d. $176,000

38. A broker enters into a listing agreement with a seller wherein the seller will receive $120,000 from the sale of a vacant lot and the broker will receive any sale proceeds over that amount. This type of agreement is called a(n)

    a. exclusive-agency listing.
    b. net listing.
    c. exclusive-right-to-sell listing.
    d. multiple listing.

39. An individual moved into a cooperative apartment after selling her house. Under the cooperative form of ownership the individual will

    a. become a stockholder in the corporation.
    b. not lose her apartment if she pays her share of the expenses.
    c. have to take out a new mortgage loan on her unit.
    d. receive a fixed-term lease for her unit.

40. A defect or a cloud on title to property may be cured by

    a. obtaining quitclaim deeds from all interested parties.
    b. bringing an action to register the title.
    c. paying cash for the property at the settlement.
    d. bringing an action to repudiate the title.

41. Discount points on a real estate loan are a potential cost to both the seller and the buyer. The points are

    a. set by FHA and VA for their loan programs.
    b. charged only on conventional loans.
    c. limited by government regulations.
    d. determined by the market for money.

42. Under the terms of a net lease the tenant would usually be responsible for paying all of the following *except*

    a. maintenance expenses.
    b. mortgage debt service.
    c. fire and extended-coverage insurance.
    d. real estate taxes.

43. The Civil Rights Act of 1866 prohibits in all cases discrimination based on a person's

    a. sex.
    b. religion.
    c. race.
    d. familial status.

44. What would it cost to put new carpeting in a den measuring 15 feet by 20 feet if the cost of the carpeting is $6.95 per square yard and the cost of laying it is an additional $250?

    a. $232
    b. $482
    c. $610
    d. $2,335

45. What is the difference between a general lien and a specific lien?

    a. A general lien cannot be enforced in court, while a specific lien can.
    b. A specific lien is held by only one person, while a general lien must be held by two or more.
    c. A general lien is a lien against personal property, while a specific lien is a lien against real estate.
    d. A specific lien is a lien against a certain parcel of real estate, while a general lien covers all of the debtor's property.

46. In an option to purchase real estate the optionee

    a. must purchase the property but may do so at any time within the option period.
    b. is limited to a refund of the option consideration if the option is exercised.
    c. cannot obtain third-party financing on the property until after the option has expired.
    d. has no obligation to purchase the property during the option period.

47. An individual seeking to be excused from the requirements of a zoning ordinance should request a

    a. building permit.
    b. certificate of alternative usage.
    c. variance.
    d. certificate of nonconforming use.

48. How many acres are there in the N½ of the SW ¼ and the NE ¼ of the SE ¼ of a section?

    a. 20 acres
    b. 40 acres
    c. 80 acres
    d. 120 acres

49. *Acceleration* is a term associated with which of the following documents?

    a. Listings
    b. Mortgages
    c. Leases
    d. Purchase contracts

50. Under the terms in the mortgage the lender must be paid in full if the property is sold. This clause is known as the

    a. acceleration clause.
    b. due on sale clause.
    c. subordination clause.
    d. habendum clause.

51. The broker receives a deposit with a written offer that indicates that the offeror will leave the offer open for the seller's acceptance for ten days. On the fifth day, and prior to acceptance by the seller, the offeror notifies the broker that he is withdrawing his offer and demanding the return of his deposit. In this situation

    a. the offeror cannot withdraw the offer—it must be held open for the full ten-day period.
    b. the offeror has the right to withdraw the offer and secure the return of the deposit at any time before he is notified of the seller's acceptance.
    c. the offeror can withdraw the offer, and the seller and the broker will each retain one-half of the forfeited deposit.
    d. the offeror can withdraw the offer, and the broker will declare the deposit forfeited and retain all of it in lieu of a commission.

52. C and L are joint tenants in a parcel of property. L sells her interest to F. What is the relationship between C and F regarding the property?

    a. They are joint tenants.
    b. They are tenants in common.
    c. They are tenants by the entirety.
    d. There is no relationship, because L cannot sell her joint tenancy interest.

53. S and W orally enter into a six-month lease. If W defaults, then S
    a. may not bring a court action because of the parol evidence rule.
    b. may not bring a court action because of the statute of frauds.
    c. may bring a court action because six-month leases need not be in writing to be enforceable.
    d. may bring a court action because the statute of limitations does not apply to oral leases.

54. On Monday T offers to sell his vacant lot to K for $12,000. On Tuesday K counteroffers to buy the lot for $10,500. On Friday K withdraws his counteroffer and accepts T's original price of $12,000. Under these circumstances
    a. there is a valid agreement, because K accepted T's offer exactly as it was made, regardless that it was not accepted immediately.
    b. there is a valid agreement, because K accepted before T advised him that the offer was withdrawn.
    c. there is no valid agreement, because T's offer was not accepted within 72 hours of its having been made.
    d. there is no valid agreement, because K's counteroffer was a rejection of T's offer, and once rejected, it cannot be accepted later.

55. The parcel of property over which an easement runs is known as the
    a. dominant tenement.
    b. servient tenement.
    c. prescriptive tenement.
    d. eminent tenement.

56. If the quarterly interest at 7.5 percent is $562.50, what is the principal amount of the loan?
    a. $7,500   c. $30,000
    b. $15,000   d. $75,000

57. Assume a house is sold for $84,500 and the commission rate is 7 percent. If the commission is split 60/40 between the selling broker and the listing broker, and each broker splits his share of the commission evenly with his salesperson, how much will the listing salesperson receive from this sale?
    a. $1,183   c. $2,366
    b. $1,775   d. $3,549

58. If the mortgage loan is 80 percent of the appraised value of a house and the interest rate of 8 percent amounts to $460 for the first month, what is the appraised value of the house?
    a. $92,875   c. $71,875
    b. $86,250   d. $69,000

59. Local zoning ordinances often regulate all of the following *except*
    a. the height of buildings in an area.
    b. the density of population.
    c. the appropriate use of the buildings.
    d. the market value of property.

60. A broker took a listing and later discovered that her client had previously been declared incompetent by the court. The listing is now
    a. unaffected, because the broker was acting in good faith as the owner's agent.
    b. of no value to the broker because the contract is void.
    c. the basis for recovery of a commission if the broker produces a buyer.
    d. renegotiable between the broker and her client.

61. A borrower defaulted on his home mortgage loan payments, and the lender obtained a court order to foreclose on the property. At the foreclosure sale, however, the property sold for only $64,000; the unpaid balance of the loan at the time of the foreclosure was $78,000. What must the lender do in an attempt to recover the $14,000 that the borrower still owes?
    a. Sue for specific performance
    b. Sue for damages
    c. Seek a deficiency judgment
    d. Seek a judgment by default

62. All of the following are exemptions to the federal Fair Housing Act of 1968 *except*

    a. the sale of a single-family home where the listing broker does not advertise the property.
    b. the restriction of noncommercial lodgings by a private club to members of the club.
    c. the rental of a unit in an owner-occupied three-family dwelling where an advertisement is placed in the paper.
    d. the restriction of noncommercial housing in a convent where a certified statement has not been filed with the government.

63. G purchases a $37,000 property, depositing $3,000 as earnest money. If he can obtain a 75 percent loan-to-value loan on the property and no additional items are prorated, how much more cash will he need at the settlement?

    a. $3,250
    b. $3,500
    c. $5,250
    d. $6,250

64. In the appraisal of a building constructed in the 1920s the cost approach would be the least accurate method because of difficulties in

    a. estimating changes in material costs.
    b. obtaining 1920s building codes.
    c. estimating changes in labor rates.
    d. estimating depreciation.

65. G sold his property to W. In the deed of conveyance G's only guarantee was that the property was not encumbered during the time he owned it except as noted in the deed. The type of deed used in this transaction was a

    a. general warranty deed.
    b. special warranty deed.
    c. bargain and sale deed.
    d. quitclaim deed.

66. S and T, who are not married, own a parcel of real estate. Each owns an undivided interest, with S owning one-third and T owning two-thirds. The form of ownership under which S and T own their property is

    a. severalty.
    b. joint tenancy.
    c. tenancy at will.
    d. tenancy in common.

67. The buyers agree to purchase a house for $84,500. The buyers pay $2,000 as earnest money and obtain a new mortgage loan for $67,600. The purchase contract provides for a March 15th settlement. The buyers and sellers prorate the previous year's real estate taxes of $1,880.96, which have been prepaid. The buyers have additional closing costs of $1,250, and the sellers have other closing costs of $850. How much cash must the buyers bring to the settlement?

    a. $19,638
    b. $17,638
    c. $17,238
    d. $16,388

68. A broker was advertising a house he had listed for sale at the price of $47,900. J, a Mexican, saw the house and was interested in it. When J asked the broker the price of the house, the broker told J $53,000. Under the federal Fair Housing Act of 1968 such a statement is

    a. legal because all that is important is that J be given the opportunity to buy the house.
    b. legal because the representation was made by the broker and not directly by the owner.
    c. illegal because the difference in the offering price and the quoted price was greater than 10 percent.
    d. illegal because the terms of the potential sale were changed for J.

69. A deed must be signed by which of the following?

    a. The grantor
    b. The grantee
    c. The grantor and the grantee
    d. The grantee and at least two witnesses

70. An appraiser has been hired to prepare an appraisal report of a property for loan purposes. The property is an elegant old mansion that is now used as an insurance company office. Which approach to value should the appraiser give the greatest weight when making this appraisal?

   a. Income approach
   b. Sales comparison approach
   c. Replacement cost approach
   d. Gross rent multiplier

71. Which of the following is true about a term mortgage loan?

   a. All of the interest is paid at the end of the term.
   b. The debt is partially amortized over the life of the loan.
   c. The length of the term is limited by state statutes.
   d. The entire principal amount is due at the end of the term.

72. J recently moved into a condominium. She has the use of many facilities there, including a swimming pool, putting green, and tennis courts. Under the typical condominium arrangement these facilities would be owned by

   a. the association of homeowners in the condominium.
   b. the corporation in which J and the other owners hold stock.
   c. J and the other owners in the condominium in the form of divided interests.
   d. all of the condominium owners in the form of percentage undivided interests.

73. Which of the following is *not* usually prorated between the seller and the buyer at the settlement?

   a. Recording charges
   b. Real estate taxes
   c. Prepaid rents
   d. Utility bills

74. T believes that he has been the victim of an unfair discriminatory practice committed by a local real estate broker. In accordance with federal regulations, how long does T have to file his complaint against the broker?

   a. 90 days after the alleged discrimination
   b. 180 days after the alleged discrimination
   c. Nine months after the alleged discrimination
   d. One year after the alleged discrimination

75. A real estate loan that uses both real estate and personal property as collateral is known as a

   a. blanket loan.
   b. package loan.
   c. growing-equity loan.
   d. graduated-payment loan.

76. All of the following are true regarding the concept of adverse possession *except*

   a. the person taking possession of the property must do so without the consent of the owner of the property.
   b. occupancy of the property by the person taking possession must be continuous over a specified period of time.
   c. the person taking possession of the property must compensate the owner at the end of the adverse possession period.
   d. the person taking possession of the property could ultimately end up owning the property.

77. What is the cost of constructing a fence six feet six inches high around a lot measuring 90 feet by 175 feet, if the cost of erecting the fence is $1.25 per linear foot and the cost of materials is $.825 per square foot of fence?

   a. $1,752   c. $2,084
   b. $2,054   d. $3,505

78. K, who desires to sell his house, enters into a listing agreement with broker E. Broker N obtains a buyer for the house, and E does not receive a commission. The listing agreement between K and E was probably a(n)
    a. exclusive-right-to-sell listing.
    b. open listing.
    c. exclusive-agency listing.
    d. multiple listing.

79. Antitrust laws prohibit all of the following *except*
    a. real estate companies agreeing on fees charged to sellers.
    b. real estate brokers allocating markets based on the value of homes.
    c. real estate companies allocating markets based on the location of commercial buildings.
    d. real estate salespersons allocating markets based on the location of homes.

80. Under the concept of riparian rights the owners of property adjacent to navigable rivers or streams have the right to use the water and
    a. may erect a dam across the navigable river or stream if the owners on each side agree.
    b. are considered to own the submerged land to the center point of the waterway.
    c. are considered owners of the water adjacent to the land.
    d. are considered to own the land to the edge of the water.

SAMPLE EXAMINATION TWO

1. The landlord of tenant D has sold his building to the state so that a freeway can be built. D's lease has expired, but the landlord is letting him remain until the building is torn down. D continues to pay the same rent as prescribed in his lease. What kind of tenancy does D have?
   a. Holdover tenancy
   b. Month-to-month tenancy
   c. Tenancy at sufferance
   d. Tenancy at will

2. When a form of real estate sales contract has been agreed to and signed by the purchaser and spouse and then given to the seller's broker with an earnest money check
   a. this transaction constitutes a valid contract.
   b. the purchasers can sue the seller for specific performance.
   c. this transaction is considered to be an offer.
   d. the earnest money will be forfeited if the purchasers default.

3. A seller gives an open listing to several brokers, specifically promising that if one of the brokers finds a buyer for the seller's property, the seller will then be obligated to pay a commission to that broker. Which of the following best describes this offer by the seller?
   a. Executed agreement
   b. Discharged agreement
   c. Unilateral agreement
   d. Bilateral agreement

4. By paying his debt after a foreclosure sale the borrower has the right to regain his property under which of the following?
   a. Acceleration
   b. Redemption
   c. Reversion
   d. Recovery

5. Which of the following is true of a sale-and-leaseback arrangement?
   a. The seller/vendor retains title to the real estate.
   b. The buyer/vendee gets possession of the property.
   c. The buyer/vendee is the lessor.
   d. This arrangement is disallowed in most states.

6. Fannie Mae and Ginnie Mae
   a. work together as primary market lenders.
   b. are both federal agencies.
   c. are both privately owned entities.
   d. are both involved in the secondary market.

7. Q decided that he could make more money from his tree farm by dividing it into small parcels and selling the parcels to numerous individuals. Subsequently Q entered into a series of purchase agreements in connection with which he agreed to continue to operate the property and distribute proceeds from its income to the buyers of the parcels. Under these circumstances Q has sold
   a. real estate, because the object of the sale was the land.
   b. securities, because the object of the purchase was the trees and the underlying land was merely incidental to the sale.
   c. real estate, because the property was subdivided before the sales ever took place.
   d. securities, because the buyers were investors relying on Q's activities to generate a profit from the premises purchased.

8. All of the following situations are in violation of the federal Fair Housing Act of 1968 *except*

   a. the refusal of a property manager to rent an apartment to a Catholic couple who are otherwise qualified.

   b. the general policy of a loan company to avoid granting home improvement loans to individuals living in transitional neighborhoods.

   c. the intentional neglect of a broker to show an Asian family any property listings of homes in all-white neighborhoods.

   d. the insistence of a widowed woman on renting her spare bedroom only to another widowed woman.

9. If a storage tank that measures 12 feet by 9 feet by 8 feet was designed to store natural gas and the cost of the gas is $1.82 per cubic foot, what does it cost to fill the tank to one-half its capacity?

   a. $685   c. $864

   b. $786   d. $1,572

10. Assume the market interest rate is 7 percent, discount points are at six, and the mortgage lender must yield 7¾ percent. If points drop to four, the interest rate will

   a. decrease by ½ percent.

   b. increase by ¼ percent.

   c. decrease by ¼ percent.

   d. increase by ½ percent.

11. When a buyer signs a purchase contract and the seller accepts, the buyer acquires an immediate interest in the property known as

   a. legal title.   c. statutory title.

   b. equitable title.   d. defeasible title.

12. Which of the following requires that finance charges be stated as an annual percentage rate?

   a. Truth-in-Lending Act (Regulation Z)

   b. Real Estate Settlement Procedures Act

   c. Equal Credit Opportunity Act

   d. Federal Fair Housing Act

13. J owns an apartment building in a large city. After discussing the matter with his advisers, J decided to alter the type of occupancy in the building from rental to condominium status. This procedure is known as

   a. amendment.   c. deportment.

   b. partition.   d. conversion.

14. In the preceding question, after checking the applicable laws, J discovered that in connection with the change to condominium status he must initially offer to sell each unit to the tenant who currently occupies the unit. If the tenant does not accept the offer, J may then offer the unit for sale to the general public. The requirement that J offer the property to the tenant in this situation is known as a

   a. contingent restriction.

   b. conditional sales option.

   c. right of first refusal.

   d. covenant of prior acceptance.

15. Which of the following real estate documents is least likely to be recorded?

   a. A standard form deed

   b. A long-term lease

   c. An option agreement

   d. A purchase agreement

16. In a township of 36 sections, which of the following statements is true?

   a. Section 16 lies to the north of Section 21.

   b. Section 18 is by law set aside for school purposes.

   c. Section 6 lies in the northeast corner of the township.

   d. Section 31 lies to the east of Section 32.

17. Broker U represented the seller in a transaction. Her client informed her that he did not want to recite the actual consideration that was paid for the house. In this situation Broker U

a. must inform her client that only the actual price of the real estate may appear on the deed.

b. may show the nominal consideration of only $10 on the deed.

c. should inform the seller that either the full price should be stated in the deed or all references to consideration should be removed from it.

d. may show a price on the deed other than the actual price, provided that the variance is not greater than 10 percent of the purchase price.

18. A broker obtained a listing agreement to act as the agent in the sale of a seller's house. A buyer has been found for the property, and all of the agreements have been signed. As an agent for the seller, the broker is responsible for the buyer's

a. completing the loan application.

b. receiving copies of all documents.

c. being qualified for the new mortgage loan.

d. inspecting the property.

19. G and M, co-owners of a corner parcel of vacant commercial property, have executed three open listing agreements with three brokers around town. All three brokers would like to place "for sale" signs on the sellers' property. Under these circumstances

a. a broker does not have to obtain the sellers' permission before placing a sign on the property.

b. only one "for sale" sign may be placed on the property at one time.

c. upon obtaining the sellers' written consent, all brokers can place their "for sale" signs on the property.

d. the broker who obtained the first open listing must consent to all signs being placed on the property.

20. In estimating the value of real estate using the cost approach, the appraiser should

a. estimate the replacement cost of the improvements.

b. deduct for the depreciation of the land and buildings.

c. determine the original cost and adjust for inflation.

d. review the sales prices of comparable properties.

21. The law that requires lenders to inform both buyers and sellers of all fees and charges is the

a. Equal Credit Opportunity Act.

b. Truth-in-Lending Act (Regulation Z).

c. Real Estate Settlement Procedures Act.

d. Real Estate Investment Trust Act.

22. If the landlord of an apartment building breaches his lease with one of the tenants and her unit becomes uninhabitable, which of the following would most likely result?

a. Suit for possession

b. Constructive eviction

c. Tenancy at sufferance

d. Covenant of quiet enjoyment

23. When the title passes to a third party upon the death of the life tenant, what is the third party's interest in the property?

a. Remainder interest

b. Reversionary interest

c. Pur autre vie interest

d. Redemption interest

24. On the settlement statement the prorations for real estate taxes paid in arrears would be shown as a

a. credit to the seller and a debit to the buyer.

b. debit to the seller and a credit to the buyer.

c. credit to both the seller and the buyer.

d. debit to both the seller and the buyer.

25. What type of lease establishes a rental payment and requires the lessor to pay for the taxes, insurance and maintenance on the property?

a. A percentage lease

b. A net lease

c. An expense-only lease

d. A gross lease

26. A conventional loan was closed on July 1 for $57,200 at 13.5 percent interest amortized over 25 years at $666.75 per month. On August 1, what would the principal amount be after the monthly payment was made?
    - a. $56,533.25
    - b. $56,556.50
    - c. $57,065.35
    - d. $57,176.75

27. In the preceding problem, what would the interest payment be?
    - a. $666.75
    - b. $643.50
    - c. $620.25
    - d. $610.65

28. The requirements of the Real Estate Settlement Procedures Act apply to any residential real estate transaction that takes place
    - a. in a state that has adopted RESPA.
    - b. involving a federally related mortgage loan.
    - c. involving any mortgage financing less than $100,000.
    - d. involving any purchase price less than $100,000.

29. Under the income approach to estimating the value of real estate the capitalization rate is
    - a. the rate at which the property will increase in value.
    - b. the rate of return the property will earn as an investment.
    - c. the rate of capital required to keep a property operating most efficiently.
    - d. the maximum rate of return allowed by law on an investment.

30. On the settlement statement the cost of the lender's title insurance policy that would be required for a new loan would usually be shown as a
    - a. credit to the seller.
    - b. credit to the buyer.
    - c. debit to the seller.
    - d. debit to the buyer.

31. An FHA-insured loan in the amount of $57,500 at 8½ percent for 30 years was closed on July 17. The first monthly payment is due on September 1. As interest is paid monthly in arrears, what was the amount of the interest adjustment the buyer had to make at the settlement?
    - a. $4,887.50
    - b. $407.29
    - c. $230.80
    - d. $190.07

32. If a home that originally cost $42,500 three years ago is now valued at 127 percent of its original cost, what is its current market value?
    - a. $33,465
    - b. $53,975
    - c. $58,219
    - d. $65,354

33. Failing to assert a right within a reasonable or statutory period of time might lead a court to determine that the right to assert it is now lost because of
    - a. laches.
    - b. novation.
    - c. rescission.
    - d. revocation.

34. When searching the public record, which of the following documents would *always* be discovered?
    - a. Encroachments
    - b. Rights of parties in possession
    - c. Inaccurate surveys
    - d. Mechanics' liens

35. A rectangular lot has an apartment structure on it worth $193,600. This value is the equivalent of $4.40 per square foot. If one lot dimension is 200 feet, what is the other dimension?
    - a. 110 feet
    - b. 220 feet
    - c. 400 feet
    - d. 880 feet

36. A broker listed widow K's property at an 8 percent commission rate. After the property was sold and the settlement had occurred, K discovered that the broker had been listing similar properties at a 6 percent commission rate. Based on this information
    - a. the broker has done nothing wrong.
    - b. the broker can lose his license.
    - c. widow K can cancel the transaction.
    - d. widow K is entitled to a refund.

37. A tenant on a long-term commercial lease is considering going out of business. Because the market rent is much greater than she is currently paying, she would most likely consider
    a. assigning the lease.
    b. subletting the property.
    c. asking the owner to rescind the lease.
    d. surrendering the premises.

38. A broker would not have to show that he was the procuring cause if the seller sells the property himself in a(n)
    a. net listing.
    b. open listing.
    c. exclusive-agency listing.
    d. exclusive-right-to-sell listing.

39. The capitalization rate on a property considers which of the following factors?
    a. The risk of the investment
    b. The replacement cost of the improvements
    c. The real estate taxes
    d. The depreciation of the improvements

40. An investment property worth $180,000 was purchased seven years ago for $142,000. At the time of the purchase the land was valued at $18,000. Assuming a 31½-year life for straight-line depreciation purposes, what is the present book value of the property?
    a. $95,071   c. $114,444
    b. $113,071   d. $126,000

41. After N purchased a property from E, they both decided to rescind the recorded sale. To do this they must
    a. return the deed to E.
    b. record a notice of rescission.
    c. destroy the original deed.
    d. make a new deed from E to N.

42. A farmer owns the W ½ of the NW ¼ of the NW ¼ of a section. The adjoining property can all be purchased for $300 per acre. Owning all of the NW ¼ of the section would cost the farmer
    a. $6,000.   c. $42,000.
    b. $12,000.   d. $48,000.

43. An offer to purchase real estate can be terminated by all of the following *except*
    a. failure to accept the offer within a prescribed period.
    b. revocation by the offeror communicated to the offeree after acceptance.
    c. a conditional acceptance of the offer by the offeree.
    d. death of the offeror or offeree.

44. A property manager would least likely
    a. handle new leases.
    b. arrange for repairs and improvements.
    c. resolve tenant disputes as to property use.
    d. prepare depreciation schedules for tax purposes.

45. The monthly rent on a warehouse was set at $1 per cubic yard. Assuming the warehouse was 36 feet by 200 feet by 12 feet high, what would the annual rent be?
    a. $3,200   c. $38,400
    b. $9,600   d. $115,200

46. A veteran wishes to refinance his home with a VA-guaranteed loan. The lender is willing but insists on 3½ discount points. In this situation the veteran
    a. can refinance with a VA loan provided there are no discount points.
    b. can refinance with a VA loan provided the discount points do not exceed 2.
    c. can be required to pay a maximum of 1 percent of the loan as an origination fee.
    d. can proceed with the refinance loan and pay the discount points.

47. All of the following are characteristics of a fee simple title *except* that it is
    a. free from encumbrances.
    b. of indefinite duration.
    c. transferable with or without valuable consideration.
    d. transferable by will or intestacy.

48. A real estate transaction had a closing date of November 15. The seller, who was responsible for costs up to and including the date of the settlement, had paid the property taxes of $1,116 for the calendar year. On the closing statement the buyer would be

    a. debited for $139.50.
    b. debited for $976.50.
    c. credited for $139.50.
    d. credited for $976.50.

49. An agreement that ends all future lessor-lessee obligations under a lease is known as a(n)

    a. assumption.
    b. surrender.
    c. novation.
    d. breach.

50. In depreciating a residential property an accountant would base the depreciable life on

    a. age-life tables.
    b. the observed condition of the property.
    c. 27½ years.
    d. 31½ years.

51. A property manager leased a store for three years. The first year the store's rent was $1,000 per month, and the rent was to increase 10 percent per year thereafter. The broker received a 7 percent commission for the first year, 5 percent for the second year and 3 percent for the balance of the lease. The total commission earned by the property manager was

    a. $840.
    b. $1,613.
    c. $1,936.
    d. $2,785.

52. Against a recorded deed from the owner of record the party with the weakest position is a

    a. party with a prior unrecorded deed who is not in possession.
    b. party in possession with a prior unrecorded deed.
    c. tenant in possession with nine months remaining on the lease.
    d. painter who is half-finished painting the house at the time of the sale and has not been paid.

53. J, age 58, sold the home he had purchased two years before and moved in with his daughter. He had purchased the property for $46,500 and sold it for $74,800. In computing his income tax, J would pay taxes on

    a. $11,320.
    b. $16,980.
    c. $28,300.
    d. nothing.

54. A man moved into an abandoned home, installing cabinets in the kitchen for his convenience and making extensive repairs. When the owner discovered the occupancy, he had the man ejected. What is the status of the kitchen cabinets?

    a. The man cannot get the cabinets back.
    b. The cabinets remain because they are trade fixtures.
    c. While the cabinets stay, the man is entitled to the value of the improvements.
    d. The man can get them back if they can be removed without damage to the real estate.

55. W, F and J are joint tenants. J sells his interest to L, and then F dies. As a result

    a. F's heirs, L and W are joint tenants.
    b. F's heirs and W are joint tenants, but L is a tenant in common.
    c. W, L and F's heirs are tenants in common.
    d. W and L are tenants in common.

56. In a settlement statement the selling price will *always* be

    a. a debit to the buyer.
    b. a debit to the seller.
    c. a credit to the buyer.
    d. greater than the loan amount.

57. The state wants to condemn a strip of land through a farm for a highway. The farm will decrease in value far more than the value of the condemned strip. The farmer should ask for

    a. inverse condemnation.
    b. severance damages.
    c. nominal damages.
    d. an injunction.

58. A man willed his estate as follows: 54 percent to his wife, 18 percent to his daughter, 16 percent to his son and the remainder to his church. The church received $79,000. The daughter received

    a. $105,333   c. $355,500
    b. $118,500   d. $658,333

59. An example of external obsolescence would be

    a. numerous pillars supporting the ceiling in a store.
    b. roof leaks making premises unusable and therefore unrentable.
    c. an older structure with massive cornices.
    d. vacant and abandoned buildings in the area.

60. Which of the following phrases, when placed in a print advertisement, would comply with the requirements of the Truth-in-Lending Act (Regulation Z)?

    a. "12 percent interest"
    b. "12 percent annual percent"
    c. "12 percent annual interest"
    d. "12 percent annual percentage rate"

61. All of the following are true regarding capitalization rates *except*

    a. the rate increases when the risk increases.
    b. an increase in rate means a decrease in value.
    c. the net income is divided by the rate to estimate the value.
    d. a decrease in rate results in a decrease in value.

62. The Equal Credit Opportunity Act makes it illegal for lenders to refuse credit or otherwise discriminate because an applicant is

    a. a single parent who cannot afford the payments and receives public assistance.
    b. a new home buyer who does not have a credit history.
    c. a single person.
    d. unemployed.

63. When P died, a signed and acknowledged but unrecorded deed was found among his effects, giving his house to a local charity. His will, however, provided that his entire estate was to go to his nephew. In this situation the house most likely will go to

    a. the charity, because acknowledgment is a presumption of delivery.
    b. the charity, because P's intent was clear.
    c. the nephew, because P died while still owning the house.
    d. the nephew, because the deed was not recorded.

64. The type of loan that features increasing payments with the increases being applied directly to the debt reduction is the

    a. SAM.   c. ARM.
    b. GEM.   d. GPM.

65. After an offer is accepted, the seller finds that the broker was the undisclosed agent for the buyer as well as the agent for the seller. The seller

    a. can withdraw without obligation to broker or buyer.
    b. can withdraw but would be subject to liquidated damages.
    c. can withdraw but only with the concurrence of the buyer.
    d. would be subject to specific performance if he refused to sell.

66. To net the owner $90,000 after a 6 percent commission is paid, the list price would have to be

    a. $95,400.   c. $95,906.
    b. $95,745.   d. $96,000.

67. Which of the following would most likely be legal under the provisions of the Civil Rights Act of 1968?

    a. A lender refusing to make loans in areas with more than 25 percent blacks
    b. A private country club where ownership of homes is tied to club membership but all members are white
    c. A church, which excludes blacks from membership, renting its nonprofit housing to church members only
    d. Directing prospective buyers away from areas where they are likely to feel uncomfortable because of their race

68. It is discovered after a sale that the land parcel is 10 percent smaller than the owner represented it to be. The broker who passed information on to the buyer is

   a. not liable as long as he only repeated the seller's data.
   b. not liable if the misrepresentation was unintentional.
   c. not liable if the buyer actually inspected what she was getting.
   d. liable if he knew or should have known of the discrepancy.

69. On a residential lot 70 feet square the side yard building setbacks are 10 feet, the front yard setback is 25 feet, and the rear yard setback is 20 feet. The maximum possible size for a single-story structure would be

   a. 1,000 square feet.
   b. 1,200 square feet.
   c. 1,250 square feet.
   d. 4,900 square feet.

70. All of the following are violations of the Real Estate Settlement Procedures Act (RESPA) *except*

   a. directing the buyer to a particular lender.
   b. accepting a kickback on a loan subject to RESPA requirements.
   c. requiring a particular title insurance company.
   d. accepting a fee or charging for services that were not performed.

71. The rescission provisions of the Truth-in-Lending Act apply to

   a. home purchase loans.
   b. construction lending.
   c. business financing.
   d. consumer credit.

72. A property has a net income of $30,000. An appraiser decides to use a 12 percent capitalization rate rather than a 10 percent rate on this property. The use of the higher rate results in

   a. a 2 percent increase in the appraised value.
   b. a $50,000 increase in the appraised value.
   c. a $50,000 decrease in the appraised value.
   d. no change in the appraised value.

73. The section of a purchase contract that provides for the buyer forfeiting any earnest money if the buyer fails to complete the purchase is known as

   a. liquidated damages.
   b. punitive damages.
   c. the safety clause.
   d. the subordination clause.

74. In one commercial building the tenant intends to start a health food shop using her life savings. In an identical adjacent building is a catalog store leased to a major national retailing chain. Both tenants have long-term leases with identical rents. Which of the following statements is correct?

   a. If the values of the buildings were the same before the leases, the values will be the same after they are leased.
   b. An appraiser would most likely use a higher capitalization rate for the store leased to the national retailing chain.
   c. The most accurate appraisal method to be used would be the sales comparison approach to value.
   d. The building with the health food shop will appraise for less than the other building.

75. An insurance company agreed to provide a developer financing for a shopping center at 11 percent interest plus an equity position. This type of arrangement is called a(n)

   a. package loan.
   b. participation loan.
   c. open-end loan.
   d. blanket loan.

76. A $100,000 loan at 12 percent could be amortized with monthly payments of $1,200.22 on a 15-year basis or payments of $1,028.63 on a 30-year basis. The 30-year loan results in total payments of what percent of the 15-year total payments?

   a. 146%   c. 171%
   b. 158%   d. 228%

77. A church has just purchased a large ranch that it intends to use for religious activities, including retreats and training. This use may impact the community by
    a. increasing the value of surrounding properties.
    b. increasing county services.
    c. lowering real estate taxes.
    d. increasing real estate taxes.

78. *Naked legal title* best describes the interest of a
    a. trustee under a deed of trust.
    b. vendee under a land contract.
    c. mortgagee under a mortgage.
    d. lessee under a lease.

79. At the settlement the lender requests $345, which will be kept in a trust account. This money is most likely
    a. a security deposit.
    b. for taxes and insurance.
    c. to insure against borrower default.
    d. to cover the expense of discount points.

80. An apartment has an annual gross income of $87,500. Annual expenses are depreciation, $8,500; debt service, $34,000, including principal of $7,200; real estate taxes, $5,100; other operating costs, $14,100. The annual cash flow is
    a. $25,800.   c. $41,500.
    b. $34,300.   d. $57,400.

Environmental Issues and the Real Estate Transaction

ENVIRONMENTAL ISSUES

Environmental issues have become an important factor in the practice of real estate. Consumers are becoming more health and safety conscious and are enforcing their right to know all the information needed to make informed decisions. Scientists are learning more about our environment; consumers are reacting by demanding that their surroundings be free of hazards. These developments affect not only sales transactions, but also appraisers, developers, lending institutions and property managers.

An increasing number of hazardous substances is being identified each year, adding to the number of property conditions that must be addressed. The government has responded to these developments by implementing additional laws and regulations that affect the usability and value of the real estate. The presence of hazardous substances significantly impacts the value of a property, requiring extensive expenditures for removal or abatement in many cases. The cost of cleaning up and removing hazards may be much greater than the actual market value of the property.

Real estate licensees must be alert to the existence of environmental hazards. While it is important to ensure the health and safety of the user of a property, the burden for disclosure and/or elimination of hazards seems to arise at the time the ownership of property transfers. This creates added liability for real estate practitioners if the presence of a toxic substance causes a health problem. If an occupant of a property suffers physical harm because of the substance, the licensee can be vulnerable to a personal injury suit in addition to other legal liability. Health issues have become real estate issues. For this reason it is extremely important that licensees not only make property disclosures but also see that prospective purchasers get authoritative information about hazardous substances so that they can make informed decisions.

Licensees should gather information from the property owner (frequently required in mandatory seller disclosure forms), utilize professionals with the scientific and technical expertise to perform tests and surveys to determine the presence of environmental hazards and be familiar with the environmental laws and the regulatory agencies. *Licensees do not have the technical expertise to determine if a hazardous substance is present.* However, they must be aware of environmental issues and take steps to ensure that the interests of all parties involved in the transactions are protected.

HAZARDOUS SUBSTANCES

Asbestos

Asbestos is a mineral that has been used as insulation because of its ability to contain heat. It is estimated that asbestos is found in 1 out of every 5 public buildings in the country today. In the majority of cases, however, it is harmless unless it is disturbed and particles become airborne. Airborne asbestos contamination is most prevalent in public and commercial buildings, including schools. Only when the asbestos material gets old and fibers crumble or it is disturbed by remodeling does it become a hazard. If the amount of asbestos fibers in a structure reaches dangerous levels, the building becomes difficult to lease, finance or insure.

Asbestos contamination can also be found in residential properties. It was used to cover pipes, ducts and heating and hot water units; in floor tile and exterior siding; and in roofing products. Though it may be easy to identify asbestos when it is wrapped around heating and water pipes, identification may be more difficult elsewhere.

Procedures. Asbestos is costly to remove, frequently further contaminating the air within the structure in the process. Encapsulation of disintegrating asbestos, rather than removal, may be a preferable remedy. Individuals who are involved with public, commercial and apartment buildings should consult the Occupational Safety and Health Administration (OSHA) and local ordinances for further guidance. Tests can be conducted to determine the level of airborne asbestos to provide an accurate disclosure in a sales transaction. A more thorough analysis of a building can be performed by an engineer who is skilled in identifying the presence of materials that contain asbestos. Either of these approaches can satisfy the concerns of a consumer. Appraisers should also be aware of the possible presence of asbestos.

Lead-Based Paint

Lead was used as a pigment and drying agent in alkyd oil-based paint. HUD estimates that lead is present in about 75% of all the private housing that was built before 1978. It may be on any interior or exterior surface, particularly on doors, windows and other woodwork. It is estimated to be present in 57 million homes, ranging from low-income apartments to million-dollar mansions.

Elevated levels of lead in the body can cause serious damage to the brain, kidneys, nervous system and red blood cells. The degree of harm is related to the amount of exposure and the age at which a person is exposed. Poisoning occurs when the body is exposed to high amounts that it is not capable of eliminating. In 1991 the Center for Disease Control lowered the threshold at which children are considered to have lead poisoning. It is estimated that as many as one in six children may have dangerously high amounts of lead in their blood.

There is a common misconception that an individual must ingest paint chips to incur lead poisoning Though infants and toddlers will ingest most anything that looks attractive, lead can enter the body from a variety of other sources. Lead dust can be ingested from the hands by a crawling infant, inhaled by any occupant of a structure or ingested from the water supply because of lead pipes or solder that was permitted in old building codes. In fact, lead particles can be present elsewhere: soil may be contaminated; the air may be contaminated from gasoline exhaust.

Procedures. Licensees who are involved in the sale, management, financing or appraisal of properties constructed before 1978 face potential liability for any personal injury that might be suffered by an occupant. A variety of legislative efforts affect licensees, sellers and landlords. There is considerable controversy about practical approaches for handling the presence of lead paint. Some suggest that it should be removed; others that it should be encapsulated; still others advocate testing to determine the amount of lead that would then be disclosed to a prospective owner or resident.

Unless specific state or local laws address lead paint, the most practical approach is to inform prospective purchasers that, if they are concerned about the presence of lead, testing is available to determine the levels, thereby enabling them to make informed decisions about a purchase. Various federal agencies, including the FHA, are implementing requirements for disclosing the presence of lead-based paint as a condition for a mortgage loan. As of December 1, 1992, a prospective buyer must sign a "Lead Disclosure" form before signing a sales contract to purchase a home built before 1978. This and other regulations will affect the practices of salespeople, lenders and appraisers. Because lead paint is currently a hot issue in the industry, licensees must keep current with legislative and regulatory developments.

Radon

Radon is a radioactive gas that is produced by the natural decay of other radioactive substances. Although it can occur anywhere, some areas are known to have abnormally high amounts of radon. If it dissipates into the atmosphere, it is not likely to cause harm. However, when it infiltrates buildings and is trapped in high concentrations, it causes health problems. There are differences of opinion as to minimum safe levels of exposure. But there is growing evidence that radon may be the most underestimated cause of lung cancer, particularly for children, individuals who smoke and those who spend a considerable amount of time indoors.

Procedures. It is impossible to detect radon without testing because it is odorless and tasteless. Care should be exercised in the manner in which tests are conducted to ensure that the results are accurate. Radon levels will vary, depending on the amount of fresh air that circulates through a house, the weather conditions and the time of year. It is relatively easy to reduce the levels of radon by installing ventilation systems or exhaust fans.

Urea-Formaldehyde

Urea-formaldehyde was first used in building materials in the 1970s, particularly in insulation. Gases leach out of the insulation as it hardens and becomes trapped in the interior of a building. In 1982 the Consumer Product Safety Commission banned its use in insulation in housing. The ban was reduced to a warning after the courts determined that there was not sufficient evidence to support the extreme action of banning its use. There is scientific evidence that it causes cancer in animals, though the evidence of its effect on humans is inconclusive.

Formaldehyde is a very common environmental allergen, causing some individuals to suffer respiratory problems and eye and skin irritations. Because it is prevalent in a number of other building products and fixtures, consumers are becoming increasingly wary of the presence of formaldehyde particularly if they are sensitive to it.

Procedures. Urea-formaldehyde foam insulation (UFFI) has received a considerable amount of adverse publicity. Buyers express concern about purchasing a property in which it was installed. Tests can be conducted to determine the level of formaldehyde gas in a house. Again, however, care should be exercised to ensure that the results of the tests are accurate and that the source of the gases is properly identified. Elevated levels could be attributed to a source other than the insulation. Licensees should be careful that any conditions in an agreement of sale that require tests for formaldehyde are worded properly to identify the purpose for which the test is being conducted, such as to determine the presence of the insulation or some other source. Appraisers should also be aware of the presence of UFFI.

Groundwater Contamination

Groundwater is the water that exists under the earth's surface within the tiny spaces or crevices in the geological formations. It should not be confused with surface water runoff or underground streams that flow as dramatically as above ground rivers. Groundwater forms the water table, which is the natural level at which the ground is saturated; this may be at the earth's surface (in areas where the water table is very high) up to several hundreds of feet below the surface. Surface water can be absorbed into the groundwater. Any contamination of the underground water, be it the groundwater or underground streams, can threaten the supply of pure, clean water for private wells or public water systems. Many experts believe that pure water could become a scarce commodity if it is not protected.

Water can be contaminated from a number of sources, including waste disposal sites, underground storage tanks, pesticides and herbicides. Because water flows from one place to another, contamination can spread far from its source. There are numerous regulations designed to protect against water contamination. Once contamination has been identified, its source can be eliminated. However, the process can be time consuming and extremely expensive. Freshwater wells may have to be relocated to protect the water from contaminates.

Underground Storage Tanks

There are approximately 3 to 5 million underground storage tanks in the United States today. No one knows how many are leaking hazardous substances into the environment. These chemicals contaminate not only the soil where they are located but also adjacent parcels and groundwater. Underground storage tanks are commonly found on sites where petroleum products are used or where gas stations and auto repair shops are located. They may be located in a number of other commercial and industrial establishments, including printing and chemical plants, wood treatment plants, paper mills, paint manufacturers, dry cleaners and food processing plants. In residential areas they are used to store heating oil. Licensees should be particularly observant for fill pipes, vent lines, stained soil and fumes or odors.

The removal of leaking tanks and the surrounding contaminated soil, which must be disposed of in a hazardous waste facility, is quite costly. However, recent federal laws impose very strict requirements on the landowner where underground storage tanks are located to detect and correct leaks in an effort to protect the groundwater. The 1984 amendment to the Resource Conservation and Recovery Act (RCRA) established a program called the *Leaking Underground Storage Tanks (LUST)*. This program established regulations for installation, maintenance, monitoring for leaks and record keeping procedures, and it requires the landowner to have sufficient financial resources to cover damages resulting from leaks.

The law generally exempts farm and residential tanks with fewer than 1,100 gallons of motor fuel that is used for noncommercial purposes, tanks storing heating oil at the premises where it is consumed and septic tanks. An important legal point is that LUST places the financial responsibility on the tank owner.

Procedures. Buyers and lenders are concerned about any undue financial burden for having to comply with federal cleanup requirements, which affect not only the property that is the source of the contamination but also any adjacent property that is contaminated. Chemical tests to determine the presence of contaminated soil prior to a purchase, or as a condition for a mortgage loan, may be requested.

Waste Disposal Sites

Because the American culture has become a "throwaway" society, landfill operations have become the main receptacle for garbage and refuse. Leakage of waste material can contaminate the local water supply. Hazardous waste disposal sites have become the receptacle for radioactive waste from nuclear energy power plants, medical procedures and scientific research. Radioactive material can have a life of thousands of years. Emissions from the waste can be extremely harmful, causing cancer and even death.

Landfill operations do not have to be a source of pollution. However, landfills at improper locations or improperly managed sites have been a source of major problems. If they are constructed on the wrong type of soil or are lined improperly, the waste will leak. Their construction and maintenance is heavily regulated by state and federal authorities. Properly designed landfills are excavated and lined with clay or a synthetic liner to prevent leakage of waste material into the water supply. Garbage is laid at the bottom of the excavation; a layer of topsoil is then compacted onto the garbage. The procedure is repeated again and again until the excavation is filled. Although there is no height limitation, the garbage is usually "capped" when it reaches several hundred feet. Capping is the process of laying 2 to 4 feet of topsoil at the very top and then planting some type of vegetation. Completed landfills have been used for such purposes as parks and golf courses. Test wells around landfill operations are installed to constantly monitor the water in the surrounding area.

While much is still to be learned about disposal techniques for radioactive waste, in most cases the only alternative is to put the material in some type of container, which is then either buried or dropped into the sea. The obvious prob-

**Figure A.1
Environmental
Issues**

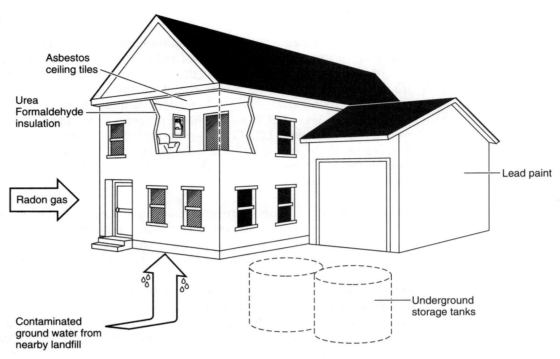

Asbestos
ceiling tiles

Urea
Formaldehyde
insulation

Radon gas

Lead paint

Underground
storage tanks

Contaminated
ground water from
nearby landfill

lem is that these containers can leak or become damaged in transit. There are numerous regulations affecting types of containers that can be used, their transportation and disposal.

Though waste disposal sites are a necessary part of life, we tolerate their existence only as long as they are located where someone else lives. It is important for real estate licensees to be aware of their locations and make proper disclosures to prospective purchasers so that they can make informed decisions.

**LEGAL
CONSIDERATIONS**

The majority of legislation dealing with environmental problems has been instituted within the last two decades. Although the Environmental Protection Agency (EPA) has been created at the federal level to oversee such problems, there are several other federal agencies whose areas of concern generally overlap. The federal laws were also created in such a way as to encourage state and local governments to prepare legislation in their own areas. All of the legislation relies on a background of common law being established by the court systems that creates liability for the seller, the buyer, the listing broker, the selling broker, the appraiser, lenders and anyone involved in the real estate business.

Federal environmental law is administered by agencies such as the United States Department of Transportation under the Hazardous Material Transportation Act; OSHA and the United States Department of Labor, which administer the standards for all employees working in the manufacturing sector; and the EPA, which administers such laws as the Toxic Substance Control Act, the Federal Clean Water Act and the Resource Conservation and Recovery Act.

The following discussion is designed to give a broad overview and a historical background to those laws affecting real estate. Increases in technology and public awareness of the problem mean that this is a dynamic area of the law with many areas of liability still being defined.

Statutory Law

The need for federal legislation was recognized after the Love Canal situation developed in New York. A hazardous waste leak created untold problems from both a physical health and property standpoint. The *Resource Conservation and Recovery Act (RCRA)* of 1976 consequently was created to regulate the generation, transportation, storage, use, treatment, disposal and cleanup of hazardous waste. However, it quickly became apparent that the legislation was not sufficiently comprehensive to cover all the situations that were quickly becoming a matter of concern.

The *Comprehensive Environmental Response, Compensation, and Liability Act (CERCLA)* was created in 1980. It established a fund of $9 billion, called the *Superfund*, to clean up uncontrolled hazardous waste dumps and to respond to spills. It created a process for identifying liable parties and ordering them to take responsibility for the cleanup action. A landowner may become liable under this act when there has been a release or a threat of release of a hazardous substance. Regardless of whether the contamination is the result of the landowner's own actions or those of others, the owner could be held responsible for cleaning up any resulting contamination. The liability includes the cleanup of the landowner's property and any neighboring property that has been contaminated. A landowner who is not responsible for the contamination can seek recovery reimbursement for the cleanup cost from previous landowners, any other responsible party or the Superfund.

In the event the Environmental Protection Agency has determined that there has been a release of hazardous material into the environment, the EPA is given the authority to begin remedial action. It will initially attempt to identify the parties responsible for the leak and approach these "potentially responsible parties" (PRP) to see if they will voluntarily cooperate in the cleanup. For a given site the potentially responsible parties may include hundreds of industrial generators of waste, previous landowners and transporters. The potentially responsible parties must then decide whether and on what terms they can fund the cleanup. If this is not done, EPA will begin work through its own contractors and charge the responsible parties for this cost. If a court determines liability after the cleanup and the potentially responsible parties refuse to pay, they could be required to pay triple damages.

Liability under the Superfund is considered to be strict, joint and several, and retroactive. *Strict liability* means that the owner is responsible to the injured party without excuse. *Joint and several liability* means that each of the individual owners is personally responsible for the damages in whole. If only one of the owners is financially able to handle the total damage, then that owner will have to pay the total and collect the proportionate share from the other owners whenever possible. *Retroactive liability* means that the liability is not limited to the person who currently owns the property but also to people who have owned the site in the past. Basically the liability provision means that all owners and operators, transporters and generators of hazardous waste are liable for the resulting cleanup cost without regard to fault. Therefore, the EPA need not prove wrongdoing to complete the cleanup or obtain recovery costs.

Superfund Amendments and Reauthorization Act (SARA). In 1986 the United States Congress reauthorized the Superfund. The amendment statute contains stronger cleanup standards for contaminated sites and five times the funding of the original Superfund, which expired in September 1985.

The amendment also sought to clarify the obligation of the lenders. As previously mentioned, liability under the Superfund extends to both the present and all previous owners of the contaminated site. Real estate lenders found themselves either as the present owner or somewhere in the chain of ownership through foreclosure proceedings. The new amendments sought to clarify the obligations of the lenders.

The amendments also created a concept called *innocent landowner immunity.* It was recognized that in certain cases a landowner in the chain of ownership had been completely innocent of all wrongdoing and therefore should not be held liable. The innocent landowner immunity clause established the criteria by which to judge if a person or business could be exempted from that liability. The criteria included that the pollution was caused by a third party, that the property was acquired after the fact, that the landowner had no actual or constructive knowledge of the damage, that "due care" was exercised when the property was purchased (the landowner made a reasonable search to determine that there was no damage to the property) and that reasonable precautions were taken in the exercise of ownership rights.

Common Law

Common law, which is created by past court decisions (as opposed to statutory law, which is created by enactment of legislation), provides a backdrop for these federal, state and local statutes to catch those situations that do not specifically fall within the law. This common law offers an important remedy for damages for personal injury or property damage that is not covered under legislation.

A good example for this is the concept of negligence. This is a field of law that defines the duty that members of the public owe to each other to take reasonable care to avoid foreseeable harm. Negligence can be defined as the failure to use such care as a reasonably prudent and careful person would use to avoid harm to others that would be foreseeable. This doctrine can be used against all owners, whether public or private, of sites and facilities who make mistakes resulting in hazardous waste being released into the environment. Negligent acts resulting in the release of chemicals to the environment are sometimes called *toxic torts.* Such torts are said to carry strict liability.

One of the most far-reaching cases was the 1986 California case of *Easton v. Strassburger.* It involved the sale of a home that had been built on an improperly designed landfill. Both the selling and listing real estate agents involved in the transaction were held liable for not providing "reasonably discoverable facts" (those that should have been known) about the property. Subsequent legislation passed and was made law in California, requiring that all real estate agents conduct a "reasonably diligent and competent inspection" of the property for sale, examining it for potential problems dealing with pollution. This inspection must be more thorough than both a casual examination of the property and a general inquiry of the seller. The law also requires and provides for the use of disclosure forms that must be presented to the prospective purchaser. Such laws are becoming more common in many states.

IMPLICATIONS OF ENVIRONMENTAL LAW

Real estate licensees must be aware of their potential liability in a real estate transaction. The other players in the transaction may have little if any knowledge of environmental issues, let alone the type of liability that they might have.

Sellers, as mentioned earlier, often carry the majority of the exposure. Innocent landowners might be held responsible even though they did not know about the presence of environmental hazards.

It is also necessary to be aware of the potential risk from neighboring properties, such as a property that abuts a gas station. The majority of lawsuits originate from the buyer. The days of "caveat emptor" (let the buyer beware) are rapidly disappearing. Both the statutes and the courts are taking steps to protect the innocent buyer whenever possible. All possible risk must be disclosed to the buyer in any situation in which there might be an environmental problem.

Liability of Real Estate Professionals

Additional exposure is created for individuals involved in other aspects of a transaction. For example, the real estate appraiser must identify and adjust for environmental problems. Adjustments to market value typically reflect that cost plus a factor of the "panic" that exists in the current market. Although the sales price can be affected dramatically, it is possible that the underlying market value would remain relatively equal to others in the neighborhood. The real estate appraiser's greatest responsibility is to the lender who depends on the appraiser to identify environmental hazards. Although the lender may be protected under certain conditions through the 1986 amendments to the Superfund Act, the lender must be aware of any potential problems and may require additional environmental reports.

The insurance carrier might also be affected in the transaction. Mortgage insurance companies will protect the lenders in their mortgage investment and might be required to carry part of the ultimate responsibility in case of a loss. More important, the hazard insurance carrier might be directly responsible for the damages if such coverage was included in the initial policy.

Environmental law is a relatively new phenomenon. Although the statutes have defined many of the liabilities involved, common law is being used for further interpretation. The real estate professional and all others associated with the real estate transaction must be aware of both actual and potential liability.

All parties to the real estate transaction should be diligent in identifying environmental hazards by obtaining professional inspections of environmental screenings prior to the purchase of the property. The environmental screening can take the form of a report or can become a complete environment audit with complete engineering and scientific tests being conducted. Examples of environmental reports that may be used are found in Figures A.2 through A.4.

Modern computer technology is now allowing the various environmental data bases to be used to effectively "screen" properties for potential problems based on the "footprint" of information regarding the subject property. Nationally, one such system, VISTA Environmental Profiles, is an example of a screening system that can be utilized by the real estate professional to prevent any environmental surprises from occurring. This system, when used by qualified individuals, can provide a key element in the environmental assessment of a property in a matter of minutes. Techniques such as this will enable real estate professionals to become more knowledgeable regarding environmental factors relating to subject properties and also will prevent large amounts of time and capital from being expended on marketing only to find an environmental problem became a "deal killer" in the final stages of negotiation.

LEGISLATIVE REFERENCES

United States Environmental Protection Agency (EPA)

The EPA was formally established as an independent agency December 2, 1970. It currently administers ten comprehensive environmental protection laws:

1. Clean Air Act (CAA)

2. Clean Water Act (CWA)

3. Safe Drinking Water Act (SDWA)

4. Comprehensive Environmental Response, Compensation and Liability Act (CERCLA)

5. Resource Conservation and Recovery Act (RCRA)

6. Federal Insecticide, Fungicide and Rodentcide Act (FIFRA)

7. Toxic Substance Control Act (TSCA)

8. Marine Protection Research and Sanctuaries Act (MPRSA)

9. Uranium Mill Tailings Radiation Control Act (UMTRCA)

10. Hazardous Solid Waste Act (HSWA)

CERCLA, known as the *Superfund*, was amended by Superfund Amendments and Reauthorization Act of 1986 known as *SARA*. SARA identifies the most common environmental risks:

*   Asbestos in building material

*   PCBs in transformers and capacitors

*   Airborne chemicals

*   Hazardous chemical storage

*   Buried waste

*   Leaking underground storage tanks

SARA places a great deal of responsibility on people who own real estate or buildings that have environmental hazards to decontaminate them. Not only the person who owns the property, but also the person who did own the property, the person who transported the hazardous material to the property, the person who disposed of the material are all jointly and severally liable for the cleanup.

Lenders are very careful not to foreclose on a contaminated property. They will then become owners and consequently will be responsible for the decontamination.

**Figure A.2
Seller's Certification—
Environmental
Hazardous Substances**

SELLER'S CERTIFICATION - ENVIRONMENTAL HAZARDOUS SUBSTANCES

Property Identification:

Address _____

City _____ State _____ Zip _____

Brief Description: _____

_____

_____

_____

Seller Identification:

Name of Owner(s) _____

Address _____

City _____ State _____ Zip _____

Telephone _____

Property Owned From _____ To _____

Seller's Certification:

I do hereby certify that to the best of my knowledge during and before my ownership of the above described property:

  a) The property was not used as a dump site or storage facility for hazardous substances.

  b) No one has received notification from a federal, state or local government in regard to pending or threatened Superfund or Superlien liability.

  c) To the best of my knowledge no environmental hazards have been identified on the subject property.

Exception to above: _____

_____

_____

_____

_____

I (we) do hereby certify that the above information is true to the best of my (our) knowledge and belief.

Date _____ Seller_____

Date _____ Seller_____

FW-70EH   Forms and Worms Inc., 315 Whitney Ave., New Haven, CT 06511   1 (800) 243-4545   Item #115200
National Association of Environmental Risk Auditors

**Figure A.3
Uniform
Environmental
History**

UNIFORM ENVIRONMENTAL HISTORY
Questionnaire and/or Certificate

File No. _____

Property Address _____
City _____ State _____ Zip _____
Name of Person Interviewed _____
Dates of Ownership From _____ To _____
Other Way Familiar With Property From _____ To _____
Interviewer _____ Date _____
Address _____
City _____ State _____ Zip _____
Telephone _____

This form is used to report the results of an interview with the current or former property owner or others familiar with the property about known Hazardous Substances or Detrimental Environmental Conditions on or around the subject property. When signed by the interviewer it becomes their certificate.

#		YES	NO	Comment on all "Yes's"
ASBESTOS				
1.	Are you aware of any asbestos on your property? Pipe covering Heating/Hot water unit covering Tile Siding Other			
2.	Are you aware of any asbestos survey being performed on your property?			
3.	Are you aware of any asbestos tests being conducted on materials from your property?			
PCBs (Polychlorinated Biphenyls)				
4.	Are you aware of any PCBs on your property?			
5.	Are you aware of any PCBs on neighboring properties that might contaminate your property?			
RADON				
6.	Are you aware of any radon tests made on the property?			
7.	If so, was radon test made more than 12 months ago?			
8.	Were the results over 4 pCi/l? (If so, report actual figures).			
9.	To the best of your knowledge do any properties within one mile have radon levels over 4 pCi/l.			
10.	Are you aware of any evidence that nearby structures have elevated indoor levels of radon or radon progeny?			
11.	Are you aware of any information that indicates the local water supplies have been found to have elevated levels of radon or radium?			
12.	Are you aware of any properties within one mile of your property of any sites that were or currently are used for uranium, thorium or radium extraction or for phosphate processing?			
UST'S (Underground Storage Tanks)				
13.	Are you aware of any underground storage tanks presently on the property?			
14.	Are you aware of any underground storage tanks which were previously removed from the property, (if so note date).			
15.	Are you aware of any site survey made by a qualified engineer which indicates the property is free of USTs.?			
WASTE DISPOSAL				
16.	Are you aware of any petroleum storage and/or delivery facilities (including gas stations) or chemical manufacturing plants located within one mile of the property?			

Page 1 of 2

Figure A.3 (continued)

File No. _____

#		Y E S	N O	Comment on all "Yes's"
17.	Are you aware of any physical testing (including on-site sampling of soil and groundwater) to determine if the property is free of waste contamination?			
18.	Do you know if the property was ever used for research, industrial or military purposes?			
19.	Do you know if the property has ever been occupied by owners or commercial tenants who are likely to have used, transported or disposed of toxic chemicals (e.g. dry cleaners, print shops, service stations, etc.)?			
20.	Do you know if there is any water provided to the property or from a well or private water company?			
21.	Do you know if the property or any site within one mile, appears on any state or federal list of hazardous waste sites (e.g. CERCLIS, HWDMS, etc.)?			
22.	Do you know of any visible evidence or documents that indicate there is or was dangerous waste handling on the property or neighboring sites (e.g. stressed vegetation, stained soil, open or leaking containers, foul fumes or smells, oily ponds, etc.)?			

(WASTE SITES)

UREA (Formaldehyde)

23.	Do you know if the property contains UREA Formaldehyde Foam Insulation? (If yes, note location and amount).			

LEAD PAINT

24.	Do you know if the property was tested for lead paint?			
25.	Do you have any reason to believe that the property contains lead paint?			

DRINKING WATER

26.	Do you know if the drinking water was ever tested for lead? (If yes, note date and results).			
27.	Do you know if any other tests were ever made on the drinking water? (If yes, describe and note results).			
28.	Do you have any reason to believe there was or is any problem with the quality and quantity of drinking water available at the property?			

AIR POLLUTANTS

29.	Do you know if the interior air was ever tested?			
30.	Do you have any reason to believe there was or is any problem with the interior or exterior air of the property?			

OTHER ENVIRONMENTAL HAZARDS

31.	Are you aware of any other hazardous substances or detrimental environmental conditions that effect the property?			

I certify that I have read the answers to the questions on this form and acknowledge that they are accurate to the best of my knowledge and belief.

Signatures   Current or former property owner(s)

_____ Date   _____ Date

_____ Date   _____ Date

Interviewer

FW-70EQ   Test Version 3A 1/90   Forms and Worms, Inc.® 315 Whitney Ave., New Haven, CT 06511 1(800)243-4545
Approved by The National Association of Environmental Risk Auditors   Item# 115250

**Figure A.4
Environmental Desk
Review**

ENVIRONMENTAL DESK REVIEW
Reviewer/Underwriter Certification
Hazardous Substances and Detrimental Environmental Conditions

Loan File No.: _____

Lender: _____

Property Identification

Address		
City	State	Zip
Type of Property		
Reviewer/Underwriter		

The following is a summary of how the property was screened for Hazardous Substances & Detrimental Environmental Conditions and the results of the screenings.

ASBESTOS   ▪ Screened   ▪ Not Screened

Name of Screener _____ Date Screened: _____
How Screened _____
Tests & Results _____

Screening Results: ☐ Acceptable   ☐ Acceptable: Requires O & M   ☐ Failed   ☐ Fail: Possible Remedy
☐ Additional Tests Required   ☐ Additional Inspections Required
Comments _____

PCBs (Polychlorinated Biphenyls)   ▪ Screened   ▪ Not Screened

Name of Screener _____ Date Screened: _____
How Screened _____
Tests & Results _____

Screening Results: ☐ Acceptable   ☐ Acceptable: Requires O & M   ☐ Failed   ☐ Fail: Possible Remedy
☐ Additional Tests Required   ☐ Additional Inspections Required
Comments _____

RADON   ▪ Screened   ▪ Not Screened

Name of Screener _____ Date Screened: _____
How Screened _____
Tests & Results _____

Screening Results: ☐ Acceptable   ☐ Acceptable: Requires O & M   ☐ Failed   ☐ Fail: Possible Remedy
☐ Additional Tests Required   ☐ Additional Inspections Required
Comments _____

USTs (Underground Storage Tanks)   ▪ Screened   ▪ Not Screened

Name of Screener _____ Date Screened: _____
How Screened _____
Tests & Results _____

Screening Results: ☐ Acceptable   ☐ Acceptable: Requires O & M   ☐ Failed   ☐ Fail: Possible Remedy
☐ Additional Tests Required   ☐ Additional Inspections Required
Comments _____

WASTE DISPOSAL   ▪ Screened   ▪ Not Screened

Name of Screener _____ Date Screened: _____
How Screened _____
Tests & Results _____

Screening Results: ☐ Acceptable   ☐ Acceptable: Requires O & M   ☐ Failed   ☐ Fail: Possible Remedy
☐ Additional Tests Required   ☐ Additional Inspections Required
Comments _____

WASTE SITES   ▪ Screened   ▪ Not Screened

Name of Screener _____ Date Screened: _____
How Screened _____
Tests & Results _____

Screening Results: ☐ Acceptable   ☐ Acceptable: Requires O & M   ☐ Failed   ☐ Fail: Possible Remedy
☐ Additional Tests Required   ☐ Additional Inspections Required
Comments _____

Page 1 of 2

FW-70ER   Test Version   ©1989 Forms and Worms, Inc., 315 Whitney Ave., New Haven, CT 06511   1(800) 243-4545   Item #115350
              #3A 1/90   Approved by The National Association of Environmental Risk Auditors

**Figure A.4
(continued)**

UREA (Formaldehyde)   ☐ Screened   ☐ Not Screened
Name of Screener _____ Date Screened: _____
How Screened _____
Tests & Results _____

Screening Results: ☐ Acceptable   ☐ Acceptable: Requires O & M   ☐ Failed   ☐ Fail: Possible Remedy
                    ☐ Additional Tests Required   ☐ Additional Inspections Required
Comments _____

LEAD PAINT   ☐ Screened   ☐ Not Screened
Name of Screener _____ Date Screened: _____
How Screened _____
Tests & Results _____

Screening Results: ☐ Acceptable   ☐ Acceptable: Requires O & M   ☐ Failed   ☐ Fail: Possible Remedy
                    ☐ Additional Tests Required   ☐ Additional Inspections Required
Comments _____

DRINKING WATER   ☐ Screened   ☐ Not Screened
Name of Screener _____ Date Screened: _____
How Screened _____
Tests & Results _____

Screening Results: ☐ Acceptable   ☐ Acceptable: Requires O & M   ☐ Failed   ☐ Fail: Possible Remedy
                    ☐ Additional Tests Required   ☐ Additional Inspections Required
Comments _____

AIR POLLUTANTS   ☐ Screened   ☐ Not Screened
Name of Screener _____ Date Screened: _____
How Screened _____
Tests & Results _____

Screening Results: ☐ Acceptable   ☐ Acceptable: Requires O & M   ☐ Failed   ☐ Fail: Possible Remedy
                    ☐ Additional Tests Required   ☐ Additional Inspections Required
Comments _____

ADDITIONAL ENVIRONMENTAL HAZARDS   ☐ Screened   ☐ Not Screened
Hazard(s) _____ Date Screened: _____
How Screened _____
Tests & Results _____

Screening Results: ☐ Acceptable   ☐ Acceptable: Requires O & M   ☐ Failed   ☐ Fail: Possible Remedy
                    ☐ Additional Tests Required   ☐ Additional Inspections Required
Comments _____

SUMMARY

I have reviewed the: (Check all that apply)
   ☐ Appraisal   ☐ Environmental Screenings   ☐ Test Results
   ☐ Seller's Certificate ☐ History   ☐ Other_____
Summary of Review _____
_____
_____
_____

They Do/Do not reveal any hazardous substances or detrimental environmental conditions,
   ☐ I recommend the property be accepted
   ☐ I recommend the following inspections, O & M and tests be conducted or reevaluated before the property is accepted
   _____

   ☐ I recommend the property not be accepted due to _____

Underwriter/Reviewer:
Signature _____   ☐ I inspected the property
Typed Name _____   ☐ I did not inspect the property
Date _____
Name of institution _____

FW-70ER   Test Version   ©1989 Forms and Worms, Inc., 315 Whitney Ave., New Haven, CT 06511 1(800) 243-4545   Item #115350
            #3A 1/90   Approved by The National Association of Environmental Risk Auditors

Glossary of Real Estate Terms

abstract of title The condensed history of a title to a particular parcel of real estate, consisting of a summary of the original grant and all subsequent conveyances and encumbrances affecting the property and a certification by the abstractor that the history is complete and accurate.

acceleration clause The clause in a mortgage or deed of trust that can be enforced to make the entire debt due immediately if the borrower defaults on an installment payment or other covenant.

accession Acquiring title to additions or improvements to real property as a result of the annexation of fixtures or the accretion of alluvial deposits along the banks of streams.

accretion The increase or addition of land by the deposit of sand or soil washed up naturally from a river, lake or sea.

accrued items On a closing statement, items of expense that are incurred but not yet payable, such as interest on a mortgage loan or taxes on real property.

acknowledgment A formal declaration made before a duly authorized officer, usually a notary public, by a person who has signed a document.

acre A measure of land equal to 43,560 square feet, 4,840 square yards, 4,047 square meters, 160 square rods or 0.4047 hectares.

actual eviction The legal process that results in the tenant's being physically removed from the leased premises.

actual notice Express information or fact; that which is known; direct knowledge.

adjustable-rate mortgage (ARM) A loan characterized by a fluctuating interest rate, usually one tied to a bank or savings and loan association cost-of-funds index.

adjusted basis *See* basis.

ad valorem tax A tax levied according to value, generally used to refer to real estate tax. Also called the *general tax.*

adverse possession The actual, open, notorious, hostile and continuous possession of another's land under a claim of title. Possession for a statutory period may be a means of acquiring title.

affidavit of title A written statement, made under oath by a seller or grantor of real property and acknowledged by a notary public, in which the grantor (1) identifies himself or herself and indicates marital status, (2) certifies that since the examination of the title on the date of the contracts no defects have occurred in the title and (3) certifies that he or she is in possession of the property (if applicable).

agency The relationship between a principal and an agent wherein the agent is authorized to represent the principal in certain transactions.

agency coupled with an interest An agency relationship in which the agent is given an estate or interest in the subject of the agency (the property).

agent One who acts or has the power to act for another. A fiduciary relationship is created under the *law of agency* when a property owner, as the principal, executes a listing agreement or management contract authorizing a licensed real estate broker to be his or her agent.

air lot A designated airspace over a piece of land. An air lot, like surface property, may be transferred.

air rights The right to use the open space above a property, usually allowing the surface to be used for another purpose.

alienation The act of transferring property to another. Alienation may be voluntary, such as by gift or sale, or involuntary, as through eminent domain or adverse possession.

alienation clause The clause in a mortgage or deed of trust that states that the balance of the secured debt becomes immediately due and payable at the lender's option if the property is sold by the borrower. In effect this clause prevents the borrower from assigning the debt without the lender's approval.

allodial system A system of land ownership in which land is held free and clear of any rent or service due to the government; commonly contrasted to the feudal system. Land is held under the allodial system in the United States.

American Land Title Association (ALTA) policy A title insurance policy that protects the interest in a collateral property of a mortgage lender who originates a new real estate loan.

amortized loan A loan in which the principal as well as the interest is payable in monthly or other periodic installments over the term of the loan.

annual percentage rate (APR) The relationship of the total finance charges associated with a loan. This must be disclosed to borrowers by lenders under the Truth-in-Lending Act.

anticipation The appraisal principle that holds that value can increase or decrease based on the expectation of some future benefit or detriment produced by the property.

antitrust laws Laws designed to preserve the free enterprise of the open marketplace by making illegal certain private conspiracies and combinations formed to minimize competition. Most violations of antitrust laws in the real estate business involve either *price-fixing* (brokers conspiring to set fixed compensation rates) or *allocation of customers or markets* (brokers agreeing to limit their areas of trade or dealing to certain areas or properties).

appraisal An estimate of the quantity, quality or value of something. The process through which conclusions of property value are obtained; also refers to the report that sets forth the process of estimation and conclusion of value.

appreciation An increase in the worth or value of a property due to economic or related causes, which may prove to be either temporary or permanent; opposite of depreciation.

appurtenance A right, privilege or improvement belonging to, and passing with, the land.

appurtenant easement An easement that is annexed to the ownership of one parcel and allows the owner the use of the neighbor's land.

assemblage The combining of two or more adjoining lots into one larger tract to increase their total value.

assessment The imposition of a tax, charge or levy, usually according to established rates.

assignment The transfer in writing of interest in a bond, mortgage, lease or other instrument.

assumption of mortgage Acquiring title to property on which there is an existing mortgage and agreeing to be personally liable for the terms and conditions of the mortgage, including payments.

attachment The act of taking a person's property into legal custody by writ or other judicial order to hold it available for application to that person's debt to a creditor.

attorney's opinion of title An abstract of title that an attorney has examined and has certified to be, in his or her opinion, an accurate statement of the facts concerning the property ownership.

automatic extension A clause in a listing agreement that states that the agreement will continue automatically for a certain period of time after its expiration date. In many states, use of this clause is discouraged or prohibited.

avulsion The sudden tearing away of land, as by earthquake, flood, volcanic action or the sudden change in the course of a stream.

balance The appraisal principle that states that the greatest value in a property will occur when the type and size of the improvements are proportional to each other as well as the land.

balloon payment A final payment of a mortgage loan that is considerably larger than the required periodic payments because the loan amount was not fully amortized.

bargain and sale deed A deed that carries with it no warranties against liens or other encumbrances but that does imply that the grantor has the right to convey title. The grantor may add warranties to the deed at his or her discretion.

base line The main imaginary line running east and west and crossing a principal meridian at a definite point, used by surveyors for reference in locating and describing land under the rectangular (government) survey system of legal description.

basis The financial interest that the Internal Revenue Service attributes to an owner of an investment property for the purpose of determining annual depreciation and gain or loss on the sale of the asset. If a property was acquired by purchase, the owner's basis is the cost of the property plus the value of any capital expenditures for improvements to the property, minus any depreciation allowable or actually taken. This new basis is called the *adjusted basis*.

bench mark A permanent reference mark or point established for use by surveyors in measuring differences in elevation.

beneficiary (1) The person for whom a trust operates or in whose behalf the income from a trust estate is drawn. (2) A lender in a deed of trust loan transaction.

bilateral contract *See* contract.

binder An agreement that may accompany an earnest money deposit for the purchase of real property as evidence of the purchaser's good faith and intent to complete the transaction.

blanket loan A mortgage covering more than one parcel of real estate, providing for each parcel's partial release from the mortgage lien upon repayment of a definite portion of the debt.

blockbusting The illegal practice of inducing homeowners to sell their properties by making representations regarding the entry or prospective entry of persons of a particular race or national origin into the neighborhood.

blue-sky laws Common name for those state and federal laws that regulate the registration and sale of investment securities.

boot Money or property given to make up any difference in value or equity between two properties in an *exchange*.

branch office A secondary place of business apart from the principal or main office from which real estate business is conducted. A branch office usually must be run by a licensed real estate broker working on behalf of the broker.

breach of contract Violation of any terms or conditions in a contract without legal excuse; for example, failure to make a payment when it is due.

broker One who acts as an intermediary on behalf of others for a fee or commission.

brokerage The bringing together of parties interested in making a real estate transaction.

buffer zone A strip of land, usually used as a park or designated for a similar use, separating land dedicated to one use from land dedicated to another use (e.g., residential from commercial).

building code An ordinance that specifies minimum standards of construction for buildings to protect public safety and health.

building permit Written governmental permission for the construction, alteration or demolition of an improvement, showing compliance with building codes and zoning ordinances.

bulk transfer *See* Uniform Commercial Code.

bundle of legal rights The concept of land ownership that includes *ownership of all legal rights to the land*—for example, possession, control within the law and enjoyment.

buydown A financing technique used to reduce the monthly payments for the first few years of a loan. Funds in the form of discount points are given to the lender by the builder or seller to buy down or lower the effective interest rate paid by the buyer, thus reducing the monthly payments for a set time.

buyer-agency agreement A principal-agent relationship in which the broker is the agent for the buyer, with fiduciary responsibilities to the buyer. The broker represents the buyer under the law of agency.

capital gain Profit earned from the sale of an asset.

capitalization A mathematical process for estimating the value of a property using a proper rate of return on the investment and the annual net operating income expected to be produced by the property. The formula is expressed as

$$\frac{\text{Income}}{\text{Rate}} = \text{Value}$$

capitalization rate The rate of return a property will produce on the owner's investment.

cash flow The net spendable income from an investment, determined by deducting all operating and fixed expenses from the gross income. When expenses exceed income, a *negative cash flow* results.

cash rent In an agricultural lease, the amount of money given as rent to the landowner at the outset of the lease, as opposed to sharecropping.

caveat emptor A Latin phrase meaning "Let the buyer beware."

certificate of reasonable value (CRV) A form indicating the appraised value of a property being financed with a VA loan.

certificate of sale The document generally given to the purchaser at a tax foreclosure sale. A certificate of sale does not convey title; normally it is an instrument certifying that the holder received title to the property after the redemption period passed and that the holder paid the property taxes for that interim period.

certificate of title A statement of opinion on the status of the title to a parcel of real property based on an examination of specified public records.

chain of title The succession of conveyances, from some accepted starting point, whereby the present holder of real property derives title.

change The appraisal principle that holds that no physical or economic condition remains constant.

chattel *See* personal property.

Civil Rights Act of 1866 An act that prohibits racial discrimination in the sale and rental of housing.

closing statement A detailed cash accounting of a real estate transaction showing all cash received, all charges and credits made and all cash paid out in the transaction.

cloud on title Any document, claim, unreleased lien or encumbrance that may impair the title to real property or make the title doubtful; usually revealed by a title search and removed by either a quitclaim deed or suit to quiet title.

clustering The grouping of homesites within a subdivision on smaller lots than normal, with the remaining land used as common areas.

code of ethics A written system of standards for ethical conduct.

codicil A supplement or an addition to a will, executed with the same formalities as a will, that normally does not revoke the entire will.

coinsurance clause A clause in insurance policies covering real property that requires the policy-holder to maintain fire insurance coverage generally equal to at least 80 percent of the property's actual replacement cost.

commingling The illegal act by a real estate broker of placing client or customer funds with personal funds. By law brokers are required to maintain a separate *trust or escrow account* for other parties' funds held temporarily by the broker.

commission Payment to a broker for services rendered, such as in the sale or purchase of real property; usually a percentage of the selling price of the property.

common elements Parts of a property that are necessary or convenient to the existence, maintenance and safety of a condominium or are normally in common use by all of the condominium residents. Each condominium owner has an undivided ownership interest in the common elements.

common law The body of law based on custom, usage and court decisions.

community property A system of property ownership based on the theory that each spouse has an equal interest in the property acquired by the efforts of either spouse during marriage. A holdover of Spanish law found predominantly in western states; the system was unknown under English common law.

comparables Properties used in an appraisal report that are substantially equivalent to the subject property.

competition The appraisal principle that states that excess profits generate competition.

competitive market analysis (CMA) A comparison of the prices of recently sold homes that are similar to a listing seller's home in terms of location, style and amenities.

comprehensive plan *See* master plan.

condemnation A judicial or administrative proceeding to exercise the power of eminent domain, through which a government agency takes private property for public use and compensates the owner.

conditional-use permit Written governmental permission allowing a use inconsistent with zoning but necessary for the common good, such as locating an emergency medical facility in a predominantly residential area.

condominium The absolute ownership of a unit in a multiunit building based on a legal description of the airspace the unit actually occupies, plus an undivided interest in the ownership of the common elements, which are owned jointly with the other condominium unit owners.

confession of judgment clause Permits judgment to be entered against a debtor without the creditor's having to institute legal proceedings.

conformity The appraisal principle that holds that the greater the similarity among properties in an area, the better they will hold their value.

consideration (1) That received by the grantor in exchange for his or her deed. (2) Something of value that induces a person to enter into a contract.

construction loan *See* interim financing.

constructive eviction Actions of a landlord that so materially disturb or impair a tenant's enjoyment of the leased premises that the tenant is effectively forced to move out and terminate the lease without liability for any further rent.

constructive notice Notice given to the world by recorded documents. All people are charged with knowledge of such documents and their contents, whether or not they have actually examined them. Possession of property is also considered constructive notice that the person in possession has an interest in the property.

contingency A provision in a contract that requires a certain act to be done or a certain event to occur before the contract becomes binding.

contract A legally enforceable promise or set of promises that must be performed and for which, if a breach of the promise occurs, the law provides a remedy. A contract may be either *unilateral,* by which only one party is bound to act, or *bilateral,* by which all parties to the instrument are legally bound to act as prescribed.

contribution The appraisal principle that states that the value of any component of a property is what it gives to the value of the whole or what its absence detracts from that value.

conventional loan A loan that requires no insurance or guarantee.

conveyance A term used to refer to any document that transfers title to real property. The term is also used in describing the act of transferring.

cooperating broker *See* listing broker.

cooperative A residential multiunit building whose title is held by a trust or corporation that is owned by and operated for the benefit of persons living within the building, who are the beneficial owners of the trust or stockholders of the corporation, each possessing a proprietary lease.

co-ownership Title ownership held by two or more persons.

corporation An entity or organization, created by operation of law, whose rights of doing business are essentially the same as those of an individual. The entity has continuous existence until it is dissolved according to legal procedures.

correction lines Provisions in the rectangular survey (government survey) system made to compensate for the curvature of the earth's surface. Every fourth township line (at 24-mile intervals) is used as a correction line on which the intervals between the north and south range lines are remeasured and corrected to a full six miles.

cost approach The process of estimating the value of a property by adding to the estimated land value the appraiser's estimate of the reproduction or replacement cost of the building, less depreciation.

cost recovery An Internal Revenue Service term for *depreciation.*

counteroffer A new offer made in response to an offer received. It has the effect of rejecting the original offer, which cannot be accepted thereafter unless revived by the offeror.

covenant A written agreement between two or more parties in which a party or parties pledge to perform or not perform specified acts with regard to property; usually found in such real estate documents as deeds, mortgages, leases and contracts for deed.

covenant of quiet enjoyment The covenant implied by law by which a landlord guarantees that a tenant may take possession of leased premises and that the landlord will not interfere in the tenant's possession or use of the property.

credit On a closing statement, an amount entered in a person's favor—either an amount the party has paid or an amount for which the party must be reimbursed.

curtesy A life estate, usually a fractional interest, given by some states to the surviving husband in real estate owned by his deceased wife. Most states have abolished curtesy.

datum A horizontal plane from which heights and depths are measured.

debit On a closing statement, an amount charged; that is, an amount that the debited party must pay.

decedent A person who has died.

dedication The voluntary transfer of private property by its owner to the public for some public use, such as for streets or schools.

deed A written instrument that, when executed and delivered, conveys title to or an interest in real estate.

deed in lieu of foreclosure A deed given by the mortgagor to the mortgagee when the mortgagor is in default under the terms of the mortgage. This is a way for the mortgagor to avoid foreclosure.

deed in trust An instrument that grants a trustee under a land trust full power to sell, mortgage and subdivide a parcel of real estate. The beneficiary controls the trustee's use of these powers under the provisions of the trust agreement.

deed of trust *See* trust deed.

deed of trust lien *See* trust deed lien.

deed restrictions Clauses in a deed limiting the future uses of the property. Deed restrictions may impose a vast variety of limitations and conditions—for example, they may limit the density of buildings, dictate the types of structures that can be erected or prevent buildings from being used for specific purposes or even from being used at all.

default The nonperformance of a duty, whether arising under a contract or otherwise; failure to meet an obligation when due.

defeasance clause A clause used in leases and mortgages that cancels a specified right upon the occurrence of a certain condition, such as cancellation of a mortgage upon repayment of the mortgage loan.

defeasible fee estate An estate in which the holder has a fee simple title that may be divested upon the occurrence or nonoccurrence of a specified event. There are two categories of defeasible fee estates: fee simple on condition precedent (fee simple determinable) and fee simple on condition subsequent.

deficiency judgment A personal judgment levied against the borrower when a foreclosure sale does not produce sufficient funds to pay the mortgage debt in full.

demand The amount of goods people are willing and able to buy at a given price; often coupled with *supply.*

density zoning Zoning ordinances that restrict the maximum average number of houses per acre that may be built within a particular area, generally a subdivision.

depreciation (1) In appraisal, a loss of value in property due to any cause, including *physical deterioration, functional obsolescence* and *external obsolescence.* (2) In real estate investment, an expense deduction for tax purposes taken over the period of ownership of income property.

descent Acquisition of an estate by inheritance in which an heir succeeds to the property by operation of law.

developer One who attempts to put land to its most profitable use through the construction of improvements.

devise A gift of real property by will. The donor is the devisor, and the recipient is the devisee.

discount point A unit of measurement used for various loan charges; one point equals 1 percent of the amount of the loan.

dominant tenement A property that includes in its ownership the appurtenant right to use an easement over another person's property for a specific purpose.

dower The legal right or interest, recognized in some states, that a wife acquires in the property her husband held or acquired during their marriage. During the husband's lifetime the right is only a possibility of an interest; upon his death it can become an interest in land.

dual agency Representing both parties to a transaction. This is unethical unless both parties agree to it, and it is illegal in many states.

due-on-sale clause A provision in the mortgage that states that the entire balance of the note is immediately due and payable if the mortgagor transfers (sells) the property.

duress Unlawful constraint or action exercised upon a person whereby the person is forced to perform an act against his or her will. A contract entered into under duress is voidable.

earnest money Money deposited by a buyer under the terms of a contract, to be forfeited if the buyer defaults but applied to the purchase price if the sale is closed.

easement A right to use the land of another for a specific purpose, such as for a right-of-way or utilities; an incorporeal interest in land.

easement by condemnation An easement created by the government or government agency that has exercised its right under eminent domain.

easement by necessity An easement allowed by law as necessary for the full enjoyment of a parcel of real estate; for example, a right of ingress and egress over a grantor's land.

easement by prescription An easement acquired by continuous, open and hostile use of the property for the period of time prescribed by state law.

easement in gross An easement that is not created for the benefit of any *land* owned by the owner of the easement but that attaches *personally to the easement owner.* For example, a right granted by Eleanor Franks to Joe Fish to use a portion of her property for the rest of his life would be an easement in gross.

economic life The number of years during which an improvement will add value to the land.

emblements Growing crops, such as grapes and corn, that are produced annually through labor and industry; also called *fructus industriales.*

eminent domain The right of a government or municipal quasi-public body to acquire property for public use through a court action called *condemnation,* in which the court decides that the use is a public use and determines the compensation to be paid to the owner.

employee Someone who works as a direct employee of an employer and has employee status. The employer is obligated to withhold income taxes and social security taxes from the compensation of employees. *See also* independent contractor.

employment contract A document evidencing formal employment between employer and employee or between principal and agent. In the real estate business this generally takes the form of a listing agreement or management agreement.

enabling acts State legislation that confers zoning powers on municipal governments.

encroachment A building or some portion of it—a wall or fence for instance— that extends beyond the land of the owner and illegally intrudes on some land of an adjoining owner or a street or alley.

encumbrance Anything—such as a mortgage, tax, or judgment lien, an easement, a restriction on the use of the land or an outstanding dower right—that may diminish the value or use and enjoyment of a property.

Equal Credit Opportunity Act (ECOA) The federal law that prohibits discrimination in the extension of credit because of race, color, religion, national origin, sex, age or marital status.

equalization The raising or lowering of assessed values for tax purposes in a particular county or taxing district to make them equal to assessments in other counties or districts.

equalization factor A factor (number) by which the assessed value of a property is multiplied to arrive at a value for the property that is in line with statewide tax assessments. The *ad valorem tax* would be based on this adjusted value.

equitable lien *See* statutory lien.

equitable right of redemption The right of a defaulted property owner to recover the property prior to its sale by paying the appropriate fees and charges.

equitable title The interest held by a vendee under a contract for deed or an installment contract; the equitable right to obtain absolute ownership to property when legal title is held in another's name.

equity The interest or value that an owner has in property over and above any indebtedness.

erosion The gradual wearing away of land by water, wind and general weather conditions; the diminishing of property by the elements.

escheat The reversion of property to the state or county, as provided by state law, in cases where a decedent dies intestate without heirs capable of inheriting, or when the property is abandoned.

escrow The closing of a transaction through a third party called an *escrow agent,* or *escrowee,* who receives certain funds and documents to be delivered upon the performance of certain conditions outlined in the escrow instructions.

escrow account The trust account established by a broker under the provisions of the license law for the purpose of holding funds on behalf of the broker's principal or some other person until the consummation or termination of a transaction.

escrow instructions A document that sets forth the duties of the escrow agent, as well as the requirements and obligations of the parties, when a transaction is closed through an escrow.

estate (tenancy) at sufferance The tenancy of a lessee who lawfully comes into possession of a landlord's real estate but who continues to occupy the premises improperly after his or her lease rights have expired.

estate (tenancy) at will An estate that gives the lessee the right to possession until the estate is terminated by either party; the term of this estate is indefinite.

estate (tenancy) for years An interest for a certain, exact period of time in property leased for a specified consideration.

estate (tenancy) from period to period An interest in leased property that continues from period to period—week to week, month to month or year to year.

estate in land The degree, quantity, nature and extent of interest a person has in real property.

estate taxes Federal taxes on a decedent's real and personal property.

estoppel Method of creating an agency relationship in which someone states incorrectly that another person is his or her agent, and a third person relies on that representation.

estoppel certificate A document in which a borrower certifies the amount owed on a mortgage loan and the rate of interest.

ethics The system of moral principles and rules that becomes standards for professional conduct.

eviction A legal process to oust a person from possession of real estate.

evidence of title Proof of ownership of property; commonly a certificate of title, an abstract of title with lawyer's opinion, title insurance or a Torrens registration certificate.

exchange A transaction in which all or part of the consideration is the transfer of *like-kind* property (such as real estate for real estate).

exclusive-agency listing A listing contract under which the owner appoints a real estate broker as his or her exclusive agent for a designated period of time to sell the property, on the owner's stated terms, for a commission. The owner reserves the right to sell without paying anyone a commission if he or she sells to a prospect who has not been introduced or claimed by the broker.

exclusive-right-to-sell listing A listing contract under which the owner appoints a real estate broker as his or her exclusive agent for a designated period of time, to sell the property on the owner's stated terms, and agrees to pay the broker a commission when the property is sold, whether by the broker, the owner or another broker.

executed contract A contract in which all parties have fulfilled their promises and thus performed the contract.

execution The signing and delivery of an instrument. Also, a legal order directing an official to enforce a judgment against the property of a debtor.

executory contract A contract under which something remains to be done by one or more of the parties.

express agreement An oral or written contract in which the parties state the contract's terms and express their intentions in words.

express contract *See* express agreement.

external depreciation Reduction in a property's value caused by outside factors (those that are off the property).

Fair Housing Act The federal law that prohibits discrimination in housing based on race, color, religion, sex, handicap, familial status and national origin.

Fannie Mae *See* Federal National Mortgage Association (FNMA).

Farmer's Home Administration (FmHA) An agency of the federal government that provides credit assistance to farmers and other individuals who live in rural areas.

Federal Deposit Insurance Corporation (FDIC) An independent federal agency that insures the deposits in commercial banks.

Federal Home Loan Mortgage Corporation (FHLMC) A corporation established to purchase primarily conventional mortgage loans in the secondary mortgage market.

Federal National Mortgage Association (FNMA) A quasi-government agency established to purchase any kind of mortgage loans in the secondary mortgage market from the primary lenders.

Federal Reserve System The country's central banking system, which is responsible for the nation's monetary policy by regulating the supply of money and interest rates.

fee simple absolute The maximum possible estate or right of ownership of real property, continuing forever.

fee simple defeasible *See* defeasible fee estate.

feudal system A system of ownership usually associated with precolonial England, in which the king or other sovereign is the source of all rights. The right to possess real property was granted by the sovereign to an individual as a life estate only. Upon the death of the individual title passed back to the sovereign, not to the decedent's heirs.

FHA loan A loan insured by the Federal Housing Administration and made by an approved lender in accordance with the FHA's regulations.

fiduciary One in whom trust and confidence is placed; a reference to a broker employed under the terms of a listing contract or buyer agency agreement.

fiduciary relationship A relationship of trust and confidence, as between trustee and beneficiary, attorney and client or principal and agent.

Financial Institutions Reform, Recovery and Enforcement Act (FIRREA) This act restructured the savings and loan association regulatory system; enacted in response to the savings and loan crisis of the 1980s.

financing statement *See* Uniform Commercial Code.

fiscal policy The government's policy in regard to taxation and spending programs. The balance between these two areas determines the amount of money the government will withdraw from or feed into the economy, which can counter economic peaks and slumps.

fixture An item of personal property that has been converted to real property by being permanently affixed to the realty.

foreclosure A legal procedure whereby property used as security for a debt is sold to satisfy the debt in the event of default in payment of the mortgage note or default of other terms in the mortgage document. The foreclosure procedure brings the rights of all parties to a conclusion and passes the title in the mortgaged property to either the holder of the mortgage or a third party who may purchase the realty at the foreclosure sale, free of all encumbrances affecting the property subsequent to the mortgage.

fractional section A parcel of land less than 160 acres, usually found at the edge of a rectangular survey.

fraud Deception intended to cause a person to give up property or a lawful right.

Freddie Mac *See* Federal Home Loan Mortgage Corporation (FHLMC).

freehold estate An estate in land in which ownership is for an indeterminate length of time, in contrast to a *leasehold estate.*

front footage The measurement of a parcel of land by the number of feet of street or road frontage.

functional obsolescence A loss of value to an improvement to real estate arising from functional problems, often caused by age or poor design.

future interest A person's present right to an interest in real property that will not result in possession or enjoyment until some time in the future, such as a reversion or right of reentry.

gap A defect in the chain of title of a particular parcel of real estate; a missing document or conveyance that raises doubt as to the present ownership of the land.

general agent One who is authorized by a principal to represent the principal in a specific range of matters.

general lien The right of a creditor to have all of a debtor's property—both real and personal—sold to satisfy a debt.

general partnership *See* partnership.

general warranty deed A deed in which the grantor fully warrants good clear title to the premises. Used in most real estate deed transfers, a general warranty deed offers the greatest protection of any deed.

Ginnie Mae *See* Government National Mortgage Association (GNMA).

government check The 24-mile-square parcels composed of 16 townships in the rectangular (government) survey system of legal description.

government lot Fractional sections in the rectangular (government) survey system that are less than one quarter-section in area.

Government National Mortgage Association (GNMA) A government agency that plays an important role in the secondary mortgage market. It sells mortgage-backed securities that are backed by pools of FHA and VA loans.

government survey system *See* rectangular (government) survey system.

graduated-payment mortgage (GPM) A loan in which the monthly principal and interest payments increase by a certain percentage each year for a certain number of years and then level off for the remaining loan term.

grantee A person who receives a conveyance of real property from a grantor.

granting clause Words in a deed of conveyance that state the grantor's intention to convey the property at the present time. This clause is generally worded as "convey and warrant," "grant," "grant, bargain and sell" or the like.

grantor The person transferring title to or an interest in real property to a grantee.

gross income multiplier A figure used as a multiplier of the gross annual income of a property to produce an estimate of the property's value.

gross lease A lease of property according to which a landlord pays all property charges regularly incurred through ownership, such as repairs, taxes, insurance and operating expenses. Most residential leases are gross leases.

gross rent multiplier (GRM) The figure used as a multiplier of the gross monthly income of a property to produce an estimate of the property's value.

ground lease A lease of land only, on which the tenant usually owns a building or is required to build as specified in the lease. Such leases are usually long-term net leases; the tenant's rights and obligations continue until the lease expires or is terminated through default.

growing-equity mortgage (GEM) A loan in which the monthly payments increase annually, with the increased amount being used to reduce directly the principal balance outstanding and thus shorten the overall term of the loan.

habendum clause That part of a deed beginning with the words "to have and to hold," following the granting clause and defining the extent of ownership the grantor is conveying.

heir One who might inherit or succeed to an interest in land under the state law of descent when the owner dies without leaving a valid will.

highest and best use The possible use of a property that would produce the greatest net income and thereby develop the highest value.

holdover tenancy A tenancy whereby a lessee retains possession of leased property after the lease has expired and the landlord, by continuing to accept rent, agrees to the tenant's continued occupancy as defined by state law.

holographic will A will that is written, dated and signed in the testator's handwriting.

home equity loan A loan (sometimes called a *line of credit*) under which a property owner uses his or her residence as collateral and can then draw funds up to a prearranged amount against the property.

homeowner's insurance policy A standardized package insurance policy that covers a residential real estate owner against financial loss from fire, theft, public liability and other common risks.

homestead Land that is owned and occupied as the family home. In many states a portion of the area or value of this land is protected or exempt from judgments for debts.

hypothecate To pledge property as security for an obligation or loan without giving up possession of it.

implied agreement A contract under which the agreement of the parties is demonstrated by their acts and conduct.

implied contract *See* implied agreement.

implied warranty of habitability A theory in landlord/tenant law in which the landlord renting residential property implies that the property is habitable and fit for its intended use.

improvement (1) Any structure, usually privately owned, erected on a site to enhance the value of the property—for example, building a fence or a driveway. (2) A publicly owned structure added to or benefiting land, such as a curb, sidewalk, street or sewer.

income approach The process of estimating the value of an income-producing property through capitalization of the annual net income expected to be produced by the property during its remaining useful life.

incorporeal right A nonpossessory right in real estate; for example, an easement or a right-of-way.

independent contractor Someone who is retained to perform a certain act but who is subject to the control and direction of another only as to the end result and not as to the way in which the act is performed. Unlike an employee, an independent contractor pays for all expenses and social security and income taxes and receives no employee benefits. Most real estate salespeople are independent contractors.

index method The appraisal method of estimating building costs by multiplying the original cost of the property by a percentage factor to adjust for current construction costs.

inflation The gradual reduction of the purchasing power of the dollar, usually related directly to the increases in the money supply by the federal government.

inheritance taxes State-imposed taxes on a decedent's real and personal property.

installment contract A contract for the sale of real estate whereby the purchase price is paid in periodic installments by the purchaser, who is in possession of the property even though title is retained by the seller until a future date, which may be not until final payment. Also called a *contract for deed* or *articles of agreement for warranty deed*.

installment sale A transaction in which the sales price is paid in two or more installments over two or more years. If the sale meets certain requirements, a taxpayer can postpone reporting such income until future years by paying tax each year only on the proceeds received that year.

interest A charge made by a lender for the use of money.

interim financing A short-term loan usually made during the construction phase of a building project (in this case often referred to as a *construction loan*).

Interstate Land Sales Full Disclosure Act A federal law that regulates the sale of certain real estate in interstate commerce.

intestate The condition of a property owner who dies without leaving a valid will. Title to the property will pass to the decedent's heirs as provided in the state law of descent.

intrinsic value An appraisal term referring to the value created by a person's personal preferences for a particular type of property.

investment Money directed toward the purchase, improvement and development of an asset in expectation of income or profits.

involuntary alienation *See* alienation.

involuntary lien A lien placed on property without the consent of the property owner.

joint tenancy Ownership of real estate between two or more parties who have been named in one conveyance as joint tenants. Upon the death of a joint tenant, the decedent's interest passes to the surviving joint tenant or tenants by the *right of survivorship*.

joint venture The joining of two or more people to conduct a specific business enterprise. A joint venture is similar to a partnership in that it must be created by agreement between the parties to share in the losses and profits of the venture. It is unlike a partnership in that the venture is for one specific project only, rather than for a continuing business relationship.

judgment The formal decision of a court upon the respective rights and claims of the parties to an action or suit. After a judgment has been entered and recorded with the county recorder, it usually becomes a general lien on the property of the defendant.

judicial precedent In law, the requirements established by prior court decisions.

junior lien An obligation, such as a second mortgage, that is subordinate in right or lien priority to an existing lien on the same realty.

laches An equitable doctrine used by courts to bar a legal claim or prevent the assertion of a right because of undue delay or failure to assert the claim or right.

land The earth's surface, extending downward to the center of the earth and upward infinitely into space, including things permanently attached by nature, such as trees and water.

land contract *See* installment contract.

law of agency *See* agency.

lease A written or oral contract between a landlord (the lessor) and a tenant (the lessee) that transfers the right to exclusive possession and use of the landlord's real property to the lessee for a specified period of time and for a stated consideration (rent). By state law leases for longer than a certain period of time (generally one year) must be in writing to be enforceable.

leasehold estate A tenant's right to occupy real estate during the term of a lease, generally considered to be a personal property interest.

lease option A lease under which the tenant has the right to purchase the property either during the lease term or at its end.

lease purchase The purchase of real property, the consummation of which is preceded by a lease, usually long-term. Typically done for tax or financing purposes.

legacy A disposition of money or personal property by will.

legal description A description of a specific parcel of real estate complete enough for an independent surveyor to locate and identify it.

legally competent parties People who are recognized by law as being able to contract with others; those of legal age and sound mind.

lessee *See* lease.

lessor *See* lease.

leverage The use of borrowed money to finance an investment.

levy To assess; to seize or collect. To levy a tax is to assess a property and set the rate of taxation. To

levy an execution is to officially seize the property of a person in order to satisfy an obligation.

license (1) A privilege or right granted to a person by a state to operate as a real estate broker or salesperson. (2) The revocable permission for a temporary use of land—a personal right that cannot be sold.

lien A right given by law to certain creditors to have their debts paid out of the property of a defaulting debtor, usually by means of a court sale.

lien theory Some states interpret a mortgage as being purely a lien on real property. The mortgagee thus has no right of possession but must foreclose the lien and sell the property if the mortgagor defaults.

life cycle costing In property management, comparing one type of equipment to another based on both purchase cost and operating cost over its expected useful lifetime.

life estate An interest in real or personal property that is limited in duration to the lifetime of its owner or some other designated person or persons.

life tenant A person in possession of a life estate.

limited partnership *See* partnership.

liquidated damages An amount predetermined by the parties to a contract as the total compensation to an injured party should the other party breach the contract.

liquidity The ability to sell an asset and convert it into cash, at a price close to its true value, in a short period of time.

lis pendens A recorded legal document giving constructive notice that an action affecting a particular property has been filed in either a state or a federal court.

listing agreement A contract between an owner (as principal) and a real estate broker (as agent) by which the broker is employed as agent to find a buyer for the owner's real estate on the owner's terms, for which service the owner agrees to pay a commission.

listing broker The broker in a multiple-listing situation from whose office a listing agreement is initiated, as opposed to the *cooperating broker,* from whose office negotiations leading up to a sale are initiated. The listing broker and the cooperating broker may be the same person.

littoral rights (1) A landowner's claim to use water in large navigable lakes and oceans adjacent to his or her property. (2) The ownership rights to land bordering these bodies of water up to the high-water mark.

loan origination fee A fee charged to the borrower by the lender for making a mortgage loan. The fee is usually computed as a percentage of the loan amount.

loan-to-value ratio The relationship between the amount of the mortgage loan and the value of the real estate being pledged as collateral.

lot-and-block (recorded plat) system A method of describing real property that identifies a parcel of land by reference to lot and block numbers within a subdivision, as specified on a recorded subdivision plat.

management agreement A contract between the owner of income property and a management firm or individual property manager that outlines the scope of the manager's authority.

market A place where goods can be bought and sold and a price established.

marketable title Good or clear title, reasonably free from the risk of litigation over possible defects.

market value The most probable price property would bring in an arm's-length transaction under normal conditions on the open market.

master plan A comprehensive plan to guide the long-term physical development of a particular area.

mechanic's lien A statutory lien created in favor of contractors, laborers and materialmen who have performed work or furnished materials in the erection or repair of a building.

meridian One of a set of imaginary lines running north and south and crossing a base line at a definite point, used in the rectangular (government) survey system of property description.

metes-and-bounds description A legal description of a parcel of land that begins at a well-marked point and follows the boundaries, using directions and distances around the tract, back to the place of beginning.

mill One-tenth of one cent. Some states use a mill rate to compute real estate taxes; for example, a rate of 52 mills would be $0.052 tax for each dollar of assessed valuation of a property.

minor Someone who has not reached the age of majority and therefore does not have legal capacity to transfer title to real property.

monetary policy Governmental regulation of the amount of money in circulation through such institutions as the Federal Reserve Board.

month-to-month tenancy A periodic tenancy under which the tenant rents for one month at a time. In the absence of a rental agreement (oral or written) a tenancy is generally considered to be month to month.

monument A fixed natural or artificial object used to establish real estate boundaries for a metes-and-bounds description.

mortgage A conditional transfer or pledge of real estate as security for the payment of a debt. Also, the document creating a mortgage lien.

mortgage banker Mortgage loan companies that originate, service and sell loans to investors.

mortgage broker An agent of a lender who brings the lender and borrower together. The broker receives a fee for this service.

mortgagee A lender in a mortgage loan transaction.

mortgage lien A lien or charge on the property of a mortgagor that secures the underlying debt obligations.

mortgagor A borrower in a mortgage loan transaction.

multiperil policies Insurance policies that offer protection from a range of potential perils, such as those of a fire, hazard, public liability and casualty.

multiple-listing clause A provision in an exclusive listing for the authority and obligation on the part of the listing broker to distribute the listing to other brokers in the multiple-listing organization.

multiple-listing service (MLS). A marketing organization composed of member brokers who agree to share their listing agreements with one another in the hope of procuring ready, willing and able buyers for their properties more quickly than they could on their own. Most multiple-listing services accept exclusive-right-to-sell or exclusive agency listings from their member brokers.

negotiable instrument A written promise or order to pay a specific sum of money that may be transferred by endorsement or delivery. The transferee then has the original payee's right to payment.

net lease A lease requiring the tenant to pay not only rent but also costs incurred in maintaining the property, including taxes, insurance, utilities and repairs.

net listing A listing based on the net price the seller will receive if the property is sold. Under a net listing the broker can offer the property for sale at the highest price obtainable to increase the commission. This type of listing is illegal in many states.

net operating income (NOI) The income projected for an income-producing property after deducting losses for vacancy and collection and operating expenses.

nonconforming use A use of property that is permitted to continue after a zoning ordinance prohibiting it has been established for the area.

nonhomogeneity A lack of uniformity; dissimilarity. Because no two parcels of land are exactly alike, real estate is said to be nonhomogeneous.

note *See* **promissory note.**

novation Substituting a new obligation for an old one or substituting new parties to an existing obligation.

nuncupative will An oral will declared by the testator in his or her final illness, made before witnesses and afterward reduced to writing.

obsolescence The loss of value due to factors that are outmoded or less useful. Obsolescence may be functional or economic.

occupancy permit A permit issued by the appropriate local governing body to establish that the property is suitable for habitation by meeting certain safety and health standards.

offer and acceptance Two essential components of a valid contract; a "meeting of the minds."

offeror/offeree The person who makes the offer is the offeror. The person to whom the offer is made is the offeree.

Office of Thrift Supervision (OTS) Monitors and regulates the savings and loan industry. OTS was created by FIRREA.

open-end loan A mortgage loan that is expandable by increments up to a maximum dollar amount, the full loan being secured by the same original mortgage.

open listing A listing contract under which the broker's commission is contingent on the broker's producing a ready, willing and able buyer before the property is sold by the seller or another broker.

option An agreement to keep open for a set period an offer to sell or purchase property.

option listing Listing with a provision that gives the listing broker the right to purchase the listed property.

ostensible agency A form of implied agency relationship created by the actions of the parties involved rather than by written agreement or document.

package loan A real estate loan used to finance the purchase of both real property and personal property, such as in the purchase of a new home that includes carpeting, window coverings and major appliances.

parol evidence rule A rule of evidence providing that a written agreement is the final expression of the agreement of the parties, not to be varied or contradicted by prior or contemporaneous oral or written negotiations.

participation mortgage A mortgage loan wherein the lender has a partial equity interest in the property or receives a portion of the income from the property.

partition The division of cotenants' interests in real property when the parties do not all voluntarily agree to terminate the co-ownership; takes place through court procedures.

partnership An association of two or more individuals who carry on a continuing business for profit as co-owners. Under the law a partnership is regarded as a group of individuals rather than as a single entity. A *general partnership* is a typical form of joint venture in which each general partner shares in the administration, profits and losses of the operation. A *limited partnership* is a business arrangement whereby the operation is administered by one or more general partners and funded, by and large, by limited or silent partners,

who are by law responsible for losses only to the extent of their investments.

party wall A wall that is located on or at a boundary line between two adjoining parcels of land and is used or is intended to be used by the owners of both properties.

patent A grant or franchise of land from the United States government.

payment cap The limit on the amount the monthly payment can be increased on an adjustable-rate mortgage when the interest rate is adjusted.

payoff statement *See* reduction certificate.

percentage lease A lease, commonly used for commercial property, whose rental is based on the tenant's gross sales at the premises; it usually stipulates a base monthly rental plus a percentage of any gross sales above a certain amount.

percolation test A test of the soil to determine if it will absorb and drain water adequately to use a septic system for sewage disposal.

periodic estate (tenancy) *See* estate from period to period.

personal property Items, called *chattels,* that do not fit into the definition of real property; movable objects.

physical deterioration A reduction in a property's value resulting from a decline in physical condition; can be caused by action of the elements or by ordinary wear and tear.

planned unit development (PUD) A planned combination of diverse land uses, such as housing, recreation and shopping, in one contained development or subdivision.

plat map A map of a town, section or subdivision indicating the location and boundaries of individual properties.

plottage The increase in value or utility resulting from the consolidation (*assemblage*) of two or more adjacent lots into one larger lot.

point of beginning (POB) In a metes-and-bounds legal description, the starting point of the survey, situated in one corner of the parcel; all metes-and-bounds descriptions must follow the boundaries of the parcel back to the point of beginning.

police power The government's right to impose laws, statutes and ordinances, including zoning ordinances and building codes, to protect the public health, safety and welfare.

power of attorney A written instrument authorizing a person, the *attorney-in-fact,* to act as agent for another person to the extent indicated in the instrument.

prepaid items On a closing statement, items that have been paid in advance by the seller, such as insurance premiums and some real estate taxes, for which he or she must be reimbursed by the buyer.

prepayment penalty A charge imposed on a borrower who pays off the loan principal early. This penalty compensates the lender for interest and other charges that would otherwise be lost.

price-fixing *See* antitrust laws.

primary mortgage market The mortgage market in which loans are originated and consisting of lenders such as commercial banks, savings and loan associations and mutual savings banks.

principal (1) A sum loaned or employed as a fund or an investment, as distinguished from its income or profits. (2) The original amount (as in a loan) of the total due and payable at a certain date. (3) A main party to a transaction—the person for whom the agent works.

principal meridian The main imaginary line running north and south and crossing a base line at a definite point, used by surveyors for reference in locating and describing land under the rectangular (government) survey system of legal description.

prior appropriation A concept of water ownership in which the landowner's right to use available water is based on a government-administered permit system.

priority The order of position or time. The priority of liens is generally determined by the chronological order in which the lien documents are recorded; tax liens, however, have priority even over previously recorded liens.

private mortgage insurance (PMI) Insurance provided by private carrier that protects a lender against a loss in the event of a foreclosure and deficiency.

probate A legal process by which a court determines who will inherit a decedent's property and what the estate's assets are.

procuring cause The effort that brings about the desired result. Under an open listing the broker who is the procuring cause of the sale receives the commission.

progression An appraisal principle that states that, between dissimilar properties. the value of the lesser-quality property is favorably affected by the presence of the better-quality property.

promissory note A financing instrument that states the terms of the underlying obligation, is signed by its maker and is negotiable (transferable to a third party).

property manager Someone who manages real estate for another person for compensation. Duties include collecting rents, maintaining the property and keeping up all accounting.

property reports The mandatory federal and state documents compiled by subdividers and developers to provide potential purchasers with facts about a property prior to their purchase.

proprietary lease A lease given by the corporation that owns a cooperative apartment building to the shareholder for the shareholder's right as a tenant to an individual apartment.

prorations Expenses, either prepaid or paid in arrears, that are divided or distributed between buyer and seller at the closing.

protected class Any group of people designated as such by the Department of Housing and Urban Development (HUD) in consideration of federal and state civil rights legislation. Currently includes ethnic minorities, women, religious groups, the handicapped and others.

puffing Exaggerated or superlative comments or opinions.

pur autre vie "For the life of another." A life estate pur autre vie is a life estate that is measured by the life of a person other than the grantee.

purchase-money mortgage (PMM) A note secured by a mortgage or deed of trust given by a buyer, as borrower, to a seller, as lender, as part of the purchase price of the real estate.

pyramiding The process of acquiring additional properties by refinancing properties already owned and investing the loan proceeds in additional properties.

quantity-survey method The appraisal method of estimating building costs by calculating the cost of all of the physical components in the improvements, adding the cost to assemble them and then including the indirect costs associated with such construction.

quiet title A court action to remove a cloud on the title.

quitclaim deed A conveyance by which the grantor transfers whatever interest he or she has in the real estate, without warranties or obligations.

range A strip of land six miles wide, extending north and south and numbered east and west according to its distance from the principal meridian in the rectangular (government) survey system of legal description.

rate cap The limit on the amount the interest rate can be increased at each adjustment period in an adjustable-rate loan. The cap may also set the maximum interest rate that can be charged during the life of the loan.

ratification Method of creating an agency relationship in which the principal accepts the conduct of someone who acted without prior authorization as the principal's agent.

ready, willing and able buyer One who is prepared to buy property on the seller's terms and is ready to take positive steps to consummate the transaction.

real estate Land; a portion of the earth's surface extending downward to the center of the earth and upward infinitely into space, including all things permanently attached to it, whether naturally or artificially.

real estate investment syndicate *See* syndicate.

real estate investment trust (REIT) Trust ownership of real estate by a group of individuals who purchase certificates of ownership in the trust, which in turn invests the money in real property and distributes the profits back to the investors free of corporate income tax.

real estate license law State law enacted to protect the public from fraud, dishonesty and incompetence in the purchase and sale of real estate.

real estate mortgage investment conduit (REMIC) A tax entity that issues multiple classes of investor interests (securities) backed by a pool of mortgages.

real estate recovery fund A fund established in some states from real estate license revenues to cover claims of aggrieved parties who have suffered monetary damage through the actions of a real estate licensee.

Real Estate Settlement Procedures Act (RESPA) The federal law that requires certain disclosures to consumers about mortgage loan settlements. The law also prohibits the payment or receipt of kickbacks and certain kinds of referral fees.

real property The interests, benefits and rights inherent in real estate ownership.

REALTOR® A registered trademark term reserved for the sole use of active members of local REALTOR® boards affiliated with the National Association of REALTORS®.

reconciliation The final step in the appraisal process, in which the appraiser combines the estimates of value received from the sales comparison, cost and income approaches to arrive at a final estimate of market value for the subject property.

reconveyance deed A deed used by a trustee under a deed of trust to return title to the trustor.

recording The act of entering or recording documents affecting or conveying interests in real estate in the recorder's office established in each county. Until it is recorded, a deed or mortgage ordinarily is not effective against subsequent purchasers or mortgagees.

rectangular (government) survey system A system established in 1785 by the federal government, providing for surveying and describing land by reference to principal meridians and base lines.

redemption The right of a defaulted property owner to recover his or her property by curing the default.

redemption period A period of time established by state law during which a property owner has the right to redeem his or her real estate from a foreclosure or tax sale by paying the sales price, interest and costs. Many states do not have mortgage redemption laws.

redlining The illegal practice of a lending institution denying loans or restricting their number for certain areas of a community.

reduction certificate (payoff statement) The document signed by a lender indicating the amount required to pay a loan balance in full and satisfy the debt; used in the settlement process to protect both the seller's and the buyer's interests.

regression An appraisal principle that states that, between dissimilar properties, the value of the better-quality property is affected adversely by the presence of the lesser-quality property.

Regulation Z Implements the Truth-in-Lending Act requiring credit institutions to inform borrowers of the true cost of obtaining credit.

release deed A document, also known as a *deed of reconveyance,* that transfers all rights given a trustee under a deed of trust loan back to the grantor after the loan has been fully repaid.

remainder interest The remnant of an estate that has been conveyed to take effect and be enjoyed after the termination of a prior estate, such as when an owner conveys a life estate to one party and the remainder to another.

rent A fixed, periodic payment made by a tenant of a property to the owner for possession and use, usually by prior agreement of the parties.

rent schedule A statement of proposed rental rates, determined by the owner or the property manager or both, based on a building's estimated expenses, market supply and demand and the owner's long-range goals for the property.

replacement cost The construction cost at current prices of a property that is not necessarily an exact duplicate of the subject property but serves the same purpose or function as the original.

reproduction cost The construction cost at current prices of an exact duplicate of the subject property.

Resolution Trust Corporation The organization created by FIRREA to liquidate the assets of failed savings and loan associations.

restrictive covenants A clause in a deed that limits the way the real estate ownership may be used.

reverse-annuity mortgage (RAM) A loan under which the homeowner receives monthly payments based on his or her accumulated equity rather than a lump sum. The loan must be repaid at a prearranged date or upon the death of the owner or the sale of the property.

reversionary interest The remnant of an estate that the grantor holds after granting a life estate to another person.

reversionary right The return of the rights of possession and quiet enjoyment to the lessor at the expiration of a lease.

right of survivorship *See* joint tenancy.

right-of-way The right given by one landowner to another to pass over the land, construct a roadway or use as a pathway, without actually transferring ownership.

riparian rights An owner's rights in land that borders on or includes a stream, river or lake. These rights include access to and use of the water.

risk management Evaluation and selection of appropriate property and other insurance.

rules and regulations Real estate licensing authority orders that govern licensees' activities; they usually have the same force and effect as statutory law.

sale and leaseback A transaction in which an owner sells his or her improved property and, as part of the same transaction, signs a long-term lease to remain in possession of the premises.

sales comparison approach The process of estimating the value of a property by examining and comparing actual sales of comparable properties.

salesperson A person who performs real estate activities while employed by or associated with a licensed real estate broker.

satisfaction of mortgage A document acknowledging the payment of a mortgage debt.

secondary mortgage market A market for the purchase and sale of existing mortgages, designed to provide greater liquidity for mortgages; also called the *secondary money market.* Mortgages are first originated in the *primary mortgage market.*

section A portion of township under the rectangular (government) survey system. A township is divided into 36 sections, numbered one through 36. A section is a square with mile-long sides and an area of one square mile, or 640 acres.

security agreement *See* Uniform Commercial Code.

security deposit A payment by a tenant, held by the landlord during the lease term and kept (wholly or partially) on default or destruction of the premises by the tenant.

separate property Under community property law, property owned solely by either spouse before the marriage, acquired by gift or inheritance after the marriage or purchased with separate funds after the marriage.

servient tenement Land on which an easement exists in favor of an adjacent property (called a *dominant estate*); also called a *servient estate.*

setback The amount of space local zoning regulations require between a lot line and a building line.

severalty Ownership of real property by one person only, also called *sole ownership.*

severance Changing an item of real estate to personal property by detaching it from the land; for example, cutting down a tree.

sharecropping In an agricultural lease, the agreement between the landowner and the tenant farmer to split the crop or the profit from its sale, actually sharing the crop.

shared-appreciation mortgage (SAM) A mortgage loan in which the lender, in exchange for a loan with a favorable interest rate, participates in the profits (if any) the borrower receives when the property is eventually sold.

situs The personal preference of people for one area over another, not necessarily based on objective facts and knowledge.

special agent One who is authorized by a principal to perform a single act or transaction; a real estate broker is usually a special agent authorized to find a ready, willing and able buyer for a particular property.

special assessment A tax or levy customarily imposed against only those specific parcels of real estate that will benefit from a proposed public improvement like a street or sewer.

special warranty deed A deed in which the grantor warrants, or guarantees, the title only against defects arising during the period of his or her tenure and ownership of the property and not against defects existing before that time, generally using the language, "by, through or under the grantor but not otherwise."

specific lien A lien affecting or attaching only to a certain, specific parcel of land or piece of property.

specific performance A legal action to compel a party to carry out the terms of a contract.

square-foot method The appraisal method of estimating building costs by multiplying the number of square feet in the improvements being appraised by the cost per square foot for recently constructed similar improvements.

statute of frauds That part of a state law that requires certain instruments, such as deeds, real estate sales contracts and certain leases, to be in writing to be legally enforceable.

statute of limitations That law pertaining to the period of time within which certain actions must be brought to court.

statutory lien A lien imposed on property by statute—a tax lien, for example—in contrast to an *equitable lien,* which arises out of common law.

statutory redemption The right of a defaulted property owner to recover the property after its sale by paying the appropriate fees and charges.

steering The illegal practice of channeling home seekers to particular areas, either to maintain the homogeneity of an area or to change the character of an area, which limits their choices of where they can live.

straight-line method A method of calculating depreciation for tax purposes, computed by dividing the adjusted basis of a property by the estimated number of years of remaining useful life.

straight (term) loan A loan in which only interest is paid during the term of the loan, with the entire principal amount due with the final interest payment.

subagent One who is employed by a person already acting as an agent. Typically a reference to a salesperson licensed under a broker (agent) who is employed under the terms of a listing agreement.

subdivider One who buys undeveloped land, divides it into smaller, usable lots and sells the lots to potential users.

subdivision A tract of land divided by the owner, known as the *subdivider,* into blocks, building lots and streets according to a recorded subdivision plat, which must comply with local ordinances and regulations.

subdivision and development ordinances Municipal ordinances that establish requirements for subdivisions and development.

subdivision plat *See* plat map.

sublease *See* subletting.

subletting The leasing of premises by a lessee to a third party for part of the lessee's remaining term. *See also* assignment.

subordination Relegation to a lesser position, usually in respect to a right or security.

subordination agreement A written agreement between holders of liens on a property that changes the priority of mortgage, judgment and other liens under certain circumstances.

subrogation The substitution of one creditor for another, with the substituted person succeeding to the legal rights and claims of the original claimant. Subrogation is used by title insurers to acquire from the injured party rights to sue in order to recover any claims they have paid.

substitution An appraisal principle that states that the maximum value of a property tends to be set by the cost of purchasing an equally desirable and valuable substitute property, assuming that no costly delay is encountered in making the substitution.

subsurface rights Ownership rights in a parcel of real estate to the water, minerals, gas, oil and so forth that lie beneath the surface of the property.

suit for possession A court suit initiated by a landlord to evict a tenant from leased premises after the tenant has breached one of the terms of the lease or has held possession of the property after the lease's expiration.

suit to quiet title A court action intended to establish or settle the title to a particular property, especially when there is a cloud on the title.

supply The amount of goods available in the market to be sold at a given price. The term is often coupled with *demand.*

supply and demand The appraisal principle that follows the interrelationship of the supply of and demand for real estate. As appraising is based on economic concepts, this principle recognizes that real property is subject to the influences of the marketplace just as is any other commodity.

surety bond An agreement by an insurance or bonding company to be responsible for certain possible defaults, debts or obligations contracted for by an insured party; in essence, a policy insuring one's personal and/or financial integrity. In the real estate business a surety bond is generally used to ensure that a particular project will be completed at a certain date or that a contract will be performed as stated.

surface rights Ownership rights in a parcel of real estate that are limited to the surface of the property and do not include the air above it (*air rights*) or the minerals below the surface (*subsurface rights*).

survey The process by which boundaries are measured and land areas are determined; the on-site measurement of lot lines, dimensions and position of a house on a lot, including the determination of any existing encroachments or easements.

syndicate A combination of people or firms formed to accomplish a business venture of mutual interest by pooling resources. In a *real estate investment syndicate* the parties own and/or develop property, with the main profit generally arising from the sale of the property.

tacking Adding or combining successive periods of continuous occupation of real property by adverse possessors. This concept enables someone who has not been in possession for the entire statutory period to establish a claim of adverse possession.

taxation The process by which a government or municipal quasi-public body raises monies to fund its operation.

tax credit An amount by which tax owed is reduced directly.

tax deed An instrument, similar to a certificate of sale, given to a purchaser at a tax sale. *See also* certificate of sale.

tax lien A charge against property, created by operation of law. Tax liens and assessments take priority over all other liens.

tax sale A court-ordered sale of real property to raise money to cover delinquent taxes.

tenancy by the entirety The joint ownership, recognized in some states, of property acquired by husband and wife during marriage. Upon the death of one spouse the survivor becomes the owner of the property.

tenancy in common A form of co-ownership by which each owner holds an undivided interest in real property as if he or she were sole owner. Each individual owner has the right to partition. Unlike joint tenants, tenants in common have right of inheritance.

tenant One who holds or possesses lands or tenements by any kind of right or title.

tenant improvements Alterations to the interior of a building to meet the functional demands of the tenant.

testate Having made and left a valid will.

testator A person who has made a valid will. A woman often is referred to as a *testatrix*, although testator can be used for either gender.

tier (township strip) A strip of land six miles wide, extending east and west and numbered north and south according to its distance from the base line in the rectangular (government) survey system of legal description.

time is of the essence A phrase in a contract that requires the performance of a certain act within a stated period of time.

time-share A form of ownership interest that may include an estate interest in property and which allows use of the property for a fixed or variable time period.

title (1) The right to or ownership of land. (2) The evidence of ownership of land.

title insurance A policy insuring the owner or mortgagee against loss by reason of defects in the title to a parcel of real estate, other than encumbrances, defects and matters specifically excluded by the policy.

title search The examination of public records relating to real estate to determine the current state of the ownership.

title theory Some states interpret a mortgage to mean that the lender is the owner of mortgaged land. Upon full payment of the mortgage debt the borrower becomes the landowner.

Torrens system A method of evidencing title by registration with the proper public authority, generally called the *registrar,* named for its founder, Sir Robert Torrens.

township The principal unit of the rectangular (government) survey system. A township is a square with six-mile sides and an area of 36 square miles.

township strips *See* tier.

trade fixture An article installed by a tenant under the terms of a lease and removable by the tenant before the lease expires.

transfer tax Tax stamps required to be affixed to a deed by state and/or local law.

trust A fiduciary arrangement whereby property is conveyed to a person or institution, called a *trustee,* to be held and administered on behalf of another person, called a *beneficiary.* The one who conveys the trust is called the *trustor.*

trust deed An instrument used to create a mortgage lien by which the borrower conveys title to a trustee, who holds it as security for the benefit of the note holder (the lender); also called a *deed of trust.*

trust deed lien A lien on the property of a trustor that secures a deed of trust loan.

trustee The holder of bare legal title in a deed of trust loan transaction.

trustee's deed A deed executed by a trustee conveying land held in a trust.

trustor A borrower in a deed of trust loan transaction.

undivided interest *See* tenancy in common.

unenforceable contract A contract that has all the elements of a valid contract, yet neither party can sue the other to force performance of it. For example, an unsigned contract is generally unenforceable.

Uniform Commercial Code A codification of commercial law, adopted in most states, that attempts to make uniform all laws relating to commercial transactions, including chattel mortgages and bulk transfers. Security interests in chattels are created by an instrument known as a *security agreement.* To give notice of the security interest, a *financing statement* must be recorded. Article 6 of the code regulates *bulk transfers*—the sale of a business as a whole, including all fixtures, chattels and merchandise.

unilateral contract A one-sided contract wherein one party makes a promise so as to induce a second party to do something. The second party is not legally bound to perform; however, if the second party does comply, the first party is obligated to keep the promise.

unit-in-place method The appraisal method of estimating building costs by calculating the costs of all of the physical components in the structure, with the cost of each item including its proper installation, connection, etc.; also called the *segregated cost method.*

unit of ownership The four unities that are traditionally needed to create a joint tenancy—unity of title, time, interest and possession.

usury Charging interest at a higher rate than the maximum rate established by state law.

valid contract A contract that complies with all the essentials of a contract and is binding and enforceable on all parties to it.

VA loan A mortgage loan on approved property made to a qualified veteran by an authorized lender and guaranteed by the Department of Veterans Affairs in order to limit the lender's possible loss.

value The power of a good or service to command other goods in exchange for the present worth of future rights to its income or amenities.

variance Permission obtained from zoning authorities to build a structure or conduct a use that is expressly prohibited by the current zoning laws; an exception from the zoning ordinances.

vendee A buyer, usually under the terms of a land contract.

vendor A seller, usually under the terms of a land contract.

voidable contract A contract that seems to be valid on the surface but may be rejected or disaffirmed by one or both of the parties.

void contract A contract that has no legal force or effect because it does not meet the essential elements of a contract.

voluntary alienation *See* alienation.

voluntary lien A lien placed on property with the knowledge and consent of the property owner.

waste An improper use or an abuse of a property by a possessor who holds less than fee ownership, such as a tenant, life tenant, mortgagor or vendee. Such waste ordinarily impairs the value of the land or the interest of the person holding the title or the reversionary rights.

will A written document, properly witnessed, providing for the transfer of title to property owned by the deceased, called the *testator*.

workers' compensation acts Laws that require an employer to obtain insurance coverage to protect his or her employees who are injured in the course of their employment.

wraparound loan A method of refinancing in which the new mortgage is placed in a secondary, or subordinate, position; the new mortgage includes both the unpaid principal balance of the first mortgage and whatever additional sums are advanced by the lender. In essence it is an additional mortgage in which another lender refinances a borrower by lending an amount over the existing first mortgage amount without disturbing the existence of the first mortgage.

zoning ordinance An exercise of police power by a municipality to regulate and control the character and use of property.

Answer Key

Following are the correct answers to the review questions included in each chapter of the text (except Chapter 13, which has no questions). In parentheses following the correct answers are references to the pages where the question topics are discussed or explained. If you have answered a question incorrectly, be sure to go back to the page or pages noted and restudy the material until you understand the correct answer.

Chapter 1
Introduction to the
Real Estate Business
  1. b (5)
  2. b (6)
  3. d (6)
  4. b (5)

Chapter 2
Real Property and
the Law
  1. c (10)
  2. b (14)
  3. c (16)
  4. c (16)
  5. d (16)
  6. d (10)
  7. a (12-13)
  8. a (15)
  9. a (13)
10. a (13)
11. c (11)

Chapter 3
Concepts of Home
Ownership
  1. d (24)
  2. b (24)
  3. a (22)

  4. b (27)
  5. c (24-25)
  6. b (21)
  7. b (25)
  8. d (25)
  9. d (26-27)
10. b (25)
11. c (25)
12. a (25)

Chapter 4
Real Estate
Brokerage and
Agency
  1. a (35)
  2. d (33)
  3. a (35)
  4. a (34)
  5. b (48)
  6. c (48)
  7. b (36-37)
  8. d (37-38, 41)
  9. b (48)
10. d (33-34)
11. b (46)
12. a (48)
13. d (47)
14. a (37-38)
15. c (38, 41)

16. d (49)
17. c (42-43)
18. b (42)

Chapter 5
Listing Agreements
  1. a (57)
  2. c (57-58)
  3. c (59-60)
  4. a (58)
  5. c (62)
  6. d (59)
  7. b (63-64, 67-68)
  8. c (61)
  9. a (57)
10. c (58)
11. b (59-60)
12. a (58)
13. b (57)
14. b (61)
15. a (62)

Chapter 6
Interests in Real
Estate
  1. b (73)
  2. a (74)
  3. c (74, 76)
  4. d (80)

  5. c (82)
  6. a (76-77)
  7. d (78-79)
  8. d (81)
  9. c (84)
10. a (72-73)
11. b (74)
12. b (80)
13. a (78)
14. b (77)
15. b (82)
16. c (78)
17. d (82)
18. a (79)
19. d (74)

Chapter 7
How Ownership
Is Held
  1. d (91)
  2. b (90)
  3. a (90, 94)
  4. b (98)
  5. b (94)
  6. d (93)
  7. b (90)
  8. a (94)
  9. b (98-99)
10. c (99-100)

11. d (90, 96)
12. d (89)
13. d (90)
14. b (99)
15. b (90)
16. c (97)
17. b (97)
18. b (90, 92)
19. d (98)
20. a (94)

Chapter 8
Legal Descriptions
1. b (108-109)
2. d (107)
3. d (108-109)
4. b (105)
5. b (108-110)
6. b (108-110)
7. d (108-110)
8. c (108-110)
9. a (108-110)
10. b (116)
11. d (111)
12. c (108)
13. d (111)
14. c (108)
15. d (109)
16. b (110)
17. b (117)
18. b (111)
19. b (116)
20. b (116)
21. b (110)
22. b (116)
23. c (110)
24. d (117)
25. b (109)
26. c (105)

Chapter 9
Real Estate Taxes
and Other Liens
1. d (123)
2. b (124)
3. b (128)
4. c (123)
5. b (129-130)
6. c (126-127)
7. c (125)
8. c (129)
9. b (126)
10. c (129)
11. d (130)

12. d (130)
13. c (128-129)
14. b (129)
15. b (129-130)
16. d (129)
17. d (128)
18. a (125)
19. b (125)
20. d (125)

Chapter 10
Real Estate Contracts
1. c (137)
2. b (136)
3. d (136)
4. b (137)
5. c (137)
6. d (140)
7. d (139)
8. d (141)
9. a (144)
10. a (146)
11. d (146)
12. b (150)
13. d (150)
14. d (150)
15. c (136)
16. b (138)
17. b (142-143)
18. a (139)
19. b (138)

Chapter 11
Transfer of Title
1. a (155)
2. a (155)
3. d (156)
4. a (157)
5. b (159)
6. c (156)
7. d (160)
8. d (161)
9. b (160)
10. c (155, 158)
11. b (156)
12. b (157)
13. b (158)
14. c (163)
15. b (163)
16. d (163)
17. a (163)
18. a (162)
19. b (164-165)
20. d (164)

21. a (164)
22. c (165-166)

Chapter 12
Title Records
1. a (170)
2. a (170)
3. c (170)
4. a (170)
5. a (171)
6. d (173)
7. d (173)
8. d (171)
9. c (172)
10. a (172-173)
11. c (170)
12. c (174)
13. b (174)
14. d (175)
15. c (174)
16. a (173-175)
17. b (175-176)

Chapter 14
Real Estate
Financing: Principles
1. d (192)
2. a (194)
3. a (188)
4. d (196)
5. d (196)
6. b (189, 192)
7. d (198)
8. d (194)
9. a (194-195)
10. a (196)
11. b (193)
12. d (196)
13. b (197)
14. a (188)
15. b (192)

Chapter 15
Real Estate
Financing: Practice
1. b (212)
2. d (212)
3. c (218-219)
4. c (207)
5. b (215-216)
6. c (215)
7. a (203)
8. a (215)
9. b (217)

10. c (206)
11. b (212)
12. c (208)
13. b (219)
14. a (207)
15. b (202-203)
16. b (218)
17. c (212)
18. a (205)
19. a (203)
20. b (218)
21. d (220)
22. c (203)

Chapter 16
Leases
1. c (237)
2. c (237)
3. d (235)
4. a (227)
5. c (226)
6. b (232)
7. d (228)
8. c (226)
9. b (234)
10. b (235)
11. b (227)
12. a (232)
13. a (233)
14. b (236)
15. d (228)
16. c (237)

Chapter 17
Property Management
1. b (256)
2. a (252)
3. d (252)
4. c (256)
5. c (252)
6. b (256)
7. b (254)
8. c (247)
9. a (252)
10. c (256)
11. c (257)
12. c (252)
13. b (254)

Chapter 18
Real Estate Appraisal
1. c (270)
2. b (262)
3. b (264)

4. b (262)

5. d (264)

6. a (264-265)

7. d (269)

8. c (272)

9. b (268)

10. d (270-271)

11. c (270-271)

12. c (270)

13. c (262-263)

14. b (270)

15. c (267)

16. b (265)

17. d (265)

18. b (270)

19. a (268)

20. b (269)

21. d (268)

Chapter 19
Control of Land Use

1. a (287)

2. a (285)

3. b (282)

4. c (282)

5. c (286)

6. b (287)

7. a (283)

8. b (285)

9. a (285)

10. d (284-285)

11. b (287)

12. a (287)

Chapter 20
Property
Development and
Subdivision

1. b (294)

2. a (292)

3. c (294)

4. b (295)

5. b (295)

6. b (287)

7. d (293)

8. d (294)

9. a (295-296)

10. a (295)

11. a (296)

Chapter 21
Fair Housing and
Ethical Practices

1. c (301-304)

2. a (300, 308-309)

3. d (300)

4. b (306-307)

5. c (307)

6. a (308)

7. b (301)

8. c (303)

9. c (307)

10. b (301)

11. a (303-304)

12. c (311)

13. d (309)

14. c (302)

15. d (307)

Chapter 22
Introduction to Real
Estate Investment

1. c (322)

2. b (323)

3. b (323)

4. a (324)

5. b (325)

6. b (325)

7. c (324)

8. d (327)

9. a (326)

10. c (324)

11. d (328)

12. a (329)

13. c (328)

14. b (328)

15. b (329)

Chapter 23
Closing the Real
Estate Transaction

1. d (343)

2. b (340)

3. d (339)

4. a (339)

5. d (335)

6. c (336)

7. c (340)

8. b (344)

9. b (344)

10. a (344-346)

11. c (344)

12. a (344)

13. b (348-351)

14. b (348-351)

15. c (341)

16. b (342)

17. d (336-337)

18. d (336-337)

Mathematics Review

1. $79,500 sales price × 6½% commission =
   $79,500 × 0.065 = $5,167.50, Happy Valley's commission
   $5,167.50 × 30% or $5,167.50 × 0.30 = $1,550.25, listing
   salesperson's commission

   b. $1,550.25

2.

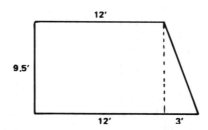

   12′ × 9.5′ = 114 square feet, area of rectangle
   ½ (3′ × 9.5′) = ½ (28.5) = 14.25 square feet, area of triangle
   114 + 14.25 = 128.25 square feet
   To convert square feet to square yards divide by 9:
   128.25 ÷ 9 = 14.25 square yards
   $16.95 carpet + $2.50 installation = $19.45 cost per square yard
   $19.45 × 14.25 square yards = $277.1625 rounded to $277.16

   c. $277.16

3. $30,000 Peters + $35,000 Gamble + $35,000 Clooney = $100,000
   $125,000 − $100,000 = $25,000 Considine's contribution
   $\dfrac{\text{part}}{\text{total}}$ = percent
   $25,000 ÷ $125,000 = 0.20 or 20%

   a. 20%

4. $391.42 × 12 = $4,697.04, annual interest
   $\dfrac{\text{part}}{\text{percent}}$ = total
   $4,697.04 ÷ 111½% or $4,697.04 ÷ 0.115 = $40,843.826
   rounded to $40,843.83

   b. $40,843.83

5. $98,500 × 5% = $98,500 × 0.05 = $4,925, annual increase in value
   $98,500 + $4,925 = $103,425, current market value

   a. $103,425

6. $95,000 × 60% = $95,000 × 0.60 = $57,000 assessed value
   Divide by 100 because tax rate is stated per hundred dollars:
   $57,000 ÷ 100 = $570
   $570 × $2.85 = $1,624.50, annual taxes

   d. $1,624.50

7.

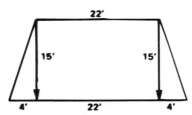

22′ × 15′ = 330 square feet, area of rectangle
½ = (4′ × 15′) = ½ (60) = 30 square feet, area of each triangle
30 × 2 = 60 square feet, area of two triangles
330 + 60 = 390 square feet, surface area to be paved
6″ deep = ½ foot
390 × ½ = 195 cubic feet, cement needed for patio   **d. 195 cubic feet**

8. $4,175 − $1,000 salary = $3,175 commission on sales
$3,175 ÷ 2.5% = $3,175 ÷ 0.025 = $127,000, value of property sold   **b. $127,000**

9. two sides of 95′ plus one side of 42′6″
95′ × 2 = 190 feet
42′6″ = 42.5 feet
190 + 42.5 = 232.5 linear feet
232.5 × $6.95 = $1,615.875 rounded to $1,615.88   **c. $1,615.88**

10. $4,500 × 12 = $54,000 annual rental
$54,000 ÷ 8% = $54,000 ÷ 0.08 = $675,000, original cost of property   **a. $675,000**

11. $1,340 ÷ 12 months = $111.667/month
$111.667 ÷ 30 days = $3.722/day
$111.667 × 2 months = $223.334
$3.722 × 15 days = $55.83
$223.334 + $55.83 = $279.164 rounded to $279.16   **b. $279.16**

12. $58,200 × 12% = $58,200 × 0.12 = $6,984
$6,984 ÷ 12 months = $582/month
$582 ÷ 30 days = $19.40/day
$19.40 per day × 11 days = $213.40   **d. $213.40**

13. $975 ÷ 12 months = $81.25/month
$81.25 ÷ 30 days = $2.708
$81.25 × 2 months = $162.500
$2.708 × 4 days = $10.832
$162.500 + $10.832 = $173.332 rounded to $173.33   **a. $173.33**

14. $61,550 × 13% = $61,550 × 0.13 = $8,001.500
$8,001.500 ÷ 12 months = $666.792/month
$666.792 ÷ 30 days = $22.226/day
$22.226 × 22 days = $488.972 rounded to $488.97   **b. $488.97**

15. 43,560 sq. ft./acre × 100 acres = 4,356,000 sq. ft.
    4,356,000 total sq. ft. × ⅛ = 544,500 sq. ft. for streets
    4,356,000 − 544,500 = 3,811,500 sq. ft. for lots
    3,811,500 sq. ft. ÷ 140 lots = 27,225 sq. ft./lot   **c. 27,225**

16. $14,100 commission ÷ 6% commission rate =
    $14,100 ÷ 0.06 = $235,000 sales price   **a. $235,000**

17. 24′ × 36′ = 864 sq. ft; entrance 2′ × 4′ = 8 sq. ft.
    864 sq. ft. − 8 sq. ft. = 856 sq. ft. + 864 = 1,720 sq. ft.   **c.**

18. 9′ × 12′ × 12′ = 1,296 divided by 27 = 48   **c.**

19. 3½% (.035) × $2,250,000.00 = $78,750.00   **a.**

20. 6½% (.065) × $325,000.00 = $21,125.00 × .65 (65%) = $13,731.25   **d.**

21. 65,340 sq. ft. divided by 43,560 sq. ft. = 1½ acres.   **b.**

22. Divide $5,800 by $145,000 = .040 or 40 mills.   **a.**

23. Divide $260,000.00 by 93% = $279,569.89, rounded to $279,600.   **c.**

24. 28% (.28) × $82,000 = $22,960 divided by 12 = $1,913.33
    (maximum monthly payment)
    Divide the yearly tax $4,200 by 12 to find the month = $350/month.
    $1,913.33 − $350.00 = $1,563.33 ÷ 11.30 = 138.3477—converted to thousands = $138,348   **c.**

25. $875,000 × 11% (.11) = $96,250   **a.**

26. $28,875 divided by $275,000 = 10½%. (.105)   **c.**

27. To convert square feet to square yards, divide by 9
    (3 × 3 = 9) to arrive at 4,570 square yards.   **b.**

28. Multiply 40″ × 72″ = 2,880 sq. in.;
    convert to square feet by dividing by 144 (12 × 12 = 144)
    to arrive at 20 square feet.   **b.**

Sample Examination
One

1. b	21. a	41. d	61. c
2. a	22. d	42. b	62. a
3. a	23. b	43. c	63. d
4. c	24. b	44. b	64. d
5. c	25. c	45. d	65. b
6. b	26. d	46. d	66. d
7. a	27. b	47. c	67. b
8. a	28. b	48. d	68. d
9. a	29. b	49. b	69. a
10. d	30. b	50. b	70. a
11. d	31. d	51. b	71. d
12. a	32. d	52. b	72. d
13. b	33. b	53. c	73. a
14. a	34. b	54. d	74. d
15. a	35. b	55. b	75. b
16. c	36. a	56. c	76. c
17. d	37. a	57. a	77. d
18. b	38. b	58. b	78. b
19. a	39. a	59. d	79. d
20. b	40. a	60. b	80. d

Sample Examination
Two

1. d	21. c	41. b	61. d
2. c	22. b	42. c	62. c
3. c	23. a	43. b	63. c
4. b	24. b	44. d	64. b
5. c	25. d	45. c	65. a
6. d	26. d	46. d	66. b
7. d	27. b	47. a	67. b
8. d	28. b	48. a	68. d
9. b	29. b	49. b	69. c
10. b	30. d	50. c	70. a
11. b	31. d	51. c	71. d
12. a	32. b	52. a	72. c
13. d	33. a	53. c	73. a
14. c	34. d	54. a	74. d
15. d	35. b	55. d	75. b
16. a	36. a	56. a	76. c
17. b	37. b	57. b	77. d
18. b	38. d	58. b	78. a
19. c	39. a	59. d	79. b
20. a	40. c	60. d	80. b

Index

unity of, 91
Title I, 209
Title II
Section 245, 209
Section 246, 209
Section 251, 209
Title II, Section 203(b), 208
Torrens system, 175
Township, 108, 110, 111
lines, 108
strip, 108
Toxic Substance Control Act, 390
Toxic torts, 392
Trade fixtures, 13-14
Transferability, 262
Transfer declaration form, 162
Transfer tax, 162, 341
Triple net lease, 236
Trust, 94-95, 96
account, 143, 195
deed, 188
Trustee, 94, 161, 188
Trustee's deed, 161
Trustor, 94, 188, 194
Truth-in-Lending Act, 219-20

Underground storage tanks, 388-89
Undue pressure, 263
Unenforceable contract, 137
Uniform Commercial Code (UCC), 175-76
Uniform Environmental History, 396-97
Uniform Limited Partnership Act, 96
Uniform Partnership Act, 96

Uniform Probate Code, 78
Uniform Residential Appraisal Report, 275-77
Uniform Residential Landlord and Tenant Act, 235
Uniform Settlement Statement (HUD Form 1), 337-38
sample, 349-50, 351
Uniform Standards of Professional Appraisal Practice, 261-62
Uniform Vendor and Purchaser Risk Act, 144
Unilateral contract, 136-37
Uniqueness, 6, 15
U.S. Geological Survey (USGS), 115-16
Unit-in-place method, 268
Units of measure, 357
Urea formaldehyde, 387-88
Usury, 189, 192
Utilities, 283, 262
Utility easements, 80, 294

VA loan, 209-11
Vacation homes, 23
Valid, 137
Value, 207, 262-63, 275
approaches to, 265-73
characteristics of, 262
final estimate, 275
principles of, 263-65
Variable lease, 237
Variance, 285
Vendee, 196
Vendor, 150, 196

Verbal lease, 226
Veterans Affairs (VA), Department of, 24
loan, 209-11
Violence, acts of, 310
VISTA Environmental Profiles, 393-94
Void, 137
Voidable, 137
Volume, 359-62
Voluntary alienation, 155-63
Voluntary lien, 123, 131

Wage levels, 7
Walk-through, 146, 339
Warehousing agencies, 218
Warranty, 67
Waste, 77
Waste disposal site, 389-90
Water rights, 83-84
Will
requirements for valid, 164
transfer of title by, 164-65
Workers' compensation acts, 256
Wraparound loan, 212
Writ of execution, 130
Written lease, 226

Zoning hearing board, 285
Zoning ordinances, 7, 283-85, 294-95
Zoning permits, 284-85